PSALMS

PETER A. STEVESON

Peter A. Steveson
PSALM 150:1-6

BOB JONES
UNIVERSITY PRESS
Greenville, South Carolina

Library of Congress Cataloging-in-Publication Data
Steveson, Peter A. (Peter Allan), 1934-
Psalms / Peter A. Steveson.
p. cm.
Summary: "An exegetical commentary on Psalms"—Provided by publisher.
Includes bibliographical references (p.) and index.
ISBN-13: 978-1-59166-687-5 (hardbound : alk. paper)
ISBN-10: 1-59166-687-2
1. Bible. O.T. Psalms—Commentaries. I. Title.

BS1430.53.S74 2007
223'.207—dc22

2006027935

Cover Photo: PhotoDisc Inc./Getty Images

All Scripture is quoted from the Authorized King James Version unless otherwise noted.

Psalms
Peter A. Steveson, PhD

Design by Nathan Hutcheon
Composition by Michael Boone

ISBN 978-1-59166-687-5

15 14 13 12 11 10 9 8 7 6 5 4 3 2 1

To Rebecca and Jim King,
my daughter and her husband,
whose spiritual growth and service
bring joy to her parents

TABLE OF CONTENTS

BOOK III

BOOK IV

BOOK V

PREFACE

Every book should have a purpose for being written. I freely admit that my purpose in writing this commentary has been selfish. I have thoroughly enjoyed the opportunity of working slowly through Psalms. At the same time, writing the book has given me a better understanding of their background and teaching. In addition to preaching and teaching from Psalms, I taught a course in the Poetical Books for over twenty years. Like most Bible teachers, I had not found other resources that completely satisfied me. This book is my effort to help others in their research.

Isaac Newton once said, “If I have seen further it is by standing on the shoulders of giants.” I feel much the same way. I have relied on “giants” in developing this book. Many of the conservative commentaries in the bibliography have given excellent help, and even those written from a theologically liberal perspective have forced me to think through my positions.

As always, I have received much help from others in developing the book. The library staffs at Bob Jones University and Furman University have greatly assisted me. My editors at Bob Jones University Press—Todd Jones, Suzette Jordan, and Marianne Appleman—have turned my spelling, grammar, and expression of the material into something more readable. Others at the Press who have helped include Mary Berg and Rebecca Wright. I also appreciate the assistance of my colleagues; Dr. Robert Bell, Mrs. Jackie Eaves, Jürgen Matthia, and Edith Smith have helped me in a variety of ways. Finally, Bob Jones University has provided a writing grant to let me complete the book.

CHIEF ABBREVIATIONS

AB	Anchor Bible
BDB	Francis Brown, S. R. Driver, and Charles Briggs, *A Hebrew and English Lexicon* (rev. 1972)
BibRev	*The Bible Review*
BibSac	*Bibliotheca Sacra*
BibThBull	*Biblical Theology Bulletin*
CTQ	*Concordia Theological Quarterly*
ET	*Expository Times*
EvQ	*Evangelical Quarterly*
G.K.C.	Gesenius' *Hebrew Grammar*, E. Kautzsch, ed., and A. E. Cowley, rev. (1970)
GTJ	*Grace Theological Journal*
HUCA	*Hebrew Union College Annual*
Interp	*Interpretation*
JBQ	*Jewish Bible Quarterly*
JBL	*Journal of Biblical Literature*
JETS	*Journal of the Evangelical Theological Society*
JQR	*Jewish Quarterly Review*
JSOT	*Journal for the Study of the Old Testament*
JSS	*Journal of Semitic Studies*
JTS	*Journal of Theological Studies*
KB	Ludwig Koehler and Walter Baumgartner, *The Hebrew and Aramaic Lexicon of the Old Testament* (rev. 1995)
LXX	Septuagint
ms, mss	manuscript, manuscripts
MT	Masoretic Text

NAB	The New American Bible
NEB	The New English Bible
NEJ	*The New Encyclopedia of Judaism*
NIB	*The New Interpreter's Bible*
NIV	The New International Version
NJB	The New Jerusalem Bible
NRSV	The New Revised Standard Version
NT	New Testament
OT	Old Testament
OTTP	A. R. Hulst, *Old Testament Translation Problems*
REB	The Revised English Bible
RevEx	*Review and Expositor*
SJOT	*Scandinavian Journal of the Old Testament*
TB	*Tyndale Bulletin*
TWOT	*Theological Wordbook of the Old Testament*
VT	*Vetus Testamentum*
WBC	*Wesleyan Bible Commentary*
ZAW	*Zeitschrift für die Alttestamentliche Wissenschaft*

INTRODUCTION

The division of the OT into three sections has long been recognized. The Prologue to Ecclesiasticus, written ca. 180 BC, refers to "the Law, the Prophets, and the other books of our ancestors."[1] The NT refers to the three areas of the OT: the Law, the Prophets, and the Psalms (Luke 24:44). The modern Hebrew name for the OT, the Jewish Bible, is *tanak*. This comes from the first letters of the names of the three sections: *torâ*, law; *nebîʾîm*, prophets; and *k*^{e}*tûbîm*, writings.[2] The third section contained the books commonly thought of today as poetical: Job, Psalms, Proverbs, Ecclesiastes, and the Song of Solomon. In addition, the Jews included several other books: Ruth, Lamentations, Esther, Daniel, Ezra, Nehemiah, and Chronicles. Since Psalms is the dominant book in this part of the OT, Luke used it to represent the group. Later authors called this section the *hagiographa*, the "holy writings."

In the OT, the book has the title of *t*^{e}*hillîm*, "songs of praises." The title of "Psalms" comes from the Greek translation of this Hebrew title. The LXX translated it as ψαλμοί, *psalmoi*, songs to be sung to the accompaniment of stringed music. The LXX was translated by the mid-third century BC, which attests to the early use of *Psalms* as a name for the book. This word also occurs in the NT, e.g., Luke 20:42; Acts 1:20; James 5:13.

The Jews used the book extensively in their rituals of worship. Fifty-five of the psalm titles mention the "chief musician." Many of the titles mention musical instruments or tunes to which the psalms should be sung. The liturgy of worship developed after the deliverance from captivity and during the intertestamental period. The Jews began to sing Psalm 24 on Sunday, the first day of the week, Psalm 48 on the second day, Psalm 82 on the third day, Psalm 94 on the

---

[1]Quoted from Patrick W. Skehan and Alexander A. Di Lella, *The Wisdom of Ben Sira*, in *The Anchor Bible*, ed. William Foxwell Albright and David Noel Freedman (New York: Doubleday, 1987), p. 8.

[2]I have used a simplified transliteration system to indicate most of the Hebrew vowels. The *a* indicates both the *qameṣ* and the *pataḥ*, the *e* indicates both the *segol* and the *ṣerê*, the *o* indicates both the *ḥolem* and the *qameṣ ḥatup*, and the *u* indicates the *qibbuṣ*. The raised *a*, *o*, or *e* indicates a *šewa*. I have used *î* to represent the *ḥireq yod*, *ê* for the *ṣere yod*, and *â* for the *qameṣ he*. The *ô* indicates the *ḥolem waw* and the *û* the *šureq*.

fourth day, Psalm 81 on the fifth day, Psalm 93 on the sixth day, and Psalm 92 on the Sabbath. The Hallel Psalms (113–118) were read during the feasts of Passover, Pentecost, Tabernacles, the New Moon observance, and Hanukkah. Other psalms were read as well throughout the year.[3]

The early church incorporated the psalms into their worship. Greek translations of the Hebrew Scriptures became the basis for many songs. Ignatius, leader of the church at Antioch, introduced antiphonal singing, such as the Jews had practiced in singing the psalms.[4] Caius, a priest in Rome, writing in the early third century, referred to "psalms and odes, such as were from the beginning written by the faithful." Words such as *alleluia*, *amen*, and *hosanna*, found in the psalms, passed over into Christian hymns. Ambrose, Bishop of Milan in the late fourth century, refers to monks "who sang the psalms by an ancient custom and practice."[5] Basil, a contemporary of Ambrose, writes of "customs now prevalent" that include "the chanting of psalms," even antiphonal chanting.[6] Augustine, Bishop of Hippo, writing near the end of the fourth century, refers to "the practice of singing of hymns and psalms."[7] Until the fourth century, many churches limited their singing to songs based on the psalms. At the same time, Christian hymns—not taken directly from Scripture but with Christian themes—began to develop.

The singing and chanting of psalms as well as the singing of hymns continued during the rise of the Roman Catholic Church. In the first half of the sixth century, St. Benedict, leader of several monastic communities in Italy, prescribed psalms to be sung during the day.[8] In the late sixth century, Pope Gregory the Great incorpo-

---

[3]*NEJ*, p. 627.

[4]Except where noted, the information on the early use of psalms in worship comes from *A Dictionary of Hymnology*, ed. John Julian. 2 vols. (London: John Murray, 1908. Reprint, Grand Rapids: Kregel Publications, 1985), II, 926–28.

[5]*Saint Ambrose Letters*, trans. Mary Melchior Beyenka, The Fathers of the Church 26 (New York: Fathers of the Church, Inc., 1954), p. 13.

[6]*Saint Basil Letters*, trans. Agnes Clare Way, The Fathers of the Church 28 (New York: Fathers of the Church, Inc., 1955), pp. 83–84.

[7]*Saint Augustine Confessions*, trans. Vernon J. Bourke, The Fathers of the Church 21 (New York: Fathers of the Church, Inc., 1953), p. 242.

[8]John Caldwell, *Medieval Music* (Bloomington, Ind.: Indiana University Press, 1978), p. 15.

rated psalms into some of the chants.[9] As the liturgy of the church developed, the music shifted more and more to trained musicians. By the ninth century, the congregation's part in the music was minimal. The choirs, however, continued to chant many of the psalms. Often, two choirs chanted them antiphonally.[10] The lack of education during these dark ages contributed to confining the music to the ritual of the church. In 1229, the Council of Toulouse issued a number of directives to the church. Canon 14 prohibited the laity from having "the books of the Old or New Testament." It did, however, allow the laity to possess the Psalter "from motive of devotion."

The Reformation stimulated the publication of several Psalters. Martin Luther continued singing the hymns he had known in the Roman Catholic Church. John Calvin, however, turned back to the Psalms for songs to be sung in the church. Calvin's approach greatly influenced the English-speaking church.[11] Scottish Psalters, published 1542–46, included several translations from Martin Luther's versions of different psalms. A French Psalter was in print by 1540. The Genevan Psalters, published about the same time, had versions of the psalms by John Calvin, Clément Marot, and Theodore Beza with melodies by Louis Bourgeois.[12]

After the death of Queen Mary, many of the refugees from England returned to their homeland. They brought with them the psalms they had been singing in Geneva. A psalter written by Thomas Sternhold and John Hopkins in 1562, called *The Whole Booke of Psalmes* and later the "Old Version," became the standard in British worship. In 1696, Nahum Tate and Nicholas Brady published a psalter that generally replaced this. Between 1414 and 1700, more than one hundred different English psalters were published. These included publications by Miles Coverdale, Queen Elizabeth I, William Kethe, Matthew Parker, and Francis Bacon.

---

[9]Caldwell, p. 38.

[10]"Psalm," *The New Grove Dictionary of Music and Musicians*, ed. Stanley Sadie (New York: Macmillan Publishers Limited, 2001), XX, 452.

[11]Benjamin Brawley, *History of the English Hymn* (New York: The Abingdon Press, 1932), pp. 35–36.

[12]*Dictionary of Scottish Church History and Theology*, ed. Nigel M. de S. Cameron *et al.*, (Downers Grove, Ill.: InterVarsity Press, 1993), p. 682.

When the church spread to the colonies in America, believers took the Psalms with them. The first book printed in America was the *Bay Psalm Book*, printed in 1640. Cotton Mather issued a psalter in 1709 that contained unrhymed psalms for singing. Several versions of the English Psalter published by Tate and Brady were printed in Boston between 1750 and 1800. Before 1800, all of the major denominations sang primarily psalms.

The book of Psalms is the favorite of many Christians. It possesses an emotional quality that speaks to the heart of its readers. The writers describe their fears, frustrations, sickness, failures, betrayal by others, dangers, and many other subjects. They speak of their faith, their devotion to the Lord, and their desire to worship Him. As you read their work, you identify with them and the book becomes more than a dry recitation of facts.

Many authors have aptly described the book. John Calvin called it "an anatomy of all the parts of the soul." He went on to say, "There is not an emotion of which any one can be conscious that is not here represented as in a mirror. . . . The Holy Spirit has here drawn to the life all the griefs, sorrows, fears, doubts, hopes, cares, perplexities, in short, all the distracting emotions with which the minds of men are wont to be agitated."[13] W. Graham Scroggie noted that many readers "have derived therefrom cheer for their tasks, strength for their burdens, courage for their battles, comfort for their sorrows, light for their journey, and hope for their ventures." He added that Psalms has

> elements which appeal, not to any one race or age, but to the heart of mankind. We are all tempted in some way or another; trouble overtakes us. . . . We are all sometimes shaken by doubt, and stricken by disappointment; and also, we all have our great days, our times of prosperity, our seasons of ecstasy. We are all creatures of moods on which circumstances play, now lifting us up to the mountain top, and now casting us down into the valley. . . . These experiences are individual and universal, and it is because they are all reflected in the Psalms that "these have been, through all the centuries, and will ever continue to be the one unique and inexhaustible treasury of devotion for the individual and for the church."[14]

---

[13]John Calvin, *Commentary on the Book of Psalms*, trans. James Anderson (Grand Rapids, Mich.: Wm. B. Eerdmans Publishing Company, 1949), I, xxxvii.

[14]W. Graham Scroggie, *The Psalms*, I, 39.

Introduction to Hebrew Poetry

Although there are many different forms of modern poetry, the traditional poem stresses the rhyming of sounds. Christians are familiar with poems such as:

> Amazing grace! How sweet the **sound**
> That saved a wretch like **me**!
> I once was lost, but now am **found**;
> Was blind, but now I **see**.

While forms such as haiku, iambic poetry, and free verse have gained in popularity in recent years, most people still think of poetry in terms of rhyme.

Parallelism. Old Testament poetry radically differs from the general idea of rhyming. Instead of rhyming the sounds of words, Hebrew poetry rhymes the thoughts being expressed. The rhythm of thought is called *parallelism.* It occurs not only in the poetical books but also widely throughout the whole of the Hebrew Scriptures. Large amounts of the OT are poetical. Even large portions of the NT express their thoughts with a poetical form.

This form of poetry is not unique to the OT. The languages of other Near Eastern nations also used parallelism to express their thoughts. The following three examples illustrate this parallelism. In the Babylonian poem *Atra-ḫasīs*, the story of the Flood begins,

> When the gods like men
> Bore the work and suffered the toil—
> The toil of the gods was great,
> The work was heavy, the distress was much—[15]

In *The Legend of Aqhat, Son of Dan'el*, an Ugaritic tablet from Ras Shamra, lines 25–30 read as follows:

> As for mortal man, what does he get as his latter end?
> What does mortal man get as his inheritance?
> Glaze will be poured out on my head,
> Even plaster upon my pate,
> And the death of all men will I die,
> Yea, I will surely die.[16]

---

[15]W. G. Lambert and A. R. Millard, *Atra-ḫasīs: The Babylonian Story of the Flood* (Oxford: Oxford University Press, 1969), p. 43.

[16]Trans. J. Gray, in D. Winton Thomas, *Documents from Old Testament Times* (New York: Harper & Row, 1958), p. 125.

The Egyptian *Hymn to Aten* begins with the following words:

> Thou dost appear beautiful on the horizon of heaven,
> O living Aten, thou who wast the first to live.
> When thou hast risen on the eastern horizon,
> Thou hast filled every land with thy beauty.[17]

In general, there are five main types of Hebrew poetry. These often occur randomly, with one verse employing one type and the next verse using a different type. In some cases, a single verse may involve more than one type. One basic form of biblical poetry uses *synonymous parallelism*. In this, the author restates the same thought with successive phrases. Psalm 2:3 illustrates this:

> Let us break their bands asunder,
> and cast away their cords from us.

Verse 4 also uses synonymous parallelism:

> He that sitteth in the heavens shall laugh:
> the Lord shall have them in derision.

With *antithetic parallelism*, the author contrasts the thought of the second phrase with the thought of the first phrase. Often, but not always, the word *but* will signal the contrast. Psalm 1:6 illustrates antithetic parallelism:

> For the Lord knoweth the way of the righteous:
> but the way of the ungodly shall perish.

Psalm 75:10 also employs antithetic parallelism:

> All the horns of the wicked also will I cut off;
> but the horns of the righteous shall be exalted.

In the third form of poetry, *synthetic parallelism*, the second phrase completes the first phrase. The form of this type varies widely. It may be relatively simple, e.g., 95:11,

> Unto whom I sware in my wrath
> that they should not enter into my rest.

Or it may be more complex, sometimes mixed with another form of poetry, e.g., 1:3,

> And he shall be like a tree planted by the rivers of water,
> that bringeth forth his fruit in his season;

---

[17]Trans. R. J. Williams, in Thomas, p. 145.

> his leaf also shall not wither; and
> whatsoever he doeth shall prosper.

With *climactic parallelism*, the second phrase restates part of the first phrase, then completes the thought, e.g., 93:3,

> The floods have lifted up, O Lord,
> the floods have lifted up their voice;
> the floods lift up their waves.

The completion often takes the poetry to a new height of thought, e.g., 29:1–2,

> Give unto the Lord, O ye mighty,
> give unto the Lord glory and strength.
> Give unto the Lord the glory due unto his name;
> worship the Lord in the beauty of holiness.

The final form of Hebrew poetry is *emblematic parallelism*. With this, one part (usually the first phrase), serves as an emblem to illustrate the other phrase, e.g., 42:1,

> As the hart panteth after the water brooks,
> so panteth my soul after thee, O God.

Psalm 73:22 illustrates this type with the emblem occurring in the second phrase,

> So foolish was I, and ignorant:
> I was as a beast before thee.

While not a separate type of poetry, the Old Testament authors sometimes use *inverted parallelism*, restating the thought by inverting the order. This requires a *quatrain*, with the four phrases occurring in an a:b::b:a order. Psalm 103:1 illustrates this:

> Bless the Lord, O my soul:
> and all that is with me, bless his holy name.

While the verse uses *synonymous parallelism*, it inverts the third and fourth phrases to create a *chiasmus*, an X-shaped parallelism. Introversion may occur with different forms of poetry—with *synonymous parallelism*, e.g., 51:3,

> For I acknowledge my transgressions:
> and my sin is ever before me.

or with *antithetic parallelism*, e.g., 15:4,

> In whose eyes a vile person is contemned;
> but he honoureth them that fear the Lord.

A more complicated *chiasmus* may also occur; e.g. 135:15–18, where the structure is a:b:c:d::d:c:b:a, or 115:4–8, where the structure is a:b:c:d:e:f:e:d:c:b:a.

There are variants of these five basic types, but these forms demonstrate the broad range of Hebrew poetry.

Meter. Due to the translation into a different language, we cannot always sense the rhythm imposed upon Hebrew poetry. It is normal, however, for the biblical writers to use a distinct *meter*. The text parallels the number of accented units in a line. For example, Psalm 46:1 follows a 2:2 meter with each part of the verse translating two Hebrew words:

> God—is our
> refuge—and strength,
> a help—in trouble
> abundantly—present.

Psalm 3:1 uses a 3:3 pattern. Each part of the verse translates three accented units.

> Lord—how many—trouble me;
> Many—rise—against me.

The dirge (or *qinah*) employs a 3:2 meter, but a 3:2 meter also occurs in other types of passages. Psalm 24:2 translates a 3:2 pattern:

> For He—upon the seas—founded it
> and upon the rivers—established it.

Although the authors are not consistent, the phrases in poetry often have a 2:2 or 3:3 meter. Other types of meter, including irregular forms, also occur. Newer translations, e.g., NASB, NIV, often translate in such a way as to bring out the meter of the verses.

Other Elements of Poetry. Several characteristics of Hebrew poetry do not appear in translation. Certain Hebrew words and phrases occur only in OT poetry, e.g., *miktam* (6 times in the psalm titles); *selâ* (71 times in the Psalms, 3 times in Habakkuk's psalm); *ʿapʿapîm* (3 times in Job, twice in Psalms, 5 times in Proverbs, once in a poetic portion of Jeremiah); *ʾal-tašḥet* (4 times in the psalm titles). There is alliteration, e.g., 63:2 (*ʾᵉlohîm ʾelî ʾattâ ʾᵃšaḥᵃreka*); 77:4 (*ʾezkerâ ʾᵉlohîm wᵉ ʾeh mayâ*). Repetition for the sake of emphasis frequently occurs, e.g., 41:13 (*ʾamen wᵉʾamen*); 150:1–6 (various forms of *halal* occur 13 times). The grammatical forms of certain words may differ between prose and poetry. Poetry may use alliteration, assonance, or an acrostic structure. As the Masoretic scribes codified the text in Job, Psalms, and Proverbs, they used accents that differed from those used elsewhere in the OT.

The Value of Poetry. The knowledge of poetry may help with the interpretation of biblical passages. Quite often, one phrase will allow an intelligent understanding of a parallel phrase. Psalm 10:4 gives a simple example. Why have the translators supplied the phrase "after God"? Literally, the Hebrew reads: "The wicked, according to the pride of his face, does not seek; there is no God in all his thoughts." The parallelism shows us that the wicked does not seek God. The translators rightly added "after God" to clarify the statement.

We can repeat this process elsewhere. In 11:4, the second phrase tells us that the "temple" in the first phrase is the heavenly temple. In 73:21, the *inverted parallelism* between the archaic word "reins" and "heart" lets us refer "reins" to the emotions. In Proverbs 8:36, the word *ḥoṭᵉʾî* can mean either "sins" or "misses." The *antithetic parallelism* with v. 35 tells us to translate it "misses." In Proverbs 14:23, antithetic parallelism contrasts the archaic word "penury" with "profit." This lets us understand "penury" as "want" or "poverty." In Isaiah 4:2, the *synonymous parallelism* with "the branch of the Lord" shows us that the phrase "fruit of the earth" is a messianic title.

These few examples illustrate the value of understanding Hebrew poetry. Over and over, the poetic form of a passage helps to guide its interpretation.

Introduction to the Psalms

The Organization of the Book. There is a unique organization of the 150 individual psalms. These are distributed into five books of unequal size (1–41, 42–72, 73–89, 90–106, 107–150). We do not know where these books came from, although it is reasonable that they represent gradual collections of the psalms. It may well be that Israel's priests collected them for use in the various worship ceremonies. Each book closes with a doxology of praise to the Lord.[18] Book II closes with the statement, "The prayers of David the son of Jesse are

[18]See 41:13; 72:19; 89:52; and 106:48. In addition, Pss. 146–150 form a grand doxology of praise that closes the whole book.

ended," 72:20. The unknown compiler of the book added the statement to reflect the influence of David in the collection.[19]

There is additional evidence of the collection process. Psalms 14 and 53, in different books, are very close in form, the primary difference being the name used for God. Psalm 40:13–17 and Psalm 70, again in different books, are almost identical. Psalm 108 combines two earlier psalms, 57:7–11 and 60:5–12. Some of the psalms were obviously collected more than once. With minimal editing, they appear in different collections of psalms.

With the exception of Psalms 1, 2, 10, and 33, all the psalms in Book I give David as their author. All of the psalms of the "Sons of Korah" (42–43, 44–49; 84–85, 87–88) are in Books II and III. Book III includes all but one (50) of the psalms attributed to Asaph (50, 73–83). The fifteen psalms with the title "A Song of degrees" (120–134) are all in Book V. A sequence of psalms that point toward the millennial reign of the Lord (95–99) occurs in Book IV. All but one of the Hallel psalms (106, 113, 135, 146, 147, 148, 149, and 150), those that begin and end with *hal^{a}lûyah* (and variant spellings), "praise ye the Lord," are in Book V. The fifty-five psalms dedicated to the "chief musician" occur in Books I, II, III, and V. None occur in Book IV.

In Book I, the name *y^{e}hwah*, "Lord," predominates, occurring about five times as often as *ʾ^{e}lohîm*, "God." In Book II the emphasis changes, with *ʾ^{e}lohîm* occurring about six times as often as *y^{e}hwah*. We do not know why the compilers of these books gave such stress to the use of these names. The two primary names of God occur about equally in Book III. In Books IV and V, *y^{e}hwah* dominates, occurring four times as often as *ʾ^{e}lohîm* in Book IV and nine times as often in Book V.[20]

---

[19]Nineteen of the thirty-one psalms in Book II name David as their author. While David also wrote psalms in the other four books, the compiler is only concerned with those in this collection.

[20]Largely on the occurrence of the divine names, Theodore H. Robinson, *The Poetry of the Old Testament*, pp. 114–18, argues that there were originally three primary collections of psalms. The second and third of these were divided to make the five collections seen today. Robinson's reasoning is selective and speculative. He draws a generalization based on the use of *y^{e}hwah* and *ʾ^{e}lohîm* but ignores the occurrence of both names in every collection. No ms evidence supports his view.

We do not know who made the collections.[21] The individual psalms cover a range of a thousand years.[22] It is reasonable that the five collections were made at different times during this period. Solomon showed his interest in literature (I Kings 4:32). Hezekiah gave his attention to earlier writings (II Chron. 29:30; Prov. 25:1). Jewish tradition refers to Ezra's involvement with the OT scriptures.[23] It is possible but unprovable that these men guided the collection of poetic writings. Whoever bears the responsibility completed the task about the time that the OT canon closed. The translation of the LXX took place 150–200 years after the writing of Malachi. The division of the Psalms into five collections had already taken place.[24]

The books give no hint of any special order or purpose.[25] The psalms are not arranged chronologically. Messianic prophecies occur

---

[21]Matthew Henry, *An Exposition with Practical Observations of the Book of Psalms*, III, 238, makes Ezra the collector of David's psalms. This does not explain why David's psalms are scattered among the five books. Franz Delitzsch, *Psalms*, I, 18, sees Solomon as collecting Books I and II and Hezekiah as responsible for Book III. The collection in Books IV and V came together during the time of Ezra and Nehemiah. In support of this, II Macc. 2:13 refers to Nehemiah's founding of "a library gathered together the acts of the kings, and the prophets, and of David, and of the epistles of the kings concerning the holy gifts." E. J. Young, *An Introduction to the Old Testament* (Grand Rapids, Mich.: Wm. B. Eerdmans Publishing Company, 1958), p. 323, suggests Hezekiah as the compiler of the first three books. Scroggie, p. 15, makes Solomon the compiler of Book I, "the men of Hezekiah" the compilers of Books II and III, and someone in "the time of Ezra and Nehemiah" the compiler of Books IV and V. No evidence lets us identify the compilers with certainty.

[22]Moses, the author of Ps. 90, wrote ca. 1400 BC. Other psalms, e.g., 129, 137, are exilic or postexilic. The range of dates thus extends about one thousand years.

[23]*NEJ*, p. 267.

[24]The final order of the psalms within the five books continued to vary until about the first century AD. The collections of psalms found in the Dead Sea scrolls show different orders in the sequence. The Jewish scribes standardized the order by the end of that century. Gerald H. Wilson, "A First Century C.E. Date for the Closing of the Book of Psalms," *JBQ* 28:2 (2000): 102–3, concludes that the first three books were fixed by the fourth century BC. The final two books were completed "some time after the mid-first century C.E." Since the LXX was completed by the mid-first century BC, Wilson's date is too late. The organization must have been completed before the Greek translation.

[25]Nancy L. deClaissè-Walford, "The Canonical Shape of the Psalms," in *An Introduction to Wisdom Literature and the Psalms*, p. 99, suggests that the order contributes to "the story of the survival of ancient Israel." It recalls "the reigns of David and Solomon in books 1 and 2; laments the dark days of oppression during the divided kingdoms and the Babylonian exile in book 3; and looks forward to and rejoices in Israel's restoration to the land and in the reign of YHWH as king in books

in all of the books. The imprecatory psalms occur randomly. We find lament psalms and psalms of praise throughout. Despite this evidence, various theories try to find some significance in the five books. Gregory of Nyssa interpreted the book as five steps to moral perfection.[26] Others suggest that the five books of the Psalms correspond to the five books of the Pentateuch.[27]

The Psalm Titles. Most of the psalms have titles. These titles may identify the author, describe the historical background, express the purpose, give musical directions, or combine these elements. The thirty-four psalms with no title are often called *orphan psalms*. Modern critics often dismiss the titles as late additions with no significant value. The psalms attributed to David become simply songs that are Davidic in style or written for David. The NT references to David refer to the book as a whole, not to specific writings of David. The historical settings in the titles merely place the psalms based on loose connections with Israel's history.[28]

---

4 and 5." The view oversimplifies the books by selectively noting those parts that support deClaissè-Walford's thesis.

[26]See Delitzsch, I, 19.

[27]*NEJ*, p. 626, gives this as the view of the Jews. Gaebelein, *The Book of Psalms*, pp. 13–14, considers Genesis as the foundation of God's revelation. So Book I "is the same for the Book of Psalms that Genesis is for the whole Bible." He illustrates this by noting that the names Jehovah and Elohim occur in Book I "just as in Genesis." He does not mention that these names also occur in the other four books. Exodus describes the sufferings of Israel and ends with the nation going toward the land of promise. He does not mention the forty years of wandering that followed. He simply notes that Book II "begins with Psalms of suffering" and closes with a psalm that "describes the reign of the King and the glories of His Kingdom." Leviticus is the book that teaches holiness. So Book III emphasizes holiness (also taught in the other books). Numbers describes the journey toward the land where Israel should find rest. Book IV includes millennial psalms (as do the other books). Deuteronomy recalls Israel's history and predicts their future. Book V begins with a psalm of history and ends with a psalm of praise. Gaebelein does not mention the wide variety of other topics found in it. His view is contrived, resting on a few isolated comparisons and neglecting the broader content of the psalms.

[28]A. F. Kirkpatrick, *The Book of Psalms*, pp. xxxi–xxxii, says that "the *authorship and occasion* of the Psalms cannot be regarded as . . . representing trustworthy traditions, and accordingly giving reliable information." He states that many of the titles "cannot be reconciled with the contents and language of the Psalms to which they are prefixed." Davidic psalms "assume situations and circumstances wholly unlike any in which he can be supposed to have been placed, or express feelings which it is difficult to attribute to a man of his position and character." J. H. Eaton, *Psalms*, p. 15, asserts that the heading "of David . . . can merely signify a connexion of

Despite this rejection of the information given in the titles, there is no persuasive argument that we should ignore them. No title goes contrary to its psalm; rather, the titles and their psalms agree. While the original authors did not include the titles, they were added early in Israel's history and reflect early beliefs regarding the individual psalms. The LXX and Vulgate include the titles although, from the translations, it is clear that they did not always understand them.[29] The titles appear in the Dead Sea Scrolls. Ancient scribes must have added the titles to prevent the loss of historical information.

The Authors.[30] In most cases, we know the author only from the titles. These tell us that David wrote seventy-three of the Psalms.[31] The NT adds Psalm 2 and, possibly, Psalm 95 to this number. From the poetry of Psalms 9–10, we can add Psalm 10 as Davidic. I Chronicles 16 suggests that David wrote Psalms 96, 105, and possibly 106. Although it is fashionable among many current writers to reject David's authorship, ample evidence in the Bible supports it.

---

some sort from the royal house which continued to be called by the ancestral name 'David.'" A. A. Anderson, *The Book of Psalms*, I, 44–45, concludes that "there is no reason to doubt that David actually composed certain psalms and songs, but it is well nigh impossible to say which of them, if any, were preserved in the Psalter. . . . Perhaps the most likely explanation is that in the majority of Psalms we should render our phrase by 'belonging to David', i.e. to the Davidic collection of songs." Despite these reservations, the psalms provide valuable information. There are no valid reasons for dismissing them as unreliable.

[29]That these titles were not understood provides a strong argument for an early date for the addition of the titles. The Captivity of Judah is the most logical time for the meanings of the musical words and phrases that later were not understood. Following the return from Babylon, the Jews once more began their worship but without completely understanding the titles. Roger T. Beckwith, "The Early History of the Psalter," *TB* 46:1 (1995): 14–17, perceptively makes this point in arguing for a preexilic dating of the titles. While some of the titles may have been added later, e.g., Pss. 126, 129 and, by extension, Pss. 120–134, the bulk of the titles should be dated earlier rather than later.

[30]Nicolaas H. Ridderbos, "The Psalms: Style-Figures and Structure," in *Oudtestamentische Studiën*, XIII, 52, suggests that the authors of the psalms were trained poets, having had "some prior sort of schooling." He bases the conclusion on the style and structure of the psalms. While the view is possible, what we know of the authors argues against it. We find no such schooling in the accounts of David or Solomon. Many of the psalms reflect a priestly background rather than that of a trained poet.

[31]The Talmud, in *Baba Bathra* 14*b*, says, "David wrote the Book of Psalms, including in it work of the elders, namely Adam, Melchizedek, Abraham, Moses, Heman, Yeduthun, Asaph, and the three sons of Korah."

His interest and ability in music is well known (I Sam. 16:23; 18:10). He directed that Israel's worship should include music (I Chron. 15:16; II Chron. 8:14). II Maccabees 2:13 refers to the "writings . . . of David." Amos 6:5 mentions people who make instruments "like David."[32] Second Samuel 23:1 refers to him as "the sweet psalmist [or 'singer'] of Israel." The titles give Solomon as the author of Psalms 72 and 127. The content of Psalm 132 suggests Solomon as its author. The descendants of Korah wrote eleven of the psalms: 42, 44, 45, 46, 47, 48, 49, 84, 85, 87, and 88. The poetry of 42–43 adds Psalm 43 to this group. Asaph and his descendants authored twelve psalms: 50, 73, 74, 75, 76, 77, 78, 79, 80, 81, 82, and 83. Psalm 88 names Heman as its author, Psalm 89 names Ethan, and Psalm 90 credits Moses. The other psalms are anonymous. While we may speculate on their authors, we cannot be dogmatic.[33]

The Types of Psalms. The book of Psalms includes a variety of styles and purposes in the individual psalms. It is impossible to give an exact number of each type, since many of the psalms have characteristics of more than one type. Further, there is no complete agreement between authors in categorizing the psalms. In general, however, there is agreement on the following groups.

The greatest number are *Lament Psalms*. There are about sixty of these, with the largest part being *Individual Laments*, e.g., 3, 31, 77. There are also *Community Laments* in which the author writes on behalf of the nation, e.g., 12, 80, 90. Both the *Individual* and *Community Laments* express the feelings of those who cry out to the Lord in some time of crisis.

In the *Lament Psalms*, the psalmist addresses God, then describes the nature of his trial—the threat of death, persecution, rejection, sickness, etc. He pleads with the Lord to deliver him and often states his trust that the Lord will meet his need. He closes with a statement of praise or a pledge to renewed service. These psalms often vary the

---

[32]J. A. Sanders, *The Dead Sea Psalms Scroll*, p. 134, notes that the Psalm scroll from cave 11 at Qumran (11QPsa) credits David with composing 3,600 psalms and 450 songs. While these figures may be inflated, they still show an early tradition that David wrote many psalms.

[33]*NIB*, IV, often refers to the psalmist as "he or she" or "himself or herself," e.g., pp. 806, 1022, 1125. It is unlikely that any of the authors were women. None of the titles suggest women authors. In addition, the Jews would not have accepted such writing as authoritative.

order of these elements and sometimes omit an element or combine one with another.

The *Penitential Psalms* come from the *Individual Lament Psalms*. In these, the psalmist laments his own sin, e.g., 6, 38, 130. When the language of a *Lament Psalm* reaches an unusually harsh level, it receives the name of an *Imprecatory Psalm*. In these, the psalmist expresses a "curse" on some foe. He expresses these curses with severe language, e.g., 35, 59, 109.[34]

About fifteen of the psalms are *Songs of Thanksgiving*. These psalms express a response to some blessing given by God. The songs include both *Individual Songs of Thanksgiving* and *Community Songs of Thanksgiving*. The *Songs of Thanksgiving* differ from the *Lament Psalms* in that they respond to some blessing *already* given by God. The *Lament Psalms* anticipate some needed future blessing.

In the *Songs of Thanksgiving*, the psalmist gives thanks to the Lord and offers praise to Him for blessings that have been given. The writer often describes the nature of these blessings—deliverance from some trial, provision of a need, etc. He will often urge others to join him in giving praise and thanksgiving to the Lord.

Thirteen of the psalms have *historical* notes in their titles: 3, 7, 18, 34, 51, 52, 54, 56, 57, 59, 60, 63, and 142. In addition, several others refer to events in Israel's history: 78, 105, 106, 135, 136, and 137. Since some of these psalms fall into other categories, e.g., *Lament Psalms*, they cannot be categorized separately. But the historical notes help to set the backgrounds to these psalms.

Fifteen of the psalms are classed as *Messianic Psalms*. In some way, these psalms point to Jesus Christ. The psalms may speak of some feature of the psalmist's life that typically portrays a part of the life of Christ, e.g., 69:7–9, 21. The psalmist may use hyperbolic language to describe something in his own life that points to the Lord, e.g., 45:3–5. Many of the psalms speak of the king in ideal terms, e.g., 72:1–20. Some psalms are directly prophetic, not featuring anything from the psalmist's own life, e.g., 110. The following list summarizes the *Messianic Psalms*:

[34]The introduction to Ps. 35 discusses the reasons that lie behind the imprecatory psalms.

2 Coronation of the King 2:7 (cf. Acts 13:33; Heb. 1:5; 5:5)
8 Dominion over the Creation 8:2 (cf. Matt. 21:16); 8:4–6 (cf. Heb. 2:6–9)
16 Resurrection of the King 16:10 (cf. Acts 2:25–28; 13:35)
22 Suffering Savior 22:1 (cf. Matt. 27:46; Mark 15:34); 22:7–8 (cf. Matt. 27:43); 22:18 (cf. Matt. 27:35; Mark 15:24; Luke 23:34; John 19:23–24)
40 Obedient Servant 40:6–8 (cf. Heb. 10:5–10)
41 Betrayal of the Savior 41:9 (cf. John 13:18)
45 Royal Wedding 45:6–7 (cf. Heb. 1:8–9)
68 Deliverance of the Captives 68:18 (cf. Eph. 4:8)
69 Rejection of the Savior 69:4 (cf. John 15:25); 69:9 (cf. John 2:17); 69:21 (cf. Matt. 27:34, 48); 69:25 (cf. Acts 1:20)
72 Kingdom of Messiah
89 Fulfillment of the Davidic Covenant
102 Eternal Savior 102:25–27 (cf. Heb. 1:10–12)
109 Betrayed Savior 109:8 (cf. Acts 1:20)
110 King-Priest 110:1 (cf. Matt. 22:43–45; Mark 12:36–37; Luke 20:41–44; Acts 2:33–35; Heb. 1:13); 110:4 (cf. Heb. 5:5–6; 6:20; 7:21)
118 Foundation of His Church 118:22–23 (cf. Matt. 21:42; Mark 12:10–11; Luke 20:17; Acts 4:11; I Pet. 2:7)

The *Enthronement Psalms* are a closely related group of psalms. These psalms speak of the Lord reigning over the earth. These include Psalms 47, 93, and 95–99. The *Songs of Praise* give an unusual emphasis to praising the Lord, with almost every verse extolling Him in some way. These include Psalms 100, 145, 148, and 150.

The New Testament Use. While the NT authors do not always refer to their source, they often quote from the Psalms. The total number of quotations from the book cannot be established with certainty.[35]

[35]Delitzsch, I, 48, makes the NT quote from the Psalms "about seventy times." Delitzsch sees this as more than any other OT book except Isaiah. Kirkpatrick, pp. 838–40, cites 93 passages from the Psalms that the NT quotes or significantly alludes to 148 times. Scroggie, *The Psalms*, IV, 277, gives 97 verses or passages quoted in the NT. Leopold Sabourin, *The Psalms: Their Origin and Meaning*, p. 164, sees about 120 NT quotations from the Psalms. Stewart Custer, "New Testament Quotations from Psalms," *BV* (1970), p. 117, sees 306 NT quotations or allusions to the book. Henry M. Shires, *Finding the Old Testament in the New* (Philadelphia: The Westminster Press, 1974), p. 126, sees 70 NT quotes introduced by formulas, 60 without an introductory formula, and 220 additional citations and references.

There are allusions to the OT that may come from different passages. There are phrases that occur in more than one place in the OT. It is clear, however, that the NT quotes from Psalms more than from any other OT book.

The Theology of the Psalms. Being such a large book, Psalms necessarily touches on many elements of theology. The following discussion gives an overview rather than a complete summary of the theology of the book.

In general, the psalms deal with God and man, and with the relationship between them. God is eternal, 90:2; 102:24*b*, 26–27. He is omniscient, 40:5; 139:1–6; 147:4–5; omnipresent, 139:7–12; and omnipotent, 62:11; 66:3; 145:11, best illustrated by His work in Creation, 8:3; 19:1; 74:16. He rules the host of heaven and earth, 24:10; 103:21; 148:2. He is holy, 47:8; 71:22; 108:7, and righteous, 11:7; 35:24; 71:19. He is merciful, 6:2; 33:22 56:1, and loving, 36:7; 42:7; 48:9. His Word to man is reliable, 19:7–11; 33:4; 117:2.

Mankind falls into one of two groups—the righteous or the wicked. The righteous accept God and His Word, 1:2; 40:8; 119:11, while the wicked reject Him and His Word, 10:4; 14:1; 106:24. The righteous trust the Lord, 13:5; 46:1; 125:1. The righteous exalt the Lord, 34:3; 57:5; 99:9; praise the Lord, 7:17; 30:1; 104:33; and rejoice in Him, 32:11; 47:1; 100:1–2. The Lord gives the righteous the privilege of prayer, a privilege illustrated several hundred times in the book, e.g., 3:4; 77:1; 141:1–2. He guides the righteous, 16:7; 23:3; 48:14.

Since the wicked reject God's Word, their manner of life is predictable. They persecute the poor, 10:2; 37:14; 82:4. They are boastful, 10:3, and proud, 10:4. They attack the godly, 11:2; 37:12; 140:4. They exalt vile men, 12:8, and work iniquity, 28:3. They do not repay debts, 37:21. They lie, 58:3; 109:2. They oppose and often persecute others, 10:2; 69:12, focusing especially on the righteous, 31:18; 37:32. They reject the Lord, 5:10; 139:20.

Life is brief for all mankind, 39:5; 89:47; 144:4. Righteous men confess their sin, 32:5; 38:18; 51:3; and the Lord forgives them, 86:5; 103:3; 130:4, 7. They will receive His blessing, 31:19; 58:11; 73:24.

R. E. O. White, *A Christian Handbook to the Psalms*, p. 5, refers to 201 quotes and 273 "more distant allusions" to the Psalms. Nestle's Greek NT lists over 200 quotations and allusions that come from 70 different psalms.

The wicked, however, will receive judgment from God, 9:17; 21:8; 110:1–2.

The psalms present many prophecies that relate both to the first and second comings of the Lord. He will be betrayed by Judas, 41:9, who will then be replaced as an apostle, 109:8. The psalms graphically portray the crucifixion of the Lord, 22:1–18; 69:21. He will, however, rise from the grave, 16:10. This sacrificial death qualifies Him to become the great High Priest of His people, 110:4.

The Father will anoint the Son as King over mankind, 2:6; 45:7. The Son will judge the heathen nations, 2:8–9. He will set up His rule over the earth, 9:7–8; 89:36–37; 99:1. He will enter into a marriage relationship with the church, 45:1–2, 8–9. All mankind will worship Him, 66:4; 68:29; 138:4–5. With David, believers have confidence that they will "dwell in the house of the Lord for ever," 23:6.

BOOK I

PSALM 1

Psalm 1 introduces the book of Psalms by drawing a contrast between the righteous and the wicked. The great test of man is his relationship to "the law of the Lord." The godly man accepts it. The ungodly man spurns it. We do not know the author of the psalm.[1] It is often dated earlier than Jeremiah, based on the similarity between v. 3 and Jeremiah 17:8.[2] From the occurrence of similar word pictures elsewhere,[3] however, it is likely that the relationship between the growth of trees and the waters of a stream or river was simply a common-sense illustration. Other dates have also been suggested.[4] Rabbinical tradition joined Psalms 1 and 2 into a single psalm.[5]

Men of all ages have found great value in Psalm 1. Charles Spurgeon said that this psalm was "the text upon which the whole of the Psalms make up a divine sermon."[6] Matthew Henry said that this psalm was placed first "because it is absolutely necessary to the acceptance of our devotions that we be righteous before God (for it is only the prayer of the upright that is his delight)."[7] Leopold Sabourin

---

[1]Stewart Custer, "Contrasts in Character," *BV* (1970): 80, Henry Morris, *Exploring the Psalms*, p. 18, and J. J. Stewart Perowne, *Commentary on the Psalms*, I, 108, hint at the authorship of Solomon. Albert Barnes, *Psalms*, I, 17, and John Calvin, *Psalms,* I, 4, give David as the author. Nothing in the psalm makes the authorship certain.

[2]Among others, Kirkpatrick, p. 1; Delitzsch, I, 83; and Carl Bernhard Moll, *The Psalms*, p. 50, date the psalm earlier than Jeremiah.

[3]See Num. 24:6; Jer. 31:12; Ezek. 31:4–5; 47:12.

[4]A. A. Anderson, I, 57, and Moses Buttenwieser, *The Psalms*, p. 451, suggest a postexilic date. They cite a resemblance to Jer. 17:5–8 to prove that Jeremiah is earlier. They also suggest that the psalm fits into a later stage of OT history. These are unsupported conclusions. Elmer A. Leslie, *The Psalms*, p. 432, views the psalm as written "around 397 BC, when the priestly law was introduced to the restored community in Jerusalem and Judah." His conclusion rests on a subjective interpretation of the psalm. W. O. E. Oesterley, I, 119, arbitrarily assigns the psalm to the mid-third century BC. W. E. Barnes, *The Psalms*, I, 2, suggests a date after Antiochus Epiphanes. He also supports this with inconclusive subjective reasoning.

[5]*Berakoth 9b* states, "Every chapter that was particularly dear to David he commenced with 'Happy' and terminated with 'Happy.'" This observation rests on the fact that Ps. 1 begins with *ʾašrê* and Ps. 2 ends with *ʾašrê* in the last phrase. There is no reason to accept this view. The two psalms have different themes.

[6]Charles H. Spurgeon, *The Treasury of David*, p. 13.

[7]Henry, III, 236.

sees the psalm, along with Psalm 2, as "a sort of preface to the whole Psalter [that brings] out some of its moral and messianic ideas."[8]

I. The Characteristics of the Righteous 1–3

A. The Avoidance of Evil Men 1

1 The godly man does not enter into close association with ungodly men. The psalmist portrays this in three ways. In the first place, the godly man does not seek "counsel" (*ᶜeṣâ*)[9] from the "ungodly" (*rašaᶜ*, better "wicked").[10] He does not "stand in the way,"[11] i.e., participate, with "sinners," those who fall short of God's standards. He does not sit "in the seat of the scornful [*leṣîm*]."[12] The godly man avoids entering into close fellowship with these persons.

There is a clear progression. The verbs "walk," "stand," and "sit" display this progress. First, there is accepting counsel from the wicked. Next, there is participation with them in their actions. Finally, there is close association with them.[13] The godly man avoids all of

---

[8]Sabourin, p. 371.

[9]Mitchell Dahood, *Psalms* in AB, I, 1, argues that *ᶜeṣâ* means "council" here. He relies on late extra-biblical evidence. The meaning of "counsel" as relating to advice or plans, however, is common in the OT.

[10]The word *rašaᶜ* is an antonym of *ṣedeq*, "righteous." It often refers generally to wicked thoughts, actions, or words.

[11]Dahood, I, 1, argues that "way" (*derek*) means "assembly," the "place where dominion is exercised." While *derek* has a broad range of meanings, it is a stretch to translate it as "assembly."

[12]The *leṣ* is the most hardened form of sinner. He scoffs at the righteous, 119:51, and will not accept correction, Prov. 13:1. The OT holds no hope that he will turn to God.

[13]A. Cohen, *The Psalms*, p. 1, describes the progression as "(a) adoption of the principles of the wicked as a rule of life; (b) persistence in the practices of notorious offenders; (c) deliberate association with those who openly mock at religion." Edward J. Kissane, *The Book of Psalms*, p. 2, describes the progression as "evil conduct, obstinacy in sin, and mockery of those who observe the Law." Joseph B. Rotherham, *Studies in the Psalms*, p. 48, sees the progression presenting "a double climax: worse and worse companions, and more and more submission to their influence." W. Ralph Thompson, *Commentary on Psalms 1–72*, in *WBC*, II, 187, classes the steps as yielding to temptation, rebelling against God, and scorning God and righteousness. John Phillips, *Exploring Psalms*, I, 18, notes "the progressions in wickedness—the ungodly, the sinner, the scornful; and the corresponding progression in backsliding—walking, standing, sitting." While phrased differently, these generally set forth the same truths.

these.[14] As a result, he is "blessed" (*ʾašrê*). This plural word indicates the intensity of the blessings that come to the godly. The phrase might be expressed, "O the blessednesses."[15] The word *ʾašrê* always refers to man, never to the Lord. It normally refers to the reward that comes as the result of some action. Here, it denotes the spiritual reward given by God to those who follow His "law," i.e., His instructions, v. 1.

B. The Association with God's Law 2

2 In sharp contrast with the negative description of v. 1, the psalmist now gives a positive description of the godly. He delights in "the law of the Lord," here the whole instruction of the Lord.[16] There is greater value in divine guidance than in human direction. The godly man will "meditate" (*hagâ*)[17] on the Word of God as he mulls it over in his mind. He does this "day and night," indicating that God's Word continually brings spiritual principles to the forefront of his thoughts, v. 2.

C. The Result of Godly Living 3

3 The godly man grows spiritually strong and bears fruit.[18] The psalmist illustrates this by comparing him to a tree. The tree serves

[14]*ʾAbodah Zarah*, in the Talmud, has a perceptive comment on v. 1: "If he did not walk [that way] at all how could he stand there? And if he did not stand there he obviously did not sit [among them], and as he did not sit among them he could not have scorned." The most important decision is to avoid walking with scorners. This keeps you from standing or sitting and subsequently scorning.

[15]Among others, Kidner, *Psalms 1–72*, p. 47, and Gaebelein, *The Book of Psalms*, p. 18, translate *ʾašrê* as "happy." This is not an apt rendering of the word. Happiness normally depends on circumstances. Blessedness depends upon obedience. The godly man is blessed with no regard to the circumstances.

[16]Robert G. Bratcher and William D. Reyburn, *A Translator's Handbook on the Book of Psalms*, p. 17, and E. W. Hengstenberg, *Commentary on the Psalms*, I, 10, understand "law" as the Torah, the first five books of the OT. At the time of the psalmist, much of the OT had been written. There is no reason, in the absence of any limitation in the text, to restrict the term to the books of Moses. Other books as well were considered as being from God.

[17]The word *hagâ* can refer to muttered words, Isa. 8:19; the growling of a lion over its prey, Isa. 31:4; or to the cooing of a dove, Isa. 38:14. This indicates some type of repetition and leads to the thought of meditating, mentally going over a thought.

[18]Note the verbs in vv. 1–3. The perfect tense in v. 1 refers to what has been done in the past. The imperfect tense in v. 2 refers to what is continuing. The *waw* consecutive that introduces v. 3 indicates the future consequences of vv. 1–2.

here to convey a picture of the godly life.[19] It is "planted" (*šatal*)[20] by "the rivers [*palgê*] of water."[21] The plural *palgê* indicates an abundant source of water. Three results come from this work of the Lord on behalf of the godly man. In the first place, he bears fruit. The fruit is not specified since the fruit differs from one godly man to another, depending on the plan of God. The important thing is not the nature of the fruit but its existence. In the second place, the leaf of the tree[22] does not "wither" (*nabel*).[23] Because the godly man relies upon divine guidance, he gives evidence of divine blessing. In the third place, the godly man is successful. Once more, the psalmist does not define his success. He accomplishes his goals in those areas to which the Lord directs him, v. 3.

II. The Characteristics of the Wicked 4–6

A. The Value of the Wicked 4

4 The psalmist directly contrasts the wicked with the godly. While the godly bring forth an abundant harvest of fruit, the wicked have no value at all. They are like "chaff" blown from the threshing floor by

---

[19]Leupold, *Exposition of Psalms*, p. 36, sees the healthy tree as a picture of good works. James G. Murphy, *A Critical and Exegetical Commentary on the Book of Psalms*, p. 54, gives "fruitfulness and growth." *NIB*, IV, 81, understands it as portraying "a stable rootedness," beside the water of "God's life-giving instruction." Weiser, *The Psalms*, p. 105, considers it as speaking of "the meaning and value of life." Delitzsch, I, 86, makes the "green foliage . . . an emblem of faith." Martin Luther, *Luther's Works*, XIV, 302, sees it as "the Word and the doctrine in general." These are possible views. Whatever application we adopt requires some subjective interpretation of the phrase.

[20]The word *šatal* may be rendered as "transplanted." The word occurs nine more times in the OT (92:13; Jer. 17:8; Ezek. 17:8, 10, 22, 23; 19:10, 13; Hos. 9:13). Each time it refers to a figurative planting by God of the godly man or Israel, often pictured as something transplanted (92:13; Ezek. 17:22, 23). God places the godly man where he receives plenty of nourishment and therefore brings forth fruit.

[21]Willem A. VanGemeren, *Psalms*, p. 56, and C. A. Briggs and Emilie Briggs, *A Critical and Exegetical Commentary on the Book of Psalms*, I, 6, understand *palgê* as an irrigation ditch, a possible view. Perowne, I, 110, argues that *palgê* refers to "different branches," not "artificial canals divided and distributed by human labour." The point of the verse does not rest on understanding *palgê* as a natural or man-made source of water. In either case, there is an abundant supply for the godly man.

[22]Kirkpatrick, p. 3, and Luther, XIV, 299, identify the tree as the palm. This is possible, but the spiritual lesson does not depend on a particular tree.

[23]The verb *nabel* often refers to divine judgment, e.g., Isa. 1:30; 24:4; Jer. 8:13.

the wind. In Israel, the farmer would thresh his harvest by having his oxen pull a threshing sledge over the kernels. In some cases, the oxen would pull a grinding-stone that would roll over the grain. The farmer would beat the lighter grains with a flail. These methods would crack the outer shell of the kernel. The farmer would then use his winnowing fan to toss the mixture into the air. Winds blowing across the threshing floor would blow the lighter husks to the side while the heavier kernels would fall almost straight down. Repeated over and over, this process produced pure and usable grain for cooking. The lighter material to the side was the chaff, which had no value to the farmer. This image occurs in the OT to picture those who have no value to God, e.g., Job 21:18; Isaiah 17:13; 29:5. The psalmist speaks of value in the eyes of God. A man may have great value in the eyes of the world and yet be as chaff in God's eyes. True value rests only in the divine evaluation of a man's worth, v. 4.

B. The Judgment of the Wicked 5

5 The wicked man will not "stand" (*qûm*)[24] in the "judgment" (*mišpaṭ*).[25] Because he has spurned righteousness in life, God will spurn him in the judgment.[26] The phrase "sinners in the congregation of the righteous" parallels the first phrase, v. 5.

C. The Destiny of the Wicked 6

6 The Lord "knoweth" (*yadaᶜ*)[27] how the righteous live. The Lord intimately knows the righteous. He therefore cares for them. In sharp contrast, He has no intimate knowledge of the ungodly. He therefore will not care for them. While not saying this explicitly, there is an

---

[24]The word *qûm* occurs broadly throughout the OT. While its basic meaning is "to rise," it also has the derived sense of "maintaining oneself" or "being established," e.g., Josh. 7:12, 13; Nah. 1:6. That is its sense here.

[25]The word *mišpaṭ* occurs widely referring to both judgment and justice. In each case, the context determines the sense.

[26]Dahood, p. 4, asserts that "the psalmist has adapted an ancient Canaanite mythological motif to his Yahwistic, ethical purposes." It is more likely that the Canaanites corrupted the truth than that the psalmist purified a corrupted myth.

[27]The verb *yadaᶜ* occurs widely. It especially refers to knowledge gained from experience but also includes knowledge coming from observation and reasoning. It may also refer to one person's intimate knowledge of another. It occurs with this last sense here.

implied judgment of the wicked. They will "perish" (*ʾabad*),[28] suffering continuing punishment. The verse develops the eternal destiny of the two ways: everlasting care of the righteous and everlasting punishment of the ungodly, v. 6.

PSALM 2

Although the psalm has no title,[29] Acts 4:25–26 (cf. vv. 1–2) indicates that David is the author.[30] This is the first of the messianic psalms.[31] In the opening stanza, David writes concerning opposition to his rule over Israel. This pictures the opposition of man to the rule of the Lord. The rest of the Psalm develops this idea. For this reason, I consider the psalm typically messianic with the spiritual lesson based on historical reality.[32]

---

[28]In general, *ʾabad* refers to destruction. In each case, the context determines whether physical or spiritual destruction is in view. With spiritual destruction, the OT never teaches annihilation. In the Psalms, many passages refer to the everlasting destruction of the wicked, e.g., 9:5; 83:17.

[29]It is common to link Pss. 1 and 2 together. McCann, p. 41, connects them on the basis of literary links. He sees the repeated *ʾašrê* in 1:1 and 2:12 as marking an *inclusio*, joining the psalms. He also takes note of repeated words and thoughts. While it possible that the collector placed the two psalms here as an introduction to the book, this view must remain speculative. The psalms have different themes.

[30]It is common to hold that "David" in Acts 4:25–26 simply refers to the Psalter. Delitzsch, I, 89, makes the psalm anonymous on the ground that no such incident as the psalm describes happened to David. Heinrich A.V. Ewald, *Commentary on the Psalms*, I, 149–50, argues that Solomon is the author. He bases this on the subjective view that the psalm is too elegant for the time of David. Buttenwieser, p. 792, makes the psalm exilic or postexilic, with the author following prophecies of Ezekiel. These views oppose the specific statement of Acts 4:25: "By the mouth of thy servant David hast said." This is more than a general reference to the Psalms as a whole.

[31]The only question about this is whether the psalm is directly messianic or typically messianic. Good men divide on this point. Leupold, p. 43, and Henry, III, 241, make the psalm typically messianic. Arthur G. Clarke, *Analytical Studies in the Psalms*, p. 28, and David Dickson, *A Commentary on the Psalms*, I, 4, consider it directly messianic.

[32]The introduction briefly summarizes the messianic psalms. There is no general agreement as to which psalms should be considered messianic. I have designated Pss. 2, 8, 16, 22, 40, 41, 45, 68, 69, 72, 89, 102, 109, 110, and 118 as messianic.

In addition to the Acts 4:25–26 quote, Acts 13:33 as well as Hebrews 1:5 and 5:5 all refer v. 7 to the Lord. The structure of the psalm is unusually regular. It divides naturally into four three-verse stanzas. Interestingly, David speaks in the first stanza, God the Father speaks in the second, God the Son continues in the third, and God the Spirit closes the Psalm in the fourth stanza.

I. Opposition to the Lord 1–3

A. Questioning of the Opposition 1

1 David asks why the heathen "rage" (*ragaš*)[33] against the Lord and His anointed king. It is appropriate here to translate, "Why are the heathen disturbed?" Why do they "imagine a vain thing" as they plot against his rule, v. 1?

B. Nature of the Opposition 2–3

2–3 These earthly rulers are plotting against the Lord and "his anointed" (*mašîaḥ*).[34] There is no great difference between "kings" and "rulers." These simply occur in poetic variation to name the leaders of nations.[35] At this point in the psalm, the "anointed" refers to David. The OT commonly refers to Israel's king as the "anointed" of the Lord (e.g., I Samuel 24:6, 10; II Samuel 19:21), v. 2. The enemies of God and His anointed try to "break their bands" and "cast away

---

While messianic prophecies occur elsewhere, these psalms uniquely portray the Lord.

[33]*TWOT*, II, 833, understands *ragaš* as "conspire." While the verb *ragaš* only occurs here, related nouns occurs elsewhere with a sense of noise, disturbance.

[34]The word *mašîaḥ* normally refers to the king in Psalms. This is the word that gives rise to the title "Messiah." Although David is in view here, the ultimate fulfillment of the *mašîaḥ* is Jesus Christ. John I. Durham, "The King as 'Messiah' in the Psalms," *RevEx* 81:3 (1984): 426, wrongly limits the word *mašîaḥ*. He notes that "*messiah* in the Psalms refers always and only to the ruling king." I object to his statement that *mašîaḥ* refers "only to the ruling king." Such NT passages as John 1:41 show that the early believers thought of the Lord as the Messiah. Heb. 1:9 quotes Ps. 45:7, where the verbal form of *mašîaḥ* occurs. In Acts 4:25–26, Peter quotes Ps. 2:1–2, where the noun occurs.

[35]G. Rawlinson, *Psalms*, I, 11, understands the "rulers" as "persons having authority, but below the rank of kings. The parallelism here argues that "kings" and "rulers" name the earthly leaders that rebel against the Lord and His anointed.

their cords." The "bands" and "cords" refer to restraining influences that keep the other nations under Israel's domination, v. 3.

II. Reaction of the Father 4–6

4–6 The Lord reacts to the rebellion with scorn. He laughs at His enemies, mocking them for their attempt to overthrow His dominion. He sits in heaven, calmly assessing the rebellion, v. 4. The time comes when He speaks to the rebels in His "wrath" (*ʾap*).[36] The OT and NT alike give many examples of prophetic warnings to the enemies of God. Further, He will "vex" (*bahal*)[37] them, bringing terror to them. This comes from His "sore displeasure" (*ḥarôn*), v. 5.[38] Despite their opposition, God Himself has "set" (better "installed") His king on the "holy hill of Zion" (or "upon Zion, My holy hill"). Just as David ruled from Zion, so the Lord will make it the center of His rule, Micah 4:1–2. Grammatically, the "king" may refer to David, the subject of the first stanza, or to Christ, the subject of the next two stanzas. Unless it is understood as introducing the next stanza, the transition is abrupt. For this reason, it is best viewed as referring to the Son of God. It is clear that the pronoun "I" refers to God the Father, v. 6.

III. Position of the Son 7–9

7–9 The Lord restates the "decree" made in II Samuel 7:14, where the Father claims David as his "son." The Davidic Covenant made there began with David, but its complete fulfillment is in Christ. The NT makes this clear by quoting this verse in Acts 13:33; Hebrews 1:5; 5:5. Acts 13:33 defines the "day" as that of the Lord's resurrection. At that point, the Atonement is complete and the Lord is appointed as the King over redeemed mankind, v. 7. The Father had also appointed the Son as King over the world. Many passages assert the Lord's rule over Gentile nations, e.g., Isaiah 11:4; 42:1–4; 45:23,

---

[36]The word *ʾap* lit. refers to the nose. Since the nose often dilates when a person becomes angry, *ʾap* came as well to represent anger.

[37]The verb *bahal* refers to the "terror" or "trouble" that comes from something that threatens disaster. This is often an unexpected danger.

[38]The word *ḥarôn* refers to the "burning" of God's wrath. The word occurs forty-one times in the OT, normally referring to God. Ps. 58:9 and Jer. 25:38 are exceptions.

v. 8. He will "break" (*ra*ʿ*a*ʿ)[39] the heathen. The "rod of iron" is a metaphorical picture of the power that shatters those who oppose Him. Revelation 12:5 and 19:15 refer the passage to the rule of Christ. The result is that the heathen are broken into pieces like the shattering of a dropped pot, v. 9.

IV. Instruction by the Spirit 10–12

10–12 The Holy Spirit now urges the kings of the earth to submit themselves to the rule of the Son of God.[40] He urges the kings and judges of mankind to receive the exhortation, v. 10.[41] They should serve the Lord with "fear" (*yir*ʾ*â*),[42] an attitude of reverence toward Him. They should also "rejoice with trembling." This phrase lends itself naturally to the thought of rejoicing in the Lord while at the same time fearing to offend Him, v. 11. They should "kiss the son [*bar*]."[43] The use of the Aramaic *bar* for "son" is unusual but not

---

[39]The Hebrew is *ra*ʿ*a*ʿ, "break." The NT follows the LXX, however, which translates ποιμανεῖς, "rule." This translates *ra*ʿ*â*, "to pasture, tend" and thus "to rule," interpreting the OT to emphasize the power of the Lord. Kidner, pp. 51–52, and Moll, p. 58, accept the change to *ra*ʿ*â*. This ignores the parallelism with v. 9*b*, "dash them in pieces like a potter's vessel."

[40]Kirkpatrick, p. 11, and Thompson, p. 188, make the poet speak here. While the human author pens these words, it is clear that he declares the divine will to the kings. The spokesman may be either the Father, as in vv. 4–6, or the Spirit, the third member of the Trinity. From a poetical point of view, it is better to see the Spirit here. Otherwise, we have here the words of the Father, Who has already spoken once.

[41]Scroggie, p. 54, relates that Henry VIII had John Lambert burned at the stake at Smithfield in 1538. Lambert admonished the king with v. 10. As he burned, he lifted his finger and said, "None but Christ, none but Christ."

[42]The word *yir*ʾ*â* is the same word that occurs elsewhere with the expression "fear of the Lord" in both Psalms and Proverbs, e.g., Pss. 19:9; 34:11; 111:10. Rather than connoting an intense dread, it refers to a reverential trust in the Lord. This is possible to those who willingly receive Him first as their Savior and then as their Lord.

[43]Among others, Kidner, p. 53, and Murphy, p. 64, understand *bar* as from *barar*, "to purify." Because of the lack of a definite article or preposition, they adopt an adverbial sense for *bar*. This gives something like "kiss purely," i.e., "give homage." The argument is grammatically correct and is supported by some early versions, but it is weakened by the fact that nowhere else does *bar* have an adverbial sense. Kissing occurs elsewhere as an act of homage, I Sam. 10:1; I Kings 19:18; Hos. 13:2. The lack of a definite article is not unusual in Hebrew. Dahood, I, 13, transfers the phrase "kiss the son" to the close of v. 11. After revocalizing, he translates, "O mortal men." There is no textual support for the change. Buttenwieser, p. 794, derives *bar* from *barar* and translates "kiss the ground." The verb *barar*, however,

unique; cf. Proverbs 31:2. The use of loan words from other languages is common in every language. The idea of "kiss[ing] the son" is that of paying homage to Him by kissing His feet; cf. I Samuel 10:1; I Kings 19:18. Failing to show respect to the Son will bring His judgment. Those who experience this will "perish" (*ʾabad*, see 1:6) when He kindles His "wrath [*ʾap*, see v. 2] . . . but a little." Rather than indicating the quantity of the Son's wrath, this last phrase refers to time, "suddenly." The Lord responds with judgment to those who refuse Him. He promises that those who "trust" (*ḥasâ*)[44] in Him, however, will be "blessed" (*ʾašrê*, see 1:1), v. 12.

PSALM 3

The title[45] sets this lament psalm at the time of Absalom's rebellion against David, II Samuel 15. According to v. 5, David writes

means "to purify, select" and thus "to winnow." The noun *bar* does not mean "ground." Jennings, *The Psalms*, pp. 12–13, suggests "chosen one." While this can rest on the verbal root, *bar* nowhere else has this meaning. William L. Holliday, "A New Proposal for the Crux in Psalm II 12," *VT* 28:1 (1978): 110–12, rejects the meaning of "son" because of the use of *bᵉnî*, "my son," in v. 7. He revocalizes the MT, a solution without textual support. Verse 7 uses *ben* because it refers back to II Sam. 7:14 where this word occurs. Since v. 12 is prophetic, not referring to David, the word changes.

[44]The verb *ḥasâ* refers directly to "taking refuge" and figuratively indicates "trust," cf. 91:14; 118:8–9.

[45]The form of the title, *lᵉdawid*, is the normal way of designating the authorship. The *lamed* preposition is the *lamed auctoris*, showing David as the author. The same grammatical construction indicates psalms belonging to other authors of the psalms, e.g., *lišlomoh* (Solomon); *lᵉʾasap* (Asaph); *libnê-qoraḥ* (sons of Korah). See G.K.C. 129 *c*; Waltke and O'Connor 11.2.10*d*. This use occurs regularly throughout the Psalms. It also appears elsewhere in the OT Song of Sol. 1:1, *lišlomoh* (Solomon); Isa. 38:9, *lᵉḥizqîyahû* (Hezekiah); Hab. 3:1, *laḥᵃbaqqûq* (Habakkuk). James D. Nogalski, "From Psalm to Psalms to Psalter," *An Introduction to Wisdom Literature and the Psalms*, pp. 38–42, discusses possible ways of understanding the *lamed* preposition in the titles. He notes that it can mean ownership, "belonging to. . . ," or indicate the destination of a psalm, as in "for the choir director." It can indicate a dedication to someone as in 18:50, "to David and to his seed for evermore." For a variety of reasons, he concludes that we must evaluate each psalm individually to determine its relation to David. While Nogalski is correct in noting the different uses of the *lamed*

this song[46] in the morning.[47] David now encourages himself with the thought of God's protection. He determines that he will not fear the army that Absalom has set against him. The Lord is able to deliver him. With these words, David illustrates the proper trust that all Christians should display as they face personal opposition.

This is a "Psalm [*mizmôr*] of David." The *mizmôr* is a song to be set to music.[48] The word *mizmôr* occurs only in psalm titles, although related words occur elsewhere in the OT. The use of the word *selâ* in vv. 2, 4, 8, also considered a musical term, further reinforces this. The term *selâ* indicates a pause for reflection upon what has just been said.[49]

I. The Lament of the Psalmist 1–2

1–2 David laments the great number involved in the rebellion against him. This agrees with the record in II Samuel, which says that Absalom "stole the hearts of the men of Israel." Then II Samuel 15:12 states, "The conspiracy was strong: for the people increased continually with Absalom." After Ahithophel advised Absalom to choose an army of twelve thousand men (17:1), Hushai persuaded him that he needed a larger army (17:11). II Samuel 18:7 mentions "a

---

preposition, the weight of Jewish tradition supports its use in the titles in identifying David as the author. Further, nothing in the Davidic psalms makes this difficult to accept. The arguments raised against David's authorship have been answered in the introductions to the individual psalms.

[46]Anderson, I, 70–71, rejects David's authorship because of the phrase "his holy hill." He asserts, "It is far from certain that Zion was thought of as Yahweh's holy mountain in the time of David." Anderson also notes that the psalm does not mention David's enemies. The phrase "his holy hill" occurs elsewhere only in Ps. 99. The shorter phrase "holy hill," however, occurs in Pss. 2, 15, both Davidic psalms. As for mentioning David's enemies, vv. 1, 2, 6, make it clear that David faced opposition. David does not always name his foes. Buttenwieser, p. 400, makes the psalm postexilic, before the Maccabean period. His reasoning, however, is subjective and therefore suspect. Rotherham, p. 58, interprets v. 7 as though the author is Hezekiah, adapting David's material to his own victory over Assyria. That verse, however, may be understood differently. There is no reason to reject David's authorship.

[47]Rawlinson, I, 17, and Fausset, III, 108, date the psalm on the evening before the battle against Absalom's army, II Sam. 18:1–8. Rawlinson explains v. 5 as referring to the previous nights in which he has slept. Hengstenberg, I, 42, sets the psalm in the first evening of David's flight from his son.

[48]For further discussion of *mizmôr*, see the introduction to Ps. 30.

[49]A brief excursus discussing *selâ* follows the commentary on this psalm.

great slaughter that day of twenty thousand men." It is no wonder that David brings his danger to the Lord's attention, v. 1. Many opposing David deny the possibility of the Lord's help for him. Shimei's curse of David in II Samuel 16:7–8 illustrates this. There were undoubtedly others who felt that God had rejected the king. David calls attention to his plight with the word "selah" (see the following excursus), v. 2.

II. The Trust of the Psalmist 3–4

3–4 The king expresses his trust in the Lord. The Lord is his "shield" (*magen*),[50] his defense from the attack of the enemy. The Lord is also David "glory," the One Who will restore glory to him.[51] He relies on the Lord as "the lifter up of [his] head." The phrase is an idiom indicating that the Lord delivers him in trials; cf. II Kings 25:27; Psalm 27:6, v. 3. David has cried out to the Lord. The imperfect verb suggests that he repeated his cry over and over as he pled with the Lord for deliverance. Thinking of the Lord's presence in the holy of holies, David states that the Lord had heard his prayer from "His holy hill." This is Mt. Zion, the location of the tabernacle. The word "selah" draws attention to the Lord's gracious work, v. 4.

III. The Confidence of the Psalmist 5–6

5–6 Although the danger was great, David lay on his pallet and slept. In the morning he woke, sustained by the Lord, v. 5. David refuses to fear the enemy. Although there may be ten thousand arrayed

---

[50]The *magen* is the small round shield carried by soldiers, II Kings 19:32; II Chron. 14:8. It often poetically pictures the defense given by the Lord, e.g., Gen. 15:1; Deut. 33:29. Dahood, I, 16, relies on Ugaritic to revocalize *magen* to *magan*, "suzerain." The argument is subjective. The word *magen* is not rare. It occurs over sixty times and fits smoothly into the verse.

[51]Bratcher and Reyburn, p. 37, reason that the word "glory" (*kabôd*) may mean "reputation." Since David's reputation depended upon victory over his enemy, they translate "victory." The reasoning is subjective. "Victory" occurs nowhere else as a translation of *kabôd*. Leupold, p. 61, relates vv. 3–4 to the past. The Lord is the source of David's glory as king of a nation. Harman, p. 76, speaks of the Lord as David's "glorious One." These views are possible. I have related the phrase to David's present troubles as being more logically on his mind. Both the previous and following phrases describe the Lord as the source of David's blessing. The Lord is the source of David's protection, his glory as a king, and his deliverance from danger.

against him, he will not "be afraid" (*yare'*, see 2:11). David is not in awe of the enemy's size because he knows that God is greater, v. 6.[52]

IV. The Deliverance of the Psalmist 7–8

7–8 David pleads with the Lord to "arise." He recognizes that the Lord has allowed the rebellion to develop. It is now time to take action against David's enemies and to "save" him, giving him victory over the rebels. He bases his prayer on the deliverances that God has given him in the past. In those cases, the Lord has "smitten" (*nakâ*) all David's enemies "upon the cheek bone." He has "broken [*šabar*][53] the teeth of the ungodly."[54] These idiomatic expressions picture the victories God has given David in the past, v. 7.[55] David recognizes that deliverance comes from the Lord. The final phrase should be phrased as a prayer: "Let thy blessing be upon thy people." In view of past deliverances, David confidently makes this plea to the Lord. Once more, he draws attention to the work of the Lord with the word "selah," v. 8.

---

[52]Rawlinson, I, 17, and Phillips, I, 34, continue the third part of the psalm to the end. They argue that the lack of the word *selâ* after v. 6 supports this. This misunderstands the purpose of *selâ*. It would be boastful for David to place a *selâ* after v. 6 since he speaks there of his personal feelings.

[53]The verb *nakâ* has a broad semantic range. It covers everything from a simple blow on someone or something to actually killing. The verb *šabar* is strong, often indicating complete destruction.

[54]The NIV translates the verbs in 7*b* as imperatives: "Strike all my enemies . . . break the teeth. . . ." The perfect tense verbs here, however, give the basis for David's prayer in 7*a*. God has delivered him in the past. David relies on this past help to give him confidence for the future. *NIB*, IV, 694, and Cohen, p. 7, understand the verbs as prophetic perfects, expressing a future so certain that David states it as having already happened. Gaebelein, p. 29, also sets the action in the future but considers the passage as messianic. This view goes beyond the context.

[55]The Talmud gives a fanciful rabbinic interpretation of v. 7*b*. *Berakoth* 54*b* refers the verse to the defeat of Og, which it relates to the casting down of "great stones," Josh. 10:11. Supposedly, Og wanted to cast a stone at the camp of Israel. He asked, "'How large is the camp of Israel? Three parasangs [about twelve miles]. I will go and uproot a mountain the size of three parasangs and cast it upon them and kill them.' He went and uprooted a mountain of the size of three parasangs and carried it on his head. But the Holy One, blessed be He, sent ants which bored a hole in it, so that it sank around his neck. He tried to pull it off, but his teeth projected on each side, and he could not pull it off. This is referred to in the text, *Thou hast broken the teeth of the wicked*." The story rests on reading *shirbabta*, "lengthened," for *shibbarta*, "broken." Aside from the fanciful nature of the interpretation, there is no textual support for the reading.

EXCURSUS: SELAH

The word "selah" occurs for the first time in Psalm 3. The word occurs a total of seventy-one times in the Psalms and three times in the psalm in Habakkuk 3. In Book I of the Psalms, it occurs seventeen times in nine psalms; in the second book, thirty times in seventeen psalms; in the third book, twenty times in eleven psalms. The fourth book does not use the term. In the fifth book, the two Davidic psalms use it a total of four times.

In general, interpretations of the word fall into three categories. These views largely depend on the derivation given to "selah."[56] The first group relates "selah" to raising the voice or music to a higher pitch. Moll, p. 31, follows this position. He derives it from *salal*, "to lift up," and refers it to "a stronger application of musical means . . . especially from the choir of priests, with their long trumpets . . . in connection with the loud sounding of harps and cithers from the choir or the Levitical orchestra." Harman, *Commentary on the Psalms*, p. 76, calls it "a technical term which probably indicates louder musical accompaniment." Delitzsch, I, 103, likewise refers it to the instruments rather than the singing. He describes it as calling for "the joining in of the orchestra, or a reinforcement of the instruments, or even a transition from *piano* to *forte*." In view of the fact that Psalms 3, 9, 24, and 46 end with "selah," it is difficult to see how it can signal a change in the voice or music, both of which would presumably close at the end of a psalm.

The second group involves an older interpretation, not widely held today. This sees the word as having a sense of "always." The Vulgate translated "selah" as *semper*, "always" or "forever." The Talmud, *Erubim 54a*, states "the process to which it refers never ceases." The Targum of Psalms routinely translates it as "forever."[57]

The third group has the largest number of advocates. In some way, the word indicates a pause for an instrumental interlude. The follow-

[56]There are a variety of other views as well. Eaton, p. 16, says that it likely indicated "the assembly of worshippers [*sic*] should bow to the ground." T. K. Cheyne, *The Book of Psalms*, I, 11, makes "selah" a corruption of אלחים. Buttenwieser, p. 45, dogmatically states, "It is nowhere a part of the text."

[57]Norman H. Snaith, "Selah," *VT* 2:56, also adopts this position but makes the word an early fourth century BC insertion. The view lacks textual support and goes contrary to the titles that indicate early authorship in many of the psalms.

ing are representative. The LXX translated it as διάψαλμα, a "musical interlude." Samuel Raphael Hirsch, *The Psalms*, I, 17, derives it from *slh*, "to the basket." He likens this to collecting the thought in the mind for meditation. Sabourin, p. 13, understands it as "a pause in the singing while the people prostrate themselves in prayer." Cyril A. Rodd, *Psalms 1–72*, p. 11, considers the word "an instrumental interlude between the strophes of a psalm." Thirtle, p. 145, suggests that it introduces new paragraphs in the psalm.[58] Fausset, p. 109, derives it from *šᵉlâ*, "rest," and therefore refers it to a pause in the singing while the instruments continue to play.

Since the OT does not define the word *selâ*, the conclusion must come from its use. The word "selah" occurs in four broad categories. By far the greatest number of passages that end with "selah" offer praise or worship to the Lord.[59] In the second category, the psalmist describes his personal need or some national need.[60] The final two categories are smaller. In the third group, the psalmist appeals to or warns others.[61] The fourth set of verses gives prayers to the Lord.[62]

I have adopted the third view based on where the word does not occur as well as where it occurs. It regularly occurs after a statement offering praise to the Lord. In many passages, "selah" concludes a statement describing a threat to the psalmist or the nation. It also concludes statements of prayer. It marks an appeal or a warning to others. In all of these cases, it is appropriate to reflect on what has been said. A brief pause is in keeping with the text. The word "selah," however, does not occur after a personal statement by the psalmist where it would be boastful to direct regard to him by calling attention to what he has said.

---

[58]There are several places where "selah" occurs in the middle of a paragraph, e.g., 57:3; 68:7, 19, 32, or at the end of a psalm, 3:8; 9:20; 24:10; 46:11. Thirtle argues that in these last four, the word may be out of place or the psalm should be joined to the following psalm. No textual evidence supports his view.

[59]"Selah" occurs in the following verses in this category: 3:8; 9:16; 21:2; 24:10; 32:5, 7; 44:8; 46:7, 11; 47:4; 48:8; 50:6; 55:19; 57:3; 60:4; 62:8; 66:4, 7; 67:4; 68:7, 19, 32; 75:3; 76:3, 9; 77:15; 81:7; 84:4; 85:2; 87:3 (praising Jerusalem as the dwelling of God); 89:4, 37; Hab. 3:3, 9, 13.

[60]This category includes the following verses: 3:2, 4; 7:5; 32:4; 39:5, 11; 46:3; 52:3; 54:3; 55:7; 57:6; 77:3, 9; 82:2; 83:8; 88:7, 10; 89:45, 48; 140:3, 5; 143:6.

[61]The following verses belong in this group: 4:2, 4; 24:6; 49:13; 52:5; 66:7.

[62]"Selah" concludes the prayer in 9:20; 20:3; 59:5, 13; 61:4; 67:1; 84:8; and 140:8.

In keeping with this purpose of "selah," it is appropriate to pause briefly in the oral reading of a psalm. This signals the hearers to think on what has been read. The other suggested uses—raising the voice to a higher pitch, something that continues forever—problems. Why should the voice be raised to a higher pitch or be changed to a new voice? How can we justify treating personal or national needs as continuing forever? Once the Lord has given deliverance, there is no need to continue dwelling on the need. The thought of an instrumental interlude seems trivial unless it is meant to stimulate reflection on what has been said. This brings us to the third view as being the most likely.

PSALM 4

This is a "psalm [*mizmôr*, see 3, intro.] of David." He assigns the psalm to the "chief musician" (*m*ᵉ*naṣṣeaḥ*).[63] This word occurs in fifty-five psalms and in Habakkuk 3:19 as a title related to worship. It refers to the leader of the temple worship. As we read the psalms, we see that their use in worship is natural. It is still appropriate to include the psalms in both personal and public expressions of devotion to the Lord.

The word "Neginoth" (*n*ᵉ*gînôt*) occurs elsewhere in the titles of Psalms 6, 54, 55, 61, 67, 76, and in Habakkuk 3:19, the musical

[63]James William Thirtle, *The Titles of the Psalms: Their Nature and Meaning Explained*, p. 13, draws on the example of Hab. 3:1–19, in which the dedication to the "chief musician" and the musical instructions come at the end of Habakkuk's psalm. From this, he concludes that the "chief musician" line "has, in every case, been placed at the beginning of THE PSALM FOLLOWING that to which it rightly belongs." While it is possible that this might have happened once or twice, it is difficult to see how the scribes could have done this fifty-five times. To further argue against this, a musical direction introduces Ps. 42, the first psalm in Book II. Thirtle finds no problem in appending it to Ps. 41. It is difficult to see how the musical notation could move to a separate collection of the psalms. The phrase "chief musician" occurs in Books I, II, III, and V. These were compiled at different times, yet Thirtle has the same error happening in all four books. This could have happened only if a single scribe repeated the error fifty-five times as he copied the book late, after all the collections had been made, and this one copy became the sole text copied in following years while all of the other copies vanished.

instructions for that book. It refers to stringed instruments.[64] We do not know the nature of the instrument. The psalm gives no indication of the background to its writing. Many authors relate it to Psalm 3.[65] If we accept this connection, the threat to David in the psalm comes naturally from Absalom's rebellion.[66] David writes Psalm 3 as a morning hymn of confidence in the Lord. Psalm 4 is an evening hymn. David prepares for sleep with these devotional thoughts expressing his continued confidence in the Lord.

I. Prayer of David 1–2

1–2 David calls upon the "God of my righteousness" (*ᵓᵉlohê ṣidqî*), i.e., "my righteous God," the God in Whom he confidently trusts.[67] This God has "enlarged" him in times of distress. David thinks of times when others have tried to shut him in but the Lord has given him freedom from their attacks; cf. 118:5.[68] He now asks the Lord[69]

---

[64]The word also occurs with different translations in 69:12; 77:6; Job 30:9; Isa. 38:20; and Lam. 3:14 and 5:14. In each of these places, the thought is of songs accompanied by stringed instruments.

[65]Delitzsch, I, 109, notes that Pss. 3 and 4 are the only psalms that use the phrase *rabbîm ᵓomrîm*, "many say" (3:2; 4:6). Harman, p. 78, notes as well the common use of the word *ṣar* ("foes," "distress"), 3:1; 4:1*b*; the word "glory," 3:3*b*; 4:2*b*; David's prayer and God's answer, 3:4; 4:1*a*, 3*b*; and the reference to lying down and sleeping, 3:5; 4:8. Clarke, I, 30, sees both as "belonging to the same crisis of [David's] life." Scroggie, I, 59, holds that the "selah" closing Ps. 3 means "Pause before going on." Ps. 4 is the continuation.

[66]Based on v. 6, Dahood, I, 23, calls the psalm "a prayer for rain." He concludes, "The 'good' par excellence in Palestine is the rain." His reasoning is doubtful.

[67]Perowne, I, 127, and Calvin, I, 38, refer the phrase *ᵓᵉlohê ṣidqî* to the God Who upholds David in his righteous cause. The grammatical structure, however, is that of an attributive genitive. The pronominal suffix modifies *ᵓᵉlohê*. So Waltke and O'Connor, p. 150.

[68]The idiom occurs again in the Psalms only at 25:17, where David refers to troubles being set loose on him. Rawlinson, I, 23, understands the idiom as being given "prosperity." This leads to the same thought, that David gains victory over his trials. W. E. Barnes, I, 17–18, rejects the thought that David has been delivered since the next clause records a prayer for mercy. David has, however, gained freedom during those critical first hours. There may be more trouble ahead, but he recognizes here the freedom given him by the Lord.

[69]Spurgeon, p. 23, aptly says, "He who has helped in six troubles will [not] leave us in the seventh. God . . . will never cease to help us until we cease to need."

to again extend "mercy" (*ḥanan*, better "grace")[70] in response to his "prayer" (*tᵉpillâ*)[71], v. 1.

David addresses his foes, "O ye sons of men [*ʾîš*]." The word *ʾîš* often refers to man generally. When there is any nuance, it is of man's greatness or dignity. The term occurs here ironically as of men who are great in their own eyes. They look down on David, turning his "glory into shame." His "glory" is his public position as Israel's king. His "shame" (or "disgrace," *kᵉlimmâ*) is his public humiliation.[72] Connecting the psalm with Psalm 3, this refers naturally to David's enforced flight to escape his son's threat. How long will they love vain things? How long will they seek "leasing" (better, "deceitful things," *kazab*)?[73] David calls attention to his plight with the word "selah," v. 2.

II. Protection from the Lord 3–4

3–4 David expresses the fact that the Lord has set apart for Himself the "godly" (*ḥasîd*) man.[74] The Lord will therefore hear David's prayer. This is not a boastful statement. David simply recognizes the many promises given by God that He will answer the prayers of those who serve Him faithfully; cf. 34:15; 55:16–17; 91:15, v. 3. David urges his foes to "stand in awe" (better "be angry," *ragaz*)[75] but

[70]The word *ḥanan* refers to freely given favor. This gracious action normally comes from the Lord but also is shown by godly men. Depending on the context, it may refer to favor, grace, extending mercy, or showing pity.

[71]The noun *tᵉpillâ* is the most common word for prayer in the OT. From the root *pll*, *tᵉpillâ* invites the Lord to intervene or to make a judgment. The word often refers to intercessory prayer.

[72]The word *kᵉlimmâ*, from the root *kalam*, has the general sense of "shame." Where the word stands by itself, it often refers to public humiliation. The context must guide in understanding the sense.

[73]The noun *kazab* refers to speaking that which is false. The word emphasizes the actual act of lying.

[74]The word *ḥasîd* has a wide range of meaning. It describes both man's responsibility to God and God's relationship to man. Such translations as "godly," "holy," "saints," "merciful," etc., occur in Psalms. There is often a sense of loyalty associated with *ḥasîd*.

[75]The verb *ragaz* has the general sense "to tremble, be agitated." Paul uses this phrase in Ephesians 4:26 (LXX), "Be ye angry, and sin not." Paul admonishes the believers to be angry against sin but to keep their anger under control. David admonishes his enemies to likewise control their anger.

"sin [*ḥaṭa*ʾ][76] not." Through they may rage against David, they should refrain from sin.[77] They should "commune with [their] own heart" (or "meditate in your heart") as they consider David's position with relation to the Lord. This would cause them to "be still," no longer making reckless accusations against David.[78] Once more, David lays stress on his statement with the word "selah," v. 4.

III. Worship of the Lord 5–6

5–6 Still speaking to his foes, David urges them to offer sacrifices to the Lord. The sense, of course, is of sincere worship; cf. 51:17. This action would show their "righteousness" and "trust" in the Lord, v. 5. David now turns to his followers. Some of them have become discouraged. They say, "Who will shew us any good?" as though there is no help for them. David, however, continues to trust the Lord for deliverance. He prays that the Lord will enlighten their way (cf. 44:3; 89:15) by looking upon them with favor, v. 6.

IV. Confidence of David 7–8

7–8 David describes the "gladness" (or "joy") the Lord has given him. This is greater than the joy that comes from the abundance his enemies possess. David refers to the situation described in II Samuel 17:26–29. Having fled for his life, he did not have adequate provisions for himself and his followers. Despite this, he finds joy in the Lord he serves, v. 7. With this confidence, he anticipates lying down for the evening's rest. He will "both" (*yaḥdaw*) lie down in peace and sleep. The adverb *yaḥdaw* here indicates a union, togetherness, bringing

---

[76]The word *ḥaṭa*ʾ is the primary term for sin in the OT. It generally has the sense of falling short of a standard, in this case the standard of God's law.

[77]*NIB*, IV, 697, refers the phrase to "the faithful" as David exhorts them "to stand firm in their identity and not be led into temptation by their opponents." While this is possible, the context better supports David's foes as the object. Verse 2 refers to those who oppose David, while vv. 4–5 naturally refer to the same group.

[78]Paul R. Raabe, "Deliberate Ambiguity in the Psalter," *JBL* 110:2 (1991): 215, gives *dmm* as an example of ambiguity. Is it *dmm* I, "be still, silent," or *dmm* II, "weep, wail"? On the basis of the parallelism with the first phrase, VanGemeren, p. 83, sees this as a call to "wail" over sin. The word *damam* occurs about thirty times. *KB* I, 226, lists three references, including this verse, where it should be taken as *dmm* II. In none of these verses is this translation demanded. Here, the thought of silence parallels the initial thought as well as that of wailing.

both the lying down and the sleeping together.[79] David's confidence in the Lord is such that he anticipates rest in the night. The Lord Himself will give him safety through the night, v. 8.

PSALM 5

David offers this morning prayer to the Lord; cf. v. 3.[80] We do not know the occasion of writing except that David faced some form of opposition. The grouping of the psalm with Psalms 3 and 4 may indicate that it also deals with Absalom's rebellion. David may also have written before taking the army into the field against some foreign threat. We do not have enough information to be certain.[81] By leaving the background unstated, the psalm sets a pattern for believers today. In times of trial, it is still appropriate to rely on the Lord.

As is done in fifty-five of the psalms, David dedicates his meditation to the "chief musician" (*m^enaṣṣeaḥ*, see 4, intro.). The psalm is to be accompanied by "Nehiloth" (*neḥîlôt*), an unknown musical direction that occurs only here.[82]

---

[79]Rawlinson, I, 24, gives a sense of time to *yaḥdaw* as though David lies down and "at once" falls asleep. The idea comes more from the union between lying down and sleeping than from the word itself. The adverb does not convey any sense of time.

[80]Weiser, p. 123, rejects David's authorship on the basis that v. 3 refers to statements made "in the Temple during the offering of the morning sacrifice." The verse is general, however, and need not be limited to the worship ritual.

[81]Some read v. 7 as though David was in Jerusalem with access to the tabernacle. This leads to speculation that David wrote the psalm shortly before Absalom's rebellion. Rotherham, p. 64, dates it "at the time when the rebellion of Absalom was being fomented by men who were yet maintaining the appearance of loyalty to the king." Hirsch, I, 31, understands David's foe as Ahithophel. Cowles, p. 23; Scroggie, I, 63; and Phillips, I, 43, also date it at this time. More generally, Cheyne, I, 14, makes the psalm a prayer of pious Jews asking "for guidance and for the overthrow of Israel's foes." We cannot be dogmatic as to the background.

[82]The meaning of *neḥîlôt* is uncertain. *TWOT*, II, 569, relates it to *ḥalîl*, "flute," but also suggests that it "may be the name of a melody." Eaton, p. 38, translates it "flutes." Leupold, p. 74, tentatively translates "the lots." He suggests that the psalm contrasts "the distinctive lot of the godly with that of the ungodly." Cohen, p. 10, offers "wind instruments." Murphy, 78, translates it as "one the heritages," and calls it an "obscure reference to the destinies of the righteous and the wicked." Delitzsch,

I. The Request of David 1–3

1–3 David asks the Lord to hear his prayer. The term "meditation" (*hagîg*) occurs only here and 39:3. The word comes from the unused root *hgg*, "to muse." The parallelism lets us see David's "words" as his meditation, v. 1. The meditation is vocalized, however, and David repeats his request that the Lord hear his "cry" (*šawʿî*). The word *šawʿî* refers to a cry for help. David comes to the Lord as his "King" and his "God." For David, the king of Israel, to recognize the Lord as his King foreshadows the time when the Lord will be the King of kings on earth. David goes beyond this in recognizing the Lord as the One will serve and the One Who deserves worship. David will "pray" (*ʾetpallal*)[83] to Him, v. 2. David states his intention to pray "in the morning" as he begins his day. He will "direct" (*ʾeʿerak*)[84] his prayer to the Lord and will "look up" (or "watch closely") to see the Lord's response to his need, v. 3.

II. The Requirement for Holiness 4–6

4–6 David recognizes God's desire for holiness in those who come to Him. The Lord has no pleasure in wickedness and will not let evil persons "dwell" (*gûr*)[85] with Him. Since the evil person has no relationship to the Lord, He cannot stay with Him, v. 4. The "foolish" (*hôlelîm*)[86] cannot stand before God. Instead, the Lord "hates"

I, 120, mentions the talmudic use of this word, "swarms," which may indicate "the beginning of a popular melody to which the Psalm is adapted." The LXX renders the term κληρονομούς, "concerning the heiress." We cannot be sure of anything more than that *neḥîlôt* is a musical notation of some kind.

[83]The verb *palal* occurs in the *hitpaʿêl* 80 out of 84 occurrences in the OT. It has the basic sense of "to intercede." It is the word most often used for prayer.

[84]The word *ʿarak* has the basic sense "to prepare." Delitzsch, I, 121, notes that it occurs elsewhere of preparing wood for the sacrifice, of arranging the pieces of a sacrifice, and of other activities related to worship. For this reason, he understands it here of preparing prayer "as a spiritual sacrifice." While a pleasant devotional thought, this goes further than the text clearly states. The word also refers to Rahab's arranging stalks of flax over the spies, to armies preparing for battle, to imposing a tax, to setting a table, and to ordering a life, none of which refer to sacrifice.

[85]The verb *gûr* refers to "sojourning," living among those whom you are not related.

[86]The participle *hôlelîm* particularly refers to those who boast of their abilities and accomplishments.

(*śaneʾ*)[87] those who work iniquity. While the Lord's love encompasses all men, the wickedness of this group makes them an abomination to Him, v. 5. He will "destroy" (*ʾabad*, see 1:6) those who speak "leasing" (or "lies," *kazab*, see 4:2). He loathes those who are "bloody," guilty of murder, and "deceitful." These final words may point directly to Absalom, David's son who leads the rebellion against him. Whomever David thinks of, his description includes seven negative terms.[88] This poetically represents David's foe as completely opposing the holiness required by God of those who come to Him, v. 6.

III. The Resolve to Worship 7–9

7–9 In contrast with the wicked, David anticipates returning to the "house," the tabernacle, for worship. This blessing will come not because of anything David has done but graciously out of the abundance of God's "mercy" (or "steadfast love," *ḥesed*).[89] In "fear" (*yirʾâ*, see 2:11), speaking of the reverence David has for the Lord, he will worship toward the "temple" (*hêkal*),[90] the earthly tabernacle where the Lord dwelled among His people, v. 7. David prays that the Lord will guide him in the ways of righteousness because of the threat from his enemies. Were they to triumph over him, he would no longer be able to follow the path of service to the Lord. David asks the Lord to make his way "straight," free from anything that would turn him aside from carrying out God's will, v. 8. David's enemies do not speak faithfully. They inwardly are "very wickedness" (*hawwôt*,

---

[87]The word *śaneʾ* expresses a broad range of negative emotions, not only hate but also such feelings as dislike, aversion, and detestation. The context in each case must determine the strength of the feeling involved.

[88]The terms are "wickedness," "evil," "foolish" (or "boasters"), "workers of iniquity," "leasing" (or "lies"), "bloody" (or "bloodthirsty"), and "deceitful."

[89]The word *ḥesed* is from the same root as *ḥasîd*, see 4:3. It is similar in meaning with the translation of "steadfast [or 'loyal'] love" normally expressing this sense.

[90]Moll, p. 75, understands the "house" as God's heavenly palace. Gaebelein, p. 34, relates it to the temple on earth during the Millennium. With the earthly tabernacle still standing at Jerusalem, David more likely looks forward to the time when he can return to worship God as he has done in the past. God's loyalty to him will bring this to pass. The noun *hêkal* refers to a place of dwelling. As such, it may refer to either the heavenly or earthly tabernacle or to the palace of a king. The context here suggests the earthly tabernacle where God dwelled with His people.

or "destruction").[91] The plural *hawwôt* intensifies the destruction they would bring upon others. Their "throat," again their speech, is an "open sepulchre" ready to encase whomever it may deceive. They use their "tongue" to "flatter," implying that they turn others from the Lord through this means. Paul uses the last half of this verse in describing the wicked, Romans 3:13, v. 9.

IV. The Renewal of the Prayer 10–12

10–12 David prays that God will "destroy" (*ʾašam*, better "hold guilty") his foes. May "their own counsels" be such as would lead them to defeat. David asks that God would thrust them away because of their "transgressions" (*pešaᶜ*) against Him. The word *pešaᶜ* expresses rebellion. David's enemies are rebellious against God, v. 10. In sharp contrast, those who "put their trust" (*ḥasâ*, see 2:12) in the Lord may rejoice. The verb *ḥasâ* refers directly to "taking refuge." It figuratively indicates "trust." Those doing this may "shout for joy" (*ranan*).[92]

The phrase "because thou defendest [*sakak*][93] them" begins a new thought that continues to the end of the verse, i.e., "and defend them so that those who love Your name[94] may exult in You." David prays not only for the destruction of his enemies but also for the protection of the godly. This will bring them to continued joy in the Lord, v. 11. The Lord will "bless" (*barak*)[95] the righteous, surrounding him with

---

[91]The word *hawâ* refers to "calamity, wickedness, destruction," with the context indicating the sense. The context here deals with the destruction that these wicked bring upon others. Delitzsch, p. 126, understands *hawwôt* as "a yawning abyss." The view is possible. It gives a picturesque description of the chasm over which those who accept their false words will fall.

[92]The verb *ranan* overwhelmingly refers to a cry of rejoicing or singing, normally directed toward the Lord.

[93]The verb *sakak* has the basic sense of "covering." This leads to the thought of defending or protecting.

[94]In Psalms, the "name" of the Lord refers most often to God's revealed nature, e.g., 9:2, 10; 18:49, but also to His reputation, e.g., 23:3; 25:11. The context determines the sense given by the word. Here, David refers to those who love God as He reveals Himself to man.

[95]The word *barak* often occurs when God blesses someone. God never uses the word *ʾašar* (see 1:1), also translated "blessing," when He blesses a person. Similarly, when someone blesses God, he uses *barak*, never *ʾašar*. The word *barak* can be used sovereignly, when man has done nothing to deserve it. The word *ʾašar* always requires that man has done something to merit blessing.

His favor as with "a shield" (*ṣinnâ*). The *ṣinnâ* is the large shield that covers the whole body. With this note of confidence, David ends his prayer, v. 12.

PSALM 6

As with many of David's psalms, we do not know the background to the writing. He has enemies, vv. 8, 10 and the threat is real enough that he sees the possibility of death, v. 5. David sees the situation as punishment for some sin, v. 1. He pleads for God to extend His mercy to him, vv. 2–3, and deliver him from the threat, vv. 4–5. He expresses his grief over the situation that he faces, vv. 6–7, but confidently anticipates the Lord's answer to his prayer, vv. 8–10. Even with this information, we cannot be certain of the time in David's life.[96]

The psalm is normally classified as a penitential psalm because of v. 1.[97] David does not mention his sin but clearly recognizes the chastisement of God for what he has done. David grieves over what he has done and pleads for the Lord to mercifully deliver him from the trial, vv. 2, 4. With his prayer for mercy, David sets an example for believers today. It is still right to turn from sin and to ask God for mercy.

David writes this for "the chief Musician" (*mᵉnaṣṣeaḥ*, see 4, intro.), the leader of the music played in the worship ceremonies. It is to be performed on "Neginoth" (*nᵉgînôt*, see 4, intro.), stringed instruments of some unknown kind. The psalm is also to be "on Sheminith" (*šᵉmînît*), a term that occurs elsewhere only in I Chronicles 15:21 and in the title of Psalm 12. From the closeness of the word to *šᵉmoneh*,

---

[96]Phillips, I, 49–50, places the psalm at the time of David's sin with Bathsheba. He makes the sickness of v. 2 leprosy. His view is speculative, without clear support from the psalm.

[97]Penitential psalms are lament psalms in which the lament comes out of the psalmist's own sin. The penitential psalms include 6, 32, 38, 51, 102, 130, and 143. The Roman Catholic Church, in its condemnation of Galileo, sentenced him for three years to "repeat once a week the seven penitential Psalms." Colin A. Roman, *Galileo* (New York: G. P. Putnam's Sons, 1974), p. 220.

"eight," the term may refer to an eight-stringed instrument or to the eight-note octave.[98] Psalm 6 is a "psalm [*mizmôr*, see 3, title] of David."

I. Plea for Mercy 1–3

1–3 David begs the Lord not to judge him with a spirit of "anger" (*ʾap*, see 2:5) or in His "hot displeasure" (*ḥemâ*).[99] While the psalm does not tell us the details, David understands that he has done wrong. The implied thought is that he hopes for loving chastisement rather than "anger" (*ʾap*).[100] Elsewhere, God punishes His enemies in anger, e.g., 21:9; 78:21. He keeps those whom He loves, 145:20, v. 1. David confesses his weakness and pleads for God to extend "mercy" (or "grace," *ḥanan*, see 4:1) to him. The phrase "my bones are vexed [or 'dismayed,' *bahal*, see 2:5]" is idiomatic, picturing the physical weakness he feels, v. 2. His soul is "sore vexed" ("greatly dismayed," *bahal*) as well. Weary with the continued suffering, David cries "How long?" In the midst of the unknown trial, David cannot see God's gracious presence. He longs for its return, v. 3.

---

[98]Steven J. Lawson, *Psalms 1–75*, p. 41, refers to "an eight-string instrument." Dahood, I, 38, relies on I Chron. 15:21 to deduce that *Sheminith* "refers to the lower octave or the bass voice." Thirtle, pp. 110–12, also refers the word to male choirs. He appends the word to Ps. 5, however, and has the choir sing this psalm. TEV translates "low-pitched harps." Phillips, II, 48, associates the number eight "with a new beginning." Calvin, I, 65–66, follows the meaning "the eighth" and conjectures that it refers to "the shrillest or loftiest note." Hengstenberg, I, 89, relates *Sheminith* to the "time" of the psalm. Casimir McCambley, "On the Sixth Psalm, Concerning the Octave by Saint Gregory of Nyssa," *Greek Orthodox Theological Review* 32:1 (1987): 39, draws on St. Gregory's view that the eighth day, following the seven days of a week, is "a symbol of eternity." The content of the psalm, however, does not support this. In a rather strange rabbinical view, *Menaḥoth* 43*b* relates the term to circumcision, which took place on the eighth day after birth. The context does not support this.

[99]The noun *ḥemâ*, "heat," occurs widely. It may refer to a fever caused by venom, 58:4, or to the fires of jealousy, Prov. 6:34. Most often, however, it poetically represents the anger of either God, as here, or man, 76:10.

[100]Leupold, p. 84, understands David's prayer as asking that God would remove all correction "because [this] is an evidence of God's anger." This is a possible view. I have chosen the view above because of the use of anger elsewhere in speaking of God's judgment.

II. Prayer for Deliverance 4–5

4–5 David now asks directly for God to return. This will relieve the sufferings of his soul and deliver him from his foes. David pleads for the "mercies" (or "steadfast love," *ḥesed*, see 5:7) of God to work on his behalf, v. 4. Otherwise, David can anticipate only victory by his enemies and his following death. But in death "there is no remembrance of thee." David does not doubt the existence of life after death. He elsewhere expresses his belief in this, 16:10. He here simply states that there will be no more "remembrance" of God's work on his behalf. The context suggests that David thinks of deliverance from those who oppose him. That ends when life ends. In the "grave" (*šᵉʾôl*, better "Sheol")[101] he will not be able to "thank" (or "praise") God for His continuing work, v. 5.

III. Grief from the Threat 6–7

6–7 David describes his sorrow. He is "weary" (*yagaᶜ*)[102] with his "groaning" (*ʾᵃnaḥâ*).[103] The context here supports an emotional trial as the source of David's weariness. He "water[s]" (*masâ*) his couch at night with his tears. The verb *masâ* picturesquely refers to dissolving the couch, i.e., a flood of tears washes across his bed, v. 6. David's eye is "consumed," not able to function properly, because of his sor-

[101]Kissane, p. 23, incorrectly states that "Sheol was a place of darkness and oblivion where the disembodied spirit endures in a shadowy existence little better than non-existence." Eaton, p. 40, similarly says that in Sheol, "he would lose his most precious possession on which all other value depends, his knowledge of God." Rodd, p. 15, views Sheol as "a dark underworld where the dead live out a shadowy existence, remembering nothing of their past life or God's goodness to them, having no opportunity to praise Him, and standing beyond the reach of His love." These views misunderstand Sheol, which is the abode of both the righteous (Ps. 16:10: 30:3) and the wicked (Num. 16:33; Ps. 9:17). The condition of the righteous and the wicked in Sheol differ (Ps. 49:14–15). The Lord will bring the righteous out of Sheol (Ps. 86:13; Prov. 15:24; Hos. 13:14). The fact that Sheol refers both to the grave and to the eternal abode contributes to the difficulty. The grave receives the dead without measure (Isa. 5:14). At other times, Sheol refers to the eternal abode. It is the home of the debased (Isa. 57:9). The dead have both a conscious existence and a personal identity (Isa. 14:9–15). There is life after death, e.g., 16:10; 139:8; Hos. 13:14.

[102]The verb *yagaᶜ* indicates labor to the point of exhaustion, thus weariness.

[103]The word *ʾᵃnaḥâ* refers to groaning that comes from either emotional or physical distress.

row. It has become "old," dimmed with age, due to the grief caused by his foes, v. 7.

IV. Confidence of David 8–10

8–10 Despite the extent of his trials, David maintains his trust in the Lord. He has prayed and he assumes the answer to his prayer. He urges the "workers of iniquity," his enemies, to turn away from him. The Lord has heard his cries of distress. The perfect tense verbs used in vv. 8–9 represent something so sure in his mind that he states it as an accomplished fact, v. 8. The Lord has heard his "supplication" (*t*ᵉ*ḥinnâ*)[104] for grace to be extended to him. The Lord will receive such a "prayer" (*t*ᵉ*pillâ*, see 4:1). The threefold statement that God will hear his prayer aptly expresses David's confidence in Him, v. 9. Let David's enemies be "ashamed [*bôš*][105] and sore vexed [or 'greatly dismayed,' *bahal*, see 2:5]." Their plans will come to nothing. They will be "ashamed" (*bôš*). The repetition of the verb in 10*b* stresses the greatness of their failure. The phrase "sore vexed" may be compared with the similar phrase in v. 3. There, David expressed his feelings. Now, trusting in the Lord, he anticipates the failure of his foes. Let his adversaries "return" (or "turn back") from their attack on him. Let them be "ashamed" (*bôš*), publicly humiliated because of the failure of their threat to the anointed king, v. 10.

PSALM 7

We cannot date this individual lament psalm with certainty other than to place it in the early part of David's life. The references to David's enemies fit into the time when David fled from Saul's attempts to kill him. David's willingness to commit the judgment of

---

[104]The noun *t*ᵉ*ḥinnâ* refers to a prayer for grace from the Lord. In the Psalms, the word occurs only here, in 55:1, and in 119:170.

[105]The word *bôš* refers to the shame that comes from failure, either a personal failure or the failure of something or someone that has been trusted. It often conveys a sense of public disgrace.

his adversaries to the Lord agrees with his actions while fleeing from Saul; cf. I Samuel 24:6–7, 12; 26:9–11. David's actions set a godly example for Christians. It is always appropriate to take life's problems to the Lord.

David calls the psalm a "Shiggaion" (*šiggayôn*).[106] The word comes from *šagâ*, "to wander, go astray." This may indicate a poem with many changes of thought such as we have here and in Habakkuk 3. While we cannot be certain, this is an attractive suggestion. In some way it refers to a song, sung by David to the Lord. The reference to "Cush the Benjamite" is obscure.[107] We know of no person by this name in the OT.

I. Confidence of David 1–2

1–2 David begins with a statement of trust in the Lord his God. The names "Lord" (*y^ehwah*) and "God" (*^[e]lohîm*) are appropriate. David refers to *y^ehwah*, the redemptive name of God that occurs regularly in referring to sacrifice or to God as He involves Himself

---

[106]The term occurs only here, although the plural "Shigionoth" occurs in Hab. 3:1. In both places, the terms likely refer to the nature of the poetry. Delitzsch, I, 139; and Moll, I, 24, both suggest this. Leupold, p. 91, rejects this view but has little better to replace it. He comments, "We may have to content ourselves with the somewhat colorless translation 'ode.'" On the basis of the Akkadian root *šegû*, he suggests that this is a complaint. Harman, p. 82, suggests that it means "a lamentation." Eaton, p. 42, considers it "an intercessory rite in time of national distress," impossible to prove because of the rarity of the term. Gaebelein, p. 38, states its meaning as "crying aloud," from danger, perplexity, or pain. This derives the word from *šag*, an improbable source. Thirtle, p. 138, suggests a root related to *ša^ag*, "to call out, cry out, sing aloud." He understands it to refer to a hymn or a song of sadness. The view is based on a speculative root. Fausset, III, 116, draws on the root *šagâ*, "to err," and refers it to the error of Saul in accusing David of plotting against him. Hirsch, I, 39, also translates the term as "error." He refers this to David's error in asking God to reveal His greatness. The view is improbable.

[107]Gaebelein, p. 40, understands "Cush" as "black" and considers this descriptive of Saul's "moral nature." Nowhere in the OT does *kûš* have the sense of "black." Eaton, p. 42, refers to Shimei, "of the clan of Kish." The OT, however, does not relate Shimei to Kish. Rawlinson, I, 42, tentatively suggests that the name refers to Saul and alludes to his father's name Kish. He says, "Such plays on words have always found much favour in the East." Thompson, p. 196, identifies him as a "close friend of Saul." Rotherham, pp. 69–70, identifies Cush as a "courtier in the court of Saul." He accuses him of slandering David to Saul by "wrongfully retaining in his own hands spoils which belonged to the king." Calvin, I, 76, identifies him as "some one of Saul's kindred." Since the name does not occur elsewhere, we can only speculate on the identity of Cush.

with man. The name *ʾᵉlohîm*, however, emphasizes the power of God. David here calls for deliverance on the God of might who involves Himself with man. David has placed his "trust" (*ḥasâ*, see 2:12) in Him, v. 1. If the Lord does not help, David's foe will "tear" David "like a lion [*ʾᵃrî*]."[108] There is no other help, v. 2.

II. Purity of the Psalmist 3–5

3–5 David's right to approach the Lord rests on his personal holiness. He denies any wickedness such as his enemies have charged to him. The word "this" looks forward to v. 4, the charge that he has returned evil for good.[109] While we do not know specifically what he refers to, this agrees with the accusation made before Saul that "David seeketh thy hurt," I Samuel 24:9. David was later accused of "the blood of the house of Saul," II Samuel 16:8; cf. 3:27; 4:8. David denies that "there be" [*yeš*][110] iniquity [*ʿawel*] in [his] hands." The root *ʿûl* refers to deviation from a right standard, here the Word of God, and often to violent wickedness, cruelty, or vicious speech rather than simple injustice, v. 3. David has not "rewarded" (*gamal*)[111] evil against anyone who "was at peace" with him. The second half of v. 4 is better "or have plundered [*ḥalaṣ*] my enemy without cause."[112] David denies that he has hurt his foe in any way, v. 4. If he has done these things, he deserves punishment. Let his enemies "persecute"

---

[108]The *ʾᵃrî* is a full-grown lion. The root word, *ʾarâ*, is "to pluck, gather." The lion is thus a "gatherer" of the prey on which he feeds.

[109]Buttenwieser, p. 417, reverses vv. 3 and 4 since *zoʾt*, "this," cannot refer to the next verse, "though separated from it by another sentence." He is virtually alone in his opinion. The word *zoʾt* regularly introduces something "about to be mentioned," Williams ¶ 113. Cf. also G.K.C. 136 *a*. Buttenwieser makes the pronoun refer back to the relocated v. 4, but nothing is lost by leaving it in place.

[110]The particle *yeš* asserts existence, something that actually is. The phrase "there be" could be rendered "there exists."

[111]The verb *gamal* has the sense "to recompense" or "to complete." The context must guide in the exact nuance given.

[112]Henry, p. 262, accepts the AV, "Yea, I have delivered him that without cause is mine enemy." On the other hand, Calvin, I, 77, supplies the negative and translates, "If I have not delivered him that persecuted me without cause." The verb *ḥalaṣ* may be translated either "deliver" or "plunder." The parallelism here supports best the thought of plundering. Delitzsch, I, 140, refers the verb to cutting the hem of Saul's robe, I Sam. 24:5. While this is possible, the statement is too general to be certain. Dahood, I, 43, goes astray by translating as "lay my liver in the mud." This requires revocalizing *kᵉbôdî* and translating *ʿapar*, "dust," as "mud," a sense it does not have.

(better "pursue") his life. Let them take his "honor" (or "glory") from him. The word "glory" contrasts with the "dust" of death.[113] The king with all his glory is brought to a shameful death. "Selah" calls attention to David's plight, v. 5.

III. Judgment of the Foes 6–8

6–8 David asks the Lord to intervene on his behalf. He calls on the Lord to arise in "anger" (*ʾap*, see 2:5) against his foes because of the "rage" (*ʿebrâ*)[114] they have directed against him. While the threat was developing, it had seemed that the Lord was sleeping. David prays that He now awake to action. The Lord has ordained judgment on all who oppose righteousness, v. 6. The "congregation [or 'assembly'] of the people [lit. 'peoples']," the nations that oppose God, will be all about Him. David thinks of the Lord coming in judgment. Afterward, He will return "on high," into the heavenlies, v. 7. David knows that the Lord will judge the "people" (again, "peoples") that oppose Him. He asks the Lord to judge him according to his righteousness and "integrity" (*tom*).[115] The request expresses David's confidence that he has walked according to God's will. He knows that there is no truth to the charge leveled against him; cf. vv. 3–4. His prayer also implies that his enemies do not carry out God's will in opposing him, v. 8.

IV. Reliance on God 9–10

9–10 David desires the "wickedness" (*raʿ*) of the "wicked" (*rašaʿ*, see 1:1) to end. The word *raʿ* indicates evil of all kinds, including physical harm, emotional problems, or spiritual wickedness. The context here supports the physical threat to David's life although, of course, sin has moved the enemy to this action. He prays that the Lord would give the "just" (or "righteous *man*") a firm posi-

[113]Alexander, p. 43, argues that "dust" refers "to present humiliation." The view is possible; however, the parallelism with the phrase "tread down my life upon the earth" seems rather to point to death.

[114]The word *ʿebrâ* carries with it a sense of overflowing anger, thus rage or fury. Depending on the context, this may describe the actions of either man or God.

[115]The noun *tom* is from the root *tamam*, "to be complete." It expresses an ethical completeness, integrity. There is no hint of self-righteousness here. The term simply describes David's actions as free from wickedness.

tion. David recognizes that the Lord examines "the hearts and reins [*kilyâ*],"[116] the inward being of a man, v. 9. To show his inward nature, David asserts his reliance on God. It is appropriate here to use the name *ᵓᵉlohîm*, the name that indicates the power of God as One Who is well able to defend David. He is David's "defence" (better "shield," *magen*, see 3:3), protecting him from those who would attack him, v. 10.

V. Power of God 11–13

11–13 The phrase "God judgeth the righteous" is better "God is a righteous judge." David recognizes God's nature as He examines man. He is angry continually at the ungodly. David likely thinks of those who oppose him, v. 11. Unless the wicked repents of his sin, the Lord will prepare judgment for him. He will sharpen His sword; cf. Deuteronomy 32:41; Isaiah 34:5. He has also "bent" (*darak*) His bow. The verb *darak* means "to tread on." The picture here is of stepping on one end of the bow in order to bend it into a position for stringing, v. 12. The Lord has prepared "instruments of death" for the wicked. He "ordaineth his arrows against the persecutors," better "makes His arrows for burning." These flaming arrows continue the poetical picture of God's power directed against His foes, v. 13.[117]

VI. Fate of the Enemy 14–17

14–17 David now describes the certain end of those who oppose God. He again considers his own foes as the enemies of God. They travail in their effort to bring forth wickedness. They have conceived

---

[116]The word *kilyâ* lit. means the "kidneys." The OT often uses this in a metaphoric sense to refer to the seat of emotions. The "heart" refers to the will, intellect, and emotions, the whole of man's inner being. The "kidneys" focus more on the emotions.

[117]On the basis of Ps. 18:14 and Zech. 9:14, Jennings, I, 30, understands "arrows" as "lightnings or thunderbolts." Alexander, p. 44, sees them as an "allusion to the ancient military custom of shooting ignited darts or arrows into besieged towns, for the purpose of setting them on fire." While these views are possible, David also refers here to God's sword and His bow, v. 12. It is more likely that all the weapons mentioned in the paragraph metaphorically picture God's power as He judges the wicked. Calvin, I, 88, makes Saul the one who prepares "instruments of death" and "arrows" against David. This shows the greatness of God's grace in delivering him from such great danger. The view does not fit into the context of vv. 11–12.

"mischief" (*ʿamal*, or "trouble")[118] and given birth to "falsehood" (or "deceitfulness"), v. 14. These actions have dug a "pit" (*bôr*),[119] a "ditch" (*šaḥat*)[120] into which they have fallen. David's confidence in the Lord is such that he speaks of the judgment of his foes as though it has already happened, v. 15. The "mischief" (*ʿamal*, again "trouble") that the wicked has planned for others will instead come upon him. His "violent dealing" (*ḥamas*, or "violence")[121] will come on his own "pate" (or "crown of his head"), v. 16. David can only respond with praise to the Lord. He is "righteous" in judging the wicked and sustaining those who follow Him. "The name of the Lord most high [*ʿelyôn*],"[122] i.e., the nature of the exalted Lord,[123] is worthy, and David will "sing praise" (*zamar*)[124] to it, v. 17.

PSALM 8

This hymn was sung at the time of harvest. The title states that it was penned for the "chief musician" (*m^enaṣṣeaḥ*, see 4, intro.) of the temple "upon ['concerning, according to'] Gittith," likely a joyful melody. The word *gittît*, from *gat*, refers to the winepress.[125] This was

---

[118]The noun *ʿamal* refers to the unpleasantness of labor and thus to "trouble."

[119]The *bôr* is normally a well or spring. It may also represent a place of captivity or the grave.

[120]The noun *šaḥat* comes from a root that means "to destroy." The noun may simply refer to a pit, as here. It may, however, go beyond this and refer to a grave or to Sheol. In each case, the context must guide the sense given to the word.

[121]The word *ḥamas* almost always indicates sinful violence rather than the violence of some natural calamity.

[122]The name "most High" (*ʿelyôn*) refers to the exalted position of God above all other heathen gods. About half of its occurrences are in Psalms.

[123]Ps. 5:11 gives a brief summary of the "name" of the Lord.

[124]The word *zamar* occurs widely in the Psalms in the context of giving praise to the Lord. Aramaic and Arabic cognates relate this to a wind instrument while an Akkadian cognate refers to singing. The biblical use embraces both singing, 30:12, and instrumental music, 33:2. In many cases, it is unclear whether the word refers to singing or to making music.

[125]Alexander, p. 46, and Murphy, p. 13, refer *Gittith* to an instrument or tune or style of performance invented or used in Gath, where David lived for a time.

a natural time for rejoicing. The psalm has this tone of joy in it here. "Gittith" occurs again in Psalms 81 and 84, both joyful psalms. Other than relating the psalm to the grape harvest, we have no information as to the time and place of its writing.[126]

The psalm is messianic.[127] Although the psalm concerns man in general as being set over nature, the NT clearly points the psalm to Christ. God has placed man over the animal world, but Christ is over the world of man. Man has a limited glory given him, but Christ possesses a fuller glory because of His nature and position. The psalm gives glory to the God Who has conceived this plan.

I. The Glory of God 1–2

1–2 David addresses his song to the "Lord [*y^{e}hwah*] our Lord [*ᵓadôn*]." The name *y^{e}hwah* refers to the redemptive God, the One Who involves Himself with man. The name *ᵓadôn* stresses the ownership of God and thus His position as Master.[128] His "name"[129]

Lawson, p. 50, calls it "a guitarlike harp associated with Gath in Philistia." Henry, p. 265, relates the word to Goliath "the Gittite," a term applied to those who lived in the Philistine city of Gath. He suggests that the psalm commemorates the slaying of the giant. Eaton, p. 45, suggests that it relates "in some way to an annual reconsecration of the Jerusalem sanctuary." These views are speculative since *Gittith* occurs only in the Psalms. No evidence supports these views. Delitzsch, I, 148, draws on the tone of joy in the psalm to conclude that the "gittith was . . . an instrument giving forth a . . . joyous melody." The view is possible although I prefer to relate *Gittith* to *gat*, "winepress." Hirsch, I, 48, relates the winepress to "bruising pressure such as occurs during the wine-pressing operation." This does not destroy but "brings out all the fine and noble essence that was locked within the crushed grape." From this, he concludes that the psalm is "a meditation upon the ennobling effect of those afflictions decreed by God for the moral betterment of mankind." Nothing in the psalm supports the view. The LXX and Vulgate support the view given above.

[126]Perowne, I, 149, and Albert Barnes, I, 66, state that David composed the psalm at night. While this view may be correct, David could as well have composed during the day while thinking of the glories of the night sky. Phillips, I, 64, transfers the title of Ps. 9 to this psalm and translates *Muthlabben* as "death of the champion." On this basis, he dates the psalm after David's victory over Goliath. See note 1, Ps. 4, for a discussion of transferring the psalm titles. In addition, it is interpretive to so translate *Muthlabben*. The word lit. refers to "the death of the son."

[127]The introduction to Ps. 2 briefly discusses the messianic psalms.

[128]The combination of *yehwah* and *ᵓadôn* occurs six times in Psalms: 8:1, 9; 97:5; 110:1; 123:2; and 135:5.

[129]Ps. 5:11 briefly summarizes the significance of the "name" of the Lord.

is "excellent" (*ʾaddîr*, or "majestic")[130] throughout the earth.[131] Rhetorically, David asks who has "set" (*tᵉnâ*)[132] the "glory" (*hôd*)[133] of God above that of the heavens, v. 1. The Lord has ordained "strength" (*ʿoz*),[134] praise, from young children.[135] Their praise to the Lord reveals the sin of His enemies. He uses "the weak things of the world to confound the things which are mighty," I Corinthians 1:27. The Lord cited this verse to the Jewish religious leaders who objected when children praised Him, Matthew 21:16.[136] With greater knowledge and ability, the wicked spurn the Lord. The Lord, however, will "still" (better "destroy") His enemies and anyone who would try to avenge himself on God, v. 2.[137]

---

[130]The word *ʾaddîr* refers to the excellence or superiority of something. The hymn "How Majestic Is Thy Name," with the words and music by Ron Hamilton, © 1978 Majesty Music, draws on this thought.

[131]Delitzsch, I, 149, understands the spokesman as the church, offering its praise to God throughout the earth. It is not necessary, however, to have spokesmen throughout the earth. David simply states that God is majestic in all places.

[132]The verb *tᵉnâ* is difficult. In form it is an imperative, which cannot follow the relative pronoun. G.K.C. 66 *h* proposes that the word should suggest *natnâ*, the *qal* 3fs, which also does not fit here. Delitzsch, I, 150, understands it as an irregular infinitive, a possible view but with almost no support from other verbs. Weiser, p. 140, revocalizes to *tānâ* and translates, "Thou whose glory is praised in the heavens." He considers the psalm as sung by the angels. I have followed Delitzsch as the most likely of the options.

[133]The word *hôd* occurs eight times in Psalms, one-third of its total appearances in the OT. When used of God, *hôd* describes His majesty and glory, e.g., 104:1. When used of man, it refers to his honor, e.g., 45:3; or dignity, Prov. 5:9. See also the discussion of *hadar* at v. 5.

[134]Leupold, p. 106, translates *ʿoz* as "stronghold." While a possible interpretation, the word *ʿoz* more directly refers to "strength."

[135]Among others, Bratcher and Reyburn, p. 79, and Dahood, I, 49, continue the thought of 1*b* with v. 2, something like "Your glory above the heavens is chanted by babes and sucklings." The translation is interpretive. The AV more closely follows the MT.

[136]Matt. 21:16 quotes the LXX, which correctly interprets "strength" as "praise."

[137]Because the words are singular rather than plural, Fausset, III, 119, understands "the enemy and the avenger" to refer to Satan. The praise of children, however, refutes the opposition of all who oppose the Lord. It is likely that the singular words here are collectives, representing all who stand against the Lord. Gaebelein, p. 46, spiritualizes the "babes and sucklings" into "new born souls" who praise God.

II. The Position of Man 3–8

3–5 David recalls the nights when he watched over his flocks under the sparkling jewels of the heavens. God's fingers had carefully shaped the heavens, ordaining for each astral body its position in the sky, v. 3. In view of this glory, why should God take note of "man" (*ᵓᵉnôš*; cf. 144:3)?[138] The "son of man" occurs in poetic variation with "man." Although man has a low position, the Lord is "mindful" of him, continually conscious of his needs. The Lord "visiteth" (*paqad*) him. The word *paqad* has a basic sense of inspecting something in order to make a decision. Sometimes the decision is simply numbering, sometimes a judgment, and sometimes exercising care. The decision here is the continuing care of God for man, v. 4. God has made man "a little lower than the angels [*ᵓᵉlohîm*]." The word *ᵓᵉlohîm* refers to might and power. Hebrews 2:6–8 quotes vv. 4–6 and rightly interprets *ᵓᵉlohîm* as "angels."[139] For a little time, man is lower than the angels. In eternity, however, man will be crowned with "glory and honour [*hadar*],"[140] holding a higher position than the angels. The ultimate fulfillment of this is in Jesus Christ. He became man, suffered and died, and now is exalted above all things, v. 5.

6–8 The Lord has given man the responsibility of ruling over nature; cf. Genesis 1:26, 28; 9:2; James 3:7.[141] All things are put "under his feet," an idiomatic expression showing his rule. Paul uses this phrase to describe the rule of Jesus Christ over this world, I Corinthians 15:27. Man's control of the earth is now partial. Only in Jesus Christ will full dominion be realized, v. 6. To illustrate this power, David mentions sheep and oxen, both domesticated animals. Man also has dominion over "the beasts of the field," wild animals, v. 7.[142] He further has dominion over fowls, fish, and other marine life, v. 8.

---

[138]The noun *ᵓᵉnôš* emphasizes the frailty and mortality of man.

[139]Cohen, p. 19, and Rodd, p. 19, translate *ᵓᵉlohîm* as "God" and see in the verse an allusion to Gen. 1:27. While the translation is possible, the NT use favors "angels."

[140]The word *hadar* indicates the splendor, honor, and glory of nature, man, and God, e.g., 21:5; 29:4. In the Psalms, *hadar* is used in connection with *hôd*, v. 1, six times (21:5; 45:3; 96:6; 104:1; 111:3; 145:5).

[141]*Nedarîm* 38*a* in the Talmud refers the "him" to Moses, but the context does not support this.

[142]Fausset, III, 120, makes "sheep" (or "flocks") represent the smaller animals and "beasts" the larger animals. He, however, omits any mention of "oxen," clearly larger

III. The Glory of God 9

9 David ends the psalm as he began, with a statement of God's glory. The Hebrew is identical to that in v. 1. The thought is therefore the same: the God Who involves Himself with man and is man's master has a majestic "name" (see v. 1) in all parts of the earth, v. 9.

EXCURSUS: ACROSTICS

The psalmists sometimes used an acrostic format. In an acrostic, sets of letters taken in order form a word, phrase, or a regular sequence of letters in the composition. Psalms 9–10, 25, 34, 37, 111, 112, 119, and 145 all use this structure. Elsewhere in the OT, Lamentations 1, 2, 3, and 4, and Proverbs 31:10–31 have an acrostic pattern. In all of these, the acrostic follows an alphabetic sequence. Babylon, the only other country of the biblical world to produce acrostic literature, used chains of letters to spell out some phrase, e.g., "God Nabû" from "I am Ashurbanipal who pray to thee; grant me life, O Marduk, and I will sing thy praise."[143] In general, biblical acrostics are shorter than their Babylonian counterparts.

The biblical writers follow different patterns in the acrostics. The simplest is the one-line acrostic seen in Psalms 111 and 112.[144] In these, each stich[145] forms a line, each beginning with a successive letter of the Hebrew alphabet. Psalms 25, 34, 145, Proverbs 31:10–31, and Lamentations 4 form two-line acrostics. In these, each line includes two stichs, with the first stich of the line beginning with the sequence of letters of the alphabet. The acrostics in Lamentations 1, 2, and 3 are three-line acrostics. In Lamentations 1 and 2, each verse has three lines, each with two stichs. The first stich in each verse

animals. The contrast seems rather between domesticated and wild animals.

[143]W. G. Lambert, *Babylonian Wisdom Literature* (Oxford: Oxford University Press, 1960), surveys the seven extant Babylonian acrostics.

[144]The discussions of the individual psalms take up the various anomalies in the biblical acrostics. The discussion here provides a general overview of acrostics.

[145] The stich is a line of Hebrew poetry. In the translation to English, this is usually but not always clear.

begins with a letter of the alphabet so that the chain of letters follows the Hebrew alphabet. In Lamentations 3, however, each verse has only one line with two stichs. In each set of three verses, every other stich begins with the same Hebrew letter. The letters follow the Hebrew alphabet.

There are three four-line acrostics, Psalms 9, 10, and 37. In these, each verse includes two lines, each with two stichs. Every fourth stich begins with a successive letter of the alphabet. Taken together, Psalms 9–10 complete the Hebrew alphabet. Psalm 9 includes the letters *ʾalep–kap* and Psalm 10 the letters *lamed–taw*. Psalm 37 follows a similar pattern.

Psalm 119 is the most elaborate acrostic in the OT, following a sixteen-line pattern. Each verse has two stichs. For eight verses, every other stich begins with the same letter of the alphabet. The titles of the paragraphs with eight verses each reflect the letter characteristic of the paragraph.

We can only speculate on the purpose of an acrostic. These may have aided memorization of the passage. They may reflect the authors' poetical efforts. They may have aided antiphonal recitation. They may have had other purposes.

PSALM 9

David consigns the psalm to the "chief musician" (*mᵉnaṣṣeaḥ*, see 4, intro.) upon "Muthlabben." This means "death of the son." We cannot be certain of the significance.[146] The psalm is an irregular

[146]Hengstenberg, I, 141, speculates that *labben* is "an anagram for *Nabal*, i.e., *a fool*" and makes the title "Upon the dying of the fool." No other psalm title follows this practice. Hirsch, I, 58–59, also conjectures a meaning. He makes *ʿal-mût*, found in many mss, mean "upon Muth," a word that he interprets as "eternal youth." This refers to the "son," Israel, as God preserves the nation. VanGemeren, p. 36, conjectures that *mût* is a variant of *alamoth,* "maidens." From this, he suggests "a female choir." Henry, III, 269, considers the word a melody or musical instrument. Murphy, p. 101, tentatively relates it to the death of "some notable man of the name of Labben." Cohen, p. 20, and Calvin, I, 109, suggest that it refers to a melody. Thompson, p. 199, makes this specific: "a well-known dirge for a son." Eaton, p. 47,

acrostic, the first of nine such psalms.[147] The first four stichs (vv. 1–2) begin with *ʾalep*. Beginning with v. 3 and continuing with some aberration to v. 18, every other verse begins with a successive letter of the Hebrew alphabet: *beth*, *gimel*, *hê*, and so forth.[148]

Interestingly, Psalm 10 continues the acrostic, again irregularly.[149] If David wrote the two songs at the same time, they were separated early. The subject matter of Psalm 10 differs so from that of Psalm 9 that they probably were separate from the time of writing.[150] They may have been written at the same time, with David carrying on the acrostic style across both. We can explain the irregularities as poetic license.

The psalm is basically a song of thanksgiving, although the final verses express David's prayer for continued deliverance. Believers today may share the same confidence that David expresses in the

---

relies on the LXX to read "secrets of the son." He refers the "secrets" to mysteries, "the hidden things of God." Gaebelein, p. 50, suggests that the phrase speaks of the death of the firstborn son in Egypt. Sabourin, p. 13, tentatively suggests "an Egyptian harp." Since this is the only occurrence of the phrase, we cannot be dogmatic as to its meaning.

[147]Pss. 9, 10, 25, 34, 37, 111, 112, 119, and 145 are acrostic in nature. We do not know the reason for this pattern in some of the psalms. Barnabas Lindars, "The Structure of Psalm CXLV," *VT* 39 (1989): 23, suggests that it is for an artistic reason. Dahood, I, 54, mentions this purpose and also the possibility that it was meant to aid the memory.

[148]There is no stich beginning with *dalet*, the section beginning with *yod* is only one line long, and the section beginning with *kap* is three lines. Moll, p. 94, and Delitzsch, I, 159, give two lines to *yod* but then make the final two lines begin with *qop*. Hengstenberg, I, 426, notes that the acrostic psalms occur "only in a particular class of Psalms,—those, namely, in which the effort is obvious to arrange a collection of individual sayings, which, from beginning to end, bear upon the same subject." He considers the alphabetical arrangement as a "symbol of completeness and compactness." The Babylonian Talmud, *Sanhedrin* 104*b*, suggests that "this alludes to the belief that the letters themselves are endowed with certain powers." While some of these views seem unlikely, the fact remains that we do not know why certain psalms (and other OT writings) have an alphabetical arrangement.

[149]John Strugnell and Hanan Eshel, "Psalms 9 and 10 and the Order of the Alphabet," *BibRev* 17:3 (2001): 41–44, argue that Pss. 9 and 10 should be reversed. Ps. 10 is a lament that should be followed by Ps. 9, a psalm of thanksgiving. As textual evidence, they cite some non-biblical texts in which alphabets were written in two parts, with the second half coming first. The evidence developed in the article, however, gives only fragments of the alphabet and may simply have been coincidental. In any case, there is no biblical evidence for such an arrangement.

[150]Among others, *NIB*, IV, 716; Weiser, p. 148; and Kissane, p. 36, consider Pss. 9–10 a single psalm which for unknown reasons was separated into two psalms.

closing verses. Man will not prevail against God; rather, God will prevail against man. Christianity will therefore gain victory over the forces of wickedness that now oppose it.

I. David's Praise for Past Deliverance 1–12

1–2 David expresses praise with all his inner being for some deliverance given from his enemies. We do not know the incident that he refers to. There were "enemies," v. 3, that were "heathen," v. 5. They had invaded Judah to destroy cities, v. 6. These circumstances could fit David's war with the Philistines, II Samuel 5:17–25, or his fight against the Ammonite-Syrian alliance, II Samuel 10:6–19. They could apply to other campaigns against the surrounding nations. The OT does not give enough information to identify the background of the psalm.[151] David purposes to declare the "marvellous" (*pala*ʾ) works of God. The participle of *pala*ʾ often refers to the works of God that are beyond the capacity of man to do. The word does not stress the miraculous nature of the works so much as it does God's care for mankind, v. 1. David will "be glad and rejoice" (or "rejoice and exult") in the Lord. He will "sing praise" (*zamar*, see 7:17) to the Lord's "name," the "most High" (*ʿelyôn*, see 7:17) God. In this context, the "name" of the Lord refers to His nature as a gracious and powerful God Who protects His children, v. 2.[152]

3–4 When David's enemies turn from him, they stumble and "perish" (*ʾabad*, see 1:6) in the Lord's presence, v. 3. David recognizes the Lord's favor in giving him victory over his foes. The Lord

[151]Phillips, I, 71–75, sets aside any historical basis for the psalm. He considers it a comprehensive prophecy of the destruction of Antichrist, the Millennium, and the Day of the Lord. The view ignores the verb tenses and historical notes. *The Scofield Reference Bible*, ed. C. I. Scofield (New York: Oxford University Press, 1945) relates the psalm to David's actions after the death of his son by Bathsheba, II Sam. 12:20. Kirkpatrick, p. 42, says that the psalm "celebrates David's victories in general." Ewald, I, 322, suggests the overthrow of Assyria. Moll, p. 93, considers the victory over Philistia the most likely basis for the psalm. Rawlinson, I, 56–57, prefers Israel's victory over Ammon and Syria. He comments, "The date of the psalm is . . . to some extent limited, since it must have been composed subsequently to the transfer of the ark to Jerusalem." While the psalm was composed after the transfer of the ark, the basis for the psalm may have come before the transfer. The reference to Zion in v. 11, then, does not help us date the psalm. Nothing in the psalm lets us be certain of its background.

[152]See note 94, 5:11, for a summary of the Lord's "name."

has maintained David's "right" (*mišpaṭ*, or "just cause," see 1:5). The Lord on His heavenly throne has judged "right" (*ṣedeq*, or "righteously") in defeating David's adversaries, v. 4.[153]

5–6 There is a progression in the Lord's work with the heathen. He first has rebuked them, then "destroyed" (*ʾabad*) them, and finally blotted out their name from memory. The wicked may flourish for a time. The Lord and His cause, however, will emerge victorious, v. 5. The enemy may have been partially successful in their invasion of Judah. They may have "destroyed [or 'uprooted'] cities."[154] But they will "come to a perpetual [or 'enduring'] end." Even the "memorial" (better "memory") of the enemy is "perished" (*ʾabad*), v. 6.[155]

7–10 In sharp contrast with David's enemy, the Lord will "endure" (*yašab*) forever. The verb *yašab* means "to sit, dwell." It refers here to the Lord sitting on His throne forever. From there, He will administer justice, v. 7. He will judge righteously and "in uprightness" (or "with equity"). Note that these verses refer to Jesus Christ, the One Who will dispense justice in the millennial kingdom, John 5:22; II Timothy 4:1, v. 8.

In addition to His role as judge, the Lord will also protect His own. He will be a "refuge" (*miśgab*)[156] not only for the "oppressed"

---

[153]The words *mišpaṭ* and *ṣedeq* occur widely through the OT. The word *mišpaṭ* refers broadly to justice or judging. In each case, the context must guide the translation. The word *ṣedeq* indicates conformity to an ethical or moral standard. This standard is often God's Word but may also refer to human relationships that come from this, i.e., love for a neighbor or acting according to truth.

[154]George Horne, *Commentary on the Book of Psalms*, p. 57, makes God the One Who destroys the cities of the enemy. It is unlikely, however, that David introduces God without a clear change in the subject. Since there is no mention of God, it is best to keep the "enemy" as the author of the destruction.

[155]Rawlinson, I, 56, understands "memorial" to refer to the cities of Judah destroyed in the enemy's invasion. It anticipates their "complete disappearance from history." Henry, p. 270, and Moll, p. 94, consider the phrase to focus on the enemy's cities that will be completely destroyed. Fausset, III, 121, refers the disappearance to the Amalekites, "who had been by this time utterly extinguished." II Sam. 8:12, however, mentions Amalek as one of the nations subdued by David. It is unlikely that they had already disappeared from history. These views overlook the masculine pronominal suffix *m* attached to "memorial." Since the word "cities" is feminine, the suffix refers back to the masculine participle "enemy." This lets the end of v. 6 parallel v. 5, both referring to the blotting out of the enemy's memory.

[156]The noun *miśgab* comes from the verb *śagab*, "to be inaccessibly high." As a "refuge," it is a place beyond the reach of enemies.

(*dak*)[157] but also for those in "times of trouble [*ṣarâ*]."[158] This oppression is crushing, a severe emotional problem for David. The Lord shelters David from those who would seek to bring him low, v. 9. Those who experientially "know" (*yadaᶜ*, see 1:6) the "name" (see v. 2), i.e., the nature of the Lord as a loving, powerful, and protecting God, will trust Him. He has never forsaken those who "seek" (*daraš*) Him.[159] David speaks from experience as one who has been hunted by his enemies, v. 10.

11–12 Having thought of the faithfulness of the Lord, David spontaneously urges "praises" (*zamar*, see 7:17) to Him. The Lord dwells "in Zion" in the tabernacle, between the cherubs over the mercy seat in the holy of holies. David urges others to speak of God's works "among the people." The word "people" is plural and likely refers to the surrounding nations. Israel is to tell the world about God, v. 11. He Who "maketh inquisition [*daraš*] for blood" (better "seeks blood") remembers them. The unusual phrase pictures the Lord avenging the blood of those who have been oppressed. He does not ignore the cry for help of the "humble" (or "afflicted," *ᶜanî*), v. 12.[160]

II. David's Prayer for Present Deliverance 13–16

13–14 Although the Lord had brought judgment upon David's enemies in the past, there was still a present threat. David pleads with the Lord to "have mercy" (or "be gracious," *ḥanan*, see 4:1) to him.[161] He asks the Lord to "consider" (or "see") the "trouble" (or

---

[157]The word *dak* comes from *dakâ*, "to be crushed." The word *dakâ* has a broad range of meanings. It may refer to emotional suffering, as here, to oppression, or even destruction. In each case, the context must guide the sense given to the word.

[158]The noun *ṣarâ* specially refers to emotional anguish.

[159]The verb *daraš* refers to seeking with care. While the Lord may forget the one who searches casually for Him, He will never desert those who earnestly seek His favor.

[160]The word *ᶜanî* may mean either "humble," "poor," or "afflicted." In every case, the context must guide in the sense given it. Here, the parallelism with the first phrase supports the idea of affliction. An alternate spelling, *ᶜanaw*, also occurs frequently in Psalms, as in v. 18.

[161]Delitzsch, I, 168, thinks that taking this passage as a present prayer destroys "the unity and hymnic character of the Psalm." He understands this as David's prayer before the deliverance described in vv. 1–12. Since David presents the prayer as a current petition to the Lord, it is more likely that he bases it on the past deliverance of vv. 1–12. There is no reason to force the entire song into the past. Bratcher and

"affliction," *ʿanî*) that comes from those who "hate" (*śane*ʾ, see 5:5) him. The danger was serious. David speaks of the Lord lifting him "up from the gates of death."[162] We do not know the specific trial that David refers to. Leaving these trials unspecified makes them general, David's response setting an example of how believers today should act when faced with difficulties, v. 13. This deliverance will let David praise the Lord openly "in the gates of the daughter of Zion." The "daughter of Zion" is Jerusalem. The "gates" of the city were the place for conducting both business and public affairs; cf. Deuteronomy 16:18; Ruth 4:11; II Kings 7:1.[163] David will rejoice in the "salvation" (or "deliverance") given him by the Lord, v. 14.

15–16 David confidently expresses his view that his enemies will sink "in the pit [*šaḥat*, see 7:15] that they made." He states this in the past tense since his confidence in God's deliverance lets him consider it an accomplished fact. He describes their fate with a second word picture. The net that they placed for his capture will instead capture them, v. 15. The phrase "The Lord is known" is better "The Lord has made Himself known." He has done this by executing judgment. He lets the wicked be "snared" (or "struck down") by his own actions. The word "Higgaion" (*higgayôn*) refers to "meditation" in 19:14 and "solemn sound" in 92:3. It may be a musical notation here telling the instruments to play while the listeners think on what David has said.[164] The word "selah" lays stress on David's words, v. 16.

Reyburn, p. 92, see "no obvious connection between this petition and the glad cry of praise of God's help in verses 11–12." Again, it is likely that David bases his prayer on past help from the Lord.

[162]Cohen, p. 22, and Harman, p. 88, go too far in making Sheol poetically regarded as a place with walls and gates. It is more likely that David simply speaks poetically of the approach to death that he had faced.

[163]Rawlinson, I, 57, understands the phrase as "within the gates" and thus "in the temple [*sic*]." There is no reason to refer to the tabernacle in such an oblique way. Rawlinson errs when he concludes that God should not be praised in daily life but rather in the place of worship. Horne, p. 59, goes to extreme by making the gates those of the New Jerusalem. There is no millennial context here.

[164]Albert Barnes, I, 83, suggests that *selah* indicates a "general pause," while *Higgaion* "denotes the particular kind of pause." Hengstenberg, I, 151, this is "a call to reflection . . . The music must cease, to afford space for calm meditation." Jennings, I, xliv, calls it "a *forte* burst of joyous music, probably upon stringed instruments." Bratcher and Reyburn, p. 94, suggest "a quiet melody." Since the word occurs so few times, we cannot be certain. Hirsch, I, 67, interprets *Higgaion* as "a

III. David's Prophecy of Final Deliverance 17–20

17–18 David's confidence that the Lord will judge his enemies leads him to a general statement regarding the future of the wicked. The Lord will turn them into "hell" (*šᵉʾôl*, see 6:5). Since David speaks here of the final judgment, the word *šᵉʾôl* refers to the eternal abode of the wicked dead.[165] The wicked involve those "nations" (or "heathen") that forget God. They will likewise go to *šᵉʾôl*, v. 17. The Lord will not always forget those in need, nor will He let the "expectation" (*tiqwâ*)[166] of the "poor" (or "afflicted," *ʿanaw*, see v. 12) "perish" (*ʾabad*, see 1:6) forever. While stated negatively, the verse expresses the confidence that the persecuted have in the Lord. The wicked will be forgotten, vv. 5–6, but the Lord will remember the godly, v. 18.

19–20 David prays again. Keep the mortal "man" (*ʾᵉnôš*, see 8:4) from prevailing. Judge the heathen, v. 19. This judgment will cause the wicked to "fear" (*môrâ*). The word *môrâ* describes a feeling of terror. The "nations" (again "heathen") will see themselves for what they are, men (*ʾᵉnôš*), not gods, and not able to stand against the power of the Lord. Once more, the "selah" calls for meditation on what David has said, v. 20.

PSALM 10

Psalm 10 continues the irregular acrostic begun in Psalm 9. It takes imagination to see the acrostic. The psalm omits *mem* and uses *nun* toward the end of v. 3 rather than at the beginning of v. 4. There is no *samek*. The psalm reverses *ʿayin* and *pê*, and both letters occur

---

thought demanding to be expressed." From this he translates "this is the truth that becomes apparent." There is no support for this in Hebrew.

[165]Delitzsch, I, 171, refers *šᵉʾôl* to the grave, since man, formed from the dust, returns to the dust. While the view is possible, it does not seem appropriate here with the emphasis on the "wicked" and "nations that forget God." A statement of judgment fits this better.

[166]The word *tiqwâ*, from the verb *qawâ*, has the sense of eager expectancy rather than a patient waiting for something.

in the middle of verses. The psalm concludes with *qôp*, *rêš*, *šîn*, and *tau* all in regular structure. David uses a great deal of poetic license in the structure of the psalm.[167]

The psalm differs from Psalm 9. Psalm 9 is basically a song of thanksgiving, while Psalm 10 is a lament over the wickedness in the land. Psalm 9 stresses the opposition of the heathen, but Psalm 10 focuses on the opposition of the wicked in Israel. Psalm 9 has musical notations while Psalm 10 does not. There are, however, several expressions and words that connect the two psalms. The phrase "times of trouble" occurs only in 9:9 and 10:1. Both psalms refer to "man" with the word *ᵓᵉnôš* (9:19, 20; 10:18). Both refer to the "oppressed" (*dak*, 9:9; 10:18) and to the "afflicted" (9:12 *ᶜanaw*/*ᶜanî*; 10:2, 12, 17). It is likely that David composed both psalms at the same time but gave each a different theme.

The LXX joins Psalms 9 and 10 into a single psalm. The Vulgate also joins the two psalms. This throws the numbers of the psalms off, generally by one, until Psalm 147.[168] Psalm 147 is divided so that vv. 1–11 become Psalm 146 and vv. 12–20 make up Psalm 147. The remaining three psalms follow the traditional numbering.

There is a practical application to the psalm. Just as David lamented the presence of wickedness and its opposition to godliness, so Christians today should hold this same attitude toward sin. Rather than joining the forces of evil, believers should take their stand against it. We grieve for those who continue in sin, and we oppose its

---

[167]Ken Burkett, *Psalm 119: A Thematic and Literary Analysis* (PhD diss., Bob Jones University, 1994), pp. 128–29, explains the disruption in the acrostic pattern "as a metaphor for order and control." Ps. 9 portrays God as "judging and avenging in righteousness (9:3–8, 11–12, 15–18) and protecting those who are His (9:9–10). The reality of God's past interventions encourages prayers for forthcoming Divine intervention—prayers that the righteous can surely expect to be answered (9:13–14; 9:19–10:2)." This part of the psalm follows the normal acrostic pattern. In 10:3–11, God drops out of sight as the psalmist "presents the world as it often appears to man. It is a world where man failed to reckon with spiritual realities and to perceive the existence of the righteous Judge." In this part, where wicked man prevails, the acrostic disappears. Only at the end does God reappear (10:12–18). It is here that the acrostic pattern resumes. While Burkett's position may be correct, it is impossible to prove.

[168]The LXX also deviates elsewhere from the numbering of the English versions. It divides Ps. 116 into two psalms and combines Pss. 114 and 115 into a single psalm. Other than these variations, the numbering of the psalms in the LXX, from Ps. 10 through Ps. 146, differs from that in the English versions by one.

presence in every area where it occurs. In doing this we rely on the Lord, Who alone has power to overcome evil.

I. David's Lament 1–11

1–2 David has faced a problem for some time. He questions why the Lord seems to stand afar off and to hide Himself from David's "trouble" (*ṣarâ*, or "distress," see 9:9), v. 1. The wicked arrogantly "persecute the poor" (or "hotly pursue the afflicted," *ᶜanî*, see 9:12). David asks that these wicked persons would fall into their own "devices" (*m^ezimmâ*, or "plans").[169] As with many of David's psalms, we do not know what trial he writes of. He has the trials of others in Judah in view. Perhaps he had seen the burdens borne by some of his nation and now takes their plight to the Lord, v. 2.

3–11 In the remainder of the section, David describes the actions of the wicked. The wicked man boasts of his "desires," in this context referring to his greed. He "blesseth" (*barak*, see 5:12) the greedy, "whom the Lord abhorreth" (or "*and* spurns the Lord"), v. 3.[170] The "pride of his countenance,"[171] his arrogance, makes him feel self-sufficient. He does not "seek" (*daraš*, see 9:10) God, nor does he include God in his "thoughts" (or "plans," *m^ezimmâ*), v. 4.[172] The phrase "His ways are always grievous" is better "His ways always endure." He is successful in what he does. This leads him to ignore the judgments of God and to look down on his foes, v. 5. He thinks that he will "never" (*l^edor wador*)[173] be moved but that he will always have success; cf. Isaiah 47:7; 56:12, v. 6.

---

[169]In Psalms, *m^ezimmâ* always refers to wicked thinking or plans; see v. 4; 21:11; 37:7; 139:20. Elsewhere, the word may refer to either good or evil thoughts.

[170]The two phrases in 3*b* stand side by side. The AV supplies the relative pronoun "whom." But supplying the copulative "and" leads more smoothly into v. 4, where David describes the wicked man's rejection of God.

[171]The phrase is lit. "height of his nose [*ᵓap*]." The word *ᵓap* normally represents anger, see 2:5. Here, however, it is the representative feature of the face, lifted up in pride.

[172]Henry, p. 273, translates 4*b* "all his thoughts are that there is no God." Cohen, p. 24, and Weiser, p. 147, are similar. Since *m^ezimmâ* in v. 2 refers to "plans," it is reasonable that it has that same meaning here. Rather than thinking, "there is no God," the wicked man simply ignores God. While unaware of the implication of this, he becomes a practical atheist by his lack of concern for the spiritual.

[173]The phrase *l^edor wador* occurs in Psalms only here and at 33:11; 49:11; 77:8; 79:13; 85:5; 89:1, 4 (with *maqqep*); 102:12; 106:31; 119:90: 135:13; 146:10. It is

At the same time, the wicked man utters "cursing" (better "oaths")[174] and deceit. While swearing to one thing, he plots devious ways of taking advantage of others. In this way, he brings about "mischief" (or "trouble," *ʿamal*, see 7:14) and "vanity" (or "oppression"). Paul quotes v. 7*a* as he describes the wickedness of mankind (Rom. 3:14), v. 7. At times, the wicked man stays in the "lurking places" where he can ambush others. From there, he kills innocent people. From the context, his purpose is robbery rather than brutality or revenge. He sets himself against the "poor" (or "unfortunate," *ḥelkâ*), v. 8.[175] David portrays him as a "lion" (*ʾarî*, see 7:2) waiting in his den. So the wicked sets himself to capture the "poor" (or "afflicted," *ʿanî*). He takes the "poor" (or afflicted, *ʿanî*) when he draws "him into his net," the web of deception that he has woven, v. 9. He "croucheth" (better "crushes," *dakâ*, see 9:9) and humbles his victims.[176] The wicked man takes the "poor" (*ḥelkaʾîm*, or "unfortunate ones") "by his strong ones" (*ʿaṣûm*), his many deceitful actions, v. 10.[177] He thinks that God will never call him to account for his actions. It is as

---

lit. "to a generation and a generation," idiomatically expressing a superlative, "through all future generations." The phrases *dor wador*, 45:17; 61:6; 100:5; *dôr wadôr*, 145:13; *dôr dôrîm*, 72:5; *bedor wador*, 90:1; *bedôr dôrîm*, 102:24; and *dôr ledôr*, 145:4, are similar in meaning.

[174]Leupold, p. 121, and Horne, p. 65, understand this as curses against others. Jennings, I, 40, views it as perjury. The word *ʾalâ*, however, refers rather to an oath, a formal promise of obligation, rather than an imprecation against another.

[175]The word *ḥelkâ* occurs only in this psalm, vv. 8, 10 (plural), 14. In each case, the translation "unfortunate" is appropriate.

[176]Henry, p. 275, refers this to the wicked man. "He *crouches* and *humbles himself*, as beasts of prey do, that they may get their prey within their reach." The word "croucheth," however, is better "crushes," a term that applies better to the emotional turmoil of the victim. Further, there is no word "himself" in the text. Leupold, p. 121, pictures the wicked as crushing his victim, then crouching again, ready for more prey. Rodd, p. 21, applies both terms to the victim, "crushed and prostrate." This ignores the context. Hirsch, I, 74, understands the wicked as acting crushed and humble to deceive his victim. I have applied both verbs to the victim rather than to the wicked man.

[177]The phrase "strong ones" is ambiguous, leading to different interpretations. Rawlinson, I, 66, refers this to "ruffians whom the wicked man employs to effect his purposes." Murphy, p. 110, considers this the "various means by which he exerts power over the weak." Leslie, p. 222, interprets the phrase as "plots." Calvin, I, 148, considers this as "the talons and teeth of the lion." These are possible views. I have referred the phrase to his actions since the adjective *ʿaṣûm* has a significant component of numerical greatness in its meaning, e.g., Ps. 35:18. It refers to "might" in the sense of number, e.g., Num. 32:1; Isa. 60:22.

though God has forgotten him or has turned His face away and cannot see him; cf. v. 13. As in v. 4, he is a practical atheist, v. 11.[178]

II. David's Prayer 12–15

12–13 Having focused on the nature of his enemies, David now commits the plight of his people to the Lord. Although he is the king, David realizes that he has no power over the evil hearts of the wicked. To this time, the Lord has seemed to stay aloof from the people; cf. v. 1. David asks Him to act on their behalf. He asks the Lord to raise His hand in preparation for striking down His foes. The hand is here a symbol of God's power; cf. 80:17; 89:13. David prays that God will not forget the "humble" (or "afflicted," *ᶜanî*, see 9:12), v. 12. Why should the wicked be allowed to "contemn" (better "spurn") God? The wicked, David reminds the Lord, has denied that God will "require" (*daraš*, see 9:10) judgment of him; cf. vv. 4, 11, v. 13.

14–15 The Lord has indeed seen the actions of the wicked. The Lord sees "mischief and spite" (or "trouble [*ᶜamal*, see 7:14] and vexation"). He will "requite" (or "take") it into His "hand," i.e., His power, to punish it. The "poor" (or "unfortunate") commits himself to God, knowing that there is no other recourse. God is "the helper of the fatherless," an illustration of His care for those without resources or strength, v. 14. David prays that the Lord will "break . . . the arm of the wicked and the evil man." The statement is poetical as David asks God to overcome those who have persecuted the helpless. The "arm" often represents strength, e.g., Job 35:9; Jeremiah 17:5. To break the arm is to overcome a person's might; cf. 37:17; Ezekiel 30:21–22. David asks the Lord to "seek out" (*daraš*) the sins of the wicked until none is left to punish, v. 15.

---

[178]Graham S. Ogden, "Translating Psalm 10.11," *BibTrans* 42:2 (1991): 233, understands the spokesman as the victim rather than the wicked oppressor. He argues that *šakaḥ*, "forgotten," in the 3ms form "consistently refers to God as having forgotten the psalmist." He also treats vv. 11–12 as a chiasmus. This, however, is a subjective view that depends on identifying the speaker as the victim. It is arbitrary to limit the use of *šakaḥ* to the 3ms *qal* perfect. The *qal* perfect also occurs in 106:13, 21; 119:139, where the wicked is the subject. Since nothing in the context signals a change in the speaker between vv. 10 and 11, it is best to see the wicked as the subject in v. 11.

III. David's Confidence 16–18

16–18 David expresses his confidence that the Lord will work on His people's behalf. He is the eternal King. The "heathen," the wicked described under his true nature, has "perished" (*ʾabad*, see 1:6) from the land. David phrases the action as complete because it is certain in his mind that God will do this, v. 16. The Lord has heard the prayer of the "humble" (or "afflicted," *ʿanî*, see 9:12). He will "prepare" (or "establish") their heart, giving them grace to trust Him. He will incline His ear to the prayers of His people, v. 17. He will "judge" (or "extend justice") to the orphan and the "oppressed" (*dak*, see 9:9), those crushed down under the brutality of the wicked. The "man [*ʾenôš*, or 'mortal man,' see 8:4] of the earth" will no longer "oppress" (or "cause terror"), v. 18.

PSALM 11

David writes this psalm for the "chief musician" (*menaṣṣeaḥ*, see 4, intro.) of the tabernacle.[179] Although there are no musical notations, David intended that the psalm be included in the nation's worship. It is a song of trust; David expresses his confidence that the Lord will overcome the wicked and sustain the righteous. With these actions, David illustrates the attitude that believers should hold today when they face the opposition of the wicked.

We do not know the incident that lies behind the psalm. From v. 2, we see that there is a threat to David's life. The statement in v. 1, "Flee as a bird to your mountain," may refer to David's escapes from Saul when first his wife and later Jonathan urged him to leave (I Sam. 19:11; 20:42).[180] It may also relate to David's flight at Absalom's

[179]The dedication to the "chief musician" coupled with the phrase "a Psalm of David" is a common title. With the supplied word "Psalm," it occurs here and in Pss. 14, 18, 36, and 70. The titles to Pss. 13, 19, 20, 21, 31, 40, 41, 51, 64, 109, 139, and 140 include the unsupplied word "Psalm."

[180]This verse was the basis for the hymn "Flee as a Bird," with the words and music by Mary Shindler, 1842.

rebellion (II Sam. 15:14; 17:16). As with most psalms, there is not enough information given to identify the setting.[181]

I. The Threat to David's Life 1–3

1–3 David states his "trust" (*ḥasâ*, see 2:12) in the Lord. Why then do others direct him to flee for his life? Although the expression "Flee as a bird to your mountain" does not occur again, it sounds proverbial. Just as a bird would fly from a threat to a safe haven in the mountains, so David must find safety in flight. This is the advice of David's friends. David, however, does not intend to flee in fear but to make a strategic retreat, still trusting the Lord to sustain him, v. 1.[182] David's foes have their weapons prepared. They "bend" (*darak*, "tread on," see 7:12) their bows, stepping on one end so that they may bend it and connect the string. They place the arrow in preparation for shooting it. They shoot at the upright "privily" (better "in darkness"), v. 2. The question "If the foundations [*šatôt*][183] be destroyed [or 'torn down,' *haras*],[184] what can the righteous do?"

[181]Cheyne, I, 36, sets the background as "the ravages of the Jerameelites," basing this on his own novel translation. Thompson, p. 202, relates the psalm to David's position in Saul's court, before his later flight. VanGemeren, p. 130, places it during David's flight from Saul.

[182]The problem in the verse lies in reconciling the question, "How say ye . . . [to] flee?" with David's actions of actual flight. Bratcher and Reyburn, p. 110, say, "The psalmist knew that his safety lay in trusting Yahweh, not in running away." Oesterley, II, 147, says that David protests "against the advice of his friends that he should take to flight." Horne, p. 66, says that "the Christian . . . in perilous times, should make God his fortress, and continue doing his duty in his station: he should not, at the instigation of those about him, like a poor, silly, timorous, inconstant bird, either fly for refuge to the devices of worldly wisdom, or desert his post, and retire into solitude, while he can serve the cause in which he is engaged." The fact is that David did flee. The flight, though, was not one of desperation but a tactical withdrawal until he was in a position to take the offensive.

[183]The source of *šatôt* is *šît*, "to put, set," which yields "something placed, a foundation." Moll, p. 108, considers this a reference to "the laws and ordinances of public justice." Henry, p. 277, relates the foundation to "principles of religion . . . on which the faith and hope of the righteous are built." Hengstenberg, I, 178, refers this to "justice and righteousness." Nothing here restricts the sense of the word. David likely thinks broadly of the dissolution of law and order by the conquest of the wicked.

[184]The verb *haras* occurs only three times in Psalms, here and at 28:5 and 58:6, although it occurs more often elsewhere. It refers to the breaking down or tearing down of something.

shows the threat to the nation. If David's enemies destroy the foundations of law and order in the nation, what will the righteous person do? The rhetorical question demands a negative answer. He will not be able to do anything, v. 3.[185]

II. The Confidence in David's God 4–7

4–7 With the eye of faith, David sees the Lord in His heavenly "temple" (*hêkal*, see 5:7). The foes of David may try to usurp control over the nation, but the Lord rules over all. He sits upon His throne in heaven (cf. Isa. 6:1). The thought is of the Son of God in His role as King of kings. He examines the actions of men.[186] The repeated reference that the Lord's sees mankind emphasizes his examination. No man acts without the Lord knowing about it, v. 4. Verse 5*a* is better "He tries the righteous and the wicked."[187] He "tries" both as He tests their loyalty to Him. He "hateth" (*śane*ᵓ, see 5:5) the one that "loveth violence," v. 5. He will punish the wicked with "snares [*paḥîm*],[188] fire and brimstone, and an horrible tempest [or 'burning wind']." These punishments are representative, not exhaustive. They poetically represent the breadth of options available to the Lord as He judges the wicked. This is their portion of the cup of judgment, v. 6. Verse 7*a* is better "For the Lord is righteous. He loves righteousness." This

---

[185]Hirsch, I, 78, understands "righteous" as the "righteous One." If the wicked prevail, what will God have accomplished? Dahood, I, 69, varies this slightly, translating, "What is the Just One doing?" While these are possible translations (so alternate translation, NIV), it is unlikely that David would ask questions such as these about God's work. Eaton, p. 50, considers "the righteous one" as Israel's king. The context is more general, referring to "the upright in heart," v. 2, and to both the righteous and wicked, v. 5. Kirkpatrick, p. 59, translates, "What hath the righteous wrought?" His efforts have availed nothing. The view is possible. The psalm goes on, however, to deal with the future. The Lord will judge the wicked. In view of this, it is reasonable to set the rhetorical question in the future. What will the righteous do? Nothing! The Lord, however, will act on his behalf.

[186]W. E. Barnes, I, 50, suggests the peculiar view that the psalmist refers to "the eyelids of the morning," with the morning dawn a sign of God's coming. This phrase occurs again only in Job 41:18, where the context makes it clear that the "eyelids" are the dawn. It is more natural here to relate it to God's vision.

[187]The AV follows the MT, with the ᵓ*atnaḥ* giving a 6:2 division to the verse. With the more common 4:4 division, most authors translate as here.

[188]There is only weak textual evidence for reading *paḥᵃmê* ᵓ*eš* or *paḥam* ᵓ*eš*, "burning coals." W. E. Barnes, I, 50, and VanGemeren, p. 134, accept the change, which the translation of Symmachus supports. The LXX and Vulgate support the MT.

continues the thought of v. 5*a*, the trying of the righteous. Rather than "his countenance" beholding the upright, v. 7*b* reads, "The upright will see His face."[189] Once more, this anticipates the privilege given to the godly to see their Savior in heaven, v. 7.[190]

PSALM 12

The title identifies the author as David, but nothing in the psalm relates it to any particular time in David's life.[191] The song is a community lament.[192] David recognizes that the wicked oppress godly persons, particularly those that are poor and without resources. He expresses his confidence that the Lord will deliver them. He states all of this generally without connecting it to any specific situation.

David intends the psalm for the "chief Musician" (*m*ᵉ*naṣṣeaḥ*, see 4, intro.). This probably indicates that David held a position of leadership such that the director of the tabernacle music would use what he had written. At the same time, he may not have been king since he seems not to have had the power to correct the situation. This points to his early life in Saul's court. The psalm is "upon Sheminith"

[189]Albert Barnes, I, 103, reads 7*b* with the AV. He explains the plural "countenance" by describing the face as having a left and a right side. While the word "countenance" is plural, due to its encompassing many parts, it does not require a plural verb. Grammatically, the face is normally an object rather than a subject. The verb is plural. This supports understanding "the upright" as a collective and making it the subject.

[190]W. H. Bellinger, Jr., "The Interpretation of Psalm 11," *EvQ* 56:2 (April 1994): 100, understands the verse as describing the accepting of "the worshipper . . . into the asylum of the sanctuary." The psalm, however, does not mention the temple. It is unlikely that this view is correct.

[191]Murphy, p. 116, dates the psalm to the "latter years of the reign of Saul." While this is possible, the psalm does not give enough information to let us be definite.

[192]Johann Sebastian Bach based his cantata "Ach Gott, vom Himmel Sieh Darein" ("O God, from Heaven Look Down") on Martin Luther's paraphrase of this psalm. Paul Hofreiter, "Johann Sebastian Bach and Scripture: 'O God, from Heaven Look Down,'" *CTQ* 59:1–2 (1995): 67–92, presents an excellent summary of this cantata and Bach's faith in Christ.

(*šᵉmînît*, see 6, intro.), a musical direction for the playing of the lament.

I. Lament for the Godly 1–2

1–2 David asks the Lord for "help" (or "deliverance") for the "godly [or 'loyal,' *ḥasîd*, see 4:3] man." He "ceaseth," coming to an end due to the oppression directed to him. The statement does not mean that there were no longer any godly among the people. Apparently something has happened to cut off a group of faithful individuals from the nation. David's lament may well have come from his own plight as others have falsely accused him, perhaps during the time of his flight from Saul. He broadens the psalm, however, to include all in the nation that face oppression, v. 1. Each one of the wicked speaks "vanity" (or "falsehood," *šawʾ*)[193] to his "neighbour" (or "friend," *reaʿ*).[194] They flatter and speak with a "double heart,"[195] knowing the truth and yet uttering falsehood, v. 2.

II. Confidence in the Lord 3–4

3–4 David expresses his confidence that the Lord will right the wrongs of this life. He will cut off those who flatter and those who speak "proud [lit. 'great'] things," who boast of themselves, v. 3. These haughty individuals have boasted of what their speech will accomplish. This may refer to persuasiveness, to verbal threats, or to debating ability. They say, "Our lips are our own" (better "Our lips are with us"), i.e., on their side to help them. The rhetorical question "Who is lord [*ʾadôn*, see 8:1] over us?" indicates their supreme confidence in themselves, v. 4.

---

[193]The noun *šawʾ* refers to that which is without substance. This may be falsehood, deceitfulness, or worthlessness. The context must determine the sense given to the word.

[194]The word *reaʿ* indicates either a close or a casual friend. The thought of "neighbour" interprets this as a more casual relationship. The thought of a "double heart" suggests betraying a closer relationship.

[195]The phrase is lit "with a heart and a heart," idiomatic for "double heart."

III. Promise of the Lord 5–6

5–6 The Lord now reveals His promise to David directly. The Lord declares that He will help the "poor" (or "afflicted," *ᶜanî*, see 9:12). He has heard the "sighing" (or "groaning) of the poor and needy, and He "will set him in safety from him that puffeth at [i.e., speaks against] him," v. 5.[196] David reassures himself by recalling the certainty of the words that God speaks. These are pure, with no blemish to hinder their fulfillment. They are like silver that has been "tried" (*ṣarap*, better "refined")[197] seven times in a "furnace" (or "crucible") made from "earth," possibly clay; cf. 18:30; 19:8; 119:140. As is often the case, the number "seven" refers to a full measure, here complete purity. The trustworthiness of God's Word is clear, v. 6. That has not changed. God's people may still rely on God's Word.

IV. Reliance on the Lord 7–8

7–8 David expresses his belief in God's promises. The Lord will keep "them," the oppressed. He will preserve "them" (lit. "him"), the individual sufferer, from the attacks of the wicked in David's own time, v. 7. David describes the present situation. The wicked walk about on every side while the "vilest" (or "worthless," *zullût*) are "exalted" (*kᵉrum*),[198] lifted up to positions of power, v. 8. While the

---

[196]KB, III, 917, recognizes *pûḥ* II, "witness," but translates v. 6 as "rage against." J. Gerald Janzen, "Another Look at Psalm XII 6," *VT* 54:2 (2004): 164, thinks that "God promises to provide a witness as deliverance." Gert T. M. Prinsloo, "Man's Word—God's Word: A Theology of Antithesis in Psalm 12," *ZAW* 110:3 (1998): 391, derives the word from *ypḥ* II, "to witness." This verb is not clearly attested in the OT. In any case, the *hipᶜil* form does not occur. The meaning "witness" is debatable. In the references given in KB, the sense is of "speaking." That idea is suitable here.

[197]The verb *ṣarap* refers to smelting or refining a metal, producing purity in the product. From this, the word came to describe something that had been tested and proved acceptable.

[198]P. Wernberg-Møller, "Two Difficult Passages in the Old Testament," *ZAW* 69:1 (1957): 70–71, understands *kᵉrum* as a variant pointing of *kerem*, "garden." He considers that the wicked "walk about (in) the vineyard with spoils belonging to (or: taken from) the children of men." In addition to repointing the verb, this view requires the supply of two prepositions and gives an unusual meaning to *zullût*. Eugene Zolli, "*Kerum* in Ps. 12:9: A Hapax Legomenon," *CBQ* 12:1 (1950): 7–9, relates *kᵉrum* to *karmîl*, "crimson." Since this biblical color comes from a worm, he translates the phrase as "despicable [*zullût*] worms to men." While the view has support in *The Targum of Psalms*, p. 43, it is an unnecessary interpretation of a common word. The word *kᵉrum* is the infinitive of *rûm* with the prefixed *kᵉ* preposition.

psalm ends on this negative thought, the promise of v. 7 gives hope for the future to the godly.

PSALM 13

In this individual lament psalm, David pleads with the Lord to deliver him from his enemy. Nothing in the psalm identifies either the time or the nature of the trial faced by David.[199] It was clearly a serious problem, since he refers in v. 3 to the possibility of death. David writes the song during the trial. He concludes with his trust in the Lord. As with many of David's psalms, he plans it for the "chief musician" (*m*^{e}*naṣṣeaḥ*, see 4, intro.) to include in the tabernacle worship. This suggests that David rules the land at the time that he writes. It is possible, of course, that he looks back to an earlier period of his life and writes of his feelings at that time.

The pattern David follows in the psalm sets an example for believers who face difficulties caused by the wicked oppression of others. David first expresses his concerns to the Lord, vv. 1–2. He follows this with his prayer that the Lord will deliver him, vv. 3–4. He concludes by stating his confidence in the Lord, vv. 5–6. Though the psalm has only a few verses, it displays a major principle for Christians to follow.

Hengstenberg, I, 195, accepts *rûm* but understands *zullût* as "depression." He translates, "Elevation is depression to the sons of men." It is, however, unlikely that *zullût* means "depression." Although the word occurs only here, it logically is a feminine noun from *zalal*, "to be light, worthless."

[199]Jennings, I, 49, and Gaebelein, p. 61, suggest that the psalm reflects David's feeling during Saul's prolonged search for him; cf. I Sam. 27:1. While this is possible, it is equally possible that the plight here may have been much shorter. Someone facing a serious trial may feel that a day or two is too long. Dahood, I, 76, sees "the lament of a man on the verge of death." Hirsch, I, 88, refers the psalm to the nation fearing that its existence "is about to come to an end." More naturally, the personal pronouns refer to an individual. Based on his subjective interpretation, Buttenwieser, p. 617, dates the psalm in 344 BC, following the Syrian conquest of Israel.

I. The Plight of David 1–2

1–2 David's questions reveal his concern. The opposition of his foe has gone on for some time. This leads David, at least for a brief time, to wonder if the Lord has forgotten him. The opening phrase is better "How long, O Lord? Will you forget me forever [or 'continually']?" The trial has gone on too long. How long will the Lord "hide [His] face," not answering David's prayers, v. 1? How long will David be shut up to his own "counsel" (*ᶜeṣâ*, see 1:1)? How long must he grieve over his situation? How long will his enemy hold the upper hand? The fourfold use of the phrase "how long" underscores the threat, v. 2.

II. The Prayer of David 3–4

3–4 Having expressed the problem he faces, David turns to the Lord in prayer. He asks the Lord to "consider and hear [better 'answer']" his requests. He prays that the Lord will "lighten [his] eyes," restoring life (cf. 19:8; Prov. 29:13) rather than letting the eyes darken with death. David will not fall before his foe, sleeping "the sleep of death." This phrase poetically pictures death as sleep, with the stretched-out corpse resembling a sleeping person, v. 3. His enemy will not boast of victory over him. Others who oppose David will not rejoice over his defeat, v. 4.

III. The Praise of David 5–6

5–6 These two verses are a single verse in the MT. David trusts in the Lord's "mercy" (or "steadfast love," *ḥesed*, see 5:7). He is confident of victory and therefore anticipates rejoicing in the deliverance the Lord will give him, v. 5. He will sing praises to the Lord because He has "dealt bountifully" (*gamal*, see 7:4), graciously rescuing David from the power of his enemy, v. 6.

PSALM 14

This individual lament is similar to Psalm 53. The titles differ slightly, and Psalm 53 describes a different situation. Psalm 53 uses *ᵓᵉlohîm* throughout, but Psalm 14 uses *yᵉhwah* in vv. 2, 4, 6, and 7.[200] David writes this psalm for a different situation than that faced in Psalm 53.[201] David is the author of this psalm, but we cannot set the circumstances for its writing with certainty.[202] It clearly comes at a time when David has no influence to stop the oppression. This may be during his flight at Absalom's rebellion. David sets forth the universal truths of the wickedness of man and the deliverance of the righteous. As with many of his psalms, David prepares the psalm for the "chief musician" (*mᵉnaṣṣeaḥ*, see 4, intro.) at the tabernacle. This suggests David's position as king at the time of writing. He likely anticipated its use in Israel's worship.

I. Rejection of the Lord 1–4

1 The "fool" (*nabal*)[203] inwardly says to himself, "There is no God." This denial of God's existence leads to his being marked by wickedness. Such fools are morally "corrupt" (*šaḥat*).[204] This leads to "abominable works," not described except generally. "None" (*ᵓên*) of

---

200The discussion at Ps. 53 takes up the individual differences in greater detail.

201I consider Ps. 53 the later composition. The notes on Ps. 53 give the reasons for this conclusion.

202Phillips, I, 107, makes the psalm David's commentary on the "universal corruption of the human race," especially in the early days of mankind and Israel. Kirkpatrick, p. 65, relates the psalm to "the days before the Flood, at Babel, in Sodom." Gaebelein, p. 64, suggests that the psalm comes from the time of David's flight from Absalom. Clarke, I, 54, relates it to the time between the capture of Jerusalem and the bringing back of the ark to the city. Murphy, p. 121, dates it at the time of II Sam. 8, as David establishes Israel's independence from heathen oppression. Ewald, II, 143, rejects Davidic authorship. On subjective grounds, he places the psalm during the Babylonian captivity. Again with subjective reasoning, Kissane, pp. 54–55, makes the psalm postexilic.

203The *nabal* opposes spiritual and moral truth. He is a hardened sinner because of his senseless rejection of divine truth, e.g., Pss. 39:8; 74:18, 22.

204While the word *šaḥat* normally refers to destruction, there is often a component of corruption. Here and in Ps. 53, the parallelism supports "corruption." In Pss. 78:38, 45 and 106:23, the only other places in Psalms that the word occurs, the thought is of destruction.

the wicked do "good," not surprising since they have rejected the One Whose very nature is good, v. 1.

2–3 The Lord sees these wicked men. David poetically calls them "the children of men," since they are born with the sinful nature of mankind. The Lord looks to see if "there" (*yeš*, see 7:3) are any that understand spiritual matters and therefore "seek" (*daraš*, see 9:10) after God, v. 2. There are none. They have "gone aside," turning away from the ways of the Lord. They are "filthy" (*ʾalaḥ*). This word occurs three times in the OT (here; 53:3; Job 15:16), always referring to moral corruption. "None" (*ʾên*) of them have done "good, no [*ʾên*], not one." The repeated *ʾên* in vv. 1 and 3 emphasizes their failure. Romans 3:12 quotes the verse to show the universal wickedness of mankind, v. 3.

4 The Lord Himself speaks through David. The question is rhetorical. Is it true that these "workers of iniquity" have no knowledge of their accountability to God? The question suggests the enormity of their sin. They devour the people of God as though they were bread, bringing them to poverty. They do not rely on the compassionate Lord, the One Who would provide their needs if they would but turn to Him, v. 4.

II. Deliverance of the Righteous 5–7

5 Suddenly, while they persecute others, "they," the wicked, are brought to "great fear" (*paḥ^{a}dû paḥad*).[205] They find that God is with His people. The implied thought is that the wicked's oppression of the righteous was at the same time an attack upon God, v. 5.

6–7 The wicked oppressors "have shamed" (better "put to shame," *bôš*, see 6:10) the "counsel" (*ʿeṣâ*, see 1:1) given to the "poor" (or "afflicted," *ʿanî*, see 9:12). This is the counsel given elsewhere that the afflicted should trust the Lord. The Lord is the great "refuge" (*maḥseh*)[206] of the oppressed. Since the wicked have rejected God,

---

[205]The word *paḥad* carries a strong emotional component. It can legitimately be translated "terror" or "tremble." The repetition of the root here emphasizes the emotional response as the wicked see themselves caught in the judgment of God.

[206]The noun *maḥseh* may refer to a literal refuge as the shelter from a storm, Job 24:8. It also has a metaphoric sense, most often of a refuge from evil. In Psalms, other than 104:18 (which refers to a shelter for animals), it always has a poetical sense.

vv. 1–4, they reject this idea as well, v. 6. David longs for the "salvation" of the nation, the completed deliverance from their oppressors.[207] When this happens, the compassionate Lord will bring back "the captivity" of the people, delivering them from their oppressors and restoring the fullness of the land. While there was undoubtedly a local fulfillment in David's mind, ultimate fulfillment will come during the millennial kingdom, when the Lord rules over the earth. Then the nation shall rejoice in the Lord, v. 7.

PSALM 15

In this psalm, David meditates on the nature of the godly person. He establishes the theme with his question in v. 1. His answer in vv. 2–5 gives twelve characteristics that every Christian should possess today. The verses alternate positive and negative characteristics, with each verse giving three qualities of the righteous.

The title is simple, relating the psalm to David but giving no musical directions, no dedication, and no hint of the circumstances leading to the writing. The first verse places the time of writing after the locating of the tabernacle at Jerusalem.[208]

The psalm is the first of eight psalms to be designated "A Psalm of David."[209] Nine more psalms have the title *l^edawid*, "belonging to David," with the word *mizmôr* supplied by the translators to give "*A Psalm* of David." Other psalms with the phrase "a Psalm of David" in their title include additional words of description or instruction.

---

[207]*NIB*, IV, 730, treats v. 7 as a "post-exilic addition." Not only is there no textual support for the view, but it ignores the natural feelings of David for deliverance from the immediate threat to the nation.

[208]Delitzsch, I, 211, speculates that David's reference to the "holy hill" places the psalm during Absalom's rebellion, "when David was cut off from the sanctuary of his God." While this is possible, the psalm may as well reflect David's meditation on the godly individual. Now that the ark of the covenant is at Jerusalem, David turns his thoughts toward the worship of Israel.

[209]These include Pss. 15, 23, 24, 29, 101, 110, 141, and 143. The heading *l^edawid*, "belonging to David," occurs elliptically for *mizmôr l^edawid*, "a Psalm belonging to David." This occurs in Pss. 25, 26, 27, 28, 35, 37, 103, 138, and 144.

I. Asking the Question 1

1 David has brought the ark of the covenant to Jerusalem (II Sam. 6:12–15) and has once more instituted the worship of the Lord (I Chron. 16:4–6, 37–42). It is a natural time for David to consider the question of worship. Whom will the Lord permit to "abide" (*gûr*, see 5:4) in His "tabernacle," the place where He receives worship? David uses the verb *gûr* appropriately. Israel had no inherent right to enter the dwelling of God. The people came only because of God's gracious hospitality. David's second question parallels the first. Who may "dwell in thy holy hill"? The phrase "thy holy hill" refers to the tabernacle's location on Mt. Zion. The "tabernacle" and the "holy hill" by metonymy represent the presence of the Lord.[210] Both questions hint at the privilege of a close relationship with the Lord. Who can enjoy this, v. 1?[211]

II. Answering the Question 2–5

2–3 As David contemplates the nature of sincere worship, he describes the worshiper both positively and negatively. He groups his description into vv. 2–3 and vv. 4–5. In each case, the first verse is positive and the second negative. The list is representative and not meant as a complete description.

In the first place, the one who worships the Lord "walketh uprightly [or 'blamelessly,' see *tom*, 7:8; cf. Prov. 10:9; 15:21]." He further "worketh righteousness," doing that which agrees with the standards set down in God's Word. Thirdly, he "speaketh the truth in [or 'with'] his heart." The preposition points to the internal nature of the truth. He not only speaks true words but also thinks true thoughts, v. 2.

David now states three negative characteristics. The godly man "backbiteth [*ragal*][212] not with his tongue." This expands the thought of speech introduced in the previous phrase by describing him as one

---

[210]Henry, pp. 285–86, spiritualizes the verse. He makes the "tabernacle" represent "the church militant" and the "holy hill" the "church triumphant." This idea is not in the OT and should be rejected.

[211]Leslie, p. 186, understands the psalm as "a Temple liturgy which was used at the moment when a company of pilgrims was on the point of entering the holy place." The view reads into the psalm what it does not explicitly say.

[212]This is the only occurrence of *ragal* in Psalms. The verb means "to go about." Doing this with the tongue, however, leads to the thought of slander or gossip.

who does not slander others. He does not do "evil to his neighbour [or 'friend,' *rea*ᶜ, see 12:2]." He further does not take up "a reproach against his neighbour [or 'kinsman,' *qarob*]"[213] by spreading evil reports about him, v. 3.

4–5 David turns back to positive characteristics. The godly man "contemn[s]" (or "despises") the "vile [or 'reprobate'] person."[214] In contrast, he honors those who "fear the Lord" (*yirᵓê yᵉhwah*).[215] When used with *yᵉhwah* as the object, the verb *yareᵓ* (see *yirᵓâ*, 2:11) has the sense of awe or reverence rather than terror or dread. Thirdly, he keeps his oath, not changing it even when it hurts him to carry out what he has sworn to do, v. 4.[216]

The final verse gives three more characteristics, expressing each negatively. The one who worships the Lord does not collect "usury" (or "interest") when he loans his money to other Israelites.[217] He does not collect a reward, i.e., take a bribe, against an innocent person (cf. Exod. 23:8; Deut. 16:19). The final characteristic sums up the passage. The godly person will "never be moved." He will be steadfast, continuing in the ways of the Lord, v. 5.[218]

---

[213]The word *qarob* often indicates a kinsman, e.g., 38:11; Lev. 21:2; 25:25; Neh. 13:4; cf. 13:28. It may also indicate a near person, i.e., a neighbor. Either kinsman or neighbor fits into the statement here.

[214]Gaebelein, p. 70, understands the phrase as "he that is little in his own eyes, despised," a statement of David's humility. This translation is not as natural as that of the AV and does not connect as well with the following phrase.

[215]This is the first of ten times that the "fear of the Lord" appears in Psalms; cf. 22:23; 25:12; 34:9; 115:11, 13; 118:4; 128:1, 4; and 135:20. The concept also appears with different phrasing in 25:14; 33:18; 34:7; 103:13, 17; and 147:11.

[216]Mitchell J. Dahood, "A Note on Psalm 15,4 (14,4)," *CBQ* 16:3 (1954): 302, argues from Ugaritic that the *lamed* preposition here has the sense of "from." He understands the verse to say, "He swore not to do wrong, and he did not retract." While the *lamed* preposition may indeed mean "away from," the context here argues against taking it so. The final three clauses all involve accepting hurt: keeping one's oath when it brings personal loss, lending money but not receiving interest, and avoiding the easy money that would come through bribery.

[217]The Law forbid taking interest on loans to other Israelites, Lev. 25:36–37; Deut. 23:19–20. Israelites could, however, collect interest on loans made to Gentiles, Deut. 23:20.

[218]Thompson, p. 212, makes the final clause express a reward to those who have the previous eleven characteristics. While this is possible, the parallelism argues that it describes a final quality of the godly person.

PSALM 16

The psalm is a "Michtam"[219] written by David. As is often the case, there is not enough information to locate the psalm precisely in David's life.[220] The psalm describes David's relationship to the Lord and his confidence in the resurrection and a coming life after death. This is the great hope of all believers. The psalm is typically messianic.[221]

I. David's Relationship to the Lord 1–6

1–2 David begins with a prayer that God will protect him. Nothing elsewhere in the psalm indicates a present peril faced by the king. He apparently states here his continuing reliance on God's care. He can pray this because of his "trust" (*ḥasâ*, see 2:12), v. 1. The phrase "*O my soul*, thou hast said" is better "I have said" with the supplied

[219]The word *miktam* is of uncertain meaning. It occurs here and in the titles of Pss. 56, 57, 58, 59, and 60, all except Ps. 16 lament psalms. The presumed verb root, *ktm*, may be related to the Akkadian *katamu*, "to cover, to close (the lips), to overwhelm," or to *kutimmu*, "goldsmith." The Arabic cognate *katam* is "to conceal." Kirkpatrick, p. xx, suggests that the word is "a musical term" with an unknown nature. Delitzsch, I, 218, offers the meaning "inscription." This leads to the idea of "an inscription-poem or epigram, a poem containing pithy sayings." Leupold, p. 147, renders the term "a mystery poem," a poem dealing with "a mysterious issue in life, like the deep mystic relation to God." Hengstenberg, I, 232, supports the sense of a "secret" that "conducts us into the mysterious depths of the divine life!" Thirtle, p. 136, refers the word to a personal psalm. Since Ps. 60 was written for the "chief musician," the view is doubtful. Eaton, p. 58, gives the view that it is a "prayer." Henry, p. 287, adopts the meaning of "golden" and makes the psalm "a very precious one, more to be valued by us than gold . . . because it speaks so plainly of Christ and his resurrection." This explanation, however, does not fit Pss. 56–60. Hirsch, I, 102–3, considers it as a "memorial," a "tenet to which [David] would adhere forever." The LXX translates Στηλογραφία, "Inscription." We do not have enough information to be certain of the sense.

[220]Gregory V. Trull, "An Exegesis of Psalm 16:10," *BibSac* 161 (2004): 305, notes that Peter refers to the Davidic Covenant, Acts 2:30, just before quoting Ps. 16:10. This supports placing the psalm early in David's life. Phillips, I, 122, sets the psalm during one of the two periods after David spared Saul's life, I Sam. 24:1–7; 26:7–11. Murphy, p. 129, dates it after the death of Saul, at the time of David's accession to the throne of Judah. Thompson, p. 212, dates it "near the close of David's life." Based on the supposed similarity of v. 4 to Isa. 57:5–6, Oesterley, I, 155, makes it postexilic. Any similarity is vague.

[221]Note 32 in the introduction to Ps. 2 briefly discusses the messianic psalms.

words omitted.[222] David describes his relationship to the Lord. The compassionate God of redemption (*y*^{e}*hwah*, see 7:1) is his Master (*ʾ*^{a}*donay*, see 8:1). The phrase "my goodness [*ṭôbâ*] extendeth not to thee" has the sense "I have no goodness besides thee." With this, David recognizes the Lord as the source of all that is good, v. 2.[223]

3–4 The grammar of v. 3 is extremely difficult.[224] If we omit the *waw* from the second half of the verse, David refers to the saints on earth as "excellent" (or "excellent ones") that he delights in. This thought follows naturally from v. 2. Because David has no good apart from the Lord, he delights in others who also follow the Lord, v. 3. As for others who "hasten" (*mahar* I)[225] after another god, their sorrows will increase. David will separate himself fully from their worship,

---

[222]Many Hebrew mss as well as the LXX, Vulgate, and Syriac support the change in persons. Both readings give the same sense, that David speaks to the Lord.

[223]Weiser, p. 171, understands *ṭôbâ* as "happiness," indicating that David has no happiness apart from God. This is a unique translation, giving a peculiar sense to the word. Calvin, I, 217, understands the phrase as "my well-doing extendeth not unto thee." With this, David recognizes that his goodness brings no advantage to God. Being all-sufficient, He needs nothing that David can bring. The view is possible, although I feel the above explanation better follows v. 1. Harman, p. 102, understands the words as spoken by "an idol worshiper who claimed allegiance to the Lord but who followed other gods." He bases this on the view that v. 3 refers to an idolater. This view is difficult to support.

[224]In the MT, the construct *w*^{e}*ʾaddîrê* governs the following clause. This leads to the translation, "To [or 'for'] the saints which are in the land, they [*hemmâ*] and [*w*^{e}] all my delight is in them." The AV supplies the conjunction "but" to obtain a contrast with v. 2. It also supplies the preposition "to," which carries the thought of the introductory *lamed* forward to the second stich. This finds the verb in the next verse, a view that does not fit well with the context. Buttenwieser, p. 511, considers that *yhwh* was abbreviated as *y*. At some point, the abbreviation was not recognized and was joined to the following *ʾaddîr* as a *waw*. While this view smoothes out the grammatical problem, it involves too many assumptions. Delitzsch, I, 221, transposes the *waw* to the first clause, a natural reading but without mss support. Several mss delete the *waw*. Leupold, p. 153, and Kidner, p. 83, adopt this approach. This gives the best explanation.

[225]Rawlinson, I, 96, translates *mahar* I as "wed themselves to" another god. Alexander, p. 75, gives it "the general sense of purchasing, by costly sacrifice or self-denial." The wide use of *mahar* I elsewhere does not support these views. Exod. 22:15, the only verse with support for these views, uses *mahar* II rather than *mahar* I. When the common view makes sense, there is no reason to look for a more obscure meaning.

not offering drink offerings of blood,[226] and not using the names of the false god (Exod. 23:13; Deut. 12:3), v. 4.

5–6 Why should David follow another god? The Lord is the portion of his "inheritance and . . . cup" (cf. Num. 18:20). The word "cup" often has a metaphorical sense of destiny, e.g., 11:6; 23:5. David is satisfied to drink deeply of the Lord since He watches over David's "lot," the circumstances of his life, v. 5.[227] The "lines" (*ḥebel*)[228] of his life, that portion which has been measured out to him, have occurred in "pleasant [or 'delightful'] places." His heritage is "goodly" (or "pleasing"), v. 6.

II. David's Consecration to the Lord 7–11

7–8 David "bless[es]" (*barak*, see 5:12) the Lord for giving him counsel. Since David makes no comment to relate this to a specific matter, he probably thinks generally of divine guidance. His "reins" (*kilyâ*, see 7:9), his emotional being, continue to instruct him at night as he reflects on the counsels of the Lord, v. 7. David has set the Lord continually before him as he recognizes His ongoing presence in his life. The Lord is at his right hand, a place of protection (73:23; 109:31; 121:5 contra 142:4). David will therefore "not be moved," overthrown by others who oppose him, v. 8.

9–11 The final paragraph relates the result of David's consecration to the Lord. His heart is "glad" (*śamaḥ*) and his "glory," from the parallelism here referring to his soul, "rejoiceth" (*gîl*).[229] His flesh rests "in hope," confident of the Lord's care. The mention of the "heart,"

---

[226]The OT does not mention drink offerings of blood elsewhere. It is not surprising, however, that the heathen might offer the blood of a human sacrifice to their god. It is also possible that "blood" occurs metaphorically here to represent wine; cf. Gen. 49:11.

[227]The Jews used the "lot" to determine a choice (e.g., Lev. 16:8; Num. 26:55). From this, it came to represent the outcome itself (e.g., 125:3; Josh. 15:1; Isa. 17:14). David uses it here to represent his portion in life.

[228]The "line" was used to measure out some portion (e.g., 78:55; II Sam. 8:2). As with "lot," so "line" came to represent the result of the measurement, the portion measured out (e.g., 105:11, "lot"; Josh. 17:5, "portions").

[229]There is little difference between *śamaḥ* and *gîl*. Unger and White, p. 322, associate *śamaḥ* with spontaneous joy. Jack Lewis, *TWOT*, I, 159, relates *gîl* to physical movements, "vigorous, enthusiastic expressions of joy." Both words refer to an emotional reaction to something that brings joy. The verb *gîl* means "to circle around." The noun form may include a physical demonstration of joy, dancing or moving to

"glory," and "flesh" brings together David's spirit, soul, and body, his whole being (I Thess. 5:23), v. 9. David's confidence comes from his certainty of the resurrection. The Lord will not leave his soul in "hell" (better "Sheol," *šᵉʾôl*, see 6:5), the grave.[230] The Lord will not allow His "Holy One" (*ḥasîd*, see 4:3), here referring to David himself,[231] to experience the "corruption" (*šaḥat*, see 7:15)[232] of the grave.[233] The NT broadens the application. The thought in Acts 2:27, 31; 13:35, is of the Lord Himself. The application proceeds from David, a type of the Lord, directly to the Lord, v. 10. The Lord will show David the path that leads to eternal "life" (*ḥayyîm*)[234] in heaven with God. In His presence is "fulness of joy," and "at [His] right hand" are everlasting "pleasures" (or "delights"). The phrase is better "in [His] right hand," not only the hand of protection (v. 8) but also the hand with the power to dispense blessings, v. 11.

---

indicate the feeling. The word *śamaḥ*, however, may also include a physical display of gladness, I Sam. 18:6. Both occur together, e.g., 14:7; 31:7; 32:11.

[230]Rawlinson, I, 97, wrongly states that "Hell (*Sheol*) is to [David] an 'intermediate state,' through which a man passes between his life in this world and his final condition in some blest abode." Albert Barnes, I, 130, describes Sheol as a "dull, gloomy abode." W. E. Barnes, I, 27, refers to it as "the place in which the dead have a kind of torpid existence." These views introduce an unneeded thought here. David thinks of the grave.

[231]Trull, pp. 307–8, summarizes five views of v. 10: (1) translation, such as that of Enoch and Elijah; (2) communion after death; (3) unbroken fellowship; (4) preservation from an untimely death; and (5) personal resurrection from the dead. The NT best supports this last idea.

[232]The word *šaḥat* may be translated either "pit" or "corruption," depending on how it is derived. The parallelism favors "pit" and many translate this way, e.g., Calvin, Perowne, NIV, NRSV. The LXX has διαφθοράν and the Vulgate *corruptionem*, both supporting "corruption." The NT use in Acts is decisive that the sense is "corruption."

[233]Rawlinson, II, 97, applies 10*b* directly to the Lord. He dismisses any reference to David by making this a rabbinical invention of "the myth that David's body was miraculously preserved from corruption." It is true that rabbis related an extreme view of David's body. It is also true that while the human body decays, the resurrection of the body will remove all traces of corruption. The parallelism of the verse, as well as the context of vv. 9, 11, argues that 10*b* refers to David.

[234]The word *ḥayyîm* is plural, "lives." The plural here intensifies the sense of "life." It is an abundant and unending life enjoyed by those who have received Jesus Christ as their Savior.

PSALM 17

This psalm has the title "A prayer of David." Although David prays in other psalms, e.g., 10:12; 13:1, there is an unusual emphasis on prayer here. In this way, the psalm gives a practical emphasis for believers. Most of the psalm refers to David's petitions and communion with the Lord, but David's mention of his enemies in v. 9 gives rise to vv. 10–12. The word "prayer" (*tᵉpillâ*, see 4:1) is the most general word for prayer in the OT. We cannot locate the background to the psalm with any certainty. It clearly refers to a threat from David's enemies, but there is no way to identify them.[235] The psalm is an individual lament.

I. David's Right to Prayer 1–4

1–2 David begins with the request that the Lord will hear "the right," the rightness of the prayer that he brings before Him.[236] His "cry" (*rinnâ*)[237] and his "prayer" (*tᵉpillâ*, see 4:1) do not come from "feigned [or 'deceitful'] lips," v. 1. He asks the Lord to let his "sentence" (or "judgment," *mišpaṭ*, see 1:5) come from Him. Knowing that his enemies are in the wrong, David confidently asks the Lord to render judgment. He asks the Lord to see "the things that are equal" (better "what is upright"), i.e., his integrity. The request again reflects David's knowledge that he is in the right, v. 2.

3–4 David now rehearses his character before the Lord. He is coming to the Lord as one who has lived in a godly manner. He therefore has the right to bring his petitions. The Lord has "proved"

---

[235]Gaebelein, p. 77, and Cohen, p. 40, locate the psalm during David's flight from Saul when he was in the wilderness of Maon, I Sam. 23:25–26. Hengstenberg, I, 255, places it more generally during "the times of Saul." Harman, p. 104, places the psalm "near the end of David's life." Phillips, I, 130–31, relates the prayer to Jesus' prayer in Gethsemane. This, however, spiritualizes the more obvious relationship of the prayer to David.

[236]Moll, p. 180, and Calvin, I, 235, understand *ṣedeq* as the "righteousness of David." He asks the Lord to hear him as a righteous person. Horne, p. 81, views *ṣedeq* as modifying *yᵉhwah* and translates, "O righteous Lord." The structure of the verse, however, parallels *ṣedeq* with "cry" and "prayer." For this reason, I prefer to make *ṣedeq* the righteous call of David.

[237]The verb *ranan*, see 5:11, refers to a ringing cry of exultation. The noun form *rinnâ* may refer either to a shout of exultation, 42:4 ("joy"); 126:2 ("singing"), or to a prayerful "cry," 61:1; 88:2.

(or "tried," *ṣarap*, see 12:6) his heart and has "visited" (*paqad*, see 8:4) him at night, a time when men's thoughts may dwell on wickedness. He has "tried" (or "refined") him and found "nothing" (or "no evil plans"). David has purposed that he will not transgress with his speech, v. 3. He has followed God's command, "the word of thy lips." He has "kept" (or "watched") the evil way of "the destroyer" (or "violent one") so as to avoid it.[238] With these comments, David does not portray himself as without sin. He rather mentions representative matters to show his desire to please the Lord with his life, v. 4.

II. David's Confidence in Prayer 5–7

5–7 Verses 5–6*a* make a statement rather than a prayer. David says, "My steps have kept your paths [*maᶜgal*]; my feet have not slipped." In the Psalms, *maᶜgal* always refers to a way of life rather than a literal path; cf. 23:3; 65:11; 140:5, v. 5. Knowing that he has walked in the ways of the Lord, David has called on Him in prayer. He is confident that the Lord will "hear" (or "answer") him. He asks the Lord to turn His ear to him, listening to his request, v. 6. He asks the Lord to show His "marvellous [*hapleh*] lovingkindness [*ḥesed*, see 5:7]." The *hipᶜîl hapleh* has the sense "to make separate." This becomes "marvellous" in that it is separate from all other actions of

---

[238]The verse is difficult. The verse reads something like "Concerning the works of man, by the word of your lips, I myself have kept [or 'observed'] the ways of the violent." The AV, NASB, and NIV supply "from" to keep David from following the wicked. Delitzsch, I, 231, is similar. He makes the verb reflexive and supplies "against." This gives "I have guarded myself against the paths of the destroyer." Hirsch, I, 111, translates *šamar* "observed." David watches the ways of the wicked and sees how these bring them into judgment. W. E. Barnes, I, 73, translates similarly but refers the phrase to David watching Saul's approach when the king sought him in the wilderness. Kidner, p. 87, translates "watched" and understands David as recognizing "the voice of God to him through Abigail," I Sam. 25:32ff, that kept "him from violence." Cohen, p. 40, inserts a comma after "the doings of men" and couples "the word of thy lips" to keeping "from the ways of the violent." This ignores the position of the *ʾatnaḥ* in the verse. *NIB*, VI, 741, takes the first half of the verse with v. 3 and the last half with v. 4. The translation becomes "My mouth has not crossed over into the deeds of others, The word of your lips, I have kept." The next thought is "[On] the violent way, my steps hold fast. On your paths, my feet are not moved." This requires paraphrasing, ignores the versification, and chooses unlikely meanings for the prepositions. Leupold, p. 156, translates *šamar* as "shunned," an unlikely sense. Other views are also held. I have translated "watched" as being the simplest solution.

human kindness. While *ḥesed* is often translated "lovingkindness," there is a strong component of loyalty in the word. It could as well be "loyalty" or "steadfast love" here. David calls on the Lord, Who saves those who rely on Him. The Lord protects by His right hand, the hand of power, those who "put their trust" (or "seek refuge," *ḥasâ*, see 2:12), v. 7.[239]

III. David's Need of Prayer 8–12

8–9 David now begins to develop the object of his prayer. He needs protection from his enemies. He asks the Lord to keep him as "the apple of the eye" (*kᵉʾîšôn bat-ʿayin*). The phrase could be translated "as the little man, daughter of the eye." This is the offspring of the eye, the reflection seen in the pupil. Each time the phrase and its close variants occur in the OT (also Deut. 32:10; Prov. 7:2), they refer to something precious. David also draws on the protection given by an eagle to her eaglets as she hides them under her wings (*kanap*).[240] The word *kanap* most often occurs to picture the protection given by the Lord to those who trust Him, e.g., 36:7; 57:1; 63:7.[241] He asks the Lord to care thus for him, v. 8. He now reveals the cause of his need

---

[239]The grammar of the verse is difficult. Literally, the verse reads, "Show your marvelous loyalty, O you who save those who seek refuge from those who rise up against your right hand [*bîmîneka*]." This requires the *bêt* preposition to introduce the object of the verb, unusual but not rare. Eaton, pp. 60–61, and Kissane, p. 69, adopt this position. The problem is that nowhere else do people rise against God's right hand. It is normal that God's right hand protects those who follow Him. Weiser, p. 181, interprets "right hand" as "power." This is possible although the interpretation rests upon the interpreter's view. Cohen, p. 41, and Oesterley, I, 160, translate with the AV as though transposing *bîmîneka* and the verb "rise up": "O thou that savest by thy right hand them which put their trust in thee." This, however, leaves only the single Hebrew word *mimmitqômmîm*, "rise up," in the second stich. Among others, Hengstenberg, I, 267; Albert Barnes, I, 138; and W. E. Barnes, I, 73, insert a comma to obtain something like "You who save those who seek refuge from those that rise up *against them*, at Thy right hand." This is awkward but better than transposing the words.

[240]This phrase was the basis for the hymn "Under His Wings," written by William Orcutt, ca. 1896, with the music by Ira Sankey.

[241]*NIB*, IV, 741, sees the wings as "originally . . . those of the seraphs that were associated with the ark in the Temple." While this is possible, it is unlikely since the people did not see the wings of the angels in the temple. The reference is more likely a proverbial thought drawn from nature.

for protection. There are wicked who "oppress" (*šadad*) him.[242] These are "deadly enemies" about him, v. 9.

10–12 David's enemies "are enclosed in their own fat [*ḥeleb*]," dull and insensitive to spiritual truth.[243] They speak with pride, v. 10. They have surrounded David in his way. They have set their eyes "bowing down" (better "to turn me down") to the ground, v. 11. They are like a lion that "is greedy of his prey" (better "longs to tear"). They are like a "young lion" (*k*ᵉ*pîr*)[244] that secretly lurks as he waits to take his prey, v. 12.

IV. David's Goal in Prayer 13–15

13–14 Having described his own faithfulness to the Lord and the threat to his life from his enemies, David now asks the Lord to intervene on his behalf. He asks the Lord to rise up to "disappoint" (better "confront") his foes and to bring them low. He asks Him to deliver him from his wicked enemy, "which is thy sword" (better "by your sword"). The "sword" here represents the various weapons at God's disposal as He exercises His power, v. 13. Continuing the thought, David develops his goal further. He asks the Lord to deliver him from men "which are thy hand" (better "with your hand") as He wields His weapons against them. David needs to be delivered from those of this "world" (*ḥeled*)[245] who find their "portion," a material goal, in this life. The Lord has gratified their desires, filling them with His treasures. They in turn focus on their children, leaving their wealth to them. David sees his enemies as trying to overcome him in order to increase their wealth, v. 14.

15 In sharp contrast with his enemies, David finds his satisfaction in the Lord. The first phrase more literally reads, "I myself in righteousness will see your face." David will continue to practice the

---

[242]The verb *šadad* is strong, referring to "ruin" or "destruction." It often refers to violent destruction, e.g., Isa. 15:1 ("laid waste"); Jer. 5:6 ("spoil").

[243]The noun *ḥeleb* normally refers to the fat of sacrifices. From this, it acquires the metaphorical sense of "the best." Underlying this, however, is the basic meaning of "fat," and the word can refer, as here, to simple fatness.

[244]The noun *k*ᵉ*pîr* widely refers to lions. Although nothing about the word inherently indicates a young lion, Ezek. 19:3, 5, and 6 suggest this.

[245]The word *ḥeled* refers first to the duration or span of life. From this it acquires the sense of a world having potential and activity but still passing away.

righteousness that will allow him to see the Lord clearly. He will be satisfied during his waking hours with the countenance of the Lord, v. 15.

PSALM 18

We know the setting of this psalm because of its lengthy title and its repetition in II Samuel 22. The two accounts are not identical. In all likelihood, the psalm is original and the parallel account in II Samuel an edited version.[246] The title indicates that the song is for the "chief musician" (*m*ᵉ*naṣṣeaḥ*, see 4, intro.). This suggests that it was for the public worship of the nation. Psalm 18 is a song of thanksgiving for the Lord's deliverance of David.[247]

The title indicates that David wrote the song "in the day that the Lord delivered him from the hand of all his enemies, and from the hand of Saul."[248] There are no significant differences between the setting given here and that in II Samuel 22:1. The title describes David as "the servant of the Lord." The title does not appear in II Samuel because of the way the author there introduces the song.

The psalm recounts the victory of David over his enemies and praises the Lord for supplying David's needs. Any outline of the

[246]The account in II Samuel seems to have been written to smooth some difficult readings in the psalm. In addition, the psalm portrays David in fellowship with the Lord. It must have been written before David's sin with Bathsheba, a sin that II Samuel includes. Cohen, p. 43, and Brevard S. Childs, "Psalm Titles and Midrashic Exegesis," *JSS* 16:2 (1971): 139, make II Samuel original and the psalm an edited version. Ewald, I, 121, and Weiser, p. 185, think that both II Samuel and Psalms borrowed from a common source. Since the debate is subjective, no certain conclusion can be made.

[247]The nine individual songs of thanksgiving include Pss. 18, 30, 34, 40:1–11; 66:13–20, 92, 116, 118, and 138. The six community songs of thanksgiving include Pss. 65, 67, 75, 107, 124, and 136.

[248]From the setting in II Sam. 22, the psalm summarizes David's gratitude to the Lord toward the end of his reign, after many deliverances from the enemy. Rawlinson, I, 115, places it between the victories of II Sam. 10 and those of II Sam. 11–12. He gives no reason for locating the psalm there. Delitzsch, I, 250, thinks that vv. 4–19 deal with David's deliverance from Saul.

psalm is arbitrary. The following suggestion breaks the account into manageable sections.

I. Devotion of David 1–2

1–2 David expresses his deep "love" (*raḥam*)[249] for the Lord, the source of his strength.[250] From the context, David thinks here of his strength in battle, v. 1. The Lord is David's "rock" (*selaᶜ*) and his "fortress," a place of defense and protection. He is David's "deliverer," the One Who watches over him to save him from his foes. He is also David's "God," the name *ᵓel* appropriately stressing the power of God. He is David's "strength" (lit., "rock," *ṣûr*),[251] the strong foundation upon which he rests. For all of these reasons, David states that he "will trust" (or "take refuge," *ḥasâ*, see 2:12), in Him. The Lord is David's "buckler" (*magen*, see 3:3), his shield of defense. He is "the horn [*qeren*][252] of [David's] salvation," a poetic term depicting the Lord as the strength that delivers David from difficult situations. He is David's "high tower" (or "refuge," *miśgab*, see 9:9), v. 2.[253]

II. Deliverance of David 3–19

3 With such a source of strength at his side, David calls for help from the Lord, Who is worthy of praise. His reliance on the Lord delivers him from his enemies. What the Lord has done in the past

---

[249]The word *raḥam* normally refers to the compassion of the Lord for man. When used with man as the subject, it refers to a deep love such as a mother has for her child or mankind has for an orphan.

[250]James L. Crenshaw, *The Psalms: An Introduction*, p. 69, is too restrictive in limiting the psalmist's love for the Lord to v. 1 and, possibly, 97:10. The psalmists also express their love for Yahweh in 31:23; 116:1; and, indirectly, in 145:20.

[251]There is no great difference between *selaᶜ* and *ṣûr*. Although *selaᶜ* may be a cliff (I Sam. 14:4) and *ṣûr* a large rock (Exod. 17:6), both may refer simply to rocks and both represent the Lord as a place of security and protection for those who follow Him. The two words occur together here and at Deut. 32:13; Judg. 6:20–21; II Sam. 22:2–3; Pss. 31:2–3; 71:3; 78:15–16; and Isa. 2:21. Elsewhere, they occur in poetic variation.

[252]The noun *qeren* often refers to a literal horn, the weapon used by animals in attacking their foes. From this idea, *qeren* came to represent power and strength, e.g. 75:4, 5, 10.

[253]The hymn "Thee Will I Love, My Strength, My Tower," written by Johann Scheffler in 1657 and translated by John Wesley, is based on vv. 1–2. Lowell Mason (1792–1872) added the music.

He will continue to do in the future. Note that David does not take the Lord's care for granted. Even though he knew that the Lord had called him to lead the people and that the Lord had promised that his line would culminate in the Messiah, David still relies on the Lord for aid, v. 3.

4–5 David now begins to describe his deliverances from past trials. While there are many of these described in the historical parts of the OT, David here sums them up as though there were a single attack. The "sorrows" (or "cords") of death had wrapped themselves about him. The "floods of ungodly men" (or "torrents of worthless [*bᵉlîyaᶜal*] men")[254] have terrified him, v. 4. The "sorrows [again, 'cords'] of hell [*šᵉʾôl*, see 6:5]" sought to turn him from safety. The "snares [*môqᵉšîm*][255] of death" confronted him. While the description is poetic, it is clear that David faced serious trials, v. 5.

6–15 David had "called upon the Lord," praying as he faced the circumstances that brought him "distress" (or "affliction"). David recalls that the Lord had heard his prayer from "his temple" (*hêkal*, see 5:7), the tabernacle where He dwelled on earth.[256] The reference to God's "ears" is anthropomorphic, describing the Lord in human terms that are easily understood, v. 6. David describes the response poetically. The Lord apparently sent an earthquake to strike fear in the hearts of David's enemies. The swaying of the mountains gave visible evidence of God's anger, v. 7. The reference to "smoke," "fire," and "coals" continues the poetic description. Smoke rises "out of [God's] nostrils." His mouth has spoken words that kindled fire to devour parts of the earth and set "coals" burning, v. 8.

The Lord "bowed" the heavens, a poetical reference to clouds touching the earth to shield the His presence as He comes (cf. 144:5;

---

[254]The word *bᵉlîyaᶜal*, often transliterated *Belial*, comes from two words, *bᵉlî*, "no," and *yaᶜal*, "worth." It thus refers to something without worth. It occurs again in 41:8 and 101:3. Other derivations have also been suggested for the word.

[255]The noun *môqᵉšîm* is from *yaqaš*, "to snare, trap." This word refers to trapping some prey but most often has a poetical sense of trapping a person, e.g., 64:5; 106:36.

[256]*NIB*, IV, 748; Perowne, I, 211; and James Luther Mays, *Psalms*, p. 92, understand the Lord as hearing from His heavenly temple. This is a possible view and, ultimately, the place from which the Lord hears all prayers. David, however, likely thought more directly of the visible tabernacle at Jerusalem, where God dwelled among His people.

Exod. 19:9, 18). "Darkness" was "under his feet" to shield His presence from the people's eyes (cf. Deut. 4:11; 5:22), v. 9. He "rode upon a cherub," the word collectively referring to the angelic beings in His presence as He flew over the earth. The cherubs are associated with the Lord in the OT (e.g., Ezek. 10:1–9, 14–20), often in a context of holiness (Gen. 3:24; Exod. 37:7–9; I Kings 6:23–35). It was as though He flew "upon the wings of the wind" in His coming to judge sin, v. 10. "Darkness" from the clouds that surrounded Him was His "secret place" where man could not see Him. "Dark waters and thick clouds," the impenetrable rain clouds, covered Him, v. 11. "Brightness," lightning, came from the clouds. Hail and "coals of fire," kindled by the lightning, accompanied Him (97:3–4; Exod. 9:23–24), v. 12. Thunder, evidence that the Lord speaks to mankind (29:3–4), came from the skies. This came from the "Highest" (*ᶜelyôn*, see 7:17). Hail and "coals of fire" again gave evidence of His power, v. 13. The "arrows" of the Lord, bolts of lightning, landed among His enemies (77:17; 144:6), v. 14. "Channels of water" filled the dry streambeds. Flashes of lightning illuminated the deepest recesses as though making the "foundations of the world" visible. All this reveals the Lord's wrath upon man for his sin, v. 15.

16–19 The previous paragraph describes the judgment on David's enemies. David now turns to his own deliverance. While the Lord was sending the waters of judgment upon His foes, He protected David, keeping him from being caught in the devastation of others, v. 16. The Lord delivered David from those who were stronger than him and "hated" (*śaneᵓ*, see 5:5) him, v. 17. They "prevented" (or "confronted") David, seeking to capture him. The Lord, however, was his "stay," a trustworthy support to keep him safe, v. 18. The Lord brought him into a "large place," an open area where there were no traps laid for him. He delivered David because He "delighted" (*ḥapeṣ*)[257] in him, v. 19.

III. Dedication of David 20–27

20–24 David now describes his dedication to the Lord, the reason the Lord has delivered him from his foes. The Lord has "rewarded"

[257]The verb *ḥapeṣ* refers to the favor or pleasure that comes from emotional involvement. It expresses itself in attitude or conduct.

(*gamal*, see 7:4) him according to his "righteousness," not sinless perfection but his basic desire to do God's will. David's hands are clean, not stained by wickedness, v. 20. He has kept God's ways without wickedly going away from Him. Note that failing to carry out God's word is the same as wickedly turning away from God, v. 21. David kept the "judgments" of the Lord, those standards by which God regulates man's conduct, before him. David did not turn away from His "statutes," the unchanging guidelines for man, v. 22. David was also "upright" (or "blameless," *tamîm*, see *tom*, 7:8) in his conduct, keeping himself from "mine iniquity [*ᶜawôn*],"[258] some unknown sin that he felt specially drawn toward, v. 23. David repeats the thought of v. 20. The Lord had rewarded him for his righteous behavior. His hands were clean, unsoiled by sin, in God's sight, v. 24.

25–27 David states the general principles by which the Lord works with mankind. With the "merciful" (or "loyal," *ḥasîd*, see 4:3), He is "merciful" (or "loyal"). With the "upright" (or "blameless," *tamîm*), the Lord will be "upright" (*tamam*, or "blameless"),[259] v. 25. With the "pure" (or "those who purify themselves"), He will show Himself "pure." With the "froward" (*ᶜiqqeš*), the Lord will show Himself "froward" (*patal*), v. 26.[260] He will "save" (or "deliver") the "afflicted" (*ᶜanî*, see 9:12), the godly who undergo oppression for their faith. In contrast, He will bring low those who are haughty, v. 27.

IV. Victory of David 28–45

28–31 David now recalls the success God has given him in his conflicts with others.[261] The Lord Himself, an emphatic construction, has

[258]The word *ᶜawôn* occurs often in parallel with other words denoting sin. The sense of *ᶜawôn* comes from the root meaning "to bend, twist." The word therefore refers to deviating from the path of righteousness.

[259]The verb *tamam*, "to be complete," is the root from which the adjective *tamîm* comes. When the verb occurs with a moral sense, the thought is of integrity or blamelessness.

[260]The previous three statements use similar words to make the comparisons. Here David uses two different words. The first, *ᶜiqqeš*, pictures the twisted and perverted ways of sin. The second, *patal*, describes the subtle actions of the Lord as He responds to the *ᶜiqqeš*.

[261]Leupold, p. 171, understands the imperfect verbs as pointing to the future. David is confident of future deliverance, vv. 28–30, based on God's past deliverance. The view is possible although we cannot be certain. In the passage, David mixes the

lighted his way through the darkness of this life, v. 28. By the Lord Himself, again stated emphatically, this has let David "run through a troop" and "leap over a wall." These word pictures may refer to literal accomplishments (conquering the Amalekites, I Sam. 30:17; entering Jerusalem, II Sam. 5:6–7) or may poetically express more generally the victories that the Lord has given him, v. 29.

Having reflected on the blessings of God, David concludes that His way is "perfect" (or "blameless," *tamîm*). David emphasizes *tamîm* in this psalm, using the word in vv. 23, 25, 30, and 32. It is a "tried" (*ṣarap*, see 12:6) way. The Lord is a "buckler" (or "shield," *magen*, see 3:3) to those who "trust" (or "take refuge," *ḥasâ*, see 2:12) in Him, v. 30. David asks "who is God [*ʾᵉlôah*][262] . . . who is a rock?" The question is rhetorical, designed to show his belief that the Lord is God. The image of a "rock" (*ṣûr*, see v. 2) occurs often to picture the Lord as a strong foundation for life, e.g., v. 46; 61:2; 62:2, v. 31.

32–36 David recounts the ways in which the Lord has prepared him for battle against his enemies. God has strengthened him and made his way "perfect" (i.e., keeping him from error, *tamîm*), v. 32. Picturesquely, David describes his swiftness and agility in war as that of "hind's [or 'doe's'] feet." The Lord has set him on "high places," inaccessible to his foes, v. 33. He has taught David the techniques of war so that "a bow of steel" (better, "a bow of bronze") is "broken" (better, "bent") by him. The statement shows David's strength for fighting his enemies, v. 34. The Lord has given him the "shield" (*magen*, see 3:3) of "salvation," delivering him from attack. The "right hand" of the Lord, the hand associated with God's power, has held David up when others tried to bring him down. The Lord's "gentleness" (or "condescension") as He stoops to notice David has made him great, giving him victory over his opponents, v. 35. The Lord has "enlarged" his steps, giving him sure footing that kept him from falling before others, v. 36.

---

imperfect with participles, infinitives, and perfect tense verbs. The final paragraph of this section, vv. 43–45, clearly looks to the future.

[262]The word *ʾᵉlôah* occurs four times in the Psalms, here and 50:22; 114:7; 139:19. *TWOT*, I, 43, suggests that the name conveys "comfort and assurance" to believers and "fear to their enemies." Robert Blake Girdlestone, *Synonyms of the Old Testament* (Grand Rapids: Wm. B. Eerdmans Publishing Company, 1951), p. 31, gives it the same sense as *ʾel*, "power or might."

37–45 David has overcome his enemies, not turning from them until he gained a complete victory (cf. II Sam. 12:29, 31; I Kings 11:15–16), v. 37. He has "wounded" (*maḥaṣ*)[263] his enemies so they could not rise against him again. In a sense, they were "under [his] feet," the picture of dominance over them (cf. 110:1; Josh. 10:24; Mal. 4:3), v. 38. David recognizes that what he has done has been done by the strength given by the Lord. He has "subdued" (or "caused to bow down") those who had risen against David, v. 39. The Lord has "given . . . the necks of mine enemies" (better "made my enemies turn their backs") as they retreated from David. This let David "destroy" (*ṣamat*)[264] those who "hate" (*śaneʾ*, see 5:5) him. Although David says nothing about this here, in hating David, his enemies expressed their hatred of God, the One Who had chosen David. This is the real reason underlying David's success, v. 40.

They "cried," apparently to their gods, but no one responded to their plea. Reflecting their view of localized gods, David's foes even cry out to the Lord as the god of Palestine. They have no success in this either, v. 41. David graphically describes his victories over his enemies. He beats them as small as dust blowing before the wind. He cast them out as he would the mire of the streets, v. 42.

The Lord has delivered David from the "strivings" (or "contentions") of his enemies. He has given David rule over the heathen (cf. the kingdom inherited by Solomon from his father, I Kings 4:21, 24). This leads into a messianic prophecy, with David foreshadowing the millennial reign of Christ. Those who have not known the Lord will serve Him (cf. Isa. 55:3–5), v. 43. When they hear of the Lord, they will yield to Him. The "strangers" (or "foreigners," *nekar*)[265] will "submit" (*kaḥaš*),[266] feigning submission to Him, v. 44. These

---

[263]The verb *maḥaṣ* refers to a severe wound. It may justly be translated "shattered."

[264]The word *ṣamat* occurs only in poetical passages. Eleven of its fifteen occurrences are in Psalms. The word refers to putting an end to someone or something, often, as here, the destruction of enemies. When used with God as the subject, the word refers to the destruction He will bring upon those who oppose Him.

[265]The noun *nekar* refers to someone or something foreign. It most often refers to foreign gods (Gen. 35:2, 4), but also to a foreigner (as here) or a foreign land (137:4).

[266]The *piʿel* of *kaḥaš* refers broadly to deception, failure, or feigned obedience. The foreigners here pretend submission to the Lord.

"strangers" (or "foreigners," *nekar*) will "fade away" (or "drop down"), fearful of standing against the Lord, v. 45.

V. Praise from David 46–50

46–48 In view of the Lord's deliverance of David and His plan to set up Messiah as king over the earth, it is appropriate to close the psalm with a note of praise. The Lord lives! David has experienced His protection and strength in his battles against his foes. David naturally "bless[es]" (*barak*, see 5:12) his "rock" (*ṣûr*, see v. 2) the strong foundation upon which he has rested his life. May "the God of my salvation," the God Who has delivered David from his enemies, be exalted among mankind, v. 46.[267] David recognizes that God "avengeth [him]" (or "brings vengeance to [him]," *n*ᵉ*qamôt*)[268] by subduing others under him. The plural *n*ᵉ*qamôt* emphasizes the completeness of the judgment, v. 47. He explains this by noting that God has delivered him from his "enemies,"[269] including both those who "rise up against" him and "the violent man," v. 48.

49–50 David announces his intention to publicly thank the Lord. He will do this "among the heathen [or 'nations']," a testimony to them of the power of David's God. He will "sing praises" (*zamar*, see 7:17) to the Lord's "name," His nature as a powerful and merciful God.[270] Paul quotes the verse in Romans 15:9 as he praises the Lord for extending salvation to the Gentiles, v. 49. God has given "great deliverance" and showed "mercy" (or "steadfast love," *ḥesed*, see 5:7) to his "anointed" (*mašîaḥ*, see 2:2), to David. Accepting God's promise (II Sam. 7:12–16) by faith, David states his confidence that God will be loyal to his "seed for evermore." While David may not have

---

[267]Fausset, p. 142, understands "the threefold blessing" as "an intimation of the Trinity." It is more likely that the repetition simply intensifies the praise offered to God by David.

[268]The ideas of avenging or revenge, from *n*ᵉ*qamâ*, do not convey the thought of getting even. Although God does not need to take revenge on anyone, He is holy; and His holiness demands that the wicked be punished. See Deut. 32:35, 41.

[269]Rawlinson, I, 121, identifies David's "enemies" as "domestic foes." He feels that "foreign foes seem never to have brought David into much peril." While the view is possible, it is difficult to see how David could have fought against any enemy without peril to himself; cf. I Sam. 21:11–12; II Sam. 18:2–3. Even Rawlinson makes the next phrase refer to "enemies of both kinds," foreign and domestic foes.

[270]See note 94, 5:11, for a brief summary of the Lord's name.

fully understood the nature of the pledge when Nathan made it, it is nonetheless a messianic promise. David's note of praise here therefore recognizes God's faithfulness to His word, v. 50.[271]

PSALM 19

The title names David as the author and dedicates the psalm to the "chief musician" (*m^e^naṣṣeaḥ*, see 4, intro.) for further use of the psalm in the worship ritual. The psalm presents a twofold description of God's self-revelation, one in nature and another in His Word.[272] Nothing in the psalm lets us date it with certainty.[273]

---

[271]Marvin E. Tate, "The Interpretation of the Psalms," *RevEx* 81:3 (1984): 364, concludes that "the titles provide little or no indication of authorship." His justification for this is that "David would hardly have written Ps. 18:49–50." While referring to himself by name is unusual, David does this again at 122:5 and 144:10. This is no reason to dismiss the authorship given in the titles.

[272]Delitzsch, I, 279; Dickson, p. 91; and Kirkpatrick, p. 101, adopt the above view. Leupold, p. 176, subordinates vv. 1–6, the glory of the lawgiver, to vv. 7–14 and makes the whole psalm praise God's Word. Fausset, III, 143, makes the single theme that of God's glory. McCann, p. 29, sees the relationship in this way: "As God is responsible for creating the heavens, the sun, and the progression of day and night [vv. 1–6], so the *torah* of God is responsible for constantly re-creating human life [vv. 7–14]." Thompson, p. 221, understands vv. 12–14 as a third revelation, that of direct revelation to the soul. For stylistic reasons, both Rodd, p. 40, and Mays, p. 170, see two independent psalms, vv. 1–6 and vv. 7–14. No manuscript evidence supports the view.

[273]Delitzsch, I, 280, suggests that the psalmist wrote in the morning, after seeing "the dawning light of day" but before preparing "for the day's work lying before him, in the light of the Tôra." While possible, it is more likely that Delitzsch strains to give a background to the writing. Albert Barnes, I, 166, suggests that David wrote "in those calm periods of his history when he led a shepherd-life, when he had abundant time to contemplate the movements of the heavenly bodies by day and by night, and to meditate on them in contrast with the higher truths which God had made known in his law." In dedicating the psalm to the chief musician, the title suggests that David is already king. He may have reflected on earlier times when he kept the flocks, but the writing occurred later.

I. The Glory of God in His Work 1–6

1–3 The creation declares God's glory. Both of the verbs, "declare" and "shew," are active participles that show the continuous nature of this revelation. The "heavens," the beauty of both the night and day skies, teach man the glory of the Creator God. It is appropriate that this first part of the psalm uses *ʾel*, a name of God that suggests His strength. In vv. 7–14, the name *yᵉhwah* occurs, the name used of God's interaction with mankind. The "firmament," the expanse in which God has placed the heavenly bodies, further shows His "handiwork" (lit. "the work of His hands"), v. 1.[274] Each day "uttereth" (*nabaᶜ*)[275] this glory; each night imparts additional knowledge of God's power, v. 2. There is no need to supply words in v. 3. It reads, "no speech, no words, their voice is not heard." There is a silent, but very eloquent, witness in nature to the glory of the God Who created the universe, v. 3.[276]

4–6 The "line" of the heavens has gone forth to measure the whole earth. Their "words" (or "utterances") witness to the farthest reaches of the world. The use Paul makes of 4*a* and 4*b* shows clearly that the "line" represents the witness to God that has gone through the earth (see Rom. 10:18). God has made a place for the sun in the heavens, v. 4. David illustrates its motion. It is like a "bridegroom" coming from his home as he goes to claim his bride. It "rejoiceth" (*śîś*)[277] like

[274]Many hymns have been based on v. 1, among them "The Heavens Declare Thy Glory." The words to this are by Isaac Watts, 1719, and use music written by Lowell Mason, 1830.

[275]The verb *nabaᶜ* is stronger than the "uttereth" of the AV. Elsewhere it refers to the rushing waters of a wadi, Prov. 18:4; the vituperative words of the wicked, Ps. 59:7; Prov. 15:28; and the babbling of a fool, Prov. 15:2. Here, the heavens "pour forth" their witness to God's glory.

[276]Luther, XII, 140, understands that "the Gospel will be preached in all lands, nations, and languages . . . in all tongues." Albert Barnes, I, 168, and Calvin, I, 311–12, are similar. The view requires the supplied words and is unnecessary since the Hebrew is sensible as it stands. Daniel G. Ashburn, "Creation and the Torah in Psalm 19," *JBQ* 22:4 (1994): 243, translates, "There is no utterance, there are no words, whose sound goes unheard." He understands the sounds of creation as being heard, "received by Creation itself." The translation, however, understands the relative pronoun "whose" rather than the personal pronoun "their." This is an unusual phrasing of the Hebrew.

[277]The verb *śîś* indicates great joy, exultation, and abundant rejoicing. It appropriately refers to rejoicing in the Lord, 40:16; 70:4; and in His Word, 119:14, 162.

a "strong man" (*gibbôr*),[278] an athlete running his race, v. 5. It moves throughout the heavens with nothing escaping the effects of its heat, v. 6.[279]

II. The Glory of God in His Word 7–14

7–11 David now turns to the praise of God's Word, a powerful declaration that reveals the glory of its Giver. While nature reveals God's power, God's Word reveals God's nature and requirements for man. David develops his praise of God's Word with a series of six thoughts. In each, the first phrase describes God's Word and the second shows its effect. God's "law" is "perfect" (or "complete," see *tom*, 7:8),[280] appropriate for "converting" (or "restoring") the soul. His "testimony" (*ᶜedût*)[281] is reliable, "making wise" (*ḥkm*) the "simple" (*petî*),[282] giving him a right way of thinking toward all of life, v. 7. His "statutes" (or "precepts") are spiritually right, bringing joy to the heart of the godly person. The "commandment" of God is morally "pure," giving light as to how one should live, v. 8. The "fear of the Lord" (*yirᵓat yᵉhwah*, see 15:4) is spiritually clean, never passing away. The final statement involving God's Word should follow the same pattern as the previous five statements. To this end, we omit the supplied *and*, translating, "The judgments of the Lord are true, altogether righteous." John may allude to this in Revelation 16:7, v. 9.

---

[278]The word *gibbôr* occurs widely to refer to a "mighty man." These may be warriors, 33:16; 127:4; greatly evil, 52:1; angels, 103:20; the Lord, 24:8; or some other mighty person. Here, an athlete is in view.

[279]While David may not have known fully what he was saying, the statement is accurate. The sun travels through the heavens at more than 700,000 miles per hour. Its orbit in our galaxy takes about two million centuries to complete. The galaxy itself is in motion through the heavens. The heat energy of the sun, carried by photons of light, goes throughout the universe. Although slight, its effects are felt by the whole of creation.

[280]Buttenwieser, p. 853, limits the "law" to the Mosaic law. There is no reason, however, to set this limit. The word has the sense of "instruction" and often refers to the full revelation of God to His people, e.g., 1:2; 119:1. See the excursus following Ps. 119 on synonyms for God's Word.

[281]The noun *ᶜedût* occurs here and 78:5; 81:5; 122:4; and nine times in Ps. 119. Its basic sense is of a "witness," bearing testimony to something. Since this is God's witness, it is accurate and therefore trustworthy.

[282]The word *petî* has a broad meaning. It may denote one who is foolish in practicing wickedness, Prov. 1:32; untaught, Prov. 1:4; or foolish in not avoiding evil, Prov. 27:12. The context must give the proper sense of the word.

God's Word is complete, reliable, right, pure, clean, and true. It restores the soul, gives wisdom to those who receive it, brings joy, guides a person through life, never passes away, and is righteous in every part. No wonder it is more desirable than "gold" and "fine [or 'refined'] gold." It is sweeter than honey or the drippings from honeycombs, v. 10. In addition, the Word of God guides man. It pricks his conscience so he is "warned" (*zahar*)[283] against sinful thoughts and acts. When man responds correctly to the Word, there is an abundant reward. While unstated, it is clear that God gives the reward to those who obey Him, v. 11.

12–14 David asks rhetorically if anyone can discern his "errors" (or "mistakes," *šᵉgîʾôt*).[284] The expected answer is no one. God's Word reveals such sins. David prays spontaneously that the Lord would cleanse him from "secret faults," i.e., inadvertent acts that he did not notice as sins, v. 12. Further, he asks the Lord to keep him from "presumptuous [or 'arrogant'] sins." These are sins done deliberately against God's Word. He asks that these sins not "have dominion" (or "rule") over him. Only then will he be "upright" (or "blameless," *tamam*, see 18:25) and innocent of committing "great transgression" against the Lord, v. 13. David closes the psalm with an additional prayer. He desires that his speech and his thoughts should please the Lord. He directs the prayer to the Lord, his "strength" (lit. "rock," *ṣûr*, see 18:2) and his "redeemer." This same combination of names occurs in 78:35, v. 14.

PSALM 20

The title directs the psalm to the "chief musician" (*mᵉnaṣṣeaḥ*, see 4, intro.). Other than that David is the author, we know little of the background to the writing. The opening part of the psalm summa-

[283]While the verb *zahar* II generally means "to warn, teach," this is likely derived from *zahar* I, "to shine, send out light." God's Word enlightens man's ways, showing him those areas that are evil.

[284]Although this is the only place that *šᵉgîʾôt* occurs, the verbal root *šgh* occurs often. The basic sense is of inadvertent sins done impulsively or through ignorance.

rizes a prayer from the people for their king.[285] It is "a day of trouble" (v. 1), but nothing lets us identify this time with certainty. The psalm mentions Zion in v. 2 and the sanctuary and offerings in vv. 2, 3. This suggests that the time of writing is after the conquest of Jerusalem and the setting up of the tabernacle there.[286] The emphasis on prayer in the psalm illustrates the needs of Christians today to take their troubles to the Lord. He is as willing to help His children today as He was in David's time.

I. The Prayer of the People 1–5

1–3 The people ask the Lord to hear David's prayer and to protect "thee," David, in the day of "trouble" (or "distress," *ṣarâ*, see 9:9), some conflict faced by the nation.[287] The "name" of God is equivalent here to His nature (cf. Ps. 5:11; 44:5; 54:1).[288] Essentially, the people ask that the God of Jacob, the one that brought the nation into being, will "defend" (*śagab*)[289] it now from its enemy, v. 1. Further, the people ask that the Lord send "help [*ᶜezer*][290] from the sanctuary" and

---

[285]Calvin, I, 333, and Jennings, I, 81, assert that David drew up this prayer for the people to pray for him. Such prayer, however, would be ritualistic rather than sincere prayer. It is more likely that the king recalls some prayer of the people that he has heard. Horne, p. 105, adopts the same view but then extends it to the prayer of the church for the Lord in His warfare against wickedness. There is, however, no messianic context to warrant the view.

[286]Delitzsch, I, 291, sets the psalm at the time of David's fall into sin with Bathsheba, II Sam. 11–12. The people pray for the king's recovery as he goes into battle against the Ammonites. Others are not specific. Eaton, p. 68, and Leslie, p. 264, view the psalm as a liturgy, prayed by the people for their king before any battle. Gaebelein, p. 93, makes it a prayer by the church for Messiah as He delivers them "in the day of trouble." The psalm, however, has no clear messianic context to support the view.

[287]Rawlinson, I, 139, and Cohen, p. 56, locate the psalm at the time of the war against Syria, II Sam. 10:17–19. Harman, p. 117, dates the psalm later, after the bringing of the ark to Jerusalem. He suggests that the people make this plea "when they leave for battle" against some foe. While either of these views is possible, the psalm does not let us be dogmatic.

[288]Note 94 at 5:11 discusses the "name" of the Lord.

[289]Rawlinson, I, 139, translates *śagab* as "exalt thee." The *piᶜel* imperfect of *śagab* normally means "to set on high," i.e., in an inaccessible place that others cannot reach, e.g., 59:1; 69:29. Metaphorically, this refers to providing defense. Other conjugations of *śagab* more frequently have the sense of "exalt."

[290]In the Psalms, *ᶜezer* generally refers to help from God Himself. The word normally refers to the Lord as being the help of the people. In 20:2, it refers to the

strengthen David from "Zion." Since the Lord dwelled among His people in the tabernacle at Jerusalem, they looked there for help (cf. 3:4; 14:7), v. 2. The people remind the Lord of David's "offerings" (or "meal offerings"). They further ask him to "accept" (*dašen*)[291] David's burnt sacrifices, finding them fat and therefore acceptable. Fatness was a sign of the best sacrifice. The people have focused their attention on the Lord by looking to Him for deliverance and noting the king's worship of Him. The word "selah" calls attention to this, v. 3.

4–5 The verbs suggest a jussive sense. This leads to "may He [the Lord] give you your heart," i.e., the desires of the heart for victory, and "fulfill [or 'satisfy'] all your counsel [*ʿeṣâ*, see 1:1]," the plans for battle, v. 4. This will let the people "rejoice" (*ranan*, see 5:11) over David's "salvation," i.e., his victory in the conflict.[292] They will set up "banners" in the Lord's "name" (see v. 1) to mark the success. The last phrase returns to the prayer as the people ask the Lord to answer the prayers of the king, v. 5.

II. The Response of the King 6–9

6–8 David expresses his confidence in the Lord.[293] He is sure that the Lord will deliver "his anointed" (*mašîaḥ*, see 2:2), David as the anointed king of the land.[294] He will "hear" (or "answer") him from

assistance given by the Lord.

[291]The verb *dašen* means "to become fat," and thus either "prosperous" or "anoint." The noun derived from this most often refers to the ashes generated by burning the fat of the sacrifices.

[292]Cohen, p. 57, and Anderson, I, 177, continue the prayer through the verse: "May we exult over the victory . . . may we unfurl our banner." While this is grammatically possible, the plural subject is a change from vv. 1–4, where the Lord is in view. For this reason, it is best to let the verse describe the reaction of the people to the victory.

[293]Perowne, I, 230, takes the singular subject as "a single Levite." Delitzsch, I, 294, sets vv. 1–5 as being sung during "the offering of the sacrifice." He then makes the speaker "one of the Levites, expressing the cheering assurance of the gracious acceptance of the offering that has been presented." These views are speculative, without supporting evidence. There is no reason to see a speaker other than David.

[294]Since the psalm does not describe "a high personality and a grand past," Ewald, I, 158, identifies the king as Asa. Kirkpatrick, p. 108, understands the "anointed" generally as "priest, or prophet, or possibly of the king himself."

heaven above.[295] He will display "saving strength" (or "mighty deeds of deliverance") with His "right hand," the hand often associated with strength (e.g., 17:7; 21:8; 44:3), v. 6. Others trust in human weapons. Israel, however, will "remember" the "name," i.e., the nature (see v. 1), of the Lord who is well able to deliver them, v. 7. The enemies of Israel "are brought down and fallen." This is so certain in David's mind that he expresses it as an accomplished fact. Israel, however, has "risen" and "stand[s] upright" (*ʿôd*, or "has been restored").[296] Again, David states this as already having taken place. With his trust in the Lord, David can confidently face his foes and anticipate success, v. 8.

9 The king concludes the psalm with a brief prayer. The NIV and several other versions translate, "O Lord, save the king! Answer us when we call." This follows the LXX which, in turn, follows the MT with the exception that it moves the *ʾatnaḥ* by one word, a minor change that does not involve the consonantal text, v. 9.

PSALM 21

David plans for the "chief musician" (*mᵉnaṣṣeaḥ*, see 4, intro.) to use the psalm in the tabernacle worship. Since worship played such a large part in Israel's national life, it is understandable that David wrote many of the psalms for this purpose. As he reflected on God's grace to him, he set down his thoughts in musical form for others to hear. Whether chanted or sung to a familiar tune, the music helped the people remember the emphases of the various psalms. The similar dedication of fifty-five psalms may seem to involve an unusually large number of the psalms. In reality, it does not. The average church hymnal has several hundred hymns. This gives the church

---

[295]Leupold, p. 187, refers the verbs to past deliverances and answers to prayer. He states that "it is unnatural to translate the verb found here in the past tense 'has helped' as though it implied a present 'saveth' or a future 'will help.'" The prophetic perfect verb, however, expressing a future act as already complete, is common in the OT. David sets the thought off with the phrase "now know I" as he expresses his faith in the Lord.

[296]The *hitpaʿel nitʿôdad* occurs only here. The related *polel* verb occurs twice (146:9; 147:6) with the meaning "restore." This supports the sense given above.

variety in its worship. Song leaders may select hymns to support an individual theme as they prepare for the sermonic emphasis in each service. The tabernacle worship needed similar variety.

The psalm commemorates some victory of David.[297] As king, v. 3, he considers his foes as the enemies of the Lord, vv. 8, 11. The threat is serious enough that David's life is in danger, v. 4, but he trusts the Lord, v. 7. The fall of his adversaries is evidence that the Lord has judged them, vv. 9–10, 12. The psalm does not clearly identify these opponents of David or set the time for their fall.[298]

The psalm often is thought to continue Psalm 20. There, David prays for victory over his enemies. Here, he gives thanks for the victory. While this is possible, it may as well be coincidental. The themes of prayer and thanksgiving are prominent in David's writings. The position of the psalms is often random. These psalms do not require a connection between them.

I. The Blessings on the King 1–7

1–2 As David reflects on the victory that the Lord has given him, he states his response. He displays "joy" (*śamaḥ*, see 16:9) in the power of the Lord and "rejoice[s]" (*gîl*, see 16:9) in the "salvation" (or "victory") given him, v. 1. The Lord has given all that David wished for, not withholding the answers to any "request" (*ʾareśet*).[299] To emphasize this thought, David adds "selah," v. 2.

3–7 The Lord "prevent[s]" (better "meets") David with "the blessings of goodness." In context, this refers to matters connected with

[297]Thirtle, pp. 87–89, transfers the musical instruction of Ps. 22, "*Aijeleth Shahar*," to follow this psalm. He spiritualizes the meaning "hind of the morning" to represent the "heart's desire," a phrase found in v. 2. He suggests, first, that this represents the prayer of David, then, secondly, that David himself is the heart's desire of the people. The view is speculative.

[298]Hengstenberg, I, 349, makes the psalm recognize the promise in II Sam. 7:16, 24–29. Rawlinson, I, 139, 144, connects it with the war against Syria, II Sam. 10:17–19. Thompson, p. 221, and Jennings, I, 83, place the battle at the conquest of Rabbah, when David set the Ammonite crown on his own head, II Sam. 12:30. Without being specific, Scroggie, I, 131, relates the psalm to the battle anticipated in Ps. 20. Among others, Harman, Hirsch, and Phillips see the psalm as continuing the theme of Ps. 20. These are possibilities although the psalm does not state explicitly the setting.

[299]The word *ʾareśet* occurs only here. In addition to the parallelism of the verse, the Akkadian cognate *erēštu*, "to desire, wish for," supports the meaning of "request."

the victory over his enemies. This includes crowning him as king over the land. As David looks back over his life, it is natural that he would see this as the climax of God's blessings to him. Taken from obscurity as a shepherd, led to become a national hero, married to the king's daughter, then forced to flee for his life, hiding in caves while Saul sought to kill him, then brought to the throne: it is a fairy tale come true, and David recognizes God's hand in his success, v. 3. The Lord has answered his prayer for life. He has given him "length of days," not letting his enemies cut off his life prematurely. That this is "for ever and ever" recognizes that the future cannot change the past. David's history will always include the "length of days" given him by the Lord, v. 4.[300]

David has received glory through the "salvation" (or "victory") given him by the Lord. Others now give him "honour [*hôd*, see 8:1] and majesty [*hadar*, see 8:5]" for his success, v. 5. He is "most blessed for ever." This is true for his role in leading the nation and also true as a type of Christ, "the son [and successor] of David," Luke 1:32. The Lord's presence, "thy countenance," has made David "exceeding glad," v. 6. He trusts the Lord. It is due to the "mercy" (or "steadfast love," *ḥesed*, see 5:7) of the "most High" (*ᶜelyôn*, see 7:17) that others have not "moved" him, v. 7.

II. The Judgment of the Enemies 8–13

8–12 David expresses his confidence that the Lord will overcome all his enemies.[301] The "hand" of the Lord, representing His power, will "find out," idiomatic for overcoming, all that "hate" (*śaneʾ*, see 5:5) Him, v. 8. The Lord will make them "as a fiery oven" as His

[300]There are other possible views of the phrase "for ever and ever." Murphy, p. 167, finds the fulfillment in "the life that comes by the new birth from above." Cheyne, I, 84, refers it to "Israel's eternity." Eaton, p. 69, suggests that it is fulfilled in the Davidic dynasty. Sabourin, p. 348, understands the phrase as "hyperbolical . . . common in ancient court etiquette." *NIB*, IV, 758, understands the words as "poetic hyperbole," not indicating "the king's divinity." *Succoth* 52*a* makes the psalm messianic.

[301]Ewald, I, 164, and Kissane, p. 93, make the second half an address to David rather than to the Lord. The content of vv. 8–12, however, goes far beyond what David could do. Making his foes "as a fiery oven" and destroying their offspring "from the earth" are works of the Lord, not David. In addition, the closing note of praise logically follows the work of the Lord.

anger consumes them. He will "swallow them up" (*bala*ᶜ I)[302] as He exercises His "wrath" (*ʾap*, see 2:5) against them. The fire of His anger will "devour them," v. 9. He will "destroy" (*ʾabad*, see 1:6) their "fruit," their offspring.[303] The statement assumes that wickedness marks the families. The Lord destroys the children for their sin, not for that of their parents, v. 10. The word "though" or "although" should introduce the verse. It refers to the evil plans of David's enemies and does not give a reason for v. 10. In plotting against David, his foes "imagined a mischievous device" (or "devised a plot") against the Lord. They "are not able to perform [it]" (or "will not prevail"), v. 11. The Lord will cause them to flee and direct His bowstring against them. This poetic description anticipates the Lord's victory over all who stand against Him, v. 12.

13 Such a God is worthy of praise. David closes the psalm by giving glory to the Lord, Who has saved David from his foes. The power of the Lord exalts Him. David pledges to sing and "praise" (*zamar*, see 7:17) the strength of the Lord, v. 13.

PSALM 22

While Psalm 22 is an individual lament psalm, it goes beyond the lament of any OT character that we know of. In general, there are four different interpretations of the psalm: personal, ideal, national, and predictive. In the *personal interpretation*, the lament comes from the experiences of some OT individual. The most common suggestion relates the psalm to some event in David's life.[304] In the *ideal interpretation*, the psalm pictures the sufferings that would occur in

---

[302]The verb *bala*ᶜ I, "to swallow," occurs regularly in the OT as a word picture of destruction, e.g., Job 2:3; 8:18; 10:8; Ps. 55:9. A related noun occurs in 52:4.

[303]Leupold, p. 193, and Horne, p. 110, refer "fruit" to the plans and actions of the wicked. The word occurs elsewhere in Psalms, normally referring to the offspring of plants, their "fruit." When used of man, 127:3; 132:11, it usually refers to children. In the Psalms, it never refers to "plans and undertakings" or to "achievements."

[304]Leslie, p. 362, gives a *personal interpretation* to the psalm. W. E. Barnes, I, 104–5, likewise adopts this view, although he rejects David's authorship by hinting that Jeremiah is the one suffering in the psalm.

the life of a person who was ideally righteous.[305] With the *national interpretation*, the sufferings described in the psalm come from the experiences of Israel.[306] In the *messianic interpretation*, the psalm is directly prophetic, pointing to Jesus Christ.[307] This is the approach traditionally adopted by believers and the view taken in the discussion that follows. While some of the sufferings mentioned in the psalm may have happened to David, the author, the Holy Spirit led him to write predictively, looking ahead to the Crucifixion.

The heading assigns the psalm to the "chief musician" (*m*ᵉ*naṣṣeaḥ*, see 4, intro.), the leader of the music used in Israel's worship. It is to be sung to the tune of "Aijeleth Shahar," better rendered "the hind of the morning." We do not know this tune today, but it was clearly known to the musicians of David's time.[308]

I. The Savior's Suffering 1–21

A. Separation from God 1–5

1–3 The initial statement "My God, my God," expresses the relationship of the Lord to His Father. Although He feels forsaken, He does not turn away from the relationship. The repetition of "My God"

---

[305]Alexander, I, 175, and Hengstenberg, I, 362, apply the psalm to the *ideal righteous person*.

[306]Cohen, p. 61, and Cheyne, I, 86, give a *national interpretation* to the psalm. Perowne, I, 238, accepts this view, although he also sees it as foreshadowing the sufferings of Christ.

[307]Gaebelein, p. 101, and Clarke, I, 72, adopt this view. Since the psalm focuses on the sufferings of Christ, the NT quotes frequently from it in describing this part of His Passion: Matt. 27:46 and Mark 15:34 from v. 1; Matt. 27:39 and Mark 15:29 from v. 7; Matt. 27:43 from v. 8; Matt. 27:35, Mark 15:24, Luke 23:34, and John 19:24 from v. 18; and Heb. 2:12 from v. 22. In addition, there are other allusions that may come from the psalm. Note 32, in the introduction to Ps. 2, briefly discusses the messianic prophecies.

[308]Clarke, I, 70, makes the expression represent "the dawn of a day." The first rays of the rising sun are likened to the horns of a deer appearing above the rising ground before its body comes into view. While possible, the view is speculative. *Yoma 29a* compares the antler with light. Just as branches of the antlers go this way and that, "so the light of the dawn is scattered in all directions." Once more, this is speculative. Alexander, p. 106, understands "Aijeleth," the hind, "a poetical figure for persecuted innocence." The addition of "Shahar," morning, suggests "deliverance after long distress." He gives several references, none of which use the words "Aijeleth Shahar." The view is subjective.

lays stress on the relationship. The Lord does not question the reason God has forsaken Him; rather, He asks in order to lament the break in the fellowship He has always known. Matthew 27:46 and Mark 15:34 quote 1*a* as the Lord experiences this breach in fellowship with His Father.

The final part of the verse is better "Far from my deliverance are the words of my roaring [or 'groaning,' *šaʾᵃgâ*]."[309] Voicing His grief has not brought deliverance from the burden He bears, v. 1. He has cried to His Father day and night, but there has been no indication that the Father has heard. The cries of the Lord to His Father include His prayers in the Garden of Gethsemane as well as His cries from the cross, v. 2.

The Lord does not criticize His Father. He recognizes that the Father is "holy," doing all things in accord with His perfect will. He addresses Him as the One "that inhabitest [*yôšeb*, 'sits,' i.e., 'is enthroned upon'] the praises of Israel," v. 3.[310]

4–5 The "fathers" of Israel have trusted the Father. We should not limit the term "fathers" to Abraham, Isaac, and Jacob. The word includes the prior generations who have trusted God and found Him faithful in their trials, v. 4. They cried out to Him in the various threats that came to them and He delivered them. They were not "confounded" (*bôš*, or "ashamed," see 6:10) of the trust that they had placed in Him, v. 5.

---

[309]Clarke, I, 73, and Fausset, III, 148, understand *šaʾᵃgâ* as the Lord's groaning on the cross. Cohen, p. 61, calls it "a shriek of agony." While *šaʾᵃgâ* can represent the lion's loud roar, it can also describe the groaning of a person undergoing trials, Job 3:24 and the verb in Ps. 38:8. Thompson, p. 226, implies that *šaʾᵃgâ* refers to the Lord's complaint. He describes the passage as "undulat[ing] between complaint and trust. . . ." There is, however, no record of the Lord complaining of His trials. The word *šaʾᵃgâ* does not refer to complaining elsewhere.

[310]B. N. Wambacq, "Psaume 22,4," *Biblica* 62:1 (1981): 99–100, views this as "une expression étrange," a strange expression. He translates "Et Toi saint, reviens, louanges d'Israël": "And you, Holy One, come back, [the] praises of Israel." The translation rests on a doubtful interpretation of the verb. Ewald, II, 38, and Jennings, I, 90, understand the phrase to refer to the Lord enthroned in the sanctuary, where He receives the praises of His people. While this is possible, it is also possible that the expression is simply a poetical description of the Lord seated upon His heavenly throne receiving the praises of those who love Him.

B. Taunts of the People 6–8

6–8 A worm is a helpless creature;[311] cf. Job 25:6; Isaiah 41:14. It is an appropriate figure for the Lord, Who is unable to defend Himself against the jeers of the crowd. He is as a worm, not as a "man" (*ʾîš*). He bears reproach from "men" (*ʾadam*),[312] and others despise Him, v. 6. Those who see Him "laugh [Him] to scorn" (or "mock" Him). They "shoot out the lip" (better "open the lip"), an idiomatic expression describing taunting or mocking.[313] They shake their head in unbelief. The NT authors describe this action in Matthew 27:39 and Mark 15:29, v. 7. The people scoff at Him, saying, "He trusted on the Lord that he would deliver him" (better "roll *your needs* to the Lord, let Him deliver him"). The NT quotes from the LXX in Matthew 27:43, giving it a past tense: "He trusted in God; let him deliver him now." The adversaries of the Lord challenge Him to have the Father deliver Him because of His "delight" (*ḥapeṣ*, see 18:19) in the Son, v. 8.

C. Trust in God 9–11

9–11 The Lord looks back to His birth, recalling the hope He has had in God since His earliest days on earth. As a baby, still nursing, He possessed confidence in God, v. 9. Even before this, when He was still in the womb, He was "cast upon" the Lord, resting upon Him as His strength, v. 10. He calls upon the Father to sustain Him now in the midst of His "trouble" (or "distress," *ṣarâ*, see 9:9). There is

---

[311]Morris, p. 113, draws on the meaning of the word *tôlaᶜ*, often translated "scarlet," to make this refer to the blood of Christ shed for mankind's sin. While the truth of this is abundantly taught elsewhere, the contrast here is between a worm and a man, not between a color and a man.

[312]There are six places in the Psalms where the word *ʾadam* and *ʾîš* occur together (22:6; 39:11; 49:2; 62:9; 80:17; 140:1). The word *ʾadam* emphasizes man's humble beginning, Gen. 2:7. In contrast, the word *ʾîš* stresses man's greatness. In 22:6, the Lord is considered *ʾadam* by the *ʾîš*. In 49:2, "low and high" are lit. "sons of *ʾadam* and sons of *ʾîš*." In 62:9, "men of low degree" are "sons of *ʾadam*," and "men of high degree" are "sons of *ʾîš*." These illustrate the contrast, which is a general one not always clear in the OT.

[313]The NRSV translates this phrase, "They make mouths at me." The REB is similar: "[They] grimace at me." Mark H. Heinemann, "An Exposition of Psalm 22," *BibSac* 147 (1990): 288, translates, "They sneer." In developing this prophecy, the NT says that the crowd "reviled him" and "railed on him," emphasizing mockery rather than the facial expression.

no one else who can help. This act of prayer is an act of faith as He looks to the Father for help in His need, v. 11.

D. Suffering of the Lord 12–18

12–13 The Lord compares His enemies to strong bulls. The plains of Bashan lay to the east and northeast of the Sea of Galilee, between the Yarmuk River and Mt. Hermon. It was a well-watered, grassy area, ideal for grazing flocks and herds. The "bulls of Bashan" were well-fed, strong animals. Idiomatically, they represent the foes of Jesus who brought about His crucifixion, v. 12. The "gaped" (or "opened") their mouths at Him. They were like "a ravening and a roaring lion [*ʾarî*, see 7:2]" attacking its prey, v. 13.[314]

14–15 The Lord uses several idioms to show the effects of the persecution that He has gone through. He is "poured out like water," emptied of physical strength. He suffers pain as if "all [His] bones are out of joint." His "heart is like wax," no longer giving Him strength of life. It is melted "in the midst of [His] bowels [or 'internal organs']," v. 14. His "strength is dried up like a potsherd," a fragment of a broken pot, brittle and easily broken. His "tongue cleaveth to [His] jaws," His mouth being so dry that His tongue sticks to the gums and roof of the mouth. He has been "brought . . . into the dust of death," anticipating the laying of His body in the grave. While these statements are poetic, they nonetheless give a vivid picture of what the Lord went through on the cross as He gave Himself as a sacrifice for the sins of man, v. 15.

16–18 The Lord continues to describe His sufferings on the cross. He is compassed about with "dogs." The biblical authors often describe degraded and defiled creatures as "dogs," e.g., Isaiah 56:10–11; Matthew 7:6; Philippians 3:2; Revelation 22:15. The Lord here compares the crowd about the cross to a pack of snarling dogs. The next phrase, "the assembly of the wicked have inclosed me," parallels the first clause and thus defines the nature of the "dogs" as wicked. These "pierced [*kaʾarî*][315] [His] hands and . . . feet," bearing

[314]James L. Mays, "Prayer and Christology: Psalm 22 as Perspective on the Passion," *Theology Today* 42:3 (1985): 326, tentatively suggests that the animals in vv. 12–16 represent demonic forces. While this is possible, it is subjective since the metaphor does not clearly occur elsewhere.

[315]If *kaʾarî* comes from *kûr*, this is its only occurrence in the OT. The LXX accepts this. While the *ʾalep* is unusual, it may simply indicate the vowel. See G.K.C. 7 *b*.

the responsibility for the action performed by the Roman soldiers. The statement points directly to the Cross; cf. Isaiah 53:5; Zechariah 12:10, v. 16.

The Lord comments that He "may tell [or 'count'] all [His] bones." This reflects His contorted position on the cross, which forces His rib cage to press outward against the skin. The crowd around the cross "look and stare" as they consider His sufferings, v. 17. "They," the Roman soldiers as part of the overall crowd, "part [His] garments among them." Not wanting to rip His coat into parts, they "cast lots upon [His] vesture [or 'clothing']." This suggests that they consider His death a foregone conclusion. Since He has no more need of clothing, they take it to themselves. The NT quotes the verse (Matt. 27:35; Mark 15:24; Luke 23:34; and John 19:23–24), v. 18.

E. Prayer for Deliverance 19–21

19–21 Despite His sufferings, the Lord continues to trust His Father to deliver Him. As in v. 10, He continues to show His faith in the Father. He prays that He will not remain "far from" Him. He calls the Father His "strength," i.e., the source of His strength, and prays again for help, v. 19. He asks the Father to deliver Him from the "sword," figurative for death, and "the power of the dog," the wicked; cf. v. 16. The word "darling" (*yaḥîd*, better "only one," cf. 35:17) occurs poetically to refer to the life that His enemies seek to take from Him, v. 20. Again speaking metaphorically, the Lord asks for deliverance from "the lion's [*ʾᵃrî*, see 7:2] mouth" as His foes try to devour Him with their speech.[316]

Among others, Hirsch, I, 164, and Alexander, pp. 110–11, understand *kaʾᵃrî* as "lion." Alexander translates, "like the lion (they have wounded) my hands and my feet." This changes the verb into a noun and requires the supply of a new verb. While this is possible, it complicates the verse. The Vulgate translates *vinxerunt*, "to bind, tie." Oesterley, pp. 177–78, follows this by reading *ʾasarû*, "bind." Weiser, p. 218, reads *kaʾabû,* and translates "my hands and my feet hurt me." There is no support for this reading. Kirkpatrick, p. 119, reads *kaʾarû*, "they digged," which he interprets with the AV. Kissane, p. 101, reads *kalû*, "to waste away." While this parallels 17*a*, the idea of hands and feet wasting away is not compelling. J. J. M. Roberts, "A New Root for an Old Crux, Ps. XXII 17c," *VT* XXIII (1973): 251–52, understands the root as *karâ* V, "to be shrunken, shriveled." This root, however, does not occur elsewhere and so is doubtful here. *TWOT*, I, 435, suggests the *hapax legomenon* root *kaʾar*, "dig, wound, pierce." This relies on the LXX and context.

[316]Phillips, I, 171, makes the lion represent Satan. This is a possible view. I have made the lion a collective singular representing the psalmist's enemies because of

He closes with a statement of confidence that the Father will deliver Him "from the horns [*qeren*, see 18:2] of the unicorn [*remîm*, or 'wild oxen']."[317] The Lord again speaks poetically of His enemies. His confidence in God is such that He speaks as though the deliverance had already happened, v. 21.

II. The Savior's Deliverance 22–31

A. Praising the Lord 22–26

22–25 The final section focuses on the work of Messiah after His deliverance by the Father. The Lord pledges to praise the "name"[318] of His Father publicly. His "brethren" are redeemed sinners, the same group as the "congregation" (or "assembly"), v. 22.[319] He calls on different classes of people to join Him in praising God. Those who "fear the Lord" (*yirʾat yᵉhwah*, see 15:4), the "seed of Jacob" and the "seed of Israel," should praise the Father. There is no significant difference between these phrases. These occur in poetic variation, v. 23. God is worthy of praise since He has not turned away from the "afflicted" (see *ʿanî*, 9:12). The term in this context refers to the Lord Himself on Calvary. The Father has not "hid his face from him" but has heard His prayers, v. 24. The praise of the Lord is "of thee," better "from you"; the note of praise that He sounds comes from the Father. He will do this openly "in the congregation [or 'assembly']." The phrase "I will pay my vows" refers to the first phrase, the praise that He intends to give before those who "fear" (see *yirʾâ*, 2:11) God, v. 25.

26 The Lord names two separate classes of society that will enjoy the blessings of God. The "meek" (or "afflicted," see *ʿanî*, 9:12) will eat until they are satisfied. Those who "seek" (*daraš*, see 9:10) the Father will praise Him. The phrase "your heart shall live for ever" has a jussive sense, "let your heart live forever." It is a benediction, pray-

---

the obvious symbolism of the dog, v. 20, and the wild oxen, v. 21.

317The animal was strong, Num. 23:22; untamed, Job 39:9–11; and had two horns, Deut. 33:17. The grouping with bullocks and bulls in Isa. 34:7 suggests a larger animal. Ewald, II, 40, understands *remîm* as "buffalo." There is no evidence that these animals were widespread in Palestine. Delitzsch, I, 321, gives "antilopes [*sic*]." Horne, p. 116, suggests "unicorn" or "oryx." The Akkadian cognate *rīmu*, "wild ox," supports the view given above.

318See note 94, 5:11, for a brief summary of the Lord's name.

319In its argument exalting the Lord, Heb. 2:12 quotes v. 22.

ing God's everlasting blessing on those who join the Lord in praising the Father, v. 26.

B. Worship of the Lord 27–31

27–31 The entire earth will remember the works of God and will turn to the Son. The second half of the verse defines this turning as "worship," v. 27. This is appropriate since the kingdom belongs to Him. He will rule over the nations. This is so sure that He states it as an accomplished fact, v. 28. Different classes of men will honor Him. The "fat [see *dašen*, 20:3] upon earth," the prosperous, will enjoy their provision as they worship the Lord. Those "that go down to the dust," that are ready to die, will bow before Him. The final phrase, "even he who cannot keep his soul alive," is in apposition to those "that go down to the dust," v. 29.

Children, a "seed" born to succeeding generations, will serve the Lord. Their service will "be accounted to the Lord" (better "be related concerning the Lord") to their generation, v. 30. They will tell of the righteousness of the Lord to generations to come. The phrase "he hath done this" refers to the salvation of man that the Lord has accomplished through the completion of His plan, v. 31.

PSALM 23

It is well said that Psalm 23 is the most beloved of the psalms. These six verses have made an immeasurable impact on people from all races, of all ages, and of all backgrounds of education and experience. This "Shepherd psalm" uniquely appeals to the heart as the reader sees himself as a sheep relying upon the shepherd for care, provision, guidance, protection, and everlasting blessing.

It is a "Psalm of David." We cannot relate it to any one experience in his life.[320] He was well versed with the responsibilities and cares

[320]Phillips, I, 175, thinks that David wrote the psalm during his shepherd days. Jack R. Lundblom, "Psalm 23: Song of Passage," *Interp* 40:1 (1986): 12, places the psalm at David's flight from Absalom. Hengstenberg, I, 398, has David writing during a period of peace in the kingdom. Albert Barnes, I, 209, thinks it is a

of the shepherd. His early experiences gave him an intimate acquaintance with the role of the shepherd; cf. I Samuel 16:11, 19; 17:15, 28, 34–37. He knew firsthand how sheep were totally dependent on their shepherd. From this background, David makes the spiritual application of the psalm. Three personal declarations by David ("I will . . .") divide the psalm.

I. The Shepherd's Provision 1–3

1–3 The Lord is David's shepherd. In the OT, a shepherd always represents a king or other civil leader; cf. I Kings 22:17; Ezekiel 34:23–24. David looks at the Lord as his King, One to command him but also to care for him. This leads David to make the first of three personal declarations in the psalm: "I shall not want," v. 1.[321] He develops this further in vv. 2–3. The Lord makes David "to lie down in green pastures." Sheep do not feed in pens but rather forage for their food in an open field. In the winter months, the sheep's coat of wool protects it from the cold. The sheep die, however, from starvation when the snow covers the grass. They need help to find food. In the summer months, the shepherd leads his flock to shady places where they may lie down. In every part of the year, the shepherd guides the sheep.[322] They are prone to graze randomly. If left alone, they will scatter widely beyond the possibility of gathering them eas-

psalm of David's old age, when he thinks back on his younger days as a shepherd. A. L. Merrill, "Psalm XXIII and the Jerusalem Tradition," *VT* 15 (1965): 359, sets the psalm during the coronation of a king. The shepherd is Israel's King, the Lord, supplying the needs of His people. Eaton, p. 77, understands the psalm as "part of a larger liturgical sequence." E. Vogt, "The 'Place of Life' of Ps. 23," *Biblica* 34 (1953): 202, places the psalm at a thanksgiving banquet of some pilgrim in the temple. This sampling of different settings given for the psalm reflects the lack of information in it.

[321]Several well-known hymns have been based on v. 1. Among these are "The Lord's My Shepherd," with the words from the Scottish Psalter and the music by William Gardiner, 1812; "The King of Love My Shepherd Is," with the words by Henry William Baker, 1868, to the tune of St. Columba, an old Irish melody; and "The Lord Is My Shepherd," with the words by James Montgomery. There are several tunes for this, with the most well known written by Thomas Koschat, 1862.

[322]The NT emphasizes the shepherding role of the Lord. He is the Chief Shepherd, I Pet. 5:4; the Great Shepherd, Heb. 13:20; the Good Shepherd, John 10:11, 14; and the only Shepherd, John 10:16.

ily. The spiritual application is clear. The Lord guides His own into pastures that will supply their needs.[323]

The shepherd also leads his sheep by "still waters" (better "waters of resting places"). The plural "resting places" intensifies the word. These are calm places. Because of their timidity, sheep will not drink from rushing waters. In addition, in barren Palestine, sheep need to be kept near places where they may find water. The shepherd has this responsibility, v. 2.

In addition, the shepherd "restore[s]" (*šûb*) the sheep, providing rest and refreshment. The *pôlel* of *šûb* has the sense of "turning back."[324] David applies this thought to the Lord, Who has turned around his "soul" (*nepeš*). While the *nepeš* can refer to the life, the desires, the emotions, even the appetite of a person, it here refers to the whole inner being of the psalmist. The last half of the verse shows the new direction. The Lord leads him in "paths [*maᶜgal*, see 17:5] of righteousness." The *maᶜgal* is lit. "a trench." Thus, this is a well-defined path.[325] The Lord leads David here "for his name's sake," i.e., for the sake of the Lord's reputation as a righteous God, v. 3.[326]

II. The Shepherd's Protection 4–5

4–5 David introduces this new thought with the word "yea" (or "even") to lend emphasis to what he is about to say. David speaks from experience; the phrase "shadow of death" (*ṣalmawet*)[327] comes

---

[323]Here and throughout the psalm, Luther, XII, 160ff., spiritualizes the text. The "green pastures" and "still waters," v. 2, the "rod" and "staff," v. 4, and the "table" and the "oil," v. 5, are pictures of God's Word and of blessings conveyed through the Word. While these are pleasant devotional thoughts, they go beyond the obvious meaning.

[324]Timothy M. Willis, "A Fresh Look at Psalm XXIII 3*a*," *VT* XXVII (Jan. 1987): 104, understands the *pôlel* of *šûb* as "He herds me in," leading the sheep into the fold. While this is a possible view, it separates 3*a* from 3*b*, which logically continues the thought.

[325]Larry G. Herr, "An Off-Duty Archaeologist Looks at Psalm 23," *BibRev* 8:2 (1992): 47, understands *maᶜgal* as "tracks running over the rolling hills." The shepherd guides his flock through a confusing "maze of paths." The use elsewhere, however, stresses *maᶜgal* as a well-defined path, e.g., I Sam. 17:20; 26:5, 7. In the Psalms, it refers to God's paths, 17:5; 65:11, also well-defined paths of righteousness.

[326]See note 94, 5:11, for a brief summary of the Lord's name.

[327]The noun *ṣalmawet* is a compound word from *ṣal*, "shadow," and *mawet*, "death." It appears ten times in Job; in Pss. 44:19 and 107:10, 14; and four times in the

from the dark wadis and caves where he had led his sheep. In the depths of a wadi or in a cave, there may be only gloom with just a faint hint of the sun. This is particularly true in the afternoon, when the sun is going down. Metaphorically, this phrase represents the unknown and therefore dangerous parts of life.[328] David bases his second personal declaration on this experience: "I will fear no evil."

Wherever David goes, the Lord's "rod" and "staff" give him comfort. The "rod" and the "staff" refer to the shepherd's crook under different names. It is the shepherd's "rod" of protection and the "staff" of guidance. The shepherd may use it as a weapon to defend the flock against marauding animals or as a tool to guide the sheep away from danger and into places of safety. The first and last pronouns in 4*b* are emphatic: "You yourself are with me . . . they themselves comfort me." No matter the situation he may face, David knows that the Lord is with him to give protection, v. 4.

The Lord had prepared David "a table [*šulḥan*] . . . in the presence of [his] enemies."[329] David thinks of times in the past when he has enjoyed fellowship with the Lord. For the shepherd, the *šulḥan* is a piece of leather rolled out on the ground.[330] Food could be placed on it. David may have thought of the incident described in II Samuel 17:27–29 or some other similar incident. Whatever he thinks of, he knows that the Lord has cared for him.

Prophets. It always refers to some kind of undesirable or dangerous situation.

[328]William G. Braude, *The Midrash on Psalms* (New Haven, Conn.: Yale University Press, 1959), I, 334, refers the phrase to "chastisement in Gehenna, whose fire God will cool." J. M. Neale and R. F. Littledale, *A Commentary on the Psalms* (London: Joseph Masters and Company, 1874), p. 319, understand this as "the grave, the fold, in which the Lord's sheep are penned safely till the morning of the Resurrection." While the Lord does give peace as death approaches, the promise includes peace in all forms of danger.

[329]Leslie, p. 283, and Weiser, p. 230, see the psalmist as taking part of a sacrificial meal in the temple. Perowne, I, 252, varies this as a "royal banquet." Aside from setting aside Davidic authorship, these views ignore the shepherding context of vv. 1–4. Only with the third personal declaration in v. 6 does the psalm turn from David's shepherding experiences.

[330]From cognate languages, the *šulḥan* is a piece of leather upon which the shepherd could place his food, i.e., a place for eating. In other places, the *šulḥan* refers to a table, also a place for eating food, e.g., I Kings 2:7; 4:27; or devoted to holding items used in Israel's worship, e.g., Exod. 25:30; 37:16.

In addition, David tells the Lord, "Thou anointest [*dašen*, see 20:3] my head with oil." The verb never refers to an anointing for office.[331] David thinks of the blessings that God has given him.[332] As he thinks of this goodness, he concludes, "My cup runneth over [*r^e^wayâ*],"[333] a metaphoric picture of the abundant blessings the Lord has given, v. 5.

III. The Shepherd's Promise 6

6 Not only has God given blessings to David in the past, but "goodness and mercy" will continue to accompany him throughout life.[334] Strictly speaking, "goodness" is open, limitless bounty from God, while "mercy" (*ḥesed*, see 5:7) is the loyal favor of God. David anticipates that both of these will remain with him. This thought climaxes with the third personal declaration of the psalm: "I will dwell in the house of the Lord for ever." No greater evidence of the "goodness and mercy" of God is available. David looks forward to unbroken fellowship with, service for, and worship of His Lord. The "house of the Lord" here differs from the tabernacle, a place David had no right to inhabit. It has instead an eschatological sense, the heavenly dwelling place of the Lord in which David anticipates spending eternity, v. 6.[335]

---

[331]Hirsch, I, 171, sees this as the anointing by Samuel as the king of the nation; cf. I Sam. 16:13. The verb used there, however, is *mašaḥ*, whereas the verb here is *dašen*, "to make fat" and metaphorically "to prosper." It never refers to anointing for an office.

[332]Fausset, III, 153, relates this to the "oil of gladness," 45:7, "the joy which the Holy Spirit imparts." Nothing here, however, brings the Holy Spirit into view. The anointing pictures spiritual blessings being poured out on David. Murphy, p. 183, sees the oil as "the symbol of sanctifying grace by which we apprehend and accept the gospel." The view goes beyond the thought of the psalm.

[333]The word *r^e^wayâ* occurs only here and at 66:12 ("wealthy"). The basic sense is of saturation. A saturated cup is one filled to abundance.

[334]John W. Peterson and Alfred B. Smith drew on v. 6 in 1958 for the words and music to the hymn "Surely Goodness and Mercy," © Singspiration Music.

[335]W. E. Barnes, I, 119, understands "the house of the Lord" as the Lord's house on Mt. Zion. Eaton, p. 78, likewise refers it to the temple. Both translate "dwell" (*w^e^šabtî*) as "return," a possible translation. The context of v. 5, however, argues for fellowship rather than a journey. Most translations adopt "dwell."

PSALM 24

This "Psalm of David"[336] was written at the time when David brought the ark of the covenant from the house of Obed-edom to the tabernacle at Jerusalem (II Sam. 6:12–15).[337] David celebrates the occasion by writing these words of praise.[338] In high church ritual today, the psalm is customarily sung or recited on Ascension Day, the Thursday that comes forty days after the Easter resurrection of the Lord. This is the time at which the Lord entered by the Spirit into the spiritual temple of His church. The Talmud refers to the singing of the psalm in the temple every Sabbath morning during the wine offering.[339]

I. The Creation by God 1–2

1–2 The psalm builds to a climax. David first expresses the Lord's ownership of the earth by right of creation. He then states the conditions that must be met by those who worship this powerful God. He ends with the entrance of the Lord into Jerusalem, where He will receive the worship of His people. The earth with all its "fulness," that which it contains, belongs to the Lord, including mankind, those "that dwell therein," v. 1.[340] This is so because God is the Creator. He

[336]With words from the 1912 *Psalter*, the song "The Earth with All That Dwell Therein" draws upon the whole psalm. The tune, AZMON, was written by Carl Gotthelf Gläser, 1829, and arranged by Lowell Mason, 1839.

[337]Delitzsch, I, 334, mentions this and also the probability that the psalm celebrates a time "when the Ark was brought back to Mount Zion, after having been taken to accompany the army to battle." Rodd, p. 52, makes it a liturgy sung as the ark "is carried in procession up mount Zion," based on the mention of "doors" and "gates," vv. 7, 9, which he assigns to the temple. Anderson, I, 200, dates the psalm after Solomon. He assigns the psalm to some "processional liturgy." The doors and gates, however, are those of the city, not the temple. There is no reason to reject David's authorship.

[338]Perowne, I, 254, assigns the whole psalm to different choirs. Rawlinson, I, 174, has vv. 7–10 sung by two choirs singing antiphonally. Josephus, *The Antiquities of the Jews* 7.4.2, says that there were seven choirs with David accompanying them on his harp. Alexander, p. 118, thinks that vv. 1–6 were sung as the ark left "its former resting-place," and vv. 7–10 "as it drew near to its new one." These views are possible but not required by the psalm.

[339]*ʾArakin* 11*b*; *Tamîd* 33*b*.

[340]Paul quotes the verse in I Cor. 10:26. This thought may have been a proverbial saying. Similar expressions occur elsewhere, e.g., Deut. 33:16; Pss. 50:12; and 89:11.

brought forth the land from the waters (Gen. 1:9–10) and established it upon the "floods" (or "rivers"), necessary to nourish the land, v. 2.

II. The Conditions for Worship 3–6

3–6 Such a Creator is worthy of man's worship. David asks, then answers his own questions as to who can give this worship. Who can "ascend into the hill of the Lord," Mt. Zion, where David erected a tent ("tabernacle," II Sam. 6:17) for the ark?[341] Who can "stand in his holy place," v. 3? Only those with "clean hands, and a pure heart" can approach the Lord.[342] David explains these idioms negatively. The one who worships God cannot lift up "his soul unto vanity [*šawʾ*, see 12:2]," the worship of vain idols.[343] He cannot deceitfully swear an oath, v. 4. The one who worships properly will receive blessing from the Lord;[344] the God Who gives salvation will judge him righteously, v. 5. Those who meet these conditions are the "generation of them that seek [*daraš*, see 9:10] him," i.e., those who worship the Lord rightly. David addresses these words to "Jacob," the nation, as if to remind them that they need righteousness.[345] He draws attention to what he has said with the word "selah," v. 6.

---

[341]Henry, III, 320, goes beyond the text by stating that "the hill of Zion . . . typified the church, both visible and invisible." This spiritualizes the thought into something never meant by David.

[342]Rawlinson, I, 173, understands v. 3 as David's warning to the Levites so "that they might purify themselves in heart and soul before venturing to take part in the solemn ceremony" of transporting the ark. This ignores the reference to lifting up of the soul in v. 4. Elsewhere, this refers to worship, 25:1; 86:4; 143:8.

[343]Cohen, p. 69, makes "vanity" the taking of the Lord's name in vain. Leslie, p. 189, understands it as longing for something worthless. Henry, III, 320, makes it refer to "the wealth of the world, the praise of men, or the delights of sense." Kissane, p. 108, relates it to "trust in power and wealth acquired by unlawful means." Hengstenberg, I, 419, translates *šawʾ* as "falsehood," possible since the phrase parallels the last part of v. 4. These are possible views since the word *šawʾ* occurs widely with a variety of senses.

[344]Moll, p. 186, limits the blessing to "Obed Edom and his house." This is too restrictive. In view of David's use of "generation" and "Jacob" later, it is better to apply the blessing to all who worship the Lord in purity.

[345]August Konkel, "The Exaltation of the Eternal King," *Didaskalia* 1:2 (1990): 21, considers the phrase "O Jacob" as "poetic ellipsis for 'God of Jacob.'" This follows the LXX translation, which is interpretive at this point. Bratcher and Reyburn, p. 241, and Rotherham, p. 139, adopt similar translations. The AV is sensible, however, and does not need to be adapted to the LXX.

III. The Coming of the Lord 7–10

7–10 David now recognizes the arrival of the ark at Jerusalem (and the accompanying presence of the Lord). Lifting the head is equivalent to being exalted, appropriate in view of the Lord's presence in the city. The "everlasting doors" are "doors of long time," i.e., ancient doors, doors that have marked the city through its history.[346] These likewise will be exalted at the entrance of the Lord, v. 7.[347] David asks rhetorically, who is this glorious king? He answers that it is the powerful Lord, the One Who defends His people in battle. David perhaps thinks of the recent victories over the Philistines that preceded the recovery of the ark (II Sam. 5:18–25), v. 8. Verse 9 is almost identical with v. 7. It differs only in the verb "lift up" with no great change in the meaning. Once again, the openings into the city are to be exalted by the entrance of the Lord through them, v. 9. David asks again the nature of this glorious King. He answers, dwelling more this time on the role of the Lord as the ruler over the hosts (*ṣᵉbaʾôt*)[348] of heaven and earth. He is indeed a glorious King. David emphasizes the thought with "selah," v. 10.

PSALM 25

The psalm is an individual lament. David faces some unknown enemy, vv. 2, 17–19. He may have felt that his sin contributed to this, vv. 7, 11, 18. In any case, he leaves no doubt that he relies on the

---

[346]Eaton, p. 80, and W. E. Barnes, I, 122, refer the doors and gates to the temple. Only by rejecting David's authorship can this be so. The temple was not built in David's time. Calvin, I, 409, thinks of the gates of the future temple. There would be no reason for opening these doors since all can worship at any time. The gates of the city were, however, often closed to protect the city from enemies.

[347]Henry, III, 321–22, is extreme in spiritualizing the entrance of the king. He first mentions the entry of the ark into David's tent. Then he suggests that it may refer to entering the Solomonic temple, to God's Word entering the heart of men, to Christ entering heaven at the Ascension, and to the Lord entering the souls of men.

[348]The word *ṣᵉbaʾôt* refers to the people of Israel, Exod. 12:41, or to angels, I Kings 22:19. The title "Lord of hosts" or "God of hosts" embraces the Lord's rule over the hosts of heaven and earth.

Lord to deliver him, vv. 2–3, 15–17, 20–21. The psalm includes two brief prayers, vv. 1–7, 15–22, separated by a description of God's work, vv. 8–14. Each of the three sections begins with a positive statement of trust in the Lord, vv. 1, 8, 15, and includes a request for forgiveness of sins, vv. 7, 11, 18. The psalm powerfully illustrates the need for Christians today to confess the sins that have drawn them from the Lord and to look to Him for guidance.

Psalm 25 is the first of nine psalms with the simple inscription *l^edawid*, all of which supply words to obtain "A Psalm of David." Eight other psalms include the fuller title *mizmôr l^edawid*, "A Psalm of David."[349] Thirty-seven more psalms include the words "a psalm of David" along with additional words of description or instruction.

The psalm has the structure of an irregular acrostic.[350] The *bêt* line has the vocative *ᵓ^elohay*, "O my God," before the *bêt* word. The *waw* line begins with *ᵓalep* with *waw* the second letter of the word. David probably chose this since the pronunciation begins with *waw*, the *ᵓalep* having no sound of its own. Two lines begin with *rêš*. David likely did not consider the second line as part of the acrostic construction. The lines all through the psalm are of irregular length. There is no *qôp* line. A second *pê* line closes the psalm. Taken as a whole, the structure suggests that David wrote the psalm over a period of time without concentrating on the acrostic. It is also possible that something distracted him during the writing.

I. The Prayer for Deliverance 1–7

1–3 David lifts up his soul in worship of the Lord, v. 1.[351] He states his trust in "God" (*ᵓ^elohîm*),[352] the name that suggests God's power,

---

349Including Pss. 25, 26, 27, 28, 35, 37, 103, 138, and 144. The heading *l^edawid*, "belonging to David," occurs elliptically for *mizmôr l^edawid*, "a Psalm belonging to David." See G.K.C. 119 *r*, 129 *b*. The fuller title *mizmôr l^edawid* occurs in Pss. 15, 23, 24, 29, 101, 110, 141, and 143.

350Pss. 9, 10, 25, 34, 37, 111, 112, 119, and 145 are acrostic in nature. An excursus discussing the acrostic psalms precedes the discussion of Ps. 9.

351See note 341, 24:4, for a brief discussion of lifting up the soul.

352The name *ᵓ^elohîm* occurs in vv. 2, 5, and 22. In each case, the context suggests David's need for the power of God to deliver him from the threat that he faces. David uses the name *y^ehwah*, the name referring to God's merciful and gracious nature as He interacts with man, in vv. 1, 4, 6, 7, 8, 10, 11, 12, 14, 15. Of these, vv. 1, 4, 6, 7, 11, and 15 refer to prayer.

then asks Him to keep him from being "ashamed" (*bôš*, see 6:10). David's concern is with some unnamed enemies that oppose him at this time. He asks the Lord to keep them from overcoming him, v. 2. David broadens his thinking. He asks that those who "wait on" (*qawâ*)[353] the Lord not be "ashamed" (*bôš*), overcome by enemies. Rather, let those who "transgress" (*bagad*, better "act treacherously")[354] be "ashamed" (*bôš*), with their plans defeated, v. 3.

4–5 David asks the Lord to show him His ways. It is not that David doesn't know the ways of the Lord (cf. v. 10) but that straying from these ways through selfish or impetuous actions is easy. David wants the Lord to keep him in the paths of righteousness, v. 4. He asks the Lord to lead him according to His truth. He recognizes that "God" (*ᵓelohîm*) is the One Who gives "salvation" (or "deliverance"). David will continue to "wait" (*qawâ*) for Him to work on his behalf, v. 5.

6–7 David continues his prayer, asking the Lord to remember His "tender mercies" (or "compassions") and "lovingkindnesses" (or "steadfast love," *ḥesed*, see 5:7). These qualities have belonged to the Lord from eternity past, v. 6. He further asks the Lord not to remember "the sins [*ḥaṭaᵓ*, see 4:4] of [his] youth" or his transgressions. The fact that David looks on past sins with regret shows his spiritual growth. He now laments what he earlier rejoiced in. He asks the Lord to extend "mercy" (or "steadfast love," *ḥesed*) to him. He bases his prayer on the goodness of God, v. 7.

II. The Path of Godliness 8–14

8–10 David recognizes that God is "good and upright," not acting wickedly. He will teach "sinners," those who fall short of God's righteous standards, "the way" in which they should walk. The "sinners" here are not David's foes but rather a general reference to mankind. Those who listen to the Lord will find that He directs them in righteous ways, v. 8. To illustrate this, David gives the example of the

---

[353]The word *qawâ* has the sense of waiting or looking for something with a spirit of eager anticipation. This may be either for a good purpose, as here, or for an evil purpose, as in 56:6. The context determines the nature of the action.

[354]The verb *bagad* refers to someone who breaks a covenant of some kind: marriage, Mal. 2:14–15; government, Judg. 9:23; and, predominantly, God's law, Jer. 5:11. This leads to a sense of "acting treacherously, deceitfully, or unfaithfully."

"meek" (or "humble," see *ʿanî*, 9:12), who humbly accept God's guidance rather than arrogantly setting their own path through life. They receive guidance in "judgment" (or "justice"), the "way" in which the Lord deals with man, v. 9. The "paths" of the Lord, His ways, involve "mercy [or 'steadfast love,' *ḥesed*] and truth" to those who obey Him. They keep His "covenant" with man and His "testimonies." Both of these terms refer to the obligations placed on man by God's Word, v. 10.

11 The thought of God's Word reminds David of his past failures. He asks the Lord to "pardon" (or "forgive") his "iniquity," his turning away from God's Word, for the sake of the Lord's "name," His reputation as a merciful God.[355] David does not minimize his sin. He calls it "great," an appropriate description of any failure to follow the teaching of the Lord, v. 11.

12–14 David asks rhetorically, who is the one that "feareth the Lord" (*yirʾê yᵉhwah*, see 15:4)? It is this one that the Lord will teach, showing him the choices that he should make in life, v. 12. He will "dwell at ease," lit. "will dwell [*lîn*] in good." The verb *lîn* refers to dwelling that is of short duration, often spending the night (e.g., Gen. 19:2; 24:54). It refers here to the brief duration of life when compared with eternity to come. The word "good" suggests the overall goodness of the godly life.[356] The offspring of this godly man will "inherit the earth." The promise assumes that the descendants will follow the godly way in which they are taught, v. 13. The Lord will reveal His "secret" (or "counsel," *sôd*)[357] to those who "fear" (or "reverence," see *yirʾâ*, 2:11) Him. He will give them His covenant, v. 14.

---

[355]Note 94 at 5:11 gives a brief summary of the Lord's "name."

[356]Rawlinson, I, 182, understands "good" as "bliss," which he defines as "blessings of every kind." Similarly, Alexander, p. 124, calls it "good fortune or prosperity." These are Pollyanna views of godliness. Even the godly may suffer reverses. In the midst of sorrow, however, they have the assurance that comes from their relationship with the Lord. Hirsch, I, 184, refers the "good" to eternal bliss. The context, however, argues for this life rather than eternal life.

[357]The noun *sôd* refers to secret counsel or intimacy. This may occur either in counsel or in a council, depending on the context. The Lord reveals His will to those who follow Him, not to mankind in general. Hengstenberg, I, 437, interprets *sôd* as "friendship" on the basis of Job 29:4 and Prov. 3:32. Both of these verses are understood better as referring to "secret" or "intimate" counsel from God.

III. The Plea for Mercy 15–22

15 David describes his reliance on the Lord. He looks continually to Him for help, knowing that He will keep him from entanglement in "the net." Giving no details as to the nature of this "net" allows a broad application that the godly may well apply to personal situations. The Lord watches over His own to keep them from the attacks of their enemies, v. 15.

16–17 David pleads for the Lord's presence in his life. He asks Him to "have mercy" (or "be gracious," *ḥanan*, see 4:1). He is "desolate and afflicted [*ᶜanî*, see 9:12]," with no one to help him in his trials. While David may have had advisors and armies at his disposal, leadership is essentially alone. The king must make the final decisions. David can thus justly feel that he is "desolate," alone, v. 16. The "troubles [*ṣarâ*, see 9:9] of [his] heart," his emotional response to the trials that he faces, are "enlarged," growing greater. He asks again that the Lord would deliver him from his "distresses" (*mᵉṣûqâ*),[358] v. 17.

18 As in vv. 7, 11, David once more seeks forgiveness for his sins. He may have felt that his "affliction [*ᶜanî*, see 9:12] and . . . pain [or 'trouble,' *ᶜamal*, see 7:14]" came from his spiritual failures. He prays that the Lord will "forgive" (*naśaᵓ*)[359] them, v. 18.

19–21 David returns to the thought of his foes. They are many, and they "hate" (*śaneᵓ*, see 5:5) him with "cruel [or 'violent'] hatred," an active hatred that seeks to overcome him, v. 19. For this reason, he asks the Lord to "keep" (or "guard") him and to deliver him from them. He prays that he may not "be ashamed" (*bôš*, see 6:10) from being overcome by his adversaries. He has put his "trust" (*ḥasâ*, see 2:12) in the Lord, v. 20. He depends on the Lord's "integrity [*tom*, see 7:8] and uprightness" to protect him.[360] He resolves to "wait" (*qawâ*, see v. 3) for the Lord, eagerly anticipating His deliverance, v. 21.

---

[358]The word *mᵉṣûqâ* occurs again at 107:6, 13, 19, and 28. It refers to either emotional or physical difficulties. In each case, the context must guide the sense taken by the word.

[359]The basic sense of *naśaᵓ* is "to lift, take." When used with the idea of forgiveness, the thought is that the Lord takes away our sins, lifting them from us and bearing them Himself at Calvary.

[360]Hirsch, I, 187, and VanGemeren, p. 232, regard "integrity and uprightness" as belonging to David. His personal qualities of godliness will deliver him. While this is possible, it seems unlikely that David would claim this for himself when he has three times confessed his wickedness, vv. 7, 11, 18.

22 David ends the psalm by once more broadening his thought; cf. v. 3. Since he is king over the land, what affects him will necessarily affect the nation. He asks that "God" (*ʾelohîm*) "redeem" (*padâ*)[361] Israel, rescuing them from their "troubles" (*ṣarâ*), v. 22.

PSALM 26

Nothing in this "Psalm of David"[362] lets us identify the date or background to its writing. David faces an unknown threat that apparently involved bribery, vv. 9–10.[363] He reminds the Lord of his faithfulness in the past and of his love for worshiping the Lord. He continues to express his need for the Lord to deliver him. In so doing, David sets a pattern for faithful believers now. We also depend on the Lord to deliver us from the trials that come in life.

I. David's Profession of Faithfulness 1–8

1–3 David speaks of the godly qualities that he has practiced. He invites the Lord to judge him, to prove the rightness of his way and, if

[361]The word *padâ* expresses the transfer of ownership by the payment of a price. The first child of a couple belonged to God but could be redeemed by paying a price, Exod. 13:13. The firstborn of unclean animals could be redeemed, Num. 18:15, but that of a clean animal could not, Num. 18:17. The payment does not always involve money. Often, the payment simply involves giving the wicked the judgment they have earned. Redemption in the OT foreshadows the redemptive work of Jesus Christ, I Pet. 1:18–19.

[362]For the heading "Psalm of David," see the introduction to Ps. 25.

[363]Rawlinson, I, 193, makes vv. 9–10 a general statement of David's practice rather than a distinct threat. He sees the psalm as expressing David's feelings as he comes to "sacrifice at God's altar." Ewald, I, 297, sets the psalm at the time of some great national plague, "perhaps a pest," leading to general suffering. Nothing in the psalm, however, clearly refers to such national suffering. Henry, III, 327, sets the psalm during the time when Saul pursued David. Spurgeon, p. 131, gives the conjecture that David writes at the time of Ish-bosheth's assassination. Perowne, I, 262, suggests the time of Absalom's rebellion. Phillips, I, 195–96, places it during the famine that occurred late in David's reign, II Sam. 21:1. Dickson, I, 136 vaguely refers to "the judges of the land, [David's] powerful adversaries." The psalm does not give enough information to let us set its background with certainty.

otherwise, to reveal his errors. He has walked in "integrity" (*tom*, see 7:8) and has trusted the Lord. The last part of the verse reads better "I have trusted the Lord without wavering," v. 1. David asks the Lord to "examine" (or "test") him and to prove him, to "try" (*ṣarap*, see 12:6) his "reins" (*kilyâ*, see 7:9) and his "heart," his inward being, v. 2. He does not assert his self-righteousness. He rather reflects the result of walking with the Lord. This becomes clear in v. 3, when David explains that the Lord's "lovingkindness" (or "steadfast love," *ḥesed*, see 5:7) has come to him. He therefore lives according to the "truth" revealed by the Lord, v. 3.

4–5 David now describes his actions negatively. He has not "sat" (or "tarried") with "vain" (or "deceitful," *šawʾ*, see 12:2) persons. He has avoided "dissemblers," those that hide the truth of their actions, v. 4. He has "hated [*śaneʾ*, see 5:5] the congregation [or 'assembly'] of evil doers" and will not spend time with the wicked. It is worth noting that ordinary life will bring contact with many such persons. David here speaks of close fellowship, not of casual encounters (cf. I Cor. 5:9–10), v. 5.

6–8 Washing was a symbolic act to show moral purity (cf. Ps. 73:13; Isa. 1:16).[364] David will wash himself in "innocency," his consciousness of freedom from guilt. This will let him "compass" (or "go about") the altar as he comes to worship, v. 6. He will cause others to hear of his "thanksgiving" (*tôdâ*, from a root meaning "to praise") to the Lord. He will declare the "works" (*palaʾ*, see 9:1) of God on his behalf, v. 7. Spontaneously, David tells the Lord of his love for the "habitation" (*maʿôn*)[365] of God's "house,"[366] the tabernacle at which David worships and where the "honour" (better "glory") of the Lord, the Shekinah glory, dwells with His people, v. 8.

---

[364]Eaton, p. 84, and Weiser, p. 243, understand the washing as a ritual act of purification at the altar. This is possible only by rejecting David's authorship and assigning the psalm to a priest. There is, however, no reason to assign the writing to an unknown person.

[365]The noun *maʿôn* is a "place of dwelling." The context may make this the lair of animals, a dwelling on earth or in heaven, or a place of safety, a refuge.

[366]In the Talmud, *Taʾanît 29a* mistakenly refers the "house" to the synagogue.

II. David's Petition for Deliverance 9–12

9–10 Although David has avoided close contact with the wicked, he recognizes the continuing threat of bad associations. Too much involvement with the ungodly could cause him to develop their attitudes. This in turn could bring him into the same judgment that the wicked suffer. He asks the Lord not to "gather" his soul with "sinners" and "bloody men [*ʾenôš*, see 8:4]," those to whom the life of others has little meaning, v. 9. This includes those who devote their hands to "mischief" (better "evil plans") and offer bribes, v. 10.

11–12 David refuses to follow such practices. He will "walk in "integrity" (*tom*, see 7:8), continuing to follow those practices mentioned in vv. 1–8. He asks the Lord to "redeem" (*padâ*, see 25:22) him, most likely here referring to deliverance from evil persons. He asks the Lord to "be merciful" (or "be gracious," *ḥanan*, see 4:1) in meeting his needs. Although David is living a righteous life, he does not depend on his godly qualities. He recognizes that his ultimate deliverance is due to the gracious work of the Lord, v. 11. David's foot stands "in an even place" (or "with uprightness," *mîšôr*),[367] a description of his godliness. He will "bless [*barak*, see 5:12] the Lord" in the "congregations" (or "assemblies") of the people, v. 12.

PSALM 27

From v. 10, David writes during his flight from Saul.[368] He has taken his parents to Moab. He now faces the attempts of Saul to capture and put him to death. Other than this, we may only speculate on

[367]The word *mîšôr* refers first to a geographical "plain," e.g., Deut. 3:10; 4:43. From this comes a metaphorical sense of "uprightness" or "justice." This is the sense in which the word occurs in the Psalms.

[368]For the title "A Psalm of David," see the introduction to Ps. 25. On weak grounds, Ewald, I, 175, rejects David's authorship. He assigns the psalm to an early Israelite king. Since the two parts differ in "mood and subject-matter," Weiser, p. 245, sees vv. 1–6 and 7–14 as written by different authors. David, however, frequently shifts from lament to praise or from confidence to prayer. There is no reason to reject his authorship of the whole psalm.

the exact circumstances that call forth the psalm.[369] David's enemies have failed in their attempts to take him, v. 2. Yet they still seek him, even lying to bring him into disrepute, vv. 11–12. Throughout these circumstances, David retains his confidence in the Lord.

Much has been made over the differing emphases of vv. 1–6 and vv. 7–14. Some have even denied that one man could write the psalm.[370] The charge makes little sense. It flies in the face of manuscript evidence. It also ignores the difficulty of explaining how such different fragments became joined. No compiler would deliberately put two such totally different themes together.

Actually, the different themes are not a serious problem. David declares his trust in the Lord in vv. 1–6. It is because of this that he goes to the Lord in prayer, vv. 7–12. The final verses urge trust upon all who follow the Lord, vv. 13–14.[371]

I. Protection by the Lord 1–6

1–3 With these familiar words, David states his confidence in the Lord as his "light," his trustworthy guide through life, and his "salvation" (or "deliverance"), saving him from the efforts of his foes to overcome him. The Lord is also David's "strength" (or "fortress," *maᶜôz*).[372] Both rhetorical questions develop the thought that David is not "afraid" (*paḥad*, see 14:5) of those who attack him, v. 1. David illustrates his reason for trust in the Lord. There was a time when the wicked came to "eat up [his] flesh," idiomatic for attempt-

---

[369]The LXX included the words πρὸ τοῦ χρισθῆναι, "before the anointing," in its title. The Latin Vulgate similarly added *priusquam liniretur*, "before he was anointed." This supports the time of Saul's persecution, before David was anointed as king. Eaton, p. 86, dates it after David's becoming the king. Perowne, I, 265, and Jennings, I, 111, place the writing during Absalom's rebellion against David.

[370]Cheyne, I, 112, sees this as two psalms "combined, the one full of calm but deep joy . . . the other . . . a psalm of anxious supplication." He makes Israel the speaker in both. Leslie, pp. 324, 353, discusses the psalm as two distinct psalms. Kissane, p. 117, asserts "there can be little doubt that Psalm 27 is composed of two originally distinct poems." The view fails to see the connection between vv. 1–6 and vv. 7–14.

[371]Mays, p. 130, argues for the unity of the psalm. He bases this on similar thoughts throughout the psalm, e.g., salvation, vv. 1, 9; adversary, vv. 2, 12; heart, vv. 3, 8, 14; life, vv. 4, 13. Thompson, p. 236, supports the unity of the psalm from its two parts, praise, vv. 1–6, and prayer, vv. 7–12, a natural order of thought.

[372]The noun *maᶜôz* refers to a place of strength, i.e., a fortress, defense, or refuge. The Lord is all of this and more to those who follow Him.

ing to overcome him. Whatever the occasion in David's mind, his foes "stumbled and fell," failing in their attempt to cast him down, v. 2. This gives him the courage to say that he will not fear even if an army should surround him. In the time of trouble, even in war, he will maintain his confidence in the Lord, v. 3.

4 David has "desired" (better "asked") one thing from the Lord, and he purposes to seek it. It is to "dwell" (or "tarry") in the tabernacle, the "house" in which the Lord dwells on earth. With this thought, David does not state a desire to dwell in the tabernacle. Only priests had the right to enter it, and no one actually lived in it. David does, however, express his love of worship. He desires this for the rest of his life. David further looks forward to beholding the "beauty [*no*^{c}*am*, or 'favor'][373] of the Lord," the evidences of His presence, as he worships. He develops the idea of favor by referring to his prayers. He will seek answers to these at the "temple" (or "tabernacle," *hêkal*, see 5:7), v. 4.

5–6 David expresses his faith that the Lord will sustain him. In "the time of trouble," again undefined, the Lord will hide him in his "pavilion" (or "covert," *sok*).[374] The Lord will hide him in "the secret [or 'secret place'] of his tabernacle," poetically describing the place of safety in which the Lord will protect him. The Lord will set him on a large "rock" (*ṣûr*, see 18:2)[375] where his enemies cannot reach him, v. 5. With this care, David confidently anticipates victory over his foes. He will offer sacrifices in the Lord's tabernacle with "joy"

---

[373]J. D. Levenson, "A Technical Meaning for $N^{C}M$ in the Hebrew Bible," *VT* 35:1 (1985): 67, takes *no*^{c}*am* as a technical form of its usual sense of "beauty." He considers it "a connection with an affirmative omen," winning a lottery (16:6) or, here, the favorable inspection of entrails. The root *n*^{c}*m* occurs several times throughout the OT, e.g., 90:17; Prov. 3:17; 15:26, regularly referring to beauty, favor, or pleasantness, and always having a clear sense of meaning. There is no need for a "technical meaning," particularly one that suggests reliance on augury rather than trust in the Lord.

[374]Properly speaking, *sok* refers to branches woven together to form a thicket or booth. The poetical sense of a place of protection comes from this.

[375]Rawlinson, I, 199, and VanGemeren, p. 245, consider the rock to be God. While this is possible, it is also possible that the rock is simply a poetic figure of safety. W. E. Barnes, I, 137, identifies the rock as Mt. Zion, an unlikely view.

(or "shouts of joy," *t^erû^câ*).[376] He will sing and "sing praises" (or "make music," *zamar*, see 7:17) to the Lord, v. 6.

II. Petition by David 7–12

7–9 Trusting in the Lord's continuing protection, David turns to Him in prayer.[377] He begins generally, asking the Lord to "hear" his "cry" (or "call") for help. He asks the Lord to "have mercy" (or "be gracious," *ḥanan*, see 4:1), by answering his requests, v. 7. Verse 8*a* is awkward to translate. It lit. reads, "To you [*l^eka*], says my heart, seek my face."[378] The phrase "my heart said unto thee" does *not* introduce v. 8*b*, "Thy face, Lord, will I seek." The key lies in understanding the *l^e* preposition. It is obviously the Lord's face David seeks, not his own. His heart echoes the call of God's heart. It speaks "in regard to you,"[379] telling David to seek God's face. He readily responds that he will indeed seek the face of the Lord, v. 8. David continues his prayer negatively, asking the Lord not to hide His face and not to "put . . . [him] away" (better "turn [him] away") in "anger" (*ᵓap*, see 2:5). By using the title "thy servant," David reminds the Lord of his relationship to Him. The Lord has helped him in the past. David asks Him not to leave or forsake him now, in the present trouble. He addresses the Lord as the "God of my salvation," the One on Whom he depends for deliverance, v. 9.

10 The word "forsake" is too strong. We have no record that David's parents ever forsook him. During Saul's search for David, he arranged asylum for them in Moab (I Sam. 22:3). This prevented Saul from threatening them in order to force David to return. This prob-

---

[376]The noun *t^erû^câ* refers to raising a noise. This may come from an instrument or, as here, from shouting.

[377]Leupold, p. 237, speaks of the "full, resonant tone of the first half" and "the plaintive cry of the second." Fausset, III, 159, refers to a "transition from triumphant confidence to mournful supplication." Briggs, writing in Moll, p. 200, says that "the triumphant strain of confidence now gives way to one of sad and earnest entreaty." These views mistake the purpose of vv. 1–6. It is because of David's confidence expressed there that he comes to the Lord with his petition in vv. 7–12.

[378]The NASB is similar to the AV. It supplies "When Thou didst say" and reverses the next two clauses, "Seek My face, my heart said to Thee." The NIV follows the word order of the MT but is free in its translation: "My heart says of you, 'Seek his [lit. "my"] face!'" Leupold, p. 237, understands secondary meanings and translates "Of thee my mind has always thought; my face has always sought thee."

[379]It is not unusual for *l^e* to follow a verb of speaking. See Bruce K. Waltke and M. O'Connor, *An Introduction to Biblical Hebrew Syntax*, 11.2.10*d*; G.K.C. 119 *u*.

ably gives us the setting for the psalm. Even though his parents have "left" him, David is confident that the Lord will sustain him, v. 10.[380]

11–12 David continues his prayer, this time more specifically. He asks the Lord to teach him so that he might follow the ways of the Lord. He wants the Lord to lead him in "a plain path" (or "uprightness," *mîšôr*, see 26:12) so that his enemies will have no way to attack him, v. 11. Negatively, he asks for deliverance for those who attack him. They have lied about him. Their very breath is cruelty, v. 12.

III. Perseverance of the Saints 13–14

13–14 The first words are supplied and are therefore subjective. Perhaps the phrase "I would have lost all hope" best expresses the thought.[381] David speaks of the goodness of the Lord, the hope that has sustained him. The "land of the living" refers to this present life, the time in which David faced the opposition, v. 13. Based on his personal experience, David concludes by urging others to trust the Lord.[382] They should eagerly "wait" (*qawâ*, see 25:3) for Him to act. They should "be of good courage" (or "be strong," *ḥazaq*).[383] The phrase "he shall strengthen [*ʾamaṣ*] thine heart" is better "and let your heart be strong." Once more, he urges others to eagerly "wait" (*qawâ*) for the Lord to work on their behalf, v. 14.

---

[380]Lawson, p. 151, understands the verse as hypothetical. If David's parents would disown him, "the love of God would still persist." Kissane, p. 120, understands this as a picture of "the closest ties of human affection." Horne, p. 134, mentions the possibility that David's parents forsook him "at their death." Kirkpatrick, p. 143, makes the verse proverbial, as though David was "forsaken as a deserted child." Weiser, p. 253, and Leslie, p. 324, assume that there was a time when David's parents actually forsook him.

[381]To show their uncertainty with the word, the Masoretes pointed *lûleʾ* ("unless") with the *puncta extraordinaria*, one of only fifteen such vowel pointings in the OT לוּלֵא הֶאֱמַנְתִּי לִרְאוֹת בְּטוּב־יְהוָה בְּאֶרֶץ חַיִּים׃ (note the dots under each of the first three consonants). The verse, however, is poetic, an example of aposiopesis with part of the sentence suppressed when the concluding thought is clear.

[382]Rawlinson, I, 200, makes the exhortation "not to others, but to himself." It is unlikely, however, that David would refer to himself in the second person, "thine heart." Leslie, p. 325, understands the verse as the speech of a priest, encouraging the one making the petition. Nothing in the context suggests a new speaker.

[383]In general, there is no great difference between *ḥazaq* and *ʾamaṣ*. The two words occur in parallel several times in the OT, e.g., Deut. 31:6, 7; Josh. 1:6, 7. The only two times that *ʾamaṣ* occurs in the *hipʿîl* theme, here and at 31:24, it refers to strength of faith.

PSALM 28

This "Psalm of David"[384] expresses his lament at some unknown situation.[385] Wicked men oppose him, vv. 3–5, and the matter threatens his life, v. 1. The plans of his enemies will affect the nation, v. 9. Despite these difficulties, David maintains his trust in the Lord. He goes to Him in prayer, vv. 1–5, 9; confidently anticipates the answer to his plea, vv. 6–7; and offers praise to the Lord, v. 8. As is so often true in the Psalms, David's actions here set a godly example for Christians today who face opposition from the wicked.

I. David's Plea for Deliverance 1–5

1–2 David calls upon the Lord. The term "rock" properly belongs to the second phrase: "My rock, be not silent to me." The name "rock" (*ṣûr*, see 18:2) suggests that the Lord is an unmovable foundation upon which David rests. He pleads with the Lord not to be "silent," to fail to act on his behalf. If the Lord fails him, he will be as others "that go down to the pit" (*bôr*, see 7:15), the grave, where there are no longer answers to prayer, v. 1.[386] He asks again that the Lord hear his "supplications" (*taḥ*^{a}*nûn*)[387] as he pleads for mercy. He lifts up his hands in prayer as though reaching out to the Lord.[388] He prays toward the "holy oracle," the most holy place in the tabernacle, where the Lord dwells among His people, v. 2.

3–5 David asks the Lord not to draw him away with the wicked, not to include him with the judgment that falls upon them. These

---

[384]For the heading, "Psalm of David," see the introduction to Ps. 25.

[385]Calvin, I, 465, places it at the time of David's "persecutions by Saul." Harman, p. 135, and Cohen, p. 81, set the psalm at the time of Absalom's rebellion. The psalm does not make clear its background.

[386]Mays, p. 135, and Oesterley, I, 198, relate the "pit" (*bôr*) to "Sheol," hell. Elsewhere, however, the word *bôr* rarely stands for *š*^{e}*ʾôl*. It normally refers to a pit. In the Psalms, it often refers to a grave, e.g., 30:3; 143:7.

[387]There is a distinct emotional component of meaning with *taḥ*^{a}*nûn*. The "supplications" describe the pouring out of a troubled heart to the Lord.

[388]Lifting the hands expressed a reaching out to God. It is a cultural expression of dependence on God, never commanded for prayer. In addition, people knelt in prayer, I Kings 8:54; Dan. 6:10; bowed their faces to the ground, Neh. 8:6; and prayed while lying down, Isa. 38:2. It is not the position of the body but the attitude of the heart that is important in prayer.

"workers of iniquity" talk of bringing peace to the land but inwardly plan "mischief" (better "evil"), v. 3. David asks the Lord to judge them for their works, according to the wickedness they have done. He repeats his prayer, asking again that the Lord would judge them for what they have done. He prays that the Lord would give them their "desert" (or "recompense"), what they have earned by their actions, v. 4. To develop this last thought, David notes that his wicked foes do not "regard" (or "consider") the works of the Lord. They care nothing for the "operation" (or "work") of His hands. David is therefore confident that the Lord will "destroy them" (better "tear them down," *haras*, see 11:3) and not build them up, v. 5.

II. David's Praise for Deliverance 6–9

6–7 David "blesse[s]" (*barak*, see 5:12) the Lord, praising Him for hearing his "supplications" (*taḥ*^{a}*nûn*, see v. 2), his pleas for mercy. David phrases his praise in the perfect tense because of his confidence that the Lord will indeed answer his prayers. While the answer is in the future, his faith allows him to regard it as already done, v. 6. He describes the Lord as his "strength" and "shield" (*magen*, see 3:3). He therefore trusts Him and finds the help he needs. For this reason, he rejoices in the Lord and pledges to praise Him in song, v. 7.

8–9 The Lord is not only David's strength but also "their strength," the strength of His people. He is the "saving strength" (or "stronghold of deliverance," *ma*^{c}*ôz*, see 27:1) for His "anointed" (*mašîaḥ*, see 2:2), referring to David, the king of the nation, v. 8. David closes the psalm by asking the Lord to deliver the nation and to "bless" (*barak*) His "inheritance." The term refers to the special position Israel held as the people of God. For this reason, David asks the Lord to supply their needs, to "feed them" (or "shepherd them") and to "lift them" from the troubles they face. While the verb "lift" does not require this, it is appropriate to think of the shepherd lifting a sheep to carry it away from some difficulty. So the Lord does for His own people today, v. 9.

PSALM 29

As with many of David's psalms,[389] nothing indicates the circumstances that led him to write.[390] There is no hint of any threat to David, only the giving of glory to the Lord. In this hymn of praise, David honors the Lord for His power. He illustrates this from the evidences of the Lord's power in nature. These encourage David that the Lord will exercise His power on Israel's behalf.[391]

The LXX added the phrase ἐξοδίου σκηνῆς, indicating that the psalm was sung on the last day of the Feast of Tabernacles.[392] While this may have once been true, the Jews do not associate the psalm with the feast today.

I. The Worship of the Angels 1–2

1–2 David calls upon the "mighty" (lit. "sons of the mighty [*ʾelîm*]") to give glory to the Lord. Elsewhere, the phrase "sons of the mighty [*ʾelîm*]" (89:6) refers to angelic beings.[393] Although they possess might far above man's, their power pales in comparison with the

[389]For the title "A Psalm of David," see the introduction to Ps. 25.

[390]Among others, Phillips, I, 217, and Lawson, p. 156, suggest that David wrote the psalm during an intense storm. While others feared, he saw the Lord exercising His power. Leupold, p. 245, suggests instead that David describes an "ideal storm," grouping features of the storm together "without necessarily claiming that all of them will be in evidence in each storm." In sharp contrast, Eaton, p. 89, sees the theme as "the worship of God as Creator-King." The storm has a Master. Oesterley, I, 199, thinks that "the awesome descriptions of the theophany on Mount Sinai" inspired the psalm. Morris, p. 39, draws on the use of *mabbûl* in v. 10 (see discussion) to make the whole psalm refer to the Noahic Flood. Gaebelein, p. 133, understands the storm as portraying God's judgment on man. These views are possible. Since the psalm does not discuss its background, we may only speculate on its source.

[391]*NIB*, IV, 792, mentions the possibility that Ps. 29 is "the oldest of the psalms." This is speculated since "it seems to be an Israelite adaptation of an ancient Canaanite hymn to Baal." David, however, draws from nature, e.g. 8:6–9; 19:1–6; 65:5–13, as he makes spiritual points. There is no reason to relate this psalm to a heathen song to Baal.

[392]*Sukkah* 55*a* states that the Jews sung Ps. 29 on the first day of the feast.

[393]Horne, p. 137, refers the phrase to the "'mighty' ones of the earth," the kings, the rich, and others of great influence. Hirsch, I, 206, understands "sons of the mighty" as "those who are endowed with strength." Leslie, p. 137, refers the phrase to the sun, moon, and stars. Since the phrase occurs elsewhere only in 89:6, it is difficult to adopt a view that has no support elsewhere. Rodd, p. 62, wrongly refers the

Lord's. They should therefore offer their glory and strength to Him, v. 1. David repeats his call to give glory to the Lord. The angels should offer Him "the glory due unto his name," the glory His nature demands.[394]

The passage ends by concluding that the angels should worship the Lord "in the beauty of holiness" (*beḥadrat-qodeš*). This cryptic phrase occurs elsewhere (96:9; I Chron. 16:29; II Chron. 20:21). A similar phrase, *beḥadrê-qodeš*, occurs at 110:3. The key lies in the understanding of *hadar*. There is no question that the verbal root underlying this means "to honor, adorn." This leads to the view that sees the Lord Himself in the phrase: worship Him in the glory of *His* holiness. This requires that we at least mentally supply the pronoun "His," but this is a minor matter. This view has the advantage of paralleling the first part of the verse.[395] It also explains the phrase where it occurs elsewhere, v. 2.

II. The Power of the Lord 3–9

3–9 Most of the psalm describes the glory of the Lord as seen in nature. The "voice of the Lord" poetically describes the thunder heard in storms. This echoes across the waters, possibly the Mediterranean Sea. David repeats this thought to emphasize that God reveals His glorious power in storms, v. 3. His voice, heard in thunder, is powerful. It is full of "majesty" (*hadar*, see 8:5), v. 4. It

---

phrase to "the divine beings who form Yahweh's heavenly court." While the angels are mighty, they are not "divine."

[394]There is a brief summary of the "name" of the Lord at 5:11, note 94.

[395]Other views are also held. The view that *beḥadrat-qodeš* means "holy attire" is often expressed. Cohen, p. 83, and Perowne, I, 276, adopt this view and refer the clothing to that of the worshipers. This is the most widely held way of understanding the phrase. Hengstenberg, I, 476, also adopts the view but refers it to the clothing of the angels in worship. We know nothing, however, of the attire of angels as they worship. Further, the phrase everywhere else refers to the worship of man. This should be continual, not limited merely to those times when attired suitably. Calvin, I, 476, and Dickson, p. 150, take the view that the phrase refers to the earthly sanctuary, a glorious place. While the word *qodeš* often refers to the sanctuary, the phrase here must refer to the heavenly sanctuary since the charge has angels in view. We can be assured of its glory, but we know nothing of angelic worship there. Do they worship in the heavenly tabernacle? Rawlinson, I, 212, and Albert Barnes, I, 248, adopt a third view by applying the phrase to the beauty of holiness itself. It is questionable that the angels should be urged to worship in holiness. The angels of heaven have no other option.

may even break down the cedar tree, a tree found in biblical times on the Lebanon Mountains, north of Palestine. The cedar is a large tree with a height up to eighty feet and a trunk that may reach forty feet in circumference, v. 5. The phrase "he maketh them also . . ." is better "he makes Lebanon skip like a calf." The trees on this mountain range sway before the storm. "Sirion" is the Sidonian name for Mt. Hermon (Deut. 3:9). This mountain is at the southern end of the Anti-Lebanon Mountains and is the highest mountain in Palestine.[396] Its trees move in the storm "like a young unicorn" (better "a young wild ox," see *remîm*, 22:21) as it gambols about, v. 6.

The thunder "divideth [*ḥaṣab*, or 'hews out'] the flames of fire" as it marks the appearance of one flash of lightning after another, v. 7.[397] It shakes the wilderness, even the wilderness found in Kadesh, south of Palestine, v. 8. The thunder "maketh the hinds to calve" (or "makes the oaks to writhe").[398] The thunder "discovereth the forest" (better "makes bare the forest"). Everyone in the "temple" (*hêkal*, see 5:7) of the Lord speaks of His glory, v. 9.

---

[396]Various heights are assigned to Mt. Hermon. Unger, p. 470, gives it a height of 9100 feet. *ISBE*, III, 1378, makes it 9200 feet. Charles F. Pfeiffer, *Baker's Bible Atlas* (Grand Rapids, Mich.: Baker Book House, 1976), p. 302, gives 9232 feet. Whatever the height, it is the highest mountain in Palestine.

[397]The action of "hewing" the lightning has puzzled some. Weiser, pp. 260, 264, translates as "the voice of the Lord flashes forth licking flames of fire." He calls this the "licking flames of fire which the mouth of God flashes down upon the earth." The sense of "licking" is a remarkably free rendering of *ḥaṣab*. Buttenwieser, p. 154, translates the verb as "hurls," also a free sense of *ḥaṣab*. Jennings, I, 114, more correctly explains the verb as "cleaveth," referring to "forked lightning-shafts." He then justifies this as a view "natural among a primitive and unscientific people." Edward L. Greenstein, "Yhwh's Lightning in Psalm 29:7," *Maarav* 8 (1992): 57, emends to *ḥṣyw* and translates "Hark! YHWH—his arrows are flames of fire." There is no textual support for the change. The use of *ḥaṣab* to indicate "hewing" is well attested in the OT, e.g., I Kings 5:15; II Kings 12:12; Isa. 10:15; 22:16.

[398]Herbert Cohn, "Hinds in Psalm 29," *JBQ* 24:4 (1996): 259, notes that the hind is timid and easily frightened. It is not therefore a good parallel to the breaking of the mighty cedars. The word translated "hinds" (*ʾayyalôt*) may be repointed *ʾeylôt*, "oaks." These "writhe," moving with the storm as it passes by. This improves the parallelism with the next phrase. Among others, Murphy, p. 205, and Dahood, I, 179, adopt the view that the storm frightens the deer into giving birth prematurely. Gaebelein, p. 136, spiritualizes the phrase, making the "hinds" refer to Israel, bringing forth "a man-child." The view rests on Gaebelein's imagination.

III. The Deliverance of the Nation 10–11

10–11 Having this display of the power of the Lord, David praises Him. He "sitteth [or 'sat'] upon the flood," a reference to the Lord's control over the "flood" (*mabbûl*). The use of *mabbûl* is significant. This is the only place it occurs outside the Genesis record of the worldwide Flood. David thinks of Noah's Flood and places it under the Lord's control. The Lord is the King, in firm control of nature "for ever," v. 10. For this reason, David now applies the psalm to Israel. The Lord will give them strength to overcome their foes. He will "bless" (*barak*, see 5:12) the nation with lasting peace, v. 11.

PSALM 30

According to the title, this is "a Psalm [*mizmôr*] and Song [*šîr*]."[399] David wrote this psalm for the dedication of the "house."[400] This refers to the dedication of the threshing floor of Araunah the Jebusite, later the location of the temple.[401] After David's sin of pride had led him to number the people, the Lord had judged him by sending

---

[399]There is not a great difference between *mizmôr* (see 3, intro.) and *šîr*. When they occur together, as they do in thirteen of the psalm titles, *mizmôr* refers to a song accompanied by musical instruments and *šîr* to a song performed by a choral group.

[400]The phrase "of David" in the title refers to "a psalm and song" rather than to "the dedication of the house."

[401]Hirsch, I, 212, and Hengstenberg, I, 482, adopt the position given above. Rotherham, p. 155, follows Perowne, I, 278, in relating the psalm to the dedication of David's house, II Sam. 5:11–12, after his capture of Jerusalem. Dickson, p. 153, more specifically refers it to "the dedication of David's house, after it was polluted by Absalom's vileness with his father's concubines." The view requires that David go through some sickness from which the Lord delivers him. VanGemeren, p. 257, considers the title as "a later addition in which the psalm was nationalized as an expression of the suffering of the nation in exile and of the restoration from exile." In this case, the "house of David" is "the second temple, dedicated in 515 B.C." The view is possible, although it goes counter to the natural understanding of the title. Weiser, p. 267, rejects David's authorship. He makes the psalm an individual's thanksgiving "on the occasion of a festival pilgrimage." Robinson, p. 124, refers the "house" to the "reconsecration of the Temple by Judas Maccabaeus," c. 165 BC. The Jews originally sang Ps. 30 in commemorating this event, but eventually they discontinued the practice. Today, Jews from the Sephardi background still use Ps. 30 at Hanukkah (*NEJ*, p. 340).

a plague on the nation, reducing the numbers he had boasted in. Realizing his sin, David purchased the threshing floor, built an altar, and offered sacrifices to the Lord (II Sam. 24:18–25). This site became the location where Solomon later built the temple (II Chron. 3:1). The psalm is one of thanksgiving to the Lord.[402]

The psalm does not mention the "house of David." It focuses instead on David's sin, v. 6; his prayer asking for divine intervention, vv. 2*a*, 8; the Lord's gracious deliverance of the people from the plague, vv. 2*b*, 5, and David's rejoicing in the Lord, vv. 4–5, 11–12. Modern Jews still recite the psalm as they observe the Feast of Dedication (John 10:22), commemorating the restoration of worship at Jerusalem by Judas Maccabaeus after defeating Antiochus Epiphanes.

I. The Devotion of David 1–5

1–3 David exalts the Lord for saving him from peril. While he does not give any detail regarding his plight, the plague sent by the Lord in judgment of David's pride fits well into the psalm (II Sam. 24:15–16). The Lord has "lifted" him from his despair and has not let his foes rejoice over his fall, v. 1. David recalls his prayer (II Sam. 24:17). The Lord has heard this and "healed" him, giving respite from the judgment (II Sam. 24:25), v. 2. The Lord has brought his "soul from the grave [*šᵉʾôl*, see 6:5]." At the time of the plague, he likely considered himself as good as dead. The Lord has graciously kept him alive and not let him "go down to the pit" (*bôr*, see 7:15), the grave, v. 3.

4–5 David climaxes this section with a call to praise the Lord. He praises the Lord himself, but he also urges all of the "saints" (*ḥasîd*, see 4:3) to "sing" (*zamar*, see 7:17) to the Lord. They should thank Him as they recall His holiness, His faithfulness to the covenant with Israel, v. 4. Yes, He has judged the nation severely, but His "anger" (*ʾap*, see 2:5) has lasted "but a moment." II Samuel 24:15 tells us that the pestilence lasted "from the morning even to the time appointed," likely the evening sacrifice. The favor of the Lord, in contrast, lasts a

---

[402]The introduction to Ps. 18 summarizes the songs of thanksgiving.

"life" (or "lifetime").[403] Sorrow may "endure" (*lîn*, see 25:13) a short time, but there will be future "joy" (*rinnâ*, see 17:1), v. 5.

II. The Deliverance of David 6–10

6–7 Looking at the prosperity of his kingdom, David had boasted that nothing could ever shake him, v. 6. He now recognizes that such stability was a gift from the Lord. The Lord had made David's "mountain," Mt. Zion, the location of Jerusalem and thus a suitable emblem to represent the kingdom, to stand firm among the kingdoms of the earth. When the Lord hid His face from David, however, David was "troubled" (or "dismayed," *bahal*, see 2:5), v. 7.

8–10 David called upon the Lord and "made supplication" ("sought grace," *ḥanan*, see 4:1), seeking favor from the Lord, v. 8. The three rhetorical questions require negative answers. There would be no gain "in [his] blood," his destruction, and in going down to the "pit" (*šaḥat*, see 7:15), the grave. Those in the "dust," the grave, cannot render praise to the Lord. They cannot declare the "truth" (or "faithfulness") of the Lord to others, v. 9. David calls upon the Lord to "have mercy upon" (or "be gracious to," *ḥanan*) him. He asks the Lord for help, v. 10.

III. The Delight of David 11–12

11–12 David celebrates the nation's deliverance from the plague. The Lord has turned his "mourning" (or "wailing," *misped*)[404] into a joyous dance. He has taken the "sackcloth" (*śaq*)[405] David wore as an outward symbol of his grief (I Chron. 21:16) and replaced it with "gladness" (or "joy"), v. 11. All of this was done that David's "glory" (*kabôd*), in a sense his "soul," the king himself with all the splendor

---

[403]While the word "life" (*ḥayyîm*) does not intrinsically refer to a lifetime, it often has this sense, e.g., 17:14; 23:6; 27:4. Alexander, p. 138, understands *ḥayyîm* as "all that makes existence desirable." The contrast with brief anger favors time rather than the quality of life. Hengstenberg, I, 488, understands "life" as a reference to deliverance. This also contrasts nicely with the brevity of the first clause.

[404]Although this is the only place *misped* occurs in the Psalms, it occurs enough elsewhere to support the sense of "wailing" or "lamenting," e.g., Est. 4:3; Jer. 6:26; 48:38.

[405]Sackcloth (*śaq*) was a coarse, dark cloth made from goat's hair. It was worn as an outward sign of inward grief; cf. Gen. 37:34; Isa. 15:3; 22:12.

of his kingdom, should "sing praise" (*zamar*, see 7:17) to the Lord.[406] The only alternative would be to remain silent and imply that his glory was due to his own accomplishments. David pledges instead to give thanks to the Lord forever, v. 12.

PSALM 31

As he does with the majority of his psalms, David writes this psalm for the "chief musician" (*m*ᵉ*naṣṣeaḥ*, see 4, intro.) to use in Israel's worship.[407] In this individual lament, David describes some threat.[408] Others have laid a net to trap him, v. 4, and he is gripped with sorrow, vv. 9–10. Others fear to be associated with him, v. 11; his foes have slandered him and plot to take his life, v. 13. Through all of this, David maintains his trust in the Lord, e.g., vv. 1, 5, 14. He is confident that the Lord will deliver him, vv. 19, 22. Just as David does here, vv. 7–8, 19, 21 23–24, so believers today should praise the Lord for deliverances from difficulty in life.

---

[406]Calvin, I, 497, views the "glory" as David's tongue, used in praising God. There is no clear place elsewhere, however, to support the view that the "glory" refers to the tongue. Phillips, I, 231, compares David's "glory" to his "crown of glory." The context, however, will not support the idea of an inanimate object praising God. Oesterley, I, 203, repoints *kabôd* to *kebedî* and translates "my heart may sing praise to thee." While the LXX supports this, the root *kbd* infrequently has this meaning, less than twenty times compared to more than two hundred times for the sense "glory."

[407]Ewald, I, 303, makes Jeremiah the author. Jer. 20:10 quotes v. 14*a*. The broken vessel, v. 12, occurs again in Jer. 22:28 and 48:38. Jer. 20:18 is close to v. 11. As Hengstenberg, I, 496, states: "The conclusion is just as valid as would be the inference that it had been composed by our Saviour, because He made use of the language of the 5th verse on the cross."

[408]Kidner, *Psalm 1–72*, p. 130, divides the psalm into two sections, vv. 1–8 and 9–24. He tentatively suggests the possibility that these refer to two different crises in David's life. Murphy, p. 212, and Cohen, p. 88, suggest that David wrote the psalm during his flight from Saul. Clarke, I, 89, makes this specific, referring to David's "experience at Keilah." Thompson, p. 245, dates it at the time of Absalom's rebellion. Statements in the psalm may support this view. David refers to his sin as the cause of his trials, v. 10; cf. II Sam. 12:10–12. He speaks of slanders, v. 13, and lies, v. 18, cf. II Sam. 15:1–4. He describes the counsel of his foes against him, v. 13; cf. II Sam. 17:1–14. For these reasons, I accept this last view although, since the psalm is not explicit, it must remain in doubt.

I. Defense of the Psalmist 1–8

1–3 David places his "trust" (better "seeks refuge," *ḥasâ*, see 2:12) in the Lord. For this reason, he asks that the Lord will not let him "be ashamed" (*bôš*, see 6:10) by falling before his foes. Let him be delivered by the Lord, the One Who is righteous and faithful to keep His covenant with David (II Sam. 7:12–16), v. 1. He asks the Lord to incline His ear to him. The anthropomorphism pictures the Lord's answer to David's prayer. He further asks the Lord to deliver him quickly from his trials. The Lord is David's "strong rock [*ṣûr*, see 18:2]," the foundation upon which he rests. He is David's "house of defence [*m^eṣûdâ*],"[409] i.e., a place from which David can gain deliverance from enemy attacks, v. 2. The Lord is David's "rock" (*selaᶜ*, see 18:2) and his "fortress" (*m^eṣûdâ*), the One on Whom he relies. David asks the Lord "for thy name's sake,"[410] i.e., for the sake of His reputation as a gracious God, to give him the direction that he needs, v. 3.

4–5 David asks the Lord to free him from the "net," the trap that others have laid for him. The Lord is his "strength" (or "stronghold," *maᶜôz*, see 27:1), again the One on Whom he relies, v. 4. David commits himself into the hand of the Lord, a picture of being held by the Lord's strength. The Lord quoted this part of the verse while on the cross, His final words, Luke 23:46. It is the Lord, the God Who is true to the "truth" of His word, Who has "redeemed" (*padâ*, see 25:22) David, v. 5.[411]

6–8 David hates (*śaneᵓ*, see 5:5) those who "regard [or 'give heed to'] lying [*šawᵓ*, see 12:2] vanities [*hebel*],"[412] worthless idols. In sharp contrast, David trusts the Lord, v. 6. He will rejoice in the Lord's "mercy" (or "steadfast love," *ḥesed*, see 5:7). The Lord has "considered" (or "seen") his "trouble" (or "affliction," *ᶜanî*, see 9:12), the opposition given by his foes. The Lord has known what "adversities"

---

[409]The word *m^eṣûdâ* comes from a root meaning "to hunt." From this derives the sense a place for hunting, i.e., a fortress or stronghold. From here, troops may go out to battle or remain behind the walls to defend themselves. The well-known fortress of the Jews, Masada, transliterates the word.

[410]See note 94, 5:11, for a brief summary of the Lord's name.

[411]Perowne, I, 284, mentions that these words were also the last words of Bernard of Clairvaux, John Huss, Jerome of Prague, Luther, Melanchthon, and others.

[412]The noun *hebel* refers to something that is empty, without substance. This leads to "vapor, breath, vanity." Since idols are not real deities, the word often describes them.

(*ṣarâ*, see 9:9) David has experienced, v. 7. He has not "shut me up" (or "delivered me") to the power of his foes. He has rather placed him in "a large room," an expanse where he was free to move about, v. 8.

II. Difficulty of the Psalmist 9–16

9–10 David continues to seek the Lord's deliverance from his trials. He asks the Lord to "have mercy" (or "be gracious," *ḥanan*, see 4:1) to him because of his "trouble" (*ṣarar*).[413] Whatever the nature of David's trouble, it had brought him emotional stress. He describes this as having his eye "consumed with grief [or 'vexation']." The emotions likewise touch his "soul" and "belly," both representing his emotional being, v. 9. Grief has consumed his life, and sighing, a response to his emotions, has affected the years of his life. David recognizes that his own iniquity underlies the problem.[414] This has caused his strength to fail and his "bones," idiomatic for his body, to waste away, v. 10.

11–13 David is a "reproach" (or "taunt") to his enemies, especially to those living nearby. The danger he faces has caused dread to those who know him. Others flee at the sight of him, fearing that they will be identified with him, v. 11. They put him out of their mind, treating him like a "broken" (*ʾabad*, see 1:6)[415] vessel that has no more use, v. 12. He has heard the slander that his adversaries have spread. This slander has caused widespread fear all about him. His foes "took counsel together" (or "sat together") as they plotted to take his life, v. 13.

14–16 Recognizing his plight, David commits himself to the Lord. He trusts the Lord and acknowledges that the Lord alone is his God, v. 14. His "times," the course of his life, are in the Lord's hand. He asks the Lord to deliver him from those foes who seek to "persecute"

[413]The word *ṣarar* refers to a place that is too narrow or restrictive. From this, it describes an emotional reaction to difficulty, the "distress" felt in times of trouble.

[414]The psalm does not tell us the nature of David's sin. II Sam. 11:2–17 describes the sin of David with Bathsheba and the subsequent murder of Uriah and other soldiers. This lay behind Absalom's rebellion, II Sam. 12:11–12, and may well be in David's mind here. If not, we can only speculate as to the nature of the wickedness.

[415]The *qal* active participle suggests a "perishing" vessel. His enemies look upon him as though his end is certain. In Psalms, this verb normally refers to the destruction of the wicked, e.g., 5:6; 92:9. David's foes may well have considered his destruction a sign of divine judgment.

(or "pursue") him, v. 15. He seeks the favorable light from the face of God to shine on him.[416] He asks once more for the Lord to deliver him for "thy mercies' sake" (or "the sake of your steadfast love," *ḥesed*, see 5:7), v. 16.

III. Deliverance of the Psalmist 17–24

17–18 David now asks that he will not "be ashamed" (*bôš*, see 6:10) by falling prey to his foes. He rather prays that they will "be ashamed" and that they will "lie silent in the grave [*šᵉʾôl*, see 6:5]." Instead of his own death, he anticipates the defeat and death of his adversaries, v. 17. Then their "lying lips" will be silenced. They will no longer speak "grievous things" (better "arrogantly") with pride and contempt against the righteous, v. 18.

19–22 David praises the Lord, Who stores great goodness for those who "fear" (or "reverence," see *yirʾâ*, 2:11) Him. He works this goodness out in the lives of those who openly "trust" (or "take refuge," *ḥasâ*, see 2:12) in Him, v. 19. He will conceal them "in the secret of [His] presence," away from the "pride" (better "conspiracies," *rokes*)[417] of men. He will hide them in a "pavilion" (or "shelter") from the strife produced by their speech, v. 20.[418] David "blesse[s]" (*barak*, see 5:12) the Lord because the Lord "hath shewed . . . his marvellous [*palaʾ*, see 9:1] kindness" (or "has wonderfully worked His steadfast love [*ḥesed*, see 5:7]"). This has taken place in a "strong city" (better "besieged city"), perhaps referring to Absalom's threat to Jerusalem (II Sam. 15:14), v. 21.[419] In his "haste" (or

---

[416]The picture of God's face shining on His people appears first in the Aaronic blessing, Num. 6:25. It occurs again in 67:1; 80:3, 7, 19; and 119:135.

[417]This is the only place that *rokes* occurs. The root *rakas*, "to bind," occurs elsewhere. This leads to the sense for the noun of people being "bound together," i.e., a conspiracy.

[418]The verse is the basis for the hymn "In the Secret of His Presence." The words of this hymn were written by Ellen Lakshmi Goreh and the music by George Coles Stebbins, both in 1883.

[419]Hirsch, I, 225, relates the "strong city" to Keilah, a city David left while fleeing from Saul. Murphy, p. 216, makes the city Ziklag, where David found shelter during his stay with the Philistines. Neither Keilah nor Ziklag, however, fit the description of "strong city." Both were relatively insignificant places. Hengstenberg, I, 506, understands the "strong city" as God Himself, "with His powerful and gracious protection." The view requires the Lord to show David His love in Himself. This is strangely phrased. Buttenwieser, pp. 565–66, concludes that the psalm should be

"alarm," *ḥapaz*),[420] David had spoken of being cut off from the Lord, but the Lord had heard his "supplications" (*taḥᵃnûn*, see 28:2) as he cried out to Him, v. 22.

23–24 The Lord has watched over David, so David now urges the "saints" (or "loyal ones," *ḥasîd*, see 4:3) to love the Lord, since He rewards those who follow Him. He "preserveth" (or "guards") the faithful and abundantly judges those who carry out their haughty plans, v. 23. David exhorts the godly; in the trials that come to all believers, they should "be of good courage" (or "be strong," *ḥazaq*, see 27:14). The Lord will "strengthen" (*ʾamaṣ*, see 27:14) those who place their "hope" (*yaḥal*)[421] in Him, v. 24.

PSALM 32

The psalm logically follows Psalm 51. Both psalms deal with David's sin with Bathsheba and the subsequent murder of Uriah, II Samuel 11:1–27. The Lord sent the prophet Nathan to rebuke David. His conviction over his sin led to his repentance and forgiveness by the Lord, II Samuel 12:1–13. He wrote Psalm 51 soon afterwards. Later, realizing more fully the grace of the Lord in forgiving him, he writes this psalm.

The psalm is a penitential psalm.[422] The title identifies David as the author and marks the psalm as a "Maschil." The root of *maśkîl* means "to be wise, understand, prosper" and, in the *hipʿîl*, "to cause to be wise," leading to the thought of a didactic psalm designed to

---

dated at the time of a Syrian attack in 344 BC when Jerusalem was besieged. It is not necessary, however, to fix the siege at that late date. Sabourin, p. 235, follows Dahood, I, 191, in reading the "strong city" as "a fortified city," poetically expressing "the heavenly abode of Yahweh." Again, this is strangely phrased.

[420]The word *ḥapaz* speaks of being alarmed or of hurrying away in alarm. The context must decide whether the thought is primarily of alarm or of haste.

[421]The thought of *yaḥal* is more than a tentative desire. It rather expresses a confident expectation. In the Psalms, this always focuses on the Lord or His word, a sure basis upon which to trust.

[422]The seven penitential psalms include Pss. 6, 32, 38, 51, 102, 130, and 143.

impart wisdom.[423] It guides the reader to reflect, to pay close attention to what follows so that he may benefit from the psalm.

Psalm 32 was Augustine's favorite psalm. As a young man, Augustine had lived a wicked life. He could identify with David over the greatness of God's forgiveness. Prior to the death of the church father, he had the "very brief penitential psalms of David" written on the wall opposite his bed. During the final days, he "read them with copious and continual weeping."[424]

When Martin Luther was asked which the best of the psalms was, he replied, "*Psalmi Paulini*," the Pauline Psalms. When asked which of the psalms fell under this description, he named "the 32nd, the 51st, the 130th, and 143rd."[425] Since that time, these have been called "the Pauline Psalms."

I. The Blessings of Forgiven Sin 1–2

1–2 As always in the Psalms, the word "blessed" (*ʾašrê*, see 1:1) is plural. This intensifies the sense. There is no greater blessing available to man than that of forgiven sin. This opens the path to heaven and removes the eternal penalty of sin. David considers his "sin" (*ḥaṭaʾ*, see 4:4) "transgression" (*pešaᶜ*, see 5:10), rebellion against God. Only because of the confession of his sin (II Sam. 12:13) can David consider himself as "forgiven" (*naśaʾ*, see 25:18). God has "covered" his sin, hidden it from view. As with all forgiveness, this

[423]The word *maśkîl* also appears in the titles of Pss. 42, 44, 45, 52, 53, 54, 55, 74, 78, 88, 89, and 142. These include a wide variety of different types. Pss. 42, 52, 53, 54, 55, 88, 89, and 142 are individual laments in which the authors cry out to the Lord for deliverance from some evil. Pss. 44 and 74 are community laments. Ps. 45 is messianic and Ps. 78 historical. Elsewhere, the *hipᶜîl* participle generally supports the meaning "wise." It occurs widely with this sense in Proverbs. The book of Daniel uses the verb nine times with the related senses of "skill, wisdom, or understanding." Since the word stands alone here, it urges the reader to reflect on what follows so that he may gain wisdom. This sense fits well into the other psalm titles. Perowne, I, 293, understands the word as "a skillfully constructed or choice poem." This leaves unanswered its absence in other skillfully constructed poems, e.g., the acrostics.

[424]The shorter penitential psalms include 6, 32, 130, and 143. Some or all of these were written on the wall. Possidius, secretary of Augustine and later Bishop of Calama in Numidia, records this story in his biography of Augustine. *Life of St. Augustine*, trans. Sister Mary Magdeleine Muller and Roy J. Deferrari, *The Fathers of the Church* (Fathers of the Church, Inc., 1952), XV, 122.

[425]Spurgeon, p. 155.

rests solely on the sacrificial work of Christ, not on the OT sacrifices (Heb. 9:14), v. 1.

The forgiveness of David's sin is of such importance that he repeats the thought. The man to whom the Lord "imputeth not [or 'does not reckon'] iniquity" (*ᶜawon*, see 18:23) is truly "blessed" (*ʾašrê*). The repetition strengthens the thought. The man who confesses his sin has no "guile" (*rᵉmîyâ*, or "deceit"),[426] because he no longer tries to hide his sin. The apostle Paul quotes vv. 1–2*a* in Romans 4:7–8 to show the blessings that forgiveness brings, v. 2.

II. The Conviction from Hidden Sin 3–4

3–4 David recalls his feelings during the time when he tried to ignore his sin. From II Samuel 11:27, we can fix this time at about one year. His "bones," idiomatic for his body, "waxed old," wasting away from the emotional impact of his sin. There was a continuing "roaring" (*šaʾᵃgâ*, see 22:1) an internal groaning as he experienced conviction over what he had done, v. 3. The Lord did not leave David alone. He felt the Lord's hand of chastisement "day and night." His "moisture" (*lašad*)[427] became a drought, a poetical picture of David's normal joyous outlook on life becoming a barren feeling (cf. Ps. 38:2–8). David's experience vividly illustrates Proverbs 28:13*a*. "Selah" draws attention to the effects of covering one's sins, v. 4.

III. The Confession of Personal Sin 5

5 David now recalls the confession of his sin. The Lord had sent the prophet Nathan to move David to action over his sin (II Sam. 12:1–14). After Nathan told the king a story of a rich man who had

---

[426]When used of speech, *rᵉmîyâ* refers to deceit. This may occur as lying, fraud, or some other form of deceitful behavior.

[427]The word *lašad* occurs elsewhere only in Num. 11:8, where the context forces a meaning of "cake," some moist baked product. The contrast here suggests "moisture," a contrast with "drought." Authors take the obvious poetical picture differently. Moll, pp. 224–25, sees peace giving way to anxiety and "the heat of Divine anger." Jennings, I, 139, refers to "drying up the vital juices." Leupold, p. 267, translates "marrow" and makes the phrase represent "total being . . . wither[ing] away under God's displeasure." Weiser, p. 84, refers to the drying up of the tongue, no longer able to speak. Phillips, I, 243, speaks of David's "vitality" being "sapped." Other views are likewise possible. Hengstenberg, I, 516, translates *lašad* as "heart," not an apt rendering.

oppressed a poor man, David became irate. Nathan then pointed out that David was the rich man who had oppressed Uriah. Upon hearing the application, David finally confessed his sin (II Sam. 12:13). There was no sacrifice, no promise of good works, no penance—only the simple confession of sin. At this, Nathan told David, "The Lord also hath put away thy sin." Notice that David does not minimize what he has done. It is "sin," falling short of God's standards. It is "iniquity," turning aside from the path of righteousness. It is "transgressions," rebellion against God. The Lord "forgave" (*naśa᾽*) this. David now reflects on this forgiveness, drawing attention to the experience with "selah," v. 5.

IV. The Safety in a Gracious God 6–7

6–7 The phrase is an exhortation. Let the "godly" (*ḥasîd*, see 4:3) man confess his sin "when [the Lord may] be found."[428] The phrase hints at what Isaiah 55:6–7 says directly. Forgiveness is available when the Lord calls to man, not when man decides to make things right with God. David illustrates the safety of God's child: to the one sheltered by the care of God, not even floods of "great waters" can overwhelm him (cf. Isa. 43:2), v. 6. The Lord is his "hiding place" and will keep him from troubles. David thinks here of those difficulties that would attack him as king, not of the many ailments that often come because man lives in a sin-cursed body. The Lord will give David songs by which he can celebrate his deliverance. Once more, the word "selah" calls upon the readers to consider what David has said, v. 7.

---

[428]The final phrase is lit. "a time of finding." Albert Barnes, I, 275, understands this as the time when the guilty find mercy. The view is possible. Barnes, however, overstates his position: "The idea is not that God is any more disposed to show mercy at one time than another." This contradicts teaching elsewhere, e.g., Jer. 11:14; 14:11–12. Hirsch, I, 228, considers the time when the guilty senses that "suffering is about to descend upon him." He should then come into a right relationship with the Lord. This is poor advice, counseling a man to wait until judgment is about to descend before repenting. Buttenwieser, p. 656, sees an ellipsis here, a time for searching the heart. The verb *meṣo᾽* refers to finding, not searching. The supply of "heart" is subjective. In the Talmud, *Berakoth* 8*a* has a trivial view, relating the "time of finding" to the finding of a wife.

V. The Instruction of Righteous Men 8–11

8–9 David[429] pledges his instruction to "thee," the singular pronoun referring to a reader of the psalm (cf. 51:13).[430] He has learned the need to confess his sins and he wants to teach this truth to others. David will guide them "with mine eye," i.e., watching over them to give counsel as needed, v. 8. David now broadens his charge by making it plural. Rather than being as animals that resist coming to man unless he controls their "mouth" (*ᶜadî*)[431] with a "bit and bridle," David urges others to respond readily to his instruction, v. 9.

10–11 David draws a contrast between the wicked and the righteous. The wicked will receive many sorrows, but those who trust the Lord will be surrounded by "mercy" (*ḥesed*, see 5:7), v. 10. For this reason, the righteous should "be glad" and "rejoice." The "upright in heart" should "shout for joy" (*ranan*, see 5:11), bring forth a ringing cry of joy as they consider the mercies of the Lord to them, v. 11.

---

[429]Rodd, p. 68, and Luther, XIV, 152, consider vv. 8–9 as the words of the Lord, quoted by the psalmist. While this is possible, nothing in the psalm indicates a change in the speaker. Further, vv. 10–11 suggest David as the speaker. Finally, the parallel thought in 51:13 supports David as the author here.

[430]There is no clear antecedent to "thee." Rawlinson, I, 237, refers it to the "godly man" of v. 6. Henry, p. 350, relates it to David's "children and family." Leslie, p. 290, sees this as "the youth of the congregation." It may just as well refer to a reader of the psalm. It may also be left indefinite, referring generally to any other individual over whom David has influence.

[431]The noun *ᶜadî* occurs in the Psalms only here and at 103:5. The root *ᶜdh* means "to adorn" and, elsewhere in the OT, *ᶜadî* has the meaning of "ornament," e.g., Exod. 33:4–5; Isa. 49:18. The LXX translates inconsistently with σιαγόνας, "jaw," i.e., mouth, here and ἐπιθυμίαν, "desire," in 103:5. The Vulgate is similar, translating *maxillas*, "jaw" here and *desiderium*, "desire," at 103:5. Cognate languages support the meaning of "ornament." Unless we consider the mouth as an ornament displayed on the face, the translation must remain interpretive. I would render it as "with bit and bridle his ornaments [i.e., the trappings of the horse] are restrained." Until he is broken to obedience, the horse avoids the rider's wishes except when controlled by the bit and bridle.

PSALM 33

Psalm 33 is a hymn of praise, most of it (vv. 4–19) summarizing why the Lord is worthy of praise. It looks forward to the millennial kingdom, when righteousness abounds and Satan is no longer free to lead the nations astray. As with many of the psalms, we do not know the author or the occasion for its writing.[432] This gives it a broad application, suggesting that God's people should praise Him at all times.

I. The Call to Praise the Lord 1–3

1–3 The psalmist calls upon the righteous to "rejoice" (*ranan*, see 5:11), a ringing cry of exultation in the Lord. It is "comely," becoming, for the upright to give Him praise, v. 1. Music may accompany the praise. The "harp" (*kinnôr*) is a lyre with its strings made from the small intestine of a sheep.[433] The people "sing" (*zamar*, see 7:17) with the "psaltery [*nebel*] and an instrument of ten strings." The phrase also occurs at 144:9. In both places, it is better read "a harp of ten strings." The *nebel* had its strings on a rounded frame, v. 2.[434] The

---

[432]The LXX assigns the psalm to David when he feigned madness before Abimelech, I Sam. 21:10–15. Moll, p. 181, makes David the author at the time of Absalom's rebellion. Nothing in the psalm forces these conclusions. *NIB*, IV, 809, pairs the psalm with Ps. 32, a Davidic psalm. It is true that some Hebrew mss join the two psalms, possibly because of the similarity of 32:11 and 33:1. In nature and content, however, the two are different psalms. Henry, p. 350, sees David as the author. He adds, "We are not told so, because God would have us look above the penmen of sacred writ, to that blessed Spirit that moved and guided them." While devotional, the comment ignores the many psalms that name their authors. Jennings, I, 142, makes the psalm postexilic because of style. Since the psalm is not definite, we cannot be certain of the date, background, or author.

[433]The *kinnôr* is the first musical instrument mentioned in the OT, Gen. 4:21. Fausset, III, 170, understands "harp" and "psaltery" as the same instrument. Both words occur in lists, however, where they cannot be the same instrument, e.g., 92:3; I Sam. 10:5; Neh. 12:27. Morris, p. 45, describes it as a four-stringed lyre." Rawlinson, I, 245, refers to an instrument with "seven strings." From archaeology, the *kinnôr* likely had differing numbers of strings.

[434]Josephus, *Antiquities* 7.12.3, describes the "psaltery" as having "twelve musical notes [that were] played upon by the fingers." Undoubtedly, there were harps with differing numbers of strings. According to the *Mishnah*, *Kinnim* 3.6, the strings were made from the large intestine of a sheep. In referring to this verse, *ᵓArakin* 13*b* says, "The harp of the world to come has ten cords."

people should sing a "new song" of praise to the Lord.[435] They play their instruments skillfully with a "loud noise" (*t^e^rûᶜâ*, better "shout of joy," see 27:6), v. 3.

II. The Cause to Praise the Lord 4–19

A. The Nature of the Lord 4–5

4–5 The first and fundamental reason to praise the Lord focuses on His nature. His word is "right" (or "upright," same word as in v. 1), with no deviousness or error. His works are "in truth" (or "in faithfulness") as He carries out His plan for this world, v. 4. He loves "righteousness and judgment [*mišpaṭ*, 'justice,' see 1:5]." The earth is full of testimonies to His "goodness" (or "steadfast love," *ḥesed*, see 5:7), v. 5.

B. The Power of the Lord 6–9

6–7 To illustrate the omnipotence of the Lord, the psalmist refers to Creation. By His "word," Genesis 1:3, 6, 9, 11, 14, 20, 24, 26, the Lord brought the creation into being. The psalmist speaks first of the "heavens." Then, to amplify the thought, he refers to "all the host of them," the sun, moon, stars, and other heavenly bodies that fill the skies. These come into being "by the breath of his mouth," the spoken commands of God, v. 6.[436] He also gathers the "waters of the sea." This refers to the Lord's work on the second day of the Creation week, when He brought the dry land out of the waters. He "layeth up" (or "puts") the deep waters in "storehouses" where the riches of the oceans still remain untouched by man, v. 7.

---

[435]The phrase "new song" occurs six times in the Psalms: 33:3; 40:3; 96:1; 98:1; 144:9; and 149:1. It also occurs at Isa. 42:10. The Greek equivalent, which may be an allusion to the phrase, occurs in Rev. 5:9 and 14:3. With the exception of Ps. 40, there is a millennial context to the phrase each time it occurs.

[436]Hengstenberg, I, 528, and Horne, p. 656, relate the phrase to the Holy Spirit. While the Spirit undoubtedly played a role in Creation, the parallelism of the verse supports the word spoken by God. Kirkpatrick, p. 166, aptly notes, "The parallelism and the addition *of his mouth* seem to exclude a reference to *the spirit of God* . . . although the word in the original is the same."

8–9 Mankind should "fear" (*yareʾ*) a God of such power. The peoples of the world should be in "awe" (*gûr*) of Him.[437] Only during the Millennium, when all know of the Lord, will this attitude be universally held, v. 8. He spoke and "it was done" (or "it came to pass"). He commanded and His word "stood fast." Both phrases include the separate personal pronoun and could be translated "He Himself spoke . . . He Himself commanded. . . ." These phrases emphatically relate creation to "the word of the Lord" (v. 6), v. 9.

C. The Wisdom of the Lord 10–11

10–11 Despite the "counsel" (*ʿeṣâ*, see 1:1) of the heathen to overthrow the work of the Lord, He causes them to fail. He causes their "devices" (*maḥšᵉbôt*, or "thoughts, plans")[438] to fail, v. 10. In sharp contrast, His "counsel" (*ʿeṣâ*) is everlasting, never being overturned. His "thoughts" (*maḥšᵉbôt*) continue "to all generations" (*lᵉdor wador*, see 10:6). The psalmist heightens the contrast between the plans of the heathen and the plans of the Lord by using identical words in the paragraph, v. 11.

D. The Choice of the Lord 12–15

12 Israel is specially "blessed" (*ʾašrê*, see 1:1) because their mighty God is also the redemptive Lord. While the statement is true of any nation that makes God their Lord, the natural emphasis here applies to Israel. He has chosen them as His special inheritance, receiving them from all nations of the earth. The fulfillment of this will take place when Israel turns to the Lord with sincere worship during the Millennium, v. 12.

13–15 To heighten Israel's privilege, the psalmist notes that the Lord sees all men. From His place in heaven, He "looketh" (*nabaṭ*) on all of humanity and "beholdeth" (*raʾâ*) them, v. 13. He "looketh"

---

[437]The verb *yareʾ* occurs widely with differing senses of fear, reverence, awe, piety, etc. In each case, the context determines the sense best understood. Here, in view of the power displayed in creation, man should be in awe of the Creator. There is no significant difference here between *yareʾ* and *gûr*.

[438]There is not a great deal of difference between *maḥšᵉbôt* and *ʿeṣâ*. Both refer to plans or advice. When they occur, the context may force a particular shade of meaning.

(*šagaḥ*) on man.[439] The cumulative effect of the three verbs is to stress the Lord's close observation of mankind, v. 14. In addition, He fashions their hearts "alike" (or "together") so that He knows them for what they are. He "considereth" (or "understands") all of their works, v. 15. Taking vv. 13–15 together, we see the great privilege that the Lord has extended to Israel. Having closely considered man, knowing both his heart and his work, He has chosen Israel from all the nations of the world.

E. The Deliverance of the Lord 16–19

16–17 The psalmist gives several illustrations to show the weakness of man. No king, for instance, can rely just on the size of his army to save him. There are many illustrations of a lesser force defeating a larger one. A "mighty man" (or "valiant man, warrior," *gibbôr*, see 19:5) cannot rely just on his strength; cf. I Samuel 17:47, v. 16. Those who trust in a horse for safety do not necessarily escape. Despite its strength, it may fail to deliver its rider. These isolated examples show that man is weak. He may have resources, but these will not always serve him well, v. 17.

18–19 The Lord, however, will never fail His own. He especially watches over those who "fear [or 'reverence,' see *yir᾽â*, 2:11] him." He looks with favor on those who "hope [*yaḥal*, see 31:24] in his mercy [or 'steadfast love,' *ḥesed*]," v. 18. He will "deliver" (or "rescue") their soul from premature "death." To illustrate this, the psalmist notes that the Lord keeps them alive during famine; cf. I Kings 17:6, 16, v. 19.

III. The Conclusion of Praising the Lord 20–22

20–22 In view of all that the Lord does for His people, the psalmist speaks of the nation's reliance on Him. "Our soul," with the soul collectively representing the souls of the godly, addressed in v. 1, waits on the Lord to meet their needs. He is their "help [*ᶜezer*, see 20:2] and . . . shield [*magen*, see 3:3]," both assisting them in times of distress and defending them from attack, v. 20. They rejoice in Him because they "have trusted in his holy name." As is often true, the

[439]The verb *nabaṭ* has the sense of "consider" as the Lord looks with insight into what He sees. The verb *ra᾽â* is the most general word for seeing. It can have the sense of "regard." The verb *šagaḥ* has the sense of looking closely at something.

"name" of the Lord refers to His nature as a loving, caring God.[440] They have trusted in Him and found Him faithful, v. 21. The psalmist closes with the prayer that the Lord will continue to extend His "mercy" (or "steadfast love," *ḥesed*) to those who "hope" (*yaḥal*) in Him, v. 22.

PSALM 34

The psalm is a song of thanksgiving,[441] arranged with an acrostic structure, possibly for help in memorizing its words.[442] It is a two-line acrostic, with every other stich beginning with a successive letter of the Hebrew alphabet. The acrostic is irregular in v. 5, with 5*a* beginning with *hê* and 5*b* with *waw*.[443] The acrostic ends with v. 21, v. 22 beginning with a *pê*.[444]

David is the author. The heading locates the background of the psalm to his capture by Abimelech, also called Achish, the Philistine king of Gath (I Sam. 21:10–15). At that time, David feigned madness, an action that caused the Philistine king to drive him out of the city. The word "Abimelech" means "the king is father."[445] The

---

[440]Note 94 at 5:11 gives a brief summary of the "name" of the Lord.

[441]The introduction to Ps. 18 discusses the songs of thanksgiving.

[442]Pss. 9, 10, 25, 37, 111, 112, 119, and 145 are also acrostics.

[443]Another way of looking at v. 5 makes it regular, with the *hê* at the head of two stichs and the *waw* not beginning a separate thought. So Rotherham, p. 165. Since *waw* is the easiest letter with which to begin a line, it shows no literary skill to use it in an acrostic pattern.

[444]Anthony R. Ceresko, "The ABCS of Wisdom in Psalm XXXIV," *VT* 35:1 (1985): 103, suggests that the addition of a line beginning with *pê* is a further literary device. This gives a sequence of twenty-three letters. The beginning letter is an *ʾalep*, the middle letter is a *lamed*, and the final letter a *pê*. These three letters name the first letter of the Hebrew alphabet, *ʾalep*. Hengstenberg, I, 32, sees v. 22 as added to form a conclusion to the psalm. While these views are possible, they must remain speculative, since this pattern does not always occur in the acrostics of the OT. Kirkpatrick, p. 136, understands v. 22 as a later "liturgical addition to the original psalm." Buttenwieser, p. 801, considers the verse an addition to avoid ending the psalm "with words of evil import." There is no textual support for either of these views.

[445]Among others, Cohen, I, 99, and Murphy, pp. 226–27, consider "Abimelech" as a title of the Philistine kings since it also refers to the king of Gerar, Gen. 20:1–18;

name "Achish," however, has a doubtful origin and thus an uncertain meaning.

The psalm portrays the proper response of God's children to trials. David praises the Lord, vv. 1–3, for the answer to his prayers, vv. 4–6. He testifies to others of God's continuing care, vv. 7–10, teaches others to live godly lives, vv. 11–14, and reassures them that the Lord protects the righteous, vv. 15–22.

I. The Praise of the Lord 1–3

1–3 David had fled from Saul's threat of death to Philistia, where he hoped to find safety. The servants of Achish knew of David's prowess as a warrior and warned the king that he would turn against them. Fearful of what Achish would do, David feigned madness, leading the king to drive him out of the city. As David recalls these circumstances, he "bless[es]" (*barak*, see 5:12) the Lord for delivering him. He purposes that he will continually praise the Lord, speaking of him openly to others, v. 1. He will "boast in the Lord," giving glory to Him. The "humble" (or "afflicted," see *ᶜanî*, 9:12) will hear of David's response to his own affliction and will rejoice, v. 2. David urges them to join him in magnifying the Lord and exalting His "name," His nature, v. 3.[446]

II. The Deliverance of David 4–6

4–6 David recalls his response at the time of the threat to his life. He earnestly "sought" (*daraš*, see 9:10) the Lord. The Lord had heard his prayer and had delivered him from the power that had caused his "fears" (*mᵉgôrâ*, or "terrors"),[447] v. 4. David includes others who joined with him in praying at the time of his imprisonment in Gath. Because they relied on the Lord, they were "lightened" (or "radiant"), their faces brightening with hope. They were no longer "ashamed" (or "confounded"), v. 5. David describes himself as a "poor [*ᶜanî*, see

---

21:22–32; 26:1–16, 26. The word, however, also occurs as a personal name, Judg. 8:31; 9:1–56; 10:1; II Sam. 11:21; and I Chron. 18:16. It is just as likely that the Philistine king was known both as Abimelech and Achish, I Sam. 21:10–15; 27:1–28:2; 29:1–11; I Kings 2:39–40.

[446]See note 94, 5:11, for a brief summary of the Lord's name.

[447]The word *mᵉgôrâ* refers to fear. It has the sense of a strong fear, terror, rather than uneasiness or simple fear.

9:12] man," lacking not wealth but rather resources to stand against the Philistine king. The Lord heard when David "cried" (*qara*ᵓ), and He delivered David from his "troubles" (*ṣarâ*, see 9:9), v. 6.

III. The Charge to the People 7–10

7–10 David takes note of the protection the Lord has given the people. The "angel of the Lord," the Lord Himself, camps around those who "fear" (or "reverence" see *yirᵓâ*, 2:11) Him, in order to deliver them from their trials, v. 7.[448] For this reason, David urges others to "taste and see that the Lord is good." Tasting here refers to experiencing the grace of the Lord. The "man" (*geber*)[449] who "trusteth" (*ḥasâ*, see 2:12) Him will be "blessed" (*ᵓašrê*, see 1:1). The blessing comes from relying on God rather than on one's own resources, v. 8. Verse 9 parallels v. 8. David urges the saints to "fear [*yare*ᵓ] the Lord," to display a reverential attitude toward Him. He will not leave them in need of any help, v. 9. As an illustration of the Lord's provision, David cites the "young lions" (*kᵉpîr*, see 17:12).[450] They may suffer hunger from the failure to take a prey. In contrast, those who earnestly "seek" (*daraš*, see 9:10) the Lord will never lack "any good thing" of the blessings that He has for them, v. 10.

IV. The Instruction of the Nation 11–22

11–14 In this final part of the psalm, David instructs the people. This first paragraph teaches them their moral responsibilities. The king urges the people to listen to him as he teaches them "the fear [or 'reverence'] of the Lord" (*yirᵓat yᵉhwah*, see 15:4), v. 11. Is there anyone who loves life and wants "many days," all the days that God

---

[448]The Talmud, *Yebamoth* 102*b*, gives the verse an eschatological application: "As a reward for those that fear him He will deliver them from the judgment of Gehenna." While this is true, there is also an application in this life.

[449]The *geber* is a mighty man, one with the skills and resources to achieve his goals.

[450]Fausset, III, 172, understands the "lion" as "the symbol of powerful oppressors of the humble saints." Nothing in the context forces the lion to be a symbol here. The verse appropriately illustrates the Lord's care for His own. While the mighty lion may suffer hunger, those who trust the Lord have their needs supplied.

wants for him, v. 12?[451] He should live morally. David stresses speech and his actions. He should avoid speaking "evil" of any kind, e.g., lying, boasting, gossip, or profanity. He should not speak "guile" (or "deceitfully"). This is an example of James 3:2. Those who control their speech have mastered the hardest area to rule, v. 13. David further urges the people to avoid evil practices and, instead, to "do good." They should seek that which promotes peace. The admonition to pursue peace shows the effort that they must put into maintaining right relationships with others, v. 14.

15–18 David now turns to the care that God gives to His own. He watches over the righteous, cf. 33:18; Job 36:7; and opens His ears to their "cry" (*šawᶜâ*) when they are in need, v. 15. He sets His face against the wicked. He sends judgment to cut them off so that those who live no longer remember them. I Peter 3:10–12 quotes vv. 12–16 in discussing the personal relationships that believers have with others, v. 16. The Lord hears the "cry" (*ṣaᶜaq*)[452] of the righteous and delivers them from their "troubles" (*ṣarâ*, see 9:9), v. 17.[453] He is near those whose hearts have been broken over their sins. He delivers those who are of a "contrite" (*dakaᵓ*, or "crushed," see 9:9) spirit, remorseful over their sin, v. 18.

19–22 The righteous person will undergo many afflictions in life. We live in a world of sin and are not immune to the problems caused by sin. The Lord, however, delivers the righteous from every afflic-

---

[451]Horne, p. 155, considers "long life" as eternal life. The context, however, focuses on this life, not on the life to come. The concept of long life cannot focus merely on age. There are too many godly people who have died young: e.g., Josiah, II Kings 23:29–30, the many martyrs of the church. Long life rather means living all the days that God has for the person. Once a Christian has fulfilled all that God has for him to do, the best thing that can happen is for the Lord to take him to heaven.

[452]The verb "cry" occurs three times in the psalm, vv. 6, 15, 17, each translating a different Hebrew word. In v. 6, the verb is *qaraᵓ*, the most common verb indicating a call or a cry. Since it occurs generally, the context describes the nature of the call. In v. 15, the verb is *šawᶜâ*, a word with a definite emotional component. This is an intense cry of anguish. The final verb in v. 17 is *ṣaᶜaq*, also a cry made under duress. It normally comes in a time of great distress.

[453]Verse 17*a* lit. reads, "They cry, and the Lord hears." Since the antecedent in v. 16 is the wicked, Kirkpatrick, p. 174, and Leupold, p. 282, move v. 17 to follow v. 15. Leslie, p. 293, and Rotherham, p. 166, move v. 15 to precede v. 17. There is no support for either change. From the context, the subject of v. 17 is clear.

tion, v. 19.[454] David picturesquely portrays this deliverance as the Lord keeping the bones of the body from being broken, v. 20.[455] The evil actions of the wicked will bring about his death. Those who "hate" (*śane͗*, see 5:5) the righteous will themselves be "desolate" (*͗ašam*, or "guilty," see 5:10). The statement implies their condemnation, v. 21. In sharp contrast, the Lord "redeemeth" (*padâ*, see 25:22) those who serve Him. Those who "trust" (*ḥasâ*, see 2:12) Him will not be "desolate" (*͗ašam*, again "guilty"), subject to condemnation, v. 22.

PSALM 35

This Davidic psalm is an individual lament.[456] David faces an unknown situation.[457] His foes have lied about him, v. 11, and betrayed his goodness to them, vv. 12–15. They have deceived those who dwell peacefully in the land, v. 20. Their opposition threatens David's life, vv. 4, 7, 17. David asks the Lord to intervene for him, vv. 1–8, 17, 22–24. He pledges to praise the Lord for His deliverance, vv. 9–10, 18, 28, with these promises closing each of the major parts of the psalm.

This is the first of the imprecatory psalms.[458] These psalms grow out of the lament psalms as the psalmist laments the oppression

---

[454]There is an understood teaching that this refers to afflictions that lie outside of God's will for His children. There are times when believers glorify God more by bearing afflictions than by being delivered from them; cf. Matt. 5:11–12; II Cor. 12:7–10; I Pet. 4:12–16.

[455]Harman, p. 155, and Clarke, I, 97, make John 19:36 a fulfillment of this verse as well as Exod. 12:46. The Lord, however, is a Passover sacrifice. This passage has nothing to do with the Passover. It is simply a poetical picture of God's care for His own, not a prophecy of the Crucifixion.

[456]For the heading "Psalm of David," see the introduction to Ps. 25.

[457]Cohen, p. 103, and Calvin, I, 574, date the psalm to the time of David's flight from Saul. Leupold, p. 284, suggests the time of Absalom's rebellion. Cheyne, I, 145, makes the psalm postexilic but does not suggest an author. *NIB*, IV, 818, tentatively suggests that it is the prayer of a sick person "whose opponents interpret this sickness as a sign of wrong doing that justifies persecution." Since the psalm does not give any information as to its background, these views must remain speculative.

[458]In the imprecatory psalms, I classify Pss. 35, 59, 69, 70, 109, and 140 as individual lament psalms. Pss. 58, 83, and 137 are community laments. J. Carl Laney, "A

of his foes. In these, the psalmist's cry for vindication receives an unusual emphasis, often phrasing his plea in words that seem startlingly cruel. There are different explanations for the extreme imprecations wished upon the wicked. In all likelihood, each of these explanations has some truth in it, with the nature of the psalm determining the reason for the imprecation.

Some of the imprecations are undoubtedly poetic, the curse involving hyperbole, e.g., 58:10; 140:10. Other imprecatory psalms show the hatred of sin, the punishment of which necessarily involves the sinner, e.g., 59:12–13; 69:27–28. In some cases, the psalmist gives over the judgment of the wicked to God, e.g., 58:6; 83:13–15. Some imprecations reflect a zeal for the Lord and His righteousness. Necessarily, this may involve the vindication of the psalmist, e.g., 35:3–4; 109:20–21. Some of the imprecatory psalms prophesy God's attitude toward sin, e.g., 109:6–16; 137:8–9. Finally, the imprecations throughout the psalms may simply reflect cultural differences between OT Israel and modern times, 109:18–19; 137:9. We see brutality elsewhere in the OT (e.g., Judg. 1:6, 7; I Kings 16:34; Dan. 3:19–21). The imprecations may relate to common OT attitudes that are no longer generally held.

I. Petition of David 1–10

1–3 David asks the Lord to "plead my cause" (better "strive," *rîb*)[459] with others who "strive" (*rîb*) with him, and to fight against those who fight with him, v. 1. He graphically asks the Lord to play the part of a soldier, taking up His "shield [*magen*, see 3:3] and buck-

---

Fresh Look at the Imprecatory Psalms," *BibSac* 138 (1981): 36, adds Pss. 7 and 139 to this list but omits 70 and 140. Alex Luc, "Interpreting the Curses in the Psalms," *JETS* 42:3 (1999): 395, classes Pss. 35, 58, 69, 83, 109, and 137 as imprecatory. Bullock, p. 228, includes Pss. 35, 55, 59, 69, 79, 109, and 139. Lewis Vaught, *A Thousand Years of Hebrew History: Psalms* (Cleveland, Tenn.: Pathway Press, 2000), pp. 69–87, recognizes Pss. 3, 7, 10, 55, 58, 69, 109, 129, 137, and 139 as imprecatory psalms. Because many of the psalms include laments and prayers for deliverance from enemies, the decision to call a psalm "imprecatory" is subjective. For this reason, the list of imprecatory psalms varies from author to author.

[459]The verb *rîb* has a primary sense of physical combat. It often, however, refers to verbal strife or quarreling. This sometimes has a legal sense of rendering a judgment. The verb occurs five times in the Psalms: here; 43:1; 74:22; 103:9; and 119:54. In each case, the psalmist refers to God's taking up the case and vindicating Himself or His people.

ler [*ṣinnâ*, see 5:12]." No soldier would use both pieces at the same time to defend himself. The picture is poetic. Equipped with both the small and large shields, the figure pictures the Lord as ready to defend David in any situation that he faces, v. 2. David asks the Lord to "draw out" His "spear" (*ḥ*ª*nît*)[460] to prepare it for use. The Lord will then be ready to stop those who "persecute" (better "pursue") David. He wants to hear the voice of the Lord assuring him that He is his "salvation" (or "deliverance"), v. 3.

4–8 David begins a series of imprecations against his enemies. He prays that the foes that seek his life will "be confounded [or 'ashamed,' *bôš*, see 6:10] and put to shame [or 'dishonored,' *kalam*]."[461] Let those who plan harm to him be "turned back and brought to confusion [or 'humiliated']," v. 4. Let them be like "chaff," the worthless husks of grain and broken straw, blown away by the wind by the threshing process in biblical times. Let the "angel of the Lord," the Lord Himself (34:7),[462] violently push them along, v. 5. Let them follow a "dark and slippery" path with the angel of the Lord "persecut[ing]" (better "pursuing") them, v. 6.

David's adversaries have opposed him "without cause," for no good reason. They have spread a "net," poetically describing a trap they have laid to snare him in a "pit" (*šaḥat*, see 7:15).[463] They have prepared this for his "soul," his life, v. 7. Once again, David prays for the defeat of his foes. Let them fall unexpectedly into "destruction" (*šô*ʾ*â*).[464] Let them be taken by the trap they had prepared for him. Let them fall into that same "destruction" (*šô*ʾ*â*), v. 8.

---

[460]The *ḥ*ª*nît* was a long, heavy spear. A soldier would normally carry it in a sling across his back.

[461]The word *kalam* often occurs in parallel with *bôš*, "to be ashamed," e.g., 44:9; 74:21. The primary sense of *kalam* is that of the public disgrace or dishonor that comes from being humiliated.

[462]Hirsch, I, 251, translates *mal*ʾ*ak*, "angel," as "decree," making the phrase "divine decree." This takes unusual liberty with the meaning of a common Hebrew word.

[463]*OTTP*, p. 99, suggests that *šaḥat* is in the wrong place for two reasons: (1) "pit of their net" has no meaning; and (2) "dig" in 7*b* has no object. It transfers *šaḥat* to the last part of the verse and reads, with the RSV, "For without cause they hid their net for me; without cause they dug a pit for my life." There is no need to formally transfer *šaḥat*. The phrase has a clear poetical sense of some type of snare set for David.

[464]The word *šô*ʾ*â* is strong, describing devastation or desolation.

9–10 David turns to his feelings at the fall of his enemies. He will "be joyful" (*gîl*, see 16:9) in the Lord and "rejoice" (*śîś*, see 19:5) in the deliverance given him, v. 9. His "bones," idiomatically representing his body, will marvel at the power of the Lord. There is no one like Him. He rescues the "poor" (or "afflicted," *ᶜanî*, see 9:12) from those who are stronger than him. He saves the "poor [again 'afflicted'] and needy" from those who would plunder what little he has, v. 10.

II. Thanklessness of the Wicked 11–18

11–16 The wickedness of David's enemies is the greater because of its nature. While David had bestowed good on them, they have returned evil. They are "false" (or "malicious" in what they say about him. They "laid to [David's] charge" (better "ask me") about matters of which he knows nothing, v. 11. They have returned "evil for good." This has resulted in the "spoiling" (better "bereavement") of David's soul, v. 12.

David recalls his treatment of them. When they were sick, he had worn "sackcloth" (*šaq*, see 30:11) to show his grief. He had "humbled" (or "afflicted," *ᶜanâ*)[465] himself with fasting. This accompanied the "prayer" (*tᵉpillâ*, see 4:1) that kept returning to his "bosom," himself, as he continually carried the burden, v. 13.[466] He considered his foes as a "friend or brother," the words occurring collectively to represent all who were arrayed against David. At their sickness, he

[465]As with *ᶜanaw* and *ᶜanî* (see 9:12), so *ᶜanâ* refers to either physical pain or emotional suffering. In each case, the context must guide the sense that the word receives.

[466]Kidner, p. 143, mentions the possibility that David's prayer returned in the sense of being unanswered. The phrase lit. reads, "And my prayer upon my bosom was returning." While it is possible to interpret this as unanswered prayer, it is more likely that the burden to pray kept impressing itself on David's heart. Jennings, I, 153, sees the prayer as "so full of good will" that David wishes himself to receive these blessings. The context does not support this. Buttenwieser, p. 451, understands that the head was continually lowered in prayer upon the breast. While the idea of continued prayer is acceptable, it is improbable that the phrase refers to the physical posture in prayer. Dahood, I, 213, wrongly draws on the NT picture of a disciple reclining on Jesus' bosom to make David's prayer "like a close friend." Hirsch, I, 253, takes the phrase as David's prayer that the good that he had asked for his enemies might now be given to him. Leslie, p. 371, understands the prayer as continually returning to the psalmist's lips. While it is possible to treat the verb as a jussive, the view turns away from the early part of the verse where David recaps his actions toward those who now oppose him.

"bowed down heavily [better 'mourning']" as though grieving for his own mother, v. 14.

His foes, however, rejoiced at David's "adversity" (or "stumbling"). These "abjects" (or "smiters") assembled themselves together to plot against him without his knowledge. They "did tear me," slandering him without ceasing, v. 15. Like "hypocritical" (or godless") mockers eating at a "feast" (or "cake," *maᶜôg*),[467] so these foes gather to bitterly assail David. In some unknown way, David hears of this wicked speech, v. 16.

17–18 Having described his plight, David now turns to the Lord. How long will He wait to deliver him? He pleads with the Lord to bring his soul back from their "destructions" (*šôʾâ*). The phrase "my darling [better 'only life'] from the lions [*kᵉpîr*, see 17:12]" poetically parallels the phrase "my soul from their destructions," v. 17. He pledges to respond to this deliverance by giving thanks to the Lord in "the great congregation," the gathering of the people at one of the feasts. He will praise the Lord there among "much people," v. 18.

III. Working of the Lord 19–28

19–21 The word "wrongfully" modifies "enemies" rather than "rejoice." David prays that those who are wrongfully his enemies, having no cause to oppose him, will not rejoice over his fall. "Winking with the eye" occurs twice in Proverbs (6:13; 10:10). It is a common way of signaling and often indicates devious actions or speech. David's foes do this without any reason to "hate" (*śaneʾ*, see 5:5) him. This last phrase is similar to 69:4. The Lord refers to one of these references in John 15:25, v. 19. Instead of speaking of peace, they have developed plans to deceive those who now dwell quietly in the land, v. 20. They open their mouths wide against David, falsely accusing him. They claim to have witnessed his evil, v. 21.

[467]The phrase is difficult. It is lit. "godless [or 'profane'] mockers [or 'stammerers'] of a cake." Clarke, I, 100, sees this as "sycophants who [make] foolish and unwholesome jests." Fausset, III, 175, and Hengstenberg, II, 8, vary this slightly. They understand it as hypocritical men who ingratiate themselves with a foe of David by scoffing and jesting at David at some meal. The word *maᶜôg*, translated here as "feast," occurs elsewhere only at I Kings 17:12, where it refers to a "cake." The corresponding verb *ᶜûg*, "to bake" (or "to bake a cake"), supports the meaning of "cake" rather than "feast."

22–24 The Lord has seen their deceit. David prays that the Lord will not "keep . . . silence" and "remain far" from him, v. 22. Rather, he asks the Lord to take action by arousing Himself to David's "judgment" (better "justice"). This will vindicate David's "cause" as being right, v. 23. He asks the Lord to "judge" him, i.e., to vindicate him according to His own righteousness, His faithfulness to the promises He made to David, II Samuel 7:12–16. David is confident, then, that his adversaries will not rejoice over his fall, v. 24.

25–28 David again asks the Lord to intervene on his behalf. Let his enemies not say, "So would we have it" (lit. "It is our desire"). May things not go as they desire. May they not be able to say that they have "swallowed" (*balaᶜ*, see 21:9) David up, v. 25. Let those who rejoice at David's problems rather be "ashamed" (*bôš*, see 6:10) and "brought to confusion" (or "confounded"). Let those who seek to make themselves greater than David be covered with "shame" (*bôšet*, see *bôš*, 6:10) and "dishonour" (*k^e^limmâ*, see 4:2), v. 26.

Positively, David prays for the Lord's blessing on those who support him. Let those who support him "shout for joy" (*ranan*, see 5:11), giving a ringing cry of exultation, and "be glad," spontaneously giving evidence of their joy. Let them continually magnify the Lord, Who Himself delights in the "prosperity" (or "peace") of his servant David, v. 27. David pledges to continually speak of the Lord's righteousness, i.e. His faithfulness to His covenant with David, and of His praiseworthiness, v. 28.

PSALM 36

David titles himself "the servant of the Lord." This thought likely comes from the nature of this lament psalm. He first describes the wickedness of the wicked, vv. 1–4, then the moral perfections of the Lord, vv. 5–9, and finally his own reliance on the Lord to deliver him from his foes, vv. 10–12. He is the Lord's servant[468] and therefore

[468]Leupold, p. 292, suggests that David speaks of himself, not "as the king of Israel, but rather in an official capacity as a leader and instructor of his people,

needs the Lord's protection. Likewise, we who have trusted Jesus Christ for salvation have the privilege of relying on the Lord for deliverance from trials.

As with most of his psalms, David plans that the "chief musician" (*m*ᵉ*naṣṣeaḥ*, see 4, intro.) use it in the tabernacle in Israel's worship. We cannot be dogmatic regarding the background of the psalm. While a good case can be made for placing it at the time of Absalom's rebellion, the psalm does not give us enough information to state this with certainty. Clearly, David has adversaries, v. 11, but he does not describe the nature or setting of their opposition.

I. The Iniquity of the Wicked 1–4

1 The opening phrase is difficult to translate. The Hebrew gives us something like "Says the transgression [or 'an oracle of transgression'] to the wicked in the midst of my heart."[469] This says that David knows in his heart what transgression says to the wicked. (Looking back on his own life, David was fully aware of the deceptive nature of sin.) This transgression leads the wicked to have "no fear of God," no reverence for the mighty God, v. 1.

2–4 The wicked man flatters himself "until his iniquity be found to be hateful [*śane*ʾ, see 5:5]" (or "concerning the finding of his iniquity and its hatefulness"). He thinks that he can act as he pleases, with no one discovering his wicked actions, v. 2. He fills his speech with "iniquity and deceit." He has ceased being wise and doing well, v. 3. He plans "mischief (better "iniquity") at night. He sets himself in a wicked way and fails to reject evil, v. 4.

---

whom he serves by serving the Lord." While this is possible, it is equally possible that David sees himself as the Lord's servant in his role as king of the Lord's people.

[469]Among others, Jennings, I, 157, and Perowne, I, 313, accept the reading of the LXX and Syriac, "his heart." They understand something like "transgression speaks to the wicked within his heart." The wicked therefore do not fear God. *NIB*, IV, 822, accepts this reading and sees the wicked as following the voice of "rebellion" as though it was their god. Hirsch, I, 257, understands the wicked as thinking that transgression "seems a pronouncement of the Lord." If God did not want evil, He would prevent man from committing it. Leslie, p. 224, considers that "transgression" is "a personified evil spirit." As a demon, it speaks to evil men, telling them that God overlooks their evil. The view expressed above sees David as knowing what wickedness says.

II. The Character of God 5–9

5–7*a* David draws a sharp contrast between the wicked and the Lord. The Lord's "mercy" (or "steadfast love" *ḥesed*, see 5:7) reaches to the heavens and His faithfulness to the clouds. This poetic description pictures the greatness of these attributes, v. 5. The Lord's "righteousness" is like the "great [or 'mighty'] mountains" (*keharrê-ʾel*).[470] His "judgments" are like a "great deep," the ocean.[471] The Lord guards both mankind and animals, v. 6. God's "lovingkindness" (or "steadfast love," *ḥesed*) is "excellent" (or "precious"), v. 7*a*.

7*b*–9 For these reasons, men place themselves "under the shadow of thy wings," placing their "trust" (*ḥasâ*, see 2:12) in God's care for them, v. 7*b*. They shall be "abundantly satisfied" (or "filled") with the "fatness" (see *dešen*, 20:3), the blessings, that come from the Lord's house where He Himself dwells.[472] He will cause them to drink from the river of His "pleasures" (or "delights"), v. 8. With the Lord is "the fountain of life," the source of abundant life. In the "light" of His presence, His children are privileged to see the "light" of His guidance, v. 9.[473]

III. The Prayer of David 10–12

10–11 David prays for a right relationship with the Lord. Positively, he asks the Lord to continue His "lovingkindness" (or

[470] Kirkpatrick, p. 185, and Alexander, p. 166, understand *keharrê-ʾel* as "the mountains of God." While the AV normally translates *ʾel* as "God," it also has the sense of "mighty," 29:1; 89:6. Here, where the phrase parallels the "great deep," it is best to take it as "mighty mountains." This agrees with other places where God's name occurs to give a superlative sense, Waltke & O'Connor, 14.5*b*.

[471] Leupold, p. 295, and Oesterley, I, 220, equate the phrase "great deep" with Gen. 7:11, where the same phrase refers to the waters of the worldwide Flood. This or similar phrases also occur in Ps. 78:15; Isa. 51:10; and Amos 7:4 where the worldwide Flood is not in view. It is therefore reasonable to understand it generally of the great ocean waters.

[472] Moll, p. 249, relates the "fatness" to the sacrificial meal that followed the peace offering. He sees this as a picture of "reconciliation with God." While possible, this would be a unique use of *dešen*. The word occurs elsewhere as a picture of blessings, 63:5; 65:11; Isa. 55:2.

[473] Dahood, I, 223, and Hengstenberg, II, 21, interpret "light" as eternal life. Anderson, I, 290, relates it to divine favor and love. Bratcher and Reyburn, p. 347, equate it with "life." While these views are possible, the word "light" often refers to guidance, e.g., 43:3; 112:4; 119:105.

"steadfast love," *ḥesed*, see 5:7) to those who have an experiential knowledge of Him. Likewise, He desires the Lord to continue His righteous actions to those who are upright in heart, accepting and practicing the guidance of God's word, v. 10. Negatively, he asks the Lord to keep the proud actions of others from touching him. He prays that the hand of the wicked will not "remove" him (or "drive [him] away"), keeping him from his proper role as king. This phrase suggests Absalom's rebellion (II Sam. 15:10–14), when David was forced to flee from Jerusalem, v. 11.

12 David displays his faith in God's protection. He describes the judgment of his foes as already having taken place.[474] In the place of God's judgment, "there," those "workers of iniquity" who have risen against David have "fallen." They are "cast down" (or "thrust down") by God's judgment. They will not be able to stand against it to continue their evil, v. 12.

PSALM 37

The psalm is a wisdom psalm written with an acrostic form.[475] It is somewhat regular in structure; sequential letters of the alphabet begin every other line.[476] In the psalm, David describes the conflict between the wicked and the righteous. A series of repetitions show that since the wicked will one day perish, the righteous should trust the Lord. That thought is still true today.

Any outline of the psalm is artificial, with overlapping points. The psalm comes from David's old age, v. 25, although nothing in the

---

[474]Moll, p. 250, understands the passage as referring "to a well known, historical example . . . in order to instruct and to comfort, or indeed to strengthen the confidence in the certainty of the Divine judgment." The view is possible. The use of the prophetic perfect, however, is common in the Psalms, e.g., 6:8–9; 20:6.

[475]Pss. 9, 10, 25, 34, 37, 111, 112, 119, and 145 are acrostics.

[476]Verses 7, 20, and 28 differ from this pattern. Verses 7 and 20, beginning with *dalet* and *kap* respectively, are tristichs rather than tetrastichs. The *ᶜayin* line, v. 28*b*, begins with a *lamed* preposition but *ᶜayin* is the second letter of the line. The *tau* line, v. 39, begins with a *waw*-consecutive. These are trivial matters in the poetic form.

psalm gives us a more precise date. The heading is simple, only identifying David as the author.[477]

I. Confidence in the Lord 1–6

1–2 David speaks generally, not directing his remarks to any one group but giving advice that applies to believers of all times. The godly should not "fret" (or "be vexed") at the seeming prosperity of the wicked. There is no reason to envy these "workers of iniquity [*ᶜawlâ,* see 7:3]," v. 1. They will soon be cut down like grass and wither like the green "herb" (or "plant"), v. 2.

3–6 Because the Lord will deal with the wicked, the believer should maintain his confidence in Him. He should trust Him and continue doing good works. He may dwell in the "land" where the Lord has placed him. The phrase "verily thou shalt be fed" is idiomatic. It reads something like "shepherd [*raᶜâ*] faithfulness." This pictures one who tends those matters associated with a faithful life, v. 3.[478] That person should delight in the Lord. The Lord, in turn, will give him the "desires of [his] heart." This is not a promise to give the godly person all he wants. It is rather a pledge to bless those desires that are centered on the Lord, v. 4. Those who follow the Lord should "commit" (*galal*)[479] their way to the Lord. They trust His power and find that He meets their needs, v. 5. He will cause their righteousness to shine brightly and their "judgment," the vindication of their godly way, to be as the noonday sun, v. 6.

II. Blessings from the Lord 7–11

7–8 David guides his readers to "rest [or 'be still'] in the Lord," patiently meditating on godly truths. They should patiently wait for Him to accomplish His work. They should not "fret" (or "be vexed,"

[477]For the heading, "Psalm of David," see the introduction to Ps. 25.

[478]W. E. Barnes, I, 184, translates "follow after faithfulness." While this gives the correct sense, "follow" is not a common translation of *raᶜâ*. Gaebelein, p. 164, and Cohen, p. 111, understand the idiom to refer to those who "feed on faithfulness." John A. Kselman, "Two Notes on Psalm 37," in *Biblica* 78 (1978): 252, suggests "feed on fidelity," a possible translation. I have taken the thought of "tending" as a better parallel to the first part of the verse.

[479]The root *gll* is first "to roll." From this comes the idea of rolling a burden on something else, thus to "commit" the burden to something or someone who can bear it.

see v. 1) when others prosper. David refers to those who bring wicked "devices" (or "schemes") to pass, v. 7. The godly person should "cease" (*rapâ*)[480] from "anger" (*ʾap*, see 2:5) and "wrath" (*ḥemâ*, see 6:1) over the success of the wicked. He should not "fret" (or "vex") himself since vexation leads to evil, v. 8.

9–11 David's reason for the patience advised in vv. 7–8 now appears. Those who do evil will be "cut off," judged by a holy God, but those who expectantly "wait" (*qawâ*, see 25:3) for the Lord to accomplish His purposes will "inherit the earth." While David undoubtedly thought of occupying the Promised Land, there is also an eschatological fulfillment. In the millennial kingdom, believers will indeed "inherit the earth," v. 9. This will take place "in a little while," a brief time in comparison with eternity. Then, the wicked will be no more. Though one should diligently seek his place, it will not be found, v. 10. The "meek" (or "humble," see *ʿanaw*, 9:12) will "inherit the earth." The Lord refers to this promise (Matt. 5:5), v. 11.

III. Judgment by the Lord 12–15

12–15 The wicked is an enemy of the godly man. He plots against the "just" (or "righteous") and gnashes his teeth at him, grinding them in anger, v. 12. The Lord laughs at him, showing scorn toward the wicked's actions; cf. 2:4. The Lord knows that the day of judgment for sin is coming, v. 13. David pictures wicked men as having drawn their "sword" and "bent [*darak*, see 7:12] their bow," poetic illustrations of their preparation to attack the "poor [or 'afflicted,' *ʿanî*, see 9:12] and needy" as well as those who are "upright" in their "conversation" (or "way of life"), v. 14. These plans will rebound upon themselves. The attack the wicked have planned on others will turn on them as the Lord breaks their weapons of attack, v. 15.

IV. Protection from the Lord 16–20

16–17 Speaking proverbially, David notes that the little amount a righteous man possesses is better than the wealth of many wicked persons (Prov. 15:16; 16:8), v. 16. The "arms" of the wicked, here metaphorically standing for his power, will be broken in the day of

[480]In the *hipʿîl*, the verb *rapâ* has the sense of "let go, abandon, relax." The believer can do this because he trusts that the Lord will take up his cause.

the Lord's judgment. In contrast, the Lord will sustain the righteous, v. 17.

18–20 The Lord knows the "days," i.e., the lives, of the "upright" (or "blameless," see *tom*, 7:8). He will reward them with an everlasting inheritance in His kingdom, v. 18. They will not be "ashamed" (or "disappointed," *bôš*, see 6:10) when evil times come. Even in a time of famine, they will be satisfied with their choice to follow the Lord, v. 19. In contrast, the wicked will "perish" (*ʾabad*, see 1:6). They will be as the "fat of lambs" (better, "splendor of meadows").[481] While the beauty of a field may be seen for a while, eventually the flowers die and the grass withers. The wicked perish; like smoke, they vanish, v. 20.

V. Guidance from the Lord 21–28

21–22 David speaks proverbially once more as he contrasts the greed of the wicked with the charity of the righteous. The one borrows but does not pay back; the other "sheweth mercy" (*ḥanan*, see 4:1) by freely giving to others in need, v. 21.[482] Those "blessed" (*barak*, see 5:12) by God will "inherit the earth," cf. v. 9, while those under God's curse will be "cut off" by everlasting judgment, v. 22.

23–24 The AV properly supplies the interpretive word "good." The Lord establishes the "steps" (or "goings") of a good mighty "man" (*geber*, see 34:8) and "delighteth" (*ḥapeṣ*, see 18:19) to see him following that way rather than relying upon himself, v. 23. Though the man may fall, he will not be "cast down" (or "cast away") because

---

[481]Among others, Murphy, p. 245, and Horne, p. 169, understand *kîqar karîm*, the "fat of lambs," as that which is burned on the altar and thus perishes. While the view is possible, it suffers from the fact that the Lord accepts the sacrificial lambs while the idea here is of rejection. The word *karîm* is also "pastures" (or "meadow"), 65:13. In the spring, the beauty appears, but this fades away in the heat of summer and the cold of winter.

[482]Leupold, p. 303, understands the verse "not so much as a contrast between the lack of moral responsibility on the part of one and the conscientiousness of the other, but rather as an indication that the one borrows and has not the wherewithal to repay, but the other is so well blessed by God that he can always repay his honest debts." While the view is possible, the thought here is of "mercy" by the righteous, not of repayment. W. E. Barnes, I, 186, misses the sense. He comments, "The great man . . . does not return the ox or the ass which he borrows to do his own work: he merely allows it to stray back (worn out) to his indigent owner." The view introduces the idea of farm animals and is too restrictive.

the Lord "upholdeth" his hand, taking it and helping him back to his feet, v. 24.

25–26 Looking back at his life, David illustrates what he has just said. The Lord is faithful and does not forsake His own. David has never seen the righteous man abandoned or his children forced to beg for survival. The parallelism explains the reference to begging. David himself had begged for food (I Sam. 21:1–6). In this, the Lord had not abandoned him but rather supplied his needs. So here David thinks of prolonged begging with no success, v. 25. The righteous are always "merciful" (or "gracious," *ḥanan*, see 4:1), and their children are blessed, v. 26.

27–28 David draws a conclusion to what he has been saying. The righteous should remain godly in their actions. They should "depart from" (or "avoid") evil actions and instead "do good." They will then "dwell for evermore," a reference to the everlasting inheritance David has mentioned before (vv. 9, 22), v. 27. The Lord loves "judgment" (better "justice") and does not forsake His "saints" (or "faithful ones," *ḥasîd*, see 4:3). They will be "preserved" (or "protected") forever. In contrast, the "seed of the wicked," presumably following the example of their wicked fathers, will be cut off in judgment, v. 28.

VI. Safety from the Lord 29–34

29–31 For the fourth time (vv. 9, 11, 22), David mentions the everlasting inheritance of the righteous, v. 29. The righteous man speaks of "wisdom" (*ḥokmâ*, see 19:7) and "judgment" (or "justice"), v. 30. God's law is in his heart, no longer an external guide but one that gives him the desire to do right. For this reason, his "steps" (or "goings") do not slip from the path of righteousness, v. 31.

32–34 The wicked spy on the righteous, looking for the opportunity of putting them to death. David uses hyperbole to make his point that the wicked seek to overcome the righteous, v. 32. The Lord, however, will neither abandon the righteous to the power of the wicked nor condemn the righteous merely at the judgment that the wicked passes. The statement gives a general principle. God may let the righteous die at the hand of the wicked. In general, however, He watches over them to deliver them from evil men, v. 33. David concludes that the righteous should "wait" (or "look expectantly," *qawâ*, see 25:3) for the Lord. They should continue to follow the way of life that pleases Him. He will reward them by letting them "inherit" the land (vv. 9, 11, 22, 29). They will see the judgment of the wicked, v. 34.

VII. Deliverance by the Lord 35–40

35–36 David makes an observation about the "wicked in great power" (or "wicked oppressor"). David has seen him spreading himself "like a green bay tree" (or "like a luxuriant tree in its native soil"), flourishing as he takes advantage of others, v. 35. This does not last. The wicked man passes away and no longer exercises power over others. Even though David sought him, he could not be found, v. 36.

37–40 David draws his final contrast in the psalm. Take note of the "perfect" (or "blameless," see *tom*, 7:8) man, the one who is "upright" judged by the standard of God's Word. This man will have a peaceful "end" (*ʾaḥᵃrît*), enjoying the everlasting blessings of heaven, v. 37. Transgressors, those who have rebelled against the Lord, will be destroyed "together." The adverb hints at the Great White Throne judgment, when the wicked will indeed be destroyed together. Their "end" (*ʾaḥᵃrît*)[483] is to be "cut off" from the future everlasting life, v. 38. The Lord, however, will deliver the righteous. In times of trial, He will be the "strength" (*maᶜôz*, see 27:1) that they need to face their "trouble" (*ṣarâ*, see 9:9), v. 39. He will help them escape the attacks of the wicked. He delivers and saves them because they "trust" (or "find refuge," *ḥasâ*, see 2:12) in the Lord, v. 40.

---

[483]Kissane, I, 167, and Cohen, p. 116, understand *ʾaḥᵃrît* as "posterity," a possible meaning. In this case, the children of the wicked follow their evil ways and are also destroyed. The word *ʾaḥᵃrît*, however, may also have an eschatological sense, 73:17; Prov. 14:12; 23:18, and I have so taken it here. However *ʾaḥᵃrît* is understood, vv. 37 and 38 must be taken in the same way.

PSALM 38

This is another of the penitential psalms,[484] a psalm in which the lament of the psalmist focuses on his own sin.[485] While we do not know the background that led to the writing of the psalm, it is clear that David is conscious of his sin, vv. 3–5, 18.[486] He writes the psalm "to bring to remembrance," a phrase that also occurs in the title of Psalm 70. In both psalms, David seeks to arouse others to spiritual truths.[487] The confession of sin and prayer for divine blessing are still needed by God's people.

I. Confession of David's Sin 1–10

Taken together, vv. 1–10 give a vivid picture of the results of sin. There are not only physical results but also emotional consequences. While neither of these is desirable, both have purpose. Where there is no reaction to sin, God has left man to his own devices. The existence

---

[484]The penitential psalms include 6, 32, 38, 51, 102, 130, and 143.

[485]This psalm has found its way into modern rituals. The high church recites it on Ash Wednesday, the first day of Lent. The day is meant as a time of sorrow and penitence. This may be symbolized by a mark on the forehead made from ashes left from the burning of palms from Palm Sunday of the previous year. As with most rituals, it is observed differently in individual churches and for most churchgoers has lost its spiritual significance.

[486]Rawlinson, I, 298, questions David's authorship due to the lack of mention of a serious illness in David's life by II Samuel. This assumes, however, that II Samuel gives a complete record of David's life, something it clearly does not do. Later, p. 299, he admits the possibility of David's writing the psalm. Delitzsch, II, 20, relates the psalm to David's sin with Bathsheba. Jennings, I, 167, connects it with Absalom's rebellion with this bringing about David's illness or Absalom taking advantage of some sickness of his father. These are possible but unprovable views.

[487]Alexander, p. 176, and Murphy, p. 245, understand the title as though the psalm brings David's circumstances to God's remembrance. While this is possible, most of the psalms cry out to the Lord. There is no reason for just two of the psalms to have this title. Hirsch, I, 283, sees the psalm as acting as a memorial, bringing these thoughts back to David. Kirkpatrick, p. xxvii, also understands the phrase as "a memorial." He makes the psalm sung at the burning of incense. While this is possible, it is speculative. The *hipʿîl* infinitive of *zakar* occurs seven other times in the OT: I Sam. 4:18; II Sam. 18:18; I Kings 17:18; I Chron. 16:4; Ps. 70:1; Ezek. 21:24; and Amos 6:10. Nowhere do these verses demand the thought of a memorial. Harman, p. 167, suggests that the title is a "later description of a psalm used by sufferers to bring their plight to God's remembrance. This is also speculative.

of physical and emotional response to sin is evidence of God's gracious call back to Himself.

1–2 Because of his trials, David feels as though the Lord has unleashed His anger toward him. He pleads with the Lord neither to rebuke him in the midst of this wrath nor to correct him in His "hot displeasure" (*ḥemâ*, see 6:1), v. 1. David feels the arrows of God's punishment sinking into him. God's hand has descended upon him, v. 2.

3–5 David sees the physical trial he is going through as resulting from God's "anger" (*zaᶜam*)[488] over his sin. The physical burden continues because of his sin, giving him "no rest" in his "bones," idiomatic here for his body, v. 3. David sees the enormity of his sins. They are as overwhelming as a flood, going over his head. They are a greater burden than he can bear, v. 4. His physical ailments "stink and are corrupt [or 'fester']" because of his "foolishness" (*ᵓwl*).[489] It is tempting to relate these trials to David's sin with Bathsheba and the subsequent murder of Uriah. While this may be the case, we do not have enough information to be certain. Whatever the sin, David felt that it was responsible for his physical trials, v. 5.

6–8 David is "troubled" (or "bent over") and "bowed down," both poetic descriptions of his grief. He mourns throughout the day, v. 6. His "loins" are full with "a loathsome disease" (or "burning"). He feels "no soundness," his body completely taken over with his physical problems, v. 7. He is "feeble" (or "numb") and "sore broken" (*dakâ*, see 9:9), emotionally overcome because of his trials. He has "roared" (better "cried in distress") because of the "disquietness" (or "groaning") of his heart, v. 8.

9–10 David knows that the Lord is aware of his burden. His desire for healing is open to the Lord. His sorrows have not hid themselves from the Lord, v. 9. His heart beats rapidly and he has no strength. The "light" of his eyes, here representing the joy in life that he normally feels, has gone, v. 10.

---

[488]The noun *zaᶜam* refers to intense anger. It occurs four times in the Psalms (see 69:24; 78:49; 102:10), always referring to God's anger. Elsewhere, it may refer to man's anger, e.g., Jer. 15:17; Hos. 7:16, but normally describes the anger of God.

[489]Different forms of *ᵓwl* occur here and at 69:5; 107:17. The word *ᵓwl* refers to a morally wicked person with no fear of God and who therefore performs wicked (and foolish) actions.

II. Supplication for Divine Deliverance 11–22

11–12 David's loved ones and friends avoid him. Even his "kinsmen," family members, turn from him, v. 11. His enemies take advantage of his physical condition by setting traps for him. They "seek" (*daraš*, see 9:10) his "hurt," to harm him in some way. They speak "mischievous things" (or "destructive words," *hawâ,* see 5:9) and plan treachery against him. Taken together, his adversaries array themselves against him with wicked actions, wicked speech, and wicked thoughts, v. 12.

13–14 Perhaps due to the knowledge that he has sinned, David likens himself to a deaf and dumb man who does not defend himself against his enemies, v. 13. He repeats this thought. He has been as one who heard nothing and who did not reprove others for their words, v. 14.

15–20 Verses 15, 16, and 17 each refer to David's prayer. Initially, David states his reliance on the Lord. Rather than defending himself, he places his "hope" (*yaḥal*, see 31:24) in the Lord. He confidently expects that the Lord will hear his prayer, v. 15. The supplied words "hear me" and "otherwise" are not necessary. David has made his prayer so that his enemies will not exult in their victory over him. If his foot should slip, they would magnify themselves over him, v. 16. He sees himself as ready to "halt" (or "stumble"). His "sorrow," his mental anguish, is continually before him, v. 17. He confesses his iniquity. He is "sorry" ("troubled") for his sin, v. 18. David reminds the Lord that his foes are active. They are "lively, and . . . strong" (or "active, and . . . mighty"). There are many who wrongfully "hate" (*śaneʾ*, see 5:5) him, v. 19. His adversaries render "evil for good," not remembering past actions of David that had benefited them. They are against him because he follows good things, v. 20.

21–22 The psalm closes with a final plea to the Lord. David states this first negatively, then positively. He asks the Lord not to abandon him, not to distance Himself from him, v. 21. He asks the Lord to speedily help him. This is the only time the title "O Lord my salvation" occurs. David uses this appropriately since he relies on the Lord to deliver him from his foes, v. 22.

PSALM 39

David prepares the psalm[490] for "the chief musician" (*m^e^naṣṣeaḥ*, see 4, intro.), then names him as Jeduthun, a name that means "praising."[491] Psalms 62 and 77 also mention Jeduthun. I Chronicles 16:41–42; 25:1–6 and II Chronicles 5:12; 35:15 name him along with Asaph and Heman as leaders of the tabernacle music. A comparison of I Chronicles 15:17, 19 with the above verses makes it likely that Jeduthun was another name for Ethan, the author of Psalm 89.

This psalm is an individual lament, perhaps concerning the same threat that faced David in Psalm 38. As there, vv. 13–14, he mentions here that he has kept quiet at the accusations by his foes, vv. 1–2, 9. He mentions there his sin, vv. 3–5, 18, also mentioned here, vv. 8, 11. Verse 10 here possibly mentions some illness, also mentioned in 38:3–5, 7. Whatever the background, David maintains his trust in the Lord, vv. 7, 12.[492]

I. Recognition of David's Plight 1–5

1–3*a* David recalls his resolve not to "sin . . . with [his] tongue," to speak angrily of his foes. He pictures this as placing a "bridle" (better "muzzle") on his speech in the presence of the wicked, v. 1.[493]

[490]On subjective grounds, Ewald, I, 201, sees the author as an unnamed prophet of the northern ten tribes. The view lacks merit.

[491]Hirsch, I, 288 rejects Jeduthun as a name. He contrives a derivation from *yadâ*, then translates as "an act of God's hand," and refers this to the providence of God. David thus dedicates the psalm to the God Who gives strength to master the "tasks set our souls by the providence of His hand." The explanation is artificial. Also, the *q^e^rê* "Jeduthun" is undoubtedly correct rather than the *k^e^tîb* "Jedithun." The same spelling occurs in I Chron. 16:38; Neh. 11:17; and the title of Ps. 77, but it is "Jeduthun" in all fourteen times it occurs elsewhere. The substitution of *yôd* for *waw* is common.

[492]Henry, III, 381, considers this a "funeral psalm," composed at the death of some friend or relative. Rawlinson, I, 304, places the psalm in David's "early life," presumably during his flight from Saul. Clarke, I, 107, puts it during the time of Absalom's rebellion. While these views are possible, the psalm does not give enough information to let us be certain of the occasion.

[493]Lawson, p. 208, is typical of most authors who refer David's resolve to keep from complaining to God: "David determined to guard his mouth as a muzzle on an animal so he would not sin against God with his tongue." This is a possible view. I have opted to refer David's statement about his speech to his foes, primarily because of the similarity between Pss. 38 and 39.

He did not speak, not even good words, but his grief "was stirred" (or "grew worse"), v. 2. He felt inward anger. As he was "musing" (or "meditating," *hagîg*, see 5:1), the anger continued, v. 3*a*.

3*b*–5 Finally David speaks, v. 3*b*, not to his enemies but to the Lord. He asks that the Lord will help him to understand his life and to recognize that his life is "frail" (better "transient"), v. 4. His life is only a few handbreadths, poetically expressing the shortness of his days on earth. His "age" (*ḥeled*, see 17:14) is as nothing in comparison with the eternity of God. Man's life is at best only "vanity" (or "a breath," *hebel*, see 31:6), short-lived. David calls attention to his plight with the word "selah," v. 5.

II. Acknowledgement of David's Sin 6–11

6–8 David recognizes that mankind goes about "as a vain shew" (*ṣelem*, or "with form").[494] The idea is that man is not what he appears. Men are "disquieted," making a commotion, but "in vain" (*hebel*), to no purpose. Man gathers riches without knowing who will use them when he is gone, v. 6. Clearly, David's hope is not in mankind. He answers his own rhetorical question, "What wait [*qawâ*, see 25:3] I for?" He eagerly waits for the Lord, placing his hope in Him, v. 7. He asks the Lord to deliver him from his "transgressions," those acts in which he had rebelled against the Lord's word. This will spare him from being scorned by the foolish, v. 8.

9–11 David has not tried to defend himself. He has been silent because he recognizes that the Lord has sent the events that have happened to him, v. 9. He asks the Lord to take His "stroke" of punishment from him. He feels that he is "consumed," completely spent, by the Lord's judgment, v. 10. The word "when" is not necessary. The statement is straightforward. The Lord uses rebuke to "correct" (or "discipline") the iniquity of a "man" (*ʾîš*, see 22:6) consuming (*ʾmasâ*, see 6:6) his "beauty" (or "what is precious") as a moth does. Repeating the thought of v. 5, "man" (*ʾadam*, see 22:6) is but "vanity" (or "a breath," *hebel*, see 31:6), only here for a brief time. Once more, David calls attention to this by adding the word "selah," v. 11.

---

[494]The word *ṣelem* refers to an "image," a shape that represents something else. It normally refers to idols, but here and at 73:20 it represents man's outward appearance.

III. Prayer for Deliverance 12–13

12–13 David now pleads with the Lord to effectually hear his "prayer" (*t^epillâ*, see 4:1) for help. He asks Him not to remain silent before his tears. He is but a "stranger," a temporary resident of this life, a "sojourner," just as his ancestors were, not having full rights in this world, v. 12. He asks the Lord to "spare" (lit. "look away from") him, no longer directing punishment to him. Then he will "recover strength" (lit. "smile"), rejoicing in his new relationship with the Lord. He desires that this will happen before his death. This suggests that David does not want others to think that his death is the result of his sin, v. 13.

PSALM 40

David assigns the psalm to the "chief musician" (*m^enaṣṣeaḥ*, see 4, intro.) for use in the temple worship. The occasion is unknown. David faced some trial that endangered his life, vv. 12, 14, and this drove him to rely on the Lord. Other than that, we may only speculate on the exact nature of the threat.[495]

The psalm is typically messianic, based on the circumstances David is going through.[496] He writes of some danger that he faces. In

---

[495]Delitzsch, II, 34, is not certain of David's authorship. If he wrote it, Delitzsch suggests the time "between Gibea of Saul and Ziklag." Leupold, p. 321, also places it during the early part of David's life "when he was an outlaw fleeing from Saul." Cohen, p. 123, places it generally during Saul's attempts to capture David. These views place the psalm before David's rule over Israel, a time that does not agree with vv. 9–10, which speak of David's speech in the "great congregation." Rotherham, p. 188, dates the psalm at the time when David becomes king. Saul's threats are gone, and David is now exalted in the eyes of man. The view does not adequately explain the references to the "innumerable evils," v. 12, that David faces. Gaebelein, p. 175, suggests that David wrote the psalm after his son Absalom usurped the throne. It seems, however, that David is still in the midst of the trial rather than looking back on it, vv. 11–15, 17.

[496]Albert Barnes, I, 356, applies this psalm directly to the Messiah. Since much of it describes events in David's life, including his "iniquities," v. 12, I see it as typically messianic. Horne, p. 184, also sees Christ as speaking throughout the psalm. He explains v. 12 as referring to "imputed sins" for which the Lord suffers. The verse

reminding the Lord of his righteous past behavior, he makes a statement that the NT applies to Christ (vv. 6–8; cf. Heb. 10:5–7). The first part of the psalm is a song of thanksgiving.[497]

I. Remembrance of Past Blessings 1–5

1–3 David thinks either of some trial in which he had relied on the Lord or of the beginning of this present trial that he refers to throughout the psalm. In either case, he meditates on the gracious provision given him by the Lord. He had "waited patiently" (*qawâ*, or "eagerly waited," see 25:3) for the Lord to intervene.[498] The Lord had "inclined" toward him, acting in such a way as to show that He had indeed heard David's cry for help, v. 1. He brought David out of the trial, poetically described as being in "an horrible pit" (*mibbôr šaʾôn*, better, "a pit of destruction," cf. 7:15; 28:1)[499] and in "miry clay" (cf. 69:14–15). The Lord had placed his feet "upon a rock" with firm footing and no danger of slipping. He "established his goings [or 'steps']," v. 2. He gave David a "new song" to sing, a song of praise to God.[500] Others will see (*raʾâ*) him singing[501] and will "fear" (or "reverence") the Lord. They will also trust the Lord to meet their needs, v. 3.

---

refers to "mine iniquities," however, rather than iniquities placed on him indirectly. Note 32 in the introduction to Ps. 2 briefly discusses the messianic psalms.

[497]The introduction to Ps. 18 discusses the songs of thanksgiving.

[498]The Hebrew repeats the verb *qawâ,* with the infinitive absolute followed by the perfect tense verb. This is a common way of emphasizing the verbal idea; cf. G.K.C. 113 *n*.

[499]The phrase *mibbôr šaʾôn* is lit. "from a pit of noise." Since this is not clear, commentators take it differently. Leupold, p. 323, understands the phrase as "awesome pit." Kidner, *Psalm 1–72*, p. 158, translates "desolate pit." Fausset, III, 187, gives "a deep of roaring." He visualizes a deep cavity into which waters rush. Henry, p. 386, interprets as a "pit of despondency and despair." *OTTP*, p. 100, suggests "wild, deserted place," which supports "desolate pit" in the RSV. Buttenwieser, p. 696, gives "yawning grave." Delitzsch, II, 35, thinks of a pit with a miry footing. I have interpreted *šaʾôn* as "destruction." Jer. 25:31 lends some support to this. The phrase is difficult, but it is clear that the Lord has delivered David from some danger.

[500]See Ps. 33:3 for a summary of the phrase "new song."

[501]The word *raʾâ* occurs widely with many nuances of meaning. One of these, seeing with favor and therefore implying acceptance, also occurs in 45:10; 49:19; 50:18. This sense fits here. Omitting the supplied object "it," others see the new song that celebrates divine deliverance, accept this, and themselves "trust in the Lord."

4–5 The mighty "man" (*geber*, see 34:8) who trusts the Lord will be "blessed" (*ʾašrê*, see 1:1). He relies on the Lord and not on his own might. His faith in the Lord leads him to turn away from proud individuals and those who "turn aside to lies" (*śaṭê kazab*) to accomplish their goals, v. 4.[502] His emotions take hold of David as he thinks of God's goodness. He utters a marvelous statement of praise. God has done many "wonderful works" (or "wonders," *palaʾ*, see 9:1). He has had many gracious "thoughts" (*maḥšᵉbôt*, see 33:10) toward man. "They cannot be reckoned up in order unto thee" (better "there is none to compare to you"). Although experiencing these mercies, David realizes that they are but faint hints of God's greatness. If he should speak of them, they could not be numbered, v. 5.

II. Summary of Past Service 6–10

6–8 Such a God is worthy to be served. David recognizes that God does not "desire" (*ḥapeṣ*, see 18:19) mere ritual "sacrifice and offering," the terms embracing both bloody and non-bloody sacrifices. The Lord has "opened" (lit. "digged") his ears,[503] boring them out so that he could hear God's Word clearly.[504] This made him realize that the Lord does not require "burnt-offering" or "sin-offering." These could be offered as a ritual, having no significance, v. 6. David responds, "Lo [or 'Behold'], I come" as if to carry out the commands of the Lord. He notes that "in the volume [or 'scroll'] of the book," a scroll having the Law written in it, "it is written of me." He recognizes that God's Word has much to say concerning him (e.g., Deut. 4:2;

---

[502]Delitzsch, II, 36, understands the participle *śaṭê* as "turners aside," i.e., apostates. He argues that *śaṭê* is intransitive and therefore gives *kazab* (see 4:2) a verbal sense. He translates "lying apostates." This unnecessarily strengthens the thought. Those who lie are not necessarily apostates nor do all apostates lie. Kissane, p. 179, and Harman, p. 173, see the "lies" as false gods, a view followed by the NIV and TEV. The parallelism with "the proud" argues against making *kazab* refer to idols.

[503]Hebrews 10:5 substitutes "a body hast thou prepared me" for the phrase here that speaks of cleaning the ears. August Konkel, "The Sacrifice of Obedience," *Didaskalia* 2:2 (1991): 6, aptly notes that "the use of 'ears' as a symbol for obedience is natural in Hebrew, which uses the word 'hear' to mean 'obey.'" This metaphor does not carry over into Greek; hence, the NT author changed the wording.

[504]Henry, p. 388, understands the boring of the ears as referring "to the law and custom of binding servants to serve for ever by boring their ear to the doorpost," Exod. 21:6. The custom of boring a hole through the servant's "ear" differs from opening the plural "ears" that occurs here.

5:3; 17:14–20; Josh. 1:8; I Sam. 15:22), v. 7. David responds that his "delight" (*ḥapeṣ*) is to do God's will. To this end, he has stored much of "the law" in his heart, v. 8.

The paragraph shows the response of godly David to the Word of the Lord. The author of Hebrews (10:5–7) applies the passage to Jesus Christ. Just as David realized that God wanted more than ritual and so dedicated himself to obeying His Word, so the Lord likewise gave Himself to obeying His Father's will completely.

9–10 As evidence of his dedication to God, David recalls that he has "preached" (or "proclaimed," *baśar*)[505] the need for righteousness. He has done this in "the great congregation," probably a meeting of the people at one of the feasts requiring men to travel to Jerusalem (Deut. 16:16).[506] David did not avoid speaking with this emphasis on righteousness, v. 9. He did not hide the need for righteousness in his heart, as though his own personal relationship was the only important thing. No! He rather declared openly the "faithfulness and . . . salvation" of the Lord. He did not conceal God's "lovingkindness [or 'steadfast love,' *ḥesed*, see 5:7] and . . . truth" from the nation, v. 10.

III. Prayer for Present Need 11–17

11–12 David turns to the crisis that he faces.[507] He asks the Lord to extend His "tender mercies" (or "compassions") to him. He asks the Lord to "preserve" (or "guard") him with His "lovingkindness [or 'steadfast love,' *ḥesed*] and truth," v. 11.[508] The reason for this request now appears: David faces "innumerable evils." He does not identify the nature of these "evils," but at least some of them have come in

[505]The verb *baśar* refers to announcing something as good news. It is often the deliverance from sin gained through the Lord.

[506]Fausset, III, 189, spiritualizes the "great congregation" as "the fully-perfected congregation of the redeemed." This can be true only if the psalm refers directly to Christ, an interpretation that cannot be true because of the reference to "iniquities" in v. 12.

[507]Verses 1–11 are often considered a song of thanksgiving. The eleventh verse properly belongs to the third section of the psalm, but if we consider only those first eleven verses, it may serve as a conclusion to vv. 5–10.

[508]Sabourin, p. 287, sees "kindness and fidelity" as personified "attendants who protect the psalmist against sundry dangers—in the present context, against the danger of wild animals." The parallelism with "tender mercies," however, suggests that "lovingkindness and . . . truth" should be understood literally.

response to his "iniquities." David sees his trials as judgment for the sins he has committed. He is "not able to look up" (or "not able to see"), i.e., to see any escape from his trials.[509] The threats to David are "more than the hairs of mine head," idiomatically showing the great number of troubles. This causes his heart to fail with fear since he sees no way to escape, v. 12.

13–15 David again asks the Lord to "be pleased" (*raṣâ*)[510] to deliver him, to hasten his escape, v. 13.[511] May his enemies be openly "ashamed" (*bôš*, see 6:10) and "confounded" (or "humiliated") by their failure to take David's life. May they be "driven backward" (or "turned back") from their attacks upon him, "put to shame" (or "disgraced," *kalam*, see 35:4) by the defeat of their plans, v. 14. May those that menace him "be desolate" (or "appalled," *šamem*)[512] as the consequence of their "shame" (see *bôš*, 6:10), their wicked actions, v. 15.

16–17 In contrast with his foes, David asks that those who seek the Lord may "rejoice [or 'exult,' *śîś*, see 19:5] and be glad" in Him. David thinks of his immediate deliverance, an act that will bring general joy to the faithful. Those who love the "salvation" given them by the Lord will continually repeat, "Let the Lord be magnified [or 'exalted']," v. 16. Now, however, David sees himself as "poor [or 'afflicted,' *ʿanî*, see 9:12] and needy [or 'in need of protection']." He looks upon the Lord as his "help and . . . deliverer" and asks the "Lord" (see *ʾadôn*, 8:1), his master, to speed his aid, v. 17.

---

[509]Hengstenberg, II, 75, understands this as "the failure of the eyesight." John S. Kselman, "A Note on LR'WT in Ps 40,13," *Biblica* 63:4 (1982): 553, makes it the failure of his sight due to tears. Delitzsch, II, 41, says that "he is closely encompassed on all sides, and a free and open view is thereby altogether taken from him." Phillips, I, 313, makes the phrase messianic, the Lord not lifting His head for the shame imposed on Him by our sin. The psalm, however, is typically, not directly, messianic. I have adopted the above view as paralleling the final phrase, "my heart faileth me."

[510]The word *raṣâ* refers generally to pleasure or delight. The word does not bring out the emotional involvement of the person involved as fully as does the synonym *ḥapeṣ* (see 18:19).

[511]Verses 13–17 are similar to 70:1–5. The differences are discussed at Ps. 70.

[512]The verb *šamem* refers to "desolation" when places or things are in view. When describing people, the verb refers to "appall, shock, or horror." Delitzsch, II, 42, understands the verb as "to become torpid, here used of outward and inward paralysis." He translates as "struck dumb," a meaning not found elsewhere.

PSALM 41

The simple title identifies the author as David and the purpose as being for the "chief musician" (*m*ᵉ*naṣṣeaḥ*, see 4, intro.) in the tabernacle worship. Other than this, we know little of the background for the writing of the psalm.[513] Within this individual lament, v. 9 gives a single messianic prophecy of the Lord's betrayal.[514] David has been ill, vv. 2*a*, 3–4. He tells of the false speech his enemies have spoken about him, vv. 5–8. One of David's friends has betrayed him, v. 9. David admits that these things have happened because of his sin, v. 4, but he commits himself to the Lord for deliverance, vv. 1, 2*b*, 10–13. The circumstances in the psalm are similar to those mentioned in Psalms 38–39. The psalm closes the first book in the Psalms.

As similar circumstances face believers today, their response should follow that of David in the psalm. He rests on the faithfulness of the Lord, vv. 1–4. Others may seek to harm him, vv. 5–9, but David turns to the Lord for deliverance, vv. 10–12. Such a God is worthy of praise, v. 13.

I. Faithfulness of David's Lord 1–4

1–2 David "bless[es]" (*ʾašrê*, see 1:1) the Lord for caring for the "poor" (or "weak," *dal*).[515] The Lord will deliver this one in troubled times, v. 1. He will "preserve" (or "protect") him, "keep him alive" (or "restore him"), and "bless" him (see *ʾašrê*, 1:1) "on the earth," in this life. He will not give him over to the will of his foes, v. 2.

3–4 The Lord is faithful to "strengthen" (or "sustain") the one who is sick in bed. The Lord will "make all his bed," lit., "turn about his bed,"[516] idiomatic for healing the sick. While David writes in the

---

[513]Murphy, p. 263, and Cohen, p. 127, place the psalm at Absalom's rebellion. Scroggie, I, 239, also sets it at the rebellion with the additional detail that David must have become "dangerously ill" as a result of his great sin. Moll, p. 277, sets it in David's old age, at the time when Adonijah attempted to take the throne.

[514]Ps. 109 also prophesies the betrayal of the Lord. The introduction to Ps. 2, note 32, briefly discusses the messianic psalms.

[515]The word *dal* refers to one who is "low." This may refer to the lack of wealth, emotional needs, physical weakness, political or social lowness, or (occasionally) a lack of spirituality. The context must guide in understanding the word.

[516]Phillips, I, 317, and Fausset, III, 190, understand the phrase as rearranging the bed to make the patient comfortable. This view, however, does not parallel 3*a* as well

third person, he likely thinks of himself since vv. 4–5 mention his illness, v. 3. David asks the Lord for "mercy" (or "grace," *ḥanan*, see 4:1) to "heal my soul" (or "heal me"). He confesses his sin, apparently seeing this as the cause of his sickness, v. 4.

II. Falseness of David's Foes 5–9

5–8 David's enemies speak of him with evil words. They wish that he die quickly and his name, his reputation, "perish" (*ʾabad*, see 1:6) as the people forget him, v. 5. If "he," one of David's enemies, likely the friend spoken of in v. 9, comes to see David, he speaks "vanity" (or "falsehood," *šawʾ*, see 12:2), pretending concern over his condition.[517] He stores up wickedness within himself, however, and when he leaves he tells others his true feelings, v. 6. Those who "hate" (*śaneʾ*, see 5:5) David "whisper together" as they stealthily plot against him. They make plans to harm him, v. 7. They tell others that an "evil disease" (*bᵉlîyaᶜal*, see 18:4)[518] has been poured out on David. They say he will never recover from his sickbed, v. 8.

9 Even David's "own familiar friend," lit., "the man of my peace," someone close to him but left unidentified, has betrayed him.[519] Though he has been a guest at David's table, he now has "lifted up his heel" against David. This is the only time this expression occurs, but the sense is clear. This "friend" has tried to place David under his foot, tried to bring him down from his position. While the event happened to David, the Lord saw it as foreshadowing His own betrayal by Judas. John 13:18 partially quotes the verse, and Matthew 26:23; Mark 14:18; and Luke 22:21 allude to it, v. 9.

---

as that of healing David.

[517]H. H. Rowley, "A Displaced Verse in Psalm XLI," *VT* 1 (1951): 65–66, notes the changes of number, from the plural in v. 6, to the singular in v. 7, and back to the plural in v. 8. He asserts also that the enemy in v. 6 would not be allowed to visit the psalmist on his sick bed. For these reasons, he transfers v. 6 to follow v. 9. There is no textual support for the view. If David's visitor was a friend, even though later proven false, he would naturally visit David during the king's sickness.

[518]While *bᵉlîyaᶜal* normally refers to a worthless person, the context here relates it to the sickness. David's enemies call it "a thing of *bᵉlîyaᶜal*," an illness given to David because of his wickedness.

[519]Among others, Rotherham, p. 193, and Murphy, p. 265, relate this to the betrayal of David by Ahithophel (II Sam. 17:1–3). While this view is possible, David does not identify here the one about whom he speaks.

III. Favor of David's Lord 10–13

10–12 David asks the Lord to show him "mercy" (again "grace," *ḥanan*, see 4:1) by raising him from his sickbed. He will then "requite" (or "recompense") his foes for their evil, v. 10. David is confident that the Lord "favour[s]" (or "delights in," *ḥapeṣ*, see 18:19) him, since He has kept David's enemies from "triumph" (or "shout in triumph," *rûaᶜ*)[520] over him, v. 11. The Lord upholds David in his "integrity" (*tom*, see 7:8), not that David is free from sin but that he wants to please the Lord. The Lord has set David before His face, in His presence, a privilege that will never cease, v. 12.

13 The psalm, and the first book of Psalms, ends with this doxology of praise to the Lord.[521] May He be "blessed" (*barak*, see 5:12) from ages past into the ages of the future. The phrase "Amen [*ᵓamen*][522] and Amen" is emphatic. May it ever be so, v. 13!

---

[520]The word *rûaᶜ* occurs widely to refer to "shouting." This may be a shout because of some victory or in praise to the Lord. It may also be a shout to attract help or to indicate distress. In each occurrence, the context determines the sense of the word.

[521]Each of the five books in Psalms ends with a doxology of praise to the Lord for His faithfulness. See also 72:19; 89:52; 106:48; and 150:6.

[522]The adverb *ᵓamen* comes from the verb *ᵓaman*, "to be faithful." The adverb has the sense of "verily" or "truly," leading to the thought "let it be so."

BOOK II

PSALMS 42–43

Psalm 42 begins the second collection of psalms (42–72). Psalms 42 and 43 were likely one psalm originally. Taken together, they form an individual lament, with Psalm 43 completing Psalm 42. The lack of a title to Psalm 43, unusual in Book II,[1] together with the repeated refrain in 42:5, 11 and 43:5,[2] argues for a close connection between the two psalms.[3]

These are the first of several psalms written by one or more of the "sons of Korah."[4] The "sons of Korah" are the descendants of the Korah involved in the rebellion against Moses (Num. 16:1–49). Although the children of Dathan and Abiram died in the judgment (Num. 16:27–33), the "sons of Korah" were spared (Num. 26:11). Descendants of Korah helped David conquer Ziklag (I Chron. 12:6). In the time of Jehoshaphat, the "sons of Korah" were temple musicians (II Chron. 20:19).

The author assigns the psalm "to the chief musician" (*m^e^naṣṣeaḥ*, see 4, intro.) for use with the nation's worship. It is a "Maschil" (*maśkîl*, see 32, intro.), urging meditation on the thoughts expressed by its writer so that the readers may gain wisdom. The repeated refrain leads to the natural divisions within the psalms. The refrains

---

[1]Only Ps. 71 is without a title in this section.

[2]All three verses begin with the identical phrase "Why art thou cast down, O my soul?" The remainder of Pss. 42:11 and 43:5 is identical in Hebrew. Ps. 42:5 differs slightly.

[3]Alexander, p. 201, calls Ps. 43 "a supplementary psalm, composed by the same person, or in imitation of him, on a different occasion." Henry, p. 398, calls Ps. 43 "an appendix" written "upon the same occasion with the former [Ps. 42]." Whether Ps. 43 is considered separate from its beginning or separated later, it serves to conclude the thought introduced in Ps. 42. The ancient versions keep the two psalms separate. The division must therefore have taken place early.

[4]These include Pss. 42–43, 44, 45, 46, 47, 48, 49, 84, 85, 87, and 88. With the exception of Ps. 88, these psalms do not identify the individual writer within the group. Delitzsch, II, 52, suggests the possible view that the descendants of Korah sought "to expiate the name of their unfortunate ancestor by the best liturgical productions." Fausset, III, 192, and Rawlinson, I, 330, make the author record the words of David. Albert Barnes, II, 2, and Calvin, II, 127, suggest that David wrote the psalm for the sons of Korah to use with the tabernacle music. Because of the similarity to other Davidic psalms, several authors suggest that the author of Pss. 42–43 was with David in the wilderness during his flight from Absalom. Cohen, p. 130, thinks that these psalms were part of a collection used by the sons of Korah.

also suggest a practical application of the psalms. Despite the difficulties that he faces, the psalmist places his confidence in the Lord. He will continue to praise Him.

I. The Longing for God 42:1–5

1–2 The psalmist pictures his desire for renewed fellowship with God.[5] The "hart" is the stag, the male deer, but occurs here as a collective referring to deer in general.[6] He "panteth after" (or "longs for") water to quench his thirst. In the same way, the psalmist longs for fellowship with God, v. 1.[7] His soul longs for the presence of God. His question, "When shall I come and appear before God?" suggests that something prevents him from worship at Jerusalem. Verse 9 and 43:1–2 make it clear that he faces some enemy. This may place the writing during Absalom's rebellion. It is equally possible that some military campaign is in view, v. 2.[8]

3–5 These circumstances have brought tears to the psalmist. They "have been [his] meat," i.e., he can taste them, "day and night." Psalm 43:1 speaks of false charges against him. Others taunt him by asking, "Where is thy God?" The question adds to the thought that he is in circumstances that require divine intervention, v. 3. Thinking on these things causes him to "pour out [his] soul" as he grieves over his situation. He recalls better times when he "went" (*dadâ*)[9] with others to worship. They had gone with the "voice of joy [*rinnâ*, see 17:1]"

---

[5]Hirsch, I, 308, understands the speaker as Israel. From the use of the first person pronoun throughout the psalm, it more likely refers to an individual.

[6]Calvin, II, 128, and Cohen, p. 130, make the "hart" a female deer, the "hind," since the verb "panteth" is feminine. Subject-verb gender disagreement, however, is not unusual in Hebrew.

[7]Verse 1 is the basis for the hymn "As the Deer," with words and music by Martin Nystrom, © Maranatha Music, 1984.

[8]Leupold, p. 337, suggests that the psalmist is separated from God by some sin. Nothing in the psalm, however, indicates a sin problem. It is rather an enemy that keeps him from worshiping at the tabernacle. In either of the above-suggested backgrounds, the psalmist must have been with David in the time when he was cut off from the tabernacle.

[9]The verb *dadâ* occurs only here (*piᶜel*) and at Isa. 38:15 (*hitpaᶜel*). From its parallel to "come," it must refer to some kind of movement. BDB, p. 186*b*, gives "lead slowly." KB, I, 214, emends to "I walk." Alexander, p. 198, translates as "march," Fausset, III, 192, "advanced," and Delitzsch, II, 50, "accompanied." The sense of all these is much the same.

to keep "holyday," one of the feasts in the land, v. 4. The psalmist asks himself the question, "Why art thou cast down, O my soul? and why art thou disquieted within me?" This is the first appearance of the refrain that occurs again in v. 11 and in 43:5. The question leads to his resolve that he will "hope" (*yaḥal*, see 31:24) in God and once more praise the Lord for the help that comes from "his countenance," His presence. The psalmist here anticipates deliverance from his enemies, v. 5.

II. The Trust in God 42:6–11

6–9 The psalmist repeats from the refrain the thought of being "cast down." He will remember the Lord as he travels throughout the land. This includes his sight of "the Hermonites" (better, "the peaks of Mt. Hermon")[10] and Mt. Mizar, v. 6.[11] The sounds of the "waterspouts" (better "waterfalls") call to one another as the streams splash over the rocks and join to form the Jordan River. The author poetically pictures himself as overwhelmed by these waters. The waves and billows of despair sweep over him, v. 7.[12] Yet he is confident that in the day, the Lord will extend His "lovingkindness" (or "steadfast love," *ḥesed*, see 5:7) to him. At night, he will meditate on songs about the Lord and will offer "prayer" (*t^epillâ*, see 4:1) to God, v. 8.

---

[10]Mt. Hermon was in the northernmost part of the land occupied by Israel in the OT across the Jordan River. It lay about ten miles northeast of Dan (Laish) and was the source for the waters of the Jordan River. The plural word "Hermonites" used here refers to the various peaks of the mountain range dominated by Mt. Hermon. See also the discussion at 29:6.

[11]We cannot identify Mt. Mizar. It apparently is also in the northern part of the land, near Mt. Hermon. From its name (*miṣ^car* = "little place"), it could not have been significant by its size. Perhaps its location gave it some importance. Kidner, p. 166, suggests that Mizar "could be an ironic reference to the mighty Hermon itself . . . in the spirit of 68:15ff., where the great peaks are made to feel insignificant beside Mount Zion, God's abode." Fausset, III, 193, similarly says, "The greatest of earthly elevations is but *little* when compared with the moral elevation of the Lord's hill of Zion." This view requires reading a mention of Zion into the thought, which is unlikely. Kissane, p. 189, proposes that Mizar is "the name of his native district in Palestine from which he is now exiled" or that it is Mt. Zion, a little mountain "in contrast with Hermon." The views are speculative.

[12]Jon. 2:3 uses the identical phrase ("All thy waves and thy billows are gone over me") to describe his plight. The psalmist uses the phrase metaphorically, picturing his distress, while Jonah uses it literally to describe his descent into the depths of the ocean.

In his prayers, he will speak of God as his "rock," the sure foundation upon Whom he rests. He will ask why God has "forgotten" him. He explains this with the next phrase. It is not that God has literally forgotten him; it only seems so since there is continuing "oppression" (or "distress," *laḥaṣ*)[13] from his "enemy," v. 9.

10–11 It is as though there is "a sword in my bones" (better "a shattering of my bones"), the psalmist says, describing the attacks of his enemies poetically. They taunt him by questioning the absence of his God, v. 10. Once more, he asks, "Why art thou cast down, O my soul? and why art thou disquieted within me?" The Hebrew of this differs slightly from that in v. 5 but expresses the same thought. Once again he resolves to maintain his "hope" (*yaḥal*) in God. He will praise God for the "health" that He gives. The psalmist thinks of the confidence and contentment that God will restore to him, v. 11.

III. The Prayer to God 43:1–5

1–2 The psalmist now turns to the Lord in prayer. He asks the Lord to "judge" him, vindicating him before others. Apparently, false charges have been made against the psalmist. He needs the Lord to "plead [his] cause" (*rîb*, see 35:1) with "an ungodly nation" (or "disloyal [*loʾ ḥasîd*, see 4:3] people"). This refers to those wicked people who have arrayed themselves against him. "The deceitful and unjust [*ʿawlâ*, see 7:3] man" likely is the leader of those opposing the psalmist, v. 1. He considers the Lord to be "the God of [his] strength [or 'defense', *maʿôz*, see 27:1]." For this reason, he does not understand the delay in delivering him. Why has God rejected him? Why must he mourn over the "oppression" (*laḥaṣ*, see 42:9) from his enemies, v. 2?

3–4 The author adds a second prayer, asking the Lord to bring him back to Jerusalem to worship Him once more. We must understand the "light" of the Lord by its parallelism with the "truth" of God. These represent the guidance that comes from following God's Word (cf. Ps. 119:105).[14] They themselves, an emphatic grammatical con-

---

[13]The noun *laḥaṣ* occurs only three times in the Psalms, here and 43:2; 44:24. The word comes from a verb meaning "to press, squeeze." This gives rise to the sense of oppression.

[14]Leupold, p. 343, understands the light "as a figure of God's mercy" and truth as "the continuance of God's mercy." Albert Barnes, II, 14, similarly makes light

struction in Hebrew, will bring him to Zion, the "holy hill" where the tabernacle is located. The word "tabernacles" is a plural of majesty, appropriate in describing the dwelling of the Lord, v. 3. The psalmist will then worship at the altar of burnt offering where sacrifice took place. He will rejoice in God, his "exceeding joy."[15] He will praise God with songs on his "harp" (or "lyre," *kinnôr*, see 33:2), v. 4.

5 The psalmist ends his meditation with a refrain identical in the MT to that in 42:11. The conclusion has a positive sense. The questions are rhetorical. There is no reason to be cast down. He resolves to confidently "hope" (*yaḥal*) in God. He expects to praise God, "the health of [his] countenance," the One Who will give him renewed confidence and deliverance from the doubts that have assailed him (cf. 42:2–3, 6–7, 9), v. 5.

PSALM 44

This is the second psalm by the "sons of Korah."[16] Like more than one-third of the psalms, it is written for the "chief musician" (*m^{e}naṣ-ṣeaḥ*, see 4, intro.) for use with Israel's worship. It is a "Maschil" (*maśkîl*, see 32, intro.), designed to impart wisdom to those hearing it. It is also a community lament. The unnamed author[17] refers first to the past activity of God on behalf of the nation, vv. 1–8; then to the

---

"favour or mercy" and truth "faithfulness." While this spiritual application is true, the context better supports something related to guidance. Anderson, I, 335, suggests that the psalmist considers light and truth "as if they were two of God's messengers or angels." Perowne, I, 354, suggests that these allude "to the Urim and Thummim." VanGemeren, p. 336, relates "the light of God" to "the fullness of his redemption" and "truth . . . of God" to "the expression of his covenantal fidelity." These views are doubtful. Gaebelein, p. 194, makes "light and truth" represent the Lord. Nothing in the psalm, however, suggests a messianic application here.

[15]The grammatical construction is also emphatic, lit., "the rejoicing of my joy." This is appropriately phrased as "my exceeding joy."

[16]See Pss. 42–43, 44, 45, 46, 47, 48, 49, 84, 85, 87, and 88. The introduction to Pss. 42–43 discusses the phrase "sons of Korah."

[17]Rotherham, p. 203, and Spurgeon, p. 210, argue for David as the writer. The title, however, identifies the author as a descendant of Korah.

present trial facing the nation, vv. 9–22;[18] and finally to the need for divine help once more, vv. 23–26.

I. Past Activity of God 1–8

1–3 The psalmist recalls the entrance of Israel into Palestine. The nation has heard from its fathers of the victories the Lord wrought then on the nation's behalf, v. 1. He drove out the heathen with His "hand," an emblem that regularly represents His power, e.g., 10:12, 14. He also "planted . . . them," i.e., established the fathers in the land. The psalmist repeats these thoughts. God overcame the heathen and at the same time "cast them out" (better, "spread them out"),[19] sending the fathers throughout the land, v. 2. The people of Israel took the land not by their own strength but by the power of God. His "right hand" and "arm," again emblems of His power, and "the light of [His] countenance," His guidance (cf. 27:1; 36:9), gave them the land. All this showed God's "favor" (or "pleasure," *raṣâ*, see 40:13) toward Israel, v. 3.

4–8 Although the psalmist speaks in the first person, the alternation with the third person shows that he still speaks for the people. God is the King. The psalmist asks Him to deliver "Jacob," here standing for the nation, v. 4. Israel will overcome their foes through the power of God. By His "name,"[20] His nature, especially seen in the display of His power, they will tread down those that oppose them, v. 5. They will not trust in their weapons, v. 6. God has saved them in

[18]Most often, the occasion for writing is set at the time of the war between Israel and the alliance of Syria, Ammon, and Edom, and Israel, II Sam. 8:13–14. So Moll, p. 289, and Clarke, I, 119. This, however, was a victorious war over the alliance, not a prolonged judgment as described in the psalm. Murphy, p. 273, sets it at "the war with the Philistines in the times of Samuel and Saul." Goldingay, *Songs from a Strange Land: Psalms 42–51*, pp. 51–52, compares the time to that of the Assyrian invasion during the reign of Hezekiah. Jennings, I, 195, and Calvin, II, 148, place it during the persecution of Antiochus Epiphanes. Hirsch, I, 315, understands the psalm as a prophecy of Israel during the years of dispersion throughout the earth. This wide variation reflects the lack of evidence in the psalm that makes its background certain.

[19]Thompson, p. 272, and Weiser, p. 356, understand the phrase "cast them out" to refer to the expulsion of the heathen from the land. It is true that *šalaḥ* can mean "cast out." The parallelism in the verse, however, argues for applying the phrase to Israel rather than to the heathen. See 80:11 for the same thought.

[20]Note 94 at 5:11 summarizes the significance of the Lord's "name."

the past, putting to "shame" (*bôš*, see 6:10) those that "hated" (*śane*ᵓ, see 5:5) them. This work of God on their behalf encourages them to trust Him now, v. 7. They "boast" (or "glory") in Him and praise His "name" (see v. 5) continually. The "selah" calls attention to this praise, v. 8.

II. Present Judgment of Israel 9–22

A. The Plight of the Nation 9–16

9–12 The psalmist now turns to the present need of the people. We cannot find with certainty elsewhere in the OT the situation that he describes. The Lord has "cast [them] off" and "put [them] to shame" (or "dishonored" them, *kalam*, see 35:4). He has not gone with Israel's armies to empower them, v. 9. No, He has rather caused them to retreat from their foes. Those that "hate" (*śane*ᵓ) the nation have plundered them, v. 10. God has let the nation be as sheep slaughtered for meat. He has let them be scattered among the heathen nations, v. 11. He has sold the people to their captors for nothing, not even enriching Himself by this, v. 12.

13–16 Israel has become a reproach. Neighboring countries scorn and deride them, v. 13. They have become a "byword" (*mašal*)[21] among the heathen, an object of their scorn equating Israel with shame and degradation, v. 14. The psalmist sees his own "confusion" (or "disgrace," *k*ᵉ*limmâ*, see 4:2). He feels his "shame" (*bôšet*, see *bôš*, 6:10), v. 15, because of the speech of the one who "reproacheth" (or "taunts") and "blasphemeth" (or "reviles") Israel, their enemy and avenger, v. 16.

B. The Problem of the Nation 17–22

17–19 The psalmist now addresses the matter that puzzles him. These trials have come upon Israel even though they been faithful to the Lord. They have not forgotten Him or been false to their covenant with Him, v. 17. They have not turned back from Him to worship of other gods. They have not turned aside from His way, v. 18. The word "though" is better "because" or "for." The psalmist recognizes that

[21]While *mašal* commonly refers to a "proverb," it has a broader meaning than this. It may also refer to a parable, a discourse, a saying, a comment, or a byword. The context must determine the sense.

the trials have come because God has ordered them. God has "sore broken" (*dak*, see 9:9) Israel in the place of "dragons" (or "jackals," *tannîm*),[22] making them a place fit for wild beasts to roam. He has covered them with the "shadow of death" (*ṣalmawet*, see 23:4), a deep-seated feeling of despair, v. 19.

20–22 If Israel had forgotten the "name" of God (see v. 5) or stretched out their hands in the worship of some "strange [or 'false,' *zûr*][23] god," v. 20, would not God know? He knows those thoughts that have been hidden away in the recesses of the mind. The psalmist implies with these verses that this is not the case, v. 21. Yet "for thy sake," because of the will of God, they continually face death. They are treated as sheep ready to be slaughtered. Paul quotes the verse in Romans 8:36 to show that tribulation has always been the lot of God's people, v. 22.

III. Future Help of the Lord 23–26

23–26 The psalmist realizes that Israel's only help lies in the intervention of the "Lord." Throughout the psalm, he has appropriately referred to "God" (*ʾᵉlohîm*, vv. 1, 4, 8, 20, 21), the name stressing the power of God. Now he refers to *ʾᵃdonay* (see 8:1), stressing God's ownership of the nation. He is their Master. The psalmist prays for Him to awaken from His inaction and not to reject them permanently, v. 23. He asks why the Lord has hidden His face from the nation. Why has He forgotten their "affliction" (*ʿanî*, see 9:12) and "oppression" (*laḥaṣ*, see 42:9)? The questions rest on the appearance of things. The Lord has not hidden His face from them, and He has not forgotten their circumstances. Because time has gone by, it appears as though He has turned from them. The psalmist does not understand the reason for this. In this, he faces the same problem that Christians have faced throughout history. God's people have always

[22]The noun *tannîm* (also spelled *tannîn*) occurs widely in the OT. It refers to "whales," Gen. 1:21; Job 7:12; a large serpent, Exod. 7:9–12; and wild animals, Jer. 14:6. It sometimes poetically describes wicked individuals or nations, Isa. 27:1; Ezek. 29:3.

[23]The word *zûr* occurs in a variety of contexts to refer to something or someone from outside the normal group, e.g., a prostitute outside of the normal group of women or an enemy outside the normal group of Israelites. Here, it refers to a god who is not Israel's God.

suffered, sometimes for their own sins but many times for matters known only to God. We may rest in the certainty that God has His reasons for allowing the persecution of His children. Our proper response is faithfulness and trust in the Lord, v. 24.

The psalmist reminds the Lord of the trauma faced by the people. They face the threat of national extinction. They are bowed down to the dust. Their "belly" (or "body") cleaves to the ground, v. 25. The psalmist pleads for the Lord to help them, to "redeem" (*padâ*, see 25:22) them, "for thy mercies' sake" (or "for the sake of your steadfast love [*ḥesed*, see 5:7]"), v. 26.

PSALM 45

This messianic psalm[24] portrays the wedding of the Lord and His bride the church.[25] There is no OT event that completely fits the details given in the psalm. There are, however, also details that do not fit the marriage of the Lord. This leads us to consider the psalm as a record of an unknown king's wedding with parts of it being purely prophetic, going beyond the earthly wedding to the heavenly event itself.[26]

---

[24]The introduction to Ps. 2, note 32, briefly discusses the messianic psalms.

[25]Spurgeon, p. 213, comments, "Some here see Solomon and Pharaoh's daughter only—they are short-sighted; others see both Solomon and Christ—they are cross eyed; well-focused spiritual eyes see here Jesus only." Despite Spurgeon's view, I am not convinced that the psalm is purely prophetic. The discussion points out those elements that do not fit into the heavenly wedding of Jesus Christ and His church.

[26]Delitzsch, II, 74, understands the psalm as having been "composed in connection with the marriage of Joram of Judah with Athaliah." Joram (or Jehoram), however, was a wicked king (cf. II Kings 8:16–18) and not an appropriate type of Christ. Moll, p. 294, and Calvin, II, 173, make the psalm refer to the wedding of Solomon and the daughter of the king of Egypt. Solomon, however, was a king of peace, and vv. 3–5 make this king a warrior. Crenshaw, p. 27, refers the psalm to a marriage between "a ruler from Israel and a bride from Tyre." Buttenwieser, p. 85, makes this specific referring to the marriage of Ahab and Jezebel. The mention of Tyre, v. 12, can be explained otherwise. Such a wicked king is not appropriate to represent the Messiah. Clarke, I, 122, and Rotherham, p. 207, suggest the marriage of Hezekiah and Hephzibah, possible types although we know little of Hephzibah. Ewald, I, 169,

The psalm is for the "chief [temple] musician" (*m*ᵉ*naṣṣeaḥ*, see 4, intro.) and is "upon Shoshannim," a word that means "lilies" and is also mentioned in Psalms 60, 69, and 80. It is likely that this refers to some tune to which the psalm was sung.[27] It is a "Maschil" (*maśkîl*, see 32, title), a psalm enjoining meditation so that the hearer may gain wisdom, written by the "sons of Korah."[28] It is further a "Song of loves." The plural "loves" (from *yadîd*)[29] is an intensive plural that points to the subject of the psalm.

I. Address to the Bridegroom 1–9

A. Description of the Bridegroom 1–2

1 The opening verse introduces the psalm. The psalmist has a full heart that "is inditing [*raḥaš*][30] a good matter" (or "stirs [with] a good matter"). He therefore speaks of these things "touching the king" (better, "to the king"). At this stage, the king is not identified. As the psalm develops, it becomes clear that the king is an unnamed earthly king. The wedding of this king foreshadows the wedding of the Lord to His bride, the church. The psalmist's tongue is as the pen

---

refers the psalm to the marriage of Jeroboam II with an unnamed daughter of another king. Again, it is unlikely that a wicked king is in view.

[27]Luther, XII, 202, translates "Shoshannim" as "roses" and spiritualizes it into "all churches gathered together in the common faith." Fausset, III, 197, sees the lilies as referring to "those possessing spiritual beauty." Alexander, p. 209, considers lilies as "a natural emblem of female beauty, the plural form implying a plurality of persons, such as we meet with in the psalm itself." C. I. Scofield, ed., *The Scofield Reference Bible* (New York: Oxford University Press, 1945), p. 620, connects the word with spring. From this he conjectures that "the Shoshannim Psalms were probably connected with the Passover season." Spurgeon, p. 835, suggests that "lilies" is "a poetical title given to this noblest of songs . . . it is easy to see the fitness of borrowing a name for so beautiful, so pure, so choice, so matchless a poem from the golden lilies, whose bright array outshone the glory of Solomon." Where the word occurs elsewhere, however, Pss. 60, 69, 80, this thought is not appropriate. Albert Barnes, II, 26, relates the word to "a musical instrument that had a resemblance to a lily." He suggests either the trumpet or cymbal.

[28]See the introduction to Pss. 42–43 for a discussion of the "sons of Korah."

[29]The word *yadîd* refers to "great love," more than mere infatuation. The name *David* comes from the same root.

[30]The word *raḥaš* occurs only here. There is, however, the related participle *marḥešet* in Lev. 2:7; 7:9, "the place of stirring," i.e., a frying pan. This leads to the sense here of "stirring, overflowing, boiling over."

of a "ready writer" (or "diligent scribe"), one prepared to set down the facts of a matter, v. 1.

2 The psalmist describes the bridegroom as "fairer [*yapyapîta*] than the children of men." The *p*^{eʾ}*alʾal* verb emphasizes the appearance of the groom; cf. Song of Solomon 5:10–16. The psalmist singles out the attractiveness of the groom's speech by saying, "Grace is poured into thy lips [or 'on your lips']," cf. Luke 4:22. While these superlatives might well refer to the Israelite king at his marriage, they also apply directly to the Lord, the Redeemer of all who trust Him for deliverance from their sins. The phrase "God hath blessed [*barak*, see 5:12] thee for ever," an eternal blessing, supports the reference to the Lord, v. 2.

B. Preparation for the Battle 3–5

3–5 The groom is a warrior. The psalmist urges him, the powerful One, to gird himself with his sword. The final phrase, "with thy glory [*hôd*, see 8:1] and thy majesty [*hadar*, see 8:5]," has no verb or preposition. It is simply "your glory and your majesty" and is a second object of the verb "gird." The warrior girds himself with "glory and . . . majesty" as he goes to war, v. 3.[31] In this "majesty" (*hadar*), he rides "prosperously [or 'successfully'] because of [or 'concerning'] truth and meekness [or 'humility'] and righteousness."[32] His "right hand," the hand with which a warrior normally strikes, will "teach" him, in the sense of showing the warrior, "terrible [or 'awesome'] things," v. 4. His arrows are sharp, causing his enemies to fall with their hearts pierced. The psalmist writes in the third person of the "king" to avoid giving a sense of over-familiarity with the Lord, v. 5.

---

[31]Fausset, III, 198, places "thy glory and thy majesty" in apposition to the warrior's "sword." It is the instrument by which "His glory and His majesty vindicate and manifest themselves." Leupold, p. 355, understands the glory and majesty as "his glorious armor." The TEV makes the phrase an independent statement: "You are glorious and majestic." Since the grammatical construction is unusual, these views are possible.

[32]Since no conjunction joins "meekness" and "righteousness," Rawlinson, I, 351, understands the construction as "meek-tempered righteousness." He comments, "Righteousness . . . to be really righteousness must be combined with meekness." While this is true, it is more likely that the construction is asyndetic; cf. G.K.C. 154 *a*, note 1(a), joining the words in thought despite the absence of a connecting *waw* before "righteousness."

We cannot certainly relate the paragraph to a specific end-time battle of the Lord. The description, however, does remind us of His conquests. At the end of the Tribulation, He will overcome the nations of the world as they join together to fight Him, Revelation 19:11–21. At the end of the millennial kingdom, He will once again defeat the forces of Satan, Revelation 20:7–9.

C. Prophecy of Messiah 6–7

6–7 The psalmist now clarifies the identify of the "king" by addressing Him as "God." The fulfillment of the psalm now comes to the forefront to replace the symbolism. The Lord will have an everlasting throne, the fulfillment of II Samuel 7:16.[33] The "sceptre" of His rule, the emblem of His royal authority, will be a "right [or 'upright,' *mîšôr*, see 26:12] sceptre" (cf. Isa. 11:3–4), v. 6. This follows naturally since He loves righteousness and "hates" (*śane*ʾ, see 5:5) iniquity. For this reason, God the Father has anointed God the Son with "the oil of gladness [or 'joy']" to set Him apart from His "fellows," i.e., fellow-kings. The anointing spoken of here is the anointing at His coronation as King of kings.[34] To make clear the messianic application of the passage, Hebrews 1:8–9 applies it to the Lord, v. 7.

---

[33]Moll, p. 296, makes *ʾelohîm* an adjective that modifies "throne." The "God-throne" is everlasting. Weiser, pp. 360, 363, is similar: "divine throne," i.e., a righteous ruler. These phrasings are awkward since the 2ms pronoun "thy" stands between "throne" and *ʾelohîm* in the MT. Hirsch, I, 326, applies *ʾelohîm* to a human ruler, "your throne, O Ruler." Rodd, p. 89, interprets the phrase as "Thy throne is everlasting like that of God." The NT use in Heb. 1:8 supports the traditional rendering of the AV. Kirkpatrick, p. 248, supplies a second "throne," translating "Thy throne [is the throne of] God." The supplied words have no textual support and are not necessary. The only justification is to avoid identifying the king as God. The LXX and Vulgate support the translation of the AV and other standard translation, e.g., NASB, NIV, NRSV. Murray J. Harris, "The Translation of Elohim in Psalm 45:7–8," *TB* 35 (1984): 87, argues that "it is a king of the Davidic dynasty who is addressed as אלהים." The NT use of the phrase, however, supports the view given above.

[34]Cohen, pp. 142–43, rejects the idea that this is the anointing "in the ceremony of coronation." Rather, he understands "that God has bestowed happiness upon the king in fuller measure than upon anybody else." While it is certain that the Son is joyous over the fulfillment of His Father's will, the context of v. 6 supports the anointing to the Son's office.

D. Ceremony of Marriage 8–9

8–9 The psalmist again speaks of the earthly king. His garments are heavily scented. Omitting the supplied word "smell," 8*a* reads "All thy garments are of myrrh, and aloes, and cassia." The scent is so pronounced that it is as though his garments have been woven from the spices themselves. "Myrrh" is a spice from Arabia that exudes from the bark of the balsam tree. The spice comes from a gummy, translucent, reddish yellow resin produced by the tree. The spice "aloes" comes from trees grown in China and India. The heart of the tree and its roots yield a fragrant resin from which the spice comes. "Cassia" is ground from the bark of several shrubs and trees.

The wealthy used ivory in decorating; cf. I Kings 10:18; 22:39; Amos 3:15; 6:4. The word "palaces" is a plural of intensity that hints at the splendor of the king's home where the wedding takes place.[35] From there, the events bring joy to the bridegroom.[36] The music comes from the palace, v. 8.[37] The attendants of the bride include the daughters of kings, likely representing nearby nations. The bride, the new queen, stands at the place of honor, the right hand of the king. Her clothing is embroidered with gold from Ophir, modern Yemen in southwest Arabia, v. 9.[38]

The wedding spoken of by the psalmist is certainly an earthly event. As with all weddings, however, it reminds us of that heavenly event which is yet to come. The NT alludes to this frequently (e.g., Rom. 7:4; II Cor. 11:2; Eph. 5:31–32; Rev. 21:9). From Revelation 19:7–9, we see that the wedding takes place during the time of the

---

[35]Moll, p. 297, understands the preposition "out of" to refer "to the palace of her father out of which a procession issues to greet the royal bridegroom." Delitzsch, II, 85, also places the wedding at the palace belonging to the bride's father. It is unlikely that a king would travel to another place to be married.

[36]The phrase "whereby they have made thee glad" is often translated "stringed instruments [*minnî*] have made you glad." Among others, Ewald, I, 170, and Goldingay, p. 83, translate similarly. This requires the word *minnî* to be a poetic form of *minnîm*, "stringed instruments," as in 150:4. The word *minnî*, however, is common, occurring more than forty times, including ten more times in the Psalms. There is no reason to understand an unusual sense here.

[37]The hymn "Out of the Ivory Palaces," the words and music written by Harry Barraclough in 1915, comes from this verse.

[38]The details in vv. 8–9 do not fit into a direct application of the psalm to the Lord. They are appropriate to an earthly wedding ceremony.

Tribulation on earth. It follows the rapture of the church and precedes the glorious appearing of Christ.

II. Address to the Bride 10–17

A. Guidance for Marriage 10–11

10–11 The psalmist now directs his words to the bride. She should "hearken . . . consider . . . incline [her] ear." The repetition of the thought stresses the importance of accepting these words of guidance. Since she is about to enter into a new relationship, she should turn from her own people, including her family. Although it is unsaid, there is an implied statement that she should turn to her new bridegroom. Spiritually, this suggests the need to leave the believer's past life of sin and to embrace wholly the Lord and His ways, v. 10. In response, the king will delight in her. He is her "Lord" (*ʾadôn*, see 8:1) and is therefore worthy of her "worship," v. 11.[39]

B. Gifts for Marriage 12

12 The "daughter of Tyre" idiomatically describes a delegation from Tyre that comes to the wedding bringing a gift; cf. 72:10. The phrase "even the rich" parallels the "daughter of Tyre." Ezekiel 26:12 refers to the wealth of Tyre. The city represents those who come to the wedding, v. 12.[40]

C. Glorious in Marriage 13–15

13–14*a* The psalmist describes the bride's gown. She is glorious in her appearance with a gown made of "wrought gold." As before, v. 9, this refers to golden threads embroidering the material. The word "within" locates this inside the king's palace (v. 8), v. 13.[41] She comes

[39]The word "worship" is lit. "bow down." This is appropriately interpreted as "worship" when speaking of the Lord. When thinking of a husband-wife relationship, the idea is better expressed as "honor." Cohen, p. 142, takes it as referring to the wife's obedience. In my judgment, this is not the best view here.

[40]Verse 12 gives additional detail that does not support a direct application of the psalm to the Lord. At the marriage of the Lamb to His bride, the church, heathen cities and nations will not send delegations to represent them.

[41]Rawlinson, I, 352, refers the word "within" to the bride. Within her heart, she is glorious. The verse, however, stresses not the bride's character but her clothing.

to the king wearing "raiment of needlework," again embroidered material, v. 14*a*.

14*b*–15 The attendants of the bride are likely the same group referred to in v. 9*a*.[42] They join her as she comes to the king at the ceremony, v. 14*b*.[43] They rejoice over their privilege of service to the king and his queen. They enter with the bride into the king's palace, the place where the wedding takes place (cf. vv. 8, 13), v. 15.

D. Outcome of the Marriage 16–17

16–17 The emphasis to this point has been on the marriage itself. The psalmist now focuses on the future of the marriage. The king and his queen will give birth to "children" (lit. "sons") that become "princes" in all the "earth" (or "land"), referring to the region occupied by the nation, v. 16.[44] The psalmist anticipates making future "generations" (*dor wador*, cf. 10:6) recall the king's "name," i.e., his nature,[45] as worthy of remembrance. They will praise him forever, v. 17. As with other parts of the psalm, the note of praise appropriately applies to the Messiah. He will indeed receive praise through eternity; cf. Revelation 5:11–14.[46]

---

[42]Moll, p. 298, identifies the "virgins, her companions" as servants belonging "to the household of the young queen." At her marriage, they are "transferred to the possession of the king." The view is possible. W. E. Barnes, II, 226, gives the unlikely view that the "virgins" represent "the cities of Judah which join in the festal celebrations."

[43]Rawlinson, I, 352, makes the attendants "symbolize the Gentile converts that should attach themselves to the original Church, and follow that Church into Christ's presence." Fausset, III, 199, is similar. In commenting at v. 8, he says that the "king's daughters are the secondary consorts; the queen is the consort of the first rank—viz., the Church of Israel, converted and re-united to her heavenly Bridegroom, and exalted to be the mother-church of Christendom." These views suggest that Gentiles will not be a part of the bride as she marries the Lord. The NT, however, makes no distinction between Jewish and Gentile converts. There is neither Jew nor Gentile in Christ, Gal. 3:28; Col. 3:11. All belong to the bride of Christ; cf. II Cor. 11:2; Eph. 5:25–27; Rev. 19:7–9.

[44]This detail is also difficult to fit into a direction application of the psalm to the Lord. There is no indication elsewhere in the Bible that children will continue to be born to the church as the bride of the Lord.

[45]Note 94 at 5:11 discusses the "name" of the Lord.

[46]*NIB*, IV, 862, refers the "I" to God and the "promise of sons [to] perpetuate the king's memory." The thought of everlasting praise more appropriately refers to praise of God.

PSALM 46

The unknown author of Psalm 46 designs it for "the chief musician" (*mᵉnaṣṣeaḥ*, see 4, intro.), indicating its intended use in Israel's worship. The author is one of "the sons of Korah."[47] The additional note "a song upon Alamoth [*ᶜᵃlamôt*]" gives musical direction (cf. I Chron. 15:20). The plural *ᶜᵃlamôt* refers to "maidens" and suggests that the psalm should be sung by a chorus of women or by soprano voices.[48]

We cannot identify the occasion for writing. The Lord has given some great victory to Israel.[49] This suggests one of several miraculous victories mentioned in the OT. The psalmist pens this psalm to commemorate this victory. The confident note the psalm strikes has made it a favorite of Christians.[50] The familiar portions of the psalm, its note of praise, and its practical teachings continue to bless believers. The word "selah" marks the divisions of the psalm.

I. The Confidence in God 1–3

1–3 Speaking on behalf of the nation, the psalmist acknowledges God as their "refuge and strength." This is the thought that led Martin Luther to write "A Mighty Fortress Is Our God."[51] In Him we find

---

[47]See the introduction to Pss. 42–43, which discusses this authorship.

[48]Sabourin, p. 13, understands *ᶜᵃlamôt* to refer to bass voices. From the derivation of the word, however, it more appropriately refers to higher voices. White, p. 24, suggests "(boy) sopranos, or viola." Thirtle, pp. 106–9, transfers the word to Ps. 45 and has the female choir sing that psalm. There is no compelling support for this view. A female choir may just as well have sung Ps. 46.

[49]Murphy, p. 287, places the psalm at "the war of David with Ammon and Aram," II Sam. 10. Delitzsch, II, 91, and Harman, p. 189, relate the victory to II Chron. 20, the record of Israel's victory over the combined forces of Moab, Ammon, and Edom. Clarke, I, 125, and Kissane, p. 202, suggest the victory of Israel over Sennacherib, II Kings 19:35. Some miraculous victory is in view (cf. vv. 1, 6, 7, 8, 9, 10, 11), but it is not possible to identify it with certainty. Cheyne, I, 206, tentatively suggests a postexilic time, but this is out of the time frame suggested by other Korahitic psalms.

[50]Among others, Henry, p. 410, and Albert Barnes, II, 39, mention that Martin Luther often suggested singing this psalm whenever he heard discouraging news.

[51]Greg C. Earwood, "Psalm 46," *ET* 86 (1989): 79, notes that Luther suffered from severe depression. He cites Kenneth Osbeck, *101 Hymn Stories* (Grand Rapids, Mich.: Kregel Publications, 1982), p. 15, which notes that "the first line of this national hymn of Protestant Germany is fittingly inscribed on the tomb of the great reformer at Wittenberg."

a place of "refuge" (*maḥseh*, see 14:6) as the storms of life swirl around us. We find help to face the "trouble" (*ṣarâ*, see 9:9) that life may bring, v. 1. There is therefore no need to fear when difficulties cause upheavals in the expected routine.[52] The psalmist poetically illustrates this with four vivid word pictures. The earth may "be removed" (or "changed") or mountains fall into the sea, v. 2. Storms may cause the waters to "roar and be troubled [or 'foam']."[53] Mountains may quake with "swelling" (or "tumult"). Even these should not bring fear. The word "Selah" draws attention to God's presence despite unusual conditions in nature, v. 3.

II. The Protection by God 4–7

4–5 The opening verses have drawn on calamitous changes in nature to illustrate the confidence in God that believers may have. The psalmist now introduces a much calmer scene from nature. The first phrase becomes clearer with the introduction of a relative pronoun: "There is a river whose streams make the city of God glad." The "city of God," Jerusalem, receives water from a stream flowing from Gihon, located outside of the city's walls. The stream flows under the city walls to the pool of Siloam (cf. Isa. 8:6).[54]

---

[52]The phrase "will not we fear" translates *lo᾽nîra᾽*. The use of *lo᾽* with the imperfect expresses an unconditional negative. This is the strongest possible way of making a negative statement. For those who trust God, it is not possible to fear since fear reflects an absence of trust. See G.K.C. 107 *o*.

[53]David Toshio Tsumura, "Twofold Image of Wine in Psalm 46:4–5," *JQR* LXXI:3 (1981): 169, understands a "twofold image of wine, which 'rages and foams' and 'gladdens' the (heart of) man, in order to describe the cosmic ocean." Tsumura relies on the association of *ḥmr* ("troubled") and *śmḥ* ("glad") with wine elsewhere, e.g., Ps. 104:15. The association proves nothing, however, since both words have other associations. In addition, nothing in the context suggests that the waters of vv. 3–4 are anything other than literal.

[54]Lawson, p. 245, identifies the "streams" as those that flow into Siloam but then makes the "river" flow "from the throne of God." Since the streams come from the river, it is better to identify the river as some underground source of water for Siloam. W. E. Barnes, II, 229, understands the river as "the Euphrates, representing the Assyrian power." When this is smitten into streams by the power of God, Jerusalem rejoices. Goldingay, p. 104, makes the river a symbol of the Lord's "unspectacular provision and protection of his people." Bratcher and Reyburn, p. 432, derive the figure of a river "from the river in the Garden of Eden" since "there was no river in the city of Jerusalem itself." They also say that the "waters suggest vitality and life, and they bring joy." *NIB*, IV, 866, sees the river as "metaphorical

The "city of God" receives its name from the presence of God there. It is the location of the "tabernacles [or 'dwelling place'] of the most High [*ᶜelyôn*, see 7:17]," the exalted God. The plural "tabernacles" is intensive, representing the dwelling of God, v. 4. Since He dwells "in the midst of her," nothing will "move" (better "overthrow") the city. God Himself will watch over her, even guarding her "right early." This phrase is lit. "at the turning of morning," a poetic description of the dawn, v. 5.

6–7 The "heathen rage" (or "the nations clamor"), the kingdoms "were moved" (or "shake"), and the earth itself melts before the power of God, v. 6. In sharp contrast, the Lord of "hosts" (*ṣᵉbaʾôt*, see 24:10), Who controls the armies of heaven and earth, is with His people. God, Who has established His covenant with Jacob, provides a "refuge" (*miśgab*, see 9:9) for His own. The word "Selah" draws attention to the protection that the Lord provides for Israel, v. 7.

III. The Exaltation of God 8–11

8–9 The thought moves beyond the present into the future. The Lord's deliverance in the psalmist's own time brings to mind the Lord's deliverance in the end time. The writer calls mankind to see what the Lord has done. He has brought "desolations" on the earth as He puts down the rebellion of man (cf. Rev. 19:15), v. 8. The Lord will make "wars to cease" throughout the earth during the millennial kingdom. The bow, the "spear" (*ḥᵃnît*, see 35:3), and the chariot, all weapons of warfare, will be done away with (cf. Isa. 2:4; Hos. 2:18; Zech. 9:10), v. 9.

10–11 The Lord now speaks directly.[55] He commands mankind to "be still" (*rapâ*, see 37:8). The *hipᶜîl* imperative here indicates something stronger than mere reflection on what God has said. It rather commands the nations to cease their strife and acknowledge Him.[56]

---

rather than geographical." It is "a life-giving stream." These views are subjective, resting on the creativity of the authors, not on the teaching of the psalm.

[55]The hymn "Be Still and Know," with the words and music by Ron Hamilton, © Majesty Music, 1989, takes its theme from v. 10.

[56]Anderson, I, 360, and Albert Barnes, II, 44, understand the command as directed to Israel. They should cease their efforts at gaining peace by war or treaty and instead depend wholly on the Lord. The context, however, refers to the nations rather than Israel.

He will be exalted among the heathen and the whole earth, v. 10. The author repeats v. 7. The Lord Who rules the "hosts" (*ṣ^e^ba'ôt*) of heaven and earth is with His people. The God of Jacob is their "refuge" (*miśgab*, see 9:9). The final "selah" calls upon the readers again to think on these things, v. 11.

PSALM 47

The psalm is by the "sons of Korah."[57] It is an *Enthronement Psalm* that praises God for His rule over the nations and for His choice of Israel for His own people. As such the psalm was appropriate for use in Israel's worship. To this end, the author writes it for the "chief musician" (*m^e^naṣṣeaḥ*, see 4, intro.). Nothing in the psalm lets us certainly locate its setting in Israel's history.[58] From its nature, the psalmist likely wrote it after some victory of Israel over the heathen. Both Israel and the church use the psalm in liturgy. Israel recites the psalm during their New Year festival in the month Tishri, either in September or October.[59] The high church recites the psalm on Ascension Sunday. These are appropriate days for offering praise to the Lord. It is also appropriate, however, to praise Him on other days, in fact, many times each day.

---

[57]See Pss. 42–43, 44, 45, 46, 47, 48, 49, 84, 85, 87, and 88. The introduction to Pss. 42–43 discusses the phrase "sons of Korah." Without arguing the point, Spurgeon, p. 223, makes David the author. Phillips, I, 371, assigns the psalm to Hezekiah.

[58]Rodd, p. 92, sets the psalm at the return of the ark of the covenant to Jerusalem, II Sam. 6:15. Jannie du Preeze, "Interpreting Psalm 47," *Missionalia* 25:33 (1997), p. 309, simply states that "one or more events during King David's reign might have led to the composition." Kissane, p. 205, finds the occasion at the defeat of the Assyrians during the reign of Hezekiah, II Kings 19:35. Alexander, p. 219, suggests "the victory of Jehoshaphat over the Ammonites and Edomites," II Chron. 20:14–26. This sampling shows the impossibility of setting the psalm's background with certainty.

[59]Cohen, p. 147, describes this: "The Psalm is recited in the Synagogue before the sounding of the *Shofar* (ram's horn) on the New Year."

I. Victory over the Nations 1–4

1–2 The psalmist urges the "people" (or "nations") of the world[60] to rejoice. They should "clap" their hands in rejoicing before their new king. They should "shout" (or "shout in triumph," *rûaᶜ*, see 41:11), and sound a "voice of triumph" (or "voice of joy," *rinnâ*, see 17:1), v. 1. The "most high" (*ᶜelyôn*, see 7:17) Lord is "terrible" (or "to be feared"), a great King Who rules over the whole earth. The statement introduces the millennial theme developed throughout the psalm, v. 2.

3–4 The psalmist now develops the theme of the Lord's conquest of the nations. He will subdue the people under Israel. The nations will be under their "feet,"[61] idiomatically showing Israel's dominion over the heathen. This will take place in the kingdom reign of Christ when Israel becomes the dominant nation in the earth, v. 3. The Lord chose Israel's inheritance, the land in which they dwell and from which they will lead the nations. The psalm writer emphasizes this with the closing "selah," v. 4.

II. Rule over the Nations 5–9

5–7 God has ascended His throne in Jerusalem[62] with a "shout" (or "shout of joy," *tᵉrûᶜâ*, see 27:6). He has risen with the sound of a "trumpet" (*šôpar*),[63] the music marking a time of joy, v. 5. The psalmist urges the people to rejoice. They should "sing praises" (*zamar*, see 7:17) to God their King, v. 6, and the King of all the earth. They should therefore "sing . . . praises" (*zamar*) to Him with "understand-

[60]Albert Barnes, II, 46, refers *ᶜammîm* to the Jews. When this word occurs in the plural elsewhere, however, it always refers to the nations of the world, e.g., 49:1; 96:3, 5. Dahood, I, 283, sees *ᶜammîm* as "heathen gods." There is no support elsewhere for this view.

[61]While not occurring often, this idiom does occur elsewhere in the Psalms, e.g., 8:6; 18:9, 38; 47:3; 91:13; 110:1.

[62]Among others, Murphy, p. 292, and Alexander, p. 220, understand this as the ascension of God into the heavens. He remains there until some new call for action moves Him to come to the earth to carry on His work. Leslie, p. 66, refers the phrase to the Lord's taking His presence in the holy of holies. Phillips, I, 374, makes the phrase refer "to the ascension of Christ to glory." The later verses in the psalm focus on the kingdom reign of the Lord. The thought here likely introduces His millennial rule.

[63]The *šôpar* was made from a ram's horn. The priests blew the *šôpar* at various times, including the time of war, Num. 10:9. It also signaled a time of rejoicing, II Kings 11:14; I Chron. 13:8.

ing" (*maśkîl*, see 32:1) as they consider His nature. The fivefold use of *zamar* in these verses emphasizes the need to praise the Lord in song, v. 7.

8–9 The psalmist now reveals the cause for rejoicing. God rules over the nations. He sits on His throne, dispensing decrees marked by holiness. The statement looks forward to the millennial kingdom, when the Lord rules the earth from Jerusalem, v. 8. The leaders of the nations now gather before the Lord. The second phrase, "the people of the God of Abraham," has no connecting word to 9*a*. The AV supplies the word "even" as though this group of leaders were from Israel. The connections with vv. 8 and 9*b* argue that these are from other nations of the world. They gather now *like* the people of Abraham, since the Lord gives the right to come into His presence. The "shields" (*magen*, see 3:3) of the earth, the defenses of the nations, have been placed under God's control.[64] He is greatly exalted, with both Gentiles and Jews claiming Him as their God, v. 9.

PSALM 48

As with the previous psalms in this section, the title names the "sons of Korah" as the authors.[65] The title mentions that this is a "song" (*šîr*, see 30, intro.) or "psalm" (*mizmôr*, see 3, intro.) for the sons of Korah" (or, "A Song. A Psalm for the sons of Korah").[66] The

[64]Phillips, I, 376, identifies the "shields" as representing the nations of the world. These "are arrayed around the temple walls." The view is speculative. Horne, p. 207, and Cohen, p. 148, see the "shields" as the princes of the nations. The view is possible and has the advantage of paralleling 9*a*. The LXX supports this view, translating as ἄρχοντες λαῶν, "rulers of the people." The word *magen*, however, normally refers to a literal shield or general defense, e.g., 7:10; 18:2, 30; 84:9, 11.

[65]See Pss. 42–43, 44, 45, 46, 47, 48, 49, 84, 85, 87, and 88. The introduction to Pss. 42–43 discusses the phrase "sons of Korah."

[66]Thirty-four psalms mention the word "song" in their title. These include Pss. 18, 30, 45, 46, 48, 65, 66, 67, 68, 75, 76, 83, 87, 88, 92, 96, 98, 108, 120, 121, 122, 123, 124, 125, 126, 127, 128, 129, 130, 131, 132, 133, 134, and 149. In the thirteen titles that include the simple phrase "a psalm or [or 'and'] song," or "a song or [or 'and'] psalm," the word "psalm" (*mizmôr*) refers to a song accompanied by musical instruments, while a "song" (*šîr*) is one performed by a choral group.

Jews chanted Psalm 48 in the temple worship on the second day of the week.[67]

The psalm is a song of praise. The author mentions no threat that would cause a lament. The song first praises Jerusalem, the nation's capital, and then closes by praising the Lord. This is an appropriate pattern: first praising what God has done, then praising God Himself. Verse 7 apparently refers to the breaking of Jehoshaphat's ships (I Kings 22:48).[68] This places the psalm later in Israel's history, c. 850 BC or after.

I. The Praise of Jerusalem 1–8

1–3 The psalmist extols the greatness of the Lord. He is worthy of praise in His city, Jerusalem, which is located in His holy mountain, Mt. Zion, v. 1.[69] It is beautiful "for situation" (better "in elevation")[70] and is the joy of the whole earth. The city of the great King is located in the heights, with its Temple Mount located on the north side of the

[67]*Tamid* 33*b*.

[68]Kidner, p. 180, relates the sinking of ships to Ezek. 27:26, which refers to the sinking of Tyre's treasure ships. Ezekiel, however, uses a metaphor, not a literal event, to portray the destruction of Tyre. Henry, III, 415, suggests the time of David for the writing. He sees the phrase as an illustration; the defeat of Israel's foes is like the breaking of ships with an east wind. Since the OT does not mention the breaking of ships in David's time, his reasoning is suspect. Rotherham, p. 222, locates it at the time of Sennacherib's defeat, II Kings 19:35, but deletes v. 7, an improbable solution. Phillips, I, 382, also dates the psalm at Assyria's defeat. The breaking of the ships is a poetic reference to the Assyrian invasion. The view requires water-based ships to picture Assyria's land-based army. Jennings, I, 220, makes the passage figurative of Israel's "proud and lofty" foes. There is no hint of this in the context.

[69]John Newton drew on vv. 1–2 in the hymn "Glorious Things of Thee Are Spoken." *Olney Hymns*, published in 1779, included this hymn.

[70]Anderson, I, 368, notes that the psalmist does not refer "so much to the actual height of Mount Zion," something over two thousand feet high. Its "theological significance" is great, however, since "it is here that, in a sense, heaven and earth meet." While Anderson's thought is devotional, nothing in the text indicates that we should take "elevation" in any way other than height. Calvin, II, 218, translates *nôp* as "situation." Michael L. Barré, "The Seven Epithets of Zion in Ps 48,2–3," *Biblica* 69:4 (1988): 562, refers *nôp* to the Egyptian city of Memphis, elsewhere called "Noph," e.g. Jer. 2:16; 44:1. It is unlikely that the psalmist would compare Jerusalem to a heathen city, elsewhere spoken of only in negative terms. The word *nôp* occurs only here. It is, however, related to cognate words and other words in the OT that have to do with height.

city, v. 2.[71] God "is known" (or "reveals Himself") in her palaces as a "refuge" (or "defense," *miśgab*, see 9:9), v. 3.

4–8 Although kings had assembled their armies, they completely passed by Jerusalem, v. 4. They saw the city but "marvelled" (or "were amazed") at it. They were "troubled [or 'dismayed,' *bahal*, see 2:5] and hasted away [or 'were alarmed']," v. 5. "Fear" (or "trembling") came on them. They knew pain like that of a woman in travail, v. 6. God had broken the "ships of Tarshish" in the time of Jehoshaphat with a fierce east wind. The phrase "ships of Tarshish" refers to ships built to carry ore to places where it was processed.[72] These were large ships, but the Lord showed His power by breaking them, v. 7.[73] Just as they have heard of God's power in breaking the ships, so they have seen His power to protect the city. It is the city of the Lord Who rules the "hosts" (*ṣᵉbaʾôt*, see 24:10) of heaven and earth. It is also the city of Israel's God, and He will therefore establish it forever. The psalmist emphasizes this thought by closing with "selah," v. 8.

II. The Praise of God 9–14

9–10 The psalmist has meditated on God's "lovingkindness" (or "steadfast love," *ḥesed*, see 5:7) while worshiping in the "temple"

---

[71]Alexander, p. 222, refers "the sides of the north" to the "northern division of the city," which joins with Zion, the southern part, to express the whole of the city. He also suggests that the "appearance of the Holy City" is elevated to an "army returning from the south." According to Kirkpatrick, p. 264, the heathen held that the gods dwelled in a sacred mountain in the north. "The Psalmist boldly calls Mount Zion *the uttermost parts of the north* with reference to this mythological idea." *NIB*, IV, 872, follows the NIV in expressing the same idea. As with *nôp* earlier, it is unlikely that the author illustrates God's dwelling by referring to a heathen idea.

[72]Kissane, p. 210, locates Tarshish at Tartessus in Spain. Although Tarshish was a place, Isa. 23:6; 66:19, the phrase "ships of Tarshish" refers to the purpose of the ships. The name likely came from ships built to carry ore from Tarshish. Later, however, it applied to ore ships in general. The use of the phrase elsewhere argues that Tarshish is not a destination but rather a type of ship. I Kings 22:48 (II Chron. 20:36) says the ships were built at Ezion-geber, on the Gulf of Aqaba. It would be well nigh impossible for ships built there to sail to Spain or Cilicia. On the other hand, ships of Tarshish would dock at Tyre after sailing on the Mediterranean and therefore grieve at its judgment, Isa. 23:1, 14. The existence of these ships in two separate bodies of water argues that the phrase "ships of Tarshish" does not refer to a location.

[73]Delitzsch, II, 105, and Moll, p. 308, understand "ships of Tarshish" as a figure for the world powers that come against Jerusalem. The view spiritualizes the text.

(*hêkal*, see 5:7), v. 9. He concludes that God's "name," referring to His nature as revealed to man,[74] demands worldwide praise. As an example of God's nature, the psalmist notes that His hand is filled with righteousness. This implies that the Lord is ready to direct His righteous actions to those who follow Him and to dispense justice upon those who oppose Him, v. 10.

11–14 Mt. Zion and the "daughters of Judah," her inhabitants, should rejoice because of the "judgments" of God on their enemies, v. 11. As they walk about Jerusalem, they should "tell" (or "count") the towers of the city, v. 12. They should note her "bulwarks" (or "ramparts") and her "palaces" (or "citadels"). They should tell their children of this preservation as evidence of God's goodness to the nation, v. 13. They will follow this God forever, letting Him guide them "unto death" (*ᶜal-mût*), the time when they die, v. 14.[75]

PSALM 49

Psalm 49 is a wisdom (or didactic) psalm, speaking to men rather than to God. It teaches that riches cannot bring salvation. The presence of this practical theme so early in the OT shows the wisdom that the Holy Spirit imparts to God's people. The theme is totally spiritual, contrary to the selfishness that marks the natural man. The "psalm" (*mizmôr*, see 3, intro.) is by one of the "sons of Korah."[76] The author prepares it for "the chief Musician" (*mᵉnaṣṣeaḥ*, see 4,

---

[74]There is a summary of God's "name" at 5:11, note 94.

[75]Since the psalm deals with national matters, some find the thought of individual death out of place. Delitzsch, II, 107, understands the phrase "unto death" as "a marginal note of the melody," similar to that in Ps. 9. It is highly unusual, however, to find the tune at the end of a psalm. Delitzsch suggests the possibility that it belongs to the following psalm. There is no evidence for this. Fausset, III, 205, understands *ᶜal-mût* as "over death," parallel to "for ever and ever" and therefore referring to eternity. He mars his interpretation by making Israel represent the church. The view is possible, although *ᶜal-mût* would be an unusual way to refer to eternity. The LXX and Vulgate joined the consonants and revocalized them to *ᶜolamôt*, "evermore." This form, however, does not occur elsewhere in the OT.

[76]See also Pss. 42–43, 44, 45, 46, 47, 48, 84, 85, 87, 88. The introduction to Pss. 42–43 discusses the phrase "sons of Korah."

intro.) for unspecified use in the temple worship. Like most psalms, it does not indicate the date or the background to its writing. The psalm divides naturally into two parts, both ending with a similar statement.

I. The Weakness of Wealth 1–12

1–4 The opening paragraph introduces the psalm without giving its theme. The psalmist calls upon "all ye people" and "all ye inhabitants of the world [*ḥeled*, see 17:14]."[77] With this, he draws the attention to all mankind, necessary since he will later develop a theme that is true with both Jews and Gentiles, v. 1. His call includes various classes of mankind—those who are "low and high" (*gam-bᵉnê ʾadam gam-bᵉnê ʾîš*)[78] as well as the "rich and poor" in material goods, v. 2.

The psalmist will speak of "wisdom" (*ḥokmâ*, see 19:7), and his heart will meditate on "understanding" (*tᵉbûnâ*).[79] Both words are intensive plurals that refer to spiritual truths, v. 3. The writer will listen intently to a "parable" (or "proverb," *mašal*, see 44:14), instruction of some kind. He will "open" (or "display, express") his "dark saying" (*ḥîdâ*)[80] with a "harp" (or "lyre," *kinnôr*, see 33:2), v. 4.

5–6 The psalmist asks rhetorically if there is any reason to fear in "the days of evil," that time when wealthy and powerful men oppress him. This is the time, he says, when "the iniquity of my heels [*ʿaqeb*, better 'of my foes']"[81] shall compass me about," v. 5. He now introduces the nature of his enemies. They are wealthy individuals who trust their riches to give them what they desire, v. 6.

---

[77]The word *ḥeled* relates to a place where activity begins and ends and thus a transitory world where things pass away. This sets the stage for the psalm.

[78]See note 312 at Ps. 22:6.

[79]The word *tᵉbûnâ* has to do with "discernment, perception, understanding." The word relates to making wise choices between different options, often between good and evil.

[80]The *ḥîdâ* is a riddle, an enigma, or a difficult matter to comprehend. This refers here to the theme of wealth dealt with in the psalm. The author has composed a melody to which he will sing his observations on wealth. With the psalm dedicated to the "chief Musician," the psalmist also looks forward to the time when the melody will be sung publicly to others.

[81]The word *ʿaqeb* refers to a "heel catcher" (Gen. 27:36; Hos. 12:3). Jacob illustrated this by trying to take his brother's place. With this sense, the psalmist's foes are deceivers who try to turn others against him.

7–10 Wealth, however, can never purchase spiritual blessings. The psalmist illustrates this by pointing out that no one can "redeem [*padâ*, see 25:22] his brother [*ʾaḥ*, another man]."[82] The phrase "by any means redeem" repeats the root *padâ* and emphasizes man's inability to redeem others. He cannot "ransom" (*koper*) them from God, v. 7.[83] The redemption of the soul is "precious" (or "costly"). The wealthy person should forever cease from trying to gain it with his material resources (cf. I Pet. 1:18–19), v. 8. Verse 9 parenthetically states the results of purchasing redemption. The person would live forever and not see "corruption" (better "the pit," i.e., the grave, *šaḥat*, see 7:15). This, of course, is unthinkable, v. 9. All men die—the "wise" (see *ḥokmâ*, 19:7), the "fool" (*kᵉsîl*), the "brutish" (*baᶜar*)[84] "perish" (*ʾabad*, see 1:6)—and leave their riches to others, v. 10.

11–12 Men act as though they would live forever. Their "inward thought" is of continued life through "their houses," their descendants. These descendants will continue to occupy "dwelling places" for "all generations" (*lᵉdor wador*, see 10:6) to come. Men give their names to lands to perpetuate their memories, v. 11.[85] All this is to no avail. Despite the honor a man may achieve in this life, he "abideth [*lîn*, see 25:13] not."[86] His life is relatively short. He is no better than the animals that are cut off from life. All will die, v. 12.

---

[82]Rawlinson, I, 378, accepts reading *ʾak* for *ʾaḥ*, and says that "'brother' is not used in the Psalms in the sense of 'fellow-man.'" There is only weak textual evidence for the change. In addition, 22:22; 122:8; and 133:1 support the sense of kinsmen, i.e., Israelites.

[83]The verbs *padâ* and *koper* are two of the great OT theological words relating to salvation. The word *padâ* describes the transfer of ownership upon the payment of a price, while *koper* refers to atonement by means of a substitutionary offering. The combination of the two words here shows the absolute impossibility of purchasing redemption. It is a gift, not something to be gained by wealth.

[84]The *kᵉsîl* refers to a person who makes foolish choices. Often, this is a moral fool, one who has gone deep into sin. The *baᶜar* is more of a stupid person or one who is dull to spiritual things. Because of this, he may also follow sinful pursuits. The emphasis here is not particularly on the spiritual. It is rather that all die.

[85]Mark S. Smith, "The Invocation of Deceased Ancestors in Psalm 49:12c," *JBL* 112:1 (1993): 107, argues that the phrase *qarʾû bišmôtam* "refers to the practice of invoking names of deceased ancestors." He cites nonbiblical evidence together with an unlikely interpretation of Ps. 16:3–4. Although the view describes the actions of the wicked, it has little to commend it.

[86]Judah Jacob Slotki, "Psalm XLIX 13, 21 (AV 12, 20)," *VT* 28:3 (1978): 361, adds the additional words from v. 21 and derives *yalîn* from *lwn*, "complain." He translates, "Man is [as] cattle and does not complain." There is no support, however,

II. The Conquest of Death 13–20

13 The men who follow the path described in vv. 7–12 are following the way of "folly" (*kesel*, see *kᵉsîl*, v. 10). Because they trust in their material wealth to supply their spiritual needs, this is indeed a foolish way. Despite this, their "posterity" (or "those who follow after"), either their descendants or others who follow their leadership, "approve" (or "delight in," *raṣâ*, see 40:13) what they say. To draw attention to the foolishness of their path, the psalmist adds the word "selah," v. 13.

14–15 The hymn writer compares these fools to sheep, animals with little common sense that simply graze with no concern for the danger about them. In the same way, these fools pass through life until they wind up in the "grave" (*šᵉʾôl*, see 6:5). Like a wild animal, "death" shall "feed" (*raᶜâ*)[87] upon these fools. The "upright," who have placed their faith in the Lord for deliverance from sin, will "have dominion" (*radâ*)[88] over this class of people in the resurrection morning (Dan. 12:2).[89] The "grave" (*šᵉʾôl*) will "consume" (or "wear out") the "beauty" (or "form," *ṣîr*) of these who trust in riches. This will take place away from their "dwelling" (*zᵉbul*, or "mansion"),[90] v. 14. The psalmist, however, has reason for confidence in the Lord. God will "redeem" (*padâ*, see 25:22) his soul from the power of the "grave" (*šᵉʾôl*). Death will not have power to consume his body; rather,

---

for reading the additional words of v. 21 in v. 13. The root *lwn* does not occur elsewhere in the Psalms. It is found elsewhere only in the early historical books.

[87]Albert Barnes, II, 64, translates *raᶜâ* as "pasture" and Rodd, p. 96, as "shepherd." Death watches over these wicked. While the translation "pasture" or "shepherd" is possible, this figure of Death goes against the OT picture of the shepherd as one who cares for his flock. The psalmist personifies death here as in Job 18:14, "the king of terrors." The OT associates the shepherd with the provision and protection of his flocks. A good shepherd provides these; cf. John 10:10*b*, 11, 14, 15, 27, 28. An evil shepherd fails to provide these and thus abandons the sheep to their own ignorance; cf. John 10:12, 13.

[88]The verb *radâ* means "rule, have dominion." During the millennial kingdom, the righteous will have dominion over those who refuse the salvation offered by Jesus Christ.

[89]Kirkpatrick, p. 273 and Leupold, p. 385, make this the morning of the day after the judgment of the ungodly. This deliverance, however, takes place after the Resurrection when the ungodly are judged and the righteous rule with the Lord; cf. I Cor. 6:2.

[90]The word *zᵉbul* carries with it the sense of an exalted dwelling. For this reason, I relate it to their dwelling place, a "mansion," rather than to the body.

the Lord will "receive" (better "take") him in the Resurrection. Once more, the word "selah" calls attention to the thought just expressed, v. 15.

16–20 The psalmist now summarizes what he has expressed in vv. 1–15. There is no need to fear the rich when he increases the splendor of his house, v. 16. It is temporary. When the rich man dies, he can take none of his glory with him. He will "descend" into the grave, but his wealth will remain behind, v. 17. While he lived, he "blessed [*barak*, see 5:12] his soul," thought well of himself, was proud of his accomplishments; cf. Luke 12:19. The psalmist parenthetically adds that others may praise you when you do well, v. 18. But "he," referring to the rich man's soul, will join his fathers in the grave. There, they will "never see light." In this context, not seeing "light" represents the lack of God's favor and blessing rather than literal darkness; con. 4:6; 89:15; 97:11, v. 19. The author of the psalm repeats the thought of v. 12 with an important qualification. It is not merely man's "honour" that brings lasting destruction. It is the honor of one who "understandeth not," who has no spiritual understanding, that brings continuing death. All men die, but some have the hope of resurrection and the blessing of God. One who dies without "understanding" has no more future than the animal that dies, v. 20.[91]

PSALM 50

This is the first of twelve psalms (50, 73–83) written by Asaph or his descendants.[92] David appointed Asaph to the position of chief musician (I Chron. 16:5). He was both a singer and an instrumentalist (I Chron. 15:19; 16:5). His family was musical; many of his sons

[91]Paul R. Raabe, "Deliberate Ambiguity in the Psalter," *JBL* 110:2 (1991): 216, translates the final phrase as "like the beasts that are dumb [*nidmû*]." He calls this "a classic case of antanaclasis, where a word is repeated [from v. 12] with a shift in meaning." The root *rmh* in the *nipᶜal*, however, routinely refers to perishing. In Isa. 15:1, where the AV reads "silence," the word is better translated "cut off."

[92]According to *Sukkah* 55*a*, the priests sang Ps. 50 on the second day of Tabernacles.

also became temple musicians (I Chron. 25:1–2). His songs were still being performed at the temple in the days of Hezekiah, and others recognized him as having had a prophetic gift (II Chron. 29:30).

The psalm is unusual in that it mainly presents the words of the Lord to the people rather than those of the psalmist. This may be a literary device meant to call the nation back to a sincere worship of God. It may also be a revelation God made to Asaph or David. Whatever the background,[93] the psalm serves a practical purpose in its spiritual challenge to its readers.

I. The Appearance of God 1–6

1–4 A triple name for God introduces the psalm: *ʾel ʾᵉlohîm yᵉhwah*, "the mighty One, God, the Lord." This combination emphasizes God's power and thus His position above all other beings that might be worshiped. It also stresses the interaction of God with His people. Both of these thoughts are necessary in a psalm that deals with the worship of the people. God has spoken to summon the earth forth in its daily motion. The "rising of the sun" is its dawning in the east and the "going down" its setting in the west; cf. 113:3, v. 1. This mighty God has shined His light upon His people in Zion, a place "perfect in beauty" because of His presence there, v. 2. He will come openly to His people, not hiding Himself behind a wall of silence. He will consume His enemies with judgment, making His presence "tempestuous" (or "stormy"), v. 3. He will call the heavens above and the earth beneath, witnesses to all that goes on among men, "that he may judge his people" (better "to judge His people"), v. 4.

5–6 God calls upon the "saints" (or "loyal ones," *ḥasîd*, see 4:3), those who have made a covenant with Him by sacrifice, to gather before Him, v. 5.[94] The heavens will declare His righteousness and,

---

[93]Clarke, I, 134, connects the psalm with David's returning the ark to Jerusalem. Rotherham, p. 232, dates it during Hezekiah's reign. Ewald, I, 311, places it during Josiah's rule. Kirkpatrick, p. 277, places it in the eighth century BC, during the ministries of Isaiah, Micah, and Hosea. Cheyne, I, 224, views it as postexilic. The psalm does not give enough information to date it clearly. Since we have no postexilic information about the family of Asaph, it is best to make the psalm early rather than late. The warnings of judgment, vv. 3, 15, 21–22, the mention of sacrifice in the temple, vv. 5, 8, 14, and of Zion, "the perfection of beauty," v. 2, support an early date.

[94]Perowne, I, 406, views the call as going forth to all Israel, not particularly godly Israel, since the Lord made His covenant with the nation. The word *ḥasîd*, however,

therefore, His qualification as judge of the earth.[95] Asaph emphasizes this thought by adding the word "selah," v. 6.

II. The Sufficiency of God 7–15

7–11 God calls on Israel to hear Him as He testifies against them. From what follows, we see that Israel's view of worship was wrong. God is indeed their God, v. 7. He does not correct them for making animal sacrifices and continual burnt offerings. They brought these in their worship, v. 8, but it was not as if God needed these sacrifices. He will not take a young bull or male goats from them, v. 9, since every wild "beast" (*ḥay*) and all "cattle" (or "domestic animals," *behemât*)[96] belong to Him, v. 10.[97] He knows the birds in the mountains, away from the vision of men, and the "wild beasts" (or "creatures of the field," *zîz*)[98] in the field, likewise hidden from man's view, v. 11.

12–15 If God were hungry, He would not reveal this to men. There would be no need to do so since He owns all that is in the world, v. 12. Rhetorically, He asks if He needs to eat the flesh of bulls or drink the blood of male goats. These were the animals often given in sacrifice. The obvious answer to the question is no, v. 13. God does not need these sacrifices. The sacrifices were for Israel's good,

---

describes loyal individuals. The idea of a covenant must refer to those who have sincerely entered into a covenant with God.

[95]Moll, p. 319, and Horne, p. 217, understand the "heavens" as angels who testify to the justice of God's judgment. The OT does not give a record of angels testifying to the justice of God. It is just as likely that the "heavens" here and the "heavens" and "earth" in v. 4 idiomatically refer to Creation's witness to God's power and therefore His ability to know truth.

[96]While neither *ḥay* nor *behemât* are specific to wild and domestic animals, this is generally their sense when the words occur together.

[97]The hymn sung so often by children, "He Owns the Cattle on a Thousand Hills," with words and music by John W. Peterson, © John W. Peterson Music Co., 1976, comes from v. 10.

[98]The word *zîz* occurs only two times in Psalms, here and 80:13. In both places, it refers to the small life of the fields, including insects. The Akkadian word *zīzāni*, "locusts," supports this. Richard Whitekettle, "Bugs, Bunny, or Boar? Identifying the *Zîz* Animals of Psalms 50 and 80," *Catholic Biblical Quarterly* 67:2 (2005): 250–64, gives an impressive argument to show that *zîz* refers to "small herbivorous terrestrial animals." The psalmist thus brings four groups together: wild beasts, domesticated animals, flying animals, and insignificant animals. God knows and owns each of these.

bringing them into favor with God. They should continue to show God their "thanksgiving" (*tôdâ*, see 26:7) by making offerings and to express their trust in the "most High" (*ᶜelyôn*, see 7:17) by making vow offerings, v. 14. In their times of "trouble" (*ṣarâ*, see 9:9) they should call on God. He will deliver them, and they should respond by giving Him glory, v. 15.

III. The Rebuke from God 16–23

16–17 God now reproves the wicked of the nation. What right did they have to declare His statutes? Why did they think that they could speak about the covenant with God? Clearly, they did not have this right. Note that these were religious without worshiping God sincerely (cf. Matt. 7:21–23), v. 16. They "hate[d]" (*śaneʾ*, see 5:5) the instruction that corrected their actions. They cast away God's words behind them, in a sense placing them where they would not see their reproof. These verses deal generally with the first part of the law, man's relationship with God, v. 17.

18–21 Asaph gives examples of the behavior of the wicked. He takes these from the second part of the law, man's relationship with other men. They "consented" (or "delighted," *raṣâ*, see 40:13) with others in their thievery, a violation of the eighth commandment. They had entered into adulterous activities, breaking the seventh commandment, v. 18. They had spoken "evil," further explained as deceitful words, forbidden by the ninth commandment, v. 19. They had spoken against their own brothers, slandering them, also breaking the ninth commandment, v. 20. God had let them go on in their wickedness, keeping silent and giving them time to repent. Instead, they concluded that God was as they were, not caring about wicked behavior. Now, however, He will reprove them. He will arrange their wicked actions openly before them, v. 21.

22–23 "God" (*ʾělôah*, see 18:31) urges those who have forgotten Him to consider the coming judgment. Otherwise, He will "tear [them] to pieces," a metaphorical picture of the sentence against them, v. 22. He holds out hope. Those who offer God "praise" (or "thanksgiving," *tôdâ*) give Him glory. The final phrase is better "And he makes a way so *that* I will show him the salvation of God." Men may continue in their wickedness and suffer the judgment of God, or they may give glory to God and experience His salvation. The choice is clear, v. 23.

PSALM 51

This "Pauline Psalm"[99] is the counterpart to Psalm 32. Both psalms recall David's sin with Bathsheba and his subsequent murder of Uriah. David writes Psalm 51 shortly after Nathan points out his sin.[100] He writes Psalm 32 later, after reflecting on the gracious forgiveness of God. Because of our knowledge of David's sin and following conduct, this psalm ranks as the greatest example of a penitential psalm. We can feel David's pain as he grieves over his sin, but we can also experience his devotion as he pledges renewed zeal in serving the Lord.

The title relates the psalm to II Samuel 11. David had entered into an adulterous relationship with Bathsheba while her husband was fighting with David's army. When Bathsheba conceived, David sent for Uriah, hoping that he would enter into normal conjugal relations with Bathsheba. Uriah, however, would not accept privileges forbidden to his fellow soldiers. David then wrote instructions to Joab, his general, to place Uriah where he would die in battle. Uriah carried his own death warrant back to the army. After Uriah's death, David took Bathsheba as his wife.

The Lord did not let David cover his sin. He sent Nathan the prophet to David to accuse David of his sin. David repented of his sin, II Samuel 12:13, but there were still consequences to his actions. The child died, and David experienced the emotions described in Psalms 32 and 51. Together, these penitential psalms give us valuable

---

[99]See the introduction to Ps. 32.

[100]Buttenwieser, p. 192, rejects David's authorship on the ground that David was not capable of such spiritual depth as is shown in the psalm. His view is subjective and not acceptable. The man "after [God's] own heart," Acts 13:22, with whom God entered into covenant, II Sam. 7:12–16, certainly possessed spiritual sensitivity. Crenshaw, p. 17, asserts that v. 18 "rules out Davidic authorship" since Jerusalem's walls were not broken until "after 587 BCE." II Sam. 5:9, however, shows that David built inside the city. This may well have included repairs or extensions of the walls.

teaching regarding the consequences of sin and the gracious forgiveness of the Lord.[101] David plans for the "chief musician" (*m^e^naṣṣeaḥ*, see 4, intro.) to use the psalm with the tabernacle worship.

I. Confession of Sin 1–6

1 David pleads for "mercy" (or "grace," *ḥanan*, see 4:1) from God. David prays to "Elohim," the name showing God's might, rather than to "Jehovah," the name by which God extends forgiveness to His people. With this, David recognizes God's power to judge him. Even though David occupies the exalted position of Israel's king, he does not rely on his authority and prestige to stand against the God of power.

David bases his confession on God's "lovingkindness" (or "steadfast love," *ḥesed*, see 5:7), i.e., His loyalty to the covenant with David, and His "tender mercies" (*raḥam*, or "compassion," see 18:1). The confession recognizes the relationship between David and the Lord as well as the compassionate nature of God. The plural noun "compassion" intensifies David's description of God's nature. David prays that God would "blot out" his transgressions, making them as though they did not exist. The plural "transgressions" includes his sins of adultery, murder, and failure to fulfill his responsibility as king of setting a godly example before the people, v. 1.

2–3 David asks God to "wash" (*kabas*) him from his "iniquity" (*ᶜawon*, see 18:23) and to "cleanse" (*ṭaher*)[102] him from his "sin" (*ḥaṭṭaʾt*). David asks to be "throughly" (better "thoroughly") washed, lit. "Multiply my washing," as though he needs repeated washing to be clean. These words express his desire to be brought back into fellowship with the Lord in order to worship Him properly, v. 2. David "acknowledge[s]" (*yadaᶜ*, see 1:6) his "transgressions" (*pešaᶜ*, see 5:10) and "sin" (*ḥaṭṭaʾt*, see 4:4). He does not minimize what he has done. His use of *ᶜawon*, *ḥaṭṭaʾt*, and *pešaᶜ* describes his wickedness from every angle. The word *ᶜawon* describes a twisting, distortion, or perversion of a standard. The word *ḥaṭṭaʾt* refers to falling short

[101]The penitential psalms include 6, 32, 38, 51, 102, 130, and 143.

[102]The verb *kabas* never refers to washing the body. It occurs with the washing of filthy clothes, and normally relates to ceremonial cleansing, e.g., Lev. 16:26, 28. The verb *ṭaher* usually refers to moral or ritual cleansing. In the Psalms, it occurs only here and in v. 7.

or missing a mark, in this case the mark of the righteousness desired by the Lord. The final word, *pešaᶜ*, carries a sense of rebellion. It is no wonder that David's sins were "ever before" him. Psalm 32:3–4 describes the conviction that David felt for his sins. The wicked may sin without conviction, but the righteous feel keenly their failure in God's sight, v. 3.

4–6 David is theologically correct in saying, "Against thee, thee only, have I sinned." One person does not have the right to set standards for another person except as God has given that right, e.g., parent-child, husband-wife, employer-employee, lawful government–citizen. Since God is man's Creator, He has the right to set moral standards. Sin therefore is fundamentally against God. David had committed adultery, he had ordered the murder of Uriah and his companions, and he had failed to provide a moral example and leadership for the nation. But his sin was against God.

David confesses his evil actions so that there would be no question of God's right to bring judgment upon him. Paul quotes this verse in Romans 3:4 as he shows God's righteousness in judging sin, v. 4. David recognizes his sinful nature, cf. 58:3; Job 14:4. The statement does not justify his sin. It rather shows that David recognizes the completeness of his sin nature. He has been sinful from his birth, v. 5.[103] The Lord, however, "desire[s]" (or "delights in," *ḥapeṣ*, see 18:19) inward truth. For this reason, He will cause David to experientially "know" (*yadaᶜ*, see 1:6) the "wisdom" (*ḥokmâ*, see 19:7) that will let him overcome temptation in the future, v. 6.

II. Plea for Forgiveness 7–12

7 David prays for cleansing. Hyssop is a fragrant member of the mint family, and the priests used it in the ceremonial sprinkling of blood (Exod. 12:22; Lev. 14:6–7, 51–52; cf. Heb. 9:19–22) or sprinkling of water (Num. 19:17–19). The association with cleansing lets David say, "Purge me [*piᶜel* of *ḥaṭaʾ*] with hyssop." While the

[103]J. K. Zink, "Uncleanness and Sin: A Study of Job XIV 4 and Psalm LI 7," *VT* 17:3 (1967): 361, refers David's statement to his "concern about cultic impurity." While it is true that women were considered unclean after the birth process, David's confession goes far beyond the statement of v. 5. Verses 2, 3, 4, and 9 make clear statements regarding his sin. Verses 1, 7, 8, 10, 11, 12, and 14 show David's desire for forgiveness and cleanings. This concerns more than mere "cultic impurity."

word *ḥaṭa᾽* is normally translated "sin," the *pi῾el* of *ḥaṭa᾽* refers to cleansing. This will leave David ceremonially clean. David's parallel request is even more picturesque. If the Lord will "wash" (*kabas*, see v. 2) him, he will become "whiter than snow," idiomatic for utmost purity (cf. Isa. 1:18; Dan. 12:10), v. 7.[104]

8–9 David has already mentioned the conviction of sin he had been carrying, v. 3. He now asks God to restore "joy and gladness." His "bones," idiomatic for his body (cf. 6:2; Job 20:11), have been "broken" (*dakâ*, or "crushed," see 9:9), but God's forgiveness will bring "rejoicing," v. 8. David repeats his request that God forgive his sins. The prayer for God to hide His face is a prayer that He will not look upon his sin in judgment. David prays that God will "blot" the sins (cf. Isa. 44:22). God must either blot out sin from a life or blot out that person's name from the Book of Life (Exod. 32:33; Ps. 69:28; Rev. 3:5; 22:19), v. 9.

10–12 David now makes a positive request. He asks God to "create" (*bara᾽*)[105] a clean heart. The verb *bara᾽* implies that a heart with this nature did not exist before. This verb is appropriate here since only God can create a clean heart. Man may change his habits, but his heart will still be wicked. In addition, David asks God to renew a "right spirit," i.e., a morally steadfast and consistent spirit in him, v. 10.[106]

David longs for renewed fellowship with the Lord. He approaches this both positively and negatively in vv. 11–12. He asks the Lord not to cast him away from His presence, where he would not enjoy fellowship with Him. The clearest example of one cast from the presence of God is Saul (I Sam. 16:1, 14; cf. II Kings 17:18; 23:27; I Chron. 28:9). David has known the guidance of the Spirit in the past (I Sam. 16:13). Knowing the effect that sin has on the Holy Spirit (Eph. 4:30; I Thess. 5:19), David prays that God would not

---

[104]In 1872, James L. Nicholson based the words to the hymn "Whiter than Snow" on the verse. The music is by William Gustavus Fischer.

[105]The verb *bara᾽* refers bringing something into existence that did not exist before. When the verb occurs in the *qal*, God is always the subject.

[106]The verse is the basis for at least two well-known hymns: "O for a Heart to Praise My God," with the words by Charles Wesley in 1742 and set to music by an anonymous writer, and "Create in Me a Clean Heart" with the words and music by Mac Lynch, © Majesty Music, 1983.

withdraw His Spirit from him, v. 11.[107] Positively, he asks that God would restore the joy that comes from "salvation," deliverance from his sins.[108] He further asks that God would sustain him by His "free" (or "willing") Spirit, v. 12.[109]

III. Dedication to Service 13–19

13–15 David recognizes that forgiveness carries responsibility with it. He pledges faithful service. He will teach others God's ways. He anticipates that this will cause sinners to "be converted" (or "turn back") to God, v. 13. For the first time, David mentions his sin specifically. He asks God to deliver him from the results of his "bloodguiltiness" (lit. "bloods"), the murder of Uriah and the other soldiers. This will let him "sing aloud" (*ranan*, see 5:11), openly praising God for His "righteousness." David thinks of "righteousness" as the Lord's faithfulness to forgive those who sincerely repent of their sins, v. 14. For the first time in the psalm, David refers to God as "the Lord." The name here, however, is *ʾadonay* (see 8:1), a title that refers to God as the "Master." This word is a plural of majesty. David asks the Lord to guide his speech so that he may praise Him, v. 15.

16–17 David senses that God "desires" (*ḥapeṣ*, see 18:19) no ritual sacrifice for his sin; cf. Matthew 9:13. He acknowledges to God, "Thou delightest [*raṣâ*, see 40:13] not" in the mere making of a "burnt-offering," v. 16.[110] David correctly sees that God wants sin-

---

[107]W. Creighton Marlowe, "Spirit of Your Holiness" (רוּח דשְׁךָ) in Psalm 51:13," *TJ* ns 19 (1998): 30, understands "spirit" as "the inner presence of a spiritual power." His translation, "spirit of your holiness," is grammatically possible. But the phrase, *rûaḥ qodeš* + a pronoun, occurs only here and at Isa. 63:10, 11, where it clearly refers to the Holy Spirit. For this reason, I support the above view.

[108]*Yoma 22b* reads into David's statement the idea that he "was stricken with leprosy" for six months. Nothing in v. 12 supports this view.

[109]Among others, Murphy, p. 309, and Clarke, I, 139, understand the "spirit" here as David's own spirit. While the view is possible, the parallelism with v. 11 favors understanding the Holy Spirit here.

[110]Rawlinson, I, 396, suggests that there were no sacrifices for adultery or murder. Had such sacrifices existed, David would have offered them. There are three problems with the view. First, Lev. 19:20–22 does give a sacrifice for some guilty of adultery. Second, while David considered himself a murderer, he had not actually killed anyone. The law regarding murderers does not consider such a case. Third, there were many sins for which the OT mentions no sacrifice. Sin and trespass offerings were available for any sin if they were sincerely offered. The teaching of the OT

cere repentance. God will not despise a "broken" (*šabar*, see 3:7) or a "contrite" (*dakâ*, or "crushed," see 9:9) spirit.[111] The Lord concerns Himself with the inward attitude toward sin more than with external actions (cf. Isa. 57:15; 66:1–2), v. 17.

18–19 It is likely that David's sin had affected the nation. He now not only pledges his personal dedication to God but also anticipates the nation's sincere worship of God.[112] He asks God to bless the nation by letting him complete his building the walls of Jerusalem.[113] Though the OT does not emphasize David's building projects in Jerusalem, Josephus says, "David . . . rebuilt Jerusalem . . . [and] made buildings round about the lower city; he also joined the citadel to it, and made it one body; and when he had encompassed all with walls, he appointed Joab to take care of them," v. 18.[114] The security of the city will let the people offer their sacrifices of praise from righteous hearts. They will offer "burnt offering and whole burnt offering [*kalîl*]."[115] The bullock was an offering for those in prominent positions (e.g., Lev. 4:3–5), for the community as a whole (e.g., Lev. 4:13–14), or for special occasions (e.g., Num. 29:20, 36). David envisions here a time when the city will make special offerings to

gives principles for worship without covering every conceivable sin that needed to be forgiven.

[111]The hymn "O Hope of Every Contrite Heart," later expanded into "Jesus, the Very Thought of Thee," draws on this verse. Bernard of Clairvaux wrote the words in the twelfth century. Edward Caswall translated it in 1849. The melody, ST. AGNES, comes from John B. Dykes, 1866.

[112]Cheyne, I, 231, and Rodd, p. 102, suggest that a later scribe added vv. 18–19. The view is speculative. The similarity of v. 7 to Isa. 1:18 and of v. 16 to Isa. 57:15 may suggest that Isaiah, who wrote after David, was familiar with the psalm. But there is nothing in these verses that does not fit into David's reign.

[113]Albert Barnes, II, 92, mentions the possibility that this is "figurative language—a prayer that God would favour and bless his people as if the city was to be protected by walls." While this is possible, the view is subjective, resting on the opinion of the interpreter. As king, David wanted a safe capital city.

[114]*Antiquities*, 7.3.2.

[115]The phrase "whole burnt offering" translates the single word *kalîl*, "entire, whole, complete." Standing in apposition to *ᶜôlâ*, "burnt offering," the word is rightly interpreted as "whole burnt offering." David may have had in mind the actions of Samuel's sons, who took for themselves part of the sacrifices meant for God, I Sam. 2:13–16. Rawlinson, I, 396, says, "Only the head, the fat, and certain portions of the interior were ordinarily burnt when a victim was offered." This was true with other sacrifices. With the burnt offering, however, the priest burned the entire animal on the altar, Lev. 1:3–17, picturing the complete dedication of the offerer to the Lord.

God in expressing devotion to Him. The Lord will then be "pleased" (*ḥapeṣ*), v. 19.

PSALM 52

The title of the psalm gives us the purpose, the author, and the background for its writing. It is a "Maschil" (*maśkîl*, see 32, intro.). David memorializes the historical event behind the psalm by assigning it to the "chief musician" (*mᵉnaṣṣeaḥ*, see 4, intro.) for the tabernacle worship.[116] I Samuel 21–22 records the event. After the warning from Jonathan, David fled from Saul's court. He went to Nob, a priestly city (I Sam. 22:19). From its grouping with other cities (Isa. 10:28–32), Nob was located a few miles north of Jerusalem. David obtained bread and the sword of Goliath there. Doeg the Edomite, head of Saul's herdsmen (I Sam. 21:7), witnessed this and later reported it to Saul (I Sam. 22:9–10). This brought about the death of the priest Ahimelech, who had assisted David innocently, as well as of the other priests who lived there with their families and animals. Eighty-five priests died (I Sam. 22:11–18).

The psalm develops its theme from a historical incident. In doing this, it makes a practical application for Christians. In this life, the wicked may prosper. They may seem to have success in persecuting believers. The time will come, however, when God will judge their wickedness. In sharp contrast, God's people will experience His blessings.

[116]*NIB*, IV, 890, takes the title "illustratively rather than historically." Buttenwieser, p. 764, directs the rebuke to a heathen king in the Persian period. Both views are subjective and go contrary to the title that reflects early tradition. Kirkpatrick, pp. 295–96, places the psalm in the eighth century BC rather than in David's time. He reasons that David cannot have written the psalm since it does not mention the murder of the priests. This assumes that David must give the details of the "mischief" mentioned in v. 1. Rodd, p. 102, makes the psalm refer to "Isaiah's denunciation of Shebna," Isa. 22:15–19. He gives no reasons for rejecting the theme expressed by the title. Jennings, I, 243, expresses doubt about the title since we do not know that Doeg was either mighty, v. 1, or rich, v. 7. The notes address these matters.

I. Rebuke of the Wicked 1–3

1–3 David rebukes Doeg, the "mighty man" (*gibbôr*, see 19:5),[117] for the slaughter of the priests at Nob.[118] Despite these wicked actions, the "goodness [or 'steadfast love,' *ḥesed*, see 5:7] of God" endures "continually" (or "every day"), v. 1.[119] Verses 2–5 develop v. 1*a*, while vv. 6–9 continue the thought of v. 1*b*. Doeg's speech had planned "mischiefs" (or "destruction," *hawâ*, see 5:9). His deceitful speech is like a sharpened razor, "deceitfully" (*r^e^mîyâ*, see 32:2) cutting those against whom it is directed, v. 2. His actions at Nob showed that he loved evil above good, and lying more than truth. To call attention to Doeg's wicked character, David adds the word "selah," v. 3.

II. Promise of Judgment 4–5

4–5 David recaps the wickedness of Doeg, focusing on his wicked speech. Either David had been told what Doeg said to Saul, or he may recall words said by Doeg while he was at Nob with David, words not recorded in the account. These were "deceitful" words, v. 4. Just as Doeg had destroyed those at Nob, so God will destroy him "for ever," an everlasting judgment. God will snatch him from his earthly "dwelling place" (lit. "tent"), taking him away from this life.[120] The

---

[117]Moll, p. 331, and Clarke, I, 143, understand the phrase "mighty man" as sarcastic since Doeg is not described as a warrior. While the view is possible, we should note that Doeg did lead the fight against the people at Nob. Though not against a fierce foe, Doeg did enter into battle. Kissane, p. 231, understands "mighty" to refer to wealth, suggested by v. 7. The word *gibbôr*, occurring 156 times, refers to might of strength or position when unmodified. Only in II Kings 15:20 and Ruth 2:1, both with a modifier, is wealth in view. Thompson, p. 288, refers Doeg's "might" to the influence of his tongue. The view requires a novel sense for *gibbôr*.

[118]Leupold, p. 419, and Fausset, III, 215, understand the denunciation as directed against Saul. They note that Doeg did not speak "lying" words," v. 3. This overlooks Doeg's statement that Ahimelech "inquired of the Lord for [David]," I Sam. 22:10, something not mentioned elsewhere. Leupold excuses Doeg's actions by noting that he carried out the command of Saul. This, however, does not justify the killing of other priests, women, and children in the city.

[119]Several newer translations, e.g., NIV, REB, NRSV, translate something like "[1]Why do you boast of evil, O mighty man; all the day [2]you plan destruction." This joins the last phrase of v. 1 with v. 2. It also omits the phrase "the goodness of God," but doing so lacks significant textual support.

[120]Weiser, p. 413, understands "tent" as the temple. He applies the verse to "expulsion from the sacred confederacy of the covenant community which would precede

word "tent" occurs appropriately since the herdsman normally lived in this. The word "selah" calls attention to David's prediction of judgment, v. 5.

III. Triumph of the Righteous 6–9

6–7 The righteous will see the judgment of Doeg. They will "fear," standing in awe of God's power, but they will also laugh at Doeg's punishment, v. 6. They will take note of this "man" (or "mighty man," *geber*, see 34:8) who failed to trust God for "strength" (*maᶜôz*, see 27:1). He trusted in his riches[121] and grew strong in his "wickedness" (or "destruction," *hawâ*, see 5:9) glorying as he overthrew others, v. 7.

8–9 David, however, is confident that he will not be taken away. He compares himself to a "green olive tree" planted in God's house. The olive tree occurs elsewhere as a picture of fruitfulness and blessing (Jer. 1:16; Hos. 14:6, cf. Ps. 92:13). David will trust the "mercy" (or "steadfast love," *ḥesed*, see 5:7) of God forever, v. 8. He will praise the Lord forever for judging the wicked. He will expectantly "wait" (*qawâ*, see 25:3) on the "name" of God, His revealed nature.[122] He will wait because the Lord's nature is good to the "saints" (*ḥasîd*, see 4:3), v. 9.

---

the . . . punishment by death." He does not apply this to Doeg, however, since the temple did not exist in David's time. The view is subjective. The parallelism argues that the "tent" refer to this life. Cohen, p. 166, considers this as rendering Doeg "homeless by forcing him into banishment." The parallelism in the verse does not support this.

[121]Apart from this verse, the OT says nothing of Doeg's wealth. "The chiefest of the herdmen that belonged to Saul" (1 Sam. 21:7) would probably have had an above-average income. Even one with a lower income may still trust in what wealth he has. Nothing in this verse is contrary to what we know of Doeg.

[122]See note 94, 5:11, for a summary of the Lord's name.

PSALM 53

Psalm 53 is similar to Psalm 14.[123] The titles differ, with that of Psalm 53 giving more detail. Psalm 53 uses *ʾelohîm* throughout, while Psalm 14 uses *yehwah* in vv. 2, 4, 6, and 7. The discussion below notes other differences between the psalms in the wording of the individual verses.

As with Psalm 14, David plans that the "chief musician" (*menaṣṣeaḥ*, see 4, intro.) will use the psalm in worship ceremonies at the tabernacle. He adds the musical direction "upon Mahalath," indicating that it is to be sung as a dirge.[124] The psalm is as well a "Maschil" (*maśkîl*, see 32, intro.), a psalm guiding the hearers to think upon the wickedness of denying God. The psalm does not indicate clearly the circumstances leading David to write the song. As with Psalm 14, we may locate it during the period before David becomes king over all Israel or during his flight during Absalom's rebellion.

I. Rejection of the Lord 1–4

1 The verse differs from 14:1 only by the addition of *waw* between the verbs and the use of *ʿawel*, "iniquity" (or "injustice," see 7:3)

[123]Leupold, p. 141, explains the similarity by assuming "that it appeared in each of two earlier collections, which were later combined." Delitzsch, I, 202, concludes that "the position of Ps. xiv. in the primary collection favours the presumption, that it is the earlier and more original composition." Later, II, 150, he attributes Ps. 53 to "a later poet, perhaps belonging to the time of Jehoshaphat or Hezekiah [who] has adapted the Davidic Psalm to some terrible catastrophe that has just taken place." Phillips, I, 107, similarly suggests Hezekiah as the editor of Ps. 53. Lawson, p. 276, makes Ps. 14 the original, with Ps. 53 "later adapted . . . as a result of a dramatic victory that God had given to his people." Sabourin, p. 395, thinks that Ps. 14 "seems to transmit more faithfully the original text than the other recension, Ps. 53."

[124]Kirkpatrick, p. 301, considers "Mahalath" as "the initial word of some well-known song, to the melody of which the Psalm was set; rather than as denoting a mournful style of music or some kind of instrument." The view is possible. Eaton, pp. 144–45, suggests that the word refers to "a plaintive ceremony of flute-playing." Gaebelein, p. 225, spiritualizes the term, referring it "to the mournful conditions of the last days of the age." Thirtle, p. 77, who attaches the musical direction to Ps. 52, understands "Mahalath" as "dancings." Oesterley, I, 17, tentatively proposes that it is a proper name, "conceivably a corruption of *Maḥli* or *Maḥali*." The same direction occurs elsewhere only in the title of Ps. 88. The word "Mahalath" (*maḥalat*) comes from *ḥalâ*, "to be weak, sick," and thus suggesting a melancholy tune. Spurgeon, p. 245, adopts this meaning but makes the psalm deal with man's disease, "the mortal, hereditary taint of sin."

rather than *ᶜᵃlîlâ*, "works." Because both psalms use the same verb, the difference is slight. Psalm 53:1 gives a bit more emphasis to the wicked actions of the "fool" (*nabal*, see 14:1). He inwardly says to himself, "there is no God." Denying the existence of the One Who has set the standards of godly behavior, the fool falls naturally into "abominable iniquity," v. 1.[125]

2–3 Except for the use of *ʾᵉlohîm* rather than *yᵉhwah* at the beginning, v. 2 is identical with 14:2. Verse 3 describes the wicked as "every one of them is gone back" (*kullô sag*) rather than as in 14:3, "they are all gone aside" (*hakkol sar*). The difference is slight, but perhaps Psalm 53 describes actions occurring later than in Psalm 14. This would suggest an explanation for the use of *ʾᵉlohîm*. With the completed apostasy of the wicked, it is no longer the compassionate *yᵉhwah* observing them. It is now the powerful *ʾᵉlohîm*, the One to Whom they must one day answer.

As in Psalm 14, God looks at mankind "from heaven," His eternal dwelling from which He sees all that man does. No man has spiritual understanding that would cause them to "seek" (*daraš*, see 9:10) after God, v. 2. Earlier, Israel had "gone aside" from godliness. They had kept the law with an evil heart. Now they have completely turned back from following godly ways. "None" (*ʾên*) of them do "good, no [*ʾên*], not one." As in 14:3, the repeated *ʾên* emphasizes the failure of the people, v. 3.

4 Psalm 14:4 refers to "all [*kol*] the workers of iniquity," while 53:4 simply says "the workers of iniquity." There is no need for David to repeat the *kol* in Psalm 53, since he has just said in v. 3 that "every one of them" has turned back. David again asks a rhetorical question: "Is it true that these "workers of iniquity" have no knowledge that they must one day give an account of themselves to God? They "eat up" the resources of the poor in the same way they would eat bread. Psalm 53:4 uses *ʾᵉlohîm* rather than the *yᵉhwah* of 14:4. The wicked rely on their oppression of the poor rather than looking to the mighty God to supply their needs, v. 4.

[125]Paul draws on this in his indictment of mankind, Rom. 3:10.

II. Deliverance of the Righteous 5–6

5 The greatest differences between Psalms 14 and 53 occur here. The opening phrase is the same. The wicked, "they," suddenly know "great fear" (*paḥadû paḥad*, see 14:5). The next phrase is unique to Psalm 53, *lo*ʾ*-hayâ paḥad*, "where no fear was." The wicked have confidently pursued their oppression of others with no qualms about their actions. God's actions, however, bring unexpected fear upon them. Psalm 14:5 relates their fear to discovering that God was with those they oppressed. Here, David relates the fear to the actions of God against them. God has "scattered the bones" of those who exploited the poor. Once more, this idiom seems to look back on the completed vindication of God's people, while Psalm 14 deals more with the ongoing process.

Verse 5*b* takes 14:6 in a new direction. Only the common thought of "shame" (*bôš*, see 6:10) is the same. In Psalm 14, David speaks of putting to shame the counsel given to the poor that they should trust the Lord. In Psalm 53, however, the mighty God brings the wicked to shame. This statement again looks back on the completed judgment of the wicked, v. 5.

6 Verse 6 is close to Psalm 14:7, with two minor changes.[126] David states his desire for the "salvations" of the nation. The intensive plural indicates the completed deliverance of the people. At this time, the mighty God will bring back "the captivity" of the people, delivering them from their oppressors and restoring the fullness of the land to them. As in Psalm 14:7, the ultimate fulfillment of this will come during the millennial kingdom, when the Lord rules over the earth. At that time, the nation shall rejoice in the Lord, v. 6.[127]

---

[126]Ps. 53 uses *ʾᵉlohîm* rather than *yᵉhwah* and makes "salvation" plural rather than construct to Israel.

[127]Phillips, I, 420, transfers the musical instruction of Ps. 54 to follow Ps. 53. He understands "Neginoth" as "smitings" and makes this refer to v. 5, where God's Son smites "the hosts of the beast at Megiddo." He can support this only by understanding it as an addition that does not appear in Ps. 14. No mss evidence supports the view; in addition, his eschatological application is forced.

PSALM 54

The detailed title gives the purpose of the psalm, musical instructions, the author, and the historical setting.[128] David intends the psalm for use in Israel's worship. To this end, he writes it for the "chief musician" (*m^e^naṣṣeaḥ*, see 4, intro.). Its singing is to be accompanied with "Neginoth" (*n^e^gînôt*, see 4, intro.), an unknown stringed instrument. The psalm is a "Maschil" (*maśkîl*, see 32, intro.), with a theme that will give wisdom as its hearers think on it.

The title sets the psalm in the time when David fled from Saul to the wilderness surrounding the town of Ziph. This town lay four miles south of Hebron in the area occupied by Judah. The inhabitants of the town sought to gain favor with Saul by informing him of David's presence.[129] Saul sent them to find David's hiding places. By the time they returned, David had moved to another area (I Sam. 23:14–24). In the psalm, David laments the faithlessness of the Ziphites and tells of his continuing faith in the Lord.

Just as David found out that others betrayed him, so there will be those today who betray Christians. The hope that we have is the same as that of David. The Lord will sustain us. He will judge the wicked and reward those who are faithful to Him.

I. The Prayer of David 1–3

1–3 David prays that the Lord will deliver him by His "name," the revealed nature of God that is powerful and well able to overcome His foes.[130] The phrase "judge me" is better "vindicate me," delivering David by God's power, v. 1. He asks God to effectually hear His "prayer" (*t^e^pillâ*, see 4:1), to listen carefully to his words, v. 2. "Strangers" (*zûr*, see 44:20), men opposed to David, have risen against him. These are "oppressors" (or "ruthless men") who seek to

[128]*NIB*, IV, 894, considers the title as an illustration rather than as a historical setting to the psalm. The view is subjective and ignores the early tradition supporting the title.

[129]Henry, III, 439, goes too far in making the inhabitants of Ziph "types of Judas the traitor." With this reasoning, anyone who fails the Lord could be regarded as a type of Judas. The Ziphites picture the betrayal of the Lord by Judas but are not types of Judas.

[130]Note 94 at 5:11 gives a brief summary of the Lord's name.

kill him. To further describe them, David notes that they have no concern for God in their actions. To emphasize his plight, David adds the word "selah," v. 3.

II. The Praise of David 4–7

4–7 In sharp contrast with his enemies, David relies on God. He looks to Him as the One Who helps him. Verse 4*b* is better "the Lord is the One Who sustains my soul."[131] In this role, the Lord preserves David's life, v. 4. He will return evil upon David's foes.[132] He will "cut them off" (*ṣamat*, see 18:40), annihilating them in His "truth" (or "faithfulness")," v. 5. In response to God's work on his behalf, David anticipates his future worship. He will make freewill sacrifices to God and praise the "name" (see v. 1) of the Lord, i.e., His nature, because it is good, v. 6. Verse 7 is a prophetic perfect, a thought so real in David's mind that he speaks of it as already accomplished.[133] The Lord will deliver him from the "trouble" (*ṣarâ*, see 9:9) that besets him. David will look upon his enemies. The AV supplies the words "his desire," as though David looks upon the work of the Lord introduced in the first half of the verse.[134] This is satisfactory although other views are also possible, v. 7.

---

[131]The AV reads "the Lord is with [*b*ᵉ] them that uphold my soul." Since the emphasis of the psalm is on the Lord's deliverance of David, it is better to treat the *b*ᵉ preposition as the *bêt essentiae*, describing the Lord as having the same character as those who uphold David. So Waltke & O'Connor 11.2.5*e*; G.K.C. 119 *i*.

[132]Kirkpatrick, p. 306, and Leupold, p. 418, follow the *kᵉtîb*, which reads, "Evil will return upon my enemies." The AV follows the *qᵉrê*, "He will return evil upon my enemies." While the difference is slight, the AV gives better parallelism with 5*b*, also spoken of God's work. Hirsch, I, 379, applies "truth" in 5*b* as though the Lord's defense of David would show that David's position agreed with God's Word. While this is possible, the word *ʾemet* may also mean "faithfulness," the view taken above.

[133]Henry, III, 439, thinks that David wrote the psalm after the threat was over. Elsewhere, however, it is clear that David writes of the future, vv. 1, 2, 5.

[134]Others suggest different supplied words: "in triumph," NIV; "with satisfaction," NASB; "calmly and leisurely," Rawlinson, I, 412; "fate," Cheyne, I, 238. Moll, p. 336, omits all supplied words, translating, "On my enemies my eye has looked," with the sense of looking without alarm on the foes. Leslie, p. 332, interprets the idea of looking by translating "my eye will gloat over my enemies."

PSALM 55

This is another of David's psalms written for performance with "Neginoth" (*n^eĝînôt*, see 4, intro.), an unknown stringed instrument. He assigns the psalm to the "chief musician" (*m^enaṣṣeaḥ*, see 4, intro.) for use in Israel's worship. The psalm is a Maschil (*maśkîl*, see 32, title). It is an individual lament in which David grieves over his betrayal by some friend. He mentions this in each of the three sections, mingling his lament with his prayer for God's deliverance. In my judgment, David wrote the psalm after Absalom's rebellion.[135]

The way David faces the problem is instructive. In each of the sections of the psalm, he prays; cf. vv. 1–2, 9, 16–17, 22. With this response to the opposition he faced, David sets an example for others who face trials. Prayer is one of the great resources the Lord has given to His followers.

I. Dismay of the Psalmist 1–7

1–3 David pleads with God to hear his "prayer" (*t^epillâ*, see 4:1) and not to hide from his "supplication" (*t^eḥinnâ*, see 6:9) for the gracious action he needs performed, v. 1. He repeats his plea that God will hear him. He "mourn[s]" (or "is restless")[136] in his "complaint" (*śîaḥ*).[137] It indicates here that David dwells on his plight, not being able to put it out of his mind. He "make[s] a noise" (or "murmurs"), continually feeling the pressure of the situation, v. 2. David now

[135]Calvin, II, 327, places the psalm during the time of Saul's persecutions. Eaton, p. 146, interprets v. 17 as though some "Judean king" were in the temple with "a background of disorder in Jerusalem." Cheyne, I, 240, makes Israel the speaker, lamenting the trials of the past. Ewald, I, 253, understands the psalm as in the last century before the fall of Jerusalem. Thompson, p. 292, concludes that the psalm does not fit into any period of David's life and that therefore "one is forced to ignore the background in this psalm's interpretation and consider it simply as an expression of religious experience." The wide diversity shows the difficulty of determining the setting of the psalm.

[136]Henry, III, 442, refers this to "weeping," then sees David as a type of Christ, "a man of sorrows and often in tears." This spiritualizes the text. The Lord wept over the sins of others, while David weeps over his own plight.

[137]The word *śîaḥ* refers to mentally repeating something, going over it in the mind, a meditation (104:34), a complaint (102:1) or, if expressed vocally, "talk" (Prov. 6:22). The context determines how the word should be understood. Both the noun and verb forms have the same basic sense.

reveals the cause of his burden. His foes speak against him. They impute iniquity to David. In their "wrath" (*ʾap*, see 2:5), they "hate" (or "bear a grudge toward," *śaṭam*)[138] him, v. 3.

4–7 David relates his reaction to the threat. His heart writhes in pain, and the dread of death consumes him, v. 4. He reacts emotionally to the problem. "Fearfulness" (*yirʾâ*, see 2:11) and trembling fill him. Horror overwhelms him, v. 5. He wishes for wings that would let him fly away from the trouble.[139] He would then settle down, at rest from the inner conflict that now grips him, v. 6. He would "wander" (or "flee") far away into the wilderness, where he could "remain" (or "lodge," *lîn*, see 25:13). The word "selah" calls attention to David's situation, v. 7.

II. Betrayal of the Friendship 8–19*a*

8–11 David continues to express his wish to escape from the trials that confront him. He would "hasten [his] escape" (or "hasten to [his] place of refuge"). This would shelter him from "the windy storm [*sʿh*][140] and tempest," a poetical description of his plight, v. 8. Once more, as in vv. 1–2, he turns to the Lord in prayer. He asks Him to "destroy" (better "confuse," *balaʿ*)[141] them and to "divide" their speech, giving them conflicting opinions. David likely draws on the events at Babel (Gen. 11:5–9). He has seen the results of the wickedness, creating strife among the people in "the city," Jerusalem, v. 9. "They," his unnamed foes, continually walk on the walls of the city. "Mischief . . . and sorrow" (or "iniquity . . . and trouble [*ʿamal*, see 7:14])" are in the city, v. 10. "Wickedness" (or "destruction," *hawâ*,

[138]The verb *śaṭam* has more of a sense of animosity or bearing a grudge than of hatred. The word occurs in describing Esau's attitude toward Jacob, Gen. 27:41, and the fear of Joseph's brothers that he would seek revenge, Gen. 50:15, both illustrating an evil attitude.

[139]The thought of flying away with "wings like a dove" is an obvious idiom that poetically pictures David's wishes.

[140]The root *sʿh* occurs only here in the OT. On the basis of a Ugaritic cognate, *KB*, II, 761, suggests "dash away, sweep away." Translations generally give something like "raging wind."

[141]The word *balaʿ* II, "to confuse," occurs here. A similar word, *balaʿ* I, "to swallow," occurs elsewhere, e.g., 21:9; 35:25. Harman, p. 210, and Dickson, p. 329, read *balaʿ* I. The parallel phrase "divide their tongues" supports reading this as *balaʿ* II.

see 5:9) is in the city. "Deceit and guile" have not left the "streets" (or "open places"), the public squares in the city, v. 11.

12–15 David now describes the source of the betrayal. Had it come from an enemy, he could have accepted that. Had it come from one who "hated" (*śane*ʾ, see 5:5) David and tried to exalt himself over him, he could simply have avoided him, v. 12. It came instead from a "man" (*ʾenôš*, see 8:4) who was an equal, David's "guide" (or "friend") and "acquaintance," one he knew closely, v. 13. They had before enjoyed "sweet counsel [*sôd*, see 25:14]," communion with one another. They joined in their worship at the tabernacle. The close acquaintance of vv. 12–13 is likely Ahithophel,[142] David's counselor whose counsel was considered an "oracle of God" (II Sam. 16:23).[143] By leaving the person unnamed, however, the psalm acquires a broad application. Anyone wronged by a friend may identify with David's situation, v. 14. Such betrayal deserves great punishment. David prays that death may "seize" (or "come deceitfully," unexpectedly)[144] upon his enemies. May they go "quick" (or "alive") into "hell" (or "the grave," *šeʾôl*, see 6:5). It is possible that David has the judgment of Numbers 16:25–33 in mind, v. 15.

16–19*a* For his part, he will commit himself to God. He is confident that the Lord will deliver him, v. 16. He will "pray" (see *śîaḥ*, v. 2) night and day.[145] He will cry out to the Lord, Who will hear him, v. 17. So confident is David of God's deliverance that he states it as an accomplished fact. The Lord has "delivered" (or "redeemed," *padâ*, see 25:22) him from the conflict, bringing peace once more to his soul. There were many "with" (or "against") him, opposed to his continuing rule, v. 18. God, the Eternal One, will hear and "afflict"

[142]Leupold, p. 420, states that Ahithophel was not David's "'equal' and his 'partner' and 'intimate acquaintance.'" David, however, may well have used these terms to reflect his high opinion of the man who had served as his counselor.

[143]We may only speculate on the motive that led Ahithophel to betray David. It is possible that he resented David's actions toward Bathsheba, his granddaughter (II Sam. 11:3; 23:34). He may have felt Absalom represented greater potential for advancement or reward. It is not possible to be certain.

[144]The *qerê yašîmawet*, "let death deceive," fits best here. The *ketîb yešîmôt*, "desolations," occurs elsewhere only as a place name, Num. 33:49; Josh. 12:3; 13:20.

[145]The order in the verse—evening, morning, noon—reflects the Jewish day, which began in the evening.

(or "respond to") the wicked plans of his enemies. Once more, David calls attention to this with the word "selah," v. 19*a*.

III. Deception by the Enemy 19*b*–23

19*b*–21 The wicked do not change and therefore have no fear of God, v. 19*b*. David's former friend has turned against the one at peace with him. In this, he has "broken" (*ḥalal* II)[146] the "covenant," the informal agreement that exists between friends, v. 20. His speech was deceitful, apparently "smoother than butter" but with war in his heart. His words were smoother than oil but were as "drawn swords" ready to cut down his friend, v. 21.

22–23 David draws the conclusion to the matter, for him and for others who face similar problems.[147] Cast the "burden" (*yᵉhab*)[148] on the Lord.[149] He will give the needed support and not let the righteous be moved. Peter quotes the verse in I Peter 5:7, v. 22. As in vv. 16–19, David expresses his confidence in God. God will bring down the wicked into the "pit [*bᵉʾar*, see *bôr*, 7:15] of destruction [*šaḥat*, see 7:15]," a poetical description of the grave.[150] These bloodthirsty and treacherous "men" (*ʾᵉnôš*, see 8:4) will die prematurely, not living half their expected days. David, on the other hand, will continue his faith in the Lord. The unstated but implied thought is that he will live a full life, v. 23.

---

[146]The word *ḥalal* II is "to profane, defile, pollute" (BDB, p. 320, sees a separate verb *ḥalal*, "to play the pipe," making this *ḥalal* III). When used of spiritual matters, it often refers to profaning them by treating them as common, not especially concerned with God. In this sense, Israel often breaks a covenant or law by treating it as unimportant, not necessary to keep.

[147]Jennings, I, 245, and Hirsch, I, 386, understand the verse as the words of David's enemy as he taunts David. While the view is possible, Peter's quote in the NT suggests more strongly that this is godly advice.

[148]The word *yᵉhab* is from a root meaning "to give." The "burden" is what has been given to the person to bear—a physical or emotional trial. No matter what the nature of this may be, the Lord will sustain you when you rely on Him. He allows the trial so that you may learn to trust Him for deliverance. Buttenwieser, p. 712, translates *yᵉhab* as "fate," a sense found nowhere else in the OT.

[149]The words to the hymn "Cast Thy Burden on the Lord" are attributed to Rowland Hill, 1783. The music is from Louis Moreau Gottschalk, 1867.

[150]Bratcher and Reyburn, p. 501, and Delitzsch, II, 165, understand the phrase to refer to Hades, the world of the dead. This is a possible view.

PSALM 56

The psalm begins a series of five "Michtam" (see 16:1) psalms. David prepares this psalm for the "chief musician" (*mᵉnaṣṣeaḥ*, see 4, intro.) to use in the nation's worship. He directs that it be performed upon "Jonath-elem-rechokim." This word means "silent [*ʾelem*][151] dove of distant places," a meaningless phrase to us.[152] It likely refers to some tune known in David's day but which has since been lost.[153]

The historical setting is early in David's career, at the time of his flight to Achish, the Philistine king of Gath (I Sam. 21:10–15). David laments the situation that he faces, and he entreats God to deliver him. While David may have written the psalm before becoming king, he later gives the psalm to the chief musician to include in occasions of worship.

It is significant that God's Word is David's great hope in this time of persecution. The prophet Samuel had anointed David to be Israel's king (I Sam. 16:13). During his flight from Saul, the Lord continually guided him (e.g., I Sam. 24:2, 4, 12; 30:8). He undoubtedly knew that God would deliver him and place him on Israel's throne. In this psalm, he recalls these words of promise, vv. 4 and 10. God's Word is still certain, and Christians may still rest on His promises to His own.

---

[151]Delitzsch, II, 166, renders *ʾelem* as "terebinths" and the phrase as "dove of the distant terebinths." *OTTP*, p. 104, adopts the same view. This requires repointing the word to *ʾelim* or *ʾelîm* (so NIV, NRSV). The view does not change the sense of the phrase significantly since it still refers to a dove in a faraway grove of trees. Eaton, p. 148, makes the phrase "equivalent to a Ugaritic phrase for the 'distant' gods of the Underworld." The view suffers in that there are no "gods of the Underworld."

[152]It is often speculated that David may refer to himself with this phrase. Murphy, p. 321, describes David "as a dove, the emblem of innocence, silent in sadness and patience, and afar off from his home among Gentiles." Henry, III, 446, is similar. He describes David as "innocent and inoffensive, mild and patient, as a dove . . . at this time driven from his nest . . . forced to wander afar off." Thompson, p. 294, sees David as a "caged dove, given a forced rest." Alexander, p. 257, sees the whole as "an enigmatical description of David as an innocent and uncomplaining sufferer among strangers." These views are possible but speculative.

[153]Scroggie, II, 31, places the title at the end of Ps. 55, arguing that 55:6–8 requires this. Kidner, p. 43, states that "the allusion in the previous psalm to a dove and to the far distance (55:6f) can hardly be a coincidence." He suggests that the heading of Ps. 56 should be read as a postscript to Ps. 55. The view is doubtful. While the musical direction follows the song in Hab. 3:19, there is no indication of this in the Psalms. The content of this psalm agrees with the heading. It is precarious to make the heading a postscript without a clear reference in the psalm itself and manuscript evidence.

I. Plea for Help 1–4

1–2 David asks God to "be merciful [or 'gracious,' *ḥanan*, see 4:1]" because of the threat facing him. Weak "man" (*ʾenôš*, see 8:4), weak in comparison to God's power, would "swallow [David] up" (or "pant after" him, *šaʾap*).[154] The subject "he" likely refers to Saul, who fights each day to place pressure on David, v. 1. David's enemies daily try to "swallow [him] up" (or "pant after" him, *šaʾap*). There are many that fight against him. The phrase "O thou most high" (*marôm*) is better taken as an adverb, "proudly" (as in 73:8), describing those who oppose David, v. 2.[155]

3–4 Despite this danger, David purposes to trust the Lord. Though he faces a fearful situation, he will place his trust in God, v. 3. Verse 11 amplifies the poetic refrain of v. 4. David purposes to praise God's word, the many promises of protection for the godly. He has placed his trust in God and will not fear man's attacks against him. Psalm 118:6 repeats the thought of the phrase, but the reception may be coincidental. The quote in Hebrews 13:6 comes from one of these two verses, v. 4.

II. Portrayal of the Problem 5–11

5–7 David describes the wicked actions of his enemies. They "wrest" his words, twisting them to mean something different from what he has said. Their "thoughts" (or "plans," *maḥšebôt*, see 33:10) are to bring evil upon him, v. 5. They "gather themselves together" (or "stir up strife"). They "hide" (or "lurk"), trying to catch him off guard. They mark his goings as they eagerly "wait" (*qawâ*, see 25:3) to kill him, v. 6. David asks rhetorically if the wicked should escape

---

[154]There are two possible roots, *šaʾap* I, "to pant after," or *šaʾap* II, "to trample." Commentators divide over the sense given to the word. Hirsch, I, 388; Albert Barnes, II, 126; and Anderson, I, 421, adopt *šaʾap* I, "pant." Alexander, p. 257; Oesterley, I, 288; and Rotherham, p. 249, adopt *šaʾap* II, "trample." I have adopted *šaʾap* I, "pant," as the more common word. The word must be taken the same way in v. 1 and v. 2.

[155]Among others, Anderson, I, 421, and Phillips, I, 446, treat *marôm* as a vocative. Anderson argues that "as the petition began with the vocative, 'O God', so also it concludes with a vocative." The NRSV translates "O Most High" but makes this introduce v. 3. The word occurs widely elsewhere but nowhere as a vocative. It regularly occurs as a descriptive word, including references to pride, 73:8; Isa. 24:4. Murphy, p. 321, understands *marôm* as "from a high place, the vantage-ground of rank and possession." The word, however, lacks a preposition to signal a phrase.

punishment.[156] No! God should exercise His "anger" (*ʾap*, see 2:5) against their iniquity and cast them down, v. 7.

8 David knows that the Lord has taken account of his wanderings as he has fled from Saul. He asks the Lord to place the tears from his sorrows in His "bottle" (better "wineskin"), keeping track of what burdens him. The Lord has already recorded these in the book where He keeps the records of men's lives (cf. Mal. 3:16), v. 8.

9–11 When David cries out to God, his enemies will turn back. He is confident that God is on his side, v. 9. He paraphrases the refrain seen earlier in v. 4. He will praise the word of the mighty God, and he will praise the word of the loving Lord, v. 10. He trusts the power of God to deliver him. He will therefore not be afraid of what men would try to do to him, v. 11.

III. Praise of the Psalmist 12–13

David closes the psalm on a note of praise to God. He has placed himself under vows to worship and serve God. He will therefore "render praises" (or "make thank offerings," *tôdâ*, see 26:7) to Him, v. 12. God has rescued him from his enemies. The next phrase should not be set in the future. It continues the thought of the first phrase: "Indeed [*hᵃloʾ*],[157] my feet from falling [or 'stumbling,' *dᵉḥî*]."[158] The Lord has provided this deliverance so that David may continue to walk before Him throughout life, v. 13.

---

[156]The phrase lit. reads, "Upon iniquity [*ʾawen*] *is* escape [*palleṭ*] to them?" Leupold, p. 428, takes *ʾawen* as "trouble" and translates, "Unto trouble set them free." This gives an unusual sense to *palleṭ*. Fausset, III, 221, supplies words to give the sense "Upon *the ground of* their iniquity *there is* to them *the hope of* escape." This requires too much speculation as to the supplied information. Kidner, p. 204, suggests that *palleṭ* is an "early miscopying for *palles*, "weigh out." There are also other views. The traditional rendering of the AV is defensible and fits into the plea of the psalmist. Murphy, p. 322, translates *ʾawen* as "vanity," a possible but infrequent meaning. This gives the wicked temporary escape. The view requires understanding thoughts that are not obvious.

[157]The use of *hᵃloʾ* introduces an affirmation rather than the simple interrogative. G.K.C. 150 *e*.

[158]The noun *dᵉḥî*, from the root *daḥâ*, "to thrust, drive out, cast down," indicates the result of stumbling or falling. Since it is connected with the feet, the idea of stumbling is prominent here.

PSALM 57

This individual lament goes back to David's flight from Saul.[159] At that time, he had escaped Saul by hiding in a cave. This happened twice, in the cave of Adullam (I Sam. 22:1) and later in the cave of En-gedi (I Sam. 24:1–3). The cave Adullam is near the city of Adullam, midway between Jerusalem and Lachish in Judah. The cave En-gedi lies near the town of En-gedi on the shore of the Dead Sea, thirty miles southeast of Jerusalem.[160] Both areas are honeycombed with caves. The phrase "Al-taschith" is a musical notation of an unknown nature.[161] David plans that the "chief musician" (*mᵉnaṣṣeaḥ*, see 4, intro.), will include the psalm in the tabernacle worship. He labels the psalm as a "Michtam" (see 16:1), a psalm worth reflecting upon.

It is appropriate that David calls on "God" (*ᵓᵉlohîm*, see 7:1) repeatedly in the psalm, vv. 1, 2, 3, 5, 7, 11. This is the name that stresses the power of God. In addition, David refers to "God" (*ᵓel*) in v. 2, most likely using the name in poetic variation with *ᵓᵉlohîm*, which also occurs in the verse. The name *ᵓel* is a related name that also emphasizes the might of God. These names remind us that God has the power to overcome His enemies. When Christians face opposition, God is still able to sustain them.

---

[159]*NIB*, IV, 905, rejects any reference to an actual historical setting and instead makes the title an illustration. The view is subjective and ignores the early tradition reflected in the title.

[160]Rawlinson, II, 6, and Gaebelein, p. 234, identify the cave as that in Adullam. Henry, III, 450, and Horne, p. 238, sees it as the cave in En-gedi. It is not possible to be certain which of the caves the title refers to, since the psalm gives no clear evidence.

[161]The phrase occurs again in Pss. 58, 59, and 75. Henry, p. 450, refers the phrase to David's words concerning Saul and to God's words concerning David. This sense cannot be sustained in the other psalms where "Al-taschith" occurs. Gaebelein, p. 234, spiritualizes the phrase into a prayer of Israel during the tribulation when Antichrist threatens their existence. Phillips, I, 444, understands the phrase as cautioning the chief musician "to take special care of this composition." This is possible although speculative. The phrase does not occur enough to let us be certain. Hengstenberg, II, 246–47, and Hirsch, I, 392, relate "Al-taschith" ("do not destroy") to David's instruction to his men when he restrained them from killing Saul (I Sam. 24:7). The placing of the phrase after the dedication to the chief musician argues for a musical sense. The phrase follows the dedication each time in the Psalms (57, 58, 59, and 75).

I. The Prayer of Faith 1–3

1–3 David asks God to be "merciful" (or "gracious," *ḥanan*, see 4:1) to him. He "trusteth" (or "takes refuge," *ḥasâ*, see 2:12) in God. Poetically, David describes the protection given as God spreads His wings over him. He will find "refuge" (*ḥasâ*) here until the "calamities" (or "destruction," *hawwôt*, see 5:9) have passed away. The intensive plural *hawwôt* calls attention to the greatness of the danger facing David, v. 1. He will cry out in prayer to the God Who is "most high" (*ᶜelyôn*, see 7:17), above all other beings in creation and therefore most powerful. This is the God Who brings about all that is necessary for David, v. 2. David is certain that God will send His hosts from heaven to deliver him from his foes. God will save him from the "reproach" (or "taunt") of those who would "swallow [him] up" (or "pant after" him," *šaʾap*, see 56:1). He draws attention to his confidence in God by adding "Selah" to his words. God will send "mercy" (or "steadfast love," *ḥesed*, see 5:7) and "truth" (or "faithfulness") to sustain him, v. 3.

II. The Threat from the Wicked 4–6

4–6 David describes himself as being among "lions," poetic for those who would attack him. He lies down in the midst of those "that are set on fire," burning in their desire to take him.[162] Their teeth are as "spears [*ḥᵃnît*, see 35:3] and arrows," weapons raised against him. Their speech is a "sharp sword" with cutting words, v. 4. The thought of his danger causes David to think of the majesty of the God on Whom he depends. He is exalted above "the heavens," His creation. David prays that God's glory will be seen as higher than "all the earth" with its resources, v. 5. Still, David's plight is dangerous. His adversaries have prepared a trap for him, and he is "bowed down" in distress. His enemies have dug a pit to trap him, but David's confidence in God is so great that he states his deliverance as an accomplished fact. His enemies have fallen into their own trap. He draws attention to this with "selah," v. 6.

[162]Fausset, p. 223, thinks that David "would not probably pass from confidence (vv. 3, 4) to complaint here." He sees the statement as David's willingness to be among "these firebrand-enemies." There is no hint, however, that this is complaint. It is rather a statement of fact. David regularly alternates his plight with his trust in the Lord; cf. vv. 5, 6.

III. The Confidence of the Psalmist 7–11

With only slight differences, verses 7–11 are at the beginning of Psalm 108, attributed to David as the original author. They are followed there by words borrowed from Psalm 60:5–12. Some later psalmist borrowed the words from here to begin Psalm 108, the later of the two songs.

7–9 In view of this deliverance, David begins to praise God. David's heart is "fixed" (or "steadfast"). He will sing and "give praise" (or "sing praises," *zamar*, see 7:17) to God, v. 7. He calls upon his "glory," his soul, to awake. He calls upon the "psaltery" (or "harp," *nebel*, see 33:2) and "harp" (or "lyre," *kinnôr*, see 33:2) to awake from their silence and bring forth music. He purposes to awake early for this. The phrase is lit. "I will awake the dawn," a picturesque way of stating his intention to rise early, v. 8. He will "praise" (or "give thanks") to the Lord in the midst of the people, and he will "sing" (or "sing praises," *zamar*) to the Lord before other nations, v. 9.

10–11 David gives the reason for his praise to God. His "mercy" (or "steadfast love," *ḥesed*) reaches the heavens above. His "truth" (or "faithfulness") extends to the clouds, v. 10. David repeats the thought earlier expressed in v. 5. The verses are virtually identical in form and are identical in meaning. God is worthy to be exalted, v. 11.

PSALM 58

This is another imprecatory psalm in which David uses strong language against his enemies.[163] Nothing in the psalm lets us clearly place it in a historical setting, although v. 1 hints at the time of Absalom's rebellion.[164] As with many of David's psalms, its general

---

[163]Within the group of imprecatory psalms, 35, 59, 69, 70, 109, and 140 are individual laments and 58, 83, and 137 are community laments. The introduction to Ps. 35 discusses the reasons for the imprecations.

[164]Dickson, p. 345, and Murphy, p. 326, set it in the time of Saul's persecution of David. Rotherham, pp. 254–55, places it early in David's reign. This is possible, although the historical books say nothing of unjust judges in David's early rule. On

nature lets us apply its principles to many different situations. The psalm is to be performed to the tune "Al-taschith" (see Ps. 57). David writes the psalm for the "chief musician" (*mᵉnaṣṣeaḥ*, see 4, intro.) to use with the tabernacle worship. The psalm is a "Michtam" (see 16:1), one worthy for its hearers to meditate on.

I. Condemnation of the Wicked 1–5

1–2 The rhetorical questions, of unknown background, demand negative answers. Apparently, some official body has condemned David, which is what leads us to place the psalm in the time of Absalom's rebellion.[165] In earlier times, during Saul's search for David, Saul did not need official sanction to move against him. Absalom, however, managed to turn a sizeable portion of the leadership against the king. The word "congregation" (*ʾelem*) is better "silence." This leads to the translation, "Do you in silence speak righteousness?" The judges remain silent rather than make righteous pronouncements, v. 1.[166] The actions of the judges reveal their inner "wickedness" (*ʿawlâ*, see 7:3). Instead of measuring out justice, they have weighed out upon the earth their violent intentions, v. 2.

3–5 David begins a poetic description of the wicked. They are "estranged" (*zûr*, see 44:20) from birth, turned aside from the practice of righteousness. They begin speaking "lies" (*kazab*, see 4:2) as soon as they are born. While the statement may seem extreme,

---

the ground that David would not have used such harsh language toward Absalom, Kirkpatrick, p. 326, places the psalm in a later period of Israelite history.

[165]Among others, Leupold, p. 435, makes the psalm a polemic against unjust judges. He argues against setting the psalm at the time of Absalom's rebellion since "David was not at all sharp in his denunciation of the wicked deed of his son, as this psalm is, but was rather far too lenient." The psalm, however, need not focus on Absalom. David directs his imprecations toward those in the nation who support his son's rebellion.

[166]Among others, *OTTP*, p. 104, and Weiser, p. 430, read *ʾelim* or *ʾelîm*, "gods," in the sense of judges or rulers: "Do you, O gods, speak righteousness?" The NASB and NIV also follow this. While this does not greatly change the sense of the phrase, it requires a change that has little support. It is also difficult to support since nowhere else does *ʾelîm* refer to gods or judges. John S. Kselman and Michael L. Barré, "A Note on *ʾelem* in Psalm LVIII 2," *VT* 54:3 (2004), p. 400, vary this by referring *ʾelîm* to "mute ones," still indicating "gods." From the development in v. 2, it is clear that "gods" are not in view. Since they do not exist, they cannot carry out the actions there mentioned. Dahood, II, 57, revocalizes and understands as "rams," metaphorical for "leaders," a doubtful view.

the self-centered conduct of babies supports the thought that at least some of their cries are for false reasons, v. 3. Their "poison" (*ḥemâ*, see 6:1), figurative for their anger, is like the poison of a serpent. It is like that of a "deaf adder" (*peten*)[167] with stopped-up ears, v. 4. Because it does not hear, it does not respond to the voice of "charmers" (or "whisperers"). The phrase "charming never so wisely" is lit. "ones charming charms from wisdom [*ḥokmâ*, see 19:7]," leading to something like "those who skillfully cast spells." So these wicked judges fail to hear any voice of righteousness as they make their evil pronouncements, v. 5.

II. Imprecation upon the Wicked 6–9

6–9 David now begins a series of imprecations as he asks God to bring the actions of his foes to naught. The "teeth" elsewhere represent the vicious speech of the wicked, e.g., 37:12; 57:4; 112:10. To "break" (*haras*, see 11:3) the teeth portrays the overcoming of the wicked words spoken against David. The figure of "lions" (*kᵉpîr*, see 17:12) elsewhere represent the wicked, e.g., 35:17; 91:13, an apt figure of those who skulk about as they wait for their prey. Breaking their teeth pictures their inability to attack others, v. 6. May the enemy "melt away" (or "flow away") like the waters of a stream. When the wicked "bendeth his bow" (*darak*, see 7:12), let his arrows be cut in pieces, becoming as headless sticks without power to pierce, v. 7.

Let these enemies be like a "snail which melteth [lit. 'as it goes']," David prays. The figure comes from the slime left by a snail as it moves, an apparent melting left as a trail. May they be as "the untimely birth of a woman," a miscarriage, not seeing life under the sun, v. 8. David climaxes this paragraph with a confident statement. Before pots placed over a fire can feel the heat from burning "thorns" (*ʾaṭad*),[168] whether green thorns or dry "burning" (*ḥarôn*, see 2:5)

---

[167]The word *peten* is often translated "cobra" (so NIV, NASB) because of the reference to "charming" in v. 5. This serpent does not occur in Palestine. Leslie, p. 231, translates it as "adder." Kissane, p. 249, gives "asp." The word may be meant generally, standing for any poisonous snake.

[168]The word *ʾaṭad* refers either to the "bramble," Judg. 9:14–15, or the "buckthorn," Gen. 50:10–11 (the name of the threshing floor coming from the bushes growing nearby). Either of these may be burned in a fire.

thorns, the living God will sweep David's adversaries away as with a whirlwind, v. 9.[169]

III. Rejoicing over the Wicked 10–11

10–11 The righteous will rejoice when God brings vengeance. Bathing their feet in the blood of the wicked vividly pictures the triumph of the righteous, v. 10. Mankind will then recognize that God rewards the righteous, that He is (*yeš*, see 7:3) a God Who judges wickedness. This says more than simply that God judges wickedness in the earth. It recognizes the existence of the God Who judges mankind, v. 11.

PSALM 59

This imprecatory psalm uses startling language in describing the judgment of the wicked in order to make a vivid point.[170] The wicked will receive judgment from a holy God. David[171] plans the psalm

---

[169]Kidner, p. 210, describes the verse as "a thoroughly tangled text." This may underestimate the difficulty. Fausset, III, 225, understands "living" (*ḥay*) as the raw contents of the pot and "wrath" (*ḥarôn*) as "sodden." He interprets, "Before your plans have come to maturity, ripe or unripe ('raw or sodden'), God will with a whirlwind carry you away." Leupold, p. 438, weaves the difficult parts together: "Before the pot actually feels the heat of the just-kindled fire, along comes a sudden gust of wind ('something like a hot anger') and sweeps away, not only the fire, but the very fuel." Delitzsch, II, 183, understands "both . . . and" (*keᵉmô. . . keᵉmô*) as "whether . . . or." The *ḥay* is uncooked meat and *ḥarôn* fierce heat. Whether the contents of the pot are raw or "in a state of heat, i.e. of being cooked through," the Lord will carry them away as with a whirlwind. The difficulty lies with the word *ḥarôn*. Everywhere else, it refers to the wrath of God. It is difficult to keep that sense here without supplying words that come, subjectively, from the translator's understanding of the verse. Since *ḥarôn* and *ḥay* are parallel, they should have parallel senses.

[170]Within the group of imprecatory psalms, 35, 59, 69, 70, 109, and 140 are individual laments and 58, 83, and 137 are community laments. The introduction to Ps. 35 discusses the reasons behind the imprecations.

[171]*NIB*, IV, 912, sees the title as an illustration rather than history. Ewald, I, 292, assigns the psalm to Josiah, writing during the invasion of Palestine by Egypt. W. E. Barnes, II, 279, attributes the psalm to Nehemiah. Buttenwieser, p. 715, dates the psalm between 318–312 BC, a time when Palestine was overrun by enemy armies. These views rest on subjective grounds.

for the "chief musician" (*m^enaṣṣeaḥ*, see 4, intro.) to use in worship. The psalm is to be sung to the tune of "Al-taschith" (see 57, intro.). The psalm is a "Michtam" (see 16, intro.) for its hearers to think on. The heading sets the time in the early life of David, when King Saul sought him at his house.[172] David escaped through the deception of his wife Michal (I Sam. 19:11–17). Later, after his accession to the throne, v. 11 ("my people"), he writes to record his feelings at the time of the trial.[173] His deliverance from Saul becomes a picture of his deliverance from the heathen nations that threaten the land, vv. 5, 8.

I. Appeal for Deliverance 1–5

1–2 David prays that God would deliver him from his enemies. He does not name them here. He is likely thinking of Saul and the servants who sought to take him captive. He asks the Lord to "defend" (*śagab*, see 20:1) him, placing him out of reach of his enemies, v. 1. He asks again for deliverance. This time, he describes his foes as "workers of iniquity" and "bloody men [*ᵓᵉnôš*, see 8:4]," would-be murderers, v. 2.

3–5 His foes "lie in wait," seeking to ambush David and take his life. These "mighty" (or "fierce") men "gather together" (or "stir up strife") against him, even though he has not committed any transgression or sin against them, v. 3. Without any "fault" (or "iniquity") on his part, his adversaries "run" against him and "prepare [or 'establish'] themselves" to take David. He therefore beseeches the Lord to rouse to help him, to see what his enemies are doing, v. 4. He calls on the "Lord God of hosts [*ṣᵉbaᵓôt*, see 24:10]," the ruler of the hosts of heaven and earth, and the God Who has specially chosen Israel as His people, to awake. David asks the Lord to "visit" (*paqad*, see 8:4) the heathen in judgment. He should not be "merciful" (or "gracious,"

[172]Thirtle, pp. 43–46, transfers this title to Ps. 58 and appends the musical instructions of Ps. 60 to the end of this psalm. He reads *ᶜedût* as the plural of *ᶜedâ*, "testimonies," and relates the psalm to the Passover celebrated under Hezekiah. The psalm, however, is one of judgment, not celebration.

[173]Delitzsch, II, 186, sets the psalm after an assumed watch by Saul of David's house in Gibeah. He explains the references to the "heathen" as "the heathen-minded in Israel," p. 188. While a possible view, this rests on an event not referred to elsewhere.

ḥanan, see 4:1) to these "wicked transgressors [*bagad*, see 25:3]" (or "who are treacherous in iniquity"). David closes the paragraph with "selah," drawing attention to his great need, v. 5.

II. Assurance of Deliverance 6–13

6–8 David describes his enemies poetically. They return to his house in the evening, hoping to find a time when they can capture him without drawing attention. They are like snarling dogs, wandering about the city seeking for their prey, v. 6. They "belch out" (or "pour out," *nabaᶜ*, see 19:2) bitter words against him. Their tongues are like "swords," weapons raised against him. They carelessly say, "Who . . . doth hear?" overlooking the fact that an omniscient God hears every word man speaks, v. 7. For this reason, the Lord will laugh at them just as He scoffs at all the heathen, v. 8.

9–13 The phrase "his strength," referring to the strength of David's foes, should be read "my strength," a vocative referring to the Lord.[174] David purposes to wait for the Lord, His "defence," to act. He has made God his "defence" (or "refuge," *miśgab*, see 9:9), v. 9. The God Who shows "mercy" (or "steadfast love," *ḥesed*, see 5:7) will "prevent" (or "go before") David. He will let David see his desire accomplished on his foes, v. 10. With an unusual request, David asks the Lord not to slay his adversaries. With no foes to face, Israel might well forget the Lord. David rather wants to see his foes scattered by God's power and brought low by the Lord, Israel's "shield" (or "defense," *magen*, see 3:3), v. 11. David mentions the wicked speech of his enemies, seen in three ways. They are arrogant, they curse, and they lie. For these reasons, he asks that they might "be taken" (or "be captured"), v. 12. He asks the Lord to "consume" (or "destroy") them in His "wrath" (*ḥemâ*, see 6:1) toward them. Because of David's request in v. 11, the phrase "that they may not be" must here be understood "that they may have no more power."[175]

---

[174]There is no need to supply words. Many manuscripts and ancient versions have "my strength" rather than "his strength." In addition, "my strength" parallels the expression in v. 17. Kidner, p. 212; Murphy, p. 333; and Moll, p. 356, adopt "my strength," as do several Hebrew mss, the LXX, and the Vulgate. Phillips, I, 472; Calvin, III, 386; and Hirsch, I, 406, follow the MT in translating "his strength."

[175]Lawson, p. 301, explains v. 11 as David's prayer that God would "spare the lives of his enemies, at least initially." This will let all see their "humiliation and defeat."

They will then know that God rules over Israel "unto the ends of the earth" and is not limited anywhere in power. David again emphasizes his words with "selah," v. 13.

III. Acclamation for Deliverance 14–17

14–15 Here David draws on the picture earlier given in v. 6. The verses are virtually identical in form, but the meanings are significantly different. There, his foes snarled over their prey; now, they growl like starving dogs looking for food. There, they sought their prey; here, they look for something to eat, v. 14. The phrase "let them wander" is simply "they wander." They look for food and "grudge" (better "growl," *lûn*)[176] when they do not find it, v. 15.[177]

16–17 His foes vanquished, David vows to "sing" of God's power. In the morning, when the brightness of peace replaces the darkness brought on by his enemies, he will "sing aloud" (*ranan*, see 5:11) of the Lord's "mercy" (or "steadfast love," *ḥesed*). David rejoices because the Lord has been his "defence" (*miśgab*, see 9:9) and "refuge" (*manôs*)[178] during his trouble, v. 16. Verse 17 repeats the thought of vv. 9–10. David will "sing" (*zamar*, see 7:17) to the One Who is his "strength." God is both David's "defence" (*miśgab*) and the God of "mercy" (or "steadfast love," *ḥesed*), v. 17.

The psalm illustrates many principles that believers should follow today. David relies on the Lord for deliverance from his trials, vv. 1, 2, 5, 11, 13. He recognizes that opposition will come to the righteous

---

Later, God will consume them, v. 13. The view is a possible way of harmonizing vv. 11 and 13.

[176]The verb *lûn* means "to murmur." Since the subjects are dogs, this is interpreted as "growling." The word occurs frequently in the Pentateuch, but this is the only occurrence in the Psalms. Fausset, III, 221, and Kirkpatrick, p. 337, understand the root as *lîn*, "to lodge, spend the night." If David's foes are not satisfied, let them "spend the night," i.e., spend the night in misery. Delitzsch, II, 192, varies this view. The enemies are not satisfied, so they spend the night looking for satisfaction. While possible, these views require more interpretation to understand and do not carry through the theme of dogs mentioned in v. 14.

[177]The NEB moves v. 15 between vv. 6 and 7 and deletes v. 14. The textual evidence does not support this. Kidner, p. 212, aptly comments, "This tells us no more than how the translators would have written the psalm themselves."

[178]There is little difference between *miśgab* and *manôs*. Both are places of refuge. The *miśgab* is a high place, unreachable by others, while the *manôs* is a place to which one flees for protection.

even though they have not sinned, vv. 3, 4. David commits his trials to the Lord in prayer, vv. 1, 2, 5, 11, 13. He calls upon the God of power ($^{\supset e}$*lohîm*), vv. 1, 5, 9, 10 (twice), 13, 17 (twice); on the merciful Lord (*y*^{e}*hwah*), vv. 3, 5, 8; and on his master ($^{\supset a}$*donay*), v. 11. He refers to the weapon of speech, v. 7. He recognizes the sins of his foes: "iniquity" and "bloody men," v. 2; "wicked transgressors," v. 5; and sins of speech seen in pride, cursing, and lying, v. 12. He speaks of God as King over the earth, v. 13, and he praises God for His power, mercy, and strength, vv. 16–17.

PSALM 60

David assigns the psalm to the "chief musician" (*m*^{e}*naṣṣeaḥ*, see 4, intro.) for use with the nation's worship. Its tune is "Shushan-eduth,"[179] which means "the lily of the testimony," likely the title of some well-known melody.[180] The psalm is a "Michtam" (see 16, intro.), a song for the hearers to meditate on. The title sets the psalm at the time of the battles between Israel and Syria (II Sam. 8:3–8; I Chron. 18:3–5). David fought with Aram-naharaim, "the Aram of the two rivers." While not clearly identified, this is probably the area controlled by Zobah between the Euphrates and Habor rivers. Shortly after David's battle here, his forces under Joab killed twelve thousand

[179]Thirtle, p. 127, transfers the musical instructions to the preceding psalm and appends those of Ps. 61 to this psalm. Because of a slightly different grammatical expression he refers the instruction to a "stringed instrument choir." While this is possible, there is only weak support for transferring them to this psalm.

[180]Alexander, p. 271, makes the "lily" an "emblem of beauty or loveliness." The psalm has a beautiful theme or subject, "most probably . . . the gracious promise cited from it." Hirsch, I, 409, translates *šûšan* as "rose." He comments, "The Lord is ready at all times to send Israel the dew of revival. Let Israel only open its heart, as the rose unfolds its petals, and turn it upward to accept the life-giving dew drops of God's word." Both of these views are devotional but require the reader or hearer of the psalm to subjectively interpret the symbol. The term "Shushan-eduth" is more commonly taken as a musical direction.

men of Edom in the Valley of Salt, on the border between Israel and Edom and south of the Dead Sea (II Sam. 8:13).[181]

I. Distress of the People 1–5

1–3 On behalf of the nation, David laments the situation he faces. It is as though God has rejected them and "scattered" (or "broken") them. God has been "displeased" (better "angry") with them. The OT does not give any details to explain this lament. Apparently, the Syrians had invaded the northern part of the land, winning several significant victories before David arrived with his army. He pleads with God: "Turn thyself to us again" (better "restore us again"), v. 1. God has caused the land to "tremble" (or "quake") and has "broken" (or "split") it; these poetically describe the reverses Israel has experienced.[182] David prays that God will heal the shaking, v. 2. God has caused the people to see "hard things" (or "difficult times"). They have drunk the "wine of astonishment [or 'staggering']," a figurative picture of Israel's confusion at these defeats, v. 3.

4–5 David now displays his faith in God. God has given a "banner" to those who "fear" (see *yirʾâ*, 2:11) Him, the godly. This is likely the promise of His presence with His people.[183] The phrase "that it may be displayed because of the truth" is better "for the flight from the face of the bow [*qošeṭ*]."[184] Although the people flee from

---

[181]II Sam. 8:13 and I Chron. 18:12 give 18,000 men killed, while the title here gives 12,000. The first passage refers to David's leadership, the second to Abishai, and the title here to Joab. David provided overall leadership, Joab served as the general, and Abishai had the delegated leadership of the troops in Edom. The numbers here likely refer to a single engagement, while the numbers in II Sam. and I Chron. refer to the whole campaign.

[182]Kissane, p. 259, and Gaebelein, p. 243, understand this as a literal earthquake that has shaken the land. While this is possible, the greater threat to the nation lay in the Syrian invasion. Poetic descriptions are normal in David's writings.

[183]Henry, III, 460, explains the "banner" as "David's government, the establishing and enlargement of it over all Israel." While this is possible, the promises of God are a greater banner to encourage God's people. VanGemeren, p. 413, considers the banner as "designating a place where the godly may find refuge under the protection of the Divine Warrior." The view also fits into the context here. Thompson, p. 302, follows the LXX, which understands the "banner" as "a signal for flight." While the view agrees with the context of vv. 1–3, it lacks support in Hebrew.

[184]The word *qošeṭ* may mean either "truth" or "bow." The first of these meanings occurs only in Prov. 22:22. While the meaning "bow" occurs only here, *qošeṭ* is thought to be a variant of *qešet*, a word that occurs several times with the meaning

the threat of Syria, they have the truth of God's promises to encourage them. To emphasize this, David adds the word "selah," v. 4. The result will be deliverance. Although the name "David" means "beloved" (*yadîd*, see 45, title), the word here refers to the nation, beloved by God. David asks God to save the nation by His "right hand," the hand of His power (e.g., 20:6; 21:8), and to hear his prayer, v. 5.[185]

II. Confidence of the Psalmist 6–12

With only minor differences, verses 5–12 appear again in Psalm 108:6–13. Since that psalm does not have a clear historical setting, it is likely that some later psalmist simply borrowed these words, joined them with other borrowed words from Psalm 57:8–12, and created a psalm of praise to God.

6–7 David now shows his confidence in God as he recalls the promises previously given. God has spoken in His "holiness," and therefore His words are true. He will "rejoice," exulting over His enemies. He will "divide" (or "apportion") Shechem, giving it to whom He will. The city of Shechem lay in the valley between Mt. Ebal to the north and Mt. Gerizim to the south. He will also measure out the "valley of Succoth," east of the Jordan River, a little more than a mile north of the Jabbok River, v. 6. Gilead, the northeastern part of Palestine primarily occupied by Gad in biblical times, belongs to God. Manasseh, here referring to the parcel east of the Jordan River and north of Gad, also belongs to Him. Ephraim, in the center of the nation and later the dominant tribe of the Northern Kingdom, is the "strength" (or "stronghold," *ma^côz*, see 27:1) of His head. This pictures Ephraim as a helmet that God puts on for protection. Judah, in

---

of "bow." Murphy, p. 336, and Alexander, p. 272, translate *qošeṭ* as "truth." Murphy considers this "a noble view of their mission on earth." This is possible, but both the context and the frequent occurrences of *qešet* support the sense given above.

[185]The AV rightly reads the *q^erê*, "hear me," repeated in 108:6, rather than the *k^etîb*, "hear us." David prays on behalf of the nation. Perowne, I, 471, and Harman, p. 223, adopt the *k^etîb*. This makes little change in the meaning of the verse. With the *k^etîb*, David prays on behalf of the nation. With the *q^erê*, he focuses on himself as the one praying.

the south and later the dominant tribe in the Southern Kingdom, is His "lawgiver" (or "giver of decrees," i.e., commander), v. 7.[186]

8 On the other hand, Moab, east of the Dead Sea, is God's "wash-pot," a pot for washing dirty hands. He will "cast out" His "shoe" (or "sandal") upon Edom, south of the Dead Sea, treating it with disdain.[187] Both of these nations were lifted up with pride (Isa. 16:6; Jer. 48:29; 49:16; Obad. 1:3), but God will humble them. The phrase "triumph thou" (*rûaᶜ*, see 41:11) is better "cry out concerning me." God will triumph over Philistia, v. 8.[188]

9–12 David asks rhetorically who will bring him into the "strong [or 'fortified'] city." The parallel half of the verse suggests that he thinks of the difficulties of overcoming Sela (now called Petra), the major city of Edom, v. 9. David answers his own question. The God Who has rejected the nation and abandoned their army will help them, v. 10.[189] David asks Him directly to deliver them from "trouble" (or "the adversary"). Other men can offer only "vain" (or "worthless," *šawʾ*, see 12:2) help, v. 11. By God's help, however, they will "do valiantly" (or "work mightily") since God Himself will "tread down" (or "trample upon") their enemies, v. 12.

---

[186]Eaton, p. 155, and Perowne, I, 473, understand *mᵉḥoqᵉqî*, "lawgiver," as "scepter" ("staff of command") from its use in Gen. 49:10 and Num. 21:18. That sense is debatable in those references. In Deut. 33:21; Judg. 5:14; and Isa. 33:22, the meaning of "lawgiver" is appropriate.

[187]Thompson, p. 302, and Henry, III, 461, suggest that the tossing of a shoe over a territory is a sign of taking possession. While this is a possible view, there is nothing clear in the OT to indicate that this was an Israelite custom. Ruth 4:7 is often cited for this purpose, but it differs significantly. In Ruth, the shoe is given to the neighbor to show the giving away of a possession. The shoe here is tossed on Edom, not given by Edom. W. E. Barnes, II, 287, describes this: "The master casts his shoes to his slave to take up; cf. Matt. iii. 11." Rotherham, p. 261, is similar: Edom is "so reduced as to become another slave to whom the master kicks off the sandals when he would have them removed to wash his feet."

[188]The idea is even clearer in 108:9, where the verb is changed slightly to bring out this sense.

[189]Hengstenberg, II, 287, and Alexander, p. 274, make David quote from 44:9. While v. 10 is similar to 44:9, it is not identical. The "sons of Korah" authored Ps. 44, while David authored Ps. 60. It is more likely that both authors paraphrased some common saying in Israel than that one author borrowed from the other.

PSALM 61

The simple heading tells us nothing about the background of the writing of the psalm. There are, however, details in the psalm that suggest the time of Absalom's rebellion. It is the work of David during his reign as king, v. 6. He laments the opposition of his foe, v. 3, commits himself to God in prayer, vv. 1–2, and declares his faith in God, vv. 4, 8. Whatever the nature of the trial, David demonstrates a right spirit in his trust of the Lord to deliver him. This is the attitude that all Christians should adopt as they face difficulties.

As is often the case, David writes for the "chief musician" (*m*ᵉ*naṣṣeaḥ*, see 4, intro.), the head of the priestly musicians. The psalm is an individual lament that David designs to be accompanied by "Neginah" (*n*ᵉ*gînôt*, see 4, intro.), music from an unknown stringed instrument.

I. The Cry of David 1–4

1–2 David asks God to hear his "cry" (*rinnâ*, see 17:1) and listen to his "prayer" (*t*ᵉ*pillâ*, see 4:1), v. 1. He calls out to God "from the end of the earth," far from his normal place of dwelling. From v. 3, it is likely that this reflects the flight from Absalom, when David is away from the tabernacle at Jerusalem.[190] His heart is "overwhelmed" (or "faint"). He asks God to lead him to the "rock" (*ṣûr*, see 18:2) that is "higher" than he is, a stable foundation upon which he may rest, v. 2.[191]

3–4 David recalls his past. God has been a "shelter" (or "refuge," *maḥseh*, see 14:6) for him. He has been a "strong tower," protecting David from his "enemy." The singular word "enemy" indicates that David thinks here of one particular enemy, likely his son Absalom, v. 3. Verse 4 should be understood as a prayer: "Let me abide in thy tabernacle . . . let me trust. . . ." David longs for access to the tab-

---

[190]Eaton, p. 157, suggests that the expression suggests "the entrance to the Underworld," as though the psalmist was about to die. The expressions of confidence throughout the psalm argue against taking the phrase in this way. W. E. Barnes, II, 289, places the psalmist "in exile." The view rejects David's authorship, a subjective conclusion.

[191]William O. Cushing based the words for his hymn "Hiding in Thee," written in 1876, on this verse. Ira D. Sankey wrote the music in 1877.

ernacle, where he may worship God for the remaining years of his life.[192] He desires to "trust" (better "take refuge," *ḥasâ*, see 2:12) in the "covert" (or "shelter") provided by God's "wings" (*kanap*, see 17:8). The picture poetically describes the protection given by God.[193] The word "selah" draws attention to David's plea, v. 4.

II. The Confidence of David 5–8

5–8 David now expresses his confidence that God will give His blessing. God has heard his vows of devotion in the past. He has given David the "heritage" (or "possession") He gives to all that "fear" (or "reverence," see *yirʾâ*, 2:11) Him. God's "name," here and in v. 8, refers to His revealed nature, v. 5.[194] The next two verses describe God's gift in a way that goes far beyond David's immediate life. God will prolong the king's life to "many generations" (*dor wador*, cf. 10:6), v. 6. He will "abide" (*yašab*) in God's presence "for ever."[195] These statements refer to Messiah's enjoyment of God's blessings upon His reign. David asks God to "prepare [or 'appoint'] mercy [or 'steadfast love,' *ḥesed*, see 5:7] and truth" as guardians to "preserve" (or "watch over") Him, v. 7. In view of what God will do, David purposes to "sing praise" (*zamar*, see 7:17) to God's "name,"

---

[192]Rawlinson, II, 17, argues that since the psalmist is in the end of the earth, "the literal 'tabernacle' cannot be intended." He understands this as "a spiritual abiding in the heavenly dwelling." David, however, prays for victory over his foe, an act of this life. The mention of prolonging his life, v. 6, shows his emphasis on the present rather than the future. The verbs here are cohortatives expressing David's wish for this life, not for the life to come.

[193]There is an unusual emphasis on the protection God gives to those who trust Him. He is a rock unreachable by man, v. 2; a refuge to give protection; a tower of strength, v. 3; a tabernacle where we may worship; and One Who spreads His wings over His own to cover them from attack, v. 4.

[194]See note 94 at 5:11 for a summary of the Lord's "name."

[195]Briggs, writing in Moll, p. 362, makes this a simple prayer for a long life, that David may see "one generation after another." This does not explain David's pledge to praise God "for ever." Bratcher and Reyburn, p. 539, understand "for ever" to refer to "the continuation of his dynasty through descendants which will succeed him on the throne." The view makes the singular subject "he" a collective. Since the singular occurs throughout the psalm, this is unlikely. It is common for psalms to focus on David and then move to an application in the life of the second David. Hengstenberg, II, 291, interprets the verb *yašab* as "sits enthroned" and makes the verse messianic, fulfilled in the Lord's reign. This is a possible view.

His revealed nature, "for ever." He will carry out his vows of devotion to God each day, v. 8.

PSALM 62

David prepares the psalm for the "chief musician" (*m^enaṣṣeaḥ*, see 4, intro.), the one responsible for the music in the nation's worship. At this time, the chief musician was Jeduthun, another name for Ethan, whom David appointed as one of the leaders of the tabernacle music.[196] The background to the psalm is not clear, but David faces opposition of some unknown kind, vv. 3, 4.[197] He maintains his confidence in the Lord, vv. 1–2, 5–8, realizing that God will judge all men, vv. 9–12.

I. Opposition of Men 1–4

1–2 In contrast with the many places where David cries out to God, here he "waiteth" (or "is silent") before God. From Him will come David's "salvation" (or "deliverance"), v. 1. He recognizes that God alone is his "rock [*ṣûr*, see 18:2] and . . . salvation," his sure foundation and deliverer. He is David's "defence" (or "refuge," *miśgab*, see 9:9); therefore, David will not be greatly "moved" (or "overthrown"), v. 2.

3–4 David now mentions those who seek to overthrow him. How long will they carry on their "mischief" (or "threaten," *hût*)[198] against

[196]The introduction to Ps. 39 discusses Jeduthun. The phrasing here differs from that in Ps. 39, *ᶜal-y^edûtûn* here rather than *lîdûtûn* there. According to Leupold, p. 458, this implies "that the psalm should be sung in a manner . . . characteristic of Jeduthun." While this may be the case, we do not know enough to be certain.

[197]Lawson, I, 311, suggests either the time of Saul or Absalom. Thompson, p. 305, and Rotherham, p. 264, suggest the time of Absalom's rebellion as the background. Weiser, p. 446, is more general: David "has been forsaken and is now persecuted by his former friends." Since David speaks with authority in the psalm (e.g., v. 8), I would place it after his accession to the throne. The psalm does not let us be certain of more than this.

[198]Although this is the only place *hût* occurs in the OT, there is an Arabic cognate that supports the sense "to shout, assail." I have interpreted this as "threaten."

him? The phrase "Ye shall be slain all of you" is better "You murder, all of you." This continues the thought of the first phrase. Like the fall of a "bowing" (or "leaning") wall or a tottering fence, v. 3, these have given counsel to bring him down from his "excellency," his high position as king of the land. They "delight" (*raṣâ*, see 40:13) in the "lies" (*kazab*, see 4:2) they have spoken about him. They "bless" (*barak*, see 5:12) him with their speech, apparently referring to words spoken in his presence, but inwardly curse him. David calls attention to their tactics with the word "selah," v. 4.

II. Trust of David 5–8

5–8 Verse 5 partially repeats the thought of v. 1. David urges himself to "wait" (or "be still") on God, meditating on Him and His promises. David's "expectation" (*tiqwâ*, see 9:18), referring here to his anticipation of deliverance, is from God, v. 5. David repeats v. 2, omitting only the final word. God alone is his "rock [*ṣûr*, see 18:2] and . . . salvation," his sure foundation and deliverer. He is David's "defence" (or "refuge," *miśgab*, see 9:9). Therefore, David will not be "moved" (or "overthrown"), v. 6. David's "salvation" (or "deliverance") and "glory" (or "reputation") depend upon God. He is "the rock [*ṣûr*] of [David's] strength," the foundation of his hope, as well as his "refuge" (*maḥseh*, see 14:6), the position of safety, v. 7. David urges the people to trust God continually. They should pour their hearts out in prayer, recognizing that He is the source of their "refuge" (*maḥseh*). The addition of "selah" lays stress on this thought, v. 8.

III. Judgment of God 9–12

9–10 Man cannot be trusted. "Men [*ʾadam*] of low degree" are "vanity" (*hebel*, see 31:6), and "men [*ʾîš*] of high degree" are "a lie" (*kazab*, see 4:2).[199] Should men of this character be placed in a balance to weigh their moral make-up, they would be less than "vanity" (or "nothing," *hebel*), with a negative moral impact on others, v. 9. Men should avoid wicked actions. They should not trust in "oppression" to gain things for themselves. They should not set their vain

[199]See the discussion contrasting *ʾadam* and *ʾîš* at 22:6.

hope in robbery. Even if they become rich, they should not set their affections on their wealth, v. 10.

11–12 The idiom of speaking once, then twice, conveys the fact that God has clearly indicated His will.[200] Power belongs to God, v. 11. Similarly, "mercy" (or "steadfast love," *ḥesed*, see 5:7) belongs to God. He will therefore "render" (or "recompense") to all men as their "work" deserves. By His power, He will judge the wicked. From His loyal love, He will extend favor to those who trust Him, v. 12.

David's conclusion in these final verses makes a powerful application. God will judge every person according to his or her work. In view of this, people today should live in accord with God's revealed will in His Word.

PSALM 63

The simple heading identifies David as the author and sets the psalm during his flight from Absalom in "the wilderness of Judah" (cf. II Sam. 15:23; 16:2). David fled from Jerusalem, first passing over the brook flowing through the Kidron Valley, between the city and the Mount of Olives. From there he passed through the northern part of the Wilderness of Judah, where he stayed the night (II Sam. 16–17). This is the region south of Jerusalem and directly west of the Dead Sea.[201] He then crossed the Jordan River and turned north to Mahanaim, about forty miles away. The timing suggests that he composed the psalm during his first night of flight (cf. v. 6), before passing over the Jordan River.[202]

---

[200]Mays, p. 216, and Jennings, I, 291, relate the two speeches to the two truths that follow, God's power and God's loyal love. This same pattern, however, occurs in Job 33:14 and 40:5, where two speeches are not in view. A similar idiomatic pattern occurs in Amos 1–2 and Prov. 30 (both "three . . . four") as well as in Job 5 and Prov. 6 (both "six . . . seven").

[201]Only Judg. 1:16 refers elsewhere to the Wilderness of Judah. It is the same as the Wilderness of Judaea in Matt. 3:1 (Mark 1:4; Luke 3:2).

[202]Anthony R. Ceresko, "A Note on Psalm 63: A Psalm of Vigil," *ZAW* 92:3 (1980), p. 435, also places the psalm as a night vigil. J. W. McKay, "Psalms of Vigil," *ZAW* 91:1 (1979), p. 231, considers the psalm a dawn vigil, "perhaps following a

Although David faces a serious threat, v. 9, the psalm displays his confidence in God. This confidence sets a marvelous example for believers today. Rather than worrying about the outcome of trials, believers should trust the Lord instead. He will work out difficult situations so that His will is done and His glory is shown. Christians should display their confidence in Him.

I. David's Longing for God 1–5

1–2 David claims the God of might (*ᵓᵉlohîm*, see 7:1) as his own God. He will seek Him "early" (or "earnestly"). To illustrate his desire, he compares it to a thirst for a cool drink. He thirsts as for a drink of water in a "dry" (or "parched") and "thirsty" (or "weary") land, one with no refreshing water, v. 1. The AV reverses the order of the clauses in the MT of v. 2. The verse is better "I have looked on you in the sanctuary to behold your power and your glory." David has seen evidences of God in the tabernacle. He has seen God manifest His power and glory, possibly in answers to prayer, v. 2.

3–5 The "lovingkindness" (or "steadfast love," *ḥesed*, see 5:7) of God is better than all that "life" has to offer.[203] For this reason, David purposes to speak words of "praise" (*šabaḥ*)[204] to God, v. 3. He will "bless" (*barak*, see 5:12) God while he lives and will lift up his hands in the "name"[205] of God, i.e., His nature, as he offers prayers, v. 4.[206] He will be satisfied with the presence of God in his life, a satisfaction compared with eating "marrow [*ḥeleb*, see 17:10] and fatness [*dašen*]," v. 5.[207]

---

night's sleep in the temple." David, however, could not have stayed in the temple, which was built later under Solomon. Hirsch, pp. 425, 430, refers v. 11 to King Saul and so relates the psalm to David's flight from Saul. Oesterley, pp. 305–6, identifies the king in v. 11 as Jehoiachin. He thus makes the psalm one of an exile in Babylon. Verse 6 supports a sleepless night, one during which David may well have composed the psalm.

[203]The plural *ḥayyîm*, "lives," lends emphasis here. David thinks of life in all of its fullness.

[204]The word *šabaḥ* has the sense of giving commendation for something. With this sense, it most often occurs of giving praise to God.

[205]See 5:11, note 94, for a brief summary of the Lord's name.

[206]See 28:2 for a discussion of lifting the hands in prayer.

[207]There is no great difference between *dašen* and *ḥeleb*. This is the only place in the OT where both words occur together. This emphasizes the poetic picture. God

II. David's Confidence in God 6–8

6–8 David states that he remembers God during the hours of the night. There were three night watches, the beginning (Lam. 2:19), middle (Judg. 7:19), and morning (Exod. 14:24). At these times, David meditates on God, consciously placing Him in his thoughts, v. 6. Because God has helped him in the past, he will continue to "rejoice" (*ranan*, see 5:11) in the "shadow of thy wings," the protection given him by God, v. 7. David's soul "followeth hard after" (better "clings to") God. At the same time, God's "right hand," the hand of God's power, upholds him, keeping him from falling before his foes, v. 8.

III. David's Triumph Through God 9–11

9–10 David is confident of eventual victory over his enemies. Those who seek to "destroy" (*šô*ʾ*â*, see 35:8) his life will die and "go into the lower parts of the earth." From the use of this phrase elsewhere (e.g., Ezek. 26:20; 31:14), the phrase idiomatically represents Sheol, v. 9. They will "fall by the sword," the phrase showing David's belief that the Lord will let his troops triumph over his foes. Their corpses will feed the "foxes" (or "jackals") who feast on the decaying flesh, v. 10.

11 David, "the king," will rejoice in God. Those who take oaths by God will glory in Him. In sharp contrast, those who "speak lies" about David, spreading false rumors and accusations about him, will "be stopped," silenced by their deaths so that they can no more speak against him, v. 11.

PSALM 64

As David normally does in his individual lament psalms, he first describes the peril that he faces, then expresses his confidence that the Lord will deliver him. We do not know the nature of the specific

---

satisfies more than the choicest of foods.

peril David faces.[208] At this time, there are multiple enemies arrayed against him, likely all joined together in some plot. They have plotted against him, vv. 2, 5, and have spread false words, vv. 3–4. They search for matters that will let them accuse him, v. 6, and the result threatens his life, v. 1. Yet he retains his confidence that God will overthrow them, vv. 7–8. The nation will honor the Lord for His deliverance, vv. 9–10.

David intends the psalm for use in the tabernacle ceremonies and so writes it for the "chief musician" (*m^enaṣṣeaḥ*, see 4, intro.). The dedication suggests that he is king, with influence over Israel's worship. The effort of his foes to plot secretly against him (v. 5) suggests the need to avoid the king's anger and retaliation. The obvious time for this is Absalom's rebellion (II Sam. 15) although, as stated above, we cannot be positive.

Because the psalm leaves the specific situation unclear, the psalm stands as a pattern for the behavior of Christians in all difficult circumstances. David's prayer asking God for deliverance and his following confidence in God set an example for believers today. God is the same today as He was in David's day. He is still able to deliver those who trust Him.

I. The Cry of David 1–6

1–6 David goes to God in prayer, pleading for deliverance from the "fear" (or "dread," *paḥad*, see 14:5) of death. The word "prayer" (or "complaint," *śîaḥ*, see 55:2) refers to the king's repetitious cry over the trials facing him, v. 1. He asks the Lord to "hide" him, protecting him from the secret plans of his foes. They are an "insurrection" (better "throng") of those who work "iniquity" (better "trouble"), men who plan evil against him, v. 2.

---

[208]Hirsch, I, 430, and Jennings, I, 296, refer the psalm to Saul's persecution of David. Leupold, p. 468, thinks the psalm is a "general prayer that was prepared for the use of individuals who encounter unprincipled foes." Clarke, I, 163, relates the psalm to Absalom's rebellion against the king. *The Midrash on Psalms*, trans. William G. Braude (New Haven: Yale University Press, 1959), I, 526, suggests that the psalm prophesies the plot to place Daniel in the lion's den. Spurgeon, III, 155, refers the psalm to the conflict between Haman and Mordecai. These widely different suggestions reflect the impossibility of finding the setting of the psalm with certainty. Whatever the setting, it comes from David's life.

These enemies have accused David falsely. Their tongues are like sharp swords and like bows that they "bend" (or "tread on," *darak*, 7:12) to string them (cf. 7:12; 11:2) in order to shoot forth their "bitter words," v. 3. They shoot their false words secretly at the "perfect" (or "innocent," *tam*, see 7:8). They do this suddenly, with no fear of reprisal, v. 4.

These foes of David plan their wickedness. They "encourage themselves in" (or "strengthen for themselves") the evil they plot. They secretly devise the trap that they lay for him. This "evil matter" refers to the false accusations of vv. 3–4. They plot to lay "snares" (*môqᵉšîm*, see 18:5) for David. Because of their secrecy, they are confident that no one will catch them. They "encourage themselves" (*ḥazaq*, see 27:14) in their wickedness, v. 5. They "search out [*ḥapaś*, or 'devise'] iniquities [*ᶜawlâ*, see 7:3]," their wicked plans. They carry out a "diligent [*ḥapaś*] search [*ḥepeś*]." The word *ḥapaś* refers to searching or planning. The threefold repetition in the verse emphasizes the plotting against the king. These thoughts are "deep" (or "unsearchable"), v. 6.

II. The Confidence of David 7–10

7–10 David earlier used the arrow to represent the evil words of his foes. He now uses this symbol to picture the poetic justice of God. God will shoot His arrow of judgment at them suddenly. They will be "wounded" (*makkôtam*), an expression that symbolizes defeat (e.g., 18:38; 68:21). The plural *makkôtam* suggests the intensity of their fall, v. 7. The tongues that formerly spoke evil of David will now "fall upon themselves," speaking divisively within their own group.[209] Others will "flee" (*nûd*, better "shake the head"), deriding them for their failure, v. 8.[210]

---

[209]The grammar here is awkward. The phrase is lit. "they cause to fall upon him, upon them their tongue." The pronoun "him" is a collective, referring to the group as a whole.

[210]The AV understands "flee" as the *hitpoᶜel* from *nadad*, "to flee." So Kissane, p. 274; Ewald, I, 263. While this is grammatically possible, the *hitpoᶜel* of *nûd* expressing the thought of derision is more natural. After the judgment has fallen, it is too late to flee. Kidner, p. 229, sees the shaking of the head as an expression of "shocked concern." This also is possible.

All who see God's overthrow of their plans will "fear," reverencing Him for His work. They will openly declare the works of God and will "wisely consider" (or "understand") what He has done, v. 9. The righteous will rejoice in the Lord. They will "trust" (or "take refuge," *ḥasâ*, see 2:12) in Him, finding all the protection they need in His care. They will "glory" in Him as they recognize His power to deliver them from their enemies, v. 10.

PSALM 65

This is "a psalm [*mizmôr*] and a song [*šîr*]"[211] of pure praise to the Lord. In addition to praising God and recognizing His mighty power, David gives one of the fullest descriptions in the OT of God's work in nature, vv. 9–13. This emphasis makes it likely that David composed the psalm in praise to God for the harvest.[212] He writes the psalm for the "chief musician" (*m*[e]*naṣṣeaḥ*, see 4, intro.) to use with the nation's worship.[213]

David sets forth multiple reasons for men to thank God. God forgives their sins and invites them to come to Him, vv. 1–4. He is a powerful God and gives men reasons to rejoice in Him, vv. 5–8. He cares for men as He provides an abundant harvest to supply their needs, vv. 8–13. For all of these reasons and more, it is still appropriate to offer thanksgiving to God.

---

[211]Ps. 65 is a community song of thanksgiving. The introduction to Ps. 18 summarizes the songs of thanksgiving. For a discussion of the words "psalm" (*mizmôr*) and "song" (*šîr*), see the introduction to Ps. 30.

[212]Kirkpatrick, p. 360, places the psalm "at the presentation of the first fruits at the Passover." He excludes Pentecost and Tabernacles because "the corn was still in the fields," v. 13. The psalm, however, may have been meant for use at the end of the harvest rather than at the beginning. Harman, p. 232, understands the psalm as one of thanksgiving "appropriate on many occasions throughout the year." The psalm, however, speaks directly of the harvest, not simply of general blessings.

[213]Perowne, I, 497, dates the psalm after Sennacherib's invasion, too late for David's authorship. Rawlinson, II, 29, rejects David's authorship because of "the mention of the temple, and especially of the 'courts' of the temple." The word "temple" (*hêkal*), however, may refer to either the tabernacle or the temple. Similarly, the "courts" may be those of the tabernacle or temple, depending on the context.

I. The Gracious Forgiveness of God 1–4

1–2 The first part of the verse should read something like "Praise is due [*dumîyâ*][214] to thee, O God, in Zion." As the nation praises God, they willingly perform their "vow." David does not define this. He may think of some specific vow, or he may use the term collectively, referring to all the vows due to God, v. 1. David recognizes God as One Who answers the "prayer[s]" (*t^epillâ*, see 4:1) of His people. This leads him to an eschatological thought. Looking forward to the Millennium, "all flesh" will come to God, v. 2.

3–4 Various "iniquities" have prevailed against David. Still, God will "purge" (better "atone for," *kapar*, see 49:7) the transgressions of the people, v. 3. Logically following the thought of forgiveness, David recognizes that the man chosen by God is truly "blessed" (*ʾašrê*, see 1:1). This man may approach God in prayer and dwell in the courts of His house, the tabernacle. He will be satisfied with the "goodness" found there in the holy "temple" (*hêkal*, see 5:7).[215] David thinks of such things as answers to prayer, fellowship, and the privilege of worshiping God, v. 4.

II. The Mighty Power of God 5–8

5–8 Still thinking of Israel's prayers, David recognizes God's faithfulness. God brings "terrible" (or "awesome") things in "righteousness," faithfulness to what He has promised the nation. The verb "wilt thou answer" is better "you answer," which expresses God's continued response to their needs. He is truly the "God of [their] salvation," the One Who has delivered them in their needs. Once again, David looks into the future millennial kingdom, when those in "all the ends of the earth" and "them that are afar off upon the sea" (better "and the farthest sea") place their confidence in God, v. 5. David illustrates God's power by giving examples from nature. God "setteth

---

[214]The accents join *dumîyâ* and "praise," *t^ehillâ*, a feminine noun. This suggests reading *dumîyâ* as *domîyâ*, the feminine participle of *damâ*. The LXX and Vulgate follow this. Delitzsch, II, 226, applies the phrase to "resignation . . . (given or presented) to Thee as praise." This understands *dumîyâ* as "resignation," a sense it does not clearly have.

[215]Thompson, p. 309, expresses his concern over "a difficult critical problem" when v. 4 refers to the temple, not built in David's reign. The word *hêkal*, however, does not necessarily refer to the temple. It rather identifies the dwelling of God. In David's time, this was the tabernacle.

fast" (or "establishes") the mountains by His strength, a natural act since He is "girded with power," v. 6. He quiets the roaring of the seas,[216] the crashing noise of its waves in the storm, and the consequent tumult of the "peoples" (or "nations"), v. 7. Those who live in "the uttermost parts" are in awe of God's "tokens" (*ʾôt*).[217] Even "the outgoings of the morning and evening," i.e., the sunrise and the sunset, "rejoice" (*ranan*, see 5:11). This pictures mankind, from east to west, singing for joy, v. 8.[218]

III. The Abundant Care of God 9–13

9–11 David concludes the psalm by giving several illustrations to show how God uses His power in caring for mankind. Ultimately, the fulfillment of this description lies in the kingdom reign of Christ over the earth. He "visit[s]" (*paqad*, see 8:4) the earth to care for it. He "water[s] it" (or "overflows it") and enriches it from "the river of God." The phrase refers to the store of waters in the heavens from which God continually brings forth rain upon the earth. He "prepar[es] corn" (or "provides grain") to the people once He has provided the needs of the land, v. 9. He abundantly waters the "ridges" (or "furrows") and levels the "furrows" (or "ridges"). He softens the ground with rain and "blessest" (*barak*, see 5:12) the crops as they spring up, v. 10. He crowns the year with His goodness in the harvest. Since this takes place in the spring, David considers the agricultural year rather than the calendar year. David pictures the abundance poetically. God's "paths," the tracks left by His chariot as He travels through the earth, "drop [or 'drip with'] fatness," the abundance of the harvest, v. 11.

12–13 "They," the paths of God, drip with fatness on the pastures where the flocks graze in the wilderness regions. The small hills of

---

[216]Fausset, p. 235, makes the sea "the emblem of the world-power." While seas may represent people elsewhere, the parallelism with "mountains" here argues that David draws his illustration from nature. God controls both the natural world and the human world.

[217]The word *ʾôt* occurs seventy-nine times in the OT. In almost every place, it refers to a religious sign, some evidence of God or of God's work.

[218]The phrase "outgoings [*môṣâ*] of the morning and evening" is unique, occurring only here. The word *môṣâ*, however, does describe the sunrise and thus the east in 75:6. This gives the sense here of east and west, i.e., people all over the world rejoicing in God and in His works.

the land are covered with rejoicing as they experience the nourishment that God supplies, v. 12. The "pastures" (or "meadows") seem to be clothed with the white of the flocks that graze in them. "Corn" (or "grain") covers the valleys. David climaxes the picture with the thought of nature's delight. The personified creation rejoices in the blessings of God. "They," the pastures and valleys, "shout for joy" (*rûaᶜ*, see 41:11) and sing to express their rejoicing, v. 13.[219]

PSALM 66

The psalm expresses praise and thanksgiving to God for His wondrous works. It begins broadly, calling upon the whole earth to praise God, vv. 1–4, then focuses on His work toward the chosen nation of Israel, vv. 5–12. The psalmist finally states his intention to worship God with offerings, vv. 13–20. The title identifies the word as "a song *or* psalm" (better "A song. A psalm").[220] The heading gives no author[221] or occasion for writing the psalm.[222] The writer prepares the

---

[219]Delitzsch, II, 231, argues that "the meadows and valleys" cannot sing. He feels that "the expression requires men to be the subject, and refers to men in the widest and most general sense." Earlier, however, Delitzsch sees the hills as personified. Nothing in the passage hints that David has moved away from this picture. The passage is highly poetic.

[220]For a discussion of the words "psalm" (*mizmôr*) and "song" (*šîr*), see the introduction to Ps. 30.

[221]Spurgeon, p. 283, makes David the author. Clarke, I, 167, suggests Hezekiah or Isaiah. Rawlinson, II, 34, assigns the psalm "to a later Judaean king, as Asa, Jehoshaphat, or Hezekiah." Kissane, p. 280, places the psalm after the Exile. These views are speculative; the psalm gives only vague clues to identify its author. From the description of the offerings that he plans to make, v. 15, the psalmist must have had access to great resources. This suggests that it is either a king or one of the highly placed priests. We cannot say more than this.

[222]Fausset, III, 236, and Cohen, p. 204, make the psalm refer to the deliverance from Sennacherib. Hengstenberg, II, 323, understands the psalm as prepared to use "generally on every occasion of deliverance from hostile power." These views are possible but tenuous since the psalm does not give information about its purpose. Dahood, II, 119, notes two sections of the psalm (vv. 1–12, 13–20) and concludes that the second part "is the thanksgiving of an affluent individual fulfilling his vows in the Temple." It is unlikely that the psalm has two authors. No ms evidence sup-

psalm for the "chief musician" (*m^e^naṣṣeaḥ*, see 4, intro.) to use with the nation's worship.

As most of the psalms do, this psalm has multiple practical applications. The writer calls others to rejoice and praise God, vv. 1–2. He acknowledges God's power and speaks of the resulting worship of mankind, vv. 3–4. He recalls God's deliverance of Israel from Egypt and mentions His continuing rule over the nations, vv. 5–7. He calls on Israel to praise God for His continuing care, vv. 8–12. He praises God for His work on his behalf, vv. 13–15. He testifies to God's answering his prayer, vv. 16–17, cautions that sin will keep God from answering prayer, v. 18, and closes with a note of praise to God, vv. 19–20. Christians should still follow this example of recalling God's work on their behalf and then praising Him for His mercy.

I. The Work of God on Behalf of Mankind 1–4

1–4 The psalmist here calls on the people of the world to "make a joyful noise" (*rûa^c^*, see 41:11), a shout of praise to God, v. 1. The people should "sing forth" (*zamar*, see 7:17) songs telling the "honor" (or "glory") of God's "name," His revealed nature.[223] They should praise God in a way that is glorious, v. 2. Verse 3 develops the reason. The people should acknowledge to God that His works are "terrible" (or "awesome"). Because of the greatness of God's power, His enemies will "submit themselves" (*kaḥaš*, see 18:44), feigning a yielded attitude for fear of His judgment, v. 3. The whole earth will worship God. They will "sing" (*zamar*) praises to God, singing of His "name," His exalted nature. Although the psalm does not emphasize it, the fulfillment of this lies in the future millennial rule of Christ. The psalmist stresses the thought of worldwide praise by adding "selah" to his statement, v. 4.

---

ports this. There is a logical progressing in the psalm as the focus shifts from the world to Israel to the psalmist himself.

[223]See 5:11, note 94, for a brief summary of the Lord's name.

II. The Work of God on Behalf of Israel 5–12

A. The Works of God 5–7

5–7 The psalmist calls on the nation to "come and see," i.e., to consider God's work among men. He is "terrible," awesome, in what He has done, v. 5. As an example of God's might, the psalmist recalls Israel's passage through the Red Sea (Exod. 14:21–22).[224] With the waters rolled back and dry ground exposed, the people passed through on foot. The Song of Moses (Exod. 15:1–19) illustrates the rejoicing of the people at that time, v. 6.[225] This God rules by His power forever and watches over the nations. For this reason, the rebellious people should not "exalt themselves."[226] Once again, the "selah" emphasizes the thought, v. 7.

B. The Response of the People 8–12

8–12 In view of God's work, Israel should "bless" (*barak*, see 5:12) and praise Him.[227] The psalmist urges the people to let their voice be heard as they praise God, v. 8. God "holdeth our soul in life," preserving them from their foes. He has not let their feet "be moved" (*môṭ*)[228] by enemy attacks, v. 9. God has "proved" (better "tried") the nation, testing them by the trials He has brought. He has "tried" (or "refined," *ṣarap*, see 12:6) them. The psalmist compares this to purging dross from silver by the fires of testing, v. 10. God has

[224]Dickson, p. 387, and Phillips, I, 528, refer the "flood" to the crossing of the Jordan River, the verse thus combining both crossings. This is possible although the only rejoicing recorded is at the crossing of the Red Sea.

[225]Numerous authors, e.g., Dahood, I, 121; Cohen, p. 205, translate as a future, "Let us rejoice in Him." The cohortative, however, may also occur euphonically without a future sense. G.K.C. 109 *g*. The use of *šam*, "there," supports the sense given above.

[226]It makes little difference whether the preposition *lamô* introduces the object, "Let not the rebellious rise up against Him" (NIV), or is reflexive, "Let not the rebellious exalt themselves" (AV, NASB). The result is the same.

[227]The word "people" (*ʿammîm*) is plural, "peoples," but the context of vv. 10–14 argues that it refers to Israel. God has "proved" the nation, v. 10, laid "affliction" on them, v. 11, and brought them through slavery and fire and water into the abundance of Palestine, v. 12. The psalmist will make offerings in God's house, v. 13, which he has vowed, v. 14. This clearly refers to Israel. Alexander, p. 287, and Murphy, p. 354, refer *ʿammîm* to the "nations," but this does not fit the context.

[228]The word *môṭ* refers to tottering or slipping, often referring to a lack of security. When this is negated, the figure reverses into a picture of great security.

brought the nation into the "net" (or "stronghold"), a place of captivity, referring to their years of slavery in Egypt.[229] He placed "affliction" (*mûʿaqâ*),[230] a crushing burden on their "loins" (or hips"), the central part of the body that often strains in carrying a heavy load, v. 11. He caused weak "men" (*ʾenôš*, see 8:4) to "ride over [Israel's] heads," putting Israel in subservience to others. They went through the fires and waters of testing. When this was complete, God brought them into "a wealthy place" (or "a place of abundance," *rᵉwayâ*, see 23:5), v. 12.

III. The Work of God on Behalf of the Psalmist 13–20

A. The Psalmist's Offering 13–15

13–15 Not only should the world see God's power, not only should Israel see God's power, but the psalmist himself has seen God's power.[231] He does not tell how God has answered his prayer. In some way, however, God had freed him from some trial. He had vowed an offering in return (Lev. 7:16; 22:21). He pledges now to go to God's house, either the tabernacle or the temple, depending on the date of writing, to fulfill his vow, v. 13.[232] The psalmist simply says that he

[229]Kidner, p. 234, states that "the ordeal . . . is probably not that of the Exodus but something more recent." This is entirely possible. If so, however, we can only speculate what it might be. The Exodus fits nicely into the context. Leupold, p. 481, sets the passage after "the deliverance wrought in Hezekiah's day." The nation, however, did not come into a place of abundance after the destruction of Assyria. They remained in the land where they already lived and, in fact, did not have a harvest until the third year, Isa. 37:30. Kissane, p. 283, suggests the Babylonian Captivity. It is difficult to see Palestine, after the Captivity, as a place of abundance. Hirsch, I, 445, speaks of "constraint" placed on Israel so that they could not move freely among other nations. We do not know of any such constraint in biblical times other than the times of captivity. Phillips, I, 530, leaps into the future, making the passage refer to the Tribulation judgments. The context does not support a prophetic view here.

[230]This is the only place in the OT that *mûʿaqâ* occurs. It comes from the root *ʿwq*, "to crush," which does occur elsewhere. The noun indicates more than light affliction. It is an oppressive burden, a crushing load.

[231]The final verses of this psalm may be considered a song of thanksgiving. The introduction to Ps. 18 summarizes the songs of thanksgiving.

[232]Fausset, III, 237, makes the psalmist speak "as personifying the elect nation." It is highly unlikely that he represents the nation. The passage uses the first person nineteen times. In addition, in v. 16, he calls upon those who "fear God," not possible if he personifies the godly in the nation.

been in "trouble" (or "distress") when he had made the vow, v. 14. He will offer "burnt sacrifices of fatlings," animals fattened especially for sacrifice. Since the burnt offering was totally consumed in the fire, it represented complete dedication to God. He will offer also the "incense" (or "smoke") from sacrificial rams. He will offer "bullocks" (or "bulls") and male "goats." The rams, bulls, and goats simply develop the nature of the "burnt offerings" mentioned earlier. For the third time (cf. vv. 4, 7), the psalmist emphasizes the point by adding "selah," v. 15.

B. The Psalmist's Testimony 16–20

16–17 The psalmist calls upon others who "fear [see *yirʾâ*, 2:11] God" to listen while he tells what God has done. The phrase "for my soul" does not necessarily suggest that his life has been at risk. It can as well simply refer to himself, i.e., he will tell what God has done for him, v. 16. He has called upon God and exalted Him with his speech. This last thought suggests that the psalmist has put his faith in God's answer to his prayer and so has offered praise to Him, v. 17.

18–20 Had the psalmist seen sin favorably within himself, the Lord would not have heard his petition, v. 18.[233] But God had certainly heard him and answered the need expressed in his "prayer" (*tᵉpillâ*, see 4:1), v. 19. In light of this, the psalmist can only say, "Blessed [*barak*, see 5:12] be God." In His faithfulness, God has not turned away from the psalmist's "prayer" (*tᵉpillâ*) nor taken His "mercy" (or "steadfast love," *ḥesed*, see 5:7) from him, v. 20.

---

[233]The author does not refer to sinless perfection. If this were required, no one would have the right of prayer. As much as possible, however, he sought to keep himself free of known sin.

PSALM 67

We do not know the author of the psalm[234] or the occasion that called forth its writing.[235] It presents a prayer of the nation, a song of thanksgiving.[236] The writer assigns it to the "chief musician" (*m^enaṣ-ṣeaḥ*, see 4, intro.). The "psalm" (*mizmôr*) and "song" (*šîr*)[237] is for performance on "Neginoth" (*n^egînôt*, see 4, intro.), unknown stringed instruments. The psalm still has a place in the worship of the Jews. They recite it before the evening service that ends the Sabbath.[238]

I. Prayer for God's Blessing 1–2

1–2 The psalmist makes a threefold request: for God to be "merciful" (or "gracious," *ḥanan*, see 4:1) to the people, to "bless" (*barak*, see 5:12) them, and to "cause [His] face to shine" on them (cf. 31:16), revealing His presence. The word "selah" draws attention to God's work, v. 1. The declaration of God's ways throughout the earth is a natural response, including the telling of His "saving health" (better "salvation") in all the nations, v. 2.[239]

II. Prayer for Mankind's Response 3–4

3–4 The prayer now broadens its focus to include the whole earth. The psalmist desires that the "people" (plural, all mankind) should

[234]Spurgeon, p. 288, makes David the author.

[235]Gaebelein, p. 263, understands the psalm as portraying the "coming age of the Kingdom." Although every OT blessing can be taken as a picture of millennial blessing, it is more likely that the psalmist wrote of his own time. Cohen, p. 207, connects the psalm to "an abundant harvest which followed soon after the victory over Assyria." That harvest, however, did not come until the third year after the victory. Many authors (e.g., Rodd, Sabourin, Weiser) understand the psalm as celebrating the yearly harvest. The broad nature of praise in it, however, focuses on making God known to all mankind.

[236]The introduction to Ps. 18 summarizes the songs of thanksgiving.

[237]For the words "psalm" (*mizmôr*) and "song" (*šîr*), see the introduction to Ps. 30. As in Ps. 66, the last part of the title is simply "A Psalm. A Song."

[238]*NEJ*, p. 669.

[239]In a real sense, v. 1 gives three steps of Christian growth: 1) receiving salvation by the gracious act of God, 2) growing in grace as God blesses you, and 3) sensing the presence of God in your life moment by moment. Verse 2 describes the witness to God that should naturally follow salvation and Christian growth.

praise God. He repeats his prayer to emphasize the thought, v. 3.[240] In v. 4, he gives reasons for this praise. The nations should be glad and "sing for joy" (*ranan*, see 5:11) because God judges them "righteously" (*mîšôr*, see 26:12) and "governs" (or "guides") them. Once more the psalmist uses "selah" to stress the thought, v. 4.

III. Prayer for Israel's Praise 5–7

5–7 Verse 5 identically repeats v. 3. There it introduces the praise to God from all the people. Here it repeats the call that all people should praise God, v. 5, then narrows the focus to Israel in the following verses. Praising God will bring His blessing. The earth will "yield" an abundant harvest.[241] The psalmist emphasizes the personal relationship with God by repeating His name: "God, our God." This God will continue to "bless" (*barak*) the nation, v. 6. The psalmist repeats the thought for emphasis. God will "bless" (*barak*) the nation. As a result, the whole earth will "fear" (or "reverence") Him, v. 7.

Without undue emphasis, the psalm presents a messianic thought. God will receive praise from the nations in the Millennium. He will also govern the nations of the earth, vv. 3–4, and the earth will bring forth an unrestrained increase. Israel will enjoy the blessings of God, and the nations of the world will reverence Him, vv. 6–7.

PSALM 68

The writer prepares the psalm for the "chief musician" (*m*[e]*naṣṣeaḥ*, see 4, intro.), the head of the tabernacle music. Verses 15–18 focus on God's choice of Mt. Zion for the place of worship. Verses 19–23 poetically describe Israel's victory over their enemies.

---

[240]It is possible that vv. 3 and 5 were to be chanted by the people in response to the priests during the reading of the psalm in the temple worship. Leslie, p. 112, adds a similar refrain after v. 7 but has no textual support for doing so.

[241]Kirkpatrick, p. 375, and W. E. Barnes, II, 213, translate as a simple past action: "The earth has yielded its increase." In light of the earlier verses of prayer, I prefer to keep the idea of a prophetic perfect. The psalmist is so certain of God's blessing that he uses a perfect-tense verb to express the thought of future blessing.

Together, these verses suggest that David wrote the psalm at the return of the ark to Jerusalem, after its capture by the Philistines and subsequent stay in the house of Obed-Edom (II Sam. 6:10–12).[242] It is a "psalm" (*mizmôr*) and "song" (*šîr*).[243] On the basis of v. 18, the psalm is often classed as messianic.

I. The Work of God 1–14

A. The Praise of God 1–6

1–2 The thought of God overcoming His enemies introduces the psalm and also occurs again in vv. 11–14, 19–23. David's conquests place the thought in his mind. He calls upon God to rise up against those who "hate" (*śane*ʾ, see 5:5) Him. The statement draws on Numbers 10:35, calling God to rise against His enemies. They then will scatter and flee, v. 1. David pictures the adversaries of God as smoke driven by wind and as wax melted by fire. So the wicked will "perish" (*ʾabad*, see 1:6) before God, v. 2.

3–4 In view of what God has done and continues to do, the righteous should be glad and rejoice. To emphasize the thought, David

---

[242]Jennings, I, 312, places its writing after the victory over the Ammonites, II Sam. 11. Moll, p. 384, varies this slightly, making the psalm an "expression of the certainty of victory" and thus giving it a prophetic sense. It is possible that this later victory gave David the reason to write. Since, however, this was the time of David's affair with Bathsheba and the subsequent murder of Uriah and his companions, it does not seem appropriate for David to sing of Israel's relationship to God. In addition, there is no biblical record of a procession after the victory over Ammon. I have chosen the earlier victory as being more significant to the nation. The return of the ark brought the ark to Jerusalem for the first time and recognized God's choice of the city as the place where He would meet with His people in their worship. Kirkpatrick, p. 375, places the psalm in the last decade of the Babylonian Captivity. Ewald, I, 200, understands it as written for the dedication of the temple after the return from Babylon. Kissane, p. 288, locates it in the time of Judas Maccabaeus, 146 BC. The mention of various tribes of Israel, v. 27, argues for a time during the United Kingdom. Delitzsch, II, 265, understands the occasion as celebrating God's victory over the whole world. Although the final part of the psalm is prophetic, the earlier context does not suggest this. Thirtle, p. 36, transfers "Shoshannim" from Ps. 69 to the close of this psalm and makes it a Passover psalm that sings of "the deliverance from Egyptian and other enemies, and the settlement in a land of prosperity." The view depends upon relocating "Shoshannim." See the introduction to Ps. 4 for a discussion of this.

[243]For the words "psalm" (*mizmôr*) and "song" (*šîr*), see the introduction to Ps. 30. As in Ps. 66, the last part of the title is simply "A Psalm. A Song."

repeats it: let them "exceedingly rejoice" (or "rejoice [*śîś*, see 19:5] with gladness"), v. 3. They should "sing" to God and "sing praises" (or "make music," *zamar*, see 7:17) to His "name," His exalted nature.[244] They should "extol" (or "raise a highway") for the One Who "rideth upon the heavens" (better "rides through the deserts"), the wilderness regions of Palestine. The phrase is similar to Isaiah 40:3; 57:14; 62:10. The people should prepare the way for the coming of the Lord. They should call Him by His name "YAH," a name that stresses God's interaction with men. They should also "rejoice" before Him, v. 4.

5–6 Verses 1–2 describe God's actions toward His enemies. David now turns to God's work on behalf of needy people. God is in His holy "habitation" (*maᶜôn*, see 26:8), His dwelling in heaven. He is a Father to those without fathers and a Judge for defenseless widows, v. 5. He places the "solitary," the lonely, in families. He releases others from captivity, possibly referring to Israel's heritage as prisoners in Egypt. He also places the stubborn in a parched land, v. 6.

B. The Settlement in the Land 7–10

7–10 David recalls Israel's march through the wilderness before coming into Palestine. God had gone before His people, leading them with the pillar of the cloud and the fiery pillar. David emphasizes the thought with the word "selah," v. 7. At Sinai, the earth "shook" (or "quaked"), and the heavens dropped rain.[245] The phrase "at the presence: even Sinai itself" is better "at the presence of God, the One of Sinai." David then repeats the thought: "at the presence of God, the God of Sinai," v. 8. He sent "rain" (*gešem*) to His people to refresh the land,[246] confirming to the nation that the land was their inheri-

---

[244]A brief summary of the Lord's "name" occurs at 5:11, note 94.

[245]Leslie, p. 68, sets the psalm just before the autumnal rains. Kidner, p. 240, relies on the similarity with Judg. 5:4 to make this reference to rain refer to the storm that defeated Sisera. The context, however, is more of Sinai and the journey into the Promised Land than of events that happened after settling the land. David quotes from Deborah's song but thinks of the events at Sinai, Exod. 19:16, 18. While that passage does not mention rain directly, it does refer to "thunders and lightnings," signs that rain is present.

[246]Henry, III, 486, draws upon 78:24, 27 to make the rain refer to the giving of manna. The word used in Ps. 78, *maṭar*, is not the same at that used here, *gešem*. Rawlinson, II, 44, states that this is "not a literal rain, but a shower of blessings—manna, quails, water out of the rock, protection against enemies, victories, etc."

tance. David does not give enough information to know what event he speaks of here. It does, however, agree with God's promise in Deuteronomy 11:11–14, v. 9. The community of Israel has dwelled in the land. God has prepared there "goodness for the poor [or 'afflicted,' *ᶜanî*, see 9:12]." Once again, we do not know to whom David refers. Elsewhere, however, the Lord makes it clear that He will meet the needs of the "afflicted" (e.g., 9:12, 18; 34:6), v. 10.

C. The Defeat of Foes 11–14

11–14 The passage pictures the announcement of some great victory, the recent defeat of an enemy or some past event when Israel came into the land.[247] The Lord delivers the "word" announcing the victory.[248] The feminine plural participle "published" (*baśśᵉrôt*, see 40:9) tells us that great companies of women declare the news.[249] Such passages as Judges 5:1–31 and I Samuel 18:7 illustrate the practice of women rejoicing at the news of a victory, v. 11.[250] While the kings of enemy armies flee in frantic haste,[251] the Israelite women at home divide the spoil from the battle, v. 12. The word "pots"

Cohen, p. 210, understands this "figuratively of the provision" made for Israel in the desert. The word *gešem* occurs over thirty times. It never has a poetic sense but everywhere else refers to literal rain.

[247]Delitzsch, II, 252–53, sets vv. 11–14 in the future. This is difficult to accept since later parts of the psalm are clearly set in the past.

[248]Since nothing relates the "word" to a specific event, it has been taken in different directions. W. E. Barnes, II, 320, understands this as the command to cross the Red Sea. Anderson, I, 488, views it as "Yahweh's voice in the thunder . . . which puts the enemies to flight." Horne, p. 273, makes it the command to engage the heathen that opposed Israel in the wilderness. Hirsch, I, 459, sees the word as a "promise," developed fully in the next verse. Phillips, I, 545, relates it to Rev. 19:15, God's Word that defeats the rebellious nations; the women then echo this word "in songs of praise." I have made the word an announcement of victory because of the celebration of the women in 11*b*. Other views are also possible.

[249]The rabbinical interpretation goes far afield from the plain sense of the verse. *Shabbath* 88*b* makes the "great company" refer to the words of the Lord "split up into seventy languages." The view is extreme.

[250]Rawlinson, II, 44, considers the women "the female choirs which took a prominent part in the war-songs of ancient days." It is possible that these were involved in declaring the victory. Nothing in the verse, however, limits the company of women to the choirs.

[251]The Hebrew emphasizes the nature of the rout by repeating the verb: "they flee, they flee."

(*šᵉpattayim*)[252] is best taken as "sheepfold." The soldiers may sleep in relatively simple surroundings.[253] But the women will enjoy the spoils, which David poetically describes as "wings of a dove covered with silver" and "feathers with yellow [or 'glistening'] gold," v. 13.[254] The "Almighty" (*šadday*)[255] has scattered the enemy. They are as snow scattered over "Salmon" (or "Zalmon"), a wooded hill near Shechem, v. 14.[256]

---

[252]The dual word *šᵉpattayim* occurs only here. Related words suggest different meanings. The denominative verb *šapat* is "to set a pot [on the fire]," while the noun *ʾašpot* is "ash heap." The NIV follows this by translating "campfires." Hirsch, I, 460, makes this "two neatly arranged rows of household vessels," i.e. "the fireside." Holladay, p. 382, advances the meaning of "saddlebags," the bags placed on either side of an animal when in use but laid out at night in the camp. Phillips, I, 546, suggests "the brick kilns of Egypt." A similar word (that should probably be pointed identically) occurs in Ezek. 40:43, which refers to a double-pronged hook set in the wall. The people here lie down among the "stakes." This suggests a "sheepfold," a place that is staked out by setting pegs in the ground. The dual form may either indicate a plural or refer to the type of stake used in defining the fold.

[253]Kissane, p. 294, understands 13*a* as based on the rebuke of Reuben in Judg. 5:16. While the word translated "sheepfolds" there is similar, it is not the same. Likewise, the verbs in the two verses differ. Finally, the particle *ʾim*, here translated "though," does not normally introduce a question. David lives long after the failure of Reuben. There is no reason to bring that thought up here.

[254]The stich does not have a subject. Calvin, III, 17–18, and Murphy, p. 364, refer it to the nation. Cohen, p. 212, sees this as "an idyllic scene of tranquility after the conquest of Canaan." Clarke, I, 173, understands the silver as redemption and the gold as "divine glory seen in the revival of nature," both received by the nation. Weiser, p. 487, suggests this is a picture of the cloud in which the Lord appeared. These views are possible, but I have understood "women" as best paralleling v. 12.

[255]The word *šadday* regularly indicates the all-powerful God. The word occurs largely in the poetical books, with three-fourths of its appearances in Job. In the Psalms, it occurs only here and at 91:1.

[256]Henry, III, 488, spiritualizes the phrase. The Almighty scatters kings for the church, and she is "purified and refined by the mercies of God." While this is true, the passage here does not teach it. Leupold, p. 494, is extreme when he relates the snow to the "bleached bones [of the kings that] lay white amid the dark trees of the forests that cover the mountainsides." The last half of the verse is lit. "It was snowing in Zalmon," which clearly has a poetical sense. I have compared it to the scattering of the fallen kings, but other views are possible. Rawlinson, II, 44, views the ground as "covered with glistering arms, armour, and garments." Delitzsch, II, 256, relates the snow to "the spoil that is dropped by those who flee." Alexander, p. 294, likens the change from war to peace "to the dazzling whiteness of snow in the midst of blackness." Calvin, III, 20, sees the covering of snow on the mountain as a picture of beauty in the nation. Hirsch, I, 461, makes the dove of v. 13 represent Israel. She now shines "snowy-white amidst the dark shadows." Kirkpatrick, p. 386, makes the falling snowflakes picture "the kings driven in pell-mell flight by the breath of the

II. The Worship of God 15–35

A. The Choice of Zion 15–18

15–16 The "hill of God" is Mt. Zion.[257] David compares it to "the hill [better 'mountain'] of Bashan." Bashan occupied the area across the Jordan, north of the Yarmuk River. Its dominant peak is Mt. Hermon. Bashan is "an high hill" (better "a mountain of *many* peaks"), v. 15. Why do these mountains "leap" (better "look with envy")? God has chosen Mt. Zion as His dwelling place. He will dwell there forever, a statement that anticipates the coming kingdom and the eternal ages, v. 16.

17–18 God's "chariots" (*rekeb*),[258] emblems of power and here likely referring to His angels, number "twenty thousand" (or "myriads").[259] The next phrase explains this: "even thousands of angels," lit. "thousands of repetitions," i.e., thousands of thousands. The Lord is in the midst of these even as He dwells among His people. In 17*b*, there is no need to supply the words "as at." The phrase reads, "Sinai is in the holy place [or 'sanctuary']."[260] The tablets of the Mosaic law, given at Sinai, now rest in the ark of the covenant, v. 17.

The Lord now has "ascended on high," into the holy place of the sanctuary located on the high hill of Zion.[261] He has "led captivity captive," taking prisoners from those who themselves had captured others. The phrase comes from the Song of Deborah, Judges 5:12, celebrating Israel's victory over the Canaanites. To lead "captivity

---

Lord." Hengstenberg, II, 350, understands the snow as the "brightness of prosperity." I have given my view above.

[257]Hengstenberg, II, 351, and Perowne, I, 526, translate literally: "A mountain of God is the mountain of Bashan." Bashan is a great mountain, one of many peaks, yet God did not choose one of these to dwell in. The phrase "mountain of God," however, refers elsewhere to Mt. Sinai, Mt. Zion, or (in Ezek. 28), the dwelling of Satan.

[258]The singular *rekeb* is a collective, "chariots."

[259]The word *ribbotayim* is dual in form. The AV translated "twenty thousand" to reflect this. The word *ribbô*, "ten thousand," may also mean "myriads," an indefinite number, Dan. 11:12. The context here supports this idea rather than a definite number. The dual form reflects a plural sense.

[260]Delitzsch, II, 242, translates, "The Lord is among them, it is a Sinai in holiness." The word "holiness" (*qodeš*) has the definite article here. This suggests "the sanctuary" rather than a moral quality.

[261]VanGemeren, p. 449, understands the Lord to ascend to heaven, where He "celebrates his kingship on earth." The context, however, suggests an ascent to the tabernacle. The "high" hill of Zion is the hill where God dwelled on earth.

captive" is idiomatic for taking many prisoners. God has "received gifts for [or 'among'] men," the spoil taken from the enemy, those who have been "rebellious" against Him. This evidence of His power gives Him the right, in the eyes of men, to dwell in their midst, v. 18.[262]

B. The Conquest of Enemies 19–23

19–21 David "bless[es]" (*barak*, see 5:12) the Lord, the One Who "daily loadeth us with benefits" (better "day by day bears our burdens"). He is indeed Israel's Savior. The word "selah" emphasizes the thought, v. 19. This God is "the God of salvation," the One Who delivers His people from their trials. To Him belong the "issues" (*tôṣaʾôt*, or "escapes") from death, v. 20.[263] The word "but" is better "surely," emphasizing the certainty that God will "wound" (or "smite," *maḥaṣ*, see 18:38) the head of His enemies, the hairy "scalp" (or "crown") of those who continue in their trespasses, v. 21.

22–23 The Lord's enemies will not escape His wrath. If they try to hide in the mountains of Bashan, He will bring them from there. There is no need to supply "people" in 22*b*. If the enemies hide in "the depths of the sea," a poetic figure, the Lord will bring them even from there, v. 22.[264] Israel's foot, then, will "be dipped in" (or "smite," *maḥaṣ*) the blood of their foes. Dogs will lick their blood, a poetic picture that these foes are no better than the refuse that often serves to feed these unclean animals, v. 23.

C. The Worship of Israel 24–27

24–27 Because God has delivered Israel, it is right that they should worship Him. David describes the procession in which the ark

---

[262]After a victory, the army might make a triumphal march to parade the captives. Paul uses this picture (Eph. 4:8) to portray the Lord ascending to heaven after capturing the powers of darkness. He bestows gifts by His Spirit, a thought Paul further develops in v. 11 by listing the gifts given for the leadership of the church. Although the bulk of the psalm refers to David, this verse has led to classifying the psalm as messianic. Note 32 in the introduction to Ps. 2 briefly discusses the messianic psalms.

[263]In the Talmud, *Berakoth* 8*a* presents a fanciful view of *tôṣaʾôt*. It relies on the numerical value of the word to conclude that there are 903 forms of death created for this world.

[264]Kidner, p. 243, understands the verse as God "reminding Israel of the periods He overcame to restore them to the promised land." While his view is possible, the imperfect-tense verbs seem rather to promise continued protection for the future.

comes back to the tabernacle.[265] "They," the people, have seen the "goings" (or "procession") of God, the nation's King, into the sanctuary (II Sam. 6:12–15), v. 24. Musicians accompany the procession. These include "singers," choral groups that could include both men and women. The players on stringed instruments follow. The women shaking tambourines accompany the procession, v. 25. David calls upon these various assemblies to bless God. "Bless[ings]" (*barak*) are to come to the Lord from the "fountain of Israel." The expression poetically represents blessings as gushing forth from the fountain that is Israel, v. 26.[266] David mentions several representative tribes, the two northernmost and the two southernmost, in the procession. "Little [*ṣaᶜîr*][267] Benjamin," one of the smaller tribes,[268] is there "with their ruler" (or "the ruler," *radâ*, see 49:14).[269] Although the tribe was insignificant in size, it was Saul's tribe and therefore has been the ruling tribe. "The princes of Judah," the ruling members of the tribe, are there, "and their council" (better "in the throng," *rigmâ*).[270] The leaders of Zebulon and Naphtali are also included, v. 27.

D. The Submission of the Nations 28–35

28–29 David now looks into the future to when the Lord sets up His kingdom and rules the earth from Jerusalem. He acknowledges

---

[265]Dahood, II, 147, sees the phrase as "God's going forth from heaven (vs. 5) to assist his people." This is possible, although it requires an abrupt change to a future event.

[266]Rawlinson, II, 46, relates the "fountain of Israel" to "the sanctuary on Mt. Zion," a fountain from which praise flows to God. The view is possible, although the tabernacle at Jerusalem has no history at this point of David's reign.

[267]The word *ṣaᶜîr* consistently has the meaning of "young" or "insignificant." Here, Benjamin is insignificant because of its small size compared to the other tribes of Israel. That the psalmist could make this statement supports the authorship of David, a time when all twelve tribes of Israel still existed.

[268]Horne, p. 279, and Jennings, I, 326, relate the term "little" to Benjamin's position as the youngest of Jacob's sons. The view is possible.

[269]Moll, p. 389, translates as "little Benjamin, their conqueror." He applies this to the conquest of the nation's enemies. Benjamin did not make up David's army alone, however, and it would therefore be wrong to give them this title.

[270]The word *rigmâ* is the noun form of *rigam*, "to stone." It acquires the meaning of "crowd, throng" from the idea of a heap of stones piled together. Fausset, III, 243, translates the phrase "the princes of Judah, their stoning," and refers it to the stoning of the enemy's forces. There is no record of this in the accounts of the victories over either Philistia or Ammon.

that it is God Who has charged the nation to be strong. To this end, he prays, "Strengthen . . . that which thou hast wrought for us" (or "Be strong, O God, in that which you have wrought for us"), v. 28.[271] Israel's role in the world is now significant. The Lord rules from His "temple" (*hêkal*, see 5:7) in Jerusalem. The kings of the nations will bring "presents," their tribute, to Him, v. 29.

30–31 David prays that God will rebuke "the company of spearmen" (better "the beasts in the reeds"). The figure likely refers to the crocodile, a symbol elsewhere of Egypt (74:14; Isa. 27:1). In addition, he asks God to rebuke the "multitude" (or "herd") of bulls with the calves of the people. The description is clearly poetic, describing the rebellious people of the earth. This rebuke will continue until the nations humble themselves and offer tribute. David now clearly states his prayer that God would scatter those who "delight" (*ḥapeṣ*, see 18:19) in battling against Him, v. 30. Egypt and "Ethiopia" (*kûš*)[272] represent the nations as they bring their gifts to the Lord. The "princes" (or "ambassadors") of Egypt come to Him. The people of Ethiopia turn to Him in prayer, v. 31.

32–35 Because of the assured future submission of the nations to God, it is right to offer praise to Him. David closes the psalm on this note. He urges the nations to "sing praises" (*zamar*, see 7:17) to God. The word "selah" draws attention to this thought, v. 32. They should praise the One Who rides His chariot over "the heaven of heavens," the highest heavens that have been since ancient times. He speaks to the world with a mighty voice, v. 33. The nations should "ascribe strength" to Him, recognizing His mighty power. He shows His "excellency" (or "majesty") in His rule over Israel. He displays His strength in the storm clouds of the sky, v. 34. David is constrained to offer his own note of praise to God. He is "terrible" (or "awesome") from His "holy places," the sanctuary, with the plural of majesty appropriate in referring to God's dwelling on earth. He is the One Who gives strength and power to His people. "Blessed" (*barak*) be such a God, v. 35.

---

[271]While the difference is slight, there is a difference in the translation. The AV shows David praying that God would strengthen the work. The suggested translation above shows David praying that God would be strong as He carries out His work.

[272]The Hebrew *kûš* is translated most often "Ethiopia" but also "Cush" (Isa. 11:11) when referring to the land south of Egypt. When referring to an individual, as in 7:1, it is generally translated "Cush."

PSALM 69

This is an imprecatory psalm. Verses 24–25, 27–28 seek strong punishment for the psalmist's enemies.[273] It is a psalm of David[274] that we cannot certainly place at a specific point in his life.[275] David's enemies seek his life, vv. 2, 4, and the threat imperils the nation, v. 35. The statement "to the chief musician" (*m^enaṣṣeaḥ*, see 4, intro.) shows that David intended the psalm for Israel's worship. To that end, David writes it for performance "upon Shoshannim." The word means "lilies," some tune familiar to the people.[276] This word also occurs in Psalms 45, 60, and 80.

While the psalm is an individual lament and imprecation, the NT also gives it a messianic application.[277] David serves as a type of Christ, with the events happening to him later taking place in the life of the Lord. The NT quotes the psalm frequently. The imprecations remind us that God will punish the wicked. While David's statements are forceful, they are mild compared to with the eternal judgment that will fall on the enemies of righteousness.

---

[273]Within the group of imprecatory psalms, 35, 59, 69, 70, 109, and 140 are individual laments and 58, 83, and 137 are community laments. The introduction to Ps. 35 discusses various reasons that justify the use of imprecations.

[274]Perowne, I, 543, states, "This Psalm could not have been written by David." He does not, however, give another author. Kirkpatrick, p. 397, identifies the author as Jeremiah or "some prophet of a kindred temper of mind under very similar circumstances." Cohen, p. 216, rejects the title and dates the psalm in the Exile. Paul's quote of v. 22 in Rom. 11:9 refers the psalm to David.

[275]Delitzsch, II, 273, sets the psalm at the time of Saul's persecution of David. A better argument can be made for placing the psalm at the time of Absalom's rebellion. It is an emotional time for David, vv. 3, 20. It involves his family, v. 8. He is subject to public ridicule by the city leaders, v. 12. A large group has come against him though he is innocent, v. 4. The dedication to the "chief musician" suggests that David is king at the time of writing. Phillips, I, 553, makes the psalm prophetic "from beginning to end." I agree that it is prophetic, but I would make it typically rather than directly prophetic.

[276]Alexander, p. 300, considers the "lilies" to represent "the delightful consolations and deliverances experienced or hoped for." While this is possible, it is strange that David would introduce the thought with the preposition *ʿal*. This normally indicates "upon," "over," "toward," or "against" and would naturally occur in suggesting a musical direction for the psalm. Murphy, p. 280, refers "lilies" to "the topic presented in the psalm." The four psalms using this term, however, reflect four different types of psalms. It is unlikely that "lilies" refers to the topics in these psalms.

[277]The introduction to Ps. 2 briefly discusses the messianic psalms in note 32.

I. David's First Prayer for Deliverance 1–4

1–3 David poetically describes his plight as though he sinks into deep waters.[278] He asks God to deliver him before his foes overwhelm his soul, taking his life, v. 1. He sinks into the mire, where there is "no standing," i.e., no place to put his feet. He is in deep waters with the flood about to flow over him, v. 2. He is weary with calling out for help. His throat is dried from his cries. His eyes fail him, seeing no deliverance during his "wait" (*yaḥal*, see 31:24) for God to intervene, v. 3.

4 David's foes "hate" (*śane*ʾ, see 5:5) him "without a cause." His enemies undoubtedly perceived a cause, but David had done nothing to merit their attack. Verse 4*a* is similar to 35:19*b*. The Lord applies one of these verses to Himself in John 15:25. Many seek to "destroy" (*ṣamat*, see 18:40) David. He idiomatically describes the number as "more than the hairs of mine head," cf. 40:12. Those who oppose him do so wrongfully, with no just reason for their enmity. Still, they are mighty. They have taken from David "that which [he] took not away [or 'did not steal']," possessions that were rightfully his, v. 4.[279]

II. David's First Expression of Grief 5–12

5–6 David's prayer flows naturally into his grief. Although he has done nothing to cause others to rebel against him, he recognizes that he has failed God. He confesses the "foolishness" (*ʾwl*, see 38:5) of his sin, knowing that it is not hid from God. Since David is not specific, we can only speculate on what sin he has in mind, v. 5. He asks the "Lord God of hosts [*ṣᵉbaʾôt*, see 24:10]" not to punish others who "wait" (*qawâ*, see 25:3) on Him because of his sin. May they not "be ashamed" (*bôš*, see 6:10) or "confounded" (*kalam*, see 35:4) because of it, v. 6.

7–9 It is for God's sake that David has borne reproach from his foes. He has been covered with "shame" (*kᵉlimmâ*, see 4:2), public humiliation, v. 7. He no longer has contact with his family. He is as a "stranger" (*zûr*, see 44:20) to his brothers, not part of the normal

[278]This is a common figure of danger, e.g., 42:7; 88:7, 17; 124:4–5.

[279]Cohen, p. 216, and Perowne, I, 546, understand the phrase "I restored that which I took not away" as proverbial, treating David as guilty of wrongs which he had not done. While this is possible, the phrase does not occur again, and the view cannot be verified.

Israelite culture, and as an "alien" (*nokrî*)[280] to his family. The thought here reflects his flight into the wilderness, no longer having normal contact with his family, v. 8.[281] His zeal for the tabernacle, the Lord's "house," has consumed him. The apostles later applied this phrase to the Lord's actions at the first cleansing of the temple, John 2:17. Others who care nothing about the Lord have reproached David for his zeal. Paul sees in this a foreshadowing of the Lord as He bore the burdens of others rather than live only for Himself (Rom. 15:3), v. 9.

10–12 David had wept and fasted, causing others to reproach him, v. 10. He showed his grief by donning "sackcloth" (*śaq*, see 30:11) to display his grief. This caused others to talk of him, making him a "proverb" (or "byword") for foolish actions, v. 11. Those who "sit in the gate," the city's leaders, repeatedly "speak" (see *śîaḥ*, 55:2) against him. Drunkards play a song (*neĝînôt*, see 4, intro.) that ridicules him, v. 12.

III. David's Second Prayer for Deliverance 13–18

13–15 David turns to the Lord in "prayer" (*tepillâ*, see 4:1) once more in "an acceptable time" (or "a time of favor"). In the abundance of God's "mercy" (or "steadfast love," *ḥesed*, see 5:7), he asks God to "hear" (better "answer") him in "the truth of . . . salvation," the sureness of God's deliverance from his trials, v. 13. David pictures himself as wallowing in mire. He asks God to keep him from sinking in it by delivering him from those who "hate" (*śaneᵓ*, see 5:5) him. He describes this as like being in "deep waters," v. 14. May these floodwaters not overflow him. May the deep waters not swallow him nor the "pit" (*beᵓer*, see *bôr*, 7:15), the grave,[282] close its mouth over him, v. 15.

---

[280]This is the only place that *nokrî* occurs in the Psalms. Elsewhere, it parallels *zûr* eleven times, with no clear difference between the words. Both words occur in all parts of the OT, although *zûr* is more common.

[281]Rawlinson, II, 53, sees here hostile feelings with Eliab. This began with Samuel's choice of David, I Sam. 16:6–13, continued at the conflict with Goliath, I Sam. 17:28, and may even have included others in the family. While this may be the case, the historical records do not mention any rebellious acts by David's brothers.

[282]Perowne, I, 548, understands the "pit" as a literal well. In the context here, where foes seek to "destroy" the psalmist, v. 4, it is better to refer it to the grave. The word has this poetic sense elsewhere, Prov. 28:17.

16–18 Since the Lord's "lovingkindness" (or "steadfast love," *ḥesed*) is good, David asks Him again to "hear" (better "answer") him. Out of the multitude of God's "tender mercies" (or "compassions"), he asks Him to turn toward him, v. 16. Negatively, he asks God not to turn away from him by hiding His face. He is in "trouble" (or "affliction, distress," *ṣarar*, see 31:9) and needs the Lord to "hear" (better "answer") him quickly, v. 17. He seeks the Lord to come near him and "redeem" (*padâ*, see 25:22) him because he faces enemies. With this thought, David sees his adversaries as adversaries of God and thus deserving judgment, v. 18.

IV. David's Second Expression of Grief 19–21

19–21 David focuses on his trial. God knows his "reproach," the taunts that others aim at him; He knows the public "shame" (*bošet*, see *bôš*, 6:10) and "dishonour" (*k^elimmâ*, see 4:2) that has been directed toward him. He knows those who have set themselves against him, v. 19. The reproach has broken David's heart, leaving him "full of heaviness" (or "weak," *nûš*).[283] His emotional reaction here supports the likely background of Absalom's rebellion. David "looked" (*qawâ*, see 25:3) expectantly for someone to extend "pity" (or "sympathy") or offer comfort to him. There is no one, v. 20. David describes his plight poetically: in place of meat, he received "gall," a bitter and perhaps poisonous herb.[284] To quench his thirst, he received "vinegar." Once again, David's experience foreshadows the action of the Lord. Matthew 27:34, 48; Mark 15:23, 36; Luke 23:36; and John 19:29–30 all refer to the Lord receiving "vinegar" while on the cross, v. 21.

V. David's Statement of Imprecations 22–28

This whole section is actually David's third prayer. Because of its nature, however, it is normally described in terms of the impre-

---

[283]The word *nûš* is a *hapax legomenon*. From the related word *ʾanaš*, it is usually translated "weak, sick." From the context, it must be an emotional reaction to David's troubles.

[284]The nature of "gall" is not known. The same word (*roʾš*) is also translated "venom" or "poison" when referred to snakes, Deut. 32:33; Job 20:16. It sometimes parallels "wormwood," a bitter tasting desert plant, e.g., Jer. 9:15; Lam 3:19.

cations. David begins with a mild request but then moves to more forceful language to express his desires.

22–23 David asks that the "table" (*šulḥan*, see 23:5) set with food may become a snare, keeping his foes from their wicked work.[285] May "that which should have been for their welfare [or 'prosperity']" become a trap, again guiding them away from further evil actions, v. 22. May the eyes of his enemies "be darkened" (or "become dim") so that they cannot see additional evil. May their loins shake with fear (cf. Dan. 5:6; Nah. 2:10) and thus turn them from further wickedness. Paul quotes vv. 22–23 in Romans 11:9–10 to show why the Jews had not followed the ways of righteousness, v. 23.

24–25 David asks God to pour out "indignation" (*zaᶜam*, see 38:3), His intense wrath, upon his foes. May God's "wrathful [or 'burning,' *ḥarôn*, see 2:5] anger [*ʾap*, see 2:5] take hold of [or 'overtake']" them, v. 24. May they then dwell in "desolate" (*šamem*, see 40:15) camps, not in their tents. Peter makes the thought of this verse apply to the situation the apostles faced at the loss of Judas. He weaves v. 25 together with 109:8 to move the apostles to select a replacement, Acts 1:20, v. 25.

26–28 David justifies his imprecations. His foes persecute the one that God Himself has already smitten. They speak about the "grief" (or "pain") of those that God has fatally "wounded," v. 26. David asks God to heap up the iniquity of his adversaries, charging them with wickedness after wickedness. May they not be permitted to enter into the righteous existence of eternal life, v. 27. Let them be blotted from the "book of the living," the record listing the names of the godly.[286]

---

[285]Henry, II, 497, sees the "table" as the "altar of the Lord . . . because in feasting upon the sacrifices they were partakers of the altar." This traps them since, by making their offerings (without turning from their sin), they become hardened in their wickedness. Cohen, p. 219, refers this to a table with guests. David's foes have "been faithless to the obligations of blood relationship; so may they suffer by the treachery of friends who share their hospitality but ignore the duties of a guest." Calvin, III, 68, makes the expression metaphorical, implying "a desire that whatever things had been allotted to them in providence for the preservation of life, and for their welfare and convenience, might be turned by God into the occasion or instrument of their destruction." These are possible views. I have adopted the above because of the parallelism with 22*b*.

[286]There are many references to the Book of Life, e.g., Exod. 32:32; Isa. 4:3; Dan. 12:1; Mal. 3:16; Luke 10:20; Phil. 4:3; Rev. 3:5; 13:8; 17:8; 20:12, 15; 21:27. Leupold, p. 506, considers the reference here a listing of those living on the earth. Blotting them from the list brings their life to an end. While this is possible, the

May they not be included with the righteous saints. While these statements seem contrary to Christianity, we must remember that the wicked deserve punishment. David may express this bluntly, but he is consumed with his desire for judgment of the wicked, v. 28.

VI. David's Praise to God 29–36

29–31 In the light of his situation, David sees himself as "poor [*ᶜanî*, see 9:12] and sorrowful [*kaʾab*]"[287] (or "afflicted and in pain"). He asks God to deliver him and to set him "on high" (*śagab*, see 20:1), safe from the attack of his enemies, v. 29. He anticipates praising the "name" of God[288] in song and giving "thanksgiving" (*tôdâ*, see 26:7) to Him, v. 30. This will please the Lord more than a sacrificial offering of an ox or a mature bullock with "horns" (*qeren*, see 18:2) and sacrificially clean, having "hoofs" (*paras*), v. 31.[289]

32–33 The "humble" (see *ᶜanî*, 9:12) will see David praising God for his deliverance. This will gladden the heart of the humble and revive the heart of the ones who "seek" (*daraš*, see 9:10) God, v. 32. The Lord hears the prayers of the needy. He does not despise those who are imprisoned for His sake, v. 33.

34–36 David calls upon the creation—the heaven and the earth—to praise God. Even the seas with their marine life should offer praise, v. 34. David's confidence now comes to the surface. God will save Zion from this threat. He will build up the "cities of Judah"[290] so the people may dwell there and possess the land, v. 35. Their descendants

---

parallel thought of not being "written with the righteous" supports the idea of judgment for sin. In any case, bringing their life to an end would surely bring them into eternal judgment.

[287]This is the only occurrence of *kaʾab* in Psalms. Elsewhere, it can refer to physical pain, e.g., Gen. 34:25; Job 14:22, but normally refers to mental anguish, e.g., Prov. 14:13; Ezek. 13:22.

[288]See 5:11, note 94, for a brief summary of the Lord's name.

[289]The verb *paras* means "divide, break in pieces." The participle here has the sense of a noun, a divided hoof. Lev. 11:3 and Deut. 14:6 set this as a requirement for clean animals that could be eaten by Israel, making bullocks acceptable for sacrifice, Lev. 1:5; 4:3.

[290]Henry, III, 499, refers the cities of Judah to churches that "shall be formed and incorporated according to the gospel model." This spiritualizes the text into something not said or implied by David, making Henry rather than Ps. 69 the authority.

will inherit the land. Those who love the "name" (see v. 30) of God will likewise settle in the land, v. 36.

PSALM 70

This psalm is unusual in that it closely repeats the MT of Psalm 40:13–17. The two are not identical, however, suggesting that David prepared this psalm to meet a specific purpose.[291] While he may have adapted previously written material, the psalm stands alone. The title suggests its purpose: "to bring to remembrance."[292] We do not know the occasion that brought forth the song. David, however, felt it important to record these words to remind him, and others hearing it in the tabernacle worship, of the need to rely upon the Lord.

This psalm is imprecatory[293] although the imprecations do not reach the blunt level found elsewhere. David merely prays here for the defeat and humiliation of his foes. By devoting the psalm to the "chief musician" (*m^e^naṣṣeaḥ*, see 4, intro.), David provides for the public instruction of Israel. Necessarily, because of the similarity to 40:13–17, the discussion here is much the same except that the differences are noted.

---

[291]Kidner, p. 249, suggests that the duplication came about "through the compiling of separate collections of psalms." Fausset, III, 248, proposes that "for the benefit of those who had not as yet received assurance of God's favour, David gives the second part of Ps. xl, in an independent form, as a prayer." Henry, III, 499, submits that the repetition is related to the title: "It may be of use sometimes to pray over the prayers we have formerly made to God." Cohen, p. 222, considers it "detached . . . for use in the temple liturgy." Delitzsch, II, 288, thinks it "obvious that David himself is not the author of the Psalm in this stunted form." He also calls this psalm "a fragment that only accidentally came to have an independent existence." Rotherham, p. 306, argues that Ps. 70 serves to introduce Ps. 71. If the two were originally one psalm, the division must have occurred early. No textual evidence supports this. In addition, there is no common refrain to signal that the two should be joined. This sampling shows that we have no idea why 40:13–17 and 70:1–5 are so close. We can only speculate.

[292]See the discussion of the phrase in the introduction to Ps. 38.

[293]Within the group of imprecatory psalms, 35, 59, 69, 70, 109, and 140 are individual laments and 58, 83, and 137 are community laments. Psalm 35 discusses possible reasons for the imprecations.

I. Defeat of the Enemy 1–3

1–3 The AV supplies the words "make haste," parallel to 1*b*, although 40:13 includes the imperative "be pleased." David seeks deliverance from his foes. He uses the name *ᵓᵉlohîm*, rather than *yᵉhwah* (40:13), perhaps to lay more stress on the power of God, v. 1. May his enemies be openly "ashamed" (*bôš*, see 6:10) and "confounded" (or "humiliated") by their failure to take his life. May they be "turned backward" from their attacks upon him. May they be "put to confusion" (or "disgraced," *kalam*, see 35:4) by the defeat of their plans, v. 2.[294] May those that menace David "be turned back"[295] as the result of their "shame" (*bošet*, see *bôš*, 6:10), their actions in scoffing at David, v. 3.

II. Deliverance of David 4–5

4–5 In contrast with his foes, David asks that those who seek the Lord may "rejoice [or 'exult,' *śîś*, see 19:5] and be glad in thee." He thinks of his immediate deliverance, an act that will bring general joy to the faithful. Those who love the "salvation" given them will continually repeat, "Let God be magnified [or 'exalted']," v. 4.[296] Now, however, David sees himself as "poor" (or "afflicted," *ᶜanî*, see 9:12) and "needy" (or "in need of protection"). He asks God to speed his aid. He looks upon God as his "help" (*ᶜezer*, see 20:2) and "deliverer" and asks the Lord not to delay, v. 5.[297]

---

[294]Ps. 40:14*a* adds the word "together" and the phrase "to destroy it" in the parallel to 2a. This gives it a 3:3 meter rather than the 2:2 here but does not change the sense.

[295]David uses the familiar *šûb*, "to turn back," rather than *šamem* as in 40:15. While this makes the prayer less vigorous, its basic sense is still that of overcoming his enemies.

[296]A *waw* consecutive introduces v. 4 here but not in 40:16, a trivial difference. More significant is David's use of *ᵓᵉlohîm*, as in v. 1, rather than *yᵉhwah*, as in 40:16. Once again, this lays stress on the power of God displayed in delivering David. Finally, v. 4 uses *yᵉšûᶜâ* rather than *tᵉšûᶜâ*, a spelling difference that makes no difference in the "salvation" given to David.

[297]More differences exist between v. 5 and its counterpart 40:17 than in any of the other verses. There is still, however, no significant difference in meaning. While 40:17 says, "Yet the Lord thinketh [*ḥašab*] upon me," v. 5 says, "Make haste [*ḥûš*] unto me, O God." We can only speculate on the difference in the verbs. In Ps. 40, David expresses his confidence in the Lord. In Ps. 70, he urges the Lord to help. David uses *ᵓᵉlohîm* in v. 5 rather than *ᵓᵃdonay* as in 40:17. In v. 5, he uses the mas-

PSALM 71

It is unusual in this section to have an orphan psalm with no indication of either the author or the occasion for writing. In my judgment, David is the author.[298] The phrase "my rock and my fortress," v. 3, occurs only elsewhere at 18:2 and 31:3, both Davidic psalms. Verses 1–3 are similar to 31:1–3; v. 12 to 22:11, 19; v. 13 to 70:2; and v. 24*a* to 35:28, all Davidic psalms. Verse 22 refers to the psalmist's use of musical instruments, a theme familiar in David's writings. The occasion may well be the rebellion of Absalom,[299] but we cannot be certain of this.

The author laments his plight and states his determination to trust the Lord for deliverance. He is older, vv. 9, 18, and has lived a godly life from his youth, vv. 5, 17. Wicked men oppose him, v. 4, even plotting to take his life, vv. 10, 13. Facing this threat, he commits himself to the Lord, vv. 1–4, 9–13, and pledges to trust Him, vv. 5–8, 14–21.[300] He closes the psalm with a triumphant note of praise, vv. 22–24.

Whatever the situation facing the psalmist, the psalm reminds us that wicked people have always opposed the righteous. Harassment, opposition, and persecution today should not surprise Christians. Until the Lord establishes His rule over the earth, believers may expect the wicked to act against them. Our resource is the Lord, not society or government.

---

culine noun *ʿezer*, while in 40:17 the feminine noun *ʿezrâ* gives the same sense. Reversing his earlier use, David uses *ʾĕlohîm* in 40:17 and *yᵉhwah* in v. 5.

[298]The LXX and Vulgate give David as the author. Leupold, p. 511, suggests Jeremiah as the possible author but admits, "Even this guess at authorship is precarious." Kirkpatrick, p. 410, interprets v. 20 as though the nation was in exile, making the author come from this later period of Israel's history. Verse 20, however, can be understood differently. Without significant argument, Oesterley, II, 333, makes the psalm postexilic.

[299]Rawlinson, II, 60, makes the occasion the attempt by Adonijah to take the throne during David's final illness. Later, however, he refers to the threat from "Absalom's party." Adonijah made no attempt on David's life as vv. 10, 11, and 13 suggest. The latter part of the psalm, vv. 18, 21–24, also indicates that David anticipates further service to the Lord.

[300]Fausset, III, 248, makes "the suffering Messiah and His people" the theme of the psalm. "The prayer not to be cast off in old age [vv. 9, 18] applies to Israel, the ancient people, whom Messiah represents." The view overlooks the fact that Israel did not live a godly life from her youth, vv. 5, 17.

I. First Prayer for Deliverance 1–4

1–4 David declares, "I put trust" (or "take refuge," *ḥasâ*, see 2:12) in the Lord. For this reason, he asks the Lord to keep him from being "put to confusion" (or "shame," *bôš*, see 6:10), v. 1. He continues his prayer, asking the Lord to deliver him "in [His] righteousness," i.e., faithfulness to His many promises to watch over the godly. He seeks to escape the threat posed by his enemies. To this end, he asks the Lord to hear him and save him from his foes, v. 2. He asks the Lord to be his "strong habitation [*maᶜôn*, see 26:8]," a secure refuge to which he may flee over and over. The Lord has given a command to save Him. This probably refers to the covenant given in II Samuel 7:12–16. The Lord is his "rock [*selaᶜ*, see 18:2] and . . . fortress," a secure refuge, v. 3. He asks for deliverance from the "unrighteous and cruel [*ḥameṣ*]"[301] man, probably the leader of his enemies, who seeks to take him, v. 4.

II. First Statement of Confidence 5–8

5–8 David now states the basis upon which he comes to the Lord. He has made the Lord his "hope" (or "expectation," *tiqwâ*, see 9:18). He has placed his trust in God from his youth, v. 5. The Lord has "holden [him] up," i.e., supported him, from his birth. The Lord is the One Who took him safely from his mother's womb. He will continually praise God, v. 6. Others consider him "a wonder" (*môpet*),[302]

---

[301]Dahood, II, 172, translates *ḥameṣ* as "robber" on the basis of an Akkadian cognate *ḥamaṣu*, "to despoil, rob." The Akkadian cognate, however, does not explain this Hebrew word. It normally refers to something leavened. The three times it occurs—here, Ps. 73:21 ("grieved"), and Isa. 63:1 ("dyed")—it has a different sense. KB, I, 329, relates it to the same Akkadian cognate, which also means "to strip, plunder" and thus "cruel." William Wilson, *Wilson's Old Testament Word Studies* (Peabody, Mass.: Hendrickson Publishers, n.d.), p. 103, sees the root sense as "to be acid," a meaning that could underlie both "leaven" and "cruel." These sources support the traditional meaning of the word.

[302]Kidner, p. 251, understands *môpet* as "portent," with "its bad sense of 'a solemn warning.'" The view is possible although it leaves us speculating on the nature of the warning. Eaton, p. 179, gives *môpet* a good sense, a sign of "God's marvellous work." Rodd, p. 132, makes the psalmist see himself "as a typical example of divine punishment." Since David praises God in the next verse, the view is doubtful. Leupold, p. 512, gives *môpet* both a good and bad sense. The *môpet* shows "the marvelous guidance of God" as well as the "heavy crosses and strange burdens" that mark David as "a victim of God's judgment." While either view is possible, *môpet* cannot have both meanings here.

a living miracle. He, however, sees himself as resting upon God, his "strong refuge" (see *maḥseh*, 14:6), v. 7. He prays that his speech will be full of praise for the Lord and that he may honor Him always, v. 8.

III. Second Prayer for Deliverance 9–13

9–11 Apparently conscious of the increasing weakness of his old age, David asks the Lord not to cast him away or abandon him, v. 9. He needs the Lord. His enemies threaten him; those who seek his life have plotted together, v. 10. Looking at the success of their efforts thus far, they conclude that God has forsaken him. They plan to "persecute" (better "pursue") and take him, since no one will deliver him from them, v. 11.

12–13 The king commits his way to God. He asks Him not to be "far" from him, i.e., not to forsake him. He needs God to "make haste" (*ḥîšâ*)[303] in helping him, v. 12. At the same time, he needs God to hinder his adversaries. He asks that those who seek his life may "be confounded" (or "ashamed," *bôš*, see 6:10) and "consumed," brought to an end. May others reproach them and bring them to public "dishonour" (*k^elimmâ*, see 4:2), v. 13.

IV. Second Statement of Confidence 14–21

14–16 David states his intention to "hope" (*yaḥal*, see 31:24) continually for the deliverance that God will give. He will multiply his praise to Him, v. 14. He will speak of the righteousness of God and of the deliverances that He has given. He will do this "all the day" since he does not know "the numbers thereof," the full scope of God's work on his behalf, v. 15. He will "go" (or "come"),[304] telling the "strength" (lit. "strengths"), the mighty acts of the Lord God. He will make known the righteousness that only God displays, v. 16.

17–18 God has taught David from his youth. David likely thinks not only of the formal instruction about God he had received from his

---

[303]While it makes no difference in the meaning, the *q^erê* correctly reads *ḥûšâ*, the form that occurs regularly elsewhere, e.g. 22:19; 38:22.

[304]Horne, p. 295, and Murphy, p. 382, follow the AV in taking the verb as "go." They refer this to going in the strength of the Lord. The verb may be translated either "go" or "come." The parallelism, however, and the plural word "strengths" support "come," giving praise to God for His works. So NASB, NIV.

parents but also of the practical lessons in life that God had led him to learn. He will now openly declare these extraordinary "works" (*palaʾ*, see 9:1), v. 17. Now that he is older, he still needs God's presence. He asks God not to abandon him before he can show God's power to his own generation as well as to generations yet to come, v. 18.

19–21 David magnifies the righteousness of God, His absolute purity and faithfulness to His Word. The phrase "who hast done great things" is not rhetorical but refers to the mighty works of God. No one is like Him, v. 19. Although David recognizes that God has brought "great and sore troubles [*ṣarâ*, see 9:9]" to "me" (better "us"), he also is confident that God will quicken "me" (again "us"), restoring the nation to normal life. He will bring them up as it were "from the depths of the earth," the abyss in which the nation would sink without divinely appointed leadership, v. 20.[305] God, however, will increase David's "greatness" (or "majesty"). David asks Him to "comfort me on every side" (or "turn yourself and comfort me"), v. 21.

V. Closing Word of Praise 22–24

22–24 In the light of the deliverance David anticipates, he purposes to praise God. He will praise Him with the "psaltery" (*nebel*, see 33:2), a ten-stringed harp. He thinks particularly of praising God's "truth" (or "faithfulness"). He will "sing" (or "make music," *zamar*, see 7:17) with the "harp" (or "lyre," *kinnôr*, see 33:2), the ten-stringed lyre, as he praises "the Holy One of Israel," v. 22.[306] He will "rejoice" (*ranan*, see 5:11), crying out with joy to the Lord as he "sing[s]" (*zamar*). His soul, "redeemed" (*padâ*, see 25:22) by the Lord, will also rejoice, v. 23. He will speak of the righteousness of God continually because his foes "are confounded" (*bôš*, see 6:10),

---

[305]Fausset, III, 250, understands "the depths [*tᵉhomôt*] of the earth" as the Great Flood. He considers that "the deliverance of godly Noah from the overflowing deluge is a pledge of the deliverance of all God's people out of the floods which threaten them." The coincidental occurrence of the singular *tᵉhôm* at Gen. 7:11; 8:2 does not support making *tᵉhomôt* here represent the Flood. The word occurs widely, including eleven others times in the Psalms, with a variety of meanings.

[306]The name "Holy One of Israel" stresses God's holy nature. The name occurs only here and in 78:41 and 89:18 in the Psalms. It occurs twice in Jeremiah (50:29; 51:5) but twenty-five times in Isaiah, a characteristic name of the Lord used by that prophet.

publicly shamed. Those who have sought to hurt David will be ashamed, v. 24.[307]

PSALM 72

This psalm closes the second book in the Psalms. All that we know of its background is that Solomon authored it.[308] A messianic psalm, it includes a vivid description of the millennial kingdom.[309] Solomon likely wrote it in the first half of his reign, when his actions show his righteous character; cf. I Kings 3:9; 8:22–53. Verse 1 asks for God's blessing on his reign. The remainder of the psalm deals with various aspects of the kingdom reign of the Lord. Solomon's rule therefore becomes a picture of the royal reign of the Messiah.

I. Prayer for the King 1

1 Solomon is both the king and the "king's son," the son of David, the great king established on the throne by God. Solomon asks God to give him His "judgments" (or "justice") and "righteousness," referring to God's faithfulness in keeping His word. Solomon may be claiming God's earlier promise to David that his son would follow him on the throne (II Sam. 7:12–16; I Chron. 22:9–10), v. 1.[310]

---

[307]The final two verbs are prophetic perfects. These reflect David's confidence that God will bring about his deliverance from his foes.

[308]W. E. Barnes, II, 342, sees an unknown psalmist writing of an "ideal king." Jennings, II, 343, offers Ethan the Ezrahite as the author. Ewald, I, 384, understands the psalm as a prayer for a "later successor of David." He suggests Josiah or a later king. Clarke, I, 182, relies on v. 20 to make David the author. There is, however, a different explanation possible for that verse. While the AV gives the title "For Solomon," this is the phrasing of the LXX. The MT has the *lamed auctoris*, regularly used throughout the book to indicate the author. G.K.C. 129 *c*.

[309]Note 32 in the introduction to Ps. 2 briefly discusses the messianic psalms.

[310]Murphy, p. 385, considers the request as asking that God give the king "the right of pronouncing judgment and administering the law." These rights came automatically to the king. Solomon does not need to ask for them. Leupold, p. 517, sees the "judgments" as "a reference to the laws and ordinances which God gave to Israel." But there is no need to ask again for these. Harman, p. 252, makes the prayer a request for character qualities of justice and righteousness. These "will enable the

II. Character of the Kingdom 2–7

2–4 Solomon now turns to the future kingdom of the Lord, the kingdom suggested by his own rule. The Lord will judge in righteousness. He will rule the "poor" (or "afflicted," *ᶜanî*, see 9:12) with "judgment" (or "justice"), v. 2. The mountains and hills occur throughout the land and so appropriately represent Palestine. From these will come peace and righteousness to the people, v. 3. The Lord will judge the "poor" (*ᶜanî*) and deliver the needy. He will "break in pieces" (better "crush," see *dakâ*, 9:9) those who oppress them, v. 4.

5–7 The people will "fear," i.e., reverence God throughout time. This will last "as long as the sun and moon endure," a poetic picture of eternity. Although the sun and the moon will fade from view in eternity (Rev. 21:23; 22:5), the parallelism with "all generations" (*dôr dôrîm*) makes it clear that this worship will continue into the ages to come.[311] Similar idioms occur elsewhere as well, v. 17; 89:36–37, v. 5. With further poetry, Solomon describes the blessings of God. He will be as the rain that makes the field grow after its harvest, thus bringing new crops. He will be as showers that refresh the earth, v. 6. In the days of His reign, the righteous will "flourish" (*paraḥ*),[312] no longer suffering for of their faith. There will be an "abundance of peace" (cf. Isa. 26:3) lasting forever, v. 7.

III. Extent of the Kingdom 8–11

8–11 Solomon now focuses on the universality of the kingdom. The Lord will have "dominion" (*radâ*, see 49:14) "from sea to sea" and "from the river unto the ends of the earth" (cf. Zech. 9:10). These two expressions poetically express the extent of Messiah's worldwide reign. It extends beyond the limits of Palestine, where He sets up His throne. It goes from the bordering sea, the Mediterranean, to the farthest sea; from the bordering river, the Euphrates (cf. Gen. 15:18;

---

king to rule well." The view is possible, but the pronoun "thy" suggests that these are qualities of God.

[311]The phrase *dôr dôrîm* is lit. "generation of generations." This is an emphatic way of saying "all generations," an unending period of time.

[312]The word *paraḥ* occurs here and at 92:7, 12, and 13. In each case, the lit. sense of "to blossom, sprout," leads to a poetical sense of "to flourish."

Josh. 1:4), to the farthest river, v. 8.[313] Those who live in the wilderness, nomads, will acknowledge Him as their King. Even His enemies "shall lick the dust," emblematic of humbling themselves before Him (cf. Isa. 49:23; Mic. 7:17), v. 9. Several kings bring tribute to Him. Tarshish is Tartessus in Spain. The "isles" (*ʾîyîm*) are the coastal areas around the Mediterranean. By extension, the word may include the regions connected to the coasts of the Mediterranean. Sheba lay on the Persian Gulf in Arabia. Seba, a province of Ethiopia, also has the name Meroë in secular history. It is thought to have been located near the confluence of the White and Blue Nile rivers in Ethiopia, v. 10.[314] Not only will these kings submit to Him, but also all the kings of the earth will humble themselves before Him. All nations will serve Him, v. 11.

IV. Compassion of the King 12–14

12–14 The king will care for those in the kingdom. He will deliver the "needy," those wanting in various areas, when they cry out for help. He will care for the "poor" (or "afflicted, *ʿanî*, see 9:12) and those who have no one to help them, v. 12. He will "spare" (or "have compassion on") the poor (*dal*, see 41:1) and the "needy" (*ʾebyôn*),[315] again those lacking in various areas. He will "save the souls" of the needy, delivering them from threats to their lives, v. 13. He will "redeem their soul," rescuing them from those who would deceive them or treat them with violence. Their lives will be precious to Him, v. 14.

While these verses seem strange in a millennial kingdom context, they teach an important truth. Men will still be sinners then and will still be subject to sinful impulses. The Lord, however, will

[313]Isaac Watts paraphrased his hymn "Jesus Shall Reign Where'er the Sun" on this psalm. The original hymn had eight verses, which were based broadly on thoughts drawn from the psalm. Watts wrote in 1719. In 1793, John Hatton wrote the music most often used for the hymn.

[314]Barry J. Beitzel, *The Moody Atlas of the Bible Lands* (Chicago: Moody Press, 1985), p. 77. "Seba," *Unger's Bible Dictionary*, confuses Seba with Sheba, in southwest Arabia, pp. 941, 990.

[315]The word *dal* describes one who is too weak to help himself. This may be due to poverty, Lev. 14:21; position, Prov. 28:15; or illness, Ps. 41:2. The word *ʾebyôn*, however, refers to one who is poor in material things, Exod. 23:11; Deut. 15:11. The words also occur together at 82:4 and 113:7.

watch over mankind. He will not let the wicked take advantage of the defenseless.

V. Tribute for the King 15

15 The phrase "he shall live" suggests that the King will prosper in every way.[316] As an example, Solomon points to the tribute of gold given from Sheba.[317] In addition, the people continually pray for Him. He should be "praised" (or "blessed," *barak*, see 5:12) each day, v. 15.

VI. Blessings of the Kingdom 16–20

16–17 To show the fruitfulness of the land, Solomon refers to corn growing on the top of the mountains, normally a barren area. There is a "handful" (or "abundance," *pissâ*)[318] there. The fruit from the mountains will "shake," i.e., wave, like the waving of the trees on the mountains of Lebanon. The inhabitants of the "city," used indefinitely to represent all the cities,[319] will "flourish" (*ṣûṣ*)[320] like the "grass" (or "plants"), v. 16. The "name" of the Lord, His exalted nature,[321] will endure forever. It will continue as long as the sun; cf. v. 5. Men will

[316]Without arguing the point, Moll, p. 407, applies the verse to the poor man of vv. 12–14. He states that the gold from Sheba is not as fine as the gold from Ophir. It therefore would not be suitable as a gift to the Lord. His argument is weak. The OT nowhere says that the gold of Ophir is the finest gold. Gold is gold, no matter what its source. Any gold may be refined to greater purity. Delitzsch, II, 304, understands the king as the one who gives gifts to a poor man, who in turn responds by praying for the king. Nothing in the text, however, calls for a change in the subject. The pronoun "him" points back to the king ("he") as receiving tribute from his subjects.

[317]Sheba occurs regularly as a source for gold. I Kings 10:10 and II Chron. 9:1, 9 refer to the gold the Queen of Sheba brought to Solomon. Isa. 60:6; Ezek. 27:22; and 38:13 also connect gold with Sheba. Diodorus (iii.12, 14) and Strabo both mention the mining of gold in the region of Arabia.

[318]This is the only time that *pissâ* occurs. Cognate words in Aramaic *ʾpassaʾ*, "spread out," and Akkadian *ʾpašašu*, "spread over, cover, anoint," support the meaning of "abundance."

[319]The Talmud, *Kethuboth* 111*b* makes the city Jerusalem. Rawlinson, II, 66, makes the city the New Jerusalem and the people citizens of "Messiah's kingdom." The passage, however, stresses the blessing of the land. The city therefore likely refers to cities throughout Palestine.

[320]The *hipʿîl* verb *ṣûṣ* means "to blossom." In each of the five times it occurs in Psalms (also 90:6; 92:7; 103:15; 132:18), it has a poetical sense of flourishing. With this, there is no special difference from *paraḥ*, v. 7.

[321]See 5:11, note 94, for a brief summary of the Lord's name.

"be blessed" (better "bless themselves," *barak*) in Him as they recognize their good fortune in having the Lord as their Savior. The nations of the earth will call Him "blessed" (see *ʾašrê*, 1:1; 5:12), v. 17.

18–19 As with the other books of the Psalms, this paragraph closes the book with a doxology of praise to the Lord.[322] The author begins by pronouncing a "bless[ing]" (*barak*) on Israel's God, the One Who has done such "wonderful things" (*palaʾ*, see 9:1), v. 18. In addition, he "blesse[s]" (*barak*) "his glorious name" (see v. 17), a summary of the glorious nature of the all-wise, all-powerful, and ever-present God. May the whole earth be filled with His glory! The doubled "Amen" (*ʾamen*, see 41:13), meaning "so be it," gives a closing emphasis to the doxology, v. 19.

20 The final verse is an addition to the psalm.[323] Occurring at the end of the second book of the Psalms, the statement serves as a closing note to the section. David is the author of most of these psalms. We do not know their compiler. It is likely, however, that he added the statement to take note of David's writings in the collection, v. 20.

---

[322]Each of the five collections of psalms ends with a benediction of praise. See 41:13; 89:52; 106:48; and 150:6.

[323]Moll, p. 408, thinks that Solomon appended the remark here to the collection of the first two books, Pss. 1–72, made under his direction. Henry, III, 510, with his view that David wrote the psalm, has him add these words "when he lay on his death-bed, and with this he breathes his last." Though dramatic, it cannot be so if we accept Solomon as the author. Rawlinson, II, 66, suggests the possibility that the collector of the third book of the Psalms added this to mark "the difference between the previous collection and his own." Since Ps. 86 in the third collection is by David, the view is unlikely.

BOOK III

PSALM 73

Psalm 73 begins Book III (73–89). Of the seventeen psalms in this section, only Psalm 86 is by David. Of the remaining sixteen, eleven are by Asaph or his descendants, four by the sons of Korah, and one by Ethan.

This psalm bears the brief title "A Psalm of Asaph."[1] It is a wisdom psalm, the second of twelve psalms written by the chief musician of the tabernacle in David's time or by his descendants.[2] Someone apparently collected the Asaphian psalms here, missing Psalm 50 in Book II. Asaph likely felt the opposition of the wicked because of his association with David. Several of his psalms, including Psalm 73, involve this theme.[3]

I. The Problem of the Wicked 1–14

1–2 Asaph acknowledges the goodness of God to Israel, especially to those whose heart is "clean" (or "pure"), v. 1. Asaph, however, has faced adversity. His feet were "almost gone," close to stumbling. His steps did not come readily, making him slip amid the trials of life, v. 2.

3–12 Asaph describes the seeming prosperity of the wicked. He had been envious of the "foolish" (or "boastful") when he had seen their "prosperity" (or "peace") despite their wickedness, v. 3. They have no "bands" (better "pangs") to cause their death, and "their strength is firm" (or "their body is fat," a poetical picture of health), v. 4. The "trouble" (*ᶜamal*, see 7:14) that so often plagues "men" (*ᵓenôš*, see 8:4) does not come to them, v. 5. As a result of their success,

---

[1]Calvin, III, 121, suggests that Asaph's name was attached to the psalm "because the charge of singing it was committed to him." He makes David the author. The *lᵉ* preposition indicates authorship, just as it does in the psalms of David. It is arbitrary to change its function.

[2]Pss. 50, 73, 74, 75, 76, 77, 78, 79, 80, 81, 82, and 83. The introduction to Ps. 50 discusses Asaph.

[3]McCann, p. 972, sees links between Pss. 73 and 74 that suggest a common authorship. There are common words: "sanctuary," 73:17 and 74:7; "violence," 73:6 and 74:20; "right hand," 73:23 and 74:11; and "ruin[s]," 73:18 and 74:3 (the only occurrences of the plural form in the OT). The view is possible although not clear enough to state dogmatically.

they wear a "chain" (better "necklace") of pride and a garment of violence, i.e., they are clothed with wickedness, v. 6.

Their eyes bulge with "fatness" (*ḥeleb*, see 17:10), a poetical description of their success. They have more than they could imagine, v. 7. They "are corrupt" (lit. "mock") and speak wickedly. They arrogantly speak of "oppression" (or "extortion"), v. 8. They speak "against" (or "in") the heavens as though having divine authority. Their speech influences the earth with its evil influence from lies, gossip, false accusations, etc., v. 9. "His people return" (better "He brings back his people"). "He," the class of wicked people, brings "his people," those practicing this evil, back to Jerusalem, where they enjoy abundant waters, a picture of their satisfaction, v. 10.[4] They reject the idea that God knows their wickedness. In effect, they are practical atheists, living as though there is no omniscient "most High" (*ᶜelyôn*, see 7:17) God, v. 11. These wicked "prosper in the world" (better "always prosper") and increase in wealth, v. 12.

13–14 Asaph gives in to the circumstances.[5] He feels that "in vain" he has "cleansed" (or "kept pure") his heart and spiritually washed his hands "in innocency," keeping them free from guilt, v. 13. He has "been plagued" (or "stricken") all day and "chastened" (or "reproved") every morning, v. 14.

[4]The verse is difficult. Gaebelein, p. 289, refers the pronoun "his" to God. His people forsake him to fall in with the ungodly. Albert Barnes, II, 256, sees God's people returning to "meditations of Divine things." They are "perplexed" over the success of the wicked. Alexander, p. 316, also understands the pronoun to refer to God. He brings His people "to survey the painful spectacle and drain the bitter draught presented by the undisturbed prosperity of wicked men." There is, however, no antecedent that refers to God. Delitzsch, II, 314, makes *ᶜammô* the subject but translates "their people" as though the suffix were plural. He further reads the *hipᶜîl* verb as a *qal* but then interprets as though "adherents . . . leave the fear of God and turn to them." The phrase lit. reads "therefore he brings back his people hither." I have given my explanation above.

[5]Moll, p. 414, and Delitzsch, II, 315, make vv. 13–14 the words of an apostate who has joined himself to the wicked. This eliminates a conflict with Asaph's words in vv. 15–28. While the view is possible, it is not necessary. Asaphian psalms often express a negative feeling followed by confidence in the Lord, e.g., 74:1, 12; 77:2–3, 11–20; 79:5, 9. The discussion of vv. 15–28 explains the apparent conflict. Nothing in the text indicates a change of spokesman in vv. 13–14.

II. Confidence in the Lord 15–28

15–20 Asaph now expresses his trust in the Lord. He realizes that the previous negative thoughts "offend[ed]" (or "acted unfaithfully," *bagad*, see 25:3) against God's people, v. 15. When he thought on these truths, it was "too painful" (or "burdensome," *ᶜamal*, see 7:14) for him, v. 16. But when he came to the "sanctuary,"[6] the tabernacle, to worship the Lord, he gained understanding of "their end" (*ᵓaḥᵃrît*, see 37:37), the judgment of God on the wicked, v. 17. The Lord has placed them "in slippery places" where they will fall. He will cast them "into destruction," likely a reference to eternal judgment in hell, v. 18.[7] They will be brought into their judgment "in a moment," quickly. Terrors will engulf them, v. 19. As the dream passes upon awakening, so when the Lord "awake[s]" (or "is roused"), He will no longer defer judgment.[8] He will despise their "image" (*ṣelem*, see 39:6), their outward appearance of prosperity, v. 20.

---

[6]Rawlinson, II, 71, regards the plural "sanctuaries" as referring to "the three subdivisions of both the tabernacle and the first temple, viz. the court, the holy place, and the holy of holies." Asaph, however, was not the high priest and would not have had access to the holy of holies. The temple was not built in his time. Leupold, pp. 528–29, refers the plural to "more than the visible Temple buildings. It can refer to the mysterious leadings of the Almighty and the understanding of them." For good reason, he gives no cross-references to support the view. Calvin, III, 142, refers the plural word to "celestial doctrine," as if the psalmist were "coming to the school of God." The view is subjective. The sanctuary elsewhere refers to the dwelling of God and should be so taken here. George Herbert Livingston, *The Book of Psalms 73–150*, in *WBC*, II, 331, suggests that the word "does not necessarily refer to the earthly temple located in Jerusalem, but it carries a deeply spiritual sense." Livingston does not further develop the thought. In normal use, the plural word "sanctuary" intensifies the thought, natural when referring to the dwelling of God on earth. The plural word elsewhere always (except in Lev. 21:22, where it refers to holy offerings) refers to the earthly sanctuary of the true God or a false god.

[7]Leupold, p. 529, refers the destruction to "a sudden and catastrophic overthrow." He gives the deaths of Pharaoh's army in the Red Sea; that of Korah, Dathan, and Abiram; and the end of Saul, Absalom, Shimei, Ahithophel, Sennacherib, and Judas as examples. The view is possible; however, the ultimate judgment is after death. The psalmist would not have needed to focus his thoughts on the Lord to be aware that some men die suddenly. This happens to the godly and ungodly alike.

[8]Fausset, III, 255, understands this as the Lord awakening the heathen; this requires the supply of the object, an unnecessary step. Calvin, III, 147, sees it as the Lord's command to man to awake. The translation does not support this. The verse is difficult; it is lit. "As a dream when one awakens, O Lord, in the city [*baᶜîr*] you despise their image." Hengstenberg, II, 411, considers that the sinful have carried on their wicked actions in the city where God judges them. On the other hand, Perowne,

21–26 Asaph recalls his former feelings (cf. vv. 2–3). His heart had been "grieved" (or "embittered") and his "reins" (or "emotions," *kilyâ*, see 7:9) pierced with the sharpness of his feelings, v. 21. He has been "foolish" (*baᶜar*, see 49:10) and ignorant, as a beast with no faith in God, v. 22. Despite this, the Lord had been faithful to him. Asaph continued to sense the Lord's presence, realizing that the Lord guided him by holding his right hand (cf. Isa. 41:13), v. 23. With renewed confidence, Asaph states his faith that the Lord will guide him with wise "counsel" (*ᶜeṣâ*, see 1:1). After his life is over, the Lord will receive him in glory, v. 24. Spontaneously, Asaph declares his devotion to God. There is no heavenly creature to trust beside the Lord, and Asaph does not "desire" (*ḥapeṣ*, see 18:19) anyone else on earth, v. 25. Even though his "flesh" and his "heart" may "fail" (*kalâ*),[9] God is still his "strength" (better "rock," *ṣûr*, see 18:2), his strong foundation. God is his chosen portion forever, v. 26.

27–28 Asaph concludes the psalm with a summary statement. The wicked, traveling through life far from the Lord, will eternally "perish" (*ʾabad*, see 1:6). The Lord "ha[s] destroyed" (or "will destroy," *ṣamat*, see 18:40) them who "go a whoring from" Him, following other gods, v. 27.[10] Asaph, however, sees that being near to God is good. For this reason, he says, "I have put my trust in the Lord God" (better, "I have made the Lord God my refuge [*maḥseh*, see 14:6]"). This lets him tell others of the marvelous works of God on his behalf, v. 28.

II, 20, argues that the verb is a contracted form of the *hipᶜîl* infinitive *beháᶜîr* (from *ᶜûr*, "to awake"); so G.K.C. 53 *q*; KB, II, 802. Although the view of Hengstenberg is possible, the parallelism supports the view that God will raise Himself to judge the wicked.

[9]The verb *kalâ* normally means "to end, finish." When expressing an emotion, it describes "exhausted with longing."

[10]The statement is a prophetic perfect, stated in the past tense because of its certainty.

PSALM 74

The psalm is a "Maschil" (*maśkîl*, see 32, title), calling the readers to reflect on the message and thereby gain wisdom. The psalm expresses the sorrow of the people. In all probability, the psalmist wrote a short time after the destruction of the temple by Babylon, ca. 586 BC.[11] He was apparently a priest left behind in the land where he could see the destruction. The situation is serious, bringing "perpetual desolations," v. 3. The "carved work" of the temple has been broken, v. 6. Prophets no longer carry on their ministries, v. 9. The enemy has attacked the "sanctuary," vv. 3, 7, and the "synagogues" in the land, v. 8. Since the entire psalm suggests a time after the Captivity, we should understand a descendant of Asaph as the author.[12]

It is appropriate to note that Israel's sin had caused the plight. God delivered them to their enemies as punishment for their sins. The psalmist laments Israel's condition under judgment (vv. 1–10). He then adopts the only proper course by recognizing God's power to deliver His people (vv. 7–11) and by interceding with God on behalf of the nation (vv. 18–23).

I. Lament for the Nation 1–10

1–3 Looking at the situation facing the nation, the psalmist grieves that God has cast off His people "for ever." God had not abandoned Israel, but from the writer's viewpoint, it seems this way. The fire of God's "anger" (*ʾap*, see 2:5) still smokes among the people. The psalmist did not understand this. Looking at the situation historically, we see that God allowed judgment to fall upon the nation

[11]Jennings, II, 7–8, and Perowne, II, 24, date the psalm after the oppression of Israel by Antiochus Epiphanes, ca. 167 BC. Both admit that the Syrians did not burn the temple, v. 7. Jennings arbitrarily refers the burning to the synagogues, while Perowne calls it "poetic exaggeration." Murphy, pp. 397–98, places the psalm at the time of Absalom's rebellion. We do not, however, have any indication in the biblical record that Absalom attacked the tabernacle in the way described by the psalm.

[12]See the introduction to Ps. 50 for information about Asaph. The name of Asaph became a family name, applied to later members of the group. Henry, III, 517, suggests that the author is an Asaph other than the one in David's time, or that Jeremiah wrote it but that the sons of Asaph delivered it to the people. While this is possible, it is wholly speculative.

that had turned from Him. While they still carried out a religious ritual, they also worshiped false gods. The judgment clearly illustrates God's punishment of those who fail to worship Him properly, v. 1. The author asks God to remember His people, those He had purchased for Himself, redeeming them from their bondage in Egypt. They are the "rod" (better "tribe") that was His "inheritance" (or "possession").[13] All of this was centered in "Zion," Jerusalem, where God Himself had dwelt among His people in the holy of holies, v. 2. The writer asks God to "lift up [His] feet," to walk through the "perpetual" (or "enduring") ruins in the land. The writer especially singles out the destruction of the sanctuary as something God should observe, v. 3.

4–8 The enemies of God roar their shouts of victory in the midst of the "congregations" (or "meeting place," *môᶜed*).[14] From vv. 3, 7, and 8, this collective word includes the temple and other places of meeting throughout the land. They have set up their "ensigns" (*ᵓôt*, see 65:8) for religious "signs" (*ᵓôt*) to show the power of their gods over Israel's God, v. 4.[15] Verse 5 is difficult to translate, since the subject is indefinite. It reads something like "It was known as from the lifting up of axes over the thicket of trees." This could refer to the cutting of trees to build the temple (I Kings 5:15) but more likely refers to the actions of the enemies, v. 5.[16] In the same way that they would attack a thicket of trees, they use their tools to smash the "carved work" of the temple. This may have been to recover gold (cf. I Kings 6:20–22, 28, 30) or may simply have been wanton destruction, v. 6. They have burned the temple (cf. II Kings 25:9). They have

[13]Fausset, III, 256, follows the AV and considers "the rod" as that by which "the inheritance is measured; then the inheritance itself." The word *šebeṭ* occurs 189 times, but never as a measuring rod. Fausset references Ezek. 40:3, but a different word occurs there. The same word elsewhere refers to the whole nation, Jer. 10:16; 51:19.

[14]The noun *môᶜed* refers to an appointed time or an appointed place for meeting. The context guides in the sense given to the word.

[15]Harman, p. 260, makes the "signs" military banners. Kissane, p. 333, likewise refers to the "standards of the victorious enemy." The word *ᵓôt* in the OT, however, overwhelmingly refers to religious signs. It occurs again in v. 9, where the context suggests a religious sign. The context of v. 3 supports that idea here.

[16]Henry, III, 518, and Calvin, III, 166, adopt the first of the above views. Other commentators and newer translations, e.g., NASB, NIV, generally follow the second.

"defiled" (*ḥalal* II, see 55:20) the dwelling of the Lord's "name"[17] by casting it down to the ground, v. 7. They planned to "destroy" (or "oppress") the people completely. They have burned the "synagogues" (or "meeting places," *môᶜed*)[18] in the land, v. 8.[19]

9–10 The psalmist laments the lack of religious "signs" (*ᵓôt*, see 65:8) in the land. The prophets no longer give God's Word to the people.[20] No one knows how long the oppression will last, v. 9. He closes this section by asking God to tell how long their enemies will reproach them. Will he be permitted to blaspheme the "name" (see v. 7) of God forever, v. 10?

II. Power of God 11–17

11–12 The psalmist now turns to the only hope available to Israel, the omnipotent God. He asks why God has withheld the "right hand" of His power from the nation. He urges Him to "pluck" (or "destroy") the foe by withdrawing His hand from the fold of His garment, v. 11. God is the psalmist's King, the One Who brings "salvation" (or "deliverance") to the earth, v. 12.

---

[17]Note 94 at 5:11 gives a brief summary of the "name" of the Lord.

[18]Synagogues did not come into use until after the OT closed. It is thought that the synagogues began during the Babylonian Captivity, and then developed in Palestine during the time of Ezra. They come into prominence only in the NT. These were not meant as places of worship but rather as places where God's Word was taught to the people.

[19]Kissane, p. 334, and Rotherham, p. 328, follow the LXX in understanding, "Cause to cease all the festivals of God in the land." The LXX, however, likely interpreted the plural *môᶜᵃdê*, which sometimes refers to time rather than a place. Since the verb in the MT is "burn," the meaning of "cause to cease" is not acceptable. Kidner, II, 267, refers the plural "meeting places" to "the Jerusalem temple as the last of God's successive meeting places . . . all of which had now been destroyed." He argues that there is no evidence of buildings used as synagogues "at this early date." While this is true, God's Word was taught throughout the land, e.g., II Chron. 17:7–9; 35:3. While this may not have been done in synagogues, there must have been places used for religious activity; cf. I Macc. 3:46. Verse 9 implies that prophets would normally have ministered throughout the land.

[20]Cohen, p. 238, and Perowne, II, 21, 28, point out that prophecy continued after the Captivity. They argue for a later date based on this fact. The prophets, however, had little freedom after the Captivity. The leaders imprisoned Jeremiah for a time and shut him up in Jerusalem. Later, he was taken to Egypt, where he died. Ezekiel's ministry was carried on in Babylon. There were few prophets moving freely throughout Palestine.

13–15 The psalmist illustrates the power of God by recalling several of God's works in the past. God divided the Red Sea, letting Israel escape from Egypt. From the parallelism, "the heads of the dragons [*tannîn*, see 44:19]" symbolically represent Pharaoh and the leaders of his army (cf. Isa. 27:1; 51:9; Ezek. 29:3), v. 13. Continuing the symbolism, "the heads of leviathan [or 'crocodile,' *liwyatan*],"[21] a reptile native to Egypt, as well represent the Egyptian leaders. Their bodies washed up on the shore become food for the "people" (*ᶜam*), i.e., the wild animals,[22] in the wilderness, v. 14. As a further example of His might, God did "cleave" (or "break open") the "fountain and the flood" (or "springs and torrents"). This refers to God's miraculous provision of water for Israel in the wilderness (cf. Exod. 17:5–6; Num. 20:11). In addition, He dried up the Jordan River while it was in its flood stage (Josh. 3:15–16), v. 15.

16–17 Moving to a different area, the psalmist illustrates God's power with the motions of the heavens. God controls the motion of the sun to give day and night (cf. Gen. 1:16–18). He has prepared the light and the sun for mankind, v. 16. He has set the bounds of the earth. The parallelism with 17*b* suggests that these are bounds of the earth's motion, bringing about the annual seasons.[23] He has established summer and winter each year (cf. Gen. 8:22), v. 17.

---

[21]The noun *liwyatan* comes from a root that means "twist, coil." This suggests a reptile or animal that moves by writhing motion. In Job 3:8 ("mourning"); 41:1, and Ps. 74:14, it indicates a crocodile. In Isa. 27:1, it is a symbol that represents the meandering Euphrates River. In 104:26, it is some sea creature, possibly a whale.

[22]Alexander, p. 324, refers *ᶜam* to "wild men living on the shores of the Red Sea." It is doubtful that such men would eat the flesh of dead soldiers washed up on the shore. While *ᶜam* normally refers to humans, it has an underlying sense of unity in a group. This may also extend to animals; cf. Prov. 30:25, 26. Kidner, p. 269, and Fausset, III, 268, understand that the Israelites spoiled the valuables of the Egyptians. Nothing in Exodus supports this speculative view. Calvin, III, 172, explains the passage poetically as "a beautiful allusion to the destruction of Pharaoh and his host." Pharaoh did not die at the Red Sea. Livingston, p. 334, suggests that the "animal figures" are "symbols of pagan nature gods," a speculative view. The literal explanation is more likely.

[23]Cohen, p. 239, and Lawson, p. 374, understand the boundaries as national boundaries. Hirsch, II, 20, varies this by calling them "the natural boundaries between countries, such as seas, mountains and rivers" and also "climatic differences." Alexander, p. 324, and Hengstenberg, II, 426, take them as the boundaries of the earth with respect to the seas. While these views are possible, the context of vv. 16, 17*b* takes up the subject of the heavenly bodies.

III. Plea for Deliverance 18–23

18–21 The psalmist now begins a series of requests to God. He asks first that God deliver His people from their trials. He reminds the Lord that the enemy has "reproached" (or "reviled") God. These foolish people have "blasphemed" (or "spurned") His "name," i.e., His nature, by rejecting any need for Him, v. 18. The psalmist asks the Lord not to deliver the "soul," i.e., the life, of His "turtledove" (*tôr*),[24] the nation, to the "multitude" (*ḥayyat*).[25] He asks Him not to forget forever the "congregation" (or "multitude," *ḥayyat*) of the "poor" (or "afflicted," *ᶜanî*, see 9:12), v. 19.

The writer reminds the Lord of the covenant between Him and the nation. The people need the Lord to consider that the "dark places of the earth," where their foes plot Israel's destruction, are filled with the abodes of "cruelty" (or "violence"), v. 20. May the "oppressed" (*dak*, see 9:9) not be left to return from their journey to God publicly "ashamed" (*kalam*, see 35:4). Rather, may the "poor" (or "afflicted," *ᶜanî*) and needy praise the "name" (see v. 7) of God, v. 21.

22–23 The psalmist calls upon God to "plead" (*rîb*, see 35:1) His own cause. God should remember how the foolish enemy "reproacheth" (or "scorns") Him throughout each day, v. 22. The psalmist asks Him not to forget the words of His enemies. The tumult caused by those who rise against God continually increases. The implication is that God needs to quiet them by judging them, v. 23.

---

[24]This is the only time that *tôr* has a symbolic sense. Everywhere else, it refers to the dove, either as a sacrifice or as a wild bird. The psalmist likely draws on the gentle nature of the dove as he uses it to represent Israel, a gentle nation in comparison to her conqueror.

[25]Among others, Fausset, III, 259, and Alexander, p. 325, understand "multitude" (*ḥayyat*) as "beasts" or "wild beasts" while understanding "congregation" (also *ḥayyat*) as the people. While the word *ḥayyat* may refer to beasts, it is unlikely that the author would use the word twice so close together with different senses. Only two words separate the two occurrences of *ḥayyat* in the MT.

PSALM 75

This "psalm" (*mizmôr*) and "song" (*šîr*)[26] is a song of thanksgiving.[27] The inscription makes "Asaph" the author.[28] As with the previous psalm, we should understand one of the "sons of Asaph" as the writer.[29] The psalm is later, after the conquest of Israel by Assyria; cf. v. 3.[30] It is to be sung to the tune of "Al-taschith" (see 57, intro.). It is prepared for the "chief musician" (*m^enaṣṣeaḥ*, see 4, intro.), the head of the priestly musicians, to use with the nation's worship.

I. Declaration of Thanksgiving 1

1 The psalmist thanks God on behalf of the nation. The repetition of "do we give thanks" lends emphasis to his statement. Verse 1*b* better reads, "And your name is near. They declare your wonderful works."[31] God's "name," i.e., His nature,[32] is near the nation. For that reason, the people speak of His marvelous works on their behalf, v. 1.

---

[26]For the words "psalm" (*mizmôr*) and "song" (*šîr*), see the introduction to Ps. 30.

[27]The introduction to Ps. 18 summarizes the songs of thanksgiving.

[28]Henry, III, 521–22, makes David the author, either by giving a speech that Asaph turned into verse or by actually writing the psalm and then giving it to Asaph. The view requires that we relate the disruption spoken of in v. 3 to some unknown event during David's reign. It also goes contrary to the nature of Book III, generally a collection of non-Davidic psalms.

[29]The introduction to Ps. 50 gives information about Asaph.

[30]*NIB*, IV, 977, tentatively dates the psalm after the Babylonian Captivity. Phillips, I, 622, places it at the time of the Assyrian defeat at Jerusalem. Hengstenberg, II, 429, makes the psalm written before the Assyrian threat. He bases this on the phrase "Al-taschith" ("do not destroy") in the title. This prayer for deliverance is followed by the confident anticipation of praise. The phrase "Al-taschith," however, occurs as well in Pss. 57, 58, and 59. It is a musical notation of some kind, not meant as a prayer. See the discussion in Ps. 57.

[31]Henry, III, 522, follows the AV, where "wonderful works" are the subject of "declare." The *nipᶜal* participle of *palaʾ*, "to be marvelous, wonderful," occurs forty-six times in the OT, always as an object or predicate adjective. Only at 139:14 is it translated as a subject, and even there it should stand as the object of the verb. See the discussion of *palaʾ* at 9:1.

[32]See 5:11, note 94, for a brief summary of the Lord's name.

II. Discussion Concerning Deliverance 2–8

2–3 God states His intentions through the psalmist.[33] The verse better reads, "For I take [i.e., select] the appointed time [*môᶜed*, see 74:4]; I myself will judge rightly." There is coming a time when the Lord will deliver His people from their oppressors, v. 2. The "earth" (or "land") and its people now "are dissolved" (lit. "melt," i.e., are fearful). In this difficult time, likely the time of Assyria's invasion of Judah (II Kings 18:17), the Lord Himself "bear[s] up" (or "measures out") the pillars that give stability to the earth. The word "selah" draws attention to the Lord's watchfulness, v. 3.

4–5 God continues to speak. He has warned the "fools" (better "boastful") against boasting, and the wicked against lifting up their "horn" (*qeren*, see 18:2), their might, against Him, v. 4. They should not raise their "horn" (*qeren*), their might, against God nor speak against Him with "a stiff neck," i.e., arrogantly, v. 5.

6–8 A nation's "promotion" (or "exaltation"), here referring to Israel's deliverance, does not come from alliances made to the east or west[34] or to the "south" (better "wilderness").[35] There is no mention of the north since that is the direction from which the invading army comes, v. 6. The deliverance of the nation comes only from God. He brings low one nation and "setteth up" (or "exalts") another, v. 7. The Lord poetically pictures His dealings with mankind. The "cup" regularly occurs as a source of either blessing, 16:5; 23:5; 116:13, or judgment, 11:6; Isaiah 51:17, 22. The cup here is filled with wine that is "red" (better "foaming," still fermenting). It is well mixed, probably with spices to flavor it. He pours "out of the same

[33] Kidner, II, 271, makes the psalmist quote the words of some prophet. This is equally possible. Albert Barnes, II, 274, considers this the language of a prince about to ascend the throne "in a time of great misrule and disorder." The context, however, suggests that the Lord speaks here. In addition, the Hebrew pronouns in vv. 2–3 are emphatic. This strongly supports the Lord as the speaker.

[34] Buttenwieser, p. 789, interprets "east" and "west" as "sunrise" and "sunset," a possible way of understanding the verse. He then goes beyond the text to refer this to sun worship, with the author admonishing "the men of his time to renounce their trust in this phantom deity." The connection with the "wilderness" argues against this view.

[35] VanGemeren, p. 493, understands "promotion . . . from the south" as "the wilderness of the mountains," representing the south and the north. He takes this as referring to universal judgment. More naturally, the phrase is "nor exaltation from the desert."

[*mizzeh*]"[36] and the wicked will "wring them out" (or "drain") and drink even the dregs of the wine. The picture is of full judgment falling upon those who oppose God, v. 8.

III. Dedication of the Psalmist 9–10

9–10 Having received revelation as to what God plans for His people, the psalmist responds with a note of praise. He will "declare for ever." The second half gives the implied object of the psalmist's intention. He will "sing praises" (*zamar*, see 7:17) to the nation's God, v. 9.[37] The psalmist will take his stand against the wicked, cutting off their "horns" (*qeren*, see 18:2), the emblems of their power.[38] At the same time, he will lift up the "horns" (*qeren*) of the righteous as he assists them, v. 10.

The pattern in this psalm involves an expression of gratitude for God's goodness, a statement of God's plan to deliver His people, and the resulting dedication of the psalmist. This is an appropriate pattern for Christians to follow now. We have abundant reason to thank the Lord for His many blessings. God has further stated in His Word His intention to deliver us from the wicked. It is only right that His people rededicate themselves to Him.

---

[36]Meindert Dijkstra, "He Pours the Sweet Wine Off, Only the Dregs Are for the Wicked. An Epigraphic Note on *mizzoeh* in Psalm 75,9," *ZAW* 107:2 (1995): 298–300, proposes to read *mz* as "sweet wine." He translates, "He pours the sweet wine off—only the dregs in it they shall drain." The word *mizzeh* is the standard preposition plus the demonstrative pronoun *zeh*. While Dijkstra cites archaeological evidence to support his suggestion, it is not clear enough to set aside the standard grammatical structure here. KB does not recognize this suggested translation. The LXX, an early witness, translated εἱς τοῦτο, clearly supporting the translation of the AV.

[37]Leupold, pp. 546–47; Hengstenberg, II, 434; and Fausset, III, 261, find the object of 9*a* in vv. 7–8, the judgments of God upon the wicked. This is equally possible. I have adopted the intention to praise as being parallel to 9*b*.

[38]Fausset, III, 261, understands the psalmist's declaration, "I will cut off," as announcing what God has done. There is no reason the psalmist should obscure his actions this way. It is more likely that God's revelation has encouraged him to also oppose wickedness.

PSALM 76

This is a "song" (*šîr*) and "psalm" (*mizmôr*).[39] It is to be performed upon "Neginoth" (*n^{e}gînôt*, see 4, intro.), unknown stringed instruments. The psalm is for use by the "chief musician" (*m^{e}naṣṣeaḥ*, see 4, intro.) with the temple worship. The background to the psalm is the defeat of Assyria, II Kings 19:35.[40] Since this took place more than two centuries after Asaph, the author is a descendant of Asaph.[41] The psalmist recognizes God's power in delivering His people.

As with many of the psalms, the pattern established here still applies. God watches over those who enjoy a right relationship with Him, vv. 1–3. He will deliver them from their enemies, vv. 4–9. All should submit themselves to God, vv. 10–11, knowing that He will judge those who oppose Him, v. 12.

I. The Relationship to God 1–3

1–3 The author states the great privilege of Judah. God has made Himself known to them so that His "name," His reputation,[42] is held in great esteem, v. 1. His "tabernacle" (or "covert," *sok*, see 27:5), where He watches over His people, is in "Salem," an early name for Jerusalem (Gen. 14:18; cf. Heb. 7:1–2). He dwells in Zion, originally one of the mountains on which Jerusalem was built but later the city itself, v. 2.[43] He broke the weapons of the enemy there. These include the "arrows of the bow" (or "flames of the bow," flaming arrows),

---

[39]For the words "psalm" (*mizmôr*) and "song" (*šîr*), see the introduction to Ps. 30.

[40]The LXX supports this by adding the phrase πρὸς τὸν Ἀσσύριον, "concerning the Assyrian." The Vulgate is similar, *ad Assyrios*. Murphy, p. 408, has the psalm describe David's victory in taking Jerusalem from the Jebusites. This, however, was a victory achieved by stealth, not direct military action as v. 3 seems to indicate.

[41]Information about Asaph may be found in the introduction to Ps. 50. The inscription here uses the family name to identify the author. Although Asaph himself did not write the psalm, it is justly related to him because of the part taken by one of his descendants.

[42]Note 94 at 5:11 discusses the "name" of the Lord.

[43]In the phrase "dwelling place [*m^{ec}ônâ*] in Zion," the word *m^{ec}ônâ* is often associated with the den of a lion, e.g., Amos 3:4; Nah. 2:12. For this reason, *NIB*, IV, 980, suggests that "God is being portrayed as divine warrior in the form of a mighty lion." But the word *m^{ec}ônâ* also refers to a dwelling place, e.g., Deut. 33:27 ("refuge"); Jer. 21:13 ("habitations"). The parallelism here with "tabernacle" argues against understanding it as "den" or "lair."

the "shield" (*magen*, see 3:3), the "sword" (the most commonly mentioned weapon in the OT), and the "battle," a summary of all that was involved in overcoming the enemy. Taken together, these poetically portray the defeat of Assyria (II Kings 19:35). The word "selah" emphasizes the work of God in delivering His people, v. 3.

II. The Deliverance by God 4–9

4–6 In the light of what God has done for His people, the psalmist declares that He is "more glorious and excellent [or 'glorious, more excellent'] than the mountains of prey." The comparison is with the mountainous region where the Assyrians became a prey. This glory spreads throughout the earth, v. 4.[44] The "stouthearted" (or "valiant of heart") have been plundered. They sleep now in the sleep of death. None of their mighty "men" (*ᵓᵉnôš*, see 8:4) can lift their hands for battle (cf. Isa. 37:33), v. 5. The God Who has chosen Jacob has rebuked both the "chariot" (or "rider") and his horse. Now they too deeply sleep, again the sleep of death, v. 6.

7–9 Having such power, God is to be feared. Rhetorically, the psalmist asks who can stand before Him when He is "angry" (*ᵓap*, see 2:5). The obvious answer is "no one," v. 7! He has caused His judgment to fall from heaven. At this, the "earth" (or "land") feared and "was still," at peace, v. 8.[45] This took place when God rose in judgment in order to deliver the "meek" (see *ᶜanî*, 9:12) of the

[44]Calvin, III, 196, sees the mountains as symbols of "kingdoms distinguished for their violence and extortion." It is true that mountains sometimes represent kingdoms, e.g., Jer. 51:25, but this is not common. In addition, the phrase "mountains of prey" is unique, not seen elsewhere. Phillips, I, 630, visualizes spoil heaped up as mountains. A heap of spoil, however, is far from being a "mountain." Leupold, p. 550, understands the phrase as "glorious from the mountains of prey." He makes God return "from some mountainous area where He engaged in battle and won much prey." He did not have to return far if this is the case, since the Assyrians camped outside the walls of Jerusalem. Gaebelein, p. 299, refers the phrase to Jerusalem, the city that has been "the prey of the enemy." The context, however, relates more to Assyria's defeat. For *ṭerep*, "prey," the LXX and Vulgate read *ᶜad*, either "prey" or "perpetuity," or *ṭerem*, an adverb relating to time. This has led some authors to translate "everlasting mountains," e.g., Anderson, II, 553, which does not change the sense of the verse.

[45]Kidner, p. 275, sees the verse as a prophetic perfect that describes end-time events. The view is possible, although the passage also applies to Hezekiah's time and the destruction of Assyria.

"earth" (or "land").[46] Once again, the "selah" draws attention to the work of God, v. 9.

III. The Submission to God 10–12

10–12 The psalmist recognizes that man's wrath shall come into submission to God. Either man will yield his will freely to God or God will judge man's sin. In either case, "the wrath [*ḥemâ*, see 6:1] of man" brings praise to the God Who is greater than man. Verse 10*b* is better, "The remainder of wrath [*ḥemâ*] you will gird on yourself." That portion of God's wrath that remains He will, in a sense, clothe Himself with as He prepares to stop wicked man from rebelling against Him (cf. Isa. 59:17), v. 10. In light of this, men should make and pay their vows of praise to the Lord. They should bring their tribute to the One Who is to be feared for His judgment of sin, v. 11. He will cut off the "spirit" (or "breath") of rebellious princes. He is "terrible" (or "to be feared") by kings, v. 12.

PSALM 77

The writer prepares this individual lament psalm for "Jeduthun,"[47] the "chief musician" (*m^enaṣṣeaḥ*, see 4, intro.). One of the descendants of Asaph authors the psalm.[48] Verse 15*b* suggests that we should date the psalm at the time of the divided kingdom. The psalmist,

---

[46]VanGemeren, p. 497, views the conquest of Assyria as relieving "all the oppressed people on the earth." This is possible, although the main emphasis is on the benefit to Judah.

[47]The *q^erê* "Jeduthun" is undoubtedly correct rather than the *k^etîb* "Jedithun." The same spelling occurs in I Chron. 16:38 and Ps. 39, title, but it is Jeduthun everywhere else in the OT. The phrasing here is similar to that of Ps. 62, *ᶜal-y^edûtûn*, rather than that of Ps. 39, *lîdûtûn*. As in Ps. 62, Leupold, p. 554, suggests that the psalm should "be rendered as Jeduthun was wont to render psalms." His view is possible, but the difference is negligible and does not require this. The introduction to Ps. 39 gives a brief summary of Jeduthun.

[48]The introduction to Ps. 50 discusses Asaph. If the historical background to the psalm is during the divided kingdom, one of the "sons of Asaph" is the author. He uses the family name for identification.

likely speaking for the nation, faces some difficult trial. He does not give enough information to let us identify the historical circumstances.[49] In this time of emotional upheaval, he finds comfort in recalling the mighty works of God.

I. Trial of the Nation 1–9

A. Cry of the Psalmist 1–3

1–3 The incomplete verse shows the emotional state of the psalmist: "My voice to God, and I will cry; my voice to God, and He will hear me." The repeated phrase gives urgency to the prayer, as does the phrase "I will cry," v. 1. In his "trouble" (*ṣarâ*, see 9:9), He has diligently "sought" (*daraš*, see 9:10) the Lord. His cries go out to Him day and night. The phrase "my sore ran in the night" is better "my hand was stretched out," referring to his pleas to God. These "ceased not" (or "did not grow numb," i.e., did not grow weak) as he continually lifted his hands to God in prayer. There was, however, no comfort for his soul, v. 2. He remembers God, but troubles still grieve him. He has "complained" (or "meditated," see *śîaḥ*, 55:2), likely on God's help, but is still "overwhelmed" (better "faint"). The "selah" calls attention to his plight, v. 3.

B. Confusion of the Psalmist 4–9

4–6 God keeps the psalmist's eyes from closing in sleep. He is so troubled that he cannot speak, v. 4. He considers the history of the nation, going back to "years of ancient times," the early days of the land when God delivered them from their enemies, v. 5. He recalls his "song" (*n^{e}gînôt*, see 4, intro.) sung in earlier times at night.[50] He

[49]Gaebelein, p. 300, makes the psalm look forward to the Tribulation. Nothing in the psalm makes this view certain; it can also refer to the psalmist's time. Hengstenberg, II, 442, sets the psalm after the deliverance from Egypt. This, however, is too early for Asaphian authorship. Murphy, p. 413, places it at some crisis in David's life. On the basis of the language, Dahood, II, 224, dates the psalm in the tenth century. Leslie, p. 238, places the author in the Northern Kingdom and dates the psalm just before its fall. Cohen, p. 246, sets the psalm at the Babylonian Captivity. We cannot be certain of the background to its writing.

[50]While *n^{e}gînôt* normally refers to a song accompanied by stringed instruments, it is difficult to find instruments here. It is possible that the psalmist had accompanied himself as he sang. He may also have sung something normally accompanied by stringed instruments. He may have remembered a song from earlier times. It is

"commune[s]" (or "meditates," *śîaḥ*) with himself and makes "diligent search" for the answers to his questions, v. 6.

7–9 The psalmist asks a series of six questions concerning the situation. Will the Lord reject His people forever? Will He never again be "favourable" (*raṣâ*, see 40:13) to them, v. 7? Has He broken off His "mercy" (or "steadfast love," *ḥesed*, see 5:7) forever? Has God's promise to care for Israel come to an end "for evermore" (*lᵉdor wador*, see 10:6), v. 8? Has God forgotten to be gracious to His people? Has God in "anger" (*ʾap*, see 2:5) shut the nation off from His tender mercies" (or "compassions")? Once more, the word "selah" draws attention to the trouble facing the nation, v. 9.

While the psalmist rightly begins with prayer, vv. 1–3, he soon turns to statements that show his perplexity with God's work on behalf of His people. The problem is Israel's sin. God allows them to suffer severe punishment. To this point, the psalmist has overlooked the justice of God's work with the nation.

II. Remembrance of God 10–20

A. The Greatness of God 10–15

10–12 The psalmist now makes the transition between doubt and faith. He admits that his questions are an "infirmity" (or "weakness," *ḥallôtî*).[51] He will think instead on "the years of the right hand[52] of the most High [*ʿelyôn,* see 7:17]," God's works in the past.[53] While there

---

equally possible that the word is broader than just music with instruments. *TWOT*, II, 551, suggests "pleasant songs," but the context here supports more of a dirge.

[51]In form, *ḥallôtî* is the *piʿel* infinitive of *ḥalâ*, "to be sick, weak." This leads to the thought of "infirmity" or "weakness." Hirsch, II, 35, derives *ḥallotî* from *ḥalal*, "to pollute." He interprets this as "becoming profane . . . for what would seem like a change in the right hand of the Most High." There is no need, however, to abandon the standard conjugation of the verb *ḥalâ*. Hengstenberg, II, 446, sees the sickness as given by the Lord and therefore to be borne patiently. This requires the "years" to be years in which suffering is borne, a thought that does not relate to the context. Buttenwieser, p. 625, is remarkably free in translating, "Because of mine infirmity the right hand of the Most High seems changed." He admits that he has "departed from the sentence structure of the Hebrew."

[52]The "right hand" of God often represents His power, e.g., 17:7; 18:35; 20:6.

[53]Weiser, p. 532, and Cohen, p. 247, understand "years" (*šᵉnôt*) as the infinitive construct of *šanâ*, "to change." They translate something like "This is my grief, that the right hand of the Most High has changed" and make it the conclusion to

is no verb in 10*b*, the verbs from vv. 11–12 suggest something like "think about" or "remember," v. 10. He will remember "the works of the Lord," i.e., the works that God has done for Israel in the past. He will also remember the miracles that God has performed in older times, v. 11. He will meditate and "talk" (or "muse," see *śîaḥ*, 55:2) on what God has done, v. 12.

13–15 God's way is "in the sanctuary" (or "in holiness"). Rhetorically, the psalmist asks if there is any other god as great as Israel's God. The obvious answer is no, v. 13. God is a God Who works miracles. He has made known His power among "the people," Israel, v. 14. To illustrate this power, the psalmist recalls the deliverance of Israel from Egypt. With His "arm," the symbol of His strength, God redeemed the nation. This included "the sons of Jacob," Judah, as well as "the sons of . . . Joseph," Israel.[54] To draw attention to God's power, the psalmist adds the word "selah," v. 15.

B. The Work of God 16–20

16–18 The psalmist continues to illustrate the power of God. He poetically describes the deliverance from Egypt. The waters of the Red Sea "were afraid" (better "writhed") as they drew back from the Lord to make an opening for Israel. The waters in "the depths" of the sea were "troubled" (or "perturbed") as they moved away from God, v. 16. The clouds poured out their water. Thunder sounded from the sky. The "arrows" of God, lightning, flashed across the skies, v. 17. The sound of thunder came from "the heaven" (better "the whirlwind," *galgal*).[55]

---

vv. 6–10. It is doubtful, however, that the psalmist would use *šanâ* one way in v. 5 and another way in v. 10. The supply of a verb is common in Hebrew. The context here makes it clear what verb is needed.

[54]After the divided kingdom, the phrase "sons of Jacob" occurs elsewhere only in Mal. 3:6, where it refers to Judah. Logically, the phrase "sons of . . . Joseph," Ephraim and Manasseh, refers to the Northern Kingdom of Israel.

[55]Kidner, p. 280, understands *galgal* as "roaring chariot-wheels" and relates the passage to the deliverance from Egypt. Perowne, II, 55, is similar, translating *galgal* as "rolling" and referring it to the chariots of God. Kissane, p. 350, refers the word to "the circuit of the horizon." Hirsch, II, 40, treats *galgal* as a verb, translating "Thy thunder rolled." The word *galgal* is a reduplicated form of *galal*, "to roll." It elsewhere refers to a "wheel" or "rolling thing." Here, however, with a context of a storm, "whirlwind" best conveys the sense.

The lightning lit up the world. The earth trembled and "shook" (or "quaked") under the impact, v. 18.[56]

19–20 The psalmist continues to describe the deliverance of Israel from Egypt. God's way, made for the nation, was in the Red Sea, and His "path" (*šᵉbîl*)[57] was in the great waters of the Gulf of Suez. Although God's clear leading was evident, there was no mark of His feet to reveal His presence, v. 19. Nonetheless, He led His people like a flock of sheep with Moses and Aaron as their shepherds, v. 20.

Although the psalmist expresses his discouragement over the nation's plight, he finds encouragement in God's power. He mentions the "right hand" of His power, v. 10; His "wonders" performed in ancient times, vv. 11, 14*a*; His "work" and "doings," v. 12; and His greatness, v. 13. He refers to God's "strength," v. 14*b*, and illustrates this by recalling Israel's deliverance from Egypt, v. 15, when God rolled back the waters of the Red Sea, v. 16. Storms at this time demonstrated His power, vv. 17–18. Like a flock of sheep, God led the nation through the waters under the leadership of Moses and Aaron, vv. 19–20. With this emphasis, the psalmist sets an example that Christians would do well to follow. It is good to dwell on the power of God and, in so doing, to remind ourselves that He is well able to meet our needs in the trials of life.

---

[56]The historical record in Exodus 14:21–31 does not describe a storm. Fausset, III, 264, suggests that Exod. 14:24, "troubled the host of the Egyptians," may imply the storm. Henry, III, 530, understands a great storm pouring water on the Egyptians while the pillar of fire, Exod. 14:19–20, "like an umbrella over the camp of Israel, sheltered it from the shower." Josephus, *The Antiquities of the Jews* 2.16.3, refers to "a torrent raised by storms of wind. . . . Showers of rain also came down from the sky, and dreadful thunders and lightning, with flashes of fire. Thunderbolts also were darted upon them." See also Ps. 81:7.

[57]The AV correctly reads the *qᵉrê šᵉbîlᵉkâ*, "path," rather than the *kᵉtîb šᵉbîlykâ*, "paths." The *qᵉrê* parallels the singular "way" in 19*a*. Fausset, III, 264, accepts the *kᵉtîb*, "paths," and refers it to the many ways in which God leads His people in difficulties. The context, however, limits the verse to the crossing of the Red Sea.

PSALM 78

This psalm is the first of five that focus on the history of Israel.[58] In particular, the psalm touches on Israel's early history, from events connected with the Exodus to the reign of David. The title names the author as Asaph, head of the tabernacle music under David, according to I Chronicles 16:5.[59] The psalm supports the statement of Asaph's authorship by mentioning nothing in Israel's history past the time of David.[60]

The psalm is a "Maschil" (*maśkîl*, see 32, title), a psalm for the reader to reflect on as he considers the nation's history and learns spiritual lessons from it. It supports setting the psalm in David's reign that the author draws from history given in Exodus, Numbers, Joshua, and I–II Samuel, but not from later books.

I. Admonition to the People 1–8

1–4 Asaph begins by exhorting the people to hear his "law" (*tôrâ*). The sense of instruction is clearly visible in the word *tôrâ*. He further urges them to hear "the words of my mouth." Either the psalm recaps a sermon preached to the people or, more probably, Asaph read the psalm to a group gathered at the tabernacle, v. 1. He declares a "parable" (*mašal*, see 44:14), his instructions drawn from Israel's history. The "parable" here differs from the short proverbial sayings in

---

[58]These include Pss. 78, 105, 106, 135, and 136. While other psalms mention Israel's history, e.g., Ps. 114, additional themes or the style of writing put them into different categories of psalms.

[59]The psalms authored by Asaph or the sons of Asaph include Pss. 50, 73, 74, 75, 76, 77, 78, 79, 80, 81, 82, and 83. See the introduction to Ps. 50 for a brief summary of Asaph's ministry.

[60]Albert Barnes, II, 291, dates the psalm after the division of the nation into Israel and Judah. He considers Ephraim, vv. 9, 67, to represent Israel in distinction from Judah. While this is possible, we may explain vv. 9 and 67 differently. The fact that the psalm ends with the choice of David as king supports the earlier date. Cohen, p. 249, understands the "sanctuary" in v. 69 as the temple and so extends the possible date to before the Babylonian captivity. He tentatively suggests Hezekiah as the author. The "sanctuary," however, refers to the Davidic tabernacle at Jerusalem, not the later temple. Dahood, II, 238, sees the rebuke of Ephraim, vv. 9–11, and the favor of Judah, vv. 67–69, as evidence of the divided kingdom. He dates the book in this period, 922–721 BC. The mentions of these tribes, however, can be explained differently. Ewald, II, 255, places the psalm in the time of Ezra and Nehemiah. The lack of any mention in the psalm of clear history after David opposes the view.

Proverbs. It is more like the longer lessons given in Ezekiel 17:2–10, 22–24; 24:3–14. Asaph further declares his intention to "utter [*naba*ᶜ, see 19:2] dark sayings [*ḥîdâ*, see 49:4] of old," lessons from the past that the people should dwell on, v. 2.[61] The "fathers," the ancestors of the people, have passed these matters on to the present generation, v. 3. They, in turn, will pass the "praises of the Lord, and his strength, and his wonderful works [*pala*ʾ, see 9:1]" to their children, "the generation to come," v. 4.

5–8 The Lord had earlier commanded that His "testimony" and "law" should be taught to the children, v. 5. Having learned the standards given to man by God, they will teach their children (Exod. 10:2; 12:26–27; 13:8, 14). These and other references make it clear that the Lord expects parents to teach their children His Word, v. 6. The result of this is that God's people will hope in the Lord rather than in man or in self. They will not forget His works on their behalf and so will keep His commands, v. 7. This knowledge of God's Word will keep them from following prior generations. These were "stubborn and rebellious" people who "set not their heart aright" (or "did not prepare their heart"). Their spirit "was not steadfast" (or "was not faithful") to God. There is an obvious spiritual lesson—God's Word makes a difference in how we live, v. 8.

II. The Failure of Ephraim 9–11

9–11 Having just mentioned the "stubborn and rebellious" nature of the fathers, Asaph now gives an illustration of this from Israel's history. The tribe of Ephraim failed the Lord several times in the OT.[62] Asaph probably refers here to the failure of that tribe to help in

[61]Matt. 13:35 calls Asaph a "prophet" in quoting v. 2. The OT prophets both foretold the future and preached God's word to the people. Asaph falls into this latter group. Matthew uses v. 2 more to illustrate the teaching of the Lord than to prophesy the nature of His ministry.

[62]Delitzsch, II, 365, accounts for the mention of Ephraim "from the special interest which the Psalms of Asaph take in the tribes of Joseph." Asaph and his descendants, however, mention these tribes in only four of their twelve psalms. Leupold, p. 564, says that this passage "is not a historical allusion to a particular event but a general statement in figurative language." There are several records of Ephraim's failure, e.g., Judg. 8:1–3; 12:1–6; I Kings 11:26. In view of this, it is reasonable that Asaph refers to a specific event. The detail that Ephraim "turned back in the day of battle" supports this. Weiser, p. 540, mentions the defeat of Saul, a battle that "paved the way for the transition of the kingship . . . from Saul to David." The record of

the time of Jephthah's fight against the Ammonites (Judg. 12:1–6). We do not know the details. Jephthah called Ephraim to the battle, but they did not join in the fight (Judg. 12:2). Their pride then led to civil war in Israel (Judg. 12:1, 3–6), v. 9. In later years, Ephraim turned from their covenant with God and failed to live by His law, v. 10. They forgot God's "wonders" (*pala*ʾ, see 9:1) on their behalf. The unstated result of this was Ephraim's adoption of idolatry (Hos. 4:17; 11:12–12:1; 12:14–13:2). Once more, there is an obvious spiritual lesson. Those who turn from God's Word will forget God and, forgetting Him, will turn to ungodly forms of worship, v. 11.

III. The Unbelief of Israel 12–41

12–13 The actions of Ephraim mirror the actions of the nation. The Lord had worked miraculously in Egypt. The "field [or 'region'] of Zoan" represents the "land of Goshen" (Gen. 45:10) in the eastern part of the Nile's delta. Zoan was the major city located in this area, v. 12. The first miracle of the Exodus was the dividing of the Red Sea and the passage of Israel through the water. The phrase "he made the waters to stand as an heap" comes from Exodus 15:8. It describes the waters standing up like a wall on the sides of the passage across the Red Sea, v. 13.

14–16 Having brought Israel to the Sinai Peninsula, the Lord now leads them with the cloudy pillar during the day and the pillar of fire at night (Exod. 13:21–22), v. 14. When the nation grew thirsty at Rephidim, the Lord caused a split in "the rocks" (*ṣurîm*, see 18:2),[63]

---

this battle in I Sam. 31 does not mention Ephraim. The *Targum*, p. 151, states that the tribe of Ephraim did not wait for the deliverance of the nation. They left Egypt thirty years earlier and were defeated in battle. Nothing in the OT supports this view. Livingston, p. 342, understands the reference as "a general allusion to the failure of the northern tribes, of which Ephraim was the leader, to conquer fully the tribal area assigned to them." Since Ephraim often stands for Israel as a whole, this is a possible view. I refer the comment to the tribe of Ephraim because of v. 67, where Asaph must refer to the tribe. VanGemeren, p. 507, suggests the Philistine victory in which the ark was lost, I Sam. 4:1–11. That account does not refer to Ephraim either although, again, Ephraim may represent the nation. Fausset, III, 266, looks ahead in the psalm and makes this refer to vv. 56–60, "followed by the rejection of Shiloh, and the election of Judah as the place of God's sanctuary." This is possible. We do not have enough details to be dogmatic.

[63]The plural word *ṣurîm* refers to both of the smitten rocks during the Exodus, at Rephidim, Exod. 17:1–6, and at Kadesh, Num. 20:7–13.

allowing water to run abundantly (*rabbâ*) from the depths of the earth (Exod. 17:1–6).[64] A similar incident took place later at Kadesh (Num. 20:7–13). Although Asaph does not stress this here, both of these incidents showed Israel's lack of faith in God. Moses named both places "Meribah" ("strife") because of Israel's contention, v. 15. Asaph now focuses on the rock at Rephidim; cf. also v. 20. He compares the abundance to waters running "like rivers," v. 16.

17–20 Asaph gives an example of Israel's lack of faith. They continued to sin against God by provoking the anger of the "most High" (*ᶜelyôn,* see 7:17) in the wilderness, v. 17. They "tempted" (or "tested") God, an action contrary to Deuteronomy 6:16. They asked for "meat" to satisfy their "lust" (or "desire"), Numbers 11:1–6, v. 18.[65] They questioned God's ability to provide food for them. The record in the Pentateuch does not mention the question "Can God furnish a table [*šulḥan*, see 23:5] in the wilderness?" This likely comes from an oral account passed down through the generations, v. 19. The people say to themselves that "he," the Lord working through Moses, struck the "rock" (*ṣûr*, see 18:2) at Rephidim to give them torrents of water. Can He give them "flesh" also? Their lack of faith is clear, v. 20.

21–25 The Lord hears the murmurings. He kindles a "fire" of judgment against the people and shows His "anger" (*ᵓap*, see 2:5) at their faithlessness. This judgment stopped only after Moses' prayer for the nation (Num. 11:1–3). We can only speculate on the source of the "fire."[66] Moses gave the name "Taberah" ("burning") to the place, v. 21. Israel did not believe that God could provide for them. They did not trust "in his salvation," the deliverance already given them

---

[64]The singular word *rabbâ* follows the plural "depths" (*tᵉhomôt*). Fausset, III, 266, follows the AV in making *rabbâ* modify *tᵉhomôt*, "great depths," a possible view although it rests on a singular word modifying a plural. It is more likely that *rabâ* adverbially modifies the verb "gave them drink." This leads to "he gave them abundant drink like the depths." The NASB and NIV understand the "depths" as the depths of the ocean or seas. I doubt Asaph would compare drinking water to an abundance of salt water. For this reason I refer the word to waters deep in the earth that gushed out when the rock was split.

[65]Among others, Cohen, p. 252, and Harman, p. 271, refer the incident to both Exod. 16:3 and Num. 11:4. There is no need to introduce a problem by bringing in Exod. 16. The incident in Exod. 16 says nothing about Israel provoking God, while Num. 11 does refer to the "anger of the Lord."

[66]Dahood, II, 241, and Alexander, p. 330, make the fire picture God's wrath. The description in Num. 11:1–3 and the name "Taberah" support the idea of literal fire.

from Egypt that continued through the wilderness, v. 22. God had shown His power in sending the Flood upon the earth (Gen. 7:11), v. 23, and in sending manna, the "corn [or 'grain'] of heaven," an idiom describing the daily manna. The Lord quotes this in John 6:31 when He introduces Himself as the "bread of life," v. 24. He gave them "angels' food," a poetic description of manna, as He supplied them from the realm of angels with food sufficient for them, v. 25.

26–33 The Lord caused winds from the east and south to bring quail from the Red Sea to the camp of Israel, v. 26, so that they had an abundance of meat, v. 27. The quail covered the camp where Israel had set up their tents. Numbers 11:31 describes the quail as lying "two cubits high" on the ground, v. 28.[67] The people ate as the Lord satisfied their desire for meat, v. 29. While "they were not estranged [*zûr*, see 44:20] from their lust," before the desires were fully satisfied, and while they were still eating, v. 30, God unleashed His "wrath" (*ʾap*, see 2:5). He slew "the fattest of them," the healthy ones, and struck down "the chosen men" (better "young men") of the nation, v. 31. Despite God's judgment, the nation continued to sin and took no notice of the "wondrous works" (*palaʾ*, see 9:1), His miracles done on their behalf, v. 32. For this reason, He "consumed" (better "ended") their days in "vanity" (or "a breath," *hebel*, see 31:6), without any substance to it. He ended their years "in trouble" (better "in sudden terror"). Asaph refers to the added years of wandering in the wilderness as God judged the nation for its sin, v. 33.

34–41 God's judgment moved the people. The nation then "sought" (*daraš*, see 9:10) Him. There are many examples of this, e.g., Numbers 21:7; Judges 3:9, 15. We cannot, however, relate the statement to a specific incident in Israel's past, v. 34. In turning to God, they remembered Him as their "rock" (e.g., Deut. 32:4, 15, 18, 31; II Sam. 22:3, 32, 47, *ṣûr*, see 18:2) and the Most High (*ʿelyôn,* see 7:17) as their "redeemer" (e.g., Job 19:25; Isa. 41:14; 43:14), v. 35. There was deceitfulness in Israel's actions. They attempted to "flatter" (better "deceive") God and they "lied" to Him, v. 36. They offered the Lord mere outward profession of loyalty when, in fact,

[67]Fausset, III, 268, states that the quails, exhausted by a long flight, flew low, only two cubits above the ground, where they might be easily caught. The account in Num. 11:31, however, says that the Lord let the quails "fall" near the camp. The people went outside the camp and gathered the birds.

their heart was not "right" (or "firmly established") and they were not "steadfast" (or "faithful") in keeping their covenant with Him, v. 37.

Being a compassionate God, He "forgave" (*kapar*, see 49:7) their iniquities and "destroyed [*šaḥat*, see 14:1] them not" (e.g., Num. 14:10–20; 16:44–48).[68] He turned His "anger" (*ʾap*, see 2:5) from them and did not let His "wrath" (*ḥemâ*, see 6:1) flare up, v. 38. He knew that the people were only weak humans. They were like a wind that blows and then is gone, cf. James 4:14, v. 39. Their actions provoked the Lord in the wilderness and caused Him to grieve for them, v. 40. They continually "turned back" from following God's ways. They "tempted [or 'tested'] God" (e.g., Exod. 17:2, 7; Ps. 95:8–9) and "limited" the work of the "Holy One of Israel"[69] on their behalf by their sin and lack of faith, v. 41.[70] This lengthy passage clearly illustrates spiritual principles. A lack of faith in the Lord brings His judgment. At the same time, He limits the punishment of His people since He knows their weaknesses. How much better it is for God's people to live wholly for Him!

IV. The Deliverance from Egypt 42–51

42–48 Asaph now shows the greatness of Israel's sin by recalling God's gracious deliverance of the nation from Egypt. The "day when he delivered [*padâ*, see 25:22] them from the enemy" was the day of the crossing of the Red Sea and the drowning of Egypt's army. Israel had forgotten God's "hand," i.e., His power, not that they knew nothing of it but that it made no difference to them, v. 42. Asaph now begins to summarize the miracles of God in Egypt. The list is not complete but is representative of the plagues. These were "signs" (*ʾôt*, see 65:8), evidences of His power. As in v. 12, the "field of Zoan" refers to the land of Goshen where Israel lived, v. 43.

---

[68]While Asaph does not mention a prayer for forgiveness or of repentance, these always accompanied God's decision to withhold His wrath.

[69]See the note at 71:22 for a brief summary of this name in the OT.

[70]W. E. Barnes, II, 380, and Cohen, p. 254, understand the limiting as Israel's view that God's power was bounded. It is difficult to see how the Creator can be limited in His power. The above view agrees better with the teaching of the OT. Israel limited God by their sin and lack of faith rather than by setting theoretical limits to His power.

The Lord turned the waters of Egypt into blood so that they had nothing to drink (Exod. 7:14–25). This was the first of the ten plagues in Egypt, v. 44. In the fourth plague, He sent "flies" (*ᶜarob*) that "devoured them," inflicting painful bites (Exod. 8:20–32).[71] The second plague involved frogs (Exod. 8:1–15), "which destroyed [or 'ruined,' *šaḥat*, see 14:1]" the Egyptians by their presence everywhere, v. 45. In the eighth plague, the "caterpillar" (*ḥasîl*) and "locust" (*ᵓarbeh*) ate their crops, destroying "their labour" (Exod. 10:12–20), v. 46.[72] The seventh plague brought hail to pound the vines and "frost" (or "sleet," *ḥᵃnamel*)[73] to destroy the sycamore trees (Exod. 9:13–35), v. 47. The seventh plague also killed cattle that had been left in the fields (Exod. 9:21–25). "Hot thunderbolts," lightning, accompanied the storm and struck the flocks in the fields (Exod. 9:23–24), v. 48.

49–51 Asaph describes the tenth plague in greater detail than the others. This shows the "fierceness" (*ḥarôn*, see 2:5) of God's "anger" (*ᵓap*, see 2:5), "wrath" (*ᶜebrâ*, see 7:6), "indignation" (*zaᶜam*, see 38:3), and "trouble" (or "distress," *ṣarâ*, see 9:9) toward the Egyptians as He sends "evil angels" to them. The destroying angels, "evil" in the destructive nature of their work, passed through the land at night to kill the firstborn sons and animals in homes without the blood applied to their doors (Exod. 12:29–30), v. 49.[74] God made

---

[71]The word *ᶜarob*, "swarms," refers to some unknown insect. The translators have supplied "flies." Cheyne, II, 21, translates "dog flies." Oesterley, II, 360, translates "locust." Henry, p. 538, gives "mixtures of insects in swarms." Rotherham, p. 342, suggests "gad-fly." Clarke, II, 200, gives "mosquitoes." Hirsch, II, 58, renders the word "beasts of the desert." Hengstenberg, II, 470, refers to "vermin." We can only speculate on the nature of the "swarms."

[72]The words *ḥasîl* and *ᵓarbeh* both refer to locusts, describing them from different aspects. The word *ḥasîl* refers to the locust's ability to eat virtually anything. The word *ᵓarbeh* refers to the many insects in a locust swarm.

[73]The word *ḥᵃnamel* occurs only here. KB, I, 334, suggests "devastating flood." W. E. Barnes, p. 381, gives "great hailstones." Without support, Cheyne, II, 24, emends to *geḥalîm*, "hot coals." Hirsch, II, 59, gives "crushing layer" but does not explain the phrase. The parallelism suggests "sleet."

[74]Delitzsch, II, 373, makes the verse describe the fifth plague, the pestilence that killed the animals of Egypt. The "evil angels" are those bringing the murrain upon the animals (Exod. 9:1–7). While this is possible, Asaph does not clearly describe a plague on animals here. The verse nicely joins with vv. 50–51 to describe the tenth plague. Archie C. C. Lee, "The Context and Function of the Plagues Tradition in Psalm 78," *JSOT* 48:84–85, refers vv. 49–50 to the destruction of Assyria in the time of Hezekiah. The context argues against this view.

a way to show His "anger" (*ʾap*). He spared none of the firstborn in the "pestilence" (or "plague"), v. 50.[75] This destroyed "the chief [or 'beginning'] of their strength," idiomatic for the firstborn (Gen. 49:3). The "tabernacles of Ham" refers to the dwellings of Egypt, the Egyptians being descended from Ham (Gen. 10:6; cf. Pss. 105:23, 27; 106:22), v. 51. These verses illustrate the power of an omnipotent God. At this time in the world's history, Egypt was the most powerful nation on earth. God, however, humbled them—not once but in several different ways—and showed His power over mankind.

V. The Defeat of Israel 52–64

52–53 This section continues the thought of the previous section. The story is familiar. God delivers Israel from Egypt, leads them through the wilderness into Canaan, and helps them conquer the heathen there. Despite this, they turn from God to serve false gods and bring judgment upon themselves. Asaph compares the nation to a flock of sheep. God, the faithful shepherd, guides them away from Egypt and through the wilderness of the Sinai Peninsula. While Asaph does not mention this, the guidance assumes the cloudy pillar by day and the pillar of fire by night (cf. v. 14), v. 52. As the Lord "led them on safely," they came to see that they had no need to fear (*paḥad*, see 14:5). Israel did show fear in the Exodus (e.g., Exod. 14:10; 16:3; 17:3). With time, however, they recognized the power of God over their enemies and in providing their physical needs, v. 53.

54–55 The Lord brought the nation to the border of his "sanctuary," the land of Canaan meant to be a haven for His people. He brought them to the "mountain," Mt. Zion, the location of the tabernacle where Asaph served, v. 54.[76] Working through Joshua's leadership, the Lord overcame the heathen that lived in the land (44:1–3). The nation then divided the land by "line" (or "measurement," *ḥebel*, see 16:6) and drew lots to assign portions to the tribes (Josh. 15–19).

[75]Rawlinson, II, 128, suggests that "pestilence" was the means used by the Lord to destroy the firstborn. While this is possible, Exod. 12 does not mention a pestilence. Verse 49 attributes the deaths to the angels.

[76]It is also possible that "mountain" is a collective, referring to the "hill country" of Palestine. I have referred the singular "mountain" to Mt. Zion because of its spiritual importance to the nation.

The people dwelled "in their tents," the living places formerly occupied by the heathen, v. 55.

56–58 Despite God's gracious provision of a land for the nation, they turned away from Him. They "tempted and provoked" the "most high [*ᶜelyôn,* see 7:17] God" by failing to keep His word, v. 56. They turned back from the Lord, acting "unfaithfully" (*bagad*, see 25:3) like their ancestors. They were like a "deceitful bow," a bow with a slack cord that has no power to send an arrow to its mark, v. 57. The people provoked the Lord to anger by worshiping false gods. They set up "high places" instead of tearing them down as the Lord had commanded (Num. 33:52). They caused jealousy in the Lord by giving their affection to "graven images," images carved from wood or stone to represent false gods, v. 58.

59–64 The Lord grew angry at the people and "abhorred" (or "rejected") them, v. 59. To show His anger, He forsook His care of the tabernacle at Shiloh. The city of Shiloh was in the area occupied by Ephraim, about twenty-four miles north-northeast of the Dead Sea. It was the first location of the tabernacle in Canaan (Josh. 18:1). From archaeology, it seems that the Philistines destroyed Shiloh ca. 1050 BC (I Sam. 4). When the ark was returned, it remained at Kirjath-jearim for twenty years (I Sam. 7:2). When David became king, he brought the ark to Jerusalem (II Sam. 6:12), v. 60. Before this, the Lord gave His "strength" and "glory," the ark of the covenant (I Sam. 4:21), to the Philistines, v. 61. He also gave the people "unto the sword." According to I Samuel 4:10, thirty thousand Israelite soldiers fell in battle when the Philistines captured the ark. In this way, the Lord showed His anger toward "his inheritance" Israel, v. 62. The "fire" of battle devoured the young men of the nation so that the maidens of Israel "were not given to marriage" (better, "did not sing [wedding] songs"), v. 63. Israel's priests fell in the battle (I Sam. 4:11). Since the bodies of these soldiers could not be recovered from the field of battle, no lamentations could be made at funerals, v. 64. How tragic! Despite the care God lavishes on His people, they spurn Him in favor of false gods. God punishes them for their wickedness. The illustration serves to show God's work today. When His people turn from Him, He judges them, often in this life but certainly in the life to come.

VI. The Choice of David 65–72

65–69 After leaving His people to their punishment by their foes, the Lord begins again to act on their behalf. Asaph compares this to awakening from sleep or the shouting of a "mighty man" (or "warrior," *gibbôr*, see 19:5) influenced by wine, v. 65. God strikes His foes "in the hinder parts," driving them backward as they retreat before Him. He causes them to lie under "a perpetual reproach," shamed by their defeat. Asaph refers to the succession of victories by Israel over Philistia that took place under Samuel, Saul, and David (I Sam. 7:10–14; 14:20–23; 17:51–53; 23:5; II Sam. 5:17–25; 8:1), v. 66. At this time, the Lord chose not to return the ark of the covenant to Shiloh in Ephraim, v. 67. He placed it on Mt. Zion, in Judah, the place He "loved" (or "desired")[77], v. 68. There He built His "sanctuary," His dwelling place among His people. It was built "like the high palaces" (better "like the heights") and like "the earth which he hath established for ever." These descriptions refer to the typology of the tabernacle that God dwells among His people. Although the OT tabernacle has been destroyed, the fulfillment remains intact. The Lord will dwell with His people throughout eternity, v. 69.

70–72 The Lord chose David to lead the nation, taking him from caring for his family's flocks, v. 70. After David had followed "ewes great with young" (better "ewes with sucking lambs"), the Lord brought him to care for the nation, v. 71. David carried out his leadership role wisely, guiding the nation with "integrity" (*tom*, see 7:8) and "skilfulness" (*teḇûnâ*, see 49:3), v. 72. These final paragraphs introduce David as both the OT king and the type of the eternal King of God's people. While the psalmist does not develop this final role of David, it is appropriate to note that God has an eternal plan for His own. God's people should learn from Israel's example. Rather than turning from the Lord and bringing in God's judgment, how much better it is to obey and to prepare for our eternal position of serving the King!

---

[77]The Hebrew has a single word (*ʾahab*) that represents the full range of positive emotions—love, like, desire, etc. In each case, the context must guide the sense given to the word.

PSALM 79

The simple heading "a psalm of Asaph" refers to the "sons of Asaph." The psalm is a community lament that comes from the fall of Judah to Babylon in the reign of Zedekiah, II Kings 25:1–21.[78] As with other psalms in this section, Asaph was a family name. Here, it identifies the descendants of Asaph.

I. Sorrow of the People 1–4

1–4 The psalmist begins by lamenting the conquest by the heathen. They have come into the land, the Lord's "inheritance."[79] They have defiled the "temple" (*hêkal*, see 5:7), a place that was meant to be holy. When the Lord departed from the temple (Ezek. 10:18; 11:23), it lost its spiritual significance. The psalmist refers to it in its historical sense, v. 1. The enemy has left the bodies of fallen Israelites in the open fields for the birds to feed on. The flesh of the "saints" (*ḥasîd*, see 4:3) serves as food for the wild beasts, v. 2. Judah's adversaries have shed the blood of God's people like water. So many have died that there is no one to bury them. The bodies are left on the ground, a disgraceful situation, v. 3. The nations around Judah look down on them with "scorn" (or "mocking") and "derision," v. 4.

Though the psalmist laments the fall of the nation, it is appropriate to note that Judah's defeat came as a just punishment for sin. The psalmist recognizes this in v. 5 where he speaks of God's "anger" and "jealousy." The people had turned from God to idols. What wor-

[78]Delitzsch, II, 378, sets the psalm at the time of the Seleucid wars. These took place during the intertestamental period and climaxed at the time of Antiochus Epiphanes in the second century BC. There are clues in the psalm, however, that fit the time of Babylon's invasion of Judah. The enemy defiled the temple, v. 1. The blood of the people was "shed like water round about Jerusalem," v. 3. The people of Judah became prisoners, v. 11. All of these fit the circumstances given in II Kings 18 at Nebuchadnezzar's conquest. In addition, I Macc. 7:17 quotes v. 3. This indicates a familiarity with the book of Psalms by the middle of the second century BC, which strongly argues for the earlier acceptance of the book. There is no need to make the psalm as late as the time of the Maccabees.

[79]While the Lord's inheritance normally refers to the people, e.g., 33:12; 94:14; 106:40, the context here argues for the land as including the people. The passage refers to the temple and Jerusalem, v. 1, and to the people, vv. 2–3.

ship they offered came as a ritualistic practice. They had ignored the warnings of the prophets. Nevertheless, the harshness of Babylon's conquest was not merited. Habakkuk 2:1–4 makes it clear that the Lord would preserve a righteous remnant from the people. Habakkuk 2:5–20 goes on to say that God would punish Babylon for its wickedness. At the time of the psalm, however, that is all future. The psalmist here puzzles over what has happened to Judah.

II. Supplication of the Psalmist 5–13

A. Judgment of the Heathen 5–7

5–7 Although the psalmist understands that the people have sinned, he does not grasp God's plan for the nation. He asks if His anger will continue forever. Will He let His jealousy for the love of the people burn like fire to consume them, v. 5? The psalmist asks God instead to exercise His "wrath" (*ḥemâ*, see 6:1) upon the heathen. They have not known God and have not called upon His "name," His nature as a forgiving God, v. 6.[80] Rather, they have consumed Jacob, the people who belong to God, and "laid waste" (or "made desolate," *šamem*, see 40:15) their dwellings. Prophesying at about the same time, Jeremiah 10:25 adapts vv. 6–7, v. 7.[81]

B. Glory of God 8–10

8–10 The psalmist begs the Lord not to hold the sins of their fathers against them. He asks that the "tender mercies" (or "compassions") of the Lord go before them. They need these since they have been brought very low by the Babylonians, v. 8. He asks for help that will glorify the God Who has delivered them in the past. He asks the Lord to deliver them from their foes and to "purge away" (*kapar*, see 49:7) their own sins for the sake of His "name" (see v. 6) as a loving God, v. 9. Why should the heathen say, "Where is their God?" This would be the natural response of people who believed in localized gods. Since they had overcome Judah, they would conclude that their

---

[80]See 5:11, note 94, for a brief summary of the Lord's name.

[81]Delitzsch, II, 379, thinks that the psalmist borrowed from Jeremiah. Since Jeremiah is the fuller version, it is more likely that he amplified the psalm than that the psalm simplified Jeremiah. Ultimately, however, we cannot be certain which is the original or if both borrowed from an unknown third source.

gods had vanquished Israel's god. The psalmist prays that the heathen around Israel will know God. This will take place as He "revenge[s]" (*n*ᵉ*qamâ*, see 18:47) the blood of those who have died at the hand of the heathen, v. 10.

C. Deliverance of Judah 11–13

11–13 May God note the "sighing" (or "groaning") of those who have been taken captive. The psalmist asks that God exercise His great power to preserve those who are "appointed to die,"[82] v. 11. May the Lord return "sevenfold," a full measure, of reproach to the "bosom" of their neighbors, the people who have reproached the Lord, v. 12. Then Judah, the "sheep of thy pasture," will give thanks to Him forever. They will praise God "to all generations" (*l*ᵉ*dor wador*, see 10:6), v. 13.

The psalmist's hope is to thank and praise the Lord. Although the situation is bleak, he turns to the Lord for deliverance. He anticipates the overthrow of the heathen and the lifting up of God's people once more. He then will offer the "sacrifice of praise" (Heb. 13:15) to God continually. Christians should still hold this attitude. No matter what the circumstances may be, we should still have the desire to praise the Lord for His sustaining grace and deliverance.

PSALM 80

This community lament psalm concerns a threat to the Northern Kingdom, likely the Assyrian invasion in 721 BC that brought about Israel's downfall. The psalm mentions Joseph, v. 1, and Ephraim and Manasseh, v. 2, together with the mention of a threat to the whole nation, vv. 6, 12, 13, 16. The temple still exists, v. 1. This argues for the time of Assyria's invasion.[83] Although Israel bore the brunt

---

[82]The phrase "appointed to die" appears only here and at 102:20. It is lit. "sons of death" and refers to the mortality of man. In both places, circumstances hasten the prospect of death, and the psalmist brings this fact to the Lord.

[83]Gaebelein, p. 310, relies on the mention of tribes in both the Northern and Southern Kingdoms to date the psalm before the division of the nation. He sees it

of the Assyrian conquest, Judah to the south also suffered terribly. On behalf of the whole community, the psalmist expresses his grief to the Lord. The author is one of the "sons of Asaph" and identifies himself by the family name.[84] He writes the psalm for the "chief musician" (*m^e^naṣṣeaḥ*, see 4, intro.) to use with the nation's worship. The psalm is to be performed upon "Shoshannim-Eduth," the "lilies of the testimony" (see 60, title), an unknown musical instruction.

I. Plea for Deliverance 1–3

1–3 The psalmist prays to the "Shepherd of Israel," the One Who cares for the flock. The phrase suggests that the people do not have the spiritual discernment or resources to care for themselves. The Lord leads "Joseph," representing the northern confederacy in Israel, like a flock of sheep. The Lord is also the One Who dwells "between the cherubims," one at each end of the ark of the covenant. In a sense, the ark was God's earthly throne. The glory of the Lord was enthroned among the cherubs. From there, He gave guidance to the people (Exod. 25:17–22), v. 1. The Assyrian threat confronts all of Palestine. Ephraim (in the middle of Israel), Benjamin (in the Southern Kingdom), and Manasseh (the northernmost tribe) represent the nation. The writer pleads with God to exercise His might and "save" (or "deliver") them, v. 2. He asks God to "turn" (or "restore") them from the actions of their enemies. If He will "cause [His] face to shine" on them (cf. 31:16; 67:1), looking favorably on them, they will be "saved" (or "delivered"). This refrain occurs again in vv. 7 and 19, v. 3.

---

as a call for God to lead the armies in battle. Solomon, however, was not involved in war, and the kingdom split shortly after Rehoboam's ascension. J. Fred McCurdy, writing in Moll, p. 447, sees the fragmenting of the nation into the Northern and Southern Kingdoms, coupled with incursions by Syria and Assyria, as the reason for writing. VanGemeren, p. 523, dates it at "the last days of Israel." Kirkpatrick, p. 483, places it after the fall of Israel, either "before the Exile or after the Return from Babylon." It is difficult to be dogmatic on the background since the psalm does not clearly state the occasion. In my judgment, the psalm best supports the view given above. The title in the LXX includes the phrase "concerning the Assyrian."

[84]See the introduction to Ps. 50 for information about Asaph.

II. Trial of the Nation 4–7

4–5 The psalmist questions the Lord, the God of the "hosts" (*ṣᵉbaʾôt*, see 24:10) of heaven and earth. How long will He be angry with the "prayer" (*tᵉpillâ*, see 4:1) of His people? While the psalmist naturally hopes for deliverance from Assyria, it is worth noting that sin causes prayers to be ineffective (66:18). While the psalmist may not have been guilty of sin, sin certainly marked the people of Israel. The punishment that came on them was due to their failure to follow the Lord, v. 4. The Lord has fed them the "bread of tears" and quenched their thirst with a "great measure" (*šalîš*)[85] of "tears." These phrases poetically describe the plight of the nation, v. 5.

6–7 The nation is now a source of "strife" (or "contention") to their neighbors, who quarrel among themselves over the spoil now available in the defeated land. Israel's foes "laugh" (or "mock") at them, v. 6. The psalmist repeats the prayer of v. 3, that the God of "hosts" (*ṣᵉbaʾôt*) would restore the nation, giving them His favor and delivering them from their enemies, v. 7.

III. History of the Nation 8–13

8–11 The psalmist now looks back over Israel's history. The thought serves as a reminder of how God had worked on their behalf in the past. The "vine" is a symbol of Israel (v. 14; Jer. 2:21; Hos. 10:1). The Lord brought them from Egypt, cast the heathen out of Palestine, and planted them there where they should have flourished, v. 8. He "prepared" (or "cleared" the ground so that it could grow. It sank roots down deep to draw nourishment from the land. It grew until it filled the land, v. 9. The shadow of the vine covered the hills and its "boughs" (or "branches" covered the "goodly [or 'mighty'] cedars."[86] Her branches spread from the Mediterranean Sea to the Jordan River. The description poetically tells of Israel's growth in the

[85]The word *šalîš*, lit. "a third," also occurs in Isa. 40:12 to refer to a "measure" of some kind. We do not know how large the *šalîš* was. The quantity "a third of an ephah," about one-fourth of a bushel, is most often suggested. The exact amount is not important. The psalmist simply conveys the thought that Israel had shed great amounts of tears over their troubles.

[86]The phrase "goodly cedars" (*ʾarzê-ʾel*) can be translated "cedars of God" (so Cheyne, Hirsch, Oesterley). I understand it rather as "mighty cedars." The word *ʾel* has this sense elsewhere, Deut. 28:32; Ps. 29:1; 89:6; Ezek. 31:11.

land. The "hills" marked the hill country of Judah to the south. The "cedars" grew in Lebanon to the north. The "sea" lay to the west and the Jordan "river"[87] to the east, vv. 10–11.

12–13 After this blessing in the past, why has God broken down Israel's "hedges," commonly planted along fields to keep marauders and wild beasts from the fruit (cf. 89:40)? Here, this represents the breaking down of Israel's defenses. Wayfarers can take spoil readily from her, v. 12. The wild boar in the "wood" (*yaᶜar*)[88] ravages it, and the "wild beast[s]" (or "creatures of the field," *zîz*, see 50:11, including all wildlife) feed upon it. Since the vine in vv. 8–11 is poetic, it is reasonable that the "boar" and "creatures of the field" are likewise poetic, probably representing Assyria and the neighboring countries around Palestine. This displays Israel's decline and inability to defend itself against those who would take spoil from it, v. 13.

IV. Petition for Deliverance 14–19

14–16 The psalm ends as it began, with a prayer that God will deliver His people. The psalmist continues poetically. He asks the "God of hosts [*ṣᵉbaʾôt*, see 24:10]" to come from heaven and "visit" (*paqad*, see 8:4) Israel, the "vine," v. 14. He asks as well that God visit the "vineyard" (or "shoot") and the "branch" (*ben*, lit. "son").[89] These terms poetically vary the symbolism for Israel. God had planted the nation and made it strong, v. 15, but it is now "burned" and "cut down" by the Assyrian onslaught. It is ready to "perish" (*ʾabad*, see 1:6) because of God's rebuke, v. 16.

---

[87]Leslie, p. 246, and Weiser, p. 550, identify the river as the Euphrates, originally given as the border of Israel, Deut. 11:24. While this is possible, Israel never occupied the territory given it by God. It is more natural to refer the river here to the area actually lived in at the time of Assyria's invasion.

[88]The *ᶜayin* is raised above the line in the MT. This *literae suspensae* signals that this is the middle letter of the book of Psalms (so *Kiddushim* 30*a*): יְכַרְסְמֶנָּה חֲזִיר מִיָּעַר וְזִיז שָׂדַי יִרְעֶנָּה׃ This is one of many ways that the Masoretic scribes tested the accuracy of their Hebrew manuscripts.

[89]The word *ben* is lit. "son." Since a "son" of the vine is a branch, the AV so translated it. The verse, however, deals with the vineyard as a symbol of the nation. The word "son" refers naturally to Israel, the nation whose father was God, I Chron. 29:10.

17–19 The "man [*ʾîš*] of thy right hand" is Israel.[90] The psalmist prays that God's "hand," His power, will bless the nation. Israel is at God's "right hand," the ceremonial position of honor, 16:8; 45:9; 110:1. God has given the "son of man [*ʾadam*]"[91] strength for his responsibilities, v. 17. The writer pledges loyalty to God. If God will "quicken" them, bringing the nation to renewed life, they will call upon His "name,"[92] v. 18. For the third time, the psalmist quotes the refrain. He asks the "Lord God of hosts [*ṣᵉbaʾôt*, see 24:10]" to "turn" (or "restore") the nation. If He will bestow His favor on them, they will be "saved" (or "delivered"), v. 19.

PSALM 81

The psalm urges the people to praise God and to worship Him. Israel had been called to this but had gone its own way instead. Despite God's gracious deliverance of the nation from their enslavement in Egypt, the people had turned from Him. Their sin brought divine judgment. The psalm closes at this point, implying but not stating the need for faithfulness on Israel's part.

The author intended the psalm for use with the Passover feast.[93] It is a time of rejoicing (vv. 2–3). God ordained this worship at the time when He passed through Egypt, v. 5, and brought the nation

---

[90]Anderson, II, 586, and Dahood, II, 260, understand the "man of thy right hand" as the king. The view is possible, although the context of vv. 15–16 concerns Israel. Fausset, III, 276, equates the phrase "man of thy right hand" with Benjamin, "son of the right hand." He concludes that the psalmist asks God to strengthen the tribe of Benjamin, a representative of Israel. The reasoning is contrived. While the phrases are similar, they are not identical, and Benjamin was part of the Southern Kingdom, not of the northern group of tribes. Phillips, I, 663, applies the verse to Jesus Christ, "the Son of God's right hand." Nothing in the context suggests a messianic application.

[91]See 22:6 for the contrast between *ʾîš* and *ʾadam*.

[92]See 5:11, note 94, for a brief summary of the Lord's name.

[93]Rodd, p. 18, and Mays, p. 266, relate the psalm to the Feast of Tabernacles. Clarke, p. 204, and Horne, p. 351, make it for the Feast of Trumpets. Buttenwieser, p. 53, and Gaebelein, p. 314, set it at the new-moon celebration. Eaton, p. 201, places it at "the autumnal New Year." Leupold, p. 587, considers that the author thinks of

out of Egypt, v. 10. It was decreed for a "solemn feast day," v. 3, and became a "statute" and "law" given by God, v. 4.

The nation of Israel later incorporated this psalm into its ritual. At the observance of the New Moon, the priests chanted this psalm during the pouring out of the drink offering. The psalm was also chanted in the temple on Thursdays.[94]

We know nothing of the date for the writing of the psalm. For this reason, it is not possible to say that the author is the Asaph who served under David as one of his chief musicians. He may be the author, or it may be one of his descendants identified with the family name. In either case, he writes the psalm for the "chief musician" (*mᵉnaṣṣeaḥ*, see 4, intro.) to use in Israel's worship "upon [or 'concerning, according to'] Gittith" (*gittît*, see 8, intro.), the time of the grape harvest and a natural time for a joyous tune.

I. Deliverance of Israel 1–5

1–3 The author begins by calling for a note of praise to God. The people should "sing" (*ranan*, see 5:11), giving forth a ringing cry of joy. They should make "a joyful noise" (*rûaᶜ*, see 41:11), shouting joyfully to God, v. 1. They should "take a psalm [*zimrâ*]"[95] accompanied with musical instruments. The "timbrel" (*top*) is a tambourine or small drum. The "pleasant [or 'delightful'] harp [or 'lyre,' *kinnôr*, see 33:2]" is a pleasant-sounding ten-stringed lyre. The "psaltery" (*nebel*, see 33:2) is a harp with ten strings, v. 2. They should blow the ram's horn "trumpet" (*šôpar*, see 47:5) at the time of the "new moon" (*ḥodeš*) and "in the time appointed" (or "at the full moon," *keseh*).[96] These times mark the month when Passover occurred. The music should take place on the "solemn feast day" (or simply "feast day," *ḥag*). The word *ḥag* occurs widely in the OT referring to vari-

---

"any and every festival that may be observed." In my judgment, the overall context of the psalm supports the time of Passover.

[94]According to *Sukkah* 55*a*, the psalm was sung on the fifth day of Tabernacles.

[95]Although the noun form of the root *zmr* occurs only here and at 98:5 in Psalms, the verb form occurs forty-one times. It refers to a song of either vocal or instrumental praise to the Lord.

[96]The word *keseh* receives little emphasis in the OT. It appears only here and at Prov. 7:20. In both places, it refers to a point of time. "Full moon" is conjectured. The use of *ḥodeš*, "new," and then "new moon" supports this.

ous feasts. The OT mentions the blowing of trumpets only in connection with the Feast of Trumpets. In light of the general rejoicing that accompanied Passover (Ezra 6:22), it is reasonable that trumpets would accompany it also, v. 3.

4–5 God gave directions to regulate Israel's worship (cf. Exod. 12:1–11, 14–28), v. 4. He appointed these as a means for Israel to establish their testimony of faithfulness to God. The reference to "Joseph" (*y^ehôsep*)[97] here denotes all Israel. God established this worship at the time when "he," God, went through the land in the time of judgment upon Egypt's firstborn.[98] At that time, "I [referring to God] heard a language that I understood not [or 'did not know,' *yada*ᶜ]." This does not refer to God's failure to understand what was said. The Creator of all languages certainly knew what the words meant. The word *yada*ᶜ often has the sense of experiential knowledge. It has that connotation here. He heard Egypt's worship of their gods but did not experientially respond to what they said, v. 5.[99]

---

[97]Over two hundred times in the OT, the spelling of "Joseph" is *yôsep*. This is the only variant spelling. The same spelling occurs often in postbiblical inscriptions. Simonis and Gesenius, *A List of the Proper Names Occurring in the Old Testament with Their Interpretations* (London: J. Wertheimer and Co., 1844), p. 55, explains the variant as an uncontracted *hip*ᶜ*îl* form of *yasap*. With no support, Cheyne, II, 36, emends to *b*ᵉ*yad-mošeh*. Since the name occurs frequently in extrabiblical material, it is difficult to accept this suggestion. Hirsch, II, 86, suggests that the added *hê*, changing the first syllable into a name of God, indicates that Joseph "had never disavowed the name of God." This follows the Talmud, *Soṭah* 10*b*, which says, "Joseph who sanctified the heavenly name in private [when he resisted Potiphar's wife] merited that one letter should be added to him from the Name of the Holy One." Scott C. Layton, "Jehoseph in Ps 81,6," *Biblica* 69:410, adopts a similar view. Since we lack evidence, we cannot be dogmatic for the variant spelling. The expansion of names which use the letter *yôd* for *yah* occurs elsewhere, e.g., Jehoshua/Joshua (Num. 13:16); Jehoash/Joash (II Kings 11:21); Jehezekiah/Hezekiah (II Chron. 29:1), and may well reflect an original name.

[98]Leslie, p. 210, and Alexander, p. 334, understand Israel as the one that goes "through . . . Egypt." They apply this to Israel's Exodus from the land. The parallelism of the verse, however, argues that "he" refers to God.

[99]Horne, p. 353, and Calvin, III, 314, see this as Israel not understanding the Egyptian language. This cannot be. The Israelites grew up in the land and were certainly able to understand their persecutors. Delitzsch, II, 396, understands that God speaks to His people in a way they had not previously known; cf. Exod. 6:3. Before, He had been the mighty God; now He is Israel's King. The pronoun "I" refers to the poet as he recalls God's expression of the change in the relationship. Moll, p. 452, also refers the pronoun to the psalmist. He hears revelation of a kind he was not accustomed to receiving. Fausset, III, 277, makes the "I" refer to the psalmist, who

II. Promise to Israel 6–10

6–7 God released His people from their bondage in Egypt. He took away the carrying of burdens. There was no longer any need for the people to carry "pots" (or "baskets"). This may refer to carrying clay for making bricks or to carrying the bricks themselves, v. 6. The people had cried out to God in their "trouble" (or "distress," *ṣarâ*, see 9:9), and He delivered them. He answered their prayers "in the hiding place of thunder," a poetic reference to the cloud leading Israel throughout the Exodus. From this, God thundered troubles upon the Egyptians (Exod. 14:24; cf. 19:16). Then He led Israel into the wilderness, where He "proved" (or "tried") the nation at Rephidim in giving them water from the rock (Exod. 17:1–7). Moses named the place "Meribah" ("strife") because of the people's response at the lack of water. The word "Selah" draws attention to God's work on behalf of Israel, v. 7.

8–10 The Lord calls upon His people to hear His words. He will "testify unto" (or "admonish") them. He has this right since He had brought the nation into being. The last phrase expresses God's desire—if they will but hear His words, v. 8! He reminds them of the first commandment of the Law: They should have no "strange" (*zûr*, see 44:20) god among them. They should not "worship" (or "bow down") before any "strange" (*nekar*, see 18:44) god, v. 9. The phrase "I am the Lord thy God" is better "I, the Lord, am your God." He alone is Israel's God. He is the One Who "brought [them] out" (better "brought you up") from Egypt. The phrase suggests bringing Israel into Palestine, the promised homeland. He has done this much for them, an indication that He wants to do more. If they will open the mouth wide, He will fill it with good things, v. 10.

III. Repentance of Israel 11–16

11–12 Despite God's gracious offer, Israel spurned His words. They would not listen to Him or accept His right to set their standards, v. 11. For this reason, He let them go after the "lust" (or "stubbornness,"

---

speaks for Israel. They hear language that "was peculiarly galling" from "a people alien . . . in sentiments." To answer these views, it is most consistent to apply the pronoun to God. The pronoun naturally refers to the same speaker throughout vv. 5–8.

šᵉrîrût)[100] of their own hearts. They then went after their own counsel, doing what they thought was best, v. 12.

13–16 The Lord expresses His desire that Israel hear Him and follow His ways, v. 13. He then would be able to bless them. He would put down their enemies and turn His hand against their foes, v. 14. The "haters" (*śaneʾ*, see 5:5) of the Lord would "have submitted" (*kaḥaš*, see 18:44) to Him, feigning submission. This will not deliver them. Their "time" of punishment will endure forever, v. 15. The Lord, however, will bless His people. Israel will feast on the "finest [*ḥeleb*, see 17:10] of the wheat." The Lord will satisfy them with "honey out of the rock [*ṣûr*, see 18:2]" (cf. Deut. 32:13), a metaphorical picture of the bounty given them by God in the land that flows with "milk and honey" (Exod. 3:8, 17), v. 16.

PSALM 82

The poet writes concerning the injustice of wicked men. We do not know the circumstances that cause Asaph to take up the subject.[101] While David, the king at this time, was a righteous leader, there may well have been wicked judges in the land.[102] Becoming aware of the problem, Asaph writes to call the matter to public attention. The Jews later chanted Psalm 82 in the temple on Tuesdays.[103]

The psalm builds toward a climax in the last verse. The first seven verses introduce the problem, and the final verse introduces its solution. In so doing, the verse sounds the only eschatological note in the psalm.

---

[100]The word *šᵉrîrût* occurs only here in the Psalms. Elsewhere it occurs in Deuteronomy and primarily in Jeremiah. A related noun means "sinew, muscle." This suggests something with strength, giving rise to the meaning of "stubbornness" here.

[101]The name of Asaph occurs in the titles of Pss. 50, 73–83. A summary of Asaph's life and ministry introduces Ps. 50.

[102]Dahood, II, 269, makes the psalm pre-monarchial. Kissane, p. 377, sees it as preexilic. Ewald, p. 140, dates the psalm toward the end of the Exile. If we accept the title, the psalm must be placed during the reign of David.

[103]*Tamid* 33*b*. According to *Sukkah* 55*a*, the priests also chanted the psalm on the sixth day of Tabernacles.

I. The Position of God 1–2

1 Asaph recognizes the position of God as judge of the wicked. God stands "in the congregation of the mighty" (lit. "in the congregation of God"). This unusual expression is similar to the phrase "congregation of the Lord" found elsewhere (e.g., Num. 27:17; 31:16). It refers to the nation of Israel. God stands among the people with power over them.[104] He judges "among the gods [*ᵓĕlohîm*]." The *ᵓĕlohîm* here cannot refer to "gods" since there is but one God (cf. Isa. 45:5, 6, 22).[105] The alternate meaning, "judges" (cf. Exod. 21:6; 22:8, 9), suits the context better, v. 1.[106]

2 Despite the power of God, wicked men on earth carry out wicked judgment. Asaph cries out to them, "How long?"[107] The question introduces the problem of injustice that marks the actions of these judges. They render unjust decisions and show favor to the wicked. While not stated, there is an underlying assumption that the judges

[104]Rawlinson, II, 177, makes the "congregation of God" a "Divine assembly" of angels. There is, however, no indication elsewhere that angels serve as judges of mankind. They carry out the will of God, which in some cases may involve judgment. They themselves are not the judges. Kenneth M. Craig Jr., "Psalm 82," *Interp* 41:3 (1995): 281, refers to "other gods" who "rule over the nations." Anderson, II, 593, considers the assembly "the divine intermediaries who formed Yahweh's heavenly court." Both of these views ignore the impossibility of multiple "gods."

[105]In addition, v. 7 states that the "gods" of v. 6 will one day die "like men." This clearly rules out the possibility of referring to superhuman beings. W. S. Prinsloo, "Psalm 82: Once Again, Gods or Men," *Biblica* 76 (1995): 227, refers to "gods who are designated as mortal." This goes against the commonly accepted view of "gods."

[106]Willa Boesak, "Psalm 82: God amidst the gods," *Journal of Theology for Southern Africa* 64:1 (1988): 67, argues that it is not necessary to choose between these positions. She then discusses the psalm as though the "gods" were human judges accorded a divine status: "The key to understanding Ps. 82 is the recognition of the state as being human but, at the same time, a servant of God. . . . The poet influenced by his Canaanitic environment, therefore sketches in mythological language the wrath of God against these 'gods' who violate the rights of the weak and the marginalised. When that happens, their elohim-status is taken away from them; they are no longer 'sons of the Most High' and they effectively lose the divine right to rule." Regardless of her attempt to combine the positions, this still understands the "gods" as human judges.

[107]Clarke, II, 61, and VanGemeren, p. 534, understand the first phrase as the Lord's speech to the wicked judges. The view is possible since it is clear that God speaks in v. 6. It is a question of determining when Asaph stops speaking for the Lord and when the Lord speaks for Himself. Since the verse concludes with "Selah," calling attention to the words, I assign v. 2 to Asaph.

accepted bribes to influence their decisions. The "selah" calls attention to the statement of the problem, v. 2.

II. The Plight of Israel 3–7

3–4 The Lord now begins to speak through the psalmist. He sets forth the proper actions of earthly judges. They should "defend" (better "judge" in the sense of vindicate) the "poor [*dal*, see 41:1] and fatherless." They should "do justice" to the "afflicted [*ʿanî*, see 9:12] and needy [*rûš*],"[108] v. 3. They should deliver the "poor [*dal*] and needy [*ʾebyôn*, see 72:13]." These groups of people have no wealth or position that will give them influence. They depend solely on the righteous actions of others. The Lord appeals to the judges to "rid them" (better "rescue them") from the power of the wicked, v. 4.

5–6 Rather than these righteous actions, the wicked proceed in their wickedness. They have no knowledge or understanding of godly behavior. They walk in spiritual darkness; cf. John 3:19. Their willful distortion of the law has caused the foundations of society to be "out of course" (or "shaken, overthrown"). The lack of justice keeps righteousness from prevailing in society, v. 5.[109] The Lord reminds the judges of their divine appointment and position. He had declared that they were "gods" (better "judges," see v. 1)[110] and His children. There is an unstated responsibility to carry out their appointment in a

---

[108]The word *rûš* occurs again in the Psalms only in 34:10, where it refers to the "lack" of food for the "young lions." When applied to men, it often suggests a destitute condition, e.g., I Sam. 18:23 (lacking in position); II Sam. 12:3–4 (the destitute man in Nathan's parable to David). The word occurs most often in Proverbs to refer to those lacking in wealth.

[109]Kidner, p. 298, applies v. 5 "to describe the plight of the misgoverned and misled, who are 'destroyed for lack of knowledge' (Hos. 4:6), and groping for lack of light or of any moral certainties (cf. Is. 59:9ff)." The view ignores the context of vv. 3–4, 6, which refers to the judges.

[110]Kidner, pp. 297, 299, refers the statement to "principalities and powers . . . the world rulers of this present darkness" and cites Isa. 24:21; Dan. 10:13, 20–21; and 12:1 in support. He states that the simile "like men," v. 7, is "fatal to the view that these are human judges." The simile, however, does not rule out humans. It simply states that these corrupt judges will face the same death that all men face. The list of responsibilities in vv. 3–4 applies to human judges. For these reasons, I prefer the view expressed above.

righteous manner and to act as befits the children of the "most High" (*ᶜelyôn,* see 7:17) God, v. 6.[111]

7 Despite their lofty position, they will die as all men die. They will fall from their position just as other leaders do. The implied thought is that these wicked judges will one day face their final judgment. They should think of that before it comes to pass, v. 7.

III. The Petition for Relief 8

8 Asaph now returns to his position as the speaker. He pleads with God to rise up to carry out His judgment of mankind. Asaph goes beyond the immediate problem of injustice. He asks God to judge "the earth," all mankind, as He rights the wrongs of this life (cf. Eccles. 5:8).[112] This is the role of the Son of God, John 5:22, 27. He will inherit the nations of the world as His own in the millennial reign over the earth, v. 8.

PSALM 83

Psalm 83 is "A Song or Psalm"[113] by the family of Asaph, their lone contribution to the imprecatory psalms.[114] It is the last of psalms

[111]The Lord quotes v. 6 in John 10:34 as He defends Himself against the charge of blasphemy because He has claimed equality with the Father. He argues that God had called others "gods." He therefore had the right to call Himself the "Son of God."

[112]Matitiahu Tsevat, "An Interpretation of Psalm 82," *HUCA* 40–41 (1970): 133, is extreme in his comment on v. 8. He understands that God had "in the distant past . . . divided mankind into nations, whose number He determined by the number of the sons of 'God/El', the minor gods; each of these gods received a nation as his portion. . . . Only one nation was not given over to these gods—Israel; that people Yhwh retained for Himself." Fearful that God will delay His rule over an "unfragmented world," the psalmist prays that God will judge the existing order and take control of what is rightfully His.

[113]For the discussion of the double title "A Song or Psalm," see the introduction to Ps. 30.

[114]The imprecatory psalms include individual laments in Pss. 35, 59, 69, 70, 109, 137, and 140 and community laments in Pss. 58 and 83. The introduction to Ps. 35 discusses the nature of the imprecatory psalms. In Ps. 83, the imprecation grows out of the desire to punish the coalition of nations that have gathered against Israel.

written by Asaph and his descendants.[115] From the psalm, we understand that several groups have joined forces against Judah. These include the nations of Edom, the Arabian descendants of Ishmael, Moab, the Hagarenes, Ammon, Amalek, Philistia, Assyria, and the cities of Gebal and Tyre. This represents the threat made during the reign of Jehoshaphat, II Chronicles 20:1–2, 10, 22–23.[116] While the historical record mentions only Ammon, Moab, and Edom, there may have been lesser support from the others groups mentioned in the psalm.

Jahaziel, a descendant of Asaph (II Chron. 20:14), may well have written the psalm. He acted as the spiritual leader at the time of the conflict between Judah and the coalition between Moab, Ammon, and Edom. He prophesied victory over the enemy without having to fight them. He uttered the well-known phrases "The battle is not yours, but God's" and "Stand ye still, and see the salvation of the Lord." His words inspired Jehoshaphat to worship the Lord. Following this, the Levites sang a chorus of praise to the Lord. If Jahaziel is the author, the title refers to the family of Asaph rather than to Asaph himself.

I. Description of Judah's Plight 1–8

1–4 The psalmist calls on God to speak and to be still no longer. From the context, it is clear that he has words and actions of judgment in mind, v. 1. It is unusual but not rare for the psalmist to identify the foes of Judah as the enemies of the Lord, e.g., 74:4; 89:10. While they move against Judah, they really attack the plans of God. Those who "hate" (*śaneʾ*, see 5:5) God "have lifted up the head," setting themselves against Him, v. 2. They have plotted against the nation, even threatening the Lord's "hidden ones." The phrase refers to those who dwell in the presence of the Lord and thus away from the common ways of life, cf. 31:20; 91:1, v. 3. The psalmist states

[115]The psalms bearing the name of Asaph include Ps. 50 and Pss. 73–83. The introduction to Ps. 50 briefly summarizes the life and ministry of Asaph.

[116]Rodd, p. 22, views the psalm as not based on history. It is "rather a cultic lament in which the onslaught of the nations . . . has been filled out with concrete detail." Weiser, p. 562, is similar. He considers the psalm as "a cultic situation in which the people deliver up to the judgment of God all their potential and actual enemies, adversaries of the past and those of the present." These views are speculative. Rotherham, pp. 366–67, argues for the time of Jeroboam II. Nothing in the OT, however, relates the combination of enemies given in the psalm to the time of this king.

clearly the goal of the enemies. They seek to overcome Israel to the point that no one will even remember them, v. 4.

5–8 The psalmist recognizes that the plans of the enemy are plans against God. They have conspired together. They "are confederate" (better, "have made a covenant") against the Lord, v. 5. The enemies include several nations and cities. The "tabernacles" (or "tents") of Edom are involved. Edom had "perpetual hatred" toward the people of God (Ezek. 35:5). The Ishmaelites continued the wilderness life of Ishmael (Gen. 21:20–21). They were a nomadic people living between Havilah and Shur (Gen. 25:17–18). Havilah was in the southern part of Arabia, while Shur (or "wall") lay east of the Nile Delta. The word "wall" refers to a barrier erected by Egypt between the delta region and the desert. Moab lay east of Jordan between the Arnon and Zered rivers. The OT often mentions them as enemies of Judah. The Hagarenes are mentioned only here and in I Chronicles 5:10, 19–20; 11:38; 27:31. They were a nomadic group living in Gilead, east of the Jordan River, v. 6.

The confederacy also included Gebal, known later by the Greeks as Byblos, a Phoenician city located on the coast about forty miles north of Sidon.[117] The Ammonites lived east of the Jordan River between the Arnon and Jabbok rivers. The Amalekites were nomads who ranged from the Negeb in the south of Judah to the Sinai Peninsula. The Philistines occupied the coastal region southwest of Judah. Tyre was an important coastal Phoenician city, v. 7. The Assyrians join the coalition. During the time of Jehoshaphat (873–848 BC), Assyria was not the powerful nation it later became. In some unknown way, they "have holpen [*hayû zᵉrôaᶜ*] the children of Lot," Moab and Ammon, called this because of their origin, Genesis 19:33–38. The phrase *hayû zᵉrôaᶜ* is lit. "become an arm," idiomatic for providing strength. The psalmist appropriately closes the stanza with "selah," calling attention to the danger, v. 8.

II. Review of Israel's History 9–12

9–12 The rest of the psalm continues the psalmist's plea. This paragraph, however, focuses on God's work on behalf of the people

---

[117]Older commentators often locate Gebal in the northern part of Edom. So Alexander, p. 361; Clarke, p. 208; and Murphy, p. 451. Greek and Assyrian writings, however, support the location in Phoenicia.

in the past. It is appropriate to separate it from the concluding verses. The psalmist asks the Lord to do again as He did to the Midianites. He refers to the victory by Israel over Midian (Num. 31:7–8).[118] The victory over Sisera and Jabin at the "brook [better 'river'] of Kishon" took place when the Lord miraculously sent torrential rain to immobilize the chariots of the Canaanites (Judg. 4:15–16; 5:4, 20–21), v. 9. The account in Judges does not mention En-dor, located between the Kishon River and the Sea of Galilee near the base of Mt. Tabor. Judges 5:19, however, does mention Taanach and Megiddo, neighboring towns; cf. Joshua 17:11. Judges 4:6, 12, and 14 mention Mt. Tabor. It is well within reason that a portion of the battle took place at En-dor. The carcasses of the Canaanites became "dung for the earth," the rotting corpses fertilizing the soil, v. 10.

In his plea, the psalmist asks that God would make the enemy like Oreb, Zeeb, Zebah, and Zalmunah, leaders of the Midianites at the time of Gideon's victory (Judg. 7:16–25; 8:10–12, 18–21), v. 11. In their arrogance, they had planned to possess "the houses [better 'pastures'] of God," the land of Israel, v. 12.

III. Prayer for Israel's Victory 13–18

13–15 The imprecation begins in v. 13. The psalmist prays that God will make Israel's enemies like a "wheel" (*galgal*, better "whirlwind," see 77:18).[119] He wants them to flee like stubble blown before the wind, v. 13. He suggests another picture. He prays that God will

---

[118]Among others, Kissane, p. 384, and Cohen, p. 273, refer the victory to that over Midian in the time of Gideon. This is possible. It is strange, however, that the psalmist would begin with Gideon's victory, move to the victory under Barak, and then return to Gideon. The listing of past victories above is sequential.

[119]Commentators take *galgal* differently. Cohen, p. 274, understands "whirling dust." Calvin, III, 348, translates "whirling ball." Moll, p. 459, adopts "whirlwind." Hengstenberg, III, 47, translates "whirl" and refers this to the whirling of stubble in the wind. Harman, p. 287, gives "tumbleweed." Henry, p. 556, accepts "wheel." He suggests either that the foes are "in continual motion, unquiet, unsettled, and giddy in all their counsels and resolves," or that they are "broken by the judgments of God" as the wheel threshes them. Oesterley, II, 377, describes this as "the dried heads of a common Palestinian weed, a wild artichoke." This has branches of equal size and length in all directions that form a sphere a foot or more across. *OTTP*, p. 110, translates "whirling thistle." Clarke, p. 208, gives "rolling thing" and refers "to the featherlight globular heads of the wild artichoke." As in 77:18 ("the heaven"), where some kind of storm is virtually demanded, so the parallelism here supports a storm.

make the defeat of Israel's foes like fire roaring through the trees or racing along the sides of a wooded mountain, v. 14. He asks God to send a tempest of judgment upon the adversaries of the people. He prays for a punishing storm so fierce that it will cause them to "be afraid" (*bahal*, see 2:5), v. 15.

16–18 It is appropriate that the psalmist now uses the name "Lord." Up to this point, he has prayed to "God," the mighty One Who has the power to judge His enemies. The psalmist here prays that the enemies "may seek thy name."[120] It is therefore right to use *y*ᵉ*hwah*, the redemptive name of God, v. 16. When the enemy is "confounded" (*bôš*, see 6:10), exposed to public disgrace, and "troubled" (or "dismayed," *bahal*); shamed and made to "perish" (*ʾabad*, see 1:6), some may well realize their need to follow Israel's God, v. 17. The psalmist's prayer is that men may experientially "know" (*yadaʿ*, see 1:6) that the God Who alone has the "name" of *y*ᵉ*hwah* is "the most high" (*ʿelyôn*)[121] above the whole earth, v. 18.

PSALM 84

This beautiful psalm expresses a longing to be in the temple to experience the presence and blessing of God. It is authored by one of "the sons of Korah,"[122] one of twelve such psalms.[123] Verses 2, 3, 4, and 10 refer to the temple, and the word "anointed" in v. 9 to the king. The author writes the psalm for use in the temple at Jerusalem by the "chief musician" (*m*ᵉ*naṣṣeaḥ*, see 4, intro.), the director of the

---

[120]Note 94 at 5:11 gives a summary of the Lord's "name."

[121]The OT often translates *ʿelyôn* as "most High," e.g., 9:2; 50:14; 91:1, 9, a personal name of God. Whether it is left as an adjective here or translated as a personal name, it clearly indicates that the Lord occupies the eminent position over the earth. He is therefore worthy of worship. See 7:17.

[122]Calvin, III, 352, and Jennings, II, 69, make David the author. The view requires that we understand the *lamed* preposition in *libnê-qoraḥ*, "for the sons of Korah," as introducing the dative of an unexpressed verb. See the introduction to Ps. 3, which discusses the *lamed auctoris*.

[123]See also Pss. 42–43, 44, 45, 46, 47, 48, 49, 85, 87, 88. The introduction to Pss. 42–43 discusses the phrase "sons of Korah."

temple music. These references suggest a date before the Babylonian captivity.[124] The singing of the psalm was "upon [or 'concerning, according to'] Gittith" (*gittît*, see 8, intro.), the time of the grape harvest. The note of joy throughout the psalm is appropriate for this time of the year.[125]

I. The Longing for God's House 1–4

1–2 The psalmist begins by extolling the loveliness of the Lord's "tabernacles" (better "dwelling"). It is "amiable" (or "lovely," *yadîd*, see 45, title). The word "dwelling" is a plural of excellence that describes the temple where the Lord dwells among His people.[126] He addresses the Lord with the title "Lord of hosts [*ṣᵉbaʾôt*, see 24:10]," a phrase that acknowledges the Lord as the King of heaven and earth, v. 1.[127]

The psalmist wants to be in the "courts of the Lord" where he may worship.[128] He "longeth [*kasap*], yea, even fainteth [*kalâ*, see 73:26]" to be in the temple.[129] He says, "My heart and my flesh," his whole being, "crieth out" (better "make a ringing cry of joy," *ranan*, see 5:11) at the thought of being in the presence of the Lord again, v. 2.

---

[124]Hengstenberg, III, 50, sets the psalm at the time of David's flight from Absalom. While this is possible, the psalm is not clear as to the background. Ewald, II, 30, and Hirsch, II, 98, date it in the Exile. Buttenwieser, p. 777, places it in the "second half of the fourth century B.C." These views are difficult to accept because of the reference to the "anointed" king and to the temple.

[125]Robert Benedetto, "Psalm 84," *Interp* 51:1 (1997): 57, suggests the Feast of Tabernacles. While this is possible, the psalm is not specific as to the time of its writing.

[126]Henry, p. 557, applies the plural "tabernacles" to the several courts, the holy place, and the holy of holies. But the psalmist, a Korahite, would have no knowledge of the holy place or holy of holies. It is unlikely that he would have extolled the beauty of the Court of the Gentiles. In addition, the Lord dwelled only in the holy of holies. I prefer to see a plural of excellence that describes the building devoted to the worship of God.

[127]See Ps. 24:10 for a discussion of the phrase "Lord of hosts."

[128]Leupold, p. 604, understands the psalmist as "apparently barred from access to the sanctuary." Weiser, p. 566, suggests a pilgrimage from a foreign land to the temple. These views are possible. The psalmist may also simply express his love for being where he may worship the Lord.

[129]The *nipʿal* verb *kasap* describes a strong desire, "yearning." The combination with *kalâ* expresses the deep longing of the psalmist to be at the temple.

3–4 Nature gives an illustration of the psalmist's desire. The "sparrow" (*ṣippôr*)[130] and the "swallow" build nests for themselves. This is their home where they raise their young. The author thinks of birds building their nests in niches found at the temple.[131] The word "altars" identifies the temple, the well-known part representing the building with which it is intimately connected. The implication is that the psalmist too desires to be at the temple. Once more, he addresses the "Lord of hosts [*ṣᵉbaʾôt*]." This time, however, he multiplies the names of the Lord, calling Him also the "King" and his own "God," v. 3.

The thought of birds making their homes at the temple causes the writer to write a spontaneous benediction for those who dwell at the temple. They are "blessed" (*ʾašrê*, see 1:1). As normal, the plural *ʾašrê* is a plural of intensity: "O the blessedness" of those who live in God's house. The statement "they will be still praising thee" is better taken as a jussive, "let them continually be praising you," a natural response to the great privilege they enjoy. The psalmist adds the word "selah" to emphasize the blessings received from the Lord, v. 4.

II. The Desire for God's Presence 5–7

5–7 "Blessed" (*ʾašrê*) is again a plural of intensity: "O the blessedness" of the man who draws his strength from the Lord. This is more than mere dwelling in the house of the Lord. This is a relationship of dependence, a man who relies upon the Lord to supply everything he needs. The phrase "in whose heart are the ways of them" is better "the highways are in their hearts." The context suggests that "highways" are those ways that lead to godly actions.[132] This leads to something like "the ways *of godliness* are in their hearts," v. 5.

When such a man passes through the "valley of Baca," he turns it into a refreshing "well" (better "spring") of water. The word *bakaʾ*

---

[130]The *ṣippôr* is a generic word for small birds. Since the sparrow occurs widely in Palestine, the word may indeed refer to the house sparrow here.

[131]Jennings, II, 71, and Hengstenberg, III, 54, consider the bird as the psalmist himself. It is difficult to understand why the psalmist would use two separate birds as pictures of himself. It is easier to have the return of the birds to their nests illustrate the psalmist's love for the temple than to make this stand for the psalmist himself. Henry, p. 557, conjectures that cages with singing birds were hung about the courts of the tabernacle to sing their songs to the Lord. There is no evidence for this.

[132]Cohen, p. 275, and Harman, p. 289, make the highways those leading to Zion where the temple stands. This does not give a good parallel to the first half of the verse.

indicates the balsam tree, a tree that exudes the gum from which balm is made.[133] The tree grows in dry regions. The "rain" (*môreh*) fills the "pools." The *môreh* is the "early rain" that ends the long dry spell of summer and prepares the ground for the sowing of seed. Together, the "spring" and the "early rain" nourish the ground and cause it to bloom. Poetically, the verse speaks of the blessings brought by the godly man, v. 6. Omitting the unnecessary supplied words, they go "from strength to strength," from one degree of strength to the next, as they rely upon the Lord to sustain them in the challenges of life, v. 7*a*. The verse better reads, "The God of gods appears in Zion," entering into fellowship with the godly, v. 7*b*.

III. The Prayer for God's Blessing 8–12

8 The psalmist goes to the Lord in "prayer" (*tᵉpillâ*, see 4:1). He gives a fuller name for the Lord than he has given before in vv. 1, 3. He now calls upon the "Lord God of hosts [*ṣᵉbaʾôt*]," again the ruler of the heavenly and earthly hosts but with the extra thought of strength coming from the addition of "God" to the name. Further, this is the "God of Jacob," the God Who has chosen Israel for Himself. The word "selah" draws attention to the psalmist's dependence on the Lord, v. 8.

9–12 Finally, the writer views God as Israel's "shield" (*magen*, see 3:3), protection against attacks by the wicked. He asks the Lord to "look upon" him, i.e., to regard him closely. The phrase "face of thine anointed [*mašîaḥ*, see 2:2]" refers to the king of the land, the one primarily responsible for guiding the nation.[134] It is possible that the nation faced a threat at this time, v. 9. The psalmist returns to the thought with which he began, the blessedness of being in the house of the Lord. Perhaps he thinks of the national threat and sees his need to spend time in the temple praying for the nation. A

---

[133]Kidner, p. 305, makes "Baca" indicate "a tree or shrub which grows in arid places." Pilgrims passing through this place "*make it a place of springs* . . . a classic statement of the faith which dares to dig blessings out of hardships." Albert Barnes, II, 342, understands *bakaʾ* as "weeping" and refers to it some lonely valley without water. I lean toward Kidner's view although I would not draw the same spiritual lesson from the verse.

[134]Gaebelein, p. 324, understands *mašîaḥ* as "God's anointed Son." The context, however, does not suggest a messianic application here.

single day at the temple has more value than a thousand days away from it. The thought is not meant as a literal comparison but rather as a poetic expression of the great benefit that comes from time in the Lord's house and, by extension, time spent with the Lord. The psalmist would rather "be a doorkeeper" (*sapap*, better "stand at the threshold") in the house of his God[135] than to "dwell" (or "heap up," referring to riches) in the tents of the wicked.[136] The Korahites were doorkeepers in the temple (I Chron. 9:19; 26:1–19), standing at the thresholds to ensure that only those with a right to enter could go through. The psalmist would rather have this simple responsibility than to lay up wealth for himself that came through wickedness, v. 10.

The Lord is a "sun and shield [*magen*]." In addition to being the psalmist's protector, the Lord is his "sun," his source of light. In the OT, light often pictures righteousness (Isa. 5:20), spiritual joy (Ps. 27:1; 97:11), or that which guides in godly ways (Ps. 119:105). The Lord is a "shield," protecting His own. He gives "grace" to live in this evil world and "glory" to reward His own. He does not withhold good from those who live "uprightly" (or "blamelessly," see *tom*, 7:8), v. 11. With this in mind, the psalmist closes by taking note of the blessings that come to those who trust the "Lord of hosts [*ṣᵉbaʾôt*]" for daily guidance and provision. They are truly "blessed (*ʾašrê*, see 1:1), v. 12.

The psalm is practical. The psalmist's love for the Lord is clear. He desires to worship Him, vv. 1–4, and to gain strength from His presence, vv. 5–7. He cries out in prayer for God's blessing, vv. 8–9. He expresses his desire to serve in the temple rather than to enjoy the company of the wicked, v. 10. The Lord is good, a thought that calls forth praise from the psalmist, vv. 11–12. Would that every Christian had this same love for the Lord and this same desire to serve Him!

---

[135]A. Robinson, "Three Suggested Interpretations in Ps. LXXXIV," *VT* 24: 380, repoints *baḥartî* to *bᵉḥûrôtay* and translates the last part of 10*a* as "a thousand days of my youth." He then translates 10*b* as "to wait in the porch of the house of my God is better than a generation in the tents of wickedness." While the change is minimal, there is no support for repointing *baḥartî*, and the view requires the supply of the verb in 10*b*.

[136]Henry, p. 560, mentions the translation "I would rather be fixed to a post in the house of my God." He applies this to a slave who "loved his master and work so well that he desired to be tied to this service for ever." While the view is devotional, the translation does not rest on the traditional meaning of *sapap*.

PSALM 85

This is one of the psalms written by the "sons of Korah."[137] The author has prepared it for the "chief musician" (*m^e naṣṣeaḥ*, see 4, intro.) to use with worship ceremonies. God has restored the people from captivity, v. 1, but there is not yet full blessing on the nation, vv. 4–7. The psalmist anticipates that God will give this in the future, vv. 8–13. This suggests a date after the return from the Babylonian captivity but before the land is fully restored to national strength.[138]

The words of the psalmist reveal his burden for the people. Though they have returned from captivity, vv. 1–3, they have not responded fully to the gracious actions of the Lord. The prayer of the psalmist in vv. 4–7 demonstrates his understanding of the need for righteousness. Only then will the nation enjoy God's full blessing, vv. 8–13. While the ultimate fulfillment of this will take place in the millennial reign of Christ, the principle should be followed today. Individuals and nations alike should follow the ways of righteousness. As they do, God's blessings will come upon them.

I. Recognition of God's Grace 1–3

1–3 The psalmist recognizes that God has been "favourable" (*raṣâ*, see 40:13) to the people. He has brought them back to the land from their Babylonian captivity, v. 1. He has "forgiven" (*nasa*ʾ, see 25:18) the iniquity of His people and covered their sins.[139] "Selah" emphasizes the gracious work of God for His people, v. 2. He has graciously removed His "wrath" (*ʿebrâ*, see 7:6) toward their sin. He has

---

[137]See also Pss. 42–43, 44, 45, 46, 47, 48, 49, 84, 87, and 88. The introduction to Pss. 42–43 discusses the phrase "sons of Korah."

[138]Spurgeon, p. 360, assigns the psalm to David, apparently making "the sons of Korah" only scribes to record his words. Fausset, III, 284, places the psalmist in Judah as he prays for the restoration of the captive northern ten tribes. Dahood, II, 286, dates the psalm before the exile. Alexander, p. 366, makes the captivity a figure for distress. Gaebelein, p. 325, sees the psalm as a prophecy of the return of the Jewish remnant to Israel in the last days. These last two views are subjective and have no textual authority behind them.

[139]Rom. 3:25 clarifies the forgiveness of sins in the OT; they were covered until the death of Christ. Although the OT saints did not know the full nature of God's plan of redemption, their faith in God was counted for righteousness. God covered their sins until Jesus Christ completed the Atonement.

turned Himself away from the "fierceness" (or "burning heat," *ḥarôn*, see 2:5) of His "anger" (*ʾap*, see 2:5) for their sin, v. 3.

II. Supplication for God's Favor 4–7

4–7 Although God has extended His favor to the nation in the past, the people still practice sin. The psalmist asks God to "turn us" (or "restore us") in order that He might end His anger toward them, v. 4.[140] The author asks two questions that make a point. Will God "be angry" (see *ʾap*) with the people forever? Will He "draw out" (or "prolong") His wrath to "all generations" (*lᵉdor wador*, see 10:6)? The psalmist implies that such wrath would bring the nation to an end, v. 5. Rather than that, he pleads that God will "revive" them, giving them new spiritual life. The people then will rejoice in the Lord, v. 6. He asks the Lord to show them His "mercy" (or "steadfast love," *ḥesed*, see 5:7) and to give them His "salvation." While this often refers to deliverance from enemies, the thought here is spiritual, of God's bringing the people into a new relationship to Himself, v. 7.

III. Anticipation of God's Blessing 8–13

8–9 The psalmist sees himself as the spokesman for God. He will hear the voice of God speaking words of peace to His "people." The parallelism clarifies this as being the "saints" (*ḥasîd*, see 4:3), those loyal to God. The psalmist adds a word of caution. These people must not return to their "folly," stupid actions that go contrary to godliness, v. 8. God's salvation comes to those who "fear" Him (see *yirʾâ*, 2:11), reverencing God with their thoughts, words, and actions. This alone will bring God's glory to the land, v. 9.[141]

---

[140]Fausset, III, 284, explains the seeming contradiction between vv. 1–3 and v. 4. He makes vv. 1–3 a prophecy stated "as an already accomplished fact." The use of prophetic perfects is common in the OT. It is just as valid, however, to explain vv. 1–3 as referring to past grace from God, and v. 4 as introducing the continuing need among the people.

[141]Kissane, p. 394, understands "glory" as "prosperity . . . in contrast with the misery which now is in the land." The word appears in the Psalms about fifty times but never refers to material prosperity. It regularly speaks of God's glory, e.g., 26:8 ("honour"); 102:16. John S. Kselman, "A Note on Psalm 85:9–10," *BQ* 46:1 (1984): 24, revocalizes *šakan* ("dwell") to a participle form so that "glory" and "salvation" are parallel. While the revocalization is relatively minor, it is not necessary. "Glory" is an unusual word to choose to convey the idea of salvation.

10–11 With a beautifully poetic picture, the psalmist portrays the land where God dwells. "Mercy" (or "steadfast love," *ḥesed*) and "truth" (or "faithfulness," *ʾemet*) meet one another at every step. Righteousness and peace have a loving relationship, v. 10. "Truth" (or "faithfulness," *ʾemet*) abounds as though the earth were sprouting it everywhere. In both verses, *ʾemet* indicates God's faithfulness to His word. Righteousness looks down from above as though preparing to rain down on the earth, v. 11.

12–13 The Lord will bless this nation. He will give it good things, the sunshine and rain, necessary so that the land may bring forth an abundant increase, v. 12. The righteousness of God goes before Him as He walks through the land. This prepares to guide man into the "way of His steps" as He goes though the land.

The fulfillment of the picture presented in vv. 10–13 is yet future, in the millennial reign of the Lord. While there have been temporary fulfillments throughout Israel's history, these have been short-lived. Only the Millennium will produce the prolonged state of righteousness that leads to material blessing in the land, v. 13.

PSALM 86

The psalm is the only psalm attributed to David in this collection.[142] It is a lament in which David cries out to the Lord for deliv-

[142]Leupold, p. 615, believes "that this psalm is pieced together by adapting sections of a number of other psalms . . . by the use of materials found in almost the same form elsewhere. In other words, it is a mosaic." While he supports David's authorship, this description takes away from the origin of the psalm. Since David faced several situations that threatened his life, it is understandable that many of his written petitions parallel one another. It is highly unlikely that David picked a verse here and a phrase there and wove them together into this psalm. Delitzsch, III, 13–14, makes the psalm Davidic only because it quotes from other Davidic psalms. This writer does not have David's "poetic capability." Kirkpatrick, p. 515, makes the psalm postexilic. He called it "an imitation of the *Prayers of David*." These views assume that David could not have written the same words in a separate psalm. There is, however, no reason to reject the accuracy of the inscription. Nothing in the psalm disagrees with what we know of David's life. The very similarity to other writings of David supports David's authorship here.

erance from an unknown threat. This threat is serious; David sees himself as "afflicted," v. 1 (see note), and facing "proud" and "violent men" who seek to kill him, v. 14. These circumstances reflect the time of Saul's attempts to take his life.[143] The inscription "a prayer [*t^e^pillâ*, see 4:1] of David" occurs again only in Psalm 17. As with that psalm, so here there is an emphasis on prayer. Verses 1, 2, 3, 4, 5, 6, 7, 11, 16, and 17 all include petitions for divine help in the trial.[144]

This emphasis on prayer gives us the major lesson from the psalm. David expresses his burden in different ways. In addition to several statements showing the content of his prayers, it is his daily cry, v. 3; the lifting up of his soul, v. 4; his "prayer" and his "supplication," v. 6; and his call in a time of trouble, v. 7. Taken together, these show the consuming burden that drove David to depend on the Lord. This is not a simple "Now I lay me down to sleep" prayer. It is a total reliance on God, the response of one who has no other hope than that his God will deliver him from his trials.

I. Prayer to God 1–7

1–4 David asks the Lord to "bow down," to incline His ear to hear David's plea. He is "poor" (or "afflicted," *ᶜanî*, see 9:12) and in need of help. As in so many other psalms, David recognizes that his only help lies in what the Lord can provide, v. 1. He asks the Lord to "preserve my soul," to spare his life, since he is "holy" (or "godly, *ḥasîd*, see 4:3). David pleads with the Lord to "save" him, delivering him from the threat to his life, because he trusts in Him, v. 2. David prays that God will "be merciful" (or "gracious," *ḥanan*, see 4:1) in response to the cry that he repeats to Him daily, v. 3. He seeks renewed joy, clearly due to deliverance from the attack on his life. Once more, David shows his reliance on the Lord by lifting up his soul to Him in prayer, v. 4.

---

[143]Hengstenberg, III, 68, and Alexander, p. 369, place the psalm during the time of Absalom's rebellion. I have placed it during the earlier period of David's life because the psalm does not mention the temple or refer to David as king. It is possible, however, that the psalm should be dated later. Phillips, I, 708–14, spiritualizes the psalm by making it a prayer of Jesus Christ.

[144]Henry, III, 563, considers the psalm as "a prayer [David] often used for himself, and recommended to others for their use, especially in a day of affliction." Nothing in the psalm, however, supports the view.

5–7 David now praises the Lord for what He is. The Lord is good, kind to all. He is forgiving, ready to restore the repentant sinner to fellowship with Himself. He bestows abundant "mercy" (or "steadfast love," *ḥesed*, see 5:7) on all who cry out to Him, v. 5. David again asks the Lord to hear his "prayer" (*tᵉpillâ*) and to give attention to his "supplications" (*taḥᵃnûn*, see 28:2), v. 6. In the day when "trouble" (*ṣarâ*, see 9:9) comes to David, he pledges to call upon the Lord, the One Who he knows will answer his prayer, v. 7.

II. Greatness of God 8–10

8–10 There is a reason for David's prayers to God. He is a great God, well able to answer the pleas of His servant. David now takes up this theme. The heathen nations all had their various "gods" (*ᵓᵉlohîm*).[145] Among all of these, none was like the Lord. Similarly, there are no works like those of God, probably referring to the creative acts of God, v. 8. The nations will one day recognize God's greatness and worship Him, a reference to the millennial reign of Christ. They will "glorify" (or "honor") His "name," His nature, v. 9.[146] God is great and does extraordinary things.[147] He alone is God, v. 10.

III. Reliance on God 11–17

11–13 David asks the Lord to teach him the way in which he should walk. He pledges to live according to the truth. David's request, "unite my heart," asks God to make his heart one, i.e., to keep it from having divided loyalties. He desires to fear God's "name" (see v. 9), to reverence the nature of God, v. 11. He will then praise God with all his heart and "glorify" (or "honor") God's nature forever, v. 12. God's "mercy" (or "steadfast love," *ḥesed*, see 5:7) is great. David illustrates this by recalling his own deliverance "from

---

[145]Kidner, p. 312, understands *ᵓᵉlohîm* here to refer to the angels. He argues that v. 10 rules out the possibility that David refers to other gods. The word *ᵓᵉlohîm*, however, refers to false gods elsewhere, e.g., 95:3; 96:4–5, where even Kidner recognizes that false gods are in view.

[146]See 5:11, note 94, for a brief summary of the Lord's name.

[147]Kidner, p. 312, limits the "wondrous things" (*palaᵓ*, see 9:1) of God to His miracles in providing salvation. The *nipᶜal* form of *palaᵓ*, however, has a broad scope. It refers to deliverance from Egypt, 106:7, 22; to the content of God's Word, 119:18; to matters not understood by man, 131:1; and to the creation of man, 139:14.

the lowest hell" (or "from the depths of the grave," *š^eʾôl*, see 6:5). He does not give any details that let us relate this to a specific deliverance. There were many cases in David's life when the Lord delivered him from the threat of death, v. 13.

14–15 David turns now to his plight. Proud men have risen against him, likely a reference to Saul (I Sam. 18:9) and others in the court who were jealous of David's success. A group of "violent men" have sought to take David's life (e.g., I Sam. 23:8, 25–26) without seeking God's will in the matter, v. 14. David finds his hope in the Lord. He is compassionate and "gracious" (see *ḥanan*, 4:1). He is "longsuffering" (or "slow to anger [*ʾap*, see 2:5]"). He is abundant in His "mercy" (or "steadfast love," *ḥesed*) and truth, v. 15.

16–17 With his final prayer of the psalm, David asks the Lord to turn toward him and extend "mercy" (or "grace," *ḥanan*, see 4:1). He asks for strength to withstand his trials and for the Lord to deliver "the son of thine handmaid." David uses the phrase twice, here and at 116:16, both times describing his mother as one devoted to the Lord. Her godly heritage had impressed itself on her son, v. 16. David asks the Lord to give him a "token" (or "sign," *ʾôt*, see 65:8) that He will accomplish good in David's life. Those who "hate" (*śaneʾ*, see 5:5) David will see it and be publicly "ashamed" (*bôš*, see 6:10) of their failure. This will show clearly that the Lord has helped and comforted David, v. 17.

PSALM 87

This song by the "sons of Korah"[148] focuses on Zion. It is lit. "a psalm [*mizmôr*], a song [*šîr*]"[149] from a descendant of Korah. The author likely wrote after Hezekiah's victory over Assyria, when the Lord devastated the Assyrian army. The psalmist mentions other

---

[148]See also Pss. 42–43, 44, 45, 46, 47, 48, 49, 84, 85, and 88. The introduction to Pss. 42–43 discusses the phrase "sons of Korah."

[149]For the words "psalm" (*mizmôr*) and "song" (*šîr*), see the introduction to Ps. 30.

nations—Egypt, Babylon, Philistia, Tyre, Cush—but not Assyria.[150] While the psalm is a song exalting Zion, it also prophesies the inclusion of Gentile nations in the kingdom of Messiah.

I. God's Love for Zion 1–3

1–3 The Lord's "foundation" is Jerusalem, the city from which He will rule in the Millennium. This is in the "holy mountains," holy because they are separated to the Lord for His purposes.[151] While the "mountains"[152] upon which Jerusalem stands are not high, they are prominent in that part of Palestine. Jerusalem is located at roughly 2,500 feet above sea level. Mt. Zion is at the southeast corner of the present-day city. Mt. Moriah (the temple mount) is in the north part of the city. The Mount of Olives is east of the temple mount. There are also other mountains around the city. Among these are the Mount of Offense, where Solomon supposedly practiced idolatry, and Mt. Scopus, north of the Mount of Olives, v. 1.

The Lord loves "the gates of Zion" more than all the dwellings scattered throughout the land. This strong statement reflects the fact that the people's worship centered in Jerusalem. The Lord loves the gates of the city where He dwells,[153] responding in love to the love He sees in the nation's worship, v. 2.[154] For this reason, glorious

[150]Clarke, p. 216, places the psalm at "the translation of the Ark to Zion." Horne, p. 376, dates it "on a survey of [Jerusalem], just after the buildings of it were finished." Murphy, p. 464, has its writing in the time of Jehoshaphat's victory over Moab and Ammon, II Chron. 20. Oesterley, II, 390, puts it in the exile. Leslie, p. 34, sets it in "the early postexilic period." Since the psalm does not clearly describe its setting, we cannot be certain of its background.

[151]Leupold, p. 623, notes that v. 1 lacks a verb. He makes the phrase "His foundation in the holy mountains" the object of the verb in v. 2. This gives a double object to the verb: "the Lord loves His foundation in the holy mountains, the gates of Zion." While this is grammatically possible, there is weak parallelism between the "foundation in the holy mountains" and "the gates of Zion." It is not uncommon to supply the verb "is" as do the AV and NASB.

[152]J. A. Emerton, "The Problem of Psalm LXXXVII," *VT* 50:2 (2000): 184, understands "mountains" as a plural of local extension. While this is possible, the city of Jerusalem embraces several mountains. There is no need to limit the word here.

[153]Hirsch, II, 113, makes the "gates" those of the temple, where "all the members of the nation enter the place of spiritual unity." The view is possible, although the parallelism with v. 3 suggests the gates of the city.

[154]Ronald B. Allen, "Psalm 87, A Song Rarely Sung," *BibSac* 153 (1996): 135, aptly notes that "the gates made it possible for people to come near to God."

words are spoken about the city that is the earthly dwelling of God.[155] Although not mentioned here, the promise that Jerusalem will continue into the millennial kingdom of the Lord is among the glorious words spoken about Jerusalem, e.g., 97:8; 110:2; 132:13, v. 3.

II. The Inclusion of Gentiles with Zion 4–6

4–6 The thought introduced in v. 3 now develops into a fuller view of the millennial kingdom. The Lord mentions Rahab and Babylon to those who know Him. The name "Rahab" (*rahab*) means "proud" or "defiant" and occurs as a poetic name describing Egypt (89:10; Isa. 51:9). In addition, He calls attention to Philistia, Tyre, and "Ethiopia" (*kûš*).[156] These five nations represent the nations of the world in the millennial kingdom, now submitted to the Lord's rule. The mention of these nations recognizes their new relationship to Him. There is still, however, a special relationship between the Lord and Zion. It will be said that individuals were born in those nations, v. 4, but special attention will be drawn to those born in Zion.[157] The "highest" (*ᶜelyôn,* see 7:17), God Himself, will establish the nation, v. 5. The Lord will "count" (or "reckon"), when He makes His listing of the people, that certain ones were born in Zion. The psalmist draws attention to the honor with the word "selah," v. 6.

[155]The hymn "Glorious Things of Thee Are Spoken" was published in John Newton's *Olney Hymns*, 1779. The first stanza draws on v. 3. The music for the hymn comes from AUSTRIA, arranged by Franz Joseph Haydn, 1797.

[156]When referring to the land south of Egypt, the word *kûš* is translated most often "Ethiopia" but also "Cush" (Isa. 11:11). When referring to an individual, it is generally translated "Cush."

[157]Kidner, p. 315, makes all of the nations represent those "of the Gentile world . . . enrolled in God's city." The writing in v. 6 is in the Lord's "book of life," giving them the right of entrance into Jerusalem during the Millennium. Fausset, III, 288, personifies Philistia, Tyre, and Ethiopia "as an ideal man" born in Jerusalem, "the mother-city of regenerated mankind." This is "their birthplace into the heavenly kingdom." I have made the phrase refer to the birth of the Gentiles in their countries. This is contrasted with the birth of Jews in Zion. Rawlinson, II, 223, notes that the word "man" is not in the MT. He prefers "this *nation* was born there" and refers it to the grafting of nations into Zion for a second birth. Salvation, however, is individual, not national. The demonstrative pronoun *zeh*, v. 4, is often "this one" or "this man."

III. The Joy of Man in Zion 7

7 The people will celebrate with music their relationship to Zion. The singers with the "players on instruments" (*ḥalal* I)[158] will perform.[159] They will announce that their "springs" (*maᶜyan*),[160] the source from which the nation springs forth, are in Zion, v. 7.

PSALM 88

This is the last of the psalms written by the "sons of Korah."[161] It is lit. "a song [*šîr*]. A psalm [*mizmôr*][162] for the sons of Korah." The psalmist writes the song for the "chief musician" (*mᵉnaṣṣeaḥ*, see 4, intro.) to use with Israel's worship. The psalm is a dirge, the word "Mahalath" (*maḥᵃlat*, see 53, intro.) indicating a mournful tune. It is performed because of "Leannoth" (*leᶜannôt*, from *ᶜanâ*, see 35:13), a term that simply means "affliction."[163] It is also a "Maschil" (*maśkîl*, see 32, intro.), a song designed to lead the hearers to greater wisdom.

---

[158]The underlying verb *ḥalal* I means "to pierce" (BDB, p. 320, sees a separate verb *halal*, "to play the pipe."). From this we get the idea of a wind instrument, a flute or some sort of pipe. Nothing in the OT gives more specific information. Hengstenberg, III, 82, and Leupold, p. 626, derive *ḥalal* from *ḥûl*, "to writhe, dance," and translate "dancers." If we repoint the participle from *ḥolᵉlîm* to *ḥolᵃlîm* with an omitted *mêm*, this is possible but unusual. The view given above is more natural.

[159]We must supply a verb to the verse. The NIV groups the "singers" and "players on instruments" as "they make music" and has them "sing." The NRSV gives "say." The mention of singers and players on wind instruments suggests something like "perform."

[160]The noun *maᶜyan* refers to a spring or fountain of running water. As in Deut. 33:28, it is figurative here, denoting a source of something. From the context of the psalm, it likely refers to Zion as the fountainhead of the nation. Kirkpatrick, p. 522, understands the "springs" as "the fountains of salvation." Anderson, II, 622, relates the phrase to "the source of blessing and joy." He admits, however, "the immediate allusion is not clear."

[161]See also Pss. 42–43, 44, 45, 46, 47, 48, 49, 84, 85, and 87. The introduction to Pss. 42–43 discusses the phrase "sons of Korah."

[162]For the words "psalm" (*mizmôr*) and "song" (*šîr*), see the introduction to Ps. 30.

[163]Without supporting his view, White, p. 24, tentatively suggests that "Mahalath Leannoth" means "antiphonal singing." Fausset, III, 289, comments that Ps. 88 "breathes gloom throughout." Since "this is without parallel in the psalms," he joins

The author is Heman the Ezrahite. He is probably the Heman of I Chronicles 2:6, a descendant of Judah.[164] This creates a minor problem since the "sons of Korah" are Levites. Heman would not have been involved with the temple worship. Heman writes this lament and dwells on his own physical weakness. The sons of Korah likely set it to music and adopted it in their temple service. The psalm shows us the example of calling upon the Lord during physical ailments.

I. Physical Weakness 1–9

1–2 Heman calls upon the Lord God, the One upon Whom he depends for "salvation," deliverance from the physical burden that afflicts him. Nothing in the psalm lets us identify the nature of his affliction,[165] giving the psalm a broad application to all who suffer from different physical problems. Heman refers to the continuing nature of the prayer that he cries out to the Lord both day and night (cf. v. 9), v. 1. He asks the Lord to receive his "prayer" (*tᵉpillâ*, see 4:1), and to hear his "cry" (*rinnâ*, see 17:1), v. 2.

---

88 and 89, having Ethan in 89 add the answer to the gloom of 88. There is, however, no other example of one writer adding to another. Fausset also argues that the word *šîr* "is always used of joy." The psalm therefore needs the addition of Ps. 89 to introduce this note. The *šîr*, however, is not always joyous. In Deut. 32:1–43 and Judg. 5:1–31, the *šîr* is a summary of Israel's history. The Song (*šîr*) of Solomon is likewise an historical record of the relationship between Solomon and the Shulamite. Scroggie, II, 215, understands "Mahalath Leannoth" as "dancings with shoutings." He attaches all of the title to this point at the end of Ps. 87. The sense of "dancings with shoutings" is unique. In addition, there is no other clear case in the Psalms where the title follows the psalm.

[164]Kidner, p. 317, makes the first part of the title identify the collection to which the psalm belongs, "the Korahite group." The second part gives the tune and author's name. Leupold, p. 628, mentions the view that Heman is the author "and that he belonged to the guild of singers called the sons of Korah." We cannot be certain of the relationship between Heman and the sons of Korah. Cheyne, II, 59, makes "the pious community" the speaker. Nothing in the psalm suggests this. Murphy, p. 468, views the psalm as "a sad memorial of the bondage of Israel in Egypt." This is possible although the theme seems rather to focus on physical and emotional matters. Roger T. Beckwith, "The Early History of the Psalter," *TB* 46:1 (1995): 8, views the first half as a dittography of the title to Ps. 87. Hengstenberg, III, 83, considers Pss. 88 and 89 as one psalm, with the title to Ps. 88 "the title of the whole." The "sons of Korah" author Ps. 88, and Heman writes Ps. 89. His view is so complex that it is not likely true.

[165]Scroggie, II, 222, identifies the psalmist's affliction as leprosy. While this is possible, the psalm does not give enough details to make it certain.

3–7 Heman now describes his affliction. It has caused him to be filled with miseries, even bringing him to the point of death, into the "grave" (*šᵉʾôl*, see 6:5), v. 3. Others consider him as near to going "down into the pit" (*bôr*, see 7:15), here a name for Sheol.[166] He has become like a "man" (or "warrior," *geber*, see 34:8) that has no strength remaining in him, v. 4. Verse 5 continues the verb in 4*b*. He is as one that lies "free among the dead." This unusual phrase refers to one forsaken by God, free from the bonds that normally connect him with the Lord.[167] Heman says this since it is as though the Lord no longer remembers his prayers. It is as though he has been cut off from God's "hand," the emblem of power, v. 5.

With poetic language, Heman describes his situation. It is as though the Lord has placed him in "the lowest pit [*bôr*]," in the depths of Sheol. It is as though he is in "darkness," hidden from God's sight, or in the "depths" of the sea, v. 6. The Lord has let His "wrath" (*ḥemâ*, see 6:1) press hard upon him. The "waves" of God break over him and have "afflicted" (*ʿanâ*, see 35:13) him. Heman emphasizes the extremity of his plight with the word "selah," v. 7.

8–9 The Lord has separated him from his friends. They see him as an "abomination," probably considering his physical trials evidence of his wickedness.[168] He is "shut up," restrained by illness so that he cannot go out, v. 8. His eye "mourneth" (or "becomes faint") with tears over his "affliction" (*ʿanî*, see 9:12). He has called daily on the Lord, stretching out his hands in prayer to Him, v. 9.

---

[166]Marvin Tate, "Psalm 88," *RevEx* 87 (1990): 91–92, understands *šᵉʾôl* as the "netherworld of the dead, equal to Sheol and Abaddon." He describes this as "a land of forgetfulness where the great saving deeds of God are not recalled or praised." This is an incorrect view of *šᵉʾôl*. See note 101 at 6:5.

[167]Leupold, pp. 629, 631, understands the phrase as semi-ironic: "Free among the dead . . . what kind of freedom do you call that?" The parallelism does not support this. Murphy, p. 469, understands the phrase as "loosened from all the ties of this life." Anderson, II, 825, relates the phrase to being free "not only from pain and trouble, but also from all that is precious and desirable." While these views are possible, I have interpreted the phrase as one cut off from God since this agrees more with the overall sense of the psalm.

[168]Cohen, p. 286, and Phillips, I, 728, consider the separation as that of a leper forced to dwell apart from others. Eaton, p. 217, suggests that others "fear the contagion of misfortune." While these views are possible, the psalm is not specific. Other causes as well may explain the phrasing.

II. Hindered Praise 10–12

Heman now begins a brief section that describes the possibility of death he faces. He will not then be able to praise the Lord or to declare His goodness. This portion of the psalm is similar to Psalms 6:5; 30:9; 115:17; Ecclesiastes 9:10; and Isaiah 38:18–19. The similarity of these passages written by different authors suggests that this was common folk wisdom in Israel.

10–12 Heman asks rhetorically if God will work miracles for the dead. Clearly, He will not. Will the "dead" (*r^{e}paʾîm*)[169] rise from their graves to praise God? Again, the answer is no. While this will indeed take place in eternity, Heman speaks here of events in their normal course in this life. The word "selah" highlights man's inability to praise God after death. What is done for the Lord must come before death, v. 10. Will the dead declare God's "lovingkindness" (or "steadfast love," *ḥesed*, see 5:7) in the grave? Will they declare God's faithfulness in the place where the body is destroyed, v. 11? Will the wonders God has performed be declared in the darkness of the grave? Will the dead speak of God's righteousness in "the land of forgetfulness," the grave in which there is no more remembering?[170] Again, Heman limits his thought to the grave. There is no hint of an eternal destruction of the body and no thought of the eternal state, v. 12.

III. Unrelieved Suffering 13–18

13–14 Heman has cried out to the Lord in prayer. In the morning, his "prayer" (*t^{e}pillâ*, see 4:1) will "prevent" (or "meet") the Lord, v. 13. He does not understand why the Lord has not answered his

---

[169]Tate, p. 92, understands *r^{e}paʾîm* in its reference to "legendary giants . . . warriors, kings, and great people of society." The word *r^{e}paʾîm* never takes this meaning in poetical settings. Both *TWOT*, II, 858, and the *New International Dictionary of Theology & Exegesis* (Grand Rapids, Mich.: Zondervan Publishing House, 1997), III, 1176, relate *r^{e}paʾîm* to the dead at Ps. 88:10.

[170]Delitzsch, III, 27, refers to "the land of forgetfulness . . . where there is an end of all thinking, feeling, and acting . . . and where the monotony of death devoid of thought and recollection, reigns. Such is the representation given in the Old Testament of the state beyond the present." He is mistaken. The Psalms speak of the Resurrection, 49:15; of the millennial reign of Christ, 89:34–37; of His priestly and kingly role, 110:1–7; of His righteous rule, 72:2; and of the glorious nature of His kingdom, 72:19. The various writers touch on other topics as well. There is no warrant for concluding that the OT has a dreary view of life after death.

prayers for healing. Why has He "cast off" (or "rejected") Heman's soul, his life, by not healing him? Why had He hid His face from him, not shining the light of His countenance on him with favor (cf. 80:3, 7, 19), v. 14?

15–18 Heman summarizes his afflictions. His problems are long-standing. He has been "afflicted" (*ʿanî*, see 9:12) to the point of being near death since his youth. He suffers from ailments that produce terrors in him. He is "distracted" (or "perplexed," *pûn*),[171] v. 15. He feels that God's "fierce wrath" (or "burning anger, *ḥarôn*, see 2:5) has swept over him. The terrors allowed by God have "cut [him] off" (*ṣamat*, see 18:40), bringing him to the end of life, v. 16. These trials surround him like a flood of water. They encompass him completely, v. 17. The Lord has removed "lover and friend" far from him. His acquaintances are in darkness, unseen by him, v. 18.

The psalm ends as it began, on a note of hopelessness. By focusing on Heman's illness, the psalm has a broad application for present-day believers who suffer from physical woes. As the psalmist cries out to the Lord, so believers today should cry out to Him. At the end of the psalm, Heman has found no relief, no occasion for rejoicing in the Lord. So, too, many today suffer without relief. It is still right to cry out to God, recognizing that relief may come only with death and its promotion to glory.

PSALM 89

This messianic psalm records the fulfillment of the Davidic Covenant.[172] It is a "Maschil" (*maśkîl*, see 32, title), suggesting that the readers should meditate on it in order to grow wiser. The author is "Ethan the Ezrahite," a name that occurs elsewhere in I Kings 4:31 as one of the wise men in Israel. The development of the psalm, however, argues that the name here refers to the founder of the family rather

[171]This is the only time that *pûn* occurs in the OT. There are no clear cognate words to suggest a meaning. From the context, it must mean something like "perplexed, feeble, despair, or overcome."

[172]The introduction to Ps. 2 briefly discusses the messianic psalms in note 32.

than to the author himself. It is probably because both authors were Ezrahites that the book groups Psalms 88 and 89 together.

From the lament in vv. 38–45, the psalm comes after the fall of Jerusalem during the Captivity. The anointed king has been "cast off and abhorred," v. 38. The Lord has "made void the covenant," and the "crown" has been brought down "to the ground," v. 39. The "hedges" (or "walls") and "strong holds" have been broken down, v. 40. Others take spoil from the land, v. 41. Judah's enemies rejoice over its fall, v. 42, and the nation's army has failed, v. 43. The "glory" of the nation no longer exists and the "throne" has been overcome, v. 44. The days of the nation's "youth" have been shortened, and the nation is covered "with shame." The description agrees with what we know of the time of Judah's fall.[173]

As is to be expected with a psalm of this length, there are multiple applications to believers in the present time. The emphasis on God's covenant with David, vv. 1–4, developed further in vv. 19–37, reminds us of His faithfulness to His word. Rejection of God's word brings judgment, vv. 38–45. The paragraph extolling the greatness of God, vv. 5–8, illustrated by His mighty works, vv. 9–14, reminds us of God's power. Christians may still anticipate God's blessings on the righteous, vv. 15–18, and approach the Lord in prayer, vv. 46–51.

I. Summary of the Covenant 1–4

1–4 Ethan pledges to sing of the Lord's "mercies" (or "steadfast love," *ḥesed*, see 5:7) the evidence of His loyalty to His people, forever.[174] He will speak of the Lord's faithfulness "to all generations" (*l^edor wador*, see 10:6). Since the theme of the psalm concerns the covenant with David, Ethan has in mind the Lord's faithfulness to

[173]Other views have been suggested. Albert Barnes, II, 362, places it during an illness of the psalmist. Moll, p. 482, locates the psalm during the reign of Rehoboam, after the conquest of Judah by Shishak, I Kings 14:25–26. Calvin, III, 418, locates it after the division of the nation into two kingdoms. Leslie, p. 274, places it during the reign of Jeroboam II and before 721 BC. Leupold, p. 632, puts it in "the days of Josiah or even of Zedekiah just before the fall of Jerusalem." Fausset, III, 297, dates it in "the third year of Jehoiakim's reign, about 607 B.C." Ultimately, the dating of the psalm depends on the interpretation given to vv. 38–45. A lesser factor but still worth considering is that the psalms in Book III tend to be later in Israel's history.

[174]The chorus "I Will Sing of the Mercies of the Lord Forever," with the music by James Fillmore (1849–1936), draws on this verse.

those promises, v. 1. Having this confidence, Ethan has testified that God's "mercy" (or "steadfast love," *ḥesed*) will be "built up" (or "brought about") forever. The Lord will establish His faithfulness in the heavens. In a sense, the Lord places His faithfulness where it can rain down upon mankind, v. 2. Ethan summarizes the promise God made to enter a covenant with the one He has chosen, His servant David, v. 3. In this, He has promised to establish David's offspring, here referring to Messiah (cf. II Sam. 7:16). The Lord will "build up" (or "bring about") Messiah's rule "to all generations" (*l^edor wador*, see 10:6). The word "selah" draws attention to this work of the Lord, v. 4.

II. Greatness of God 5–8

5–8 The "heavens," i.e., the angels in the heavens, will praise the wonderful works of the Lord and His faithfulness among the gathering of the "saints," the holy angelic host (cf. Deut. 33:2),[175] v. 5. Who in the "heaven" (or "skies") compares to the might of the Lord? Who among "the sons of the mighty," the angelic hosts, is like Him? The obvious answer to these rhetorical questions is that no one measures up to the Lord, v. 6. God should be "greatly feared," i.e., held in awe, in the "assembly" (or "council," *sôd*, see 25:14) of the "saints," again the angels. He is to be reverenced by all around Him, v. 7. Ethan rhetorically asks the Lord God of the "hosts" (*ṣ^eba᾽ôt*, see 24:10), in this context referring to the angels in heaven, if there is any other like Him, a strong Lord and surrounded by faithfulness. Once more, the answer is that no one is like the Lord, v. 8.

III. Works of God 9–14

9–11 Ethan begins a series of illustrations to demonstrate the greatness of God. He quiets the raging sea, calming its tossing waves (cf. 65:7; 93:3, 4), v. 9. He has "broken . . . in pieces" (or "crushed," see *dak*, 9:9) Rahab (*rahab*, see 87:4), the name representing Egypt.[176]

---

[175]Henry, III, 574, understands the "saints" as the godly on earth. While this is possible, the parallelism with 5*a* supports understanding these as the angels. Verse 6 likewise refers to angels.

[176]Crenshaw, p. 33, understands "Rahab" as "the monster representing primeval chaos." There is no need to introduce a fanciful notion here, since Rahab refers to Egypt elsewhere; cf. 87:4; Isa. 51:9.

This land now lies smitten as though dead.[177] The Lord has scattered His foes with His "strong arm," the emblem of His power (e.g., Exod. 15:16; Jer. 21:5), v. 10. The heavens and the earth belong to Him. The world with all that is in it likewise is His since He is its creator, v. 11.

12–14 The Lord has created the north and south. The mountains that He has "created" (*baraʾ*, see 51:10) will "rejoice" (*ranan*, see 5:11) at His name. Tabor and Hermon, while not large, were likely among the largest mountains known to the psalmist. Mt. Tabor, which is 1,843 feet high, is on the border between Issachar and Zebulon, about six miles southeast of Nazareth. Mt. Hermon is the dominant mountain in the north. It is 9,232 feet above sea level and was the northern boundary of the land Israel occupied.[178] These elements of creation poetically rejoice in the Lord's "name," His powerful nature, v. 12.[179] The Lord is mighty. His "arm," again representing His power, is strong. His "hand" is also an emblem of strength, 73:23; 78:42. His "right hand" is "high" (or "exalted") in its power, 17:7; 18:35, v. 13. The "habitation" (or "foundation") of His throne rests upon "justice and judgment" (or "righteousness and justice"). "Mercy [or 'steadfast love,' *ḥesed*, see 5:7] and truth" go before Him, v. 14.

IV. Blessings of the Godly 15–18

15–18 Having such a God as Ethan has described, those who worship Him with "the joyful sound" (or "shout of joy," *teruʿâ*, see 27:6) are truly "blessed" (*ʾašrê*, see 1:1). They walk through life with God's favor, "the light of [His] countenance," attending their way, v. 15. They continually rejoice in God's "name" (see v. 12), here representing His nature. "In" (or "by") God's righteousness they will receive

---

[177]Shortly after Israel's exile, Egypt fell to the Persians. For the next century, under the successive leadership of Cambyses, Darius I, Xerxes, and Artaxerxes, Egypt remained under Persian control. Even after regaining its independence, it did not regain its former glory.

[178]Among others, Alexander, p. 380, and Horne, p. 387, see Tabor and Hermon as representing the west and east respectively. This gives all four of the directions in the verse. While Hermon lies to the east of the Jordan River, it is too far north to serve as a good symbol of the east. Similarly, Tabor lies west of the Jordan but not significantly. It lies in the center of the nation and is not a good symbol of the west. Anderson, II, 637, sees a chiasm in the verse: north, south, Tabor (south of Hermon), and Hermon (in the north). The view is possible but not necessary.

[179]See 5:11, note 94, for a brief summary of the Lord's name.

exaltation, v. 16. The strength of the Lord is the glorious focus of their strength. By means of His favor, the "horn" (*qeren*, see 18:2) of the people, their strength, is exalted, v. 17.[180] Verse 18 should be read, "For to [*l*ᵉ] the Lord is our shield, and to [*l*ᵉ] the Holy One of Israel is our king." In both cases, the *l*ᵉ preposition indicates "belonging to." The parallelism with 18*b* suggests that the "defence" (or "shield," *magen*, see 3:3) is the Davidic king. The nation's king belongs to the "Holy One of Israel," v. 18.[181]

V. Exaltation of David 19–37

The thought that the king belongs to the Lord, v. 18, makes the transition to this section. The Lord has placed David and David's offspring on the throne of the nation. Ultimately, the Son of God, Who is also the Son of David, will fill this position.

A. The Choice of David 19–28

19–21 In time past, the Lord spoke in a vision to His "holy one" (or "saints," *ḥasîd*, see 4:3), both Samuel and Nathan, telling them that He had given "help" (*ᶜezer*, see 20:2) to "one that is mighty [*gibbôr*, see 19:5]." This refers to God's pronouncements of a divinely appointed king (I Sam. 16:1, 12–13; II Sam. 7:12–16). He has exalted this one chosen from among the people, v. 19. He has found David to be His servant and has anointed him to be king (I Sam. 16:13; II Sam. 2:4; 5:3), v. 20. The Lord's "hand," again an instrument of power (cf. v. 13), will be firmly established with him. He will strengthen David with His arm (cf. vv. 10, 13), v. 21.

22–23 David's foes will not "exact" (or "exact usury") from him, defeating him and collecting yearly tribute. The "son of wickedness," his heathen foe, will not "afflict" (*ᶜanâ*, see 35:13) him, v. 22. The Lord will "beat down" (or "crush") David's enemies before him. He will "plague" (or "strike down") those that "hate" (*śaneʾ*, see 5:5) David, v. 23.

24–28 The faithfulness of the Lord to His covenant (II Sam. 7:12–16) and His "mercy" (or "steadfast love," *ḥesed*) will continue

[180]While it does not make a great difference in the sense, I read the *qᵉrê tarûm* rather than the *kᵉtîb tarîm*. In addition to support from the LXX, v. 24 reads *tarûm*.

[181]A brief note at 71:22 summarizes the use of this name in the OT.

to be with David. "In" (or "by") the "name" (see v. 12) of the Lord, His nature as a faithful God, David's "horn" (*qeren*, see 18:2), his strength, will be exalted, v. 24. The Lord will set David's "hand," his strength, "in" (better "on") the Mediterranean Sea. His "right hand," also representing his strength, will be on the rivers of Palestine. Poetically, the promise is of David's control over the land, v. 25. David will come to the Lord as his spiritual father, his God, and his "rock" (*ṣûr*, see 18:2), the foundation upon Whom he rests, v. 26. The Lord will make him His "firstborn." This position carried with it certain privileges. Among these were the leadership of the family (II Chron. 21:2–3) and the position as the family priest (Gen. 22:9, 13; 35:7). The fulfillment of this will come when Jesus Christ begins His rule (cf. 2:7; Col. 1:15, 18). He will lead the people and be "higher" (*ᶜelyôn,* see 7:17) than all other kings. While not mentioned here, His position as the firstborn gives Him the position as the Great High Priest to all who accept His atoning work at Calvary, v. 27. The Lord will keep "mercy" (or "steadfast love," *ḥesed*, see 5:7) for Him forever. The Davidic Covenant (II Sam. 7:12–16) will "stand fast" (or "be confirmed") with Him, v. 28.

B. The Offspring of David 29–37

29–32 Returning to David as the focus of His thought, the Lord will "make" (or "establish") his family line continue forever.[182] His "throne," the rule over the nation, will last as long as "the days of heaven." This idiom portrays the continuing nature of his rule, v. 29. The psalmist sounds a note of caution. Should David's offspring forsake the law of God and not live according to His judgments, v. 30, or should they "break" (or "profane," *ḥalal* II, see 55:20) His statutes and fail to keep His commands, v. 31, they will suffer judgment. God will "visit" (or "punish," *paqad*, see 8:4) them with the rod. He will judge their iniquity with stripes, v. 32.

33–37 Even if judgment should become necessary, the Lord will not reject the nation. He will not "utterly take" (or "make ineffectual")

[182]Fausset, III, 295, understands the verse as a promise to the Messiah. The "seed" here are the "believing people, who shall endure for ever." The view faces the problem that vv. 30–32 deal with unbelieving offspring who suffer judgment. Fausset explains this as those who suffer for their sins but are not utterly cast off. While his view is possible, I prefer to apply the verse to David and his offspring, continuing forever in Christ.

His "lovingkindness" (or "steadfast love," *ḥesed*, see 5:7) from David's seed. He will not "suffer [His] faithfulness to fail" (or "deal falsely") toward them, v. 33. He will not "break" (*ḥalal* II) His covenant with David nor change the promises He has made regarding David's seed, v. 34. The Lord has taken an oath, based on His holiness, that He will not "lie unto" (or "fail") David, v. 35. David's offspring will continue forever, and his rule will continue as long as the creation endures. The scope of this promise includes the reign of Jesus Christ, v. 36. His rule will be established like the sun, "a faithful witness in heaven [or 'the sky']" in its regular periodic movements (Gen. 1:14–16).[183] Ethan calls attention to the promise of God with the word "selah," v. 37.

VI. Rejection of the Covenant 38–45

38–45 Tragically, the situation warned against in vv. 30–32 has come to pass. The Lord has turned away from Israel. He has rejected, despised, and been furious with their "anointed" (*mašîaḥ*, see 2:2) king. There is an implied reference to the nation's sin that has brought this judgment on the nation, v. 38. The Lord has "made void" (or "spurned") the covenant made with David. He has "profaned" (or "dishonored," *ḥalal* II) the crown of the king, bringing it "to the ground." This idiom speaks of dishonoring the rule God conferred upon David and his descendants.[184] While this is an everlasting covenant, the sin of the people brings a judgment that temporarily suspends the monarchy, v. 39. God has broken down the "hedges" (better

---

[183]E. Theodore Mullen, Jr., "The Divine Witness and the Davidic Royal Grant: Psalm 89:37–38," *JBL* 102:2 (1983): 218, understands the sun or moon, "two of the olden gods so often called upon as witnesses to treaties" in the ancient near east. While the sun may be the witness, it is inconceivable that the psalmist would have called on heathen gods as witnesses. Paul G. Mosca, "Once Again the Heavenly Witness of Ps 89:38," *JBL* 105:1 (1986): 37, makes "the throne of David" the witness. This makes David's throne witness to David's throne, a doubtful relationship. Timo Veijola, "The Witness in the Clouds: Ps 89:38," *JBL* 107:3 (1988): 416, rejects both Mullen and Mosca and sees God as the faithful witness. Hirsch, II, 132, sees the moon as the faithful witness. This repeats 37*a* and is unlikely. Horne, p. 391, understands the "faithful witness" as the rainbow. This is possible although it is an abrupt introduction of the thought.

[184]The idiom draws on the literal casting of something "to the ground" e.g., 74:7; 147:6, to develop the metaphor of degrading something, e.g., I Sam. 3:19; Dan. 8:12. The idiom occurs again in v. 44.

"walls") of Jerusalem and has ruined the strongholds of the nation, v. 40.[185] Those who pass by take spoil. Israel is an object of scorn to its neighbors (cf. 80:6), v. 41. The Lord has "set up" (or "lifted up") the "right hand," the hand of strength, of Israel's foes. He has brought rejoicing to their enemies, v. 42. The Lord has turned away the "edge" (lit. "rock," here representing strength, *ṣûr*, see 18:2)[186] of the swords wielded by Israel's soldiers. He has not given them the courage needed to stand against the enemy, v. 43. He has taken away Israel's glory and dishonored the king, v. 44. He has "shortened the days of his youth," cutting off the nation.[187] In light of its forecast future during the millennial reign of the Lord, Israel's past history is justly compared by the psalmist to that of a youth. "Shame" (*bôš*, see 6:10) covers the nation. The psalmist emphasizes the nation's plight with the word "selah," v. 45.

Note that the psalmist sees the work of God in Israel's downfall. As v. 49 shows, he does not understand it. Still, he recognizes that God is in control of the circumstances that confront the nation. God often uses difficult circumstances to judge His people's sin.

VII. The Prayer of the Psalmist 46–51

46–48 The psalmist asks the Lord how long He will let these trials continue. Will He hide Himself forever? Will He let His "wrath" (*ḥemâ*, see 6:1) burn like fire, v. 46? He reminds the Lord how "short" (or "transitory," *ḥeled*, see 17:14) his life is and asks if the Lord has "made" (*bara᾿*, see 51:10) all men "in vain" (*šaw᾿*, see 12:2), to no purpose. The men of Israel have lived their lives to no purpose if the covenant with God is annulled, v. 47. Rhetorically, he

[185]Calvin, III, 450, and Anderson, II, 645, understand the "hedges" and "strong holds" as the defenses guarding the borders of the land. This is a possible view although the record in II Kings 24:11–15; 25:14 stresses the fall of Jerusalem.

[186]Delitzsch, III, 43, derives *ṣûr* from another root *ṣûr*, "to cut off with pressure," thus a knife or blade. He supports this with an Arabic cognate *ṣar*. This word does not occur elsewhere in the OT and therefore is not likely the word here.

[187]Fausset, III, 296, applies the phrase to the overthrow of Jehoahaz at the age of twenty-three, II Kings 23:31–33. Cohen, p. 295, relates it to the captivity of Jehoiachin at the age of eighteen, II Kings 24:8–15. Delitzsch, III, 44, who dates the psalm in the reign of Rehoboam, sees this as a reference to the king "becoming prematurely old" through the experiences that he faces. The context argues for applying the verse to the nation.

asks if any mighty "man" (*geber*, see 34:8) will escape death. Can anyone deliver his own life from "the hand of the grave [*šᵉʾôl*, see 6:5]"? Clearly, no man can escape death. The word "selah" draws attention to this profound thought. The implied thought of the psalmist is that the people need divine help. Since death comes on them rapidly, the Lord must intervene to deliver them, v. 48.

49–51 The psalmist asks the Lord where His "lovingkindnesses" (or "expressions of steadfast love," *ḥesed*, see 5:7), sworn to David in "truth" (or "faithfulness"), have gone. Clearly, the psalmist does not understand the impact of sin on the nation's relationship to the Lord. He has not forgotten the covenant He made with David. Israel's sins, however, have made it necessary that they undergo severe judgment, v. 49. The psalmist asks the Lord to remember the "reproach" that has come upon His "servants," the nation in their covenant relationship to the Lord. The psalmist bears in his "bosom," himself,[188] the taunts from the "mighty people" (or "many people") of the surrounding nations, v. 50. These enemies have taunted the "footsteps" of the "anointed" (*mašîaḥ*, see 2:2) king, hurling their gibes at him wherever he goes, v. 51.

Closing Benediction 52

The final verse of the psalm is separate from the psalm itself. The tone of blessing differs radically from the previous paragraph. We do not know when the blessing was added, although the ms evidence we have shows that it was joined to the psalm at an early date. The collection closes with the prayer that the Lord may be "blessed" (*barak*, see 5:12) forever. While the verse does not say who gives these blessings, the likely thought is that mankind will bless the Lord throughout eternity. The double "Amen" (*ʾamen*, see 41:13) accentuates the benediction, v. 52.[189]

---

[188]Fausset, III, 297, refers the word "bosom" to the "midst" of the land. Only in I Kings 22:35 does this word have this sense. It normally refers literally to the breast or poetically to the person himself, e.g., 35:13; Isa. 65:6, 7; Jer. 32:18.

[189]Each of the five collections of psalms ends with a doxology of praise to the Lord for His faithfulness. See also 41:13; 72:19; 106:48; and 150:6.

BOOK IV

PSALM 90

Psalm 90 is the only psalm attributed to Moses.[1] The title recognizes it as the "prayer" (*t^epillâ*, see 4:1) of a "man of God."[2] It is a community lament that recognizes God's judgment upon the sins of the people. The psalm displays the faith of Moses. He begins by recognizing the greatness of the Lord in His creation. In the closing paragraph, he asks the Lord to bless the people again. The psalm may well have been written by Moses near the end of his life. He looks back over forty years of wandering and sees the eternal nature of God and the weakness of men. Having suffered for their sins, the nation now approaches the Promised Land. Moses prays for God's blessings upon them.[3]

I. The Eternality of God 1–2

1–2 Moses recognizes the Lord as Israel's "dwelling place [*ma^côn*, see 26:8] in all generations [*b^edor wador*, cf. 10:6]."[4] Though Moses led Israel's first generation of freedom, the patriarchs and Israel in its Egyptian bondage had gone before him. All these found their refuge

---

[1]Kirkpatrick, p. 547, argues that v. 1 suggests "a long period of national existence." For this reason, he places the psalm at the time of the Exile. On the basis of style, a subjective matter, Ewald, I, 211–12, makes the author an unknown eighth-century BC writer from the northern ten tribes. It is not strange that Moses should have written. Deut. 32:1–44 records what is commonly called the "Song of Moses." Rev. 15:3 tells us that a song of praise written by Moses will be sung in heaven.

[2]Moses receives this title in Deut. 33:1; Josh. 14:6; Ezra 3:2; I Chron. 23:14; II Chron. 30:16. The title also occurs with other godly men in the OT: Samuel (I Sam. 9:6–10), Shemaiah the prophet (I Kings 12:22; II Chron. 11:2), an unknown prophet (fifteen times in I Kings 13:1–31; II Kings 23:16–17), David (II Chron. 8:14; Neh. 12:24, 36), another unknown prophet (II Chron. 25:7, 9), and Elijah (five times in II Kings 1:9–13). It is the characteristic title given to Elisha (thirty-one times in II Kings 4:7–8:11 and 13:19).

[3]Henry, III, 582, dates the psalm just after the unbelief of Israel and the sentence to wander forty years in the wilderness. He suggests that Moses wrote this prayer for use "by the people in their tents, or, at least, by the priests in the tabernacle-service, during their tedious fatigue in the wilderness." While possible, the psalm does not give any background to its writing.

[4]*Megillah 29a* mistakes the verse as teaching that God dwelled in the "synagogues and houses of learning." The verse does not deal with God's dwelling but with the nation's.

in the presence of the Lord, v. 1.[5] God is everlasting. Moses pictures the creation of the mountains as being "brought forth" (lit. "born"), as though God gave birth to them. God "formed [or 'travailed'] the earth." This describes the birth of the earth, with all of its parts, and the forming of the dry land of the "world." Even before this, He had existed as God. He will further exist into the everlasting future, v. 2.

II. The Weakness of Man 3–6

3–6 God causes frail "man" (*ᵓᵉnôš*, see 8:4) to turn to "destruction" (or "dust").[6] This fulfills His saying that mankind should return to dust (Gen. 2:17; 3:17–19), v. 3. God's time is not as man's time. A thousand years to God are but as a day that has passed. They are like a "watch in the night," a brief four-hour period of time, v. 4.[7] Man, however, passes swiftly away from life. God carries them away like floodwaters that sweep things away.[8] The life of man is like a night's sleep. In the morning of his life, he is like grass that "groweth up" (or "sprouts"), v. 5. The grass "flourisheth" (*ṣûṣ*, see 72:16) in the morning. In the evening, men cut it down and it withers, v. 6.

---

[5]Isaac Watts drew on the thought of several verses in writing "O God, Our Help in Ages Past" in 1719. The song uses the tune ST. ANNE, written by William Croft, 1708.

[6]*Pesaḥim* 54*a* translates "destruction" (*dakaᵓ*) as "contrition" and concludes on the basis of v. 2 that God created repentance before He created the world. While *dakaᵓ* may be translated "contrition," it also refers to crushing someone, e.g., Job 4:19; 5:4; Lam. 3:34. Verse 2 refers to the creation of the material world, not repentance which was unneeded until Adam's sin. Verses 5 and 7 support the thought of judgment here.

[7]There were three night watches: the beginning (Lam. 2:19), middle (Judg. 7:19), and morning (Exod. 14:24). The apostle Peter quotes this verse in II Pet. 3:4–8. Some had rejected the thought that the Lord would return. "It has been years," they say, "but He has not come yet." Peter argues that the Lord's time is not like man's time, using this verse to prove his point.

[8]The verb *zaram* occurs only here and at 77:17, where it refers to clouds pouring out water. The noun form *zerem* ("rain"), however, occurs frequently, e.g., Isa. 4:6; 25:4, so that the meaning is not in doubt. Charles Whitley, "The Text of Psalm 90,5," *Biblica* 63:4 (1982): 557, develops the translation "Their offspring changeth, as grass undergoing change." This, however, requires great freedom with the MT and is not necessary. N. H. Tur-Sinai, "Unverstandere Bibelworte I," *VT* 1 (1951): 309, asserts that the poet sought "den unreinen Ursprung des Menschen in Zeugung und Geburt zu beschreiben" ("to describe the impure origin of man in procreation and birth"). The view also requires great liberty with the Hebrew.

III. The Judgment of Sin 7–12

7–10 Moses now turns to the sins of the nation, sins that have brought judgment to the people. They are consumed by God's "anger" (*ʾap*, see 2:5) and "troubled" (or "dismayed," *bahal*, see 2:5) by His "wrath" (*ḥemâ*, see 6:1); cf. Numbers 14:22–23, 27–30, 35, v. 7. God has set the iniquities of the nation before Him. The sins they have committed in secret now stand revealed in the light of His "countenance" (or "presence"), v. 8. All of their days pass away within the sphere of His "wrath" (*ʿebrâ*, see 7:6) toward their sin. They "spend" (or "finish") their lives "as a tale that is told" (better "like a moan"), a brief action, v. 9. Their expected life is seventy years. If there is unusual strength, life might extend to eighty years. In all of this, their "strength" (better "pride"), what they boast in, is still "labour [*ʿamal*, see 7:14] and sorrow," a difficult life. It soon ends and they "fly away," an idiom drawn from the flight of a startled bird, from this world, v. 10.

11–12 Who can understand the strength of God's "anger" (*ʾap*, see 2:5)? According to the greatness of the "fear" (or "reverence," *yirʾâ*, see 2:11) God deserves, so is the greatness of His "wrath" (*ʿebrâ*, see 7:6). If reverence is withheld, the same degree of wrath will be received, v. 11. In view of this, Moses asks the Lord to make the people know the value of their days. Then they will "apply [their] hearts unto wisdom [*ḥokmâ*, see 19:7]" (or "gain a wise heart"), v. 12.

IV. The Prayer for Blessing 13–17

13–14 Moses now anticipates the end of the journey. He prays for the Lord's blessings upon the nation as they come to the border of the Promised Land (Gen. 12:7). He begins by asking the Lord to "return" (or "turn back") from His anger toward the nation. The phrase "how long?" suggests that Moses feels that Israel has been under God's judgment for a long time. He asks God to "let it repent [Him]" (or "have compassion") concerning His "servants," the nation of Israel, v. 13. If the Lord will satisfy them "early" (or "in the morning," poetically representing the beginning of the new relationship) with His "mercy" (or "steadfast love," *ḥesed*, see 5:7), they will "rejoice" (*ranan*, see 5:11) and be glad for the rest of their days, v. 14.

15–17 Moses asks the Lord to make the nation glad. The phrase "according to the days wherein thou hast afflicted [*ʿanâ*, see 35:13] us" does not ask for a mere forty years of gladness. The thought is that God should give many years of blessing just as He had given many years of judgment, v. 15. May the Lord show His work openly to His servants. May He show His "glory" (or "majesty," *hadar*, see 8:5) to their children, v. 16. May the "beauty" (or "favor") of the Lord their God be upon them. May He establish the work of their hands, not letting it be swept away in judgment but giving it permanence, v. 17.

In the psalm, Moses recognizes God's greatness, vv. 1–2, and man's weakness, vv. 3–6. This weakness has led man into sin, a position that has brought God's judgment, vv. 7–12. Moses anticipates relief from this punishment. He prays that the nation will indeed turn back to God and experience His blessings, vv. 13–17. In a sense, the nation pictures the return of a backslider as he abandons his sin to live for God's glory. Only this will bring God's blessings upon his life.

PSALM 91

This orphan psalm expresses confidence in the protection of the Lord.[9] The unknown author[10] does not relate his words to any specific incident. His illustrations ("the snare of the fowler . . . noisome pestilence," v. 3; "terror . . . arrow . . . pestilence . . . destruction," vv. 5–6; attack by the wicked, vv. 7–8) all give the opportunity to show the Lord's care for those who worship Him.[11] It is in this that the psalm has gained its major value to believers. Many have found comfort here in the midst of the difficulties that life has brought them.

---

[9]Asher Eder, "Psalm 91 as Responsory," *JBQ* 28:2 (2000): 117–18, suggests that the psalm was a "choral reading, with a Levite choir welcoming pilgrims making their way to the Temple." The view is possible but unprovable.

[10]Clarke, p. 228, sees Moses as the author, writing "at the beginning of the thirty-eight years of the wilderness wanderings." Morris, p. 57, and Murphy, p. 488, assign the psalm to David or an earlier writer. Eaton, p. 223, identifies the author as "a Temple minister." Kissane, p. 426, places the psalm during the Exile. Nothing in the psalm lets us be certain of the author.

[11]In the Talmud, *Shebuʾoth* 15*b* designates the psalm as one that guards against "evil occurrences," i.e., a song of protection against "evil spirits or demons."

I. Trust in the Lord 1–4

1–2 The psalmist states a general principle. The one who dwells "in the secret place of the most High [*ᶜelyôn*, see 7:17]," in a position of fellowship with the Lord, will enjoy protection given by the "Almighty" (*šadday*, see 68:14). Similar phrases occur elsewhere to describe a shelter in times of trouble, e.g., 27:5; 31:20; 32:7 ("hiding place"). This man will "abide" (*lîn*, see 25:13) under the "shadow" cast by the Almighty God. The verb *lîn* implies that troubles will not last long. The godly have the anticipation of an eternity free from the attacks of the wicked. The "shadow" of the Almighty is the shade He casts to protect His own from the heated wrath of His enemies. The word "shadow" also indicates elsewhere a place of protection, e.g., 17:8; 36:7; 121:5 ("shade"), v. 1. The writer claims the Lord as his "refuge" (see *maḥseh*, 14:6) and "fortress." The Lord is his God, the word *ʾᵉlohîm* reemphasizing the Lord's power to protect. The psalmist therefore trusts in Him, v. 2.

3–4 The author begins setting forth examples of the Lord's care for His own. He will deliver "thee," the pronoun referring generally to those who belong to the Lord. The "snare of the fowler," a man-made threat, and "the noisome pestilence" (or "disastrous plague"), a natural disaster, both picture attacks upon God's people, v. 3. In these trials, the Lord will "cover" (*sakak*, see 5:11) His own "with his feathers" (cf. Deut. 32:11–12). They will "trust" (or "seek refuge," *ḥasâ*, see 2:12) "under his wings." Both figures poetically picture the Lord's protection. As a bird shelters her young under her wings, so the Lord protects His own.[12] His "truth" (or "faithfulness") is a large "shield" (*ṣinnâ*, see 5:12) and a "buckler" (*soḥerâ*)[13] defending those who follow Him, v. 4.

[12]The hymn "Under His Wings" draws its theme from the verse. William O. Cushing (1826–1902) wrote the words to this hymn, with Ira D. Sankey, 1899, writing the music.

[13]This is the only place that *soḥerâ* occurs. An Akkadian cognate suggests the idea of "going around, encircling," which supports the idea of a buckler, a round shield. A. A. Macintosh, "Psalm XCI 4 and the root סחר," *VT* 23 (1973): 61, suggests the idea of "(supernatural) protection." While this carries out the idea of encirclement, early witnesses, e.g., LXX, *Targum*, support the traditional rendering of "buckler."

II. Confidence from the Lord 5–13

5–6 Knowing that the Lord watches over His own gives confidence. The psalmist gives several random examples to illustrate situations God's people do not need to fear. They need not fear attacks from their enemies, terrors that come at night or arrows they face in the day, v. 5. They may face trials with confidence, whether life-threatening sicknesses, pestilence that moves about in darkness,[14] or destructive ailments that come in broad daylight, v. 6.

7–8 With poetic hyperbole, the psalmist describes the success of God's people in danger. Although a great number may attack God's people, the attack will fail.[15] The promise does not guarantee that no evil will touch the righteous. The Lord often uses trials to prepare His children for the future. The promise here assures the godly that no harm will come outside of God's will, v. 7. The believer will look on as God gives a "reward" (*šillumâ*)[16] to the wicked. This is a general statement; in many cases, the wicked seem to succeed without punishment. Their judgment will come after death. There are also, however, instances where the Lord delivers His children from seemingly impossible situations and causes the wicked to fail, v. 8.

9–10 Such protection comes to those who make the Lord their defender. They have adopted the psalmist's "refuge" (*maḥseh*, see 14:6), the "most High" (*ᶜelyôn*, see 7:17), as their "habitation" (or "dwelling," *maᶜôn*, see 26:8), v. 9. In this position, no "plague" will "come nigh" their dwelling." Once more, the "plague" poetically represents harm that comes apart from God's will, v. 10.

---

[14]Delitzsch, III, 63, and Kirkpatrick, p. 556, relate the pestilence and sickness to "destroying angels" who pass through the nation. Leslie, p. 408, and Rodd, p. 40, are similar in making these demons. Livingston, p. 369, suggests "evil omens or curses . . . carried out by demons." It is just as reasonable to understand them as various forms of ill health from which the Lord delivers. The thought occurs again in v. 10. Rawlinson, III, 268, sees "the plague-god" personified, "represented as stalking through the land in the hours of darkness." There is no need, however, to see a god at this point. The word occurs here with a general sense of any destructive force that shrikes the nation. Horne, p. 400, understands "pestilence" to refer to "concupiscence," a meaning the word does not have elsewhere.

[15]*Berakoth 6a* refers the "thousand" and "ten thousand" to unseen demons that surround God's people. The context, however, deals with battles against human foes.

[16]Although the word *šillumâ* occurs only here, the root *šlm* occurs widely. A related word suggests the sense of "recompense."

11–13 The means of divine protection now comes into view. The Lord will send angels to care for those who trust Him. This refers to guardian angels, sent by the Lord to watch over His own (cf. 34:7; II Kings 6:16–17; Heb. 1:14), v. 11.[17] They will sustain believers, keeping them from even such minor trials as stubbing their toe against a rock. While Satan used this passage when he tempted the Lord (Matt. 4:6; Luke 4:10–11), it is also a general promise that relates to all who follow God. It is worth noting that this care comes "in all . . . ways," understanding that these are godly ways. There is no warrant for recklessly tempting the Lord by godless living, v. 12. The godly individual will overcome the "lion" (*šaḥal*),[18] the "adder" (*peten*, see 58:4), the "young lion" (*kᵉpîr*, see 17:12), and the "dragon" (*tannîn*, see 44:19), all poetic representations of evils faced in this life.[19] The Lord may well have based the promise of Luke 10:19 on this verse, v. 13.

III. Promise by the Lord 14–16

14 The Lord now speaks through the psalmist with a series of "I will" promises.[20] Because this one has "set his love upon" the Lord, the Lord will pour blessing upon blessing upon him. First, He will

[17]Alexander, p. 393, and Perowne, II, 302, reject the notion of guardian angels watching over individuals. They understand that all of the angels minister on behalf of the saints. This is a matter of semantics. Whether a single angel watches over each believer or God calls upon one from the whole company when a believer needs supernatural care, the believer is still guarded by angels.

[18]This is the only time that *šaḥal* occurs in Psalms. Elsewhere in the OT, it consistently refers to a lion. From an Akkadian cognate, the root likely refers to a roaring noise. The thought of a "lion" comes naturally from this.

[19]Cohen, p. 303, makes the lions represent "open attack." The serpents display "underhand scheming." Henry, p. 589, lets the animals stand for the devil since he is called "a roaring lion, the old serpent, the red dragon." Paul repeats the promise of treading Satan underfoot in Rom. 16:20. Moll, p. 494, innocuously makes vv. 1–10 refer to "God's protection of the righteous dwelling in his tent" and vv. 11–13 to "the dangers of the traveller." Since the interpreter can take the symbolism in any direction, it is best to give it a general sense that covers all of the dangers faced by believers.

[20]There are seven imperfect verbs in vv. 14–16: "I will deliver [or 'rescue'] him . . . I will set him on high . . . I will answer him . . . I will deliver him . . . honour [or 'I will honor' him] . . . will I satisfy him . . . shew [or 'I will show'] him my salvation." Although the phrase "I will be with him in trouble" does not use a verb, the grammatical construction clearly supports an eighth promise to the godly.

rescue him from his enemies. The context suggests that these are the attacks of the wicked poetically described in v. 13. In the second place, the Lord will "set him on high" (*śagab*, see 20:1), securely placing him where no enemy can overcome him. This security comes to the godly, the Lord says, "because he hath known my name." As is often the case, the "name" here reflects the nature of God.[21] The godly knows of God's nature by experience because he has walked in fellowship with Him over a period of time, v. 14.

15–16 With a third promise, the Lord gives to this person the right of answered prayer. In context, the promise relates to the godly person's need in times of danger. In the fourth place, the Lord will be with him in "trouble" (or "distress," *ṣarâ*, see 9:9), not abandoning him to his own resources. With the fifth promise, the Lord will deliver him from his trials. Sixth, He will "honour" the godly. This probably refers to exaltation in the eyes of others as they see God's presence in his life, v. 15. The seventh promise involves satisfying the godly person with a "long life," giving him all the days that God desires him to enjoy in this life. The eighth and final promise states that God will give him "salvation," the glorious end for all who love the Lord, v. 16.

PSALM 92

This "psalm" (*mizmôr*) or "song" (*šîr*)[22] is written for the "sabbath day."[23] The Jews adopted it in the temple ritual for the Sabbath,[24] but we do not know when this practice began. We know little of the back-

[21]Note 94 at 5:11 summarizes the meaning of the Lord's "name."

[22]For the words "psalm" (*mizmôr*) and "song" (*šîr*), see the introduction to Ps. 30.

[23]Delitzsch, II, 66, understands the "sabbath" as the "final Sabbath of the world's history . . . the day that is altogether Sabbath." More probably, David simply meant it for Sabbath-day worship at the tabernacle.

[24]*Tamid* 38*b*. This rabbinical comment also gives an eschatological sense to the psalm, saying that it is "a song for the time to come, for the day that will be all Sabbath and rest for everlasting life." Ashkenazi Jews, generally Reformed Judaism, recite this psalm (along with Pss. 93, 95–99) in the Friday evening service that begins the Sabbath. *NEJ*, p. 668.

ground to the psalm. It is a song of thanksgiving,[25] but we have no knowledge of the occasion for its writing. It is written at a time when the psalmist faces enemies, v. 11, but also while the "house of the Lord" is standing, v. 13. In my judgment, David is the author.[26] The vocabulary and style are similar to that of his other psalms.[27]

As is so often the case, the background of the psalm is not described. This lets the psalm represent different trials that may come upon men. In praising the Lord, vv. 1–4, and in expressing his confidence in the Lord, vv. 9–15, the psalmist sets an example that Christians would do well to follow in every trial.

I. Praises of the Lord 1–4

1–4 David introduces the psalm with a note of praise. It is good to thank the Lord for His mercies and to "sing praises" (*zamar*, see 7:17) to the "name"[28] of the "most High" (*ᶜelyôn*, see 7:17), v. 1. This leads one to "shew forth" (or "declare") God's "lovingkindness" (or "steadfast love," *ḥesed*, see 5:7) in the morning and His faithfulness at night. The joining of "morning" and "night" suggests that praise to the Lord should be unending, v. 2. Appropriate for the worship rituals of the nation, music accompanies this praise from "an instrument of ten strings," the "psaltery" (*nebel*, see 33:2), and the "harp" (or "lyre," *kinnôr*, see 33:2). These instruments produce a "solemn sound" (or "resounding music") as praise ascends from the worshipers to the Lord, v. 3. Since the Lord has made the psalmist glad by His "work" on his behalf, the psalmist will "triumph" (*ranan*, see 5:11), giving a ringing cry of exultation over the "works" done by the

---

[25]The introduction to Ps. 18 discusses the songs of thanksgiving.

[26]Scroggie, II, 256, places the psalm in either the time of Hezekiah or Zerubbabel. Leupold, p. 658, tentatively locates it after the return from exile. We cannot be dogmatic as to the authorship and background of the psalm.

[27]In the psalms that name an author, only David mentions the "instrument of ten strings" and "the psaltery" together elsewhere, 144:9. Of the psalms that name their author, only David mentions the "house of the Lord" elsewhere, v. 13, cf. 23:6; 27:4; 122:1, 9. Only David uses the phrase "workers of iniquity," v. 7, cf. 5:5; 6:8; 14:4; 28:3; 36:12; 37:1; 53:4; 59:2; 64:2; 141:9. Only David mentions the "unicorn," v. 10, cf. 22:21; 29:6. In addition to the use of Davidic vocabulary, the reference to anointing, v. 10, likely refers to the anointing of the king.

[28]Note 94 at 5:11 gives a summary of the Lord's "name."

Lord. While "work" and "works" are two different Hebrew words, there is no great difference between them, v. 4.[29]

II. Wickedness of Man 5–9

5–9 The psalmist repeats his praise of the Lord for His works. In addition, he recognizes that God's "thoughts" (*maḥšᵉbôt*, see 33:10) are profound, "very deep," v. 5. The wicked do not understand this. A "brutish man" (*baᶜar*, see 49:10) does not have experiential knowledge of spiritual truth. The "fool" (*kᵉsîl*, see 49:10) likewise does not understand. Both of these phrases look forward to what is about to be said, v. 6.[30] When the wicked "spring" (or "sprout," *paraḥ*, see 72:7) like grass, when those who work iniquity "flourish" (*ṣûṣ*, see 72:16), they will be destroyed forever, v. 7. In sharp contrast, the Lord is "high," exalted forever, v. 8. The enemies of the Lord will "perish" (*ᵓabad*, see 1:6). The repetition of the phrase "thine enemies" gives stress to this fact. All those who work iniquity will be scattered, driven away from their attempts to work evil toward the people of God, v. 9.

III. Confidence of the Psalmist 10–15

10–11 Understanding that the wicked will be judged, the psalmist now expresses his own confidence for the future. The Lord will exalt his "horn" (*qeren*, see 18:2), the emblem of his strength, like that of a "unicorn" (or "wild ox," see *remîm*, 22:21). "I shall be [or 'I have been'] anointed with fresh oil" refers to his divine appointment as king (I Sam. 16:13; II Sam. 2:4; 5:3). Symbolically, this portrayed the

[29]Fausset, III, 303, goes too far in making the "work" of God "the final redemption of His people." Nothing in the psalm suggests limiting God's work to a future event. It is more likely that the psalmist looked at present deliverance from some threat and praised the Lord for that. W. E. Barnes, II, 448, understands "the works of thy hands" as God's creative work. This does not give good parallelism to "work." Kissane, p. 432, limits the works to "the miracles wrought on behalf of Israel in the past, particularly the deliverance from Egypt and the conquest of Canaan." There is, however, no reason to restrict here the scope of God's works.

[30]Kidner, p. 335, argues that v. 6 refers to v. 5, that the wicked do not understand the greatness of God. He argues that *zoᵓt* + *bᵉ* preposition is normally backward looking and gives six illustrations, none of which involve the *bᵉ* preposition. The demonstrative pronoun *zoᵓt* can refer backward but normally looks forward to something new. So G.K.C. 136 *a*; Williams ¶ 113.

divine leading of the king by the Spirit of God, v. 10. He will look on his foes and hear of others rising against him. The implied thought is that he anticipates victory over his enemies, v. 11.

12–15 The righteous person will "flourish" (*paraḥ*, see 72:7) like the date palm, a tree that grows up to eighty feet, lives up to two centuries, and may bear several hundred pounds of fruit each year. The righteous will grow like a cedar on Mt. Lebanon. The trunk of this tree grows up to seventy or eighty feet and as much as forty feet around. These trees live for centuries, v. 12. The righteous people who take root in the "house of the Lord" will "flourish" (*paraḥ*) in God's courts, v. 13. They will bear spiritual fruit even in old age. They will be "fat" (see *dašen*, 20:3) and "flourishing" (or "luxuriant"), v. 14. This prosperity reveals that the Lord is "upright" (or "righteous," keeping His covenant). He is the psalmist's "rock" (*ṣûr*, see 18:2) , a secure foundation, and there is no "unrighteousness" (*ᶜawlâ*, see 7:3) with Him, v. 15.

PSALM 93

This brief hymn of praise has no background information on its author or the occasion of writing.[31] The mention of God's "house" in v. 5 suggests that the psalm comes from the period when the tabernacle or temple was still standing. The Jews sang it in their worship on the sixth day of the week, before the Sabbath.[32] The psalm looks forward to the coming kingdom reign of the Lord over the earth. As such, it is an *Enthronement Psalm*.

---

[31]The LXX gives the title "For the day before the Sabbath, when the land was settled, a song of praise by David." The Talmud, *Rosh Hashanah* 31*a*, also follows this view. Leupold, p. 664, and Phillips, II, 46, make the psalm postexilic. While either of these views may be true, nothing in the psalm lets us be certain.

[32]*Tamid* 33*b*. In our times, Ashkenazi Jews, generally identified with Reformed Judaism, recite this psalm (along with Pss. 92, 95–99) in the Friday evening service that begins the Sabbath. *NEJ*, p. 668.

I. The Reign of the Lord 1–2

1–2 The psalmist begins by announcing the rule of the Lord. As the ruling monarch of the earth, He has put on both majesty and strength like a garment.[33] The world under His control is firmly "established," not disrupted but stable and unmovable, v. 1.[34] This throne has been set up from "of old," from eternity past. The world may think that it governs itself. In reality, the Lord has given the world time to prove itself incapable of ruling itself in righteousness. His reign is eternal, however, and the day will come when He will exercise His rule, v. 2. This is the great hope that should still motivate believers to faithful service.

II. The Exaltation of the Lord 3–5

3–5 The psalmist uses nature to illustrate the power of the Lord. The mighty waters lift up their voice, heard in the crashing of the waves.[35] This hints at the power of the waters, v. 3. The Lord "on high," the exalted Lord, is mightier than these crashing waters. He is

---

[33]The psalmist doubles words throughout the psalm to give emphasis. Here, the doubled verb *labeš*, "is clothed," stresses the characteristics that mark the Lord. In vv. 1*c* and 2, he repeats the root *kûn*, "established," to emphasize the permanence of His reign. In v. 3, the psalmist repeats the phrase *naś'û nᵉharôt*, "the floods have lifted up." The final part of the verse changes the form of the verb to a perfect tense but still repeats the root *nś'* along with *nᵉharôt*. The adjective "mighty" reappears in v. 4.

[34]Compare with 96:10, which emphasizes the righteous judgment of the Lord in keeping the earth from being moved. Here, the emphasis is on the strength of the Lord in checking the forces of nature. The world will become much like the Garden of Eden without the effects of the curse to shake it. There will be no earthquakes, no hurricanes or cyclones or tornados, no raging forest fires, no tidal waves, or other phenomena of nature to disrupt the peace of mankind.

[35]Among others, Clarke, p. 233, and Hirsch, II, 161, see the waters as representing the world powers. It is true that the word *nahar*, here translated "floods," often represents nations, e.g., Isa. 8:7; 59:19. In the Psalms, however, *nahar* does not have this symbolism. Fausset gives Ps. 46:2–3, but this more readily illustrates nature's power. *Nahar* may represent nations here, but the psalm does not require it. Bratcher and Reyburn, p. 815, understand the "floods" as "the powers defeated [by the Lord] at creation." This symbolism is not clear. Paul Nadim Tarazi, "An Exegesis of Psalm 93," *St Vladimir's Theological Quarterly* 35 (1991): 143–44, understands the verse as proclaiming God's victory over "the 'primeval sea,' also known under its mythological figure of Leviathan/Rahab/dragon." He supports this from Pss. 74:12–14, 16*b*; 89:9–10, 11*b*, 13. Both of these passages better refer to Egypt. There is no need to find symbolism here. VanGemeren, p. 608, translates *nᵉharôt* as "rivers." While this is a possible rendering elsewhere, the context of v. 4 argues for floodwaters.

mightier than the breakers of the sea, v. 4. In view of this power possessed by the Lord, His "testimonies," here referring to His promises of an everlasting kingdom, are "very sure," fully reliable. Such holiness, seen in the fulfillment of His words, is appropriate to the house where He will be worshiped forever, v. 5.

PSALM 94

This lament psalm interrupts a series of hymns that celebrate the kingship of the Lord (93, 95–99). The nation here faces a serious threat, vv. 3–6, possibly the invasion of Assyria under Sennacherib (II Kings 18:13, 17–37).[36] We do not know certainly the psalmist or the date.[37] Whoever it is, he maintains his faith in the Lord, v. 14. He expresses his confidence that the Lord will overthrow the wicked, vv. 22–23. The LXX makes the psalm one for the fourth day of the week.[38]

The pattern of the psalm is a familiar one. The psalmist laments to the Lord the continuing success of the wicked, vv. 1–3. He describes their wicked actions, vv. 4–6, their living as though God will never notice them, v. 7. Despite this, the psalmist maintains his confidence in the Lord. He rebukes the wicked, vv. 8–11, and describes God's blessings on His own, vv. 12–15. He states his intention to rely on the Lord, vv. 16–19, and he expresses his confidence that God will give him victory, vv. 20–23. With this approach, the psalmist sets a proper

---

[36]Clarke, p. 235, and Cohen, p. 308, see the threat as an internal one, coming from wicked Israelites. Verses 5–6 rather refer to an external oppression of the people.

[37]The LXX assigns the psalm to David. Rotherham, p. 412, sees the psalm as "written by Hezekiah himself or at his dictation." Kirkpatrick, p. 566, makes it exilic or postexilic. Delitzsch, III, 79, calls it "one of the latest, but not necessarily a Maccabaean Psalm." These views are possible since the psalm does not give enough information to let us be certain about its origin.

[38]The title in the LXX is "A psalm of David, for the fourth day of the week." This reflects the Jewish use of the psalm (*Tamid* 33*b*). According to *Sukkah* 55*a*, the priests sang 94:16–23 on the third day of Tabernacles. On the fourth day of this feast, they recited 94:8–15.

example for Christians today who face various problems. It is always right to trust the Lord in the middle of difficult circumstances.

I. Lament of the Psalmist 1–7

A. Prayer of the Psalmist 1–3

1–3 The psalmist prays that the God Who takes "vengeance" (*n*^{e}*qamâ*, see 18:47) on sinners (cf. Rom. 12:9) will show Himself to the nation. In the repeated phrases, the plural *n*^{e}*qamôt* stresses the completeness of God's judgment, v. 1. The psalmist asks the "judge of the earth" to give a "reward" (better "recompense") to the proud, a judgment against them for their wickedness, v. 2. His question, "How long shall the wicked triumph [or 'exult']?" suggests that they have oppressed the nation for a prolonged period of time, v. 3.

B. Description of the Wicked 4–7

4–7 The psalmist begins to speak of the sins of Israel's foes. They "utter" (or "pour out," *naba*^{c}, see 19:2) and speak "hard things" (or "arrogantly"). These "workers of iniquity" are proud, speaking boastfully, v. 4. They "break in pieces" (or "crush," see *dak*, 9:9) those who belong to the Lord. They "afflict" (^{c}*anâ*, see 35:13) the inheritance of God, v. 5. This oppression has included the murder of widows, "the stranger" (a foreigner in the land), and orphans, v. 6. Despite the heinousness of their actions, they say that the Lord of Israel will not see what they have done. He will not "regard" (or "consider") it. They think that Israel's God is weak, not able to defend His people. While this attitude may seem strange, it is the same attitude sinners hold today. They live as though God will never take note of them, v. 7.

II. Confidence of the Psalmist 8–15

A. Rebuke of the Wicked 8–11

8–11 Despite the oppression that has come upon the nation, the psalmist maintains his trust in the Lord. He urges the "brutish" (or "stupid") among the enemy to understand the nature of Israel's God. The "fools" (*k*^{e}*sîl*, see 49:10) should become "wise" in their behavior, v. 8. He Who "planted" (or "established") man's ear, can He not hear what they say of Him? He Who formed the eye, can He not see their work, v. 9? He Who chastens the "heathen" (or "nations"), will He not "correct" (or "rebuke") them? Does the One Who gives knowledge to man not have knowledge Himself, v. 10? The Lord knows that man's "thoughts" (*maḥšᵉbôt*, see 33:10) are "vanity" (or "a breath," *hebel*, see 31:6), insubstantial. Taken together, these rhetorical questions show God to be the Creator, the Holy One, and the Omniscient One. How foolish of man to pit himself against God, v. 11!

B. Blessings of the Godly 12–15

12–15 The strong "man" (*geber*, see 34:8) whom God chastens is "blessed" (*ʾašrê*, see 1:1). Not only does the Lord's chastening keep him from going farther down the wrong path of life, but it also teaches him the truth of God's Word, v. 12. This gives him "rest" (or "quietness"), emotional peace, until God finally digs a "pit" (*šaḥat*, see 7:15) into which the wicked fall in judgment, v. 13. The Lord will not abandon His own. He will not forsake those whom He will one day inherit as His own people, v. 14. The injustice that now prevails will not last. Judgment will once more return to righteousness. The upright in heart will follow righteous practices, v. 15.

III. Reliance of the Psalmist 16–23

A. Provision of the Lord 16–19

16–19 The psalmist asks rhetorically, Who will help him against the wicked? Who will stand up for him against those who practice iniquity, v. 16? He answers himself by recalling the past. Unless the Lord had helped him, his soul would have dwelled in the silence of death, v. 17.[39] When he had said that his foot had slipped, the Lord in His "mercy" (or "steadfast love," *ḥesed*, see 5:7) had held him up, v. 18. Though he has many "thoughts" (i.e., anxious thoughts, *śarʿap*),[40] the "comforts" (or "consolations") of the Lord give him delight, v. 19.

---

[39]Rawlinson, II, 301, refers the phrase "to the abyss of Sheol, the silent land." Nothing in the Bible suggests that Sheol is silent. Pss. 18:5 and 116:3 mention the "sorrow" of Sheol. Isa. 14:9–11 refers to the taunt of Babylon's king in Sheol. Luke 16:23–31 relates a conversation in Hades, the NT equivalent of Sheol. Since the verse does not use the word "sheol," it is better to limit the thought here to the grave.

[40]The word *śarʿap* occurs only here and in 139:23. An Arabic cognate suggests "anxious thoughts," a sense that fits well into both passages.

B. Anticipation of Victory 20–23

20–21 Once more, the psalmist asks rhetorical questions to make his point. Will those who occupy a throne that causes "iniquity" (better "destruction") be joined with the Lord? Can those who cause "mischief" (or "trouble") by their "law" (or "statute") enjoy fellowship with Him? The parallelism suggests that the second question makes the same point as the first. Will these wicked rulers be united with the Lord, v. 20? They unite with others of like mind to oppose "the soul of the righteous," seeking to take their lives. They condemn the innocent man to death, v. 21.

22–23 In such adversity, the psalmist turns to the Lord as his "defense" (or "refuge," *miśgab*, see 9:9). God is the "rock" (*ṣûr*, see 18:2) that provides "refuge" (see *maḥseh*, 14:6) for him, v. 22. The Lord will bring back upon Israel's enemies their own iniquity. What they had planned for others shall happen to them instead. He will "cut them off" (*ṣamat*, see 18:40), destroying them in their "wickedness" (or "evil").[41] He will "cut them off" (*ṣamat*), v. 23.

PSALM 95

This *Enthronement Psalm* sounds a clear note of praise to the Lord. In addition, the psalm closes with a sobering warning that neglecting God's Word will bring severe judgment. Since the early days of the church, the psalm has been known by the name *Venite*, "O Come," the opening word in the Vulgate and a call to worship. The LXX makes this a "song of David."[42] In modern times, Ashkenazi

[41]*ʾArakin* 11*b* and *Taʾanith* 29*a* teach that the first temple was destroyed on Sunday at the end of a Sabbatical year while the priests and Levites were chanting this verse. They were overwhelmed before the final phrase. While this is an interesting historical note, it goes contrary to the context. The verse refers to the enemies of Israel.

[42]Quoting vv. 7–8, Heb. 4:7 reads "in David." There is debate over whether this refers to the book of Psalms or to David, the author of Ps. 95. Jennings, II, 136, and Perowne, II, 190, refer the phrase to the entire book; but Henry, III, 600, and Phillips, II, 62, refer it to David. Either view is possible. The twin thoughts of praise to the Lord and obedience to His words are Davidic in nature, whether the author of the psalm is David or not.

Jews, generally Reformed Judaism, recite this psalm (along with Pss. 92–93, 96–99) in the Friday evening service that begins the Sabbath.[43]

I. Praise to the Lord 1–5

1–2 The psalmist calls upon others to "sing" (*ranan*, see 5:11) to the Lord. The verb *ranan* refers to a ringing cry of joy or exultation, an appropriate act of praise to the Lord. They should "make a joyful noise" (*rûa*ᶜ, see 41:11) to God, the "rock [*ṣûr*, see 18:2] of [their] salvation." The verb *rûa*ᶜ is broader in meaning than *ranan* but still occurs often as a "shout" of praise to the Lord. The Psalms refer to the Lord sixteen times as a "rock," a strong foundation upon which to build a godly life, e.g., 28:1; 62:2, 6, 7, v. 1. His people should come to Him with "thanksgiving" (*tôdâ*, see 26:7). They can make there "a joyful noise" (*rûa*ᶜ) as they sing "psalms," songs of praise, to Him, v. 2.

3–5 The Lord is worthy to receive our praise. He is a "great God, and a great King above all gods." The Psalms elsewhere tell us that "his greatness is unsearchable," 145:3. He further rules over all that men set as gods in this life, v. 3. He holds the "deep places of the earth" in His hand. He also owns "the strength [better 'eminences'] of the hills." From the lowest parts of the earth to the tips of the mountains, all belongs to Him, v. 4. The "sea," the oceans of the world, belongs to Him by right of its creation. The "dry land," which He brought forth from the waters, is also His creation, v. 5.

II. Obedience to the Lord 6–11

6–7a Because of God's greatness, the psalmist calls the people to worship Him. They should "bow down" and "kneel" to the Creator God as they express their submission to Him, v. 6. He is Israel's God. They, in turn, are as people enjoying His pasture and as sheep cared for by His hand, v. 7*a*.

7b–11 The psalmist now warns against disobedience to the revealed will of God. Hebrews 3:7–11 quotes this passage as the author challenges his readers to continue obeying God's Word.

[43] *NEJ*, p. 668.

In addition, Hebrews 3:15 and 4:7 quote the shorter challenge in vv. 7*b*–8. The word "today" establishes this as an immediate action. Positively, the people should give heed to God's revealed Word, v. 7*b*. Negatively, they should not harden their hearts against it.

The psalmist gives an extended illustration of disobedience to God. Israel had disobeyed Him in the "provocation," better transliterated as Meribah, and in the day of "temptation," better transliterated as Massah. The statement refers to Exodus 17:2–7, which describes the complaining of the people at Rephidim. Moses called the place "Massah, and Meribah" (Exod. 17:7). "Massah" means "strife," and "Meribah" means "testing." The psalmist recalls this as he warns the people not to harden their hearts, v. 8. Their fathers tested God, they "proved" Him, and "saw [His] work" (better, "although they had seen [His] work"). Despite seeing God's miracles in Egypt, despite seeing the waters of the Red Sea rolled back miraculously, despite seeing God provide daily manna, and despite seeing the miracle at Marah where the bitter waters were made sweet, they still complained of God's treatment, v. 9. As a result, they wandered forty years until the generation under God's judgment died in the wilderness. They erred "in their heart" and did not know God's ways, v. 10. For this reason, the Lord swore in His "wrath" (*ʾap*, see 2:5) that the generation twenty years and above would not enter Canaan, the land of rest (cf. Numbers 14:22–23, 26–29, 31–34), v. 11.[44]

The author of Hebrews makes an important application of this passage. Just as Israel suffered judgment for rejecting the promises of God, so we too may miss the blessings of God by rejecting His Word. Canaan was meant to be a land of rest. Because of their disobedience to the Lord, however, Israel never experienced this rest. There is a rest that remains for God's people, Hebrews 4:9. Only those who receive and obey God's Word can enter that rest.

---

[44]Strictly speaking, the pronouncement of judgment followed Israel's rebellion after the negative report of the ten spies, not after the incident of Massah and Meribah. The psalmist joins Israel's acts of rebellion together as he recites God's judgment in keeping them from their promised rest. All of the rebellious acts reflected the nation's testing of God and the strife involved with their actions.

PSALM 96

A similar song occurs in I Chronicles 16:23–33 with David as the author. Because of differences between the two versions, it is debated whether David is the author here.[45] If David authored the psalm, the occasion was the return of the ark of the covenant to Jerusalem. Under the guidance of the Holy Spirit, David later modifies his original psalm to create an *Enthronement Psalm* that looks forward to the millennial reign of Christ over the earth; cf. vv. 10, 13.[46]

I. The Lord as the Creator 1–6

A. The Call to Worship 1–3

1–3 The psalmist urges that the nations sing a "new song" to the Lord.[47] This new song is a song of praise, an action that greatly differs from the rebellious mutterings so often heard from mankind. "All the earth" should sing this song. This suggests a millennial context, the only time when the whole earth will look upon the Lord as worthy of praise, v. 1.[48] In addition to the new song, they should "bless [*barak*, see 5:12] his name,"[49] giving praise to Him. One way of carrying out this command is to "shew forth [*baśar*, see 40:9] his salvation" each day, v. 2. His glory should be proclaimed to the heathen. All "people" (or "nations") of the earth should hear of His "wonders" (*pala*ʾ, see 9:1), His miraculous powers, v. 3.

---

[45]Hengstenberg, III, 172, thinks that the author "was stimulated by the second part of Isaiah to compose this poem." Moll, p. 507, and Cohen, p. 315, assign the psalm to an unknown postexilic author. Both make the passage in Chronicles a revision of the psalm. These views fail to account for David being called the author in Chronicles. Calvin, IV, 359; Gaebelein, p. 359; and Henry, p. 603, accept David's authorship.

[46]In modern times, Ashkenazi Jews, generally identified with Reformed Judaism, recite this psalm (along with Pss. 92–93, 95, 97–99) in the Friday evening service that begins the Sabbath. *NEJ*, p. 668.

[47]There is a brief summary of the phrase "new song" at 33:3.

[48]Leupold, p. 682, aptly states, "The Lord is so great and His works so wonderful that it takes 'all the earth' to do justice to such a theme."

[49]Note 94 at 5:11 gives a summary of the Lord's "name."

B. The Cause for Worship 4–6

4–6 The mention of the Lord's extraordinary powers leads the psalmist to speak of His greatness. The Lord is not only "great" but greatly worthy of praise. He is more to be feared than any other one or any other thing that is worshiped as a god, v. 4. Other gods are but "idols" (*ʾᵉlîlîm*),[50] false and without substance. The Lord, however, is the Creator of the heavens, v. 5. Before Him go "honour [*hôd*, see 8:1] and majesty [*hadar*, see 8:5]," reflecting His innate splendor. In His sanctuary are "strength [or 'power'] and beauty [or 'glory']," again describing His nature.[51] The "sanctuary" here is the millennial temple, Isaiah 60:13.[52] The people will worship the Lord there in the Millennium with their feasts, Isaiah 33:20*a*, and sacrifices, Isaiah 56:7; 60:7, v. 6.

II. The Lord as King 7–10

A. The Call to Worship 7–9

7–9 The psalmist calls upon the nations to "give" (in the sense of "ascribe")[53] to the Lord "glory and strength [or 'power']," v. 7. They should ascribe to Him "the glory due unto his name" (better "the glory of His name," see v. 2). They should bring an "offering" (*minḥâ*) for sacrifice as they enter the courts of the millennial kingdom. The *minḥâ* was a grain offering. Malachi 1:11 and 3:3–4 note

---

[50]The word *ʾᵉlîlîm* refers to something worthless, weak, or feeble, Job 13:4 ("no value"); Jer. 14:14 ("a thing of nought"). By extension, it refers to an idol.

[51]Fausset, III, 310, understands "strength" as "the *power* obtained by prayer" while beauty is "the *glory* of God's presence." While the suggestion is devotional, it cannot be sustained. Both strength and beauty occur elsewhere in contexts that do not agree with this, e.g., strength, 28:7; beauty ("honour"), 71:8.

[52]Kirkpatrick, p. 577, makes this the rebuilt sanctuary after the Captivity. Barnes, III, 42, spiritualizes the sanctuary to find the ultimate fulfillment in "the Church of God." Rawlinson, II, 319, refers the passage to "the glory of God seated between the cherubim in the first temple." Kidner, II, 348, makes the sanctuary both earthly and heavenly since the earthly one was a copy of the heavenly. Kissane, p. 446, sees this as "the heavens where He reigns as king over all the whole world."

[53]Scroggie, II, 280, notes that the verb "sing" occurs three times in vv. 1–2, and the verb "give" three times in vv. 7–8. He makes this "an unconscious intimation of the Holy Trinity." It is more likely a coincidence. What significance can be attached to the one occurrence of "bless," v. 2; the twofold occurrence of "gods," vv. 4, 5; the fourfold occurrence of "earth," vv. 1, 9, 11, 13; or the fivefold occurrence of "people," vv. 3, 5 ("nations"), 7, 10, 13? Scroggie's view is selective spiritualizing.

that Gentiles will offer this to the Lord in the Millennium. With such an offering, the nations will recognize the position of the Lord as deserving of their worship, v. 8. The psalmist calls upon the nation to worship the Lord in "the beauty of holiness." We understand the phrase to speak of worshiping the Lord in the "beauty of *His* holiness."[54] Since He deserves this, the whole earth should reverence the Lord, v. 9.

B. The Cause for Worship 10

10 The nations should worship the Lord because He is the King Who rules over them. This looks forward to the Millennium, when the Lord takes His position as ruler of the nations. In addition, He will establish the world so that no evil forces will move it. He will judge the questions and conflicts of men with righteousness, v. 10.

III. The Lord as Judge 11–13

A. The Call to Worship 11–12

11–12 Having mentioned the coming of the Lord to establish His rule over the earth, the psalmist now calls nature itself to worship Him. Nature's cooperation with the righteous rule of the Lord is vital in establishing peace throughout the earth. The heavens and the earth are joyful without any upset of the natural order. The sea "and the fulness thereof," all it contains, roars as its waves crash on the beach. The "roar" of the oceans is its voice speaking to the Lord that all is well, v. 11. The fields with all that grows in them will likewise be jubilant; cf. Isaiah 14:7–8; 44:23; 55:12. All of the trees in the forests will "rejoice" (*ranan*, see 5:11), v. 12.

B. The Cause for Worship 13

13 The first three words finish v. 12. Nature expresses its joy "before the Lord." The remaining words give the cause for this: the Lord is coming to judge the earth. The repeated phrase "for he cometh" gives

[54]The phrase occurs again in 29:2 (see discussion); 110:3; I Chron. 16:29; and II Chron. 20:21. Clarke, p. 239, suggests that the phrase refers to vestments worn by the priests in their temple service. Nowhere in the OT, however, are worshipers told to wear special clothing when worshiping the Lord. In addition, II Chron. 20:21 does not support the view.

emphasis to the fact. He will indeed come! He will then carry His responsibility with "righteousness," cf. v. 10, as He performs all things in accord with the Father's will. He will judge the "people" (better "world," the nations of the earth) "with his truth" (or "faithfully"), v. 13.

The second coming of the Lord and His reign over the kingdoms of this world are still the hope of the believer (Titus 2:13). As the psalmist here demonstrates, so there should be continual praise and worship of the Lord by His followers. He is still worthy to receive the adoration of those who have accepted Him as their Savior and Lord.

PSALM 97

This *Enthronement Psalm* is another of pure praise to the Lord as the psalmist looks forward to His millennial reign.[55] He describes the Lord as King, exalted above all the false gods of the heathen, victorious over all His foes, righteous in all His ways, and caring for all His people. The psalmist weaves these themes together to magnify the Lord. There is no information in the psalm to guide us in setting the background for its writing, its date, or its author.[56]

I. The Power of the Lord 1–5

1–2 The Lord reigns as King. While stated as a present fact, this is a prophecy as well of the future kingdom when the Lord rules the earth from Jerusalem. In light of this glorious future, the people of the earth should rejoice. The "multitude of the isles," the coastal areas around the Mediterranean Sea,[57] should be glad, v. 1. The Lord

[55]In modern times, Ashkenazi Jews, generally identified with Reformed Judaism, recite this psalm (along with Pss. 92–93, 95–96, 98–99) in the Friday evening service that begins the Sabbath. *NEJ*, p. 668.

[56]The LXX assigns the psalm to David. Spurgeon, p. 406, follows this view. Kirkpatrick, p. 579, and Kissane, p. 447, make the psalm postexilic. Either view may be correct. We cannot, however, be certain of the author, background, or the date of writing for this psalm.

[57]Rotherham, p. 414, refers the "isles" (*ʾîyîm*, see 72:10) to "the West," including Europe and possibly America as well. The biblical focus is on the biblical world.

veils Himself with clouds and "darkness" (or "thick darkness"). The description speaks of His holiness that separates Him from sinful mankind. "Righteousness and judgment [or 'justice']" serve as the "habitation" (better "foundation") of His throne, v. 2.

3–5 The fire of His judgment goes out from Him and burns up His enemies (cf. II Thess. 1:8), v. 3. He sends forth "lightnings" that light up the world. This display of His might brings fear to the people of the earth, v. 4. The "hills" (or "mountains") melt like wax at His presence.[58] The phrase suggests a return to the original creation when a semitropical climate covered the earth. The high mountains, now responsible for much of the weather patterns of the earth, will disappear when the Lord, the "Lord" (*ʾadôn*, see 8:1) of the whole earth, comes to rule, v. 5.

II. The Exaltation of the Lord 6–9

6–7 In the day of the Lord's reign over the earth, the angels in the "heavens" will declare His righteousness (cf. 89:5). On earth, the "people" (or "nations") will see His glorious nature, v. 6. Those who seek to serve false gods, represented by "graven images," and who boast in their idols, will be "confounded" (*bôš*, see 6:10), publicly humiliated for their misplaced trust. The false gods of mankind—anyone or anything with glory or renown that might call forth worship—should themselves worship the Lord, v. 7.[59]

8–9 The people of Zion hear of the righteous rule placed over them, and they are glad (cf. Zech. 9:9). The people in the cities of

There is no warrant for broadening this emphasis.

[58]Leupold, p. 688, understands the phrase as describing the eruption of volcanoes, a further display of God's power. Henry, III, 607, describes this as the "fire of divine wrath . . . [that] will even melt the hills themselves like wax." W. E. Barnes, II, 465, suggests "the earthquake" at Sinai during the giving of the law. Fausset, III, 311, has the unlikely view that the hills "symbolize the heights of man's self-exalting pride of intellect, wealth, and power." These views neglect the future changes of the earth during the millennial kingdom, e.g., Isa. 40:4; 41:18; 43:19.

[59]Kidner, p. 350, and Fausset, III, 312, understand the "gods" as angels as in 96:4–5. They support this view by appealing to Heb. 1:6. The verse in Hebrews, however, quotes the LXX version of Deut. 32:43. It does not refer to this psalm. The "gods" in psalms may refer to false gods, angels, or judges. In each case, the context must guide the sense that the word takes. The earlier part of v. 7 argues that the word refers to false deities. Hirsch, II, 185, picturesquely describes this: "All that men had worshipped heretofore shall now lie prostrate before the One God."

Judah rejoice in the "judgments" (or "justice") of the Lord, v. 8. The phrase "thou, Lord, art high" is better "thou art the Lord most High [*ᶜelyôn*, see 7:17]." He is greatly exalted above all "gods," again the false deities worshiped by man, v. 9.

III. The Protection from the Lord 10–12

10–12 Those who love the Lord should "hate" (*śaneʾ*, see 5:5) evil. The Lord shows His hatred for evil by "preserv[ing]" (or "guarding") the "saints" (*ḥasîd*, see 4:3) from the attacks of the wicked. The Lord delivers them from their "hand," the power of evil men, v. 10. In the psalms, "light" often represents God's presence, e.g., 4:6; 89:15, which in turn may lead to divine guidance, e.g., 43:3; 119:105. This is sown like seed in the life of the righteous, where it will grow to maturity. Gladness as well grows in the lives of the upright, v. 11. In view of these blessings, the righteous should rejoice in the Lord and be thankful at the "remembrance"[60] of His holiness in His dealings with mankind, v. 12.

The psalm appropriately offers praise to the Lord. In view of His reign over the earth, vv. 1–2, His judgment of the wicked, vv. 3–4, and His power as seen in the changes to the earth, v. 5, it is right to exalt Him, vv. 6–9. He will protect those who are His own, v. 10, and will guide them through life, v. 11. In response, it is right to rejoice and to express gratitude to Him, v. 12. This was true of mankind in the day of the psalmist and still is true today.

PSALM 98

Psalm 98 is another *Enthronement Psalm*[61] that looks forward to Christ in His millennial role as King, v. 6. The heading is simply

[60]Leupold, p. 661, follows BDB, p. 271, in equating *zeker*, "remembrance," with *šem*, "name." The NASB translates similarly, "give thanks to his holy name." This has the support of the Targum but only weak support elsewhere.

[61]In modern times, Ashkenazi Jews, generally identified with Reformed Judaism, recite this psalm (along with Pss. 92–93, 95–97, 99) in the Friday evening service that begins the Sabbath. *NEJ*, p. 668.

"A Psalm" (*mizmôr*, see Psalm 3, title), the only psalm with such a simple title. The LXX attributes the psalm to David.[62] There is no way of knowing whether or not he is the author except that the tone of the psalm is similar to Psalm 96, some of the verses being extremely close in wording. I Chronicles 16:23–33 suggests David as the author of Psalm 96, and he may also have written this psalm. Psalm 98 occupies itself totally with praise but gives us no clue as to the occasion being celebrated. We best take it as a prophetic look into the future.[63]

I. The Call for Man's Praise to the Lord 1–3

1 The psalmist urges the people to sing a "new song" of praise to the Lord.[64] He then begins to list the actions of the Lord that merit such a song of praise. The Lord has done "marvellous things" (*pala^ɔ*, see 9:1) as He has cared for the people. His "right hand," here the emblem of strength, cf. 17:7, and His "holy arm," the arm wielding a sword in a just cause, cf. Isaiah 52:10, have gained a victory. He does not give here any significant details of this deliverance. From what occurs later in the psalm, the verse describes prophetically what God is going to do on behalf of His people. He will put down the nations of the earth at the end of the Tribulation.[65] Since it is certain that this will be done, the psalmist speaks of it as already accomplished, v. 1.

---

[62]The Vulgate also attributes the psalm to David. Fausset, III, 313, dates the psalm to the rule of Jehoshaphat. He finds similarities to Pss. 47 and 48, which he dates at the same time. Any similarities are due to the similar themes of praise to the Lord, which can occur at any time. Kirkpatrick, p. 583, and Leupold, p. 691, locate the psalm after the deliverance of the people from their Babylonian captivity. Ewald, II, 200, sees the psalm as composed for the consecration of the postexilic temple.

[63]Tremper Longman III, "Psalm 98: A Divine Warrior Victory Song," *JETS* 27:3 (1984): 267–68, identifies the thesis of the psalm as "a Divine Warrior victory song celebrating the return of Yahweh the commander of the heavenly hosts who is leading the Israelite army home after waging victorious holy war." Later, however, p. 273, Longman recognizes the involvement of the church. While the idea of "Divine Warrior" is acceptable, it is too restrictive to limit the army to Israel. The end-time battle will include all believers. While David may have thought in terms of Israel, his prophecy goes beyond the nation.

[64]See 33:3 for a discussion of the phrase "new song." As is normal, the "new song" here looks forward to the millennial reign of the Lord that follows His conquering the nations at the end of the Tribulation.

[65]VanGemeren, p. 628, places the victories of the Lord in the past history of the nation. The many victories of the Lord are here summed up as a single event. While

2–3 Others will know of the deliverance given by the Lord. He will show the heathen His righteousness in faithfully upholding His promises to His people, v. 2. This deliverance shows that the Lord remembers His "mercy" (or "steadfast love," *ḥesed*, see 5:7) and "truth" (or "faithfulness") to Israel. All the earth sees the salvation of Israel that God accomplishes, v. 3.

II. The Nature of Man's Praise to the Lord 4–6

4 The psalmist calls upon the whole earth to rejoice in the Lord.[66] This now makes clear the timing of God's work on behalf of His people. Only in the millennial reign of Christ will all of the nations praise Him. They should "make a joyful noise" (or "joyful shout," *rûaᶜ*, see 41:11). They should "make a loud noise [better 'break forth'], and rejoice [*ranan*, see 5:11]." They should "sing praise" (*zamar*, see 7:17) to the Lord for delivering the earth from sin, v. 4.

5–6 Musical instruments should accompany their rejoicing. They "sing" (*zamar*) with the "harp" (or "lyre," *kinnor*, see 33:2) and a "psalm" (*zimrâ*, or "song," see 81:2), v. 5. They play "trumpets" (*ḥaṣoṣerâ*) and the "cornet" (*šôpar*, see 47:5). The *ḥaṣoṣerâ* was the straight metal trumpet of the priests, while the *šôpar* was made from a ram's horn. With their musical instruments accompanying their vocal praise, the people make a "joyful noise" (or "joyful shout," *rûaᶜ*), a jubilant note of praise to the Lord, Who has now been crowned "King" over the earth, v. 6.

III. The Joining of Nature's Praise to the Lord 7–9

7–8 Verses 7–9 are similar to Psalm 96:11*b*–13. There are enough differences, however, to let us know that one psalm does not come from the other. Nature also rejoices in the Lord. Since the ravages of sin no longer exist, nature gives forth an untainted voice of praise to God. The sea roars as its waves crash on the beach. This is its voice that offers a note of praise to God. The "fulness thereof" refers to all

---

the view is possible, the use of the phrase "new song," together with the clear context of vv. 3, 7–9, argues for a prophetic sense.

[66]In 1719, Isaac Watts wrote what has become a Christmas song, "Joy to the World," drawing upon the psalm from this point on for the verses. Lowell Mason published the music sung today in 1836.

that lives within the sea. The world of inhabited mankind joins with nature in giving praise to the Lord, v. 7. The "floods [better 'rivers'] clap their hands." The babbling of the flowing waters is pictured as the clapping of hands, a pleasant sound offered to the Lord.[67] The "hills" (or "mountains") are "joyful" (*ranan*, see 5:11). This sound reflects the blowing of breezes through the trees on the mountains, a noise that is pleasing to the Lord, v. 8.

9 As in 96:13, the first three words of v. 9 finish the previous verse. Nature expresses its joy "before the Lord." The remaining words develop the work of the Lord as He comes to rule. He will judge mankind, carrying out this responsibility with "righteousness" as He makes decisions in accord with the Father's will. He will judge the "people [better 'world,' the nations of the earth] with equity [or 'uprightness,' with no deviation from true justice]," v. 9. Matthew Henry aptly ends his discussion of Psalm 98 with the comment, "If all rejoice, why should not we?"[68]

PSALM 99

This psalm closes the series of *Enthronement Psalms*[69] that exalt the Lord as King over the earth. As with Psalms 93:1; 96:10; and 97:1, the phrase "the Lord reigneth" points to a millennial context.

---

[67]Delitzsch, III, 98, explains the clapping of hands as "high waves, which flow into one another like clapping hands." The view is possible although rivers do not normally have high waves. *NIB*, IV, 1072, sees the sea, v. 7, and floods, v. 8, as "chaotic forces that oppose in battle the sovereignty of the supreme creator-God." The verses thus "call to mind the image of God as divine warrior." From the context, which also mentions the world, those who dwell in it, and the hills, it is more likely that the sea and floods are simply elements of nature, not meant as symbols.

[68]Henry, p. 611. Ellen F. Davis, "Psalm 98," *Interp* 46:2 (1992): 175, similarly states, "If indeed every one of God's works is specifically designed for glorification, then the praise of God cannot be viewed as an activity in which human beings engage occasionally or even electively. Rather, praise is woven into the very web of reality, as the primary mode of communication between Creator and creature."

[69]In modern times, Ashkenazi Jews, generally Reformed Judaism, recite this psalm (along with Pss. 92–93, 95–98) in the Friday evening service that begins the Sabbath. *NEJ*, p. 668.

The refrain in vv. 5 and 9 closes each of the two sections of the psalm.[70] There is not enough information in the psalm to tell us the author or the occasion that brings forth this hymn of praise to the Lord.[71] The mention of the cherubim in v. 1, God's "footstool" in v. 5, and the command to worship at God's "holy hill" in v. 9 suggest that the psalmist writes before Judah's exile.[72] We cannot be more specific as to the time.

As with other psalms that focus on the rule of Christ over the earth, the psalm strikes a note of praise. The Lord is great, vv. 1–5, and worthy of man's worship. In view of this, praising God is appropriate for believers in all ages.

I. The Greatness of the Lord 1–5

1–3 The psalmist calls attention to the Lord's position as King over the "people" (better "nations") of the world. As with other occurrences of the phrase "the Lord reigneth," it is a prophetic perfect, so certain that the psalmist states it as a present fact. In view of the Lord's position as King, the people should tremble with fear lest they offend Him. The OT picture of the Lord, dwelling in the holy of holies between the cherubs on the ark of the covenant, portrays His future position on the throne with living creatures about Him (Rev. 4:1–6).[73] The nations of the earth should be "moved" (*nûṭ*)[74] with anxiety over the possibility that they should incur His wrath, v. 1. The Lord is a great King in Zion, His own people. He is also exalted above all the "people" (again "nations"), v. 2. They should therefore

---

[70]While the Hebrew text of the two verses is not identical, they are identical in thought. Among others, Delitzsch, III, 99, and Phillips, II, 90, divide the psalm into three parts. They base this on the repeated phrase "he is holy," vv. 3, 5, and "the Lord our God is holy," v. 9. Delitzsch waxes eloquent, calling this "an earthly echo of the trisagion of the seraphim," cf. Isa. 6:3. Phillips sees the three parts as describing Jesus Christ as the King, Priest, and Prophet.

[71]The LXX and Vulgate assign the psalm to David. This is possible but not clear from the psalm. Kirkpatrick, p. 585, and Leupold, p. 695, place the psalm after the rebuilt temple. This requires that the "footstool," v. 5, be explained. See the notes on v. 5.

[72]While the psalm is prophetic, looking forward to the millennial reign of the Lord, the psalmist draws his thought from the temple worship in his day.

[73]Kirkpatrick, p. 585, places the Lord in heaven, surrounded by the cherubs. He requires this since he dates the psalm after the Captivity.

[74]The word *nûṭ* is a *hapax legomenon*. Similar words in cognate languages give no clear sense, but the parallelism requires something similar in meaning to "tremble."

praise the great and "terrible [or 'awesome'] name"[75] of the Lord, i.e., His nature. It is holy and therefore worthy of praise, v. 3.

4–5 The first phrase is better "The king is mighty; He loves justice." For this reason, He has established "equity" (or "uprightness"). He has brought about "judgment" (or "justice") and righteousness among His people, v. 4. Because of these actions, we should praise Him. The psalmist commands the people to exalt Him. They should "worship" Him, bowing toward the temple at Jerusalem, the location of His footstool,[76] as a sign of respect as they give homage to the Lord. He is a holy God and worthy of worship, v. 5.

II. The Worship of the Lord 6–9

6–7 The final phrase of v. 5 leads naturally to an emphasis on the worship of the Lord. The psalmist recalls Israel's history and the Lord's answers to prayer. Such men as Moses and Aaron were among the priests. While we do not normally think of Moses as a priest, he did perform priestly duties (e.g., Exod. 24:6–8; Lev. 8:15–21). God answered the prayers of both Moses (Exod. 15:25; 32:11–14) and Aaron (Lev. 16:21, "confess"; cf. Num. 16:22). Samuel also was among those that called on the "name" (see v. 3) of the Lord and saw Him answer prayer (I Sam. 7:5; 12:23), v. 6. The Lord spoke to the people in the cloudy pillar (Exod. 19:9; 33:9; Num. 12:5). They responded by keeping His testimonies and "ordinances" (or "statutes"), v. 7.

8–9 The writer recalls God's dealings with the nation. God answered their prayers. He also "forgave" (*nasa*ᵓ, see 25:18) them for their sins after punishing them for their wicked actions, v. 8. He therefore deserves praise. As in v. 5, the psalmist calls upon the people to exalt the Lord and to bow down in worship. Rather than using the term "footstool," which may be taken in different directions, he this time specifically directs the worship toward the "holy hill" of Mt. Zion, the location of the temple. God is holy and worthy of such worship, v. 9.

---

[75]Note 94 at 5:11 gives a summary of the Lord's "name."

[76]The "footstool" of God may be the earth, Isa. 66:1, or the ark of the covenant, I Chron. 28:2. The parallel comment in v. 9 requires that the footstool refer to the ark here. Cf. 132:7. Leupold, p. 696, makes the footstool "the very throne of God in heaven before which the devout worshiper feels that he steps when he rightly worships the Lord." The parallelism between vv. 5 and 9 suggests the earthly temple. Since there was no ark in the second temple, this must be the first temple.

PSALM 100

The title, "A Psalm of praise [or 'thanksgiving,' *tôdâ*, see 26:7]," aptly describes this psalm. In liturgical circles, the psalm has the name *Jubilate*, Latin for "O be joyful!" It is the basis for the hymn "All People That on Earth Do Dwell," written by William Kethe and included in the *Genevan Psalter*, 1561, and now sung to the tune popularly known as OLD HUNDREDTH.

The five verses of the psalm praise the Lord without a single negative thought. Such praise is still natural for believers today. We do not know its author or the occasion for its writing.[77] Whatever its background, there is a call to praise the Lord. The author likely intended the song for use in the worship of the Lord.

I. Service with Praise 1–3

1 The song begins with a call to "make a joyful noise" (or "shout joyfully," *rûaᶜ*, see 41:11) to the Lord. The command goes to "all ye lands [*ʾereṣ*]," a disputed group. The word *ʾereṣ* is singular, leading either to the "land" of Palestine, the Jewish nation, or to the "earth," all nations. The Jewish context in the psalm (coming into His presence, v. 2; His people and sheep in His pasture, v. 3; and entering into the gates and courts of the temple, v. 4) suggests a call to the Jews to praise the Lord, v. 1.[78]

2–3 The people should serve the Lord with "gladness" (or "joy"). His service is not burdensome but joyful. This lets His servants come into His presence with "singing" (or "a joyful shout"), v. 2. They

---

[77]Rodd, p. 54, suggests that the psalm "was sung at the entrance to the temple as a procession approached on a festival day." Sabourin, p. 183, sees the psalm as sung antiphonally by a priestly choir and the congregation. These views are possible although nothing compels them. Delitzsch, III, 104, with no strong evidence, makes the psalm "deutero-Isaianic." He concludes this from its note of praise, p. 90, which compares to the "one chief aim of Isa. ch. xl.–lxvi. to declare the pinnacle of glory of the Messianic apostolic mission." Isa. 40–66, however, is not the only part of the OT to praise the Lord. Fausset, III, 315, sets the psalm at the ascension of Messiah to His throne because of the "shout of acclamation" at "Messiah's coming visibly to reign (Ps. ii. 6, 8, 11, 12)." This is closer to the correct view, although the word *rûaᶜ* ("joyful noise") does not occur in Ps. 2. The command "make a joyful noise" also appears in other settings, Pss. 66:1; 81:1; 95:1–2; 98:4, 6.

[78]Among others, Perowne, II, 210; and Alexander, p. 413, translate *ʾereṣ* as "earth."

should experientially "know" (*yada*^{c}, see 1:6) that the redemptive "Lord" (*y*^{e}*hwah*), the One Who involves Himself with mankind, is also the powerful "God" ($^{\supset e}$*lohîm*). God's people can have this experiential knowledge because they have proved Him. They have relied on Him for redemption and have sought help from His power. As evidence of His power, He is Israel's Creator, "and not we ourselves" (*w*^{e}*lo*$^{\supset}$ $^{\supset a}$*naḥnû*). The last part of the verse supports reading this phrase *w*^{e}*lô* $^{\supset a}$*naḥnû*, "and we are His."[79] We belong to the Lord because He has created us. We are as sheep grazing in His pasture, v. 3.

II. Worship with Praise 4–5

4 The people should come into the gates of the temple; cf. II Kings 15:35; I Chronicles 9:19, 23. They come to worship with "thanksgiving" (*tôdâ*, same word as in the title). They come into the courts of the temple with "praise." They are "thankful" (*yadâ*, the root underlying *tôdâ*) to Him and they "bless" (*barak*, see 5:12) His "name,"[80] ascribing praise to Him, v. 4.

5 The psalmist mentions several reasons for worshiping the Lord. In all that He is and all that He does, He is "good." To illustrate this, the psalmist notes that His "mercy" (or "steadfast love," *ḥesed*, see 5:7) lasts for ever. His "truth" (or "faithfulness") continues throughout "all generations" (*dor wador*, cf. 10:6). As God's people respond to the Lord, praise and gratitude is natural, v. 5.

[79]The *q*^{e}*rê* reads *lô*, "to him," for *lo*$^{\supset}$, "not.' Calvin, IV, 83; Dickson, II, 195; and the LXX all accept the MT. Cohen, p. 324; Perowne, II, 211; and the Vulgate all accept the *q*^{e}*rê*. In my judgment, the parallelism supports the *q*^{e}*rê*. Joe O. Lewis, "An Asseverative לא in Psalm 100 3?" *JBL* 86:2 (1963): 216, argues from Ugaritic that the *lo*$^{\supset}$ is an asseverative. He translates, "He has made us, and, indeed, we are the sheep of his pasture." While this gives a reasonable sense, it is doubtful that the Ugaritic use stands in the Hebrew. The overwhelming sense of *lo*$^{\supset}$ is as a negative or, in the numerous *q*^{e}*rê* readings, a prepositional phrase, "to him."

[80]See 5:11, note 94, for a summary of the Lord's "name."

PSALM 101

This brief psalm of David expresses his dedication to the Lord.[81] The psalm comes from the early years of David's reign before the harsh realities of life set in.[82] It reflects his idealism early in his rule. He pledges to walk "in a perfect way" and with a "perfect heart," v. 2. He will cut off the wicked, vv. 3–5, 7–8, and will have only those who live "in a perfect way" to serve him, v. 6.

I. Dedication of the King 1–2

1–2 David pledges to sing of the Lord's "mercy" (or "steadfast love," *ḥesed*, see 5:7) and His "judgment" (or "justice").[83] He will "sing" (*zamar*, see 7:17) his song to the Lord, v. 1. David will seek these same qualities in his reign. He will "behave . . . wisely" (or "act circumspectly") in a way that is "perfect" (or "blameless," see *tom*, 7:8). The rhetorical question conveys David's desire for fellowship

[81]Delitzsch, III, 107, refers to a story told by "Eyring, in his *Vita* of Ernest the Pious (Duke of Saxe-Gotha, b. 1601, d. 1675)." The story tells that the Duke "sent an unfaithful minister a copy of the 101st Psalm, and that it became a proverb in the country, when an official had done anything wrong: He will certainly soon receive the prince's Psalm to read."

[82]Scroggie, III, 6, and Jennings, II, 160, date the psalm before the return of the ark to Jerusalem, II Sam. 6. Both mention the similarity of David's question in v. 2 to II Sam. 6:9. This assumes that, for David, the presence of the Lord was equivalent to the presence of the ark. While this is possible, it rests on the somewhat vague resemblance of two questions. Albert Barnes, III, 58–59, suggests that David wrote this "when he was entering on domestic life." Calvin, IV, 86, considers it before being "put in possession of the kingdom." Cohen, p. 326, places it "at the beginning of his reign." Perowne, II, 213, dates it during "the early part of David's reign." Ewald, I, 86, makes it shortly after the capture of Jerusalem. This sampling shows the impossibility of dating the psalm to a specific time.

[83]J. Emmette Weir, "The Perfect Way, A Study of Wisdom Motifs in Psalm 101," *EvQ* 53:1 (1981): 55–56, understands "mercy and judgment" as David's own practice. David declares that "his is to be a life marked by integrity of the highest order. Nothing base or degrading is to be tolerated." The parallelism with 1*b*, however, supports the view that these are the marks of God's dealings with man. In addition, it is unlikely that David would sing of his own qualities. David rather praises the Lord, the One Who has thus wrought on his behalf. Only in v. 2 does David indicate his desire to rule in a godly manner.

with the Lord.[84] He will live at home, hidden from the eyes of others, with a "perfect" (*tom*) heart, v. 2.

II. Separation of the King 3–8

3–5 David will avoid temptation by placing no "wicked" (or "worthless," *beliyaᶜal*, see 18:4) thing where he can fix his mind on it. He "hate[s]" (*śaneʾ*, see 5:5) the work of those who "turn aside" (or "fall away") and will not let it cling to him, v. 3.

David spends the remaining verses in developing the last thought stated in v. 3. He will not entertain "a froward [or 'perverse,' *ᶜiqqeš*, see 18:26] heart," nor will he become involved with "a wicked *person*" (or, omitting the supplied word, simply "evil"), v. 4. He will "cut off" (or "put to silence," *ṣamat*, see 18:40)[85] one who secretly slanders a "neighbor" (*reaᶜ*, see 12:2). He will have nothing to do with haughty individuals, v. 5.

6–8 In contrast with his avoidance of wickedness, David purposes to cultivate his association with righteousness. He will look favorably on the faithful as he encourages them to remain in the land. He will choose those who walk in a "perfect" (or "blameless," see *tom*, 7:8) way to serve him, v. 6. He will not let the deceitful dwell in his household. He will not let liars "tarry" (or "be established") in his presence, v. 7. "Early" (or "every morning"), he will "destroy" (*ṣamat*, see 18:40) the wicked from the land so that he may cut them off from access to Jerusalem, the city devoted to the worship of the Lord, v. 8.

Such was David's goal. As things turned out, he was not able to carry out these practices. His own sin with Bathsheba brought judgment from God. The deceitfulness of his son brought him rebellion and heartache. David's idealism will be fulfilled, however, when the Son of David, the Lord, sets up His rule over the earth. At that time, righteousness will prevail and the sinfulness of men will be cut off.

---

[84]Th. Booij, "Psalm CI 2—'When Wilt Thou Come to Me?'" *VT* 38:4 (1988): 460, interprets the question as the request for "a revelatory dream or vision of a special kind." While this is possible, such appearances of God to man were sovereignly granted, not given in response to man's desires.

[85]While *ṣamat* may refer to destruction, the context here does not warrant such an extreme action. The idea of bringing something to an end leads to the thought of silencing the slanderer.

Although David failed to reach the goals stated in the psalm, those goals remain desirable for believers in this life. David seeks, positively, to praise the Lord, v. 1, and to enter in fellowship with Him, v. 2, and with the righteous, v. 6. Negatively, he will avoid worthless things, v. 3, and wicked persons, vv. 4–5, 7–8. Dedication to the Lord still involves a positive separation *to* Him and a negative separation *from* evil.

PSALM 102

This lament psalm is both penitential and messianic. The classification as a penitential psalm is unusual in that there is no confession of the psalmist's sin to mark his repentance.[86] He does, however, allude to his sin, v. 10. The lament of the psalmist gives rise to the promise of ultimate victory by the Lord. The title is appropriate. The psalmist is "afflicted" (*ᶜanî*, see 9:12); he is "overwhelmed" (or "faint") from what he faces. In this condition, he turns to the Lord, pouring out his "complaint" (*śîaḥ*, see 55:2) to the Lord in "prayer" (*tᵉpillâ*, see 4:1).

Verses 25–27 supply the messianic prophecy in the psalm.[87] The Messiah is the Creator, the eternal One and the unchanging One. Hebrews 1:10–12 cites this as the author shows the superiority of Jesus Christ to the angels. This glorious description is still true and, therefore, remains a source of comfort to believers. We have a powerful and unchanging God!

We do not know the author.[88] There are hints in the psalm that suggest that it may have been written toward the end of the Captivity. The laments of the psalmist reflect his Babylonian exile. Verse 13

[86]The penitential psalms include Pss. 6, 32, 38, 51, 102, 130, and 143.

[87]Note 32 in the introduction to Ps. 2 briefly discusses the messianic psalms.

[88]Gaebelein, p. 372, makes David the author. While this is possible, the psalm allows for a later date. Murphy, p. 524, places the author "in the beginning of Hezekiah's reign." Jennings, II, 165, tentatively suggests Jeremiah. Cohen, p. 328, understands the author as "an individual captive who details his wretched plight." Phillips, II, 116, accepts Daniel as the author. We cannot be certain.

mentions the "set time," possibly the time appointed for ending the nation's exile. Verse 14 likely mentions the ruined city of Jerusalem. Verse 20 refers to the prisoner and those who are condemned to death, again possibly referring to the time in Babylon. If we take these references as mentions of the Babylonian captivity, the author is an unknown Jew, probably a priest, who expresses his feelings through the psalm.

I. The Fretfulness of the Psalmist 1–11

1–2 The psalmist asks the Lord to hear his prayer and to let his "cry" (or "cry for help") come to Him, v. 1. He pleads with the Lord not to hide from him when he is in "trouble" (or "distress"). He asks the Lord rather to hear him and to answer his prayer quickly, v. 2. These petitions set an example for believers today. Rather than trying to solve life's problems with our own ability and resources, we should respond first with prayer. We turn to the Lord because He has commanded us to rely upon Him (e.g., Luke 18:1; I Thess. 5:17).

3–7 The psalmist poetically describes the distress that has overtaken him. His days are consumed as if a fire giving off smoke were eating them away. His "bones," the framework of his body, are "burned" (or "scorched") like the hearth of a fireplace, v. 3. He compares his heart, the seat of his emotions, to grass that has been "smitten" (or "blighted") and withered. The sorrow causes him to lose his appetite, v. 4. Under the influence of the "voice of [his] groaning" (or "noise of [his] sigh"), his "bones cleave to [his] skin." He feels like skin and bones, wasted away and weak, v. 5. He is like a "pelican" (*qaʾat*)[89] that dwells alone in the wilderness. He is like an "owl" (or "little owl") in the "desert" (or "waste places"), v. 6. He "watch[es]" (or "lie[s] awake"). He is like a "sparrow" (or "bird," *ṣippôr*, see 84:3) alone on a housetop. The point of all these birds is that they dwell

[89]The *qaʾat* is an unknown bird. It is unclean, Lev. 11:18, and lives in a lonely place, Isa. 34:11, or a high place, Zeph. 2:14. Horne, p. 434, identifies it as a pelican. Henry, III, 618, suggests the bittern. Bratcher and Reyburn, p. 862, give "vulture." Hirsch, II, 203, uses the generic "bird." Buttenwieser, p. 383, translates "screech owl." VanGemeren, p. 647, follows the NIV in rendering "desert owl." Kissane, p. 464, offers "raven." This variety shows the impossibility of dogmatically identifying the *qaʾat*.

in lonely places. Their loneliness portrays the loneliness felt by the psalmist, v. 7.

8–11 The author's enemies have continually reproached him. Those that "are mad against [him]" (or "consider [him] a fool") curse him, v. 8. His grief has brought him to eat the ashes, which show his sorrow, as if they were bread. He has mixed his tears with his drink, v. 9. He sees the hand of the Lord in this. He is the subject of the Lord's "indignation" (*zaᶜam*, see 38:3) and wrath. Apparently, he is conscious of some sin that has brought judgment upon him. This has caused the Lord to raise him up in order to cast him down, v. 10. He sees his life as a lengthened shadow, with the sun about to set. He is like withered grass, v. 11.

II. The Favor of the Lord 12–22

12–17 Despite the burdens the psalmist carries, he retains his trust in the Lord. In contrast to his own mortality, the Lord will "endure" (or "abide," *yašab*)[90] forever. There will be a remembrance of the Lord to "all generations" (*lᵉdor wador*, see 10:6), v. 12. He will rise up and show "mercy" (or "compassion") to His people in Zion. It is time to extend "favor" (or "grace," *ḥanan*, see 4:1) to her. The "set [or 'appointed'] time" (*môᶜed*, see 74:4) has come for once more exalting her among the nations. The psalmist refers to the end of the seventy-year captivity and to the subsequent restoration, both prophesied by Jeremiah (25:12; 27:22; 29:10), v. 13. Those who serve the Lord have "pleasure" (*raṣâ*, see 40:13) in the stones that make up the walls of the city. They "favour" (or "pity," *ḥanan*) the dust of the ruined city, v. 14.[91] When the Lord moves on behalf of His people, the "heathen" (or "nations") will fear His "name," here representing His nature as a powerful God.[92] The kings of other nations will "fear" (or "stand in awe of") His glory, v. 15. At that time, the Lord

---

[90]The verb "endure" (*yašab*) occurs over one thousand times. It may be translated "to dwell" or "to sit." Hirsch, II, 205, and Clarke, p. 249, understand it as "sit" and apply the verse to God's sitting upon His throne when He reigns. The NIV also translates this way: "You, O Lord, sit enthroned forever." The view is possible, although it requires interpreting the idea of sitting as sitting on a throne. The sense of dwelling is more common elsewhere.

[91]The verse was the basis for Pharisaical legalism. Rabbi Hiyya ben Gamda rolled himself in the dust of Palestine to show his love for the land. *Kethuboth* 112*b*.

[92]Note 94 at 5:11 summarizes the Lord's "name."

will have built up Zion. He will appear in glory to mankind, v. 16. In addition to His work on behalf of the nation, He will also care for the downtrodden. He will hear the "prayer" (*t*^{e}*pillâ*, see 4:1) of the destitute. He will not despise their prayer (*t*^{e}*pillâ*), v. 17.

18–22 This history will be recorded for generations to come. People yet to be "created" (*baraʾ*, see 51:10) will praise the Lord, v. 18. The psalmist writes confidently, as though these future events have already happened. The Lord looks from His dwelling on high to see the earth, v. 19. He hears the groaning of the prisoner and frees those who are "appointed to death" (lit., "sons of death," cf. 79:11), v. 20, so they may tell of the "name," i.e., the nature (cf. v. 15), of the Lord in Zion. They will tell of His praiseworthiness in Jerusalem, v. 21, when the "people" (or "nations") and kingdoms come together to serve the Lord, v. 22.

III. The Future of the Nation 23–28

23–24*a* The author returns once more to his own situation. The Lord has "weakened" (*ʿanâ*, see 35:13) him in his way and has shortened his days, v. 23. He pleads with God not to take him away "in the midst of [his] days," before the end of his expected life, v. 24*a*.

24*b*–27 In contrast with his own expected end (cf. v. 12), the psalmist acknowledges the eternality of the Lord Who continues through "all generations" (see *l*^{e}*dor wador*, 10:6), v. 24*b*. In olden times, He created the earth and the heavens. These are the work of His "hands," which are the emblem of God's power, 89:13; 106:26, v. 25. They will "perish" (Isa. 51:6) when the Lord brings "new heavens and a new earth" (II Pet. 3:12–13; cf. Rev. 21:1) to replace this present sin-cursed universe. The Lord, however, will remain. The universe will wear out like well-worn clothing. The Lord will cause it to pass away, a change that will indeed come about, v. 26.

The Lord, however, is unchanging. There is no end to His existence. Hebrews 1:10–12 quotes vv. 25–27 as a proof of Christ's superiority over the angels. He is the Creator, and He alone is eternal and without change, v. 27.

28 The psalmist now draws a conclusion. God will not abandon His covenant with His people (II Sam. 7:12–16). In view of the eternality of the Lord, there will always be those who serve Him. While generations may pass away, coming generations will serve the Lord. Their descendants will be established as His servants, v. 28.

PSALM 103

This "Psalm of David"[93] is a hymn of praise to the Lord, with a special emphasis given to the grace of God. Rather than mentioning some specific threat from which he trusts the Lord to deliver him, David simply extols the grace of God in many different areas. Because there are no personal references in the psalm, it is not possible to relate it certainly to any one time in David's life.

> After the first communion service with natives in Calabar, present-day Nigeria, the congregation sang Psalm 103,
>
> All thine iniquities who doth
> Most graciously forgive
> Who thy diseases all and pains
> Doth heal, and thee relieve.
>
> Who doth redeem thy life, that thou
> To death mayst not go down
> Who thee with lovingkindness doth
> And tender mercies crown.[94]

I. Illustrations of God's Grace 1–5

1–2 David begins with his personal feelings. He ascribes blessings to the Lord. Emphasizing his determination, he dedicates "all that is within me" to "bless" (*barak*, see 5:12) the "holy name" of the Lord. As usual, the "name" of the Lord refers to the Lord Himself and thus

---

[93]For the heading "Psalm of David," see the introduction to Ps. 25. Moll, p. 525, and Kirkpatrick, p. 599, reject David's authorship on the grounds of some rare Aramaic forms found in the psalm. While these are unusual forms, it is still possible to accept David's authorship. Every language receives influence from the languages of surrounding countries. *Berakoth* 10*a*, in the Talmud, identifies David as the author.

[94]Basil Miller, *Mary Slessor: Heroine of Calabar* (Uhrichsville, Ohio: Barbour Publishing, Inc., 1998), pp. 95–96.

reflects His nature.[95] In this psalm, David emphasizes the graciousness of God toward man, v. 1. Once more, David "bless[es]" (*barak*) the Lord. This time, however, he gives the reason that is uppermost in his mind. The Lord has given "benefits," gifts that David summarizes in the next few verses, v. 2.

3–5 The Lord forgives man's "iniquities"[96] and heals his "diseases." The parallelism with 3*a* and the context of v. 4 argue that these diseases are spiritual in nature (cf. Isa. 33:24), v. 3.[97] He redeems the life of men from "destruction" (or "the pit," *šaḥat*, see 7:15), the place of judgment for sinners. While not an explicit statement, the phrase implies the resurrection of the believing dead. The Lord bestows "lovingkindness" (or "steadfast love," *ḥesed*, see 5:7) and "tender mercies" (or "compassions") as He cares for man, v. 4. He satisfies the "mouth" (or "soul," *ᶜadî*, see 32:9)[98] with good things. The result is that youth is refreshed, renewed like the soaring eagle (cf. Isa. 40:31), v. 5.[99]

---

[95]Note 94 at 5:11 summarizes the Lord's "name."

[96]David here gives a brief summary without developing the basis upon which the Lord forgives man's wickedness. In the OT, forgiveness rested on man's faith in God. This faith let the Lord "cover" man's sins until Christ's great sacrifice at Calvary, which atoned for the sins of the OT saints, Rom. 3:25.

[97]Cohen, p. 333, and Harman, p. 336, understand "diseases" literally. The view is possible, since the Lord often heals men from their physical problems. This does not always happen, however, while the other benefits mentioned in vv. 3–5 are constant. For this reason, I have relied on the parallelism to refer the "diseases" to the spiritual diseases that the Lord always forgives when sinners repent.

[98]The noun *ᶜadî* is lit. "ornament." David uses the term metaphorically here to represent something highly desirable. Weiser, p. 656, follows the LXX in giving "desire." Livingston, p. 387, suggests "old age." VanGemeren, p. 652, accepts the emendation BHS suggests: *ᶜodekî*, "your being." Kirkpatrick, p. 601, remains close to the sense by interpreting the stich as "who adorneth thee to the full with goodliness." W. E. Barnes, II, 486, argues for "health" on the basis of the emphasis in 5*b*. Cohen, p. 333, gives "godliness." Calvin, IV, 128, argues for "mouth." There is room for difference of opinion here. I have referred it to the soul as naturally continuing v. 4.

[99]Joachim Neander based his hymn "Praise Ye the Lord, the Almighty," written in the last half of the seventeenth century and published after his death in 1680, on vv. 1–6 and Ps. 150. Catherine Winkworth translated the hymn from German in 1863. Neander also selected the music for the hymn from a tune current in his day. William Sterndale Bennett and Otto Goldschmidt modified this in 1863. In 1834, Henry Francis Lyte wrote a free paraphrase of the psalm, preserved today in the hymn "Praise, My Soul, the King of Heaven." John Goss composed music for it in 1869, and Queen Elizabeth II requested this hymn as the processional at her wedding at Westminster Abbey in 1947.

II. Forgiveness by God's Grace 6–14

6–10 The Lord "executeth" (or "performs") righteous actions and "judgment" (or "justice") for all who are oppressed, v. 6. David's thought is primarily of his own people. He develops this idea next. The Lord began this work for Israel when He revealed His will to Moses and showed His deeds to the nation, v. 7. He is "merciful" (or "compassionate") and "gracious" (see *ḥanan*, 4:1). He is slow to unleash His "anger" (*ʾap*, see 2:5) and abounding in "mercy" (or "steadfast love," *ḥesed*, see 5:7), v. 8. David recognizes that the Lord will not withhold His judgment forever. He will not continue to "chide" (*rîb*, see 35:1), verbally contending with the people. He will not restrain His judgment for their sin forever, v. 9. To this point, however, He has not dealt with Israel as their sins deserved. He has not "rewarded" (i.e., "punished," *gamal*, see 7:4) the nation as their iniquities would suggest, v. 10.

11–14 The "mercy" (or "steadfast love," *ḥesed*) of the Lord is toward those who "fear him" (see *yirʾâ*, 2:11), reverencing Him as their God. This love is immeasurable, "as the heaven is high above the earth," v. 11. He has put far away the transgressions of the godly. The picturesque phrase "as far as the east is from the west" conveys the thought that the separation is total and complete, v. 12. Like a father "pitieth" (or "has compassion on") his children, so the Lord has compassion on those who "fear" (or "reverence," see v. 11) Him, v. 13. He knows what we are and is mindful that we are created from dust, v. 14.

III. Need for God's Grace 15–18

15–18 With the last verse, David has introduced man's frailty. He now develops this further to show man's need for God's grace. The life of "man" (*ʾenôš*, see 8:4) is like grass, soon to be cut down and withered (cf. 37:2; 90:5–6). He is like a flower. It "flourisheth" (*ṣûṣ*, see 72:16) for a time, v. 15, but then the wind blows from the desert and withers the flower. It dies and the plant gives no sign that it has ever bloomed, v. 16. God, however, extends His "mercy" (or "steadfast love," *ḥesed*) to frail man. He gives everlasting mercy to those who "fear" (or "reverence," see v. 11) Him. He bestows His righteousness upon their descendants, v. 17, to those who keep His covenant with them and carry out His "commandments" (or "precepts"), cf. Deut. 7:9, v. 18.

IV. Praise to the God of Grace 19–22

19–22 In view of what God has done, both for David and for the godly in the nation, it is appropriate to close on a note of praise. David introduces this thought by recognizing that the Lord has "prepared" (or "established") His heavenly throne. From His kingdom, He rules over "all." From the development of this in the remaining verses, it is clear that David includes both the living and inanimate things in this, v. 19. The angels that "excel [*gibbôr*, see 19:5] in strength" and carry out the commands spoken by the Lord should "bless" (*barak*, see 5:12) Him, v. 20. The "hosts" (*ṣᵉbaʾôt*, see 24:10) of mankind,[100] His earthly "ministers" (or "servants"), doing that which pleases Him, should "bless" (*barak*) the Lord, v. 21. The works of the Lord throughout the universe should likewise "bless" (*barak*) Him. David himself will "bless" (*barak*) the Lord, v. 22.

The psalm has an unusual emphasis on the grace of God. This includes forgiveness, v. 3, and deliverance from judgment, v. 4*a*, both illustrating His steadfast love (also v. 11) and compassions (also v. 13), v. 4*b*. He refreshes mankind, v. 5. He works righteousness and justice for the oppressed, v. 6. He revealed His will to Israel, v. 7. He is compassionate, gracious, patient, and steadfastly loyal in love, v. 7. He has withheld judgment, allowing time for repentance, vv. 9–10, allowing complete forgiveness of sin, v. 12. He knows that man is weak, vv. 14–16, but still extends steadfast love and righteous actions, v. 17, to those who obey Him, v. 18. In view of this, it is still appropriate for His followers to "bless the Lord," vv. 20–22.

---

[100]Cohen, p. 336, and Leslie, p. 49, refer the word "hosts" to the heavenly bodies. Dahood, III, 30, and Perowne, II, 230, refer it to the angels. Anderson, II, 717, includes both angels and stars. Rawlinson, II, 383, refers v. 20 to the archangels and v. 21 to the lesser angels. Clarke, p. 252, refers it to "all the powers of nature." While it is true that the word may refer to the creation, e.g., Deut. 4:19, it is also true that it refers to angels, I Kings 22:19; or to Israel, Exod. 12:40–41; Josh. 5:14. The focus here is on mankind. David has just mentioned the heavenly hosts in the previous verse and will mention the works of God in the next verse.

PSALM 104

This beautiful psalm does not name its author and, for that reason, cannot be certainly assigned to anyone.[101] It is a hymn that praises the God of Creation. With poetic license, the psalm parallels the Creation account in Genesis 1–2 as it relates in order the various parts of the psalm to the days of the Creation. Then, having established the power of God, the psalm closes with a note of praise to the Lord. This gives a simple but powerful message to the psalm: God is great and is therefore to be praised!

I. The First Day: Creation of Light 1–2*a* (Gen. 1:3–5)

1–2*a* In view of the great subject, it is appropriate that the psalmist both begin and end with a note of praise to the Lord Who has created all things. The psalmist himself purposes to "bless" (*barak*, see 5:12) the Lord. He is "very great" and, as such, is covered with "honour" (*hôd*, see 8:1) and "majesty" (*hadar*, see 8:5). This statement anticipates the account of Creation to follow. The glory of the creation brings honor and majesty to its Creator, v. 1. With this verse, the psalmist begins to describe the creative work of the Lord. The Lord has created light. Since this light fills the universe, in a sense it is a garment that covers Him. Although the works of God reveal His presence, the creation does not see the Lord directly because He has veiled Himself from its vision, v. 2*a*.[102]

II. The Second Day: Creation of the Firmament 2*b*–4 (Gen. 1:6–8)

2*b*–4 The psalmist poetically describes the creation of the firmament, the expanse that originally divided the waters on the earth from the watery covering that surrounded it. The Lord has stretched out the "heavens" like the curtain of a tent, spreading them over the

---

[101]Clarke, p. 252, and Hirsch, II, 221, give it to David. Spurgeon, p. 431, sees either David or Solomon as the author. Oesterley, II, 440, sees it as preexilic. Kissane, p. 471, makes it postexilic. We cannot be dogmatic about the authorship.

[102]In the early 1800s, Robert Grant adapted an earlier work by William Kethe into the hymn "O Worship the King." The hymn draws on vv. 1–2 in its second stanza. The music for the hymn is credited to Johann Michael Haydn.

earth. The heavens in view here are the atmospheric heavens, created on the second day by the Lord, v. 2*b*. He lays the support beams of his "chambers" (or "upper chambers") in the waters above the heavenly expanse. From this exalted dwelling, He sends rain to the earth (cf. v. 13). He uses the clouds as His chariots and walks on the "wings of the wind." Both of these poetic pictures convey God's presence as He moves throughout the creation, v. 3. He makes "his angels [*mal*ᵓ*ak*] spirits" (better "His angels winds") and "his ministers a flaming fire." The author of Hebrews quotes the verse in 1:7 as he shows the superiority of the Son of God to angels. The passage states that angels are servants. God made them "spirits" (or "winds") and flames of fire. Where man sees only the works of nature, angels often carry out God's will. Jewish readers would possibly have thought of the giving of the Law (Exod. 19:16, 18; Gal. 3:19), v. 4.[103]

III. The Third Day

A. Creation of the Land and Water 5–13 (Gen. 1:9–10)

5–9 The psalmist now turns to the creation of the land masses.[104] Breaking through the waters, the Lord brings forth the continents. The Lord "laid" (or "established") the earth on its foundations so it will never be "removed" (or "shaken"). The "foundations" are those interior parts of the planet that allow the continents to rise above the waters.[105] Although minor changes may take place in the landmasses,

---

[103]Livingston, p. 389, translates *mal*ᵓ*ak* as "messengers," an alternate translation that avoids the presence of spiritual beings here. The NT use in Heb. 1:7, however, supports "angels." Morris, p. 68, understands the passage to refer to the creation of angels at this point. Since the angels witnessed the creation of the earth (Job 38:4–7), here taken up in v. 5, this is a possible view.

[104]David G. Barker, "The Waters of the Earth: An Exegetical Study of Psalm 104:1–9," *GTJ* 7:1 (1986): 57–80, refers this passage to the Noahic Flood rather than to the Creation. If the passage is considered by itself, this view might be possible. When, however, it is taken in relation to the surrounding context, it better describes the third day of Creation.

[105]Bratcher and Reyburn, p. 880, accept the blatantly false idea that this "reflects the idea that the earth was a flat disk that rested on pillars under the ground which reached down to the underworld." Cowles, p. 422, relates the "foundations" to the "law of gravitation" that keeps the earth in its orbit. Moll, p. 529, considers this a poetic statement showing "the stability of the earth as suspended in space." Hengstenberg, II, 240, considers the earth held up "by the omnipotence of God,

the earth itself remains, v. 5. Initially, the waters are like clothing that covers the earth. The waters are above the mountains, v. 6. At the reproof of the Lord, like a thundering noise, the waters flee, hurrying away from their position that covers the ground, v. 7. The phrase "they go up by the mountains" is lit. "the mountains go up," rising above the waters. The waters find their natural level in the valleys that result from the creation of the mountains, v. 8.[106] The Lord sets boundaries to keep them from covering the earth, v. 9.[107]

10–13 As a result of God's work, springs of water now run through valleys between the "hills" (or "mountains"), v. 10. "Every beast [or 'creature'] of the field," the wild animals, created on the sixth day, drinks from the springs. The "wild asses" serve as an example, v. 11. Anticipating the creation of shrubs and trees, the psalmist notes the birds that dwell beside the springs. They sing among the branches of the trees, v. 12. The Lord waters the "hills" (or "mountains") from His upper chambers (cf. v. 3). The earth is satisfied with the results of God's works, v. 13.[108]

B. Creation of the Vegetation 14–18 (Gen. 1:11–13)

14–18 Naturally following the creation of the land, the Lord now brings forth varying forms of vegetation. He causes grass to grow to meet the needs of the "cattle," here referring to the domesticated animals. The "herb" (or "vegetation") grows for the "service" (or "work") of "man" (*ᵓ*ͤ*nôš*, see 8:4), letting him harvest food, v. 14. The grapes serve to make "wine" to cheer mankind. Men apply "oil," generally made from olives and a sign of prosperity (cf. Deut.

---

without a foundation, as if it had one." I have understood v. 5 as a summary statement, with vv. 6–9 giving the details of God's creative work.

[106]Edmund F. Sutcliffe, "A Note on Psalm CIV 8," *VT* 2:2 (1952): 179, suggests that the psalmist had in mind "the three sources of the Jordan" in the mountains north of Israel. He writes of the waters high in the mountains that naturally flow downward. The view ignores the Creation context of the psalm.

[107]While the Genesis Flood is an exception to this, the psalmist writes from the perspective of one covered by the Noahic Covenant. In this, the Lord promises never again to send waters to cover the earth, Gen. 9:11.

[108]Th. Booij, "Psalm 104,13b: 'The Earth is Satisfied with the Fruit of Thy Works,'" *Biblica* 70:3 (1989): 410, argues that the "earth" here includes "the creatures upon it." He cites Pss. 69:34 and 96:11 in support. While not necessary, the view is possible. The context speaks of "mountains" and "valleys," "springs," "beasts," "wild asses," "fowls," "branches," and "hills," but not of humans.

33:24; Job 29:6), to make their faces glisten. They make bread that "strengtheneth" (or "sustains") their heart with nourishment, v. 15. Trees, brought forth by the Lord, "are full of sap" (better "are satisfied," i.e., well watered). The "cedars of Lebanon" (see 92:12) serve as an example of the Lord's provision, v. 16. The birds nest in the trees. The stork, an unclean bird found in Palestine (Lev. 11:19), dwells in the fir trees, v. 17. The mention of the trees growing throughout the land leads the psalmist to mention animals that also dwell in the land. He will develop this more in vv. 27–28. The wild goats find their "refuge" in the "high hills" (or "high mountains"). The "conies" (or "rock badgers")[109] dwell in the rocks, v. 18.

IV. The Fourth Day: Creation of the Heavenly Bodies 19–24 (Gen. 1:14–19)

19–22 Although the Lord also creates the stars and other heavenly bodies at this time, the psalmist focuses on the creation of the moon and sun. He mentions one purpose given in Genesis for the creation of the heavenly bodies. The Lord made the moon to establish the "seasons" (*môᶜed*, see 74:4).[110] Even today, men mark times within a month by referring to the new moon, the crescent moon, the quarter-moon, the half-moon, the gibbous moon, and the full moon. At special times of the year, we speak of the harvest moon or the hunter's moon. The focus here, developed in vv. 20–24, is on the night and day being designed to meet the needs of the animals and man.[111] The sun knows the place where it sets, v. 19. This brings the darkness of the night, the time when the creatures (cf. v. 11) come out of their dens, v. 20. The "young lions" (*kᵉpîr*, see 17:12) roar to frighten their prey as they seek the meat God has prepared for them, v. 21. When the sun rises, the animals return to their dens for sleep. The mention

[109]The rock badger, *Hyrax syriacus*, is a small mammal with short legs and ears. It has large front teeth and heavy, broad nails on its padded feet. It lives in crevices among the rocks.

[110]There are three remaining reasons for the heavenly bodies. They divide the day from the night, act as signs to remind man of the power of God, and give light to the earth. See Gen. 1:14–15.

[111]Merrill F. Unger, ed., *Unger's Bible Dictionary*, p. 757, refers the "seasons" to "the great religious festivals of the Jews." Since the Lord did not give directions for these until 2,500 years after the Creation, it is unlikely that the word "seasons" refers to them here.

of animals in vv. 20–22 and man in vv. 23–24 merely illustrates activities during the night and day, v. 22.

23–24 In contrast with the animals, man goes to his work, where he labors until night, v. 23. This design of the Lord is marvelous. The psalmist praises Him. His works are "manifold" (or "many") and brought forth by means of divine "wisdom" (*ḥokmâ*, see 19:7). The earth is full of His "riches" (or "possessions," *qinyan*), v. 24.[112]

V. The Fifth Day: Creation of Marine Life and Birds 25–26 (Gen. 1:20–23)

25–26 While the fifth day includes the creation of birds, the psalmist mentions here only the sea creatures. He has referred to birds earlier, vv. 12, 17. The phrase "great and wide sea" is stated unusually. It is lit. "there is the sea, great and wide of hands." The "hands" are the sides of the sea that extend broadly to the right and left hands. Numbers of large and small sea creatures are in it, v. 25. The ships sail through the seas. The need for ships to traverse the waters suggests the waters' great size. The great sea creature "leviathan" (*liwyatan*, in 74:14 a crocodile but here possibly a whale with no adversaries to fear) plays in the waters, v. 26.

VI. The Sixth Day

A. Creation of the Animals 27–28 (Gen. 1:24–25)

27–28 The psalmist has mentioned the wild animals, including "wild asses," in vv. 11, 21–22, and the domesticated animals in v. 14. He focuses here on the provision that the Lord makes for the animal kingdom. They wait for the Lord, and He gives them their "meat" (better "food") in "due season" (or "its time"), v. 27. The animals gather what the Lord has provided. He opens His hand and they are "filled" (or "satisfied") with good things (cf. 145:16), v. 28.

---

[112]Cohen, p. 341, and Dahood, III, 44, translate *qinyan* as "creatures." The word *qinyan* basically refers to "possessions," which may or may not include animals. In the only other occurrence in the Psalms, 105:21, it refers to "possessions." Since v. 23 discusses man and his work, it is unlikely that v. 24 returns to the animals of vv. 20–22.

B. Creation of Man 29–30 (Gen. 1:26–31)

29–30 As with the animals, the psalmist has already introduced man, vv. 14–15, 23. He now turns to man once more.[113] Apart from the presence of the Lord, man is "troubled" (or "dismayed," *bahal*, see 2:5). When the Lord takes away their breath, they die and return to the dust from which they were created. All of this relates to man's sin and the subsequent judgment (Gen. 3:16–19), v. 29. New life comes when the Lord sends His "spirit" (or "breath") and life is "created" (*bara*ᵓ, see 51:10). He renews the face of the earth as He provides food for mankind to gain (Gen. 3:19), v. 30.

VII. The Seventh Day: Recognition of the Creator 31–35 (Gen. 2:1–3)

31–32 As in the Genesis account the final day was set aside to recognize the Lord, so the psalmist closes his account by taking note of what the Lord has done. In view of this great creation, he praises the Lord. The jussive verb suggests that v. 31 should be translated, "May the glory of the Lord endure forever; may the Lord rejoice in His works," v. 31. The earth's reaction to God shows His greatness. A mere glance at the earth from God causes it to tremble. He "toucheth" (or "strikes") the hills and they belch forth smoke. Passages like Nahum 1:5–6 and Habakkuk 3:10 illustrate the verse, v. 32.

33–35 In view of God's greatness, the psalmist can only praise Him. He pledges to sing to the Lord throughout his life. He will "sing praise" (*zamar*, see 7:17) to God while he is alive, v. 33. Once more, the jussive verbs suggest a wish: "May my meditation [*śîaḥ*, see 55:2] of Him be sweet." This will lead to his rejoicing in the Lord, v. 34. The psalmist hopes for a godly world. To this end, he prays that sinners may be consumed and that the wicked would exist no more. He closes the psalm as he began it, "bless[ing]" (*barak*, see 5:12) the Lord and giving praise to Him, v. 35.[114]

---

[113]Bratcher and Reyburn, p. 887, apply vv. 29–30 to the animals. The emotional response of v. 29 and the emphasis on breath in v. 30 suggests rather that the passage refers to man; cf. Gen. 2:7. This agrees with the pattern of the psalm as it parallels the Genesis record of the Creation.

[114]Scroggie, III, 104, and Weiser, p. 671, transfer the closing *halᵉlû·yah* to the beginning of Ps. 105. There is no textual support for this.

PSALM 105

The psalm does not name its author. The comparison of vv. 1–15 with I Chronicles 16:8–22, however, makes it certain that David expanded his earlier song into this psalm.[115] The fact that David gave the psalm to Asaph (I Chron. 16:7) suggests that he meant it for use in Israel's worship. The psalm praises the God Who has brought the nation into existence and given them the land in which to dwell.[116] With this note of praise, the psalm sets an example for all believers. It is still right to praise the Lord for His works on our behalf.

I. The Praise of the Mighty God 1–15

A. The Exhortation to Praise 1–5

1–5 David calls upon the people of Israel to thank the Lord. They should call on His "name,"[117] His nature as a gracious God, as they express their devotion to Him. They should also declare the works of the Lord among the various peoples with whom they interact, v. 1. They should sing to the Lord. They should "sing psalms" (or "make music," *zamar*, see 7:17) to Him. They should "talk . . . of" (or "meditate on," see *śîaḥ*, 55:2) His "wondrous works" (*pala*ʾ, see 9:1), v. 2.

The people should glory in the holy "name" (see v. 1) of the Lord. As is often the case, the name of the Lord represents His nature as revealed to His people. In view of all that He has meant to the nation, this is truly something worthy of glory. Those who "seek" (*baqaš*) Him should rejoice in His willingness to be found by them, cf. 40:16; 70:4, v. 3. They should "seek" (*daraš*, see 9:10) the Lord and the strength He exercises on behalf of His people. They should "seek" (*baqaš*)[118] His presence continually, v. 4. They should remember the

---

[115]Phillips, II, 140, dates the psalm after the Exile. This ignores the passage in I Chron. 16:8–22 that assigns it to David. Hirsch, II, 232, 234, accepts David as the author but makes the psalm for "Israel in exile." This requires the psalm to be a prophecy, an improbable view.

[116]The introduction to Ps. 78 briefly discusses the historical psalms.

[117]See note 94 at 5:11, which summarizes the "name" of the Lord.

[118]The alternation of *baqaš* and *daraš* reflects poetic license. While both *baqaš* and *daraš* stress the carefulness of a search, *daraš* sometimes emphasizes more the mental aspect of a search. David does not emphasize any difference here.

"marvellous works" (*pala'*) He has done for Israel. These include His "wonders" (or "miracles") and the "judgments" He has pronounced upon their enemies.[119] From the later development in vv. 28–36, the psalmist likely thinks of God's works in Egypt to free Israel from their bondage, v. 5.

B. The Fulfillment of the Covenant 6–15

6–15 David now introduces the theme that he develops in the rest of the psalm. He speaks to the Jews, the descendants of Abraham, the servant of God (cf. v. 42; Gen. 26:24; Exod. 32:13). They were also the descendants of Jacob, chosen by God to be His own nation, v. 6. It is the Lord, Israel's God, Who has sent His judgments throughout the earth as He shaped human history to bring Israel forth as a nation, v. 7. He remembers His covenant with them forever. The phrase "to a thousand generations" idiomatically illustrates God's faithfulness to His covenant (cf. Deut. 7:9; I Chron. 16:15), v. 8.[120]

The Lord first made this covenant with Abraham (Gen. 12:2–3) and then confirmed it later with Isaac (Gen. 26:2–4), v. 9. Still later, He confirmed it with Jacob (Gen. 28:13–15) and to the entire nation (Exod. 6:2–8), v. 10. In the covenant, the Lord promised to give Canaan to Israel as their "lot" (*ḥebel*, see 16:6), the portion of their inheritance, v. 11. He did this when they were "but a few men in number" and "strangers" in the land, an apt description of Abraham's camp in Palestine, v. 12. As time went by, Israel went from "one nation to another," a reference to the wanderings of Abraham, Isaac, and Jacob in the early years, v. 13. Despite these travels, the Lord allowed no one "to do them wrong" (or "oppress them"), punishing them beyond what they deserved. From time to time, God rebuked kings based on their treatment of His people, v. 14. He told these rulers not to touch

[119]Kidner, p. 374, refers to his *Psalms 1–72*, p. 147, where he relates "judgments" to the revelation of God's will. While this is possible, the later development of God's judgments upon Egypt supports the view given above.

[120]In the Talmud, *Ḥagigah* 13*b* says that God had originally intended to give His Law at the end of a thousand generations, "but foreseeing their wickedness, God held back nine hundred and seventy-four generations, and gave the Torah at the end of twenty-six generations from Adam." The view is fanciful, overlooking the omniscience of God, Who knew the end from the beginning.

His "anointed" (*mašîaḥ*, see 2:2) ones.[121] In context, David refers to the patriarchal leaders. The command "Touch not mine anointed" paraphrases the prohibition given to heathen kings.[122] They should likewise do no harm to His "prophets." From the parallelism of the verse, the word also refers to the patriarchs, v. 15.[123]

II. The Work of the Mighty God 16–45

A. The Preparation through Joseph 16–22

16–22 David now gives some of the details by which God worked on behalf of the covenant people. He begins with Joseph. The Lord sent a famine to Palestine, so severe that there was no bread for the people to eat, v. 16. Before this, He had arranged for Joseph to go into Egypt. Joseph had been sold by his brothers to be a "servant" (or "slave," Gen. 37:27–28, 36), v. 17. After being falsely accused by his master's wife, Joseph was put in prison. The Genesis account makes no mention of fetters to "hurt" (*ᶜanâ*, see 35:13) his feet or that he himself was kept in "irons." It is reasonable, however, that this would have taken place at this time (Gen. 39:20). David mentions here what has been preserved in Israel by oral tradition, v. 18.

Eventually, the word Joseph had brought to his family (Gen. 37:7, 9) came to pass. The Lord's word, which governed Joseph's circumstances, "tried" (or "tested," *ṣarap*, see 12:6) him, v. 19. To show his wisdom, the Lord allowed Joseph to interpret Pharaoh's dream. After this, the king released him from prison, v. 20, and made him the "lord" (*ʾadôn*, see 8:1), i.e., governor, over Egypt (Gen. 41:38–44), even over the "substance" (or "possessions," *qinyan*, see 104:24) of Pharaoh, v. 21. David illustrates the power given to Joseph. He had the authority to imprison members of royalty and to teach his "senators [better 'elders'] wisdom [*ḥokmâ*, see 19:7]." This refers

---

[121]The word *mašîaḥ* in the Psalms normally refers to a king, e.g., 18:50; 132:10, 17. While the patriarchs were not kings, they exercised leadership over the developing nation.

[122]See, for example, Gen. 20:3–7; 26:25–31; 35:5.

[123]The biblical record calls only Abraham a prophet, Gen. 20:7. Isaac serves prophetically as a type, Gen. 22:7–14, and also prophesies the future of his sons, Gen. 27:37–40. Jacob likewise foretells the future of his sons, Gen. 48:13–20; 49:1–28.

to Joseph's plans in preparing for the seven-year drought that was to come, v. 22.

B. The Deliverance of Israel 23–38

23–27 The exaltation of Joseph brought Jacob and his family to Egypt, the land descended from Ham (Gen. 10:6, "Mizraim"), v. 23. Over time, Jacob's family grew in size, developing into the nation of Israel, a power greater than the Egyptian nation, v. 24. The Egyptian rulers, fearing that this nation might overthrow their own rule, developed a "hate" (*śane*ʾ, see 5:5) for Israel. One of the later Pharaohs dealt "subtilly" (or "deceitfully") with them, putting them into slavery.[124] God, in His wisdom, brought this relationship to pass in order to prepare Israel to leave Egypt, v. 25. After more than four hundred years in Egypt (Exod. 12:41), the Lord sent Moses and Aaron to lead the nation out of Egypt, v. 26. Under the leading of the Lord, they performed "signs" (*ʾôt*, see 65:8) and miracles in Egypt, v. 27.

28–36 David illustrates these signs and miracles by randomly recalling several of the plagues. In the ninth plague, the Lord sent darkness into the land (Exod. 10:21–23).[125] Moses and Aaron did not rebel at God's command.[126] Moses stretched out his hand toward

[124]It is a reasonable conjecture that this was one of the early Hyksos kings. These overthrew Bebnem, the last king of the fourteenth dynasty, and ruled Egypt ca. 1670–1570 BC. Little historical and archaeological evidence survives from this period. Being usurpers themselves, they may well have feared the power of another foreign group in Egypt, Exod. 1:8.

[125]Fausset, pp. 330–31, calls the darkness "figurative," a reference to the dark cloud of God's wrath that confronted Egypt throughout the plagues. If the remaining plagues are literal, it is difficult to see how this can be explained as figurative. Alexander, p. 441, adopts a similar view. He argues that the rest of the plagues come in order, "the only deviation being very trivial compared with this." He refers with this statement to v. 31, which reverses the third and fourth plagues. Trivial or not, it is a change in order that refutes Alexander's argument.

[126]The logical antecedent of "they" is Moses and Aaron, mentioned in v. 26 and referred to in v. 27. Kidner, pp. 376–77, sees an allusion to the Egyptians in Exod. 11:3 as they respond to Israel's request for gifts. David mentions this clearly in v. 37. It is therefore unlikely that he alludes to it here. Th. Booij, "The Role of Darkness in Psalm CV 28," *VT* 39:2 (1989): 211–12, argues that darkness is the subject. The Lord "sent darkness, which made it dark." The darkness, therefore, did not rebel against His Word. This is possible but unusually phrased. Henry, III, 637, suggests that Israel did not rebel at God's command "to circumcise all among them that had not been circumcised." The three days of darkness protected them during the healing period. This is pure speculation since the OT gives no such command at this

heaven to initiate the miracle, v. 28.[127] In the first of the plagues, the Lord turned the waters of the land into blood, killing the fish in the rivers (Exod. 7:20–21), v. 29. In the second plague, frogs covered the land, even finding their way into the chambers of the Egyptian "kings"[128] (Exod. 8:3–14), v. 30. In the fourth plague, Moses warned Pharaoh and "flies" (or "swarms," *ᶜarob*, see 78:45)[129] invaded the land (Exod. 8:21–24). In the third plague, Moses commanded Aaron to strike the dust. From this symbolic act, "lice" sprang up throughout Egypt (Exod. 8:16–18),[130] v. 31. In the seventh plague, severe hail and ball lightning struck the land, causing the death of men caught in it and destroying the flax and barley crops (Exod. 9:22–32), v. 32. Continuing the effects of the seventh plague, David describes the destruction of vines, fig trees, and trees in their "coasts" (or "territory"), v. 33. The eighth plague brought an innumerable host of

---

time. Bratcher and Reyburn, p. 900, and W. E. Barnes, II, 505, follow some mss of the LXX and omit the word "not." They refer the phrase to the rebellion of Egypt to God's word. While this does not greatly change the passage, the textual evidence for the change is not strong.

[127]These miracles not only judged Egypt for their refusal to do God's will in freeing Israel but also displayed the power of God and the weakness of Egypt's gods. The ninth plague judged the sun god, v. 28. The first plague brought judgment on the Nile, deified by the Egyptians as Hapi, one of the chief gods in their pantheon, v. 29. The second plague caused the frog god Hekt to be a curse to Egypt, v. 30. The fourth plague of "flies" showed God's power as He placed "a division," Exod. 8:23, between Israel and Egypt. The third plague revealed the weakness of Pharaoh's magicians, Exod. 8:18, v. 31. The seventh plague gave the Egyptians the opportunity to believe in the power of Israel's God, Exod. 9:20, vv. 32–33. The eighth plague of locusts devastated the land. It also showed God's omnipotence in bringing the plague from a distance, Exod. 10:13, and taking it away, Exod. 10:19, vv. 34–35. The tenth plague struck the firstborn. The selective nature of this plague showed God's power in judging Egypt. It also showed the weakness of Egypt's gods. Other plagues had showed this weakness one god at a time. In this plague, the Lord takes on all of the living creatures worshiped by Egypt. From the son of Pharaoh to the firstborn of the animals, all suffered death, v. 36.

[128]The plural "kings" either includes the king and others in the royal family or is a plural of majesty, referring to the Pharaoh alone.

[129]Clarke, p. 258, suggests "gadflies" for *ᶜarob*. Cheyne, II, 126, gives "dog-flies." Hengstenberg, III, 264, translates as "vermin." Hirsch, II, 242, understands "beasts of the wilderness." Leslie, p. 163, offers "gnats." Horne, p. 461, renders it "a mixture." We cannot be certain of the nature of the *ᶜarob*.

[130]As with the "flies," we can only speculate on the nature of the "lice." These are generally thought to be some kind of gnat with a bite that causes irritation. Perowne, II, 255, suggests mosquitoes. Jennings, II, 195, translates "stinging-flies." Hirsch, II, 242, gives "vermin." Hengstenberg, III, 264, refers this to "midges."

"locusts" (*ʾarbeh*, see 78:46) and "caterpillars" (or "young locusts"), v. 34. These destroyed those crops that had matured since the earlier plague of hail (Exod. 10:12–15), v. 35. The tenth plague brought death to the firstborn male offspring of both men and animals. These were the "chief of all their strength," anticipated successors to their fathers, v. 36.[131]

37–38 Egypt's will to resist is gone. They urge the Israelites to leave (Exod. 12:31–33). Following the Lord's instructions, the Israelites ask the Egyptians for gifts of silver and gold, to be needed later for the adorning of the tabernacle and its service for worship (Exod. 12:35–36). There are no Israelites that are "feeble" (or that "stumble"). The Lord gives good health so Israel can travel, v. 37.[132] The Egyptians rejoice to see them go because they have come to "fear" (or "dread") them, v. 38.

C. The Exodus from Egypt 39–42

39–42 The nation now leaves Egypt. Pharaoh changes his mind and sends troops to bring them back (Exod. 14:5–9). The Lord, however, sends the cloudy pillar of His presence between Israel and Egypt. This "covering" gave darkness to Egypt, keeping them from pursuing. At the same time, it was a fire giving light to Israel to let them cross the Red Sea (Exod. 14:19–20), v. 39. After entering the wilderness of Sinai, the people ran out of food. The Lord sent them quails in the evening and the "bread of heaven," manna, in the morn-

---

[131]*NIB*, IV, 1105, notes that "the number and order of the plagues differ . . . from both Exod 7:14–12:32 and Ps 78:44–51, perhaps reflecting a different tradition and illustrating that the poet's purpose was not historical accuracy." The comment assumes that the writer seeks completeness in describing the plagues. It is more likely that he simply summarizes the work of God without trying to follow precisely the account in Exodus. Even *NIB* recognizes this with Ps. 78: "The order of plagues differs in Psalm 78 from the Exodus account, but this matters little since the psalmist's concern is less with the past than with the present and future," p. 992.

[132]Leupold, p. 741, notes Deut. 25:17–18 to conclude that this passage presents an idealized view. Deut. 25:17 refers to Exod. 17:8 and the conflict with Amalek. The Amalekites preyed on the sick and elderly at the rear of Israel. Joshua led the nation to fight with them at Rephidim. This was well after the crossing of the Red Sea. Israel had murmured at Marah, Exod. 15:23–24; accused Moses of leading them into the wilderness to starve, Exod. 16:2–3; violated God's commands regarding the manna, Exod. 16:27; and accused Moses of taking them into an area where they would die of thirst, Exod. 17:2–3. The physical problems mentioned in Deut. 25:17–18 came in response to Israel's sin.

ing (Exod. 16:12–13), v. 40. Still later, he provided water gushing from a "rock" (*ṣûr*, see 18:2) struck by the rod of Moses (Exod. 17:5–6), v. 41. In all of these matters, the Lord was faithful to His promise to Abraham that He would free Israel from their bondage (Gen. 15:14–15), v. 42.

D. The Entrance into Palestine 43–45

43–45 The Lord brought Israel from their bondage with joy and "gladness" (*rinnâ*, see 17:1), v. 43. As their possession, He gave them the land He had long before promised to Abraham (Gen. 12:7). They took it from the heathen who had lived there before, which allowed them to inherit the results of the "labour" (*ʿamal*, see 7:14) of the former occupants, v. 44. This land was meant to give the people a place where they might worship God through obedience to His word. This thought leads David to close his song on a note of praise, v. 45.[133]

PSALM 106

This orphan psalm is the first of the "Hallelujah" psalms, those beginning with the word *halᵉlûyah*, "Praise ye the Lord."[134] Although the psalm does not name an author, it is likely that David wrote it. Verses 1 and 47–48 are close to I Chronicles 16:34–36, a Davidic passage. If this is the case, the writing took place when David had the ark of the covenant brought to Jerusalem.[135] He draws spiritual

---

[133]Anthony R. Ceresko, "A Poetic Analysis of Ps 105, with Attention to Its Use of Irony," *Biblica* 64:1 (1983): 21, transfers the "Alleluia" from 104:35 to 105:1 so that "it forms a perfect inclusion with Ps cv 45, *halᵉlū·yah*, 'Praise Yah!'" There is, however, no textual evidence to support this. There is also no literary evidence. The phrase *halᵉlū·yah* occurs often in psalms where it does not form an inclusio with another *halᵉlū·yah*, e.g., 111:1, 112:2; 116:19; 117:2.

[134]While the phrase "Praise ye the Lord" (*halᵉlû·yah* or *halᵉlû yah*) occurs twenty-four times in the Psalms, it begins only ten of them: 106, 111, 112, 113, 135, 146, 147, 148, 149, and 150. Of these, all but 111 and 112 begin and end with the phrase. The phrase *halᵉlû·yah* occurs only in the Psalms.

[135]Alexander, p. 444, sees the psalm as a paraphrase of Daniel's prayer, Dan. 9. *NIB*, IV, 1110, and Leslie, p. 165, make the psalm exilic or postexilic. These views require the Chronicler to put these words into David's mouth. Nothing of the history

lessons from the up-and-down history of Israel.[136] He briefly summarizes several of Israel's failures that illustrate God's patience with the nation and His mercy toward His people. This psalm ends the fourth division in the book of Psalms.

I. The Desire for Blessing 1–5

1–3 David gives praise and thanks to the Lord for His goodness. As evidence of this, he recognizes that the Lord's "mercy" (or "steadfast love," *ḥesed*, see 5:7) is everlasting, v. 1. With two rhetorical questions, he shows the impossibility of recounting all that God has done. No one can describe the mighty works of the Lord. No one can adequately proclaim the praise He deserves, v. 2. "Blessed" (*ʾašrê*, see 1:1) by God are those who continually practice "judgment" (better "justice") and righteous deeds, v. 3.

4–5 David prays that the Lord will remember him as He extends favor to His people. The thought is not that the Lord has forgotten him but that he wants the Lord to include him in the blessings He bestows. The parallel request, "visit [*paqad*, see 8:4] me with thy salvation," is similar to David's words in I Chronicles 16:35. In both places, the words refer to God's continuing deliverance of His people, not to a specific crisis faced by the nation, v. 4.[137] This deliverance will let him see the "good of thy chosen," the blessings that will come upon God's people. He will rejoice in the joy of the nation and glory together with the Lord's "inheritance" (or "possession"), v. 5.

II. The Confession of Sin 6–43

David now recalls the sin-prone history of the nation. He summarizes eight times in which Israel turned from the Lord to its own ways. The account is generally chronological.

---

in the psalm comes after David. The mere fact that v. 47 refers to being among the heathen proves nothing. Israel's sins caused them to have captives in almost every generation.

[136]The introduction to Ps. 78 briefly discusses the historical psalms.

[137]Henry, p. 640, understands the "salvation" as the salvation of the soul. The overall context of the psalm, however, refers to the nation. David thinks generally of the continuing favor of God toward Israel.

A. Egypt 6–12

6 David introduces this portion with a general confession of the nation's sin. As their ancestors have sinned, so have the people. The three words "sinned," "iniquity," and "wickedly" describe the many-sided failures of Israel. They "have sinned," falling short of God's standards. They have "committed iniquity," rebelling against the Lord. They have "done wickedly," carrying out evil activities, v. 6.

7 David introduces the first of the illustrations that show the nation's bent to sin. The ancestors of Israel "understood [or 'considered'] not" God's "wonders [*palaʾ*, see 9:1] in Egypt," the miraculous plagues brought upon Egypt, as showing that God could deliver them. They did not remember these "mercies" (or "steadfast loves," *ḥesed*) but instead "provoked" God by their faithlessness at the Red Sea. Despite all that the Lord had done to bring about their deliverance from Egyptian bondage, they accused Moses of bringing them into the wilderness to die from the attack of the Egyptian army (Exod. 14:10–12). As it consistently appears in Exodus, the "Red sea" (*yam sûp*) is literally "reed sea." This does not suggest that the waters were shallow. It merely represents the name given to the body of water because of the plants growing nearby, v. 7.

8–12 Despite Israel's lack of faith, the Lord saved them "for his name's sake," His reputation as a powerful God.[138] Had the Lord let the Egyptians take the nation captive once more, He would have appeared to be a weak God. To prevent this, He delivered Israel. This openly showed His "mighty power" (or "power"; no need for the adjective since all of God's power is mighty), v. 8. In Israel's deliverance, the Lord "rebuked" the Gulf of Suez so that it no longer opened into the Red Sea. Israel passed through the waters on the dried-up bed of the waters (Exod. 14:22) just as if it were the wilderness they later traversed, v. 9. This miraculous work delivered the people from "them that hated [*śaneʾ*, see 5:5] them," Egypt. He "redeemed" (*gaʾal*, see 19:14) them from the power of Egypt, v. 10. None of the Egyptian army that followed them into the waters survived (Exod. 14:27–28), v. 11. Then Israel believed God's words of deliverance and sang praise to Him (Exod. 15:1–19), v. 12.

---

[138]Note 94 at 5:11 summarizes the Lord's "name."

B. Wilderness 13–15

13–15 David continues to illustrate Israel's lack of faith in the Lord. Despite God's continuing care of the nation, they "soon," in a few days, "forgat" His miracles and failed to seek His "counsel" (*ᶜeṣâ*, see 1:1), v. 13. He refers to Israel's rejection of the manna provided for them (Num. 11:4–9, 31–33). They longed for the leeks, onions, and garlic of Egypt and criticized Moses for bringing them out of their bondage. This was a direct challenge to God, the One Who had led Moses in his actions, v. 14. The Lord gave the nation food but also "sent leanness into their soul," a wasting disease that took many lives. This illustration describes the pattern that occurs often in the OT. Forgetting God's mercy brings sin, and sin brings judgment. The principle remains true today, v. 15.

C. Rebellion 16–18

16–18 Some time later, a group led by Dathan and Abiram envied the positions of Moses and Aaron (Num. 16:1–40).[139] Despite God's appointment of Moses and Aaron, this group felt that they should have some of the leadership. The phrase "saint [or 'holy one'] of the Lord" refers to Aaron's position rather than to his personal holiness, v. 16. God judged the rebels by sending an earthquake that caused the earth to open and close over them and their families, v. 17.[140] He then sent fire to consume the rest of the rebels, v. 18.

---

[139]Num. 16:1 also mentions Korah and On as rebels. On is not mentioned again in any of the passages dealing with the incident. Julius H. Greenstone, *Numbers* (Philadelphia: Jewish Publication Society of America, 1948), p. 167, suggests that his part was minor or that he withdrew before taking part. *Unger's Bible Dictionary*, p. 809, refers to a rabbinical tradition that his wife persuaded him to withdraw from the others. Rawlinson, II, 426, excludes Korah from the judgment of v. 17 since he is not mentioned. He includes him in the judgment by fire that followed. Num. 26:10, however, makes it clear that the supernatural judgment of being swallowed by the earth included Korah. David may have omitted Korah's name out of consideration for his descendants, still associated with David in his reign. The introduction to Pss. 42–43 discusses "the sons of Korah."

[140]*Baba Bathra* 74*a* relates a fanciful story regarding those who were swallowed by the earth. Supposedly, smoke still issues from the spot. If you bend down, you hear voices saying, "Moses and his Torah are truth and we are liars." On the thirtieth day of the month, "Gehenna causes them to turn back here, as [one turns] flesh in a pot, and they say this: Moses and his law are truth and we are liars."

D. Mt. Sinai 19–23

19–22 David now recalls Israel's sin at the time when God gave the law to Moses (Exod 32:1–14). Despite the "thunders and lightnings, and a thick cloud upon the mount . . . and the smoke thereof . . . as the smoke of a furnace" (Exod. 19:16–18), evidences of God's presence, the people tired of waiting after forty days. They persuaded Aaron to make a golden calf, an image to remind them of the Lord. Rather than worshiping the invisible God by faith, they worshiped this visible image. This followed the pattern of worship they had seen in Egypt. It also violated the law the Lord had already given orally (Exod. 20:4–5). In some way, Horeb refers to Mt. Sinai. It is either a particular peak of the mountain or a general name for the mountain range, v. 19. This idolatry degraded Israel. Rather than the "glory" of worshiping by faith, they required an image of "an ox that eateth grass," the golden calf. Paul quotes from the LXX version of this verse in Romans 1:23, v. 20. They forgot the God Who had saved them from Egypt by performing "wondrous works" (*pala*ʾ, see 9:1), miracles on their behalf. These were done in "the land of Ham" and "the Red sea." Ham, the youngest son of Noah, was the progenitor of Mizraim (Gen. 10:6), from whom Egypt was settled. Rather than following God's will, the people turned to their own will, vv. 21–22.

23 God pronounced judgment on the nation (Exod. 32:9–10). Initially, He announced His plan to destroy the nation and begin anew with Moses. Only the intercession of Moses on the people's behalf turned the Lord from unleashing His "wrath" (*ḥemâ*, see 6:1) to "destroy" (*šaḥat*, see 14:1) them. Moses noted that such judgment would make God appear weak, unable to fulfill the covenant He had given to Abraham, Isaac, and Jacob (Exod. 32:11–14). This concern for His glory kept God from carrying out such complete judgment, v. 23.

E. Kadesh-barnea 24–27

24–25 David now turns to Israel's failure to go into the Promised Land. From Kadesh-barnea, the nation sent spies into the land. These brought back a negative report that made the people weep and decide to return to Egypt. Despite the positive report from Caleb and Joshua, the nation refused to obey God's leading (Num. 14:1–10*a*), v. 24. They murmured against Moses and Aaron, saying that it would have been better had they died in Egypt or in the wilderness, v. 25.

26–27 Once again, the Lord "lifted up his hand," taking an oath that He would destroy the nation in the wilderness (Num. 14:11–12). Once more, Moses interceded for the nation (Num. 14:13–17). In response, the Lord pardoned them (Num. 14:20). But because of their sin, He pronounced a forty-year judgment that would bring about the death of Israel's adults (Num. 14:29–35), v. 26. Verse 27 extends the judgment beyond the immediate context of Israel's sin at Kadesh-barnea. In later times, Israel's continued sin brought the destruction of their children and their dispersion among foreign nations, v. 27.

F. Moab 28–31

28–29 Numbers 25 records Israel's sin with the heathen nation of Moab. After first intermarrying with the heathen, the people joined the Moabites in worshiping Baal-peor. The Moabites worshiped this Baal god on Mt. Peor (Num. 25:1–3), a peak whose location is uncertain. They "ate the sacrifices of the dead," sacrifices offered to the false and therefore dead Moabite gods, v. 28.[141] Their "inventions" (or "deeds") provoked God to anger, causing Him to send a "plague" upon the people (Num. 25:4–5). The plague is the judicial decree of Moses that the idolaters should be slain, v. 29.

30–31 In the midst of God's judgment, an Israelite man named Zimri openly brought a heathen woman, Cozbi, to his tent. In the midst of their liaison, the priest Phinehas killed them by plunging a spear through both of them. God was so pleased at this concern for maintaining the purity of the nation that He stayed the "plague," the judgment that had begun. Paul refers to this incident in I Corinthians 10:8, v. 30. The Lord saw the action of Phinehas as evidence of his righteousness. He rewarded him by making him the high priest with that office to continue through his descendants "for evermore" (*l^{e}dor wador*, see 10:6), as long as the Levitical priesthood would last, v. 31.

G. Meribah 32–33

32–33 David remembers an earlier sin of Israel, one that involved Moses as well as the people. The nation had come to the region of

[141]Kidner, pp. 380–81, understands the phrase to refer to sacrifices to the dead, cf. Deut. 26:14. Perowne, II, 264, sees the phrase as speaking of sacrifices offered in connection with "necromantic rites." Horne, p. 469, mentions the possibility of sacrifices offered to men "deified after death." Num. 25:2, however, refers to the sacrifices as those offered to the "gods" of Moab. This suggests the view given above.

Kadesh, where they lacked water (Num. 20:11–13). As they normally did, the people blamed Moses for the problem. After Moses prayed, the Lord told him to "speak" to a large rock in the area and it would gush forth a river of water to meet the needs of the nation. Moses, however, allowed the attitude of the people to anger him. For this reason, the place is called "the waters of strife [or 'Meribah,' the name given in Num. 20:13]." Rather than speaking to the rock, Moses struck it twice with his rod. This violated the typical meaning of the rock. The rock having been struck once earlier (Exod. 17:6), a picture of Christ smitten once for the sins of mankind (John 7:37–39; I Cor. 10:4), it did not need to be smitten again (Heb. 10:12). Striking the rock disobeyed God's command and brought judgment on Moses. This was the time that God confirmed to Moses that he would not enter the land of promise, v. 32. The actions of the people provoked Moses' spirit[142] so that he "spoke unadvisedly [or 'rashly']" as he rebuked the people. His actions brought judgment, v. 33.

H. Promised Land 34–43

34–39 After Israel came into the land of God's promise, they ignored His commands to rid the land of the heathen (e.g., Deut. 7:16, 23–26). The book of Judges records instance after instance to show Israel's disobedience. Rather than driving out the heathen, Israel put them to tribute (e.g., Judg. 1:21, 28–33, 35), v. 34. The placing of earthly riches above obedience to God brought Israel under heathen influence. The people of God learned the evil practices of the heathen, v. 35, and began to serve their false gods. These were a "snare" to Israel, leading them away from the true God and into a system of false worship, v. 36. They even fell so far into degradation that they sacrificed their children to "devils" (or "demons," e.g., II Kings 16:3; 17:17; 21:6), v. 37. This sin is so great that David emphasizes it by repeating his statement of Israel's actions. The people shed the innocent blood of their children by sacrificing them to the heathen idols. So frequent was this that the land was considered "polluted with blood," v. 38. Israel became spiritually unclean with these evil deeds. They committed spiritual fornication with their practice of worshiping the gods of the heathen, v. 39.

---

[142]Among others, Calvin, IV, 235, and Clarke, p. 261, refer the phrase "his spirit" to God's spirit. There is, however, no antecedent to support this. The natural reference is to Moses. This makes v. 33*a* parallel with v. 32*a*.

40–43 The sin of Israel caused God's "wrath" (*ʾap*, see 2:5) to burn toward them. He regarded the people of His inheritance as an abomination, v. 40. To punish them, He gave them into the power of the people whose gods they had worshiped. The people that "hated" (*śaneʾ*, see 5:5) Israel ruled them, v. 41. Their foes oppressed them, subjecting them to their power, v. 42. The Lord delivered them from this oppression "many times," an act seen regularly in the book of Judges. Israel, however, soon forgot God's mercy and turned back to the false gods. They "provoked" (better "rebelled against") the Lord with their "counsel" (*ʿeṣâ*, see 1:1) and were brought low in their iniquity, v. 43.

III. The Need of Mercy 44–48

44–46 Despite the need for judging Israel's sin, when they cried out to God for mercy, He heard their "cry" (*rinnâ*, see 17:1), e.g., Judg. 3:9, 15; 4:3, v. 44. He remembered the covenant that He had made with Abraham, Isaac, and Jacob (cf. Ps. 105:8–10). He "repented" (or "had compassion"), no longer extending punishment but now giving them abundant "mercies" (*ḥesed*, see 5:7), v. 45. He caused them "to be pitied," to be extended compassion, by their captors, v. 46.[143]

47–48 Anticipating times when the nation will face enemy opposition, David prays that the Lord will do for them in the future what He has done in the past. They then will offer thanks to the "name" (see v. 8) of God for His deliverance, and they will "triumph" (better "boast," *šabaḥ*, see 63:3) in their praise to Him, v. 47. David "bless[es]" (*barak*, see 5:12) the Lord with an everlasting blessing. He urges the people to say "Amen" (*ʾamen*, see 41:13) an affirmation of what has been said. He ends the psalm as he began: *halᵉlû·yah*, "Praise ye the Lord," v. 48.[144]

---

[143]On the basis of v. 46, many authors make the psalm postexilic, with Cyrus the king who deals compassionately with Israel, Isa. 44:28. The view requires that vv. 1, 47–48, be put into David's mouth by the author of I Chron. 16:34–36. This, of course, means that David did not speak what the passage attributes to him. It is better to refer v. 46 to other historical incidents in Israel's history, e.g., the willingness of their captors to put them to tribute or slavery rather than death. Since the OT gives only a summary of the nation's history, we cannot dogmatically refer v. 46 to the Babylonian captivity.

[144]The closing phrase may have been added later. Each of the five books in Psalms ends with a doxology of praise to the Lord for His faithfulness. See also 41:13; 72:19; 89:52; and 150:6.

BOOK V

PSALM 107

The psalm begins Book V, the final collection of psalms. It is a song of thanksgiving,[1] marked by the refrain "O that men would praise the Lord for his goodness, and for his wonderful works to the children of men." These words occur toward the end of the first four sections of the psalm (vv. 8, 15, 21, 31). There is no indication of the author or the date of writing other than that it must have been post-exilic, following the deliverances from danger mentioned. The psalm remembers various deliverances of the nation, but it is not possible to identify them with certainty.[2]

There is a pattern in the first four deliverances. The psalmist first describes the people's **plight** (vv. 4–5, 10–12, 17–18, 23–27). This causes them to cry out to the Lord in **prayer** (vv. 6*a*, 13*a*, 19*a*, 28*a*). In response, He provides **preservation** from their dangers (vv. 6*b*–7, 13*b*–14, 19*b*–20, 28*b*–30). The people acknowledge His gracious deliverance by offering Him **praise** (vv. 8–9, 15–16, 21–22, 31–32). The final deliverance (vv. 33–43) changes the pattern as the psalmist summarizes God's **provision** for the nation. Even here, the passage ends with a note of praise, v. 43.

It is still right to follow this pattern. When Christians find themselves in some plight, their great resource is prayer. God's gracious preservation as He responds to our prayers should lead believers to sound a chorus of praise to Him.

---

[1]The introduction to Ps. 18 summarizes the songs of thanksgiving.

[2]Henry, III, 647, sees the psalm as describing God's "providential care of the children of men in general." Nothing in the psalm, however, forces us to expand its scope to the nations as a whole. It would be unusual to see this emphasis in the psalms. On the basis of the deliverance from storms (vv. 23–32), Moll, p. 545, dates the psalm in the Maccabean period (con. the discussion of vv. 23–27). McCurdy, writing in Moll, pp. 545–46, understands the psalm as not being historical but a "broad and varied record of human experience." Neither of these views is common in the Psalms. Kidner, p. 383, suggests that the descriptions of deliverance are "four different ways of depicting the plight from which the nation had been delivered." He makes this the return from the Exile in Babylon. His approach requires us to spiritualize the descriptions. The wilderness wanderings, the captivity, the sickness, and the storm all become pictures of the Exile. Eaton, p. 256, considers the four deliverances as "imaginary examples illustrating deliverance from extreme danger." How can actual deliverances from Israel's history be "imaginary"? It is just as reasonable to understand the psalmist as praising God for His care of the nation over the years of its history. The different parts of the psalm then illustrate His care.

I. Deliverance from the Wilderness 1–9

1–3 The psalmist begins by praising the Lord. He anticipates a description of several different times in which the Lord has delivered His people. In view of this, it is appropriate to begin with a note of praise. The thought occurs widely. The opening phrase, "O give thanks unto the Lord," also occurs in 105:1; 106:1; 118:1, 29; and 136:1. The final phrase, "His mercy endureth for ever," occurs (with differing translations) in 100:5; 106:1; 107:1; 117:2; 118:2, 3, 4, 29; and twenty-six times in Psalm 136. The full verse occurs with minor variations elsewhere in 106:1; 118:1, 29; 136:1, 2, 3, 26; and I Chronicles 16:34, 41.

The psalmist thanks the Lord, a good God Who extends His "mercy" (or "steadfast love," *ḥesed*, see 5:7) to the nation forever, v. 1. The ones He has redeemed should speak freely of His deliverance. Without being specific, the psalmist refers to some deliverance from an enemy of the nation, v. 2.[3] At that time, the Lord gathered exiles from different areas. If the psalmist thinks of the gathering of the people from Egypt, the four directions ("east . . . west . . . north . . . south [or 'sea'])[4] refer to their coming together from all parts of the land in preparation for the Exodus, v. 3.

[3]Hengstenberg, III, 285–86, sets the psalm at the celebration of the Feast of Tabernacles, after the return from the Captivity. While the psalm may refer to Israel's deliverance from captivity, it is difficult to fit vv. 4–7 into the return from Babylon. The road from Babylon, through Israel, and on to Egypt, was a well-defined trail. There would have been no reason to leave it to wander in the wilderness. It is more likely that the psalmist thinks of the Exodus from Egypt and the subsequent forty-year wandering in the wilderness.

[4]The word translated "south," *yam*, is so rendered because of its contrast to *ṣapôn*, "north." The word *yam*, however, nowhere else refers to the south. The word occurs more than three hundred times referring to the "sea" or to the "west." Dahood, III, 81, refers it to the Gulf of Aqabah, south of Palestine. In the context here, it likely refers to the Nile River, elsewhere called a "sea," Nah. 3:8, and which flows from the south in Egypt. Jennings, II, 213, relates *yam* to the "southern sea," the Red Sea, also a possible view. Delitzsch, III, 165, refers *yam* to the southwest where the Mediterranean meets Egypt. He sees the directions as referring to exiles from "all countries" that have come to join the returned exiles from Babylon. There is, however, no record of people coming from this region. Several translations, e.g., NRSV, NIV, accept an emendation to *yamîn*, "west," with no textual evidence. John Jarick, "The Four Corners of Psalm 107," *CBQ* 59:2 (1997): 274, relates the four words to the first four sections of the psalm. The "east" represents the eastern desert in Palestine, vv. 4–9; the "west" is the place where the sun sets, thus standing for the darkness of vv. 10–16; the "north" is the place from which evil often comes, e.g., Jer.

4–7 As the Israelites returned, they wandered in the wilderness "in a solitary place" (or "in a wasted place") where there were no cities in which to dwell, v. 4. They grew hungry and thirsty and became discouraged, v. 5. In their trouble, they cried to the Lord in prayer. In answer, He delivered them from their "distresses" (*m*ᵉ*ṣûqâ*, see 25:17), e.g., Exodus 15:25; 16:13; 17:6, v. 6. He led them in the right way to "a city of habitation," the phrase collectively representing the cities where the nation settled after entering Canaan, v. 7.

8–9 The psalmist now uses for the first time the refrain that will recur throughout the psalm. He had hinted at this in v. 1, where the phrase "O give thanks unto the Lord" (*ḥodû layhwah*) is similar to "Oh that men would praise the Lord" (*yôdû layhwah*). In addition, "mercy" in v. 1 is identical to "goodness" in v. 8. He urges men to "praise" (or "give thanks to") the Lord for His "goodness" (or "steadfast love," *ḥesed*) and for His "wonderful works" (*pala*ʾ, see 9:1) as He cares for His people, v. 8. He summarizes this provision during the Exodus. At that time, the Lord satisfied the "longing" (or "thirsty") person and filled the hungry person with "goodness" (or "good things"), v. 9.

II. Deliverance from the Captivity 10–16

10–12 The phrase "such as sit in darkness" is better translated as independent from v. 9: "There were those dwelling in darkness." The psalmist turns to the deliverance of Israel from their Babylonian bondage. They knew the gloom of captivity, and the shadows of death[5] surrounded them. They were bound by "affliction" (*ʿanî*, see 9:12) and by iron chains. Luke 1:79 quotes the verse as a picture of spiritual bondage, v. 10. This punishment came on the nation because of their sin. They had rebelled against God's word, which had been given them by godly leaders and by the prophets. They had "contemned" (or "spurned") the "counsel" (*ʿeṣâ*, see 1:1) given them by "the most High [God]" (*ʿelyôn*, see 7:17), v. 11. For this reason, the Lord had "brought [them] down" (or "humbled" them) with hard

---

1:13–14; 50:41–42, and so pictures the illness of vv. 17–22; the "sea" is the place under discussion in vv. 23–32. Since all of these words—east, west, north, sea—elsewhere stand for good as well as bad, Jarick's position is not likely here.

[5]For the phrase "shadow of death" (*ṣalmawet*), see 23:4.

"labour" (*ʿamal*, see 7:14). When they "fell down" (or "stumbled"), no one helped them, v. 12.

13–16 The troubles caused them to cry out to the Lord. He responded to their prayer by delivering them from their "distresses" (*mᵉṣûqâ*, see 25:17), v. 13. He brought them from the gloom of captivity and the "shadow of death" (*ṣalmawet*, see 23:4); cf. v. 10. He broke apart the bands that held them in captivity, v. 14. Once more, the psalmist urges men to "praise" (or "give thanks to") the Lord for His "goodness" (or "steadfast love," *ḥesed*) and for His "wonderful works" (*palaʾ*) on behalf of the people, v. 15. He has broken the gates of "brass" (or "bronze")[6] and the iron bars that held them in Babylon, v. 16.

III. Deliverance from Sickness 17–22

17–18 The psalmist turns to an area that cannot be related certainly to any OT event although some of the national plagues satisfy the circumstances (e.g., Num. 16:44–48; 25:1–9). Those "fools" (*ʾwl*, see 38:5) who have committed transgressions and iniquities are "afflicted" (*ʿanâ*, see 35:13). The next verse shows that physical afflictions are in view, v. 17. The illness causes them to lose their appetite and brings them near to death, v. 18.

19–22 Verses 19 and 13 are identical in the MT. When these afflicted ones cry out in prayer to the Lord, He delivers them from their "distresses" (*mᵉṣûqâ*), v. 19. He sends His word, the command that the sickness should depart, and the sickness disappears. He delivers them from their "destruction" (*šᵉḥît*),[7] v. 20. The psalmist again urges men to "praise" (or "give thanks to") the Lord for

---

[6]Herodotus described Babylon, "The wall contains a hundred gates in the circuit of the wall, all of bronze, with posts and lintels of the same." *The Histories* 1.179. Isa. 45:2 uses the same phrasing in prophesying the destruction of Babylon by Cyrus.

[7]The word *šᵉḥît* occurs only here in the Psalms. In Lam. 4:20, it is translated "pits," a rendering that lies behind the NIV translation here of "grave." The root *šḥh* means "to bow down." It occurs with this sense in polite greeting, Gen. 19:1; 23:7, in falling down, Isa. 45:14; and in worship of God, Pss. 5:7; 66:4; or of idols, Jer. 1:16; 8:2. Used here of sickness, it refers to the unexpected falling down of the soul, i.e., early death. The plural here intensifies the thought. Delitzsch, III, 168, gives the possible view that the "pits" were the "deep afflictions into which they were plunged." Weiser, p. 687, suggests that this is "a priestly oracle foretelling future salvation." While possible, the view goes against the context that describes past events.

His "goodness" (or "steadfast love," *ḥesed*) and for His "wonderful works" (*palaʾ*) to them, v. 21.[8] Let them also make offerings to express "thanksgiving" (*tôdâ*, see 26:7) and openly declare with "rejoicing" (*rinnâ*, see 17:1) what the Lord has done for them, v. 22.

IV. Deliverance from the Storm 23–32

23–27 The psalmist now turns to a general danger faced by mariners. Again, he shows the power of the Lord to deliver His people from dangers. Those whose trading ventures send them out "in great waters," the Mediterranean Sea and beyond,[9] v. 23, see the power of God displayed. They see His works and "wonders" (*palaʾ*, see 9:1) in the waters, v. 24. He commands, and the storms bring powerful waves, v. 25.[10] The psalmist describes the height of the waves and the troughs between them. They seem to rise up into heaven and sink down deeply. The soul of the mariners "is melted" (or "becomes faint") as they face the storm, v. 26. They reel to and fro, staggering like drunken men as they make their way along the deck of the ship. They are "at their wit's [*ḥokmâ*, see 19:7] end," having no wisdom to help them overcome their danger, v. 27.

[8]For an unknown reason, the Masoretes placed an inverted *nun* before vv. 21–26 and v. 40 to indicate that these verses were misplaced. The inverted *nun* at v. 40 is similar to those in vv. 21–26:

׆ יוֹד֣וּ לַיהוָ֣ה חַסְדּ֑וֹ וְנִפְלְאוֹתָ֗יו לִבְנֵ֥י אָדָֽם׃
׆ וְ֭יִזְבְּחוּ זִבְחֵ֣י תוֹדָ֑ה וִיסַפְּר֖וּ מַעֲשָׂ֣יו בְּרִנָּֽה׃
׆ יוֹרְדֵ֣י הַ֭יָּם בָּאֳנִיּ֑וֹת עֹשֵׂ֥י מְ֝לָאכָ֗ה בְּמַ֣יִם רַבִּֽים׃
׆ הֵ֣מָּה רָ֭אוּ מַעֲשֵׂ֣י יְהוָ֑ה וְ֝נִפְלְאוֹתָ֗יו בִּמְצוּלָֽה׃
׆ וַיֹּ֗אמֶר וַֽ֭יַּעֲמֵד ר֣וּחַ סְעָרָ֑ה וַתְּרוֹמֵ֥ם גַּלָּֽיו׃
׆ יַעֲל֣וּ שָׁ֭מַיִם יֵרְד֣וּ תְהוֹמ֑וֹת נַ֝פְשָׁ֗ם בְּרָעָ֥ה תִתְמוֹגָֽג׃

Rosh Hashanah 17*b* states that the psalmist inserted the extra letters "to indicate that if they cried before the final sentence they were answered, but if they cried after the final sentence they were not answered." This explanation is contrived and goes counter to the teaching on prayer elsewhere. We can only speculate on the rabbinical purpose for this.

[9]Jacob's dying blessing referred to Zebulon as a "haven of ships" (Gen. 49:13). Moses spoke of trade with Egypt by ships (Deut. 28:68). The historical and prophetic sections of the OT have many references to trade by ships. Jon. 1:3–5 describes the storm that confronted Jonah when he tried to flee from the Lord's commission.

[10]The vivid description of the storm in Acts 27:14–41 illustrates the power of storms on the Mediterranean. Storms on the ocean may exceed the strength of storms on the Mediterranean.

28–32 Having come to the end of their own resources, the mariners cry out to the Lord. He delivers them from the storms that bring "distresses" (*m^e ṣûqâ*), the fear they experience as they face the storm, v. 28. He calms the waters so that the waves no longer beat against the ship, v. 29. The mariners rejoice that the waters are quiet. The Lord now brings them to their "haven" (*maḥôz*),[11] their intended port, v. 30. For the final time, the psalmist calls upon men to "praise" (or "give thanks to") the Lord for His "goodness" (or "steadfast love," *ḥesed*) and for His "wonderful works" (*pala*ᵓ) to them, v. 31. They should openly exalt Him in public assemblies of the people and their "elders," the civic leaders, v. 32.

V. Deliverance from Judgment 33–43

33–34 The final portion of the psalm gives two illustrations of deliverance from judgment, vv. 33–38 and vv. 39–43. The first illustration focuses on the effects of God's judgment on nature. This happened several times in the OT (Gen. 19:24–25; I Kings 17:1; Isa. 19:5–10). The Lord dries up rivers, turning them into wilderness. The springs of water become dry parcels of dirt, v. 33. The land that had been fruitful becomes "barrenness" (or "a salt waste"). All of this comes because of the wickedness of those dwelling in the land, v. 34.

35–38 After satisfying His judgment, the Lord begins to bless the land. He changes the wilderness into "standing [or 'a pool of'] water." The parched ground becomes springs of water, v. 35. The Lord leads the hungry to dwell there, where they can establish a city in which to live, v. 36. They can sow the fields and plant vineyards that will bring forth "fruits of increase" (or "a fruitful harvest"), v. 37. He "bless[es]" (*barak*, see 5:12) them with children so that their families multiply. He keeps their "cattle," the domestic farm animals, from decreasing, v. 38.

39–40 The second illustration focuses on the people. It likely comes from the Babylonian conquest of Judah, although enemies conquered the people at other times also (e.g., Judg. 6:3–6; II Kings 10:32–33; 25:4–6). They are "minished" (or "diminished") and "brought low" (or "bowed down") through the trials they face. These

---

[11]The word *maḥôz* occurs only here. An Akkadian cognate means "city, town." The LXX translated λιμένα, "harbor," and the Vulgate *portum*, also "harbor."

include oppressions from others, "affliction" (or "calamity"), and the resulting sorrow that comes upon them, v. 39. The "princes" (or "nobles") suffer contemptuous treatment. They wander through the wilderness region, where there is no road to follow, v. 40.

41–43 The Lord is able to restore prosperity in the land. He makes the "poor" (or "needy") dwell on "high" (*śagab*, see 20:1), safe from "affliction" (*ᶜanî*, see 9:12). The Lord multiplies his family with as many children as a flock of sheep or goats, v. 41. The righteous sees these things and is glad. In contrast, "iniquity" (or "unrighteousness," *ᶜawlâ*, see 7:3) shuts its mouth, no longer able to boast of its success, v. 42. The psalmist closes with an appeal. If there is a "wise" (see *ḥokmâ*, 19:7) man, let him "observe" (or "give heed") to these things. Let him "understand" (or diligently consider") the "lovingkindness" (or "steadfast love," *ḥesed*, see 5:7) of the Lord, v. 43.

PSALM 108

This is a "song" (*šîr*) or "psalm" (*mizmôr*)[12] written originally by David. Either David or some later psalmist combined the thought from two previous psalms. Verses 1–5 come from Psalm 57:8–12 and vv. 6–13 from Psalm 60:5–12. The text is not identical but is close enough that the connection is clear. We may explain the differences as the psalmist's attempt to draw on memory in joining the two portions.

The background of Psalm 57 places it early in David's life, while the setting of Psalm 60 is within a few years of David's becoming king over the united nation. There is no historical information in this psalm to date it.[13] The nation clearly faced some crisis, vv. 6, 13, due to God's judgment, v. 11. The psalmist writes to express praise to the Lord, vv. 1–5, and the nation's reliance on His mercy, vv. 12–13. The

[12]For the words "psalm" (*mizmôr*) and "song" (*šîr*), see the introduction to Ps. 30.

[13]Fausset, III, 341, places it during the return from the Babylonian captivity. If so, the title reflects David's authorship of Pss. 57 and 60.

fact that Psalm 108 is a conflation of the two other psalms makes it later than the others.[14] For comments, see 57:8–12 and 60:5–12.

PSALM 109

David, the author, prepares the psalm for the "chief musician" to use in the nation's worship. In this individual lament, David pronounces imprecations on his enemies, vv. 6–15, 17–20.[15] These wicked and deceitful men have lied about David, v. 2, and fought against him though he is innocent of wrongdoing, v. 3. David sees himself as righteous and therefore asks that God extend His steadfast love to him, vv. 21, 27. He will respond with open praise to the Lord, v. 30.

We cannot be certain of the situation. David's enemy held some office, v. 8. This may support Saul's persecution, the accusation of Doeg, or some other peril in David's life.[16] The opposition is prolonged, involving repeated lies, expressions of hatred, vv. 2, 3, 20, 28, and betrayal of friendship, vv. 4, 5. The fact that David does not mention either the tabernacle or his position as king suggests the earlier part of his life.[17]

The curses David invokes here involve some of the harshest imprecations in the Psalms. This has brought about several attempts

---

[14]Kidner, *Psalms 73–150*, p. 387, argues its later date based on its use of the name "God" by itself. It occurs here in vv. 1, 5, 7, 11, and 13. He notes that the name occurs by itself "in only one other place in this Fifth Book of the Psalter (144:9)." The argument is trivial. The name occurs numerous times with only the personal pronoun, e.g., 115:2, 3; 147:1, 7, 12, or in connection with the name "LORD."

[15]Within the group of imprecatory psalms, 35, 59, 69, 70, 109, and 140 are individual laments and 58, 83, and 137 are community laments. The introduction to Ps. 35 discusses reasons that may have justified the imprecations.

[16]Henry, III, 654, mentions the possibility that David wrote the psalm "when his son Absalom rebelled against him." While this is possible, the psalm does not clearly identify its setting.

[17]Oesterley, II, 458, rejects David's authorship and makes the psalm "late post-exilic." The view ignores Peter's comment in Acts 1:16–20. Peter conflates Pss. 69:25 and 109:8 and specifically refers them to "the mouth of David."

to explain the passage.[18] There is no serious problem here. We find imprecations throughout the Bible, even in the teaching of the Lord (Matt. 23:13–36). David sees himself as righteous and his enemies as wicked, guilty of great sin. His pronouncement of judgment is a vivid reminder that the ungodly will face divine retribution for their sin. David uses illustrations drawn from life to portray this judgment. Because of v. 8, the psalm may be considered as typically messianic.[19] The apostles relied on this verse in deciding to replace the betrayer Judas, Acts 1:20*b*.

I. Plight of David 1–5

1–5 The phrase "hold not thy peace" is better "be not silent." David approaches the God Whom he praises, v. 1, concerning those that oppose him. Wicked and deceitful men have spoken "against" him.[20] They have lied about him, v. 2. They have surrounded David with their hatred. They fight him although there is no cause for their opposition, v. 3. These foes are former friends to whom David has shown love. In response, they have become his adversaries. He, however, continues to offer his "prayer" (*t^epillâ*, see 4:1) for deliverance, v. 4.[21] They have set evil in place of his good to them. They have

[18]Alexander, III, 92–93, sees the sufferings of David as those of Israel and a type of Messiah's "sufferings . . . from the treachery of Judas." The imprecations are stronger than they would have been "in reference to ordinary criminals." Leupold, p. 764, understands an "unspoken presupposition . . . [that] should the wicked opponent turn from his ungodliness and seek the Lord, no one would be happier than the writer of the psalm." Since this is not likely, David prays "for the total overthrow of these men and what they stood for." Henry, III, 654, refers to the imprecations as being "not of passion, but of the Spirit of prophecy." Phillips, II, 182, and Leslie, p. 388, make the imprecations those spoken by David's foes against him, an unnatural view of vv. 6–19. Rawlinson, III, 20, comments that "the spirit of Christian love must ever shrink from such utterances, which belong to an earlier and less perfect dispensation." The inspiration of Scripture argues against this view.

[19]The introduction to Ps. 2, note 32, briefly discusses the messianic psalms.

[20]Kidner, p. 388, understands *ᶜalay*, "against me," as "to my face." The preposition *ᶜal* normally refers to "over" or "upon." This leads to the speech being "concerning me" or "against me." The parallelism with 2*b* and the context of v. 3 support this. Words of hatred and lies are rarely spoken directly to a person. See G.K.C. 119 *dd*; Williams ¶ 289; Waltke and O'Connor 10.2.1*c*; 11.2.13.*g*.

[21]Kidner, p. 388, argues that "the three surrounding expressions of kindnesses betrayed" argue that David prayed for his enemies. The problem with this is that

given hatred in return for his love. David does not go into the details of the opposition, but it is clear that he faces a difficult matter, v. 5.

II. Pronouncement of Imprecations 6–20

6–10 David prays for judgment on the leader of his enemies. He asks the Lord to set a wicked man to take vengeance on him. May "Satan" (or "an adversary." The same root *śṭn* occurs in vv. 4, 20, 29 in the word "adversaries") be at his "right hand." This is normally a place of protection (see v. 31; 16:8; 121:5). Here, however, it is an adversary standing by David's enemy, v. 6.[22] When the Lord judges him, let him be "condemned" (or "guilty"). May the Lord consider the "prayer" (*tᵉpillâ*) of David's foe as "sin" (cf. 66:18; Prov. 28:9), v. 7. May his life be shortened and another take his office. The apostles saw in this verse a commission to replace Judas after he betrayed the Lord and died (Acts 1:20), v. 8. The curse on the family of David's enemy reflects his wish that the Lord will put his foe to death. His children then will be without a father, and his wife will be a widow, v. 9.[23] The children will "be . . . vagabonds" (or "wander about"), begging for food. They will diligently "seek" (*daraš*, see 9:10) food and money from their "desolate places," homes that have fallen into ruin without the means to keep them up, v. 10.

11–16 David prays that his enemy will have financial reverses. May an "extortioner" (or "creditor"), someone to whom he owes money, "catch" (or "seize") all that he has. May "strangers" (or "enemies," *zûr*, see 44:20) plunder the results of his labor, v. 11. May no one extend "mercy" (or "steadfast love," *ḥesed*, see 5:7) to him. May no one grant "favour" (*ḥanan*, see 4:1) to his children after his death, v. 12. This will lead to the cutting off of the family, and thus the reputation, of David's foe. May the family's name be blotted out

---

David later calls down severe imprecations upon his enemies. It is not likely that he would manifest such a sharp change of attitude toward them.

[22]Dahood, III, 101, and Fausset, III, 343, understand *śaṭan* literally, as Satan standing on the right of David's enemy to deceive him. While this is possible, nothing in the passage requires the word to refer to Satan. The occurrences of this root in vv. 4, 20 and 29 argue against it.

[23]Leupold, p. 767, suggests that the children and wife of David's foe have "given evidence of having the same spirit that controlled their father." While this is possible, the curse does not require this. David's words would naturally come to pass without a husband and father in the home to supply the financial needs.

in the next generation. It was important to the Israelites to have children (cf. Gen. 24:60; 30:1; I Sam. 1:11). The lack of a family was considered a mark of divine punishment (cf. Gen. 16:2; 30:2; I Sam. 1:6). David's prayer thus reflects the Jewish culture, v. 13.

David prays that the Lord will not pass by the iniquity of the father and mother of his adversary, v. 14. Let the Lord keep their actions before Him continually as He brings judgment on them. May He cut off their memory from the earth. The judgment of the parents of David's foe would also help to blot out his name, v. 15. David prays that this will come to pass because "he," David's enemy, showed no "mercy" (or "steadfast love," *ḥesed*) on the "poor" (*ᶜanî*, see 9:12) and needy. He even sought to put the brokenhearted to death, v. 16.

17–20 David prays for poetic justice for his enemy. This enemy loves "cursing" that focuses on others; may these curses come on him. Negatively, David's foe has not "delighted" (*ḥapeṣ*, see 18:19) in bringing blessing to others. May he not receive blessing, v. 17. He has vilified others so much that it is as though he has clothed himself with cursing. May this cursing come into his "bowels" (or "inner being") like a drink of water. May his "bones," idiomatically representing his body, be anointed with the "oil" of his curses, v. 18. May his curses cover him like a garment. May they be a "girdle" (better "belt") that is tied continually about him, v. 19. David now broadens his imprecations to include all his foes. May the curses that David has pronounced on one come on all his adversaries, those who have spoken against his "soul" as they plotted to take his life. David resigns the "reward," the judgment, of his enemies to the Lord (cf. Rom. 12:19), v. 20.

III. Plea for Help 21–29

21–25 David now turns from his enemies to himself. He asks the Lord to help him "for thy name's sake," for the sake of the Lord's reputation.[24] Because the Lord's "mercy" (or "steadfast love," *ḥesed*) is good, he prays for deliverance, v. 21. In comparison to the resources and power of his foes, he is "poor" (*ᶜanî*) and needy. His

[24]Note 94 at 5:11 gives a summary of the Lord's "name."

heart is wounded with the treatment he has received, v. 22.[25] He is passing away like the gradual motion of a shadow that lengthens due to the sun's motion; cf. 102:11; 144:4. He is "tossed up and down" (or "shaken off") like a "locust" (*ʾarbeh*, see 78:46), an undesirable insect, v. 23. His knees have grown weak through fasting as he has sought God's blessing. His flesh "faileth" (or "becomes lean") and is no longer fat, v. 24.[26] He is a reproach to his foes. Upon seeing him, they "shaked" (or "wagged") their heads in derision, v. 25.

26–29 David asks the Lord, out of His "lovingkindness" (or "steadfast love," *ḥesed*), to "save" him, to deliver him, v. 26. The word "that" does not occur in the Hebrew. David simply asks the Lord to show his adversaries that the deliverance comes from His "hand," i.e., power, 102:25; 106:26. They will then know that the Lord has brought about David's escape from their plans, v. 27. They may curse, but let the Lord "bless" (*barak*, see 5:12) David. When they rise against him, let them be "ashamed" (*bôš*, see 6:10), publicly humiliated. As the servant of the Lord, David will rejoice then, v. 28. May his adversaries be covered with "shame" (or "disgrace," *kᵉlimmâ*, see 4:2). May they cover themselves with "confusion" (or "shame," *bošet*, see *bôš*, 6:10) as though they had put on a "mantle" (or "robe"), v. 29.

IV. Praise to God 30–31

30–31 David closes the psalm with a note of praise. This reflects his confidence that the Lord will deliver him from the threat he faces. He will greatly "praise" (or "give thanks") with his speech. He will do this openly, in the midst of many people, v. 30. The Lord "shall stand" (or "stands") at the "right hand" to protect the poor; cf. 16:8; 73:23; 110:5; 121:5; con. 142:4. David likely thinks of himself as

---

[25]Henry, III, 657, understands the wounded spirit to include "a sense of guilt." There is nothing in the psalm, however, to indicate that David sees himself as guilty of unconfessed sin.

[26]Hengstenberg, III, 311, translates, "My flesh deceives from want of oil," referring to the absence of anointing oil to make the flesh shine. Rawlinson, III, 22, refers to abstaining from anointing, "which has still further weakened" the speaker, an unlikely picture. While the word *šemen* may refer to oil, as in v. 18, it may also refer to fatness, Isa. 25:6; 28:1, 4. This naturally continues 24*a*, while the idea of deceitful flesh is not clear. W. E. Barnes, II, 532, relates the phrase to "involuntary fasting caused by a sick man's distaste for food." The view is speculative.

"poor," without resources to oppose those that "condemn" (or "execute judgment on") him, v. 31.

It is clear from the psalm that David relies on the Lord to deliver him from his situation. While his language reflects his unique situation and the culture of his day, we still see his reliance on the Lord. It is in this that the psalm guides Christians in our day. We too should depend on the Lord when difficult circumstances confront us.

PSALM 110

This messianic psalm[27] is familiar because of its use in the NT. Matthew, Mark, Luke, and the author of Hebrews quote it frequently. There are also additional allusions to words and phrases in the psalm.[28] It is theologically important since it points to Jesus Christ. It teaches His deity, His eternality, His resurrection, the judgment of His enemies, His kingship, and His priesthood.[29] While David is the author, nothing in the psalm hints at the background of its writing.[30] From the nature of the psalm, it is best to understand it as pure prophecy as the Holy Spirit leads David to speak of messianic truths.

---

[27]Note 32 in the introduction to Ps. 2 briefly discusses the messianic psalms.

[28]David M. Hay, *Glory at the Right Hand: Psalm 110 in Early Christianity* (Nashville, Tenn.: Abingdon Press, 1973), p. 15, identifies 33 quotations and allusions to Ps. 110 in the NT. Even granting that some of the allusions are debatable, this is a significant number of references to the psalm.

[29]Martin Luther said of the psalm, "It describes the kingdom and priesthood of Jesus Christ, and declares him to be the King of all things, and the intercessor for all men; to whom all things have been remitted by his Father, and who has compassion of us all. 'Tis a noble psalm." *The Table Talk of Martin Luther*, Thomas S. Kepler, ed. (New York: The World Publishing Company, 1952), p. 20.

[30]Matt. 22:42–46; Luke 20:42–44; and Acts 2:34–35 confirm David's authorship. Delitzsch, III, 187, places the psalm after David's conquest of Ammon, II Sam. 10, the climax of his conquering works. While this is possible, no evidence makes it certain. Hirsch, II, 281, arbitrarily rejects Davidic authorship, assigning the psalm to "some other author."

I. The Lord as King 1–3

1–3 David speaks prophetically, referring directly to God the Father and God the Son. The "Lord" (*y*ᵉ*hwah*, see 7:1), the Father, speaks to the "Lord" (*ʾadôn*, see 8:1), the Son, the master, the sovereign ruler of mankind.[31] The Son is to take the position of honor at the Father's right hand (cf. I Kings 2:19; Ps. 45:9) until His enemies have been humbled (cf. Josh. 10:24; I Cor. 15:25).[32] Daniel 7:13–14 describes the fulfillment of the prophecy, v. 1. The Father will send "the rod of [His] strength" (better "your mighty scepter")[33] from Zion, Jerusalem, the center of the Lord's "rule" (*radâ*, see 49:14). This will take place at the end of the Tribulation, when the Lord returns to the earth to put down His enemies. He will set up His kingdom "in the midst of [His] enemies," overcoming them and beginning His millennial reign, v. 2. The psalmist speaks of the Lord's "people." Although David may have had Israel in mind, in this context the word refers to all believers who willingly join with the Lord[34] as He sets up His reign. The "day of thy power" is that day when the Lord puts down

[31]Authors differ as to the spokesman and the recipient of the statement. Kirkpatrick, p. 664, has the spokesman direct his words to David. Eaton, p. 261, understands them as spoken to a Davidic king. Elliot E. Johnson, "Hermeneutical Principles and the Interpretation of Psalm 110," *BibSac* 149 (1992): 450, sees David speaking to Solomon. The NT, however, strongly argues that David spoke these words prophetically of the Lord. Cf. Matt. 22:44; Luke 20:42; Acts 2:34.

[32]The NT refers to this in numerous quotations and allusions, e.g., Matt. 22:43–44 (Mark 12:35–36; Luke 20:42–43); Acts 2:34–35; Heb. 1:13. *NIB*, IV, 1130, notes that the word "footstool" normally refers to "God's footstool, probably the ark." From this, it suggests that "the king's coronation involved a visit to the ark, to stand symbolically at God's right hand." The view is impossible. The king had no right to enter the holy of holies.

[33]Henry, III, 659, mentions the possibility that the rod is the "shepherd's crook." This suggests "the tender care Christ takes of his church." Alexander, p. 465, asserts that "rod," *maṭṭeh*, "never means a sceptre." While *maṭṭeh* has a wide variety of meanings, it does refer to a scepter in Isa. 14:5 and Ezek. 19:11. The parallelism with 2*b* ("rule") suggests that the rod is the scepter of the king. Fausset, III, 346, makes the rod "not a sceptre, but a rod of slaughter and punishment." He further takes "rule" (*radâ*) as "lord it over." The verb *radâ*, however, regularly occurs with the sense of ruling. Horne, p. 491, spiritualizes the rod into Christ's "Word, accompanied by his Spirit." Livingston, p. 404, refers the strong rod to emissaries sent by the king. This also spiritualizes the text.

[34]Kidner, p. 394, goes too far in understanding "willing" as "freewill offerings." He makes this anticipate "the Pauline pictures of a 'living sacrifice'" of Rom. 12:1. The word *n*ᵉ*dabot* may mean "freewill offering." The thought here, however, is of the saints coming with the Lord, not of a lifetime of willing service.

the kingdoms of this world (Matt. 25:31–46). It closes the Tribulation and begins the Millennium. The saints return with the Lord at this glorious appearing. They come "in the beauties [or 'splendors,' *hadar*, see 8:5] of holiness." The phrase refers to the "splendors of *His* holiness."[35] The saints come from "the womb [*reḥem*, better 'dawn']][36] of the morning," the beginning of the millennial rule. The Lord comes with "the dew of . . . youth," a freshness and purity that does not fade away, v. 3.[37]

II. The Lord as Priest 4

4 In addition to His position as King, the Son is also the Great High Priest of His people. The "Lord" (*y^ehwah*), here God the Father, has sworn that the Son is a priest "after the order of Melchizedek." The significance of this is that the priesthood will no longer involve the tribe of Levi. The OT mentions Melchizedek only here and in Genesis 14:18–20. The NT commentary on him (Heb. 5:5–6; 6:20; 7:1–10, 17, 21) proves that Melchizedek is one of the most complete OT types of Jesus Christ. He is both king and priest (Heb. 7:1), something not permitted to the OT kings (I Sam. 13:8–13; II Chron. 26:16–21). He is the king of righteousness and the king of peace (Heb. 7:2). He is the eternal one (implied by Heb. 7:3). He gained his position by divine appointment, not by the mere chance of birth (Heb. 7:4–6). He is positionally superior to the Levitical priests (Heb. 7:7–10), v. 4.

---

[35]See the discussion at 29:2.

[36]Gary Rendsburg, "Hebrew *rḥm* = 'Rain,'" *VT* 33:3 (1983): 357, and "Psalm CX 3*b*," *VT* 39:4 (1999): 550, argues that *reḥem* means "rain" here and in a number of OT references. This word occurs twenty-five times in the OT, always translated "womb" or a parallel term. The mere fact that it could mean "rain" does not mean that it should mean "rain." The "womb" of the morning is that place from which the morning comes forth, i.e., the dawn.

[37]Weiser, p. 695, understands the "dew" as a picture of abundance. The "dew of thy youth" then refers to a numerically abundant army. Hirsch, II, 283, refers to "the spiritual aspect of the education of the young." Perowne, II, 308, refers the phrase to the vigor of youthful warriors. Eaton, p. 262, sees it as "the divine power to give life." These views are possible. The Hebrew is lit. "to you, the dew of your youth." The phrasing is ambiguous and leads to different views. Murphy, p. 581, sees the dew as a symbol of the Holy Spirit, Who empowers the Son. While this is possible, it gives "dew" a symbolism not found elsewhere.

III. The Lord as Judge 5–7

5–7 The "Lord," again God the Father, is at the "right hand" of the Son to support His conquest of the kings of the earth. As in v. 3, "the day of his wrath [*ʾap*, see 2:5]" refers to the closing battle of the Tribulation. The Lord will "strike through" (or "shatter," *maḥaṣ*, see 18:38) the kings who array themselves against Him, v. 5. This judgment of the "heathen" (or "nations") will fill "the places" with "dead bodies." The word "places" is supplied. From elsewhere, this conflict takes place throughout Israel with the action centered in Megiddo (Zech. 12:2–11; 14:2–3).[38] At this time, the Lord will "wound [or 'shatter,' *maḥaṣ*] the heads [*roʾš*]" of the nations. The word *roʾš* is singular but stands here as a collective, denoting the kings that oppose the Lord, v. 6.[39] Drinking of the "brook in the way" pictures the refreshing pause that follows the Lord's victory. He will "lift up the head," comforting and sustaining others that are weary, v. 7.[40]

---

[38]Henry, III, 662, refers the filling to "the filling of hell . . . with damned souls." While it is true that hell will receive the lost, the passage here refers to an earthly conquest.

[39]Rawlinson, III, 29, refers the singular *roʾš* to either Satan or the "central power of the whole confederacy of evil." The parallelism with v. 5 rather supports taking *roʾš* as a collective. Leslie, p. 103, sees *roʾš* as the summits of hills, now red with blood. He is, however, too free in translating *maḥaṣ* as "makes" and *roʾš* as "summits."

[40]Henry, III, 662, understands "the brook" as the Crucifixion, the "bitter cup which the Father put into his hand." Following this, Christ lifts up His own head "by his own power in the resurrection." Phillips, II, 201, makes the brook a "mud puddle." In drinking of this, the Lord shows His humiliation. Rawlinson, III, 29, calls the brook "the well-spring of truth and righteousness." The Lord draws from this "as he advances on his career of victory." Gaebelein, p. 415, sees this as a picture of the Lord's humiliation. These views ignore the context, which deals with an earthly battle against the heathen. Clarke, p. 274, and Harman, p. 362, considers drinking from the brook as the Lord pausing to refresh Himself, then moving on to complete the victory. While possible, it is difficult to think of the Lord needing refreshment at the time of His glorious appearing at the end of the Tribulation. Cohen, p. 373, sees the psalm reverting to David, as if he is "tired and thirsty" and so "refreshes himself at a stream." There is no reason for the psalm to turn to David when the emphasis throughout has been on the Lord. Th. Booij, "Psalm CX: 'Rule in the Midst of Your Foes!'" *VT* 41:4 (1991): 404–5, identifies the brook as "the stream that flows from the mountain of the gods." This relates the psalm to Canaanite tradition, an unacceptable view. VanGemeren, p. 700, considers the drink "ceremonial, as the psalmist expresses his confidence in the Lord in the presence of his troops." This abandons the prophetic view of the psalm. We also have no example elsewhere of a ceremonial drink other than at the temple. Murphy, p. 583, makes the water of the brook represent the Holy Spirit. The verse, however, mentions not "water" but a "brook."

While the world may scoff at the thought of the Lord's return, Christians should maintain their hope in it (Col. 3:4; I John 3:2–3). This hope will help believers remain pure in a sinful world, and it is the only hope that this world will ever be freed from the domination of evil. Only Christ can defeat the forces of wickedness.

PSALM 111

The psalm is an acrostic.[41] After the opening *hal^{e}lu yah*, "praise ye the Lord," the unknown author begins each stich with successive letters of the alphabet. The first eight verses include two letters each. The last two verses include three letters each.[42] The psalm is a hymn of pure praise with no stress on any threat to the psalmist or the nation. Nothing in the psalm indicates either the background or the date for writing.[43] The acrostic nature of the psalm governs its structure. The following outline roughly describes the contents.

I. Praise for Material Blessings 1–6

1 The psalmist begins with the phrase *hal^{e}lu yah*, "praise ye the Lord." The psalmist purposes to "praise" (or "give thanks to") the Lord with his whole heart. He will do this publicly, together in an

[41]Pss. 9, 10, 25, 34, 37, 111, 112, 119, and 145 are acrostics.

[42]Moll, p. 560, suggests that the psalmist limited the song to ten verses "due to an unwillingness that the verses should exceed ten, the number of completeness." Since the verse numbers were added after the original writing, it is unlikely that the author had this in mind. In any case, the number ten occurs as a round number, an approximation, see Gen. 31:7, 41; Num. 14:22; Neh. 4:12, rather than showing completeness. Had the last two verses been divided into three verses, the acrostic would be regular.

[43]Leupold, p. 779, makes the psalm postexilic. He suggests that the psalmist wrote to encourage the discouraged people who had returned to Palestine from their captivity in Babylon. Fausset, III, 348, places the psalm just before the return from Babylon. On the other hand, Henry, III, 662, attributes the song to David. Rawlinson, III, 36, does not date the psalm but makes it, along with 112, an introduction to the "chant sung at the Passover, at Pentecost, and at the Feast of Tabernacles, Pss. 113–118. These views are possible but must remain speculative since the psalm gives no firm evidence of its date or purpose.

"assembly" (or "council," *sôd*, see 25:14) of others who are upright in heart and in the "congregation" (or "assembly") of the people, v. 1.

2–6 The psalmist begins to describe the works of God on behalf of His people.[44] They are great works. Those who delight in them have "sought" (*daraš*, see 9:10) them earnestly, v. 2. The work of the Lord is "honourable and glorious" (or "glorious and majestic," *hôd* and *hadar*, see 8:1, 5) in comparison to man's accomplishments. The Lord's work also displays His continuing righteousness, v. 3. The Lord causes men to remember His "wonderful works" (or "wonders," *pala*ʾ, see 9:1). By performing them on man's behalf, the Lord shows that He is "gracious" (see *ḥanan*, 4:1) and compassionate, v. 4. To illustrate the Lord's care, the psalmist mentions that He has given "meat" (*ṭerep*), food,[45] to those who "fear" (or "reverence," see *yir*ʾ*â*, 2:11) Him. The context of v. 6 suggests that this refers to the food Israel received in the wilderness. This showed the Lord's faithfulness to His covenant with the people. Though the Israelites were inconsistent and fainthearted in the wilderness, they were the covenant people, fearing the Lord as they kept His laws, v. 5. He "hath shewed" (or "declared") to His people His power "that he may give them" (better "by giving them") the "heritage of the heathen," the land of Palestine, v. 6.

II. Praise for Spiritual Blessings 7–10

7–9 The psalmist now emphasizes the spiritual works of the Lord. His works are marked by "verity and judgment" (or "truth and justice"). His "commandments" (or "precepts") are reliable, v. 7. They "stand fast" continually, sustained by His power. He carries them out in truth and uprightness as the marks of His character are transferred to His works, v. 8. He sent redemption to Israel. This probably refers to their deliverance from Egyptian bondage, a picture of spiritual

[44]Kidner, p. 397, understands the "works of the Lord" as those of Creation since, in Psalms, they refer most often to the heavens and the earth. On the other hand, Anderson, II, 773, says that "works" refers to His "mighty deeds in history and, apparently, does not include the works of creation." While this word often refers to Creation, cf. 8:3; 19:1; 102:25, it also refers to other works; cf. v. 6; 33:4; 104:13; 139:14. There is no need to limit the word.

[45]Fausset, III, 349, suggests that *ṭerep* refers to "booty" or "spoil" brought out of Egypt at the Exodus. W. E. Barnes, II, 540, refers the word to "the spoils of Canaan." The word *ṭerep*, however, generally refers to "prey" or "food" elsewhere, e.g., 104:21; Prov. 31:15.

redemption. He has "commanded" (or "ordained") His covenant with them forever. His "name,"[46] representing His nature, is holy and "reverend" (or "awesome"), v. 9.

10 The "fear of the Lord" (*yirʾat yᵉhwah*, see 15:4), a reverence for the Lord, is "the beginning of wisdom [*ḥokmâ*, see 19:7; cf. Prov. 1:7; 9:10]." Putting this negatively, no person can be wise who does not reverence the Lord. Those who obey His "commandments" (or "precepts," cf. v. 7) have good understanding of what the He wants from His followers. The praise of the Lord will endure forever, v. 10.

With these few words, the psalmist illustrates for believers today a proper attitude of praise. God is the giver of all good gifts (Jas. 1:17), including both material provisions and spiritual blessings. It is right that He be praised.

PSALM 112

The psalm follows the acrostic of Psalm 111 with its own acrostic.[47] The acrostic structure here is identical to that of Psalm 111. There is an opening *halᵉlû yah*, "praise ye the Lord." Following this, the unknown author begins each stich with successive letters of the alphabet. The first eight verses each include two of the letters. The last two verses include three letters each.

The emphasis in this psalm is on the godly man. Because of the similarity in form and the logical progression from praising the Lord (Ps. 111) to praising the godly, the two psalms were likely written around the same time by the same author. As with Psalm 111, nothing in this psalm lets us set its background or date of writing.[48] Although the acrostic guides the structure of the psalm, the following outline approximates its contents.

---

[46]Note 94 at 5:11 gives a summary of the Lord's "name."

[47]The acrostics in the book include Pss. 9, 10, 25, 34, 37, 111, 112, 119, and 145.

[48]As with Ps. 111, speculations on the date of Ps. 112 vary widely. Kissane, p. 461, places it "before the end of the exile." Clarke, p. 276, makes it "early postexilic." Leslie, p. 423, dates it "probably not earlier than the fourth century B. C."

I. Blessings on the Godly 1–4

1–4 The phrase *halᵉlû yah*, "praise ye the Lord," opens the psalm. The psalmist turns immediately to his theme of the godly person. This person is "blessed" (*ʾašrê*, see 1:1), the plural indicating the intensity of the blessings. These come because he "feareth the Lord," maintaining a holy reverence, and because he "delighteth" (*ḥapeṣ*, see 18:19) in the commandments given by the Lord to His people, v. 1. As an example of the Lord's blessing, the psalmist notes that the offspring of the godly person will be "mighty" (*gibbôr*, see 19:5), having strong influence over others. The "generation of the upright," those marked by godliness, will be "blessed" (*barak*, see 5:12), v. 2. The godly person will have material blessings with great "wealth," possessions, and riches. He will also have spiritual blessings, and his righteousness will continue forever, v. 3. The light of God's presence arises to guide His children through the darkness of trials. The Lord, represented by the light, is "gracious" (*ḥannûn*, see *ḥanan*, 4:1), compassionate (*raḥûm*), and righteous in His care for the godly, v. 4.[49]

II. Characteristics of the Godly 5–10

5–9 The phrase "a good man" is better "good is the man," i.e., matters go well with the godly man. He shows "favour" (or "grace," *ḥanan*, see 4:1) and lends his resources to meet the needs of others. He maintains his affairs with "discretion" (or "justice"), v. 5. His foundation of delight in God's Word, cf. v. 1, is such that he will never be "moved" (or "shaken") by matters in this life. The Lord will remember the righteous forever, v. 6. The psalmist illustrates the stability of the righteous. He will not fear when evil tidings come. His heart is "fixed," steadfast in its trust of the Lord, v. 7. His heart is "established," sustained amid the trials of life. Throughout his trials, he will not fear until he looks in victory over those who afflict him,

[49]Verse 4*b* has no subject. It simply says "gracious, and compassionate, and righteous." Some refer the "light" to the influence of the godly and make 4*b* describe his character. So Eaton, p. 264, and Albert Barnes, III, 147. Others see "light" as hope of varying kinds for the godly in trials but make 4*b* describe the upright. So among others, Harman, p. 366, and VanGemeren, p. 709. Horne, p. 498, speaks of a "threefold 'light;' the light of truth, the light of comfort, and the light of life." The words *ḥannûn* and *raḥûm*, however, always describe the Lord elsewhere. For that reason, it is best to understand "light" in 4*a* to refer to the Lord and to make Him the subject of 4*b*.

v. 8. The godly man has "dispersed" (or "scattered") his goods, giving to others in need. His righteousness remains forever. The "horn" (*qeren*, see 18:2) of the godly man, his power,[50] will be exalted with honor, v. 9.

10 The wicked will grieve over the exaltation of the righteous. He will "gnash with his teeth," grinding them together in his anger. This will do him no good. He will eventually "melt away," his opposition fainting. His desire for dominance over the godly will "perish" (*ʾabad*, see 1:6), being vanquished completely by the continued blessing of God on those who follow Him, v. 10.

Like Psalm 111, this psalm sets an example for believers today. The godly man enjoys God's blessings, vv. 1–4. He therefore lives in a way that reflects God's presence in his life. He is gracious, meeting the needs of others, and just, v. 5. He is confident amid the trials of life, knowing that God remembers him, v. 6. He is not fearful but trusts in the Lord, v. 7. He is victorious over his foes, v. 8. He is charitable, persistent in righteousness, and honored by the Lord, v. 9. God will overcome the wicked, v. 10. In light of these blessings showered upon the righteous, we have every reason to continue in righteousness as we live for the glory of our Saviour.

PSALM 113

We do not know either the author or the background for this psalm.[51] It occupies, however, a position as one of the major psalms in the Jewish ritual of worship. It is the first of the "Hallel" psalms, Psalms 113–118, which take their name from the theme of praise that appears in them. Psalms 113–118 are also called the "Egyptian Hallel" from their use in the temple at the Feast of Passover, a feast

---

[50] The "horn" occurs frequently as a symbol of power or strength, e.g., 75:10; 148:14.

[51] Leupold, p. 789, makes the psalm postexilic. He bases this on vv. 7–9, comparing Israel after her return from Babylon to a "poor man sitting on the ash heap" or to "the childless mother of the household." These verses, however, can readily be explained in other ways.

commanded by the Lord when Israel was in Egypt. In the temple, the priests chanted the Hallel during the killing of the lamb. At the Passover meal, the people chanted Psalms 113 and 114 before the meal and 115–118 after the meal.[52] The priests also chanted these psalms after the morning sacrifices during the Feasts of Passover, Pentecost, Tabernacles, the New Moon, and Dedication (*ḥannukâ*).[53]

I. The Praise of God 1–3

1 The psalm begins with a clear command: "Praise ye the Lord." This translates the familiar *halᵉlû yah*. For the sake of emphasis, the imperative *halᵉlû*, "praise," occurs twice more in the verse.[54] The participle *mᵉhullal*, "praised," occurs in v. 3, and the command *halᵉlû·yah*, "praise ye the Lord," closes the psalm in v. 9. The phrase "servants of the Lord" includes all of mankind who serve God.[55] Verse 3 extends the call to praise the Lord throughout the earth, indicating that both Jews and Gentiles are in view. The "name of the Lord"[56] refers to the nature of the Lord (a theme developed more fully in vv. 4–6), v. 1.[57]

2–3 The psalmist calls for the Lord's "name," the self-revelation of His nature, to be "blessed" (*barak*, see 5:12). This blessing should be perpetual, both now and into eternity. The emphasis here is that the Lord should receive praise throughout time. In the next verse,

---

[52]Without mentioning the specific psalms, Matt. 26:30 and Mark 14:26 refer to chanting Pss. 115–118. Pss. 113–114 would have been sung before the Passover meal.

[53]*NEJ*, p. 627.

[54]While there is no object for the first imperative "praise," the parallelism of the verse indicates that the thought is to "praise Him."

[55]Henry, III, 668, includes angels among the "servants of the Lord" who praise Him. Although the angels do praise the Lord, it is doubtful that the psalmist had them in mind with his call here to offer praise. Kissane, p. 589, and Kirkpatrick, p. 678, limit the servants to Israel, a possible view. I include Gentiles since the rest of the psalm has a worldwide emphasis.

[56]See note 94 at 5:11 for a summary of the Lord's "name."

[57]Spurgeon, p. 485, relates the threefold mention of the Lord to the Trinity. There is nothing here, however, to support this. It would be just as appropriate to praise the God of space, of time, and of redemption, or the God of the past, present, and future. When we go beyond the statements of Scripture, we become the authority and make the Bible subject to our views. Repetition normally emphasizes some thought. Single repetition is common but double repetition is rare. Double repetition occurs in Isa. 6:3; Jer. 7:4; 22:29; and Ezek. 21:27. A close parallel occurs in II Sam. 18:33. There is a NT parallel in Rev. 4:8.

the emphasis is that He should receive praise throughout space, v. 2. From "the rising of the sun" in the east to "the going down of the same" in the west, man should offer praise to the "name" (see v. 1) of the Lord.[58] The combined thought is that there is no limit to praising the Lord. Whenever we have the opportunity and wherever we are, we should praise the Lord. He is worthy of this, v. 3.

II. The Nature of God 4–6

4 The psalmist now turns to the reason for praising the Lord. He is exalted above His creation. He is "high [*rûm*] above all nations." It is understandable then that the nations of the earth should seek to exalt Him. Satan's influence has turned the nations of the world away from the Lord. The time will come, however, when they will give Him the praise He deserves (Isa. 42:10, 12; 61:11). The Lord is not only above the nations but above "the heavens" also. The Creator is higher than His entire creation (cf. 8:1; 57:11), v. 4.

5–6 With a startling question, the psalmist introduces the humiliation involved in the Lord's condescending to involve Himself with sinful man. Rhetorically, the writer asks, "Who is like unto the Lord our God, who dwelleth [or 'sits enthroned'] on high [*gabâ*]?"[59] Obviously, no one is like the Lord, v. 5. Yet this exalted Being lowers Himself to take note of the heavens and the earth.[60] The Lord does not turn away from the polluted creation or from sinful man. With this thought, the author introduces the final section of the psalm, v. 6.

---

[58]Gaebelein, p. 421, and Oesterley, II, 469, make the phrase refer to time. Verse 2 has already referred to time. Verse 3 refers to direction. The phrase "rising of the sun" occurs elsewhere where it can refer only to a direction, Num. 2:3; Josh. 12:1; Isa. 59:19.

[59]While both *rûm* and *gabâ* have the sense of "high," the author makes a slightly different emphasis. In v. 4, the Lord is exalted, worthy of receiving praise. Verses 5–6 are comparative, with the Lord above His creation but taking note of the things lower than Himself.

[60]A *b*^{e} preposition introduces both "heavens" and "earth." This is normal following the verb *raʾâ*, "to see." The more unusual grammar of the verse involves the *ḥireq compaginis* ("joined *ḥireq*"), a *ḥireq yôd* added to several of the *hipʿîl* verbs in vv. 5, 6, 7, 8, and 9. This is an archaic ending that occurs only rarely. This is the only place that the construction occurs repeatedly. It is a connecting vowel that joins the word with its context; hence, the name.

III. The Work of God 7–9

7–9*a* The psalmist gives three examples to show the Lord's care for mankind. He raises the "poor" (*dal*, see 41:1) from "the dust" and the "needy" (*ʾebyôn*, see 72:13) from the "dunghill" (better "ash heap"). The picture comes from Hannah's song, I Samuel 2:8. Elsewhere in the OT, sitting in the dust pictures humiliation and sorrow (Job 2:12; Isa. 47:1; Lam. 2:10). Likewise, sitting in ashes portrays abasement and grief (cf. Lam 4:5). The Lord lifts this man out of his degradation, v. 7. He "set[s]" (*lᵉhôšîbî*)[61] him "with the princes of his people," giving him an exalted position. The examples of Joseph (Gen. 41:14–43), Jephthah (Judg. 11:1–11), Saul (I Sam. 10:22–24), and David (I Sam. 16:11–13) illustrate the Lord's ability to raise a person from a low position to one of leadership, v. 8. The Lord gives children to the barren woman. This phrase also comes from Hannah's words (I Sam. 2:5). These illustrations do not give an exhaustive list of God's gracious interaction with man. They do, however, portray the grace of God in meeting the needs of sinful man, v. 9*a*.

9*b* The psalm ends as it began, with *halᵉlû·yah*, "Praise ye the Lord."[62] The principle remains true today; God's people should be quick to praise the Lord. In the difficulties of life—physical problems, financial reverses, decisions, family problems—look beyond the problem to the God Who gives grace for every challenge, v. 9*b*.

---

[61]This is the only place where the *ḥireq compaginis* occurs with an infinitive. Since vv. 5, 6, 7, and 9 attach the *ḥireq* to a participle, many authors emend *lᵉhôšîbî* to *lᵉhôšîbô*. So Delitzsch, III, 204; Kirkpatrick, p. 679. Since this construction occurs only rarely, we do not have enough information to rule out its connection to an infinitive. There is no need to emend since the sense of the MT is clear.

[62]The final word, *halᵉlû·yah*, introduces Ps. 114 in the LXX, Vulgate, and several other older versions. Virtually all commentators discuss the word with Ps. 113. It is not unusual for psalms to end this way, e.g., 115, 116, 117. In addition, its presence here brings the psalm to a fitting conclusion.

PSALM 114

This brief hymn recalls the work of the Lord in delivering Israel from bondage in Egypt.[63] It poetically summarizes the miracles that aided the people in their journey to Palestine. It is one of the Hallel psalms, Psalms 113–118, sung by the Jews at the Feasts of Passover,[64] Pentecost, Tabernacles, the New Moon, and Dedication (*ḥannukâ*).[65] During Passover, Psalms 113 and 114 were sung before the Passover meal and Psalms 115–118 afterwards. We do not know its author or the occasion for its writing.[66]

I. Deliverance of Israel 1–4

1–2 The psalmist looks at the Exodus. The phrase "house of Jacob" refers to Israel as it leaves the land populated by "a people of strange language [*loᶜez*],"[67] Egyptian rather than Hebrew, v. 1. Compressing history, the psalmist next sees the nation in the land of promise. In the Promised Land, Judah lay to the south. This was the location of the temple, the "sanctuary," the holy dwelling of the Lord. The nation of Israel became God's "dominion," dwelling in the land over which He ruled, v. 2.

3–4 Looking back at the Exodus, the Red Sea saw Israel approaching and "fled," the waters rolling back to let them pass (Exod. 14:21–22). The Jordan River also "was driven back" to let the people pass over on dry ground (Josh. 3:13–17), v. 3. The psalmist poetically describes the quaking of Mt. Sinai and the region around

---

[63]For no good reason, the LXX, several mss, and some ancient versions join Pss. 114 and 115. The two psalms differ in their emphasis, however, and should remain separate.

[64]According to *Sukkah* 47*a*, the Jews sang Ps. 114 at the sacrifice on the eighth day of the Passover celebration.

[65]*NEJ*, p. 627.

[66]Rodd, p. 78, gives the possibility that the psalm "was sung at the sanctuary at Gilgal during one of the feasts which were celebrated there." Dahood, III, 134, thinks it describes a setting in the ninth century BC. Among others, Kirkpatrick, p. 680, dates the psalm following the Babylonian captivity. It was written "to encourage the downhearted people in those gloomy days that followed . . . after the captives had come back home." Nothing in the psalm lets us date it certainly.

[67]The word *loᶜez* occurs only here. The meaning of "strange [or 'unintelligible'] language" comes from cognate words. The LXX and Vulgate also have this sense.

it. He compares the quaking to the skipping of rams along the sides of the mountains. Smaller nearby hills moved like the unstable tottering of young "lambs" (lit. "sons of small cattle," usually goats or sheep; 68:8; Exod. 19:18), v. 4.

II. Power of God 5–8

5–6 The psalmist asks a series of four rhetorical questions that bring out the power of the Lord. Why had the Red Sea fled to let Israel cross? Why did the Jordan River let itself be driven back, v. 5? Why did the mountains of Sinai skip about like rams? Why did the hills in the region totter like lambs? There are no answers given to the questions. From the development in vv. 7–8, it is clear that the Lord brought these physical miracles to pass, v. 6.

7–8 The earth should tremble in the presence of the "Lord" (*ʾadôn*, see 8:1), its master. Such trembling will indeed happen again (cf. Rev. 6:12, 14; 11:13; 16:18, 20) during the Tribulation at the end of this age, v. 7. The psalmist gives one more example of the power of the "God [*ʾelôah*, see 18:31] of Jacob." God turned the "rock" (*ṣûr*, see 18:2) to "standing [or 'a pool of'] water" (107:35; Exod. 17:5–6). The phrase "the flint into a fountain of waters" expands on the first half of the verse. This gives additional details as to the nature of the rock (Deut. 8:15) and the gushing forth of the waters (105:41) before they formed the pool in a low-lying area nearby. The God Who graciously provided for Israel's needs still provides for His people, v. 8.

In looking back at Israel's deliverance from their bondage in Egypt, the psalmist looks briefly at the power of God. This power is still evident as God works on behalf of His people. Although trials may confront those who serve the Lord, God is able to overcome the opposition. We have every reason to maintain our confidence in Him.

PSALM 115

This psalm[68] was one of the "Hallel Psalms" used in Jewish liturgy. In Jewish homes, at the Passover meal, the people chanted Psalms 113 and 114 after drinking the first cup of wine.[69] Later, after the meal and the fourth cup of wine, the family chanted the second part of the Hallel Psalms. This included Psalms 115–118. These psalms were also sung at other feasts during the year: Pentecost, Tabernacles, the New Moon, and Dedication (*ḥannukâ*).[70]

There is also a significant occurrence of the psalm in history. At the Battle of Agincourt, Henry V of Great Britain defeated the French army in a major victory. After the battle, Henry commanded his soldiers to kneel and sing Psalm 115 in thanks to the Lord. Such a note of praise is still appropriate.

We know nothing of the author or the occasion for writing the psalm.[71] From the content, we can conclude that Israel faced some threat from the heathen. The psalmist condemns those who worship idols and urges the nation to trust the Lord. He ends the psalm by expressing Israel's intention to praise the One Who has blessed His people.

I. The Futility of Worshiping Idols 1–8

1–3 Anticipating the following emphasis on idols, the psalmist begins by giving glory to the Lord. The nation does not deserve glory. The psalmist emphasizes this by repeating the phrase "not unto us."

---

[68]The LXX, Theodotion's translation of the OT, Jerome, the Syriac, and several Hebrew mss join Pss. 114 and 115 together. There is, however, no common theme to the psalms. In addition, the Jews made a distinction by singing 114 before the Passover meal and 115 after it.

[69]Among others, Ewald, II, 181, and Cohen, p. 382, suggest that groups chanted different parts of the psalm. While this may have been so, the NT references to singing after the Passover meal argue that smaller groups sang it as well. Without mentioning the specific psalms, Matt. 26:30 and Mark 14:26 refer to chanting Pss. 115–118.

[70]*NEJ*, p. 627.

[71]Dahood, III, 139, sees vv. 9–12 as indicating "that Israel still had a king," which would make a preexilic date likely. Rotherham, p. 481, dates it in the reign of Jehoshaphat. Rodd, p. 79, suggests a postexilic date. As is often the case, the psalm does not give enough information to let us fix its date.

The glory should go to the "name" of the Lord. As is customary, the "name" of the Lord refers to His revealed nature.[72] To illustrate His nature, the psalmist refers to His "mercy" (or "steadfast love," *ḥesed*, see 5:7) and "truth," v. 1.

Why should the heathen be permitted to say of Israel, "Where is now their God?" This suggests that the nation has suffered some reverse, perhaps the defeat that led them into the Babylonian captivity, v. 2. The psalmist recognizes the sovereignty of God. He has done what He "pleased" (*ḥapeṣ*, see 18:19), v. 3.

4–8 As a sharp contrast with the sovereignty of God, Who does what He will, the psalmist now shows the weakness of idols. Psalm 135:15–18 repeats the thought of the passage in similar words. The passage is a chiasm:

A Their [the heathen's] idols are silver and gold,[73]
 B the work of men's hands, v. 4.
  C They have mouths, but they speak not:
   D eyes have they, but they see not, v. 5.
    E They have ears, but they hear not:
     F noses have they, but they smell not, v. 6.
    E[1] They have hands, but they handle not:
   D[1] Feet have they, but they walk not:
  C[1] neither "speak" [or "mutter"] they through their throat, v. 7.
 B[1] They that make them are like unto them:
A[1] so is every one that trusteth in them, v. 8.

This poetic passage shows the weakness of idols. They cannot speak, see, hear, smell, or use their hands and feet. They are the products of man's work. The idols have no ability to do anything. Those who worship them, therefore, gain no profit from their worship.[74]

---

[72]Note 94 at 5:11 summarizes the Lord's "name."

[73]Henry, III, 672, appropriately notes that the silver and gold which the idols come from is dug from the earth and thus dirty. While these are "proper things to make money of," they are "not to make gods of."

[74]Leslie, p. 195, and W. E. Barnes, II, 549, suggest that v. 8 may be a prayer: "May they . . ." The verbs in the verse are participles rather than jussives, which supports making the verse a statement rather than a wish.

II. The Blessing of Worshiping the Lord 9–18

9–11 Once more using a poetic structure, the psalmist exhorts others to trust the Lord.[75] He begins with the broad group, the nation of Israel. He next moves to the priests and temple workers, the "house of Aaron." He then focuses on those that "fear the Lord" (*yirᵓê yᵉhwah*, see 15:4), a phrase that likely includes Gentiles who worshiped Israel's God. The psalmist here urges others to "trust the Lord." In a time of trial, when the nation has undergone a defeat, the Lord alone is a "help" (*ᶜezer*, see 20:2) and a "shield" (*magen*, see 3:3). The psalmist repeats this thought to each of the three groups addressed in vv. 9–11.

12–13 Following the same pattern used in vv. 9–11, the psalmist now affirms his confidence in the Lord's blessing of His people. The Lord has not forgotten them. He remembers them and will "bless" (*barak*, see 5:12) them. The psalmist again speaks first to Israel, then to the house of Aaron, v. 12, and finally to those that "fear the Lord" (*yirᵓê yᵉhwah*). With the last group, he adds the thought "both small and great," referring to their social position and influence.[76] He states his conviction that the Lord will "bless" (*barak*) each group, v. 13.

14–15 As a specific example of the Lord's blessing, the psalmist refers to the "increase" that God will give the people and their children. By leaving the nature of the "increase" undefined, it becomes a general promise of blessing in every area, v. 14. The final statement is a prayer. May the Lord, Who made "heaven and earth," i.e., the powerful Lord, bless (*barak*) the nation, v. 15.

---

[75]Kidner, p. 405, suggests revocalizing the verbs to the third person, following the LXX, Vulgate, and Syriac. This would give something like "Israel trusts in the Lord . . . the house of Aaron trusts in the Lord . . . ye that fear the Lord trust in the Lord." Aside from the needless repetition this introduces in v. 11, it would also require revocalizing 135:19–21, where a similar thought occurs. Despite the textual support, it is unlikely that the change is necessary.

[76]Kissane, p. 529, and Henry, III, 673, refer the phrase "small and great" to the young and the old. The view is possible. The combination of "small" and "great" refers to size or amount, Ps. 104:25; Isa. 54:7; to age, Gen. 27:15, 42; Ezek. 16:46, 61; to importance, Exod. 18:22; I Sam. 20:2; or to position and influence, Deut. 1:17; I Chron. 12:14. Any of the last three views will fit here. Alexander, p. 478, and Livingston, p. 410, consider "small and great" an idiom for all people with no emphasis on any kind of groups within the whole. While the view is possible, the phrase normally refers to contrasting groups.

16–18 The heavens belong to the Lord; they vividly display His power.[77] In addition, they testify to the omniscience of the One Who designed them and serve as witnesses to His glory. He has given the earth to mankind to use as he will, v. 16. From the number of times that the OT refers to the fact that the dead cannot openly praise the Lord,[78] the statement must have been proverbial in Israel. Those who go into the "silence" of death cannot give open praise to the Lord, v. 17. The living, however, can praise the Lord on earth. The psalmist pledges that "we," those who fear the Lord, will pronounce "bless[ings]" (*barak*) on Him forever. This thought leads the psalmist to close the song with *hal^{e}lû·yah*, "praise the Lord," v. 18.

PSALM 116

Psalm 116[79] is another song of thanksgiving as the psalmist expresses his gratitude for the blessings the Lord has given him.[80] The psalm is anonymous. The similarity to David's writing elsewhere, vv. 3–4 and 18:4–6; vv. 8–9 and 56:13, leads some to suggest David's

[77]Fausset, III, 354, calls attention to the lit. sense of the MT, "'the heavens, heavens;' the latter without the article." He refers the first "heavens" to the visible heavens, and the second "heavens" to "the general name for all that is above the earth." It is more likely that we should supply the verb, "the heavens *are* the heavens of the Lord," or treat the phrase as a superlative, "the highest heavens," or as giving emphasis, "the heavens themselves." The phrase occurs only here, but nothing suggests that we should give different meanings to *šamayim* because it occurs twice. Albert Barnes, III, 158, supplies the copulative but translates "the heavens are heavens for Jehovah" as if the heavens were "a home for himself, or as his peculiar possession and abode." Calvin, IV, 355, understands the phrase as "the heavens are enough for God." God is independent of the earth and its resources. These are possible views. Since the phrase does not occur elsewhere, we cannot be certain of the sense.

[78]Similar statements appear in 6:5; 30:9; 88:10–12; Eccles. 9:10; and Isa. 38:18–19.

[79]For unknown reasons, the LXX divides the psalm into two psalms. Verses 1–9 are Ps. 114, and vv. 10–18 are Ps. 115. See the introduction to Ps. 10 for a summary of the numbering of the psalms by the LXX.

[80]The introduction to Ps. 18 summarizes the songs of thanksgiving.

authorship.[81] Whoever the author may have been, it is clear that the Lord has delivered him from the threat of death; cf. vv. 3, 8–9. We do not know the specific incident that the psalmist has in mind. By leaving the psalm general, we see a picture of the deliverance that the Lord gives His own in every threat they face.

The psalm is part of the Hallel Psalms, 113–118, and was included in the Jewish liturgy during the feasts of the year. It was sung at the Journey Feasts of Passover, Pentecost, and Tabernacles. It was also included in the New Moon worship, and the Feasts of Dedication (*ḥannukâ*).[82]

I. Declaration of the Psalmist's Love 1–2

1–2 The psalmist states his love for the Lord because of the Lord's faithfulness in hearing his prayers and "supplications" (*taḥᵃnûn*, see 28:2), his cries for mercy. While he does not describe the nature of his prayers, they undoubtedly relate to the threat that he mentions later, v. 1. The Lord has heard him in the past. This gives him the confidence to pledge continued prayer for the rest of his life, v. 2.

II. Proclamation of the Psalmist's Deliverance 3–11

3–4 These two verses are similar to Psalm 18:4–6. This suggests three possibilities: (1) David may have written both psalms; (2) the psalmist was familiar with David's writings; or (3) both David and this author used cliches that were common in Israel. Although I lean toward the first, it is not certain which one is correct.

The psalmist laments that "the sorrows [lit. 'cords'] of death" and the "pains [or 'anguish,' *meṣar*][83] of hell [*šᵉʾôl*, see 6:5]" have compassed him. He visualizes death as having tied him so that it

---

[81]Henry, p. 674, and Calvin, IV, 360, make David the author. Scroggie, III, 129, and Rotherham, p. 484, assign the psalm to Hezekiah. Oesterley, II, 475, sets the time of writing as "late post-exilic." He notes the presence of "Aramaisms" and "the term *Ḥasidim*" in v. 15. These are not conclusive, however, since both occur where the date is clearly early, e.g., Aramaisms, Gen. 24:26; Num. 11:20; *Ḥasidim*, I Sam. 2:9; Prov. 2:8. Although it is not possible to be dogmatic, I lean toward David's authorship. Not only is it similar to Pss. 18 and 56, the phrase "son of thine handmaid," v. 16, occurs elsewhere only in Ps. 86, also a Davidic psalm.

[82]*NEJ*, p. 627.

[83]The word *meṣar* occurs in Psalms only here and at 118:5. It refers to emotional pressures.

pulls him toward itself. His anguish is bringing him to *šᵉʾôl*, here best understood as the grave.[84] He faces "trouble [or 'distress,' *ṣarâ*, see 9:9] and sorrow," v. 3. In his adversity, the psalmist calls on the "name of the Lord,"[85] the Lord's nature as a merciful God, to deliver him, v. 4.

5–6 The Lord has answered the psalmist's prayer. The psalmist therefore pauses to praise Him. He is "gracious" (see *ḥanan*, 4:1), giving favor to those who do not deserve it. He is "righteous," keeping His promises to hear the prayers of His own. He is "merciful" (or "compassionate"), helping those without strength, v. 5. The psalmist now describes his own situation. The Lord preserves the "simple" (*petî*, see 19:7), here one with no knowledge of how to face his enemy. The enemy had brought the psalmist low, a poetical picture of weakness, but the Lord had delivered him, v. 6.

7–11 The psalmist urges his soul to "return unto [its] rest," to a state of peace. He recognizes that the Lord has "dealt bountifully" (*gamal*, see 7:4) with him in delivering him from the threat, v. 7. The Lord has delivered him from death, cf. v. 3, answering the prayer of v. 4. As a related matter, his eyes have been delivered from tears so that he no longer needs to grieve. His feet have been delivered from that which would trip them to keep him from "falling" (*dᵉḥî*, or "stumbling," see 56:13), v. 8. He will now be able to walk in the sight of the Lord openly in "the land of the living," populated areas. This implies his freedom from fear of attack by others, v. 9.[86] He "believed," trusting in the Lord, when he had "spoken" in prayer, reminding the Lord that he "was greatly afflicted [*ʿanâ*, see 35:13]." The apostle Paul quotes from the LXX translation of this verse, II Corinthians 4:13. Just as the psalmist did, so Paul also believed and therefore spoke, v. 10.[87] In his "haste" (*ḥapaz*, or "terror," see 31:22),

---

[84]Leslie, p. 306, understands *šᵉʾôl* as "the realm of the departed." Henry, p. 675, relates the pains of *šᵉʾôl* to the "terror of conscience arising from sense of guilt." Jennings, II, 257, refers *šᵉʾôl* to "Hades." The parallelism with "death" rather identifies *šᵉʾôl* here with the grave.

[85]Note 94 at 5:11 gives a summary of the Lord's "name."

[86]Verses 8–9 are similar to 56:13, a psalm authored by David.

[87]Leupold, p. 806, understands "that the writer had said some things during the time of his great trouble, words that might have been construed as though he had been driven to the point of abandoning his faith." He here defends himself from

the psalmist had reminded the Lord of the deceitfulness of others. This undoubtedly relates to the threat he faced, v. 11.

III. Consecration of the Psalmist's Life 12–19

12–15 In view of the Lord's gracious "benefits" (*tagmûlôhî*)[88] in deliverance, the psalmist naturally asks how he can show his gratitude to the Lord, v. 12. He immediately answers his own question by making several pledges. In the first place, he will "take the cup of salvation [or 'deliverance']." The phrase "cup of salvation" idiomatically represents the deliverance given him by the Lord.[89] He will continue to call upon the "name" of the Lord (see v. 4) in prayer, v. 13. Secondly, the psalmist pledges to pay his vows openly so that others may see his devotion. From the identical repetition of this verse in v. 18, it likely refers to the vow of prayer just made, v. 14.[90]

Verse 15 again refers to the threat of death that the psalmist faces. He recognizes that death is not a light matter. The death of the "saints" (or "holy ones," *ḥasîd*, see 4:3) is "precious," of great value, in the sight of the Lord.[91] Since it is of such value, the Lord orders its

---

others who might accuse him of unbelief. Paul's use of the verse better supports the view given above.

[88]The word *tagmûlôhî* has a 3ms Aramaic suffix. Alexander, p. 481, and Delitzsch, III, 215, see this as evidence of a late date for the psalm. This may or may not be so. In all ages, neighboring countries exert an influence on language.

[89]The phrase is similar to the "cup of . . . fury," Isa. 51:17, 22, and "cup of consolation," Jer. 16:7. Cf. also 11:6; 75:8. It is as though the subject lifts the cup and drinks the contents of it. The psalmist has drunk of the deliverance provided by the Lord.

[90]Barnes, II, 163, equates the "vows" with promises made to the Lord by the psalmist while sick. Anderson, II, 794, notes that v. 14 is missing in some mss. While this is true, the majority include the verse. We gain nothing significant by omitting it. Anderson considers the vows fulfilled in offering a thanksgiving sacrifice. J. P. Fokkelman and Gary A Rendsburg, "נגדה נא לכל עמו (Psalm CXVI 14B, 18B)," *VT* 53:3 (2003): 328–36, note the *he locale* added to the preposition and the particle נא following a preposition, the only time both of these constructions occur in the OT. They locate נגדה as an imperative from נגד. This verb normally means "to tell," but cognates suggest a meaning of "guide, lead." The Hebrew word *nagîd*, "leader," supports this. This leads to translating the verse either as "I will lead now, for the benefit of all his people" or as "I will lead now his entire people." While the view is acceptable, it requires reliance on the grammar of cognate languages.

[91]Babylas, bishop of Antioch and martyred under Roman persecution of Christianity, went to his death while reciting v. 15.

occurrence. He had delivered the psalmist because it was not yet time for him to die, v. 15.[92]

16–19 The psalmist acknowledges his position as a servant of the Lord. He further is the "son of [the Lord's] handmaid," an indication of his godly heritage. He acknowledges that the Lord has loosed his "bonds," probably the constraints placed upon him by his foes, v. 16. He pledges to offer a thank offering to the Lord, a sacrifice made to express "thanksgiving" (*tôdâ*, see 26:7) for some blessing already received. He will also continue his reliance on the "name" (see v. 4) of the Lord in prayer, v. 17. As in v. 14, the psalmist pledges to pay his vow in the sight of others, v. 18. He will do this in the tabernacle courtyard in Jerusalem, where other worshipers will see him. He ends the psalm with a note of praise. The phrase "Praise ye the Lord" translates the well-known *halᵉlû-yah* "Hallelujah," v. 19.

PSALM 117

Some consider this shortest of all the psalms (and all chapters in the Bible) to be a conclusion for Psalm 116 or an introduction to Psalm 118.[93] It is separate, however, in many of the Hebrew manuscripts, as well as in the LXX and Vulgate. It is likely that

[92]There is no reason to apply the death of the saints to anything other than the death of individuals. Even Fausset, who at first makes this refer to the captivity of the nation, p. 354, later makes it speak of "the Lord's zealous care for His people's lives." Buttenwieser, pp. 643–44, rearranges the text, concluding with v. 15 as a question from the psalmist. There is no textual support for the rearrangement. The translation as a question is grammatically possible, but nothing in the text signals a question. Bratcher and Reyburn, p. 963, understand "precious" as "costly," thus paining the Lord when it takes place. Since the Lord controls death, the view is not likely. J. A. Emerton, "How Does the Lord Regard the Death of His Saints in Psalm CXVI. 15?" *JTS* 34:1 (1983): 155, relates *yaqar* to its Aramaic cognate and translates "grievous in Yahweh's sight is the death of his saints." Although *yaqar* occurs over thirty times in the OT, it does not have this sense elsewhere. In addition, since the Lord controls death, the view is suspect.

[93]Fausset, III, 354, and Hengstenberg, III, 367, consider Ps. 117 as the conclusion to Ps. 116. Oesterley, II, 479, tentatively supports it as introducing Ps. 118. With only weak support, Buttenwieser, p. 360, makes it the conclusion of Ps. 148.

Hebrew scribes joined it to either 116 or 118 to keep from losing it. Psalms 116 and 118 are songs of thanksgiving for deliverances from unknown circumstances. Psalm 117 is a brief hymn of unrestrained praise to the Lord. It is one of several synagogal psalms. These are chanted antiphonally in synagogues, the congregation repeating the first verse after every verse chanted by the precentor.[94] Here, of course, there are only two verses to chant antiphonally. The psalm is also one of the Hallel Psalms sung at the Feasts of Pentecost, Tabernacles, the New Moon, and Dedication (*ḥannukâ*).[95]

It is an "orphan psalm" with its author left anonymous and no background or setting given for its writing.[96] These two verses do, however, make an important eschatological emphasis, the worldwide praise that will one day come to the Lord. For this reason, it is well worth meditation.

I. The Source of Praise to the Lord 1

1 The psalmist call the "nations" (*gôyim*) of the earth to "praise" (*halᵉlû*) the Lord. While the word *gôyim* is translated most often as "nations," the apostle Paul quotes this verse in calling the Gentiles to praise the Lord, Romans 15:11. This looks forward to the millennial kingdom, when the nations of the world will indeed give praise to the Lord. While it would be appropriate now for the Gentile nations to praise Him, the ultimate fulfillment is yet future.

The repeated call to "praise" (*šabaḥ*, see 63:3) uses a different word from the initial command to "praise" (*halᵉlû*). The word *šabaḥ* has the sense of giving commendation for something. The command *halᵉlû* occurs most widely of all the words for giving praise. As such it has many components that make up its meaning. It may refer to giving glory to someone or something, to giving thanks, to express

[94]Jacob Zallel Lauterbach, "Psalms," *The Jewish Encyclopedia*, ed. Isidore Singer (New York: KTAV Publishing House, Inc.), X, 247–48.

[95]*NEJ*, p. 627.

[96]Kissane, p. 535, states that the psalm commemorates "the fulfillment of the promise made to Israel by the settlement in Canaan as God's chosen people." Jannie du Preez, "The Missionary Significance of Psalm 117 in the Book of Psalms and in the New Testament," *Missionalia* 27:3 (1999): 370, suggests that the psalm is post-exilic. The disparity in these dates reflects the lack of information in the psalm.

satisfaction or general delight. All of these are appropriate when we offer praise to the Lord.

This command goes forth to the "people" (*ᵓummîm*). The word occurs only here, but related words occur elsewhere. The combination of *gôyim* and *ᵓummîm* brings together all people on the earth.[97] Without exception, all should praise the Lord, v. 1.

II. The Cause for Praise to the Lord 2

2 There are two reasons stated for praising the Lord. In the first place, He is worthy of man's praise because of His "merciful kindness" (or "steadfast love," *ḥesed*, see 5:7). In all of His dealings with man, the Lord shows His love, a love that expresses loyalty to His Word and to His redeemed people. This is "great to us."[98]

The second cause for giving praise to the Lord is the reliability of His Word. His truth is forever, never changing, never failing, and always reliable. The God Who can give such guidance is worthy of man's praise. The psalmist ends with a spontaneous note of praise, *halᵉlû-yah*, "Praise ye the Lord." Because of the greatness of His love and the faithfulness of His Word, all mankind should give Him praise, v. 2.

PSALM 118

This psalm is the final psalm sung during the Passover celebration.[99] It is also sung during the Feasts of Pentecost, Tabernacles,

---

[97]The word *gôyim* is the most general word for "peoples, nations" and seems to have a horizontal stress, all people everywhere. The word *ᵓummîm* comes from a root meaning "mother." It does not occur widely to refer to "people" but may have a vertical sense, all descendants; cf. Gen. 25:17.

[98]Clarke, p. 285, understands the phrase as "prevails over us," a possible rendering. With this sense, the phrase refers to God's love that draws men away from their sin to Him. He prevails over them in winning them to Himself and to His cause.

[99]See the introduction to Ps. 113 for a discussion of the Hallel psalms. The introduction to Ps. 18 summarizes the songs of thanksgiving.

the New Moon, and Dedication (*ḥannukâ*).[100] It is a song of thanksgiving[101] as the psalmist celebrates his deliverance from dangers.[102] He had called on the Lord in prayer for help, v. 5. He faced a threat from others who hated him, v. 7. This may have been a coalition from various nations, v. 10, that had surrounded him, v. 11. The Lord had delivered him, vv. 13, 15*b*–16, 18, and he praises Him for it, vv. 21, 28. The fact that the psalmist faced the opposition of other nations suggests that the author was a leader of the people.

These circumstances appear to fit the time when Zerubbabel led the nation to rebuild the temple.[103] After he rejected the Samaritans' offer to help, a coalition from various nations opposed him, Ezra 4:8–10. The rebuilding of the temple stopped until the preaching of Haggai and Zechariah moved the nation to complete it, Ezra 5:1–2. Once more opposition arose, Ezra 5:7–17. This time, however, the Jews received permission to finish the building, Ezra 6:3–14. A joyful dedication of the building took place, Ezra 6:15–18. The joy-filled

---

[100]*NEJ*, p. 627.

[101]The psalm was the favorite of Martin Luther. He wrote, "This is my own beloved psalm. Although the entire Psalter and all of Holy Scriptures are dear to me as my only comfort and source of life, I fell in love with this psalm especially. Therefore I call it my own. When emperors and kings, the wise and the learned, and even saints could not aid me, this psalm proved a friend and helped me out of many great troubles. As a result, it is dearer to me than all the wealth, honor, and power of the pope, the Turk, and the emperor. I would be most unwilling to trade this psalm for all of it." *Luther's Works*, XIV, 45.

[102]Kidner, II, 412, thinks that the psalm "may have pictured . . . the rescue of Israel at the Exodus, and the eventual journey's end at Mount Zion." He does not, however, date its writing. Spurgeon, p. 503, assigns the psalm to David. Dahood, III, 156, and Eaton, p. 271, make the psalm pre-exilic. Rawlinson, III, 88, sets the psalm "in the time of Nebuchadnezzar, when not only the Babylonians but the Syrians, the Moabites, the Ammonites, and the Edomites took part in hostilities against Israel." Gaebelein, p. 434, and Ewald, II, 177, think the occasion for writing was the first celebration of the Feast of Tabernacles after the completion of the second temple. In this case, the pronoun "I" refers to the nation of Israel. Kirkpatrick, p. 693, dates it at the dedication of the rebuilt temple or the Passover that followed it. From the psalm, it is not possible to be dogmatic on the exact time of writing.

[103]Ezra 3:10–11 refers to thanking the Lord because "his mercy endureth for ever." Because this is close to the first and last verses of Ps. 118, Spurgeon, p. 503, concludes "that the people chanted the whole of this sublime song." On the other hand, Livingston, p. 412, calls the psalm "liturgical with indications that at least portions were chanted antiphonally." While either view may be true, they go beyond anything clearly recorded.

Feast of Tabernacles followed, Ezra 6:22. It may be that the author wrote the psalm for one of these occasions.[104]

Primarily because of vv. 21–22, we may consider the psalm messianic.[105] While the author undoubtedly thought of his own time, the NT makes Jesus Christ the fulfillment of the passage. The Gospels do so (Matt. 21:42; Mark 12:10–11; Luke 20:17). Luke refers to it again in Acts 4:11. Both Paul and Peter mention it (Eph. 2:20–21; I Pet. 2:4–8). This NT emphasis leaves no doubt regarding the messianic nature of the psalm.

I. Call to Give Thanks 1–4

1–4 The psalmist announces the theme of thanksgiving. The Lord is good, extending His "mercy" (or "steadfast love," *ḥesed*, see 5:7) to the nation forever. This call to express gratitude may have been a standard call to worship. It occurs again in v. 29; 106:1; and 107:1. It also occurs with variations in 136:1, 2, 3, and 26 and in the mouth of David in I Chronicles 16:34, v. 1. The psalmist directs his call to three groups, the same groups mentioned twice in 115:9–13. He speaks first to "Israel," the nation as a whole; then to "the house of Aaron," the priests and temple workers; and finally to those "that fear the Lord" (*yirʾê yehwah*, see 15:4), the godly in the land. This group may well have included Gentiles who worshiped the Lord. The psalmist urges all of these to speak of the Lord's continuing "mercy" (or "steadfast love," *ḥesed*), vv. 2–4.

II. Confidence in the Lord 5–9

5–9 As the result of his "distress" (or "anguish," *meṣar*, see 116:3), the psalmist has called on the Lord. The Lord has answered his prayer by setting him "in a large place," a place free of the pressures that had closed about him, v. 5. With the Lord on his side, the psalmist need not fear. His rhetorical question states his confidence that man cannot harm him, v. 6.[106] The Lord has helped him, along

[104]Kissane, pp. 537, 543, refers it to the Passover feast. Most authors, however, e.g., Cohen, p. 389; Gaebelein, p. 434, associate it with Tabernacles.

[105]Note 32 in the introduction to Ps. 2 briefly discusses the messianic psalms.

[106]Verse 6 repeats the thought of 56:4, but this may be coincidental. The quote in Heb. 13:6 comes from one of these verses.

with others who have given him aid. He is confident that he will look with victory on those that "hate" (*śane*ʾ, see 5:5) him, v. 7. Having this assurance, the psalmist states his belief that it is better to "trust" (*ḥasâ*, see 2:12) the Lord than to rely on men in general, v. 8, or "princes," the leaders of men, v. 9.

III. Characterization of the Threat 10–14

10–14 The psalmist refers to the nations that have surrounded him. In referring to "me," he thinks of himself as the leader of the nation. If he wrote the psalm after the situation described above, the nations included the Dinaites, Apharsathchites, Tarpelites, Apharsites, Archevites, Babylonians, Susanchites, Dehavites, and Elamites (Ezra 4:9). The Assyrians settled these groups of people in Syria after defeating them in their homelands. The enemies of Israel also appealed to Artaxerxes, leader of the dominant nation in the world at that time. Israel truly faced a large group of nations. The psalmist, however, has "destroy[ed] them" (or "cut them off")[107] by "the name of the Lord,"[108] His revealed nature, v. 10. The adversaries of Israel have surrounded them, but he has "destroy[ed] them" (or "cut them off") in the Lord's "name," v. 11. They have been like bees buzzing around the psalmist, but by the Lord's "name" they have been "quenched" (or "consumed") like thorns burned in the fire. He has "destroy[ed] them" (or "cut them off"), v. 12. They violently thrust at "me," the psalmist as the leader of the nation. They thought that he "might fall" in defeat. The Lord, however, has helped him, v. 13. Drawing on Moses' song in Exodus 15:2, the psalmist describes the Lord as the source of his strength and joy and as his deliverer from the adversaries of the nation, v. 14.

---

[107]The passage uses both perfect and imperfect verbs. The overall picture is that of expressing thanks for the deliverance given by the Lord to the nation. This requires us to understand the imperfect verbs to describe past actions. See G.K.C. 107 *a–d*; Waltke and O'Connor 31.2. Delitzsch, III, 226, translates the perfects as "hypothetical." Should the heathen attack, the psalmist will overcome in the name of the Lord. Verse 14, however, lends itself more to a deliverance already accomplished.

[108]See note 94 at 5:11 for a summary of the Lord's "name."

IV. Commemoration of the Deliverance 15–18

15–16 The psalmist describes the joy of Israel at the victory over their foes. There is a cry of "rejoicing" (*rinnâ*, see 17:1) and of "salvation" (or "victory") that comes from the "tabernacles" (or "tents") of the righteous. The right hand of the Lord, the hand representing His strength, has worked "valiantly" (or "powerfully") on their behalf, v. 15. His right hand is exalted among the people. It has worked powerfully for them, v. 16.

17–18 The psalmist speaks with confidence. His enemies will not prevail by bringing about his death. He will live and openly tell of the Lord's work, v. 17. The opposition he had faced had "chastened [him] sore," bringing severe discipline. The Lord, however, had chastened him in measure, not letting his foes take his life, v. 18.

V. Celebration of the Deliverance 19–21

19–21 The "gates of righteousness" are the entrances to the temple area through which the righteous enter as they come to worship. We have no archaeological information about the temple built in the time of Ezra and Zerubbabel. The original temple, however, had an inner and an outer court with gates for entrance. We assume that the psalmist faced a similar arrangement. He plans to enter into the temple area where he will praise the Lord, v. 19. Adding the verb yields, "This *is* the gate of the Lord." The righteous enter through the gate as they come to worship, v. 20. The psalmist will praise the Lord for answered prayer and for his "salvation," his deliverance from his foes, v. 21.

VI. Consequence of the Deliverance 22–23

22–23 The psalmist gives a poetical picture of what has happened. The "builders," those who would establish their own kingdom, had rejected the divinely appointed cornerstone of the kingdom, the nation of Israel. Despite this rejection, Israel has become the "head stone of the corner," the major stone at the top of the building of God's kingdom. The NT draws on this in referring to Jesus Christ as the chief stone in the building of the church (Matt. 21:42; Mark 12:10–11; Luke 20:17; Acts 4:11; I Pet. 2:7), v. 22. The psalmist marvels at the work of the Lord in building His house. This spiritual fulfillment of this thought comes in the Resurrection, when God the Father unmistakably declares His satisfaction with the redeeming work of the Son, v. 23.

VII. Commendation of the Deliverer 24–29

24–25 The "day" is that time when God restores the nation to its position.[109] The psalmist urges others to rejoice[110] in this mighty work of the Lord, v. 24.[111] He asks the Lord to "save now," to deliver the nation in times of future need. Specifically, he asks the Lord to send them "prosperity."[112] Since Israel was still a weak nation that faced opposition from the surrounding people, that needed to sow crops and reap a harvest, and that needed to build homes, the request for prosperity was appropriate, v. 25.

26–27 Honoring the Lord is necessary in these perilous times. The priests bless (*barak*, see 5:12) the one who comes to worship the Lord in the temple.[113] All four of the Gospels refer to v. 26*a* in describing the triumphal entry of the Lord into Jerusalem (Matt. 21:9; Mark 11:9–10; Luke 19:38; John 12:13).[114] As a nation, Israel will not see the Lord again until they acknowledge Him as the One coming in the "name" (see v. 10) of God (Matt. 23:39). The nation in the time of the psalmist has pronounced blessings on "you," the Lord

---

[109]Adele Berline, "Psalm 118:24," *JBL* 96:4 (1977): 567–68, argues that the translation should be "This is what the Lord has done today," emphasizing the work of the Lord rather than the day of His work. The MT, however, supports the traditional translation found in most Bibles.

[110]The verbs "rejoice" and "be glad" should be translated as jussives: "Let us rejoice and be glad in it." The psalmist looks back to an accomplished event, not forward to something anticipated.

[111]The chorus "This is the Day," © 1967, Scripture in Song, a division of Integrity Music, Inc., ASCAP, with the music by Les Garrett, comes from v. 24.

[112]Jakob J. Petuchowski, "'*Hoshiᶜah Na*' in Psalm CXVIII 25, — A Prayer for Rain," *VT* 5 (1955): 271, relates *ṣalaḥ* to rain. This is interpretive and does not explain why v. 25 uses *ṣalaḥ*, routinely "prosperity," and not *gešem* or *maṭar*, used elsewhere in the Psalms for "rain."

[113]Fausset, III, 359, refers the pronoun to Zerubbabel. The priests bless him for his part in the rebuilding. While this is possible, the verse is too general to let us be certain as to whether or not any specific person is in view.

[114]Matthew, Mark, and John introduce the quotation with the word "Hosannah." This transliterates ὡσαννά, the Greek equivalent of *hôšîᶜâ naʾ*, translated "save now" in v. 25.

Himself, from the temple where they worship, v. 26. The mighty God is also the gracious Lord. He has given the light of His guidance. The people should "bind the sacrifice [*ḥag*, see 81:3] with cords." Since at a festival time, many sacrifices might be offered (Num. 29:12–34), it was necessary to bind the animals until the time of their offering.[115] Thus bound, the animals could be slain and sacrificed in gratitude to the Lord. The use of *ḥag* suggests that the psalmist has a festival sacrifice in mind, one of the feast days in which Israel would offer sacrifice to the Lord, v. 27.

28–29 The psalmist acknowledges the Lord as his God. He praises and extols Him, v. 28. He ends the psalm using the same words with which he began. He calls upon the nation to thank the Lord for His goodness and "mercy" (or "steadfast love," *ḥesed*), v. 29.

Although the trying circumstances of believers today may differ from those of the psalmist, it is still right to bring those problems to the Lord in prayer. Feelings of gratitude, vv. 1–4, and confidence in the Lord, vv. 5–9, underlie the psalmist's reliance on Him in prayer. After describing his trial to the Lord, vv. 10–14, he states his confidence that God will deliver him, vv. 15–18. He anticipates a celebration at the temple, vv. 19–21. His recognition of God's work serves as a backdrop to the Resurrection, vv. 22–23. He praises the Lord, vv. 24–29. The psalm serves as a general pattern for giving praise to the Lord for deliverance from trials.

PSALM 119

Psalm 119 is one of the most widely known psalms. Its unique emphasis on the Word of God gives it a prominence that is easy to remember. For this reason, Philip Henry, father of the well-known

[115]The phrase might also be translated, "Order the feast day with foliage." The Talmud, *Sukkah 45b*, refers this to binding boughs of foliage to the altar at the Feast of Tabernacles, as the priests brings sacrifices and apply the blood to the "horns" of the altar of burnt offering. While Lev. 23:40 refers to branches of trees, these were used for building the booths in which the people lived. Nothing suggests that boughs should be bound to the horns of the altar.

Matthew Henry and, like his son, a seventeenth-century English pastor, recommended taking a verse of the psalm "every morning to meditate upon, and so go over the psalm twice in the year."[116] Thomas Sternhold and John Hopkins, authors of the first English Psalter, recommended, "If thou woudest live a godly life, if thou woudest replynysh thy mynde with goo[d]ly preceptes, and thereby obtayne immortalitie, and eternal felicitie: Study diligently the .119. Psalme."[117] When properly translated, only vv. 84, 90, 121, 122, and 132 do not clearly refer to the word of God.[118] Martin Luther described it as "The Christian's golden ABC of the praise, love, power and use of the word of God."[119]

We do not know the author or the occasion that led him to focus on God's Word.[120] The author was apparently a relatively young man (vv. 9, 100), yet mature enough that he could speak of knowing God's Word from "of old" (v. 152). He was undergoing persecution (vv. 42, 61, 110) that included opposition from those in high places (vv. 23,

---

[116]J. B. Williams, ed., *The Lives of Philip and Matthew Henry* (Carlisle, Penn.: The Banner of Truth Trust, 1974), p. 247.

[117]Quoted by Donald P. Hustad, "The Psalms as Worship Expression: Personal and Congregational," *RevEx* 81:3 (1984): 422.

[118]Even in these verses, there may be veiled references to God's Word. Verse 84 refers to God's judgment on the wicked, an act carried out in accord with His word. Verse 90 refers to God's "faithfulness," a truth we know only by comparing His actions with His word. In v. 121, the psalmist states his own "judgment and justice" (or "justice and righteousness"). On the basis of the blessings God's Word promises to the righteous, he prays for deliverance. Verse 122 asks for deliverance from the proud, a prayer based on the psalmist's obedience to God's Word. Verse 132 refers to those who "love thy name," an attitude that can be seen only in obedience to the Word.

[119]Trans. from microfiche, *Early American Imprints 1639–1800*, American Antiquarian Society.

[120]Horne, p. 519, identifies David as the author of the psalm. Rotherham, p. 514, assigns the psalm to Hezekiah. Leupold, p. 822, dates the psalm to "the days of Ezra and Nehemiah" when the nation faced persecution from their enemies. Cohen, 394, sees a follower of Ezra as the author. Delitzsch, III, 245, does not name an author but concludes, "It is at least probable that the . . . Psalm . . . is the work of one in prison, who whiled away his time with the plaiting together of his complaints and his consolatory thoughts." Will Soll, *Psalm 119: Matrix, Form, and Setting*, in *The Catholic Biblical Quarterly Monograph Series*, no. 23, p. 152, dates the psalm during the Babylonian captivity and identifies Jehoiachin as the writer. Phillips, II, 260, tentatively advances Daniel as the author. R. E. O. White, "The Student's Psalm?" *ET* 102:2 (1990): 71, places it "late in Israel's post-exilic period." White, p. 72, considers the psalm the exercise of a student scribe, "a pupil's set assignment in poetic composition." This variety shows the impossibility of identifying the author with certainty.

46, 161). This suggests that he was a highly placed leader, perhaps the king of the nation. The more I study the psalm, the more David seems to be the author. I cannot prove this, so I have left the authorship general in the discussion.[121]

The psalmist uses ten different words to describe God's Word.[122] An excursus on these words follows the discussion of the psalm. Together, they convey the many-sidedness of God's revelation to man. The rabbis noted that the use of ten words pointed to the Decalogue.[123] We do not know whether the number is significant or not. In any case, the words point to the rich depth of meaning that comes from God's Word. As believers apply this Word to their lives, it gives eternal results.

The psalm is an acrostic with twenty-two stanzas of eight verses each. Each stanza begins with a successive letter of the Hebrew alphabet, beginning with *alep* and concluding with *tau*. Each stanza has eight lines, each line comprising two stichs. Every other stich begins with the same letter of the Hebrew alphabet. This makes the psalm a sixteen-stich acrostic. It is by far the most elaborate such poetical arrangement in the OT.

The organization of the psalm revolves around God's Word. The psalmist expresses his obedience to the Word as well as his meditation on it and love for it, and he also appeals to its promises. All of this, however, is woven together with a secondary theme of prayer for the Lord's deliverance from enemies.[124] The mention of God's Word

---

[121]In support of David's authorship, all of the other acrostic psalms (9–10, 25, 34, 37, 111, 112, 145) except the anonymous 111 and 112 are authored by David. Verse 103 recalls 19:10. Other Davidic psalms duplicate the numerous references to his enemies and his trust in the Lord.

[122]*NIB*, IV, accepts only the eight words used most often, omitting *derek* and *ʾoraḥ*. In the comments on v. 3, however, *NIB* recognizes that *derek* indicates God's revelation. It also refers to v. 15 where *ʾoraḥ* does the same. Bratcher and Reyburn, pp. 998, 1002, are similar but recognize *derek* and *ʾoraḥ* as synonyms in the commentary. Kissane, p. 545, and Bridges, II, 415, assume that the eight words originally occurred in each of the strophes but that textual errors have created exceptions. Without mss support, both emend in order to restore the perceived original text.

[123]So Delitzsch, III, 243, and Kirkpatrick, p. 703.

[124]Morris, pp. 148–157, gives a theme for each section, relating each one differently to the Word of God. His applications are artificial, however, as he picks a word or phrase here and there to characterize each paragraph. Delitzsch, III, 243–44, also gives a theme for each section. Together, these support the general theme of "a prayer for steadfastness in the midst of an ungodly, degenerate race, and in the midst

establishes the author's right to prayer. Over one-third of the verses relate to prayer in some way.[125]

ʾ*Alep*

The opening four verses state the believer's responsibility to God's Word. The psalmist begins with two beatitudes that pronounce a "bless[ing]" (*ʾašrê*, see 1:1) on those who follow God's word. In both verses, the word *ʾašrê* is an intensive plural, emphasizing the spiritual blessing God gives to these people. It may rightly be rendered, "O the blessedness of . . ." Verse 1 states the result before the action: "Blessed are the undefiled [or 'blameless,' see *tom*, 7:8]." Their freedom from the blemishes of sin comes from walking through life in accord with the "law" (*tôrâ*, see excursus) given by the Lord. This refers to the whole revelation of God, not merely the Ten Commandments, v. 1. Once more, "blessed" (*ʾašrê*) are those who keep the "testimonies" (*ʿedût*, see excursus) of the Lord. As evidence of this, they "seek" (*daraš*, see 9:10) Him with all of their heart. The use of *daraš*, indicating a careful search, suggests that the search includes time spent in meditating on His Word, v. 2. Once again, the psalmist gives the result before the action. The godly person will not commit "iniquity" (*ʿawlâ*, see 7:3) by turning from God's Word. He walks according to God's "ways" (*derek*, see excursus), v. 3. God has commanded His followers to keep His "precepts" (*piqqudîm*, see excursus). The subject is emphatic, "thou thyself." The godly person

---

of great trouble, which is heightened by the pain [the psalmist] feels at the prevailing apostasy, and a prayer for ultimate deliverance." While Delitzsch's view seems forced and artificially constructed, he does recognize prayer as the theme. Soll, pp. 59, 144, considers the psalm a prayer for the restoration of Jehoiachin's rule. Ken Burkett, *Psalm 119: A Thematic and Literary Analysis* (PhD diss., Bob Jones University, 1994), pp. 62, 85, sees the general theme of personal prayer in the psalm.

[125]Seventy-seven petitions occur in sixty-two verses. These predominantly use the imperative, vv. 12, 17, 18, 22, 25, 26, 27, 28, 29, 33, 34, 35, 36, 37 (twice), 38, 39, 40, 49, 58, 64, 66, 68, 73, 86, 88, 94, 107, 108 (twice), 116*a*, 117, 121, 122*a*, 124 (twice), 125, 132 (twice), 133*a*, 134, 135 (twice), 144, 145, 146, 149 (twice), 153 (twice), 154 (twice), 156, 159 (twice), 169*b*, 170*b*, 176. Eighteen petitions use the jussive with both negative requests, vv. 8, 10, 19, 31, 43, 116*b*, 122*b*, 133*b*, and positive requests, vv. 41, 43, 77, 78, 79, 80, 169*a*, 170*a*, 175 (twice). Two petitions use infinitives to make their request, vv. 76, 173. In addition, in three verses the psalmist talks to the Lord without making a petition, vv. 5, 82, 84.

is to keep these "diligently," exercising great care to observe the Lord's directions, v. 4.

The psalmist expresses his desires for consistency. This begins a series of four verses in which the author gives his personal response to the Lord and His Word. He wishes to keep the Lord's "statutes" (*ḥoq*, see excursus), the unchangeable Word of God, v. 5. He will not then be publicly "ashamed" (*bôš*, see 6:10) by his failure in spiritual matters. He will "have respect unto" (or "regard") the Lord's "commandments" (*miṣwâ*, see excursus), v. 6. This obedience to the Lord will lead naturally to praise. The psalmist will offer this by "uprightness of heart," living in accord with God's Word. It is worth noting that obeying God praises Him. It acknowledges the truth of His Word, adopts its wisdom, and accepts its power. For these reasons, the psalmist looks forward to learning more of the "righteous judgments [*mišpaṭ*, see excursus]" of the Lord, v. 7.[126] The psalm writer pledges to keep God's "statutes" (*ḥoq*) but recognizes his need of divine help. He pleads with the Lord not to "forsake" him, v. 8.

Beth

The author poses a question in v. 9 and answers it in v. 10. In view of man's sinful nature, how can a young man "cleanse his way" (or "make his way pure")? Verse 9*b* continues the question: in order to live in accord with God's "word" (*dabar*, see excursus), v. 9.[127] In view of his youth, the psalmist displays unusual spiritual maturity with his answer.[128] He has earnestly "sought" (*daraš*, see 9:10) the Lord with all of his heart. He asks the Lord not to let him "wander"

[126]The psalmist's desire to learn God's Word is a recurring theme throughout the psalm; cf. vv. 12, 26, 64, 66, 68, 71, 73, 108, 124, 135, 171.

[127]There is debate over the translation of the second half of the verse. Among others, Ewald, II, 259, and Dahood, III, 161, follow the AV in answering the question. It may also continue the question: "How shall a young man cleanse his way to keep it according to your word?" The grammar supports the second approach. The infinitive in 9*b*, *lišmor*, with the *lamed* prefix would normally express purpose or motives or would occur epexegetically, G.K.C. 114 *g*, *o*. The identical construction occurs in vv. 4, 5, 57, 60, and 106. In none of these can we translate the infinitive in the same way as the AV does in v. 9. In addition, the same construction occurs thirty times elsewhere in the OT with this sense.

[128]Rawlinson, III, 103, states that the author is older and gives advice here to young men. The inclusion in the psalm of vv. 99, 100, argues for the relative youth of the author.

(*šagâ*, see 7, intro.) from His "commandments" (*miṣwâ*). The psalmist states his need of the Lord's help to keep him from falling into unthinking deviation from God's Word, v. 10. In all likelihood, he thinks now of the potential sin he has just mentioned. He has "hid" (or "treasured") God's "word" (*ᵓimrâ*, see excursus) in his heart to keep him from falling into mindless sin against God, v. 11. With renewed appreciation for the Word of God, the psalmist "bless[es]" (*barak*, see 5:12) the Lord. In the OT, pronouncing a blessing on God is a way of expressing gratitude and praise. The writer asks the Lord to teach him His "statutes" (*ḥoq*). The request recognizes the need for God's guidance in understanding His Word, v. 12.

The psalmist continues to express his relationship to God's Word. He has openly "declared" (or "recounted") to others the "judgments" (*mišpaṭ*) God has spoken, v. 13. He has "rejoiced" (or "exulted," *śûś*, see 19:5) in the way directed by God's "testimonies" (*ᶜedût*). To show the extent of his joy, he notes that it is greater than rejoicing over "riches," v. 14. Because of this great value, he plans to "meditate" (*śîaḥ*, see 55:2) on the "precepts" (*piqqudîm*) of God. He will "have respect unto" (or "consider") the "ways" (*ᵓoraḥ*, see excursus) of the Lord, v. 15. He will delight himself in the "statutes" (*ḥoqqîm*) of God and not "forget" (or "ignore") His "word" (*dabar*), v. 16.

Gimel

The psalmist prays that the Lord will "deal bountifully" (*gamal*, see 7:4) with him, doing good for him so that he may live and keep God's "word" (*dabar*), v. 17. He also asks the Lord to open his eyes, clearing away the cloudy veil created by sin. This will let him see "wonderful things" (*palaᵓ*, see 9:1), extraordinary truths, from the "law" (*tôrâ*), v. 18. He considers himself a "stranger," a sojourner in the earth while he awaits his heavenly home (cf. Heb. 11:13–16; I Pet. 2:11). He asks the Lord not to hide His commands (*miṣwâ*) from him. The request implies the psalmist's awareness that he needs guidance from the Lord in order to live properly, v. 19. For this reason, his soul "breaketh" (better "is crushed") with the desire to have the "judgments" (*mišpaṭ*) of the Lord continually with him, v. 20.

The writer notes that the Lord has "rebuked" those "proud" (or "arrogant") people who are under God's curse because they "err" (*šagâ*, see v. 10), ignorantly going away from God's "commandments" (*miṣwâ*), v. 21. He asks the Lord to take from him the "reproach" (or "scorn") and "contempt" that others would direct to him. He has kept the "testimonies" (*ᶜedût*) of the Lord, separating from the world, v. 22. Although "princes" (or "rulers") speak against the psalmist, this does not cause him to change his ways. He continues to "meditate" (see *śîaḥ*, 55:2) on God's "statutes" (*ḥôq*), v. 23. The Lord's "testimonies" (*ᶜedût*) are his "delight" (*šaᶜaᶜšuᶜay*)[129] and his "counsellors." The MT lit. reads, "men [*ᵓenôš*, see 8:4] of my counsel [*ᶜeṣâ*, see 1:1]." The psalmist has replaced human advisors, who might lead him astray, with God's "testimonies" that will always give him right guidance, v. 24.

Dalet

The psalmist feels great pressure from the attacks of his foes. So heavy is this burden that he feels as if his soul lies buried in the ground. He prays that the Lord will "quicken" him,[130] reviving his spirit according to His "word" (*dabar*). The writer refers here to the many promises of God gives to bless those who obey Him, v. 25.[131] He has declared his ways to the Lord in prayer, seeking divine help for his problems.[132] The Lord has heard his plea. In response, the psalmist asks the Lord to teach him His "statutes" (*ḥôq*) so that he may continue to live correctly, v. 26. He also asks the Lord to help him understand His "precepts" (*piqqûdîm*). In response, the psalm writer pledges to "talk" (*śîaḥ*, see 55:2) of the "wondrous works" (*palaᵓ*, see 9:1) of the Lord, v. 27. Again referring to the burdens he

[129]The form *šaᶜaᶜšuᶜay* is unusual but not rare. It is an intensive plural that appropriately conveys here the extreme delight of the psalmist. The word occurs again at vv. 77, 92, 143, and 174.

[130]This is one of the author's most frequent requests. The word *ḥayâ* occurs sixteen times in the psalm, translated either "live" or "quicken." See vv. 17, 25, 37, 40, 50, 77, 88, 93, 107, 116, 144, 149, 154, 156, 159, 175.

[131]Moll, p. 590, refers the "reviving . . . not to the strengthening of the spiritual, but to the restoration of the physical life, welfare, and prosperity, by deliverance from distress and danger." Cohen, p. 395, likewise refers to restoration of "fresh strength." As I read the verse, I see a restoration of the emotional side of life rather than of the physical or material. The Lord could bring this about by delivering the psalmist from his foes or by encouraging him in the midst of his trials.

[132]Henry, p. 691, mentions the possibility that the psalmist here confesses his sins to the Lord. The verb "declared," however, never refers to confession elsewhere in the Psalms.

bears, the psalmist describes his soul that "melteth" (or "weeps") for heaviness. He asks the Lord to give him strength from His "word" (*dabar*), v. 28.

The author asks the Lord to take the "way of lying" (or "deceitful way") from him.[133] Instead, he desires the Lord to "graciously" (*ḥanan*, see 4:1) show him the way of the "law" (*tôrâ*), v. 29. He has chosen "the way [*derek*] of truth [or 'faithfulness']," i.e., the way that faithfully carries out the will of God as expressed in His Word. He has "laid [*šawâ*] before [himself]" (or "agreed with")[134] God's "judgments" (*mišpaṭ*), v. 30. He has "stuck" (or "clung") to the "testimonies" (*ᶜedût*) of the Lord. On this basis, he asks the Lord not to put him to open "shame" (*bôš*, see 6:10). He apparently thinks of the public shame of having his foes overcome him, v. 31. He will "run" in the way defined by the "commandments" (*miṣwâ*) of the Lord. The idea of running expresses the psalmist's desire to obey the Word of the Lord quickly. The phrase "when thou shalt enlarge my heart" is better "for you have enlarged my heart." The Lord has given him the spiritual understanding to see the value of hurrying to follow His Word, v. 32.[135]

Hê

The writer prays that the Lord will teach him the "way" (*derek*) marked out by His "statutes" (*ḥoq*). This prayer occurs seven times

[133]Hengstenberg, III, 389, limits "the way of lying" to apostasy, departing from God. While this is possible, nothing in the context suggests this narrow view. In contrast with "the way of lying," the psalmist chooses "the way of truth," the "judgments" of God, the "testimonies" of the Lord, and the "commandments" of God, vv. 30–32. These cover every false way.

[134]There is debate as to whether the verb is *šawâ* I, "to agree with," or *šawâ* II, "to set, place" (so AV). If we adopt *šawâ* II, the words "before me" must be supplied to make sense of the verse. Kirkpatrick, p. 710; Soll, p. 158; and Alexander, p. 493, adopt *šawâ* I. Hirsch, II, 337; Horne, p. 528; and Cohen, p. 398, adopt *šawâ* II. I have opted for *šawâ* I as occurring more often in the OT and as giving the simpler view.

[135]Delitzsch, III, 248, understands the enlarged heart as one that is free from the burden of persecution. He states that God widens the psalmist's heart "by granting and preserving to the persecuted one the joyfulness of confession and the confidence of hope." Hirsch, II, 337, similarly says that the enlarging of the heart expresses freedom "from the constricting effect of suffering upon my spirit." The psalmist's desire, however, is to keep God's commands. Increased spiritual understanding would enable this more than freedom from an emotional burden would.

in the psalm (vv. 12, 26, 33, 64, 68, 124, 135), the repetition showing the psalmist's deep desire to know God's Word. He pledges his obedience to "the end" (*ᶜeqeb*), throughout the remainder of his life, v. 33.[136] The poet prays that the Lord will help the psalmist understand His truth. In response, he will keep His "law" (*tôrâ*) with his "whole heart," not with a divided loyalty, v. 34. He asks the Lord to make him go in the path defined by His "commandments" (*miṣwâ*). It would be possible to stray from this path through ignorance or impulsive behavior. The psalmist, however, asks the Lord to keep him from this since he has a deep emotional "delight" (*ḥapeṣ*, see 18:19) in the Lord's Word, v. 35.

The author gives two examples to illustrate the prayer he has just made. He wants the Lord to "incline" (or "turn") his heart to His "testimonies" (*ᶜedût*) and away from "covetousness" (or "unjust gain"), v. 36. Next, the writer asks the Lord to turn his eyes from "vanity" (or "worthless things," *šawᵓ*, see 12:2) and to "quicken" him, cf. v. 25, making him responsive, to His "way" (*derek*). These requests show the greater value of spiritual truth as compared to material prosperity and things without eternal significance, v. 37.

Rather than devoting himself to matters with no lasting value, the psalmist prays that the Lord will "stablish" His "word" (*ᵓimrâ*), causing it to take a firm stand in his life. The next phrase, "who is devoted to thy fear [*yirᵓâ*, see 2:11]," is better "which belongs to your fear," i.e., which underlies reverence for the Lord.[137] The psalmist recognizes that God's Word will produce a reverence in him for the Lord, v. 38. He asks the Lord to turn away from him the "reproach which [he] fear[s]," the reproach that would come on him if he spurned God's Word. He has no fear of being guided by the "judgments" (*mišpaṭ*) of God, those laws that establish justice among mankind, since they are good, v. 39. He longs for the "precepts" (*piqqudîm*) of the Lord. He asks the Lord to "quicken" him, cf. v. 25, to make him live, in His ways of righteousness, v. 40.

---

[136]Harman, p. 3854, and Soll, p. 159, give the possibility that *ᶜeqeb* refers to "reward" as in 19:11 (also 40:15; 70:3). Hirsch, II, 337, refers *ᶜeqeb* "to the utmost." The basic sense of *ᶜeqeb* is "consequence." The word occurs again in v. 112, where it completes *ᶜôlam*, "alway," thus supporting the idea of "end."

[137]Soll, p. 160, understands the psalmist as praying that he may establish the fear of the Lord "in Israel and among the 'nations.'" The parallelism with 38*a*, however, suggests a more personal application.

Waw

The letter *waw* is the easiest letter to use in beginning a line. The writer introduces the paragraph with *waw*. In each of the following lines, he shows his literary skill by beginning with a *waw-alep* combination. He continues to plead with the Lord. He asks that the "mercies" (or "steadfast love," *ḥesed*, see 5:7) of the Lord may come to him. He then defines this as "salvation," here referring to deliverance from his foes. This will come according to God's "word" (*ʾimrâ*), the promises that God will protect those who obey Him, v. 41. This deliverance will let the psalmist answer anyone who reproaches him. He makes this prayer because he trusts in God's "word" (*dabar*), v. 42. He also asks the Lord not to "take . . . utterly"[138] from his mouth the "word" (*dabar*) that is true. He reminds the Lord that he has placed his "hope" (*yaḥal*, see 31:24) in the Lord's "judgments" (*mišpaṭ*), v. 43.

The psalmist now recites five steps he will take. He has purposed to keep God's "law" (*tôrâ*) to the end of time, v. 44. Further, he anticipates walking "at liberty" (lit. "in a broad place"). The idea of walking in a wide area refers to the freedom given to those who limit themselves only by the word of God. The poet feels this liberty because he carefully "seek[s]" (*daraš*, see 9:10) the "precepts" (*piqqudîm*) of the Lord, v. 45. He will speak of the Lord's "testimonies" (*ʿedut*) before kings without feeling "ashamed" (*bôš*, see 6:10) of his position, v. 46. He will delight in the Lord's "commandments" (*miṣwâ*), which he loves (cf. vv. 48, 127), v. 47. He will lift up his hands to God's "commandments" (*miṣwâ*), an act of worship focused on God's Word, since this reflects the character of God.[139] He will also "meditate" (see *śîaḥ*, 55:2) on the Lord's "statutes" (*ḥoq*), v. 48.

Zayin

The psalmist continues to express his devotion to the Word of God. He asks the Lord to remember the "word" (*dabar*) given to His servant, the promise that has him "hope" (*yaḥal*, see 31:24). There is

---

[138]The expression "take . . . utterly" translates a combination of words with the sense "take . . . exceedingly." This expresses taking something to the highest degree, i.e., "utterly take."

[139]W. E. Barnes, p. 576, and VanGemeren, p. 745, treat the lifting of the hands as prayer. While this is true elsewhere, e.g., 63:4; 141:2, prayer is not appropriate here. We pray not to the Word of God but to the God of the Word.

no specific communication given that we can point to. The psalmist's prayer likely refers to the general promises of care and protection in God's Word, v. 49.[140] He finds comfort in the midst of "affliction" (*ʿanî*, see 9:12), the opposition from his enemies. God's "word" (*ʾimrâ*) has "quickened" him, reviving his spirits; cf. v. 25, v. 50. The "proud" (or "arrogant") have held the psalmist "greatly in derision" (or have "greatly scorned me"). Despite this opposition, he has not turned from the "law" (*tôrâ*) of the Lord, v. 51. He finds comfort in the "judgments" (*mišpaṭ*) of the Lord given in the past, v. 52.[141]

The psalmist feels "horror" (better "burning indignation") because of wicked men that turn from God's "law" (*tôrâ*), v. 53. In sharp contrast, the "statutes" (*ḥoq*) of God have been the theme of his songs in "the house of [his] pilgrimage [or 'sojournings']." The author has been fleeing from his foes, but the word of God becomes the theme of his songs wherever he lodges, v. 54.[142] He remembers the "name"[143] of the Lord, His nature, at night. Expressing satisfaction with the Lord he serves, he keeps His "law" (*tôrâ*), v. 55. The phrase "this I had" is lit. "this is to me," i.e., "this is my practice." He refers to his keeping of the Lord's "precepts" (*piqqudîm*), v. 56.

Ḥêt

The Lord is the "portion" of the psalmist. For this reason, he has promised to keep the Lord's "words" (*dabar*), v. 57. He has entreated the "favour" (lit. "face") of the Lord with an undivided heart. He entreats the Lord to "be merciful" (or "be gracious," *ḥanan*, see 4:1) to him according to the promises in His "word" (*ʾimrâ*), v. 58. At some point in the past, he considered the ways that he was following in life. He realized his errors and turned to follow the "testimonies"

---

[140]Perowne, II, 355, refers to some "special word of promise which had been [the writer's] stay in his affliction." This is possible although we have no evidence of it elsewhere in the psalm.

[141]Anderson, II, 824, and Alexander, p. 497, understand *mišpaṭ* to refer to acts of judgment mercifully given to Israel and imposed on their enemies. While this is a possible view, the greater emphasis in the psalm is on the ordinances given by God to guide His people.

[142]Moll, p. 591, refers the "house of my pilgrimage" to the earthly sojourn of the believer. The view is possible, but the psalmist probably thinks of his own flight from his enemies.

[143]Note 94 at 5:11 gives a summary of the Lord's "name."

(*ᶜedut*) of the Lord, v. 59. He made these changes speedily, with no delay in keeping the Lord's "commandments" (*miṣwâ*), v. 60.

The phrase "the bands of the wicked robbed [*ᶜûd*] me" is better "the cords [i.e., 'snares'] of the wicked surround me."[144] Despite this threat, the psalmist has not forgotten God's "law" (*tôrâ*), v. 61. In the middle of the night, he will thank the Lord for His "righteous judgments [*mišpaṭ*]." The poet thinks once more of the righteous ordinances of the Lord, v. 62.[145] He is a companion of others who "fear" (*yareᵓ*, see 2:11) the Lord and who keep His "precepts" (*piqqûdîm*). The parallelism suggests that those who fear the Lord also keep His Word, v. 63. The psalmist sees that the Lord's "mercy" (or "steadfast love," *ḥesed*, see 5:7) fills the earth. As more evidence of this loyal love, he asks the Lord to teach him His "statutes" (*ḥoq*), v. 64.

Ṭêt

Despite the threat the psalmist feels, he acknowledges that the Lord has been good to him. The Lord has dealt with him according to the promises of care and protection in His "word" (*dabar*), v. 65. He asks the Lord to teach him "good judgment" (or "sound discernment") and experiential "knowledge" (*daᶜat*, see *yadaᶜ*, 1:6). The request implies that God's Word will be the basis for these aspects of wisdom. The author states his personal belief in the "commandments" (*miṣwâ*) of the Lord, v. 66. In the past, before he was "afflicted" (*ᶜanâ*, see 35:13), he had gone astray from the Lord. The affliction has been good for him since it has driven him to keep the "word" (*ᵓimrâ*); cf. Hebrews 12:11, v. 67. The psalmist recognizes that the Lord is good in His nature and in His work. He asks again that the Lord teach him His "statutes" (*ḥoq*); cf. vv. 12, 26, 33, 64, 124, 135, v. 68.

"The proud [or 'arrogant'] have forged [*ṭapal*] a lie" against the writer. The verb *ṭapal* is "to smear, plaster over." It gives the poetic picture of plastering over the psalmist with so many lies that his true character cannot be seen. Even then, he pledges to keep the Lord's

---

[144]Horne, p. 539, and Calvin, IV, 416, follow the AV translation of *ᶜûd*, "robbed." The verb, however, never has this sense elsewhere. The basic sense of *ᶜûd*, "to return, go around, repeat," occurs only here in the *piᶜel* as "surround."

[145]Fausset, III, 306, relates "midnight" to the judgment of God on Egypt, Exod. 11:4; 12:29. Israel therefore "at midnight remembers this deliverance and rises to give thanks." The author of the psalm, however, is an individual, not the nation.

"precepts" (*piqqûdîm*), v. 69. The heart of his foes is "as fat [*ṭapaš*][146] as grease [*ḥeleb*, see 17:10]" or, perhaps better, "covered with fat." The portrayal picturesquely describes hearts that are insensitive to spiritual truth. The psalmist, however, will delight in God's "law" (*tôrâ*), v. 70. Returning to the thought of v. 67, he admits that it has been good for him to be "afflicted" (*ᶜanâ*, see 35:13). The affliction has helped him learn the "statutes" (*ḥoq*) of the Lord, v. 71. The "law" (*tôrâ*) spoken by God is better to the writer of the psalm than great wealth is, v. 72.

Yôd

The psalm writer acknowledges God as the Creator. The reference to God's "hands" is anthropomorphic, describing the Lord in human terms to provide an understandable picture. Since, however, the Lord has "made . . . and fashioned [or 'established']" him, the author asks that He also would give him spiritual understanding of His "commandments" (*miṣwâ*), v. 73. Others who "fear" (see *yirʾâ*, 2:11) the Lord will rejoice when they see the psalmist, because he has "hoped" (*yaḥal*, see 31:24) in God's "word" (*dabar*). As in v. 63, there is a relationship between fearing the Lord and keeping God's Word, v. 74.

The psalmist knows that the "judgments" (*mišpaṭ*) of the Lord are "right" (or "righteous"). As in vv. 52 and 62, the author refers once more to the righteous ordinances of the Lord. He also knows that the Lord has "afflicted" (*ᶜanâ*, see 35:13) him "in faithfulness," for a just purpose (cf. vv. 67, 68, 71), v. 75.

The psalmist now makes five separate requests of the Lord. Rather than affliction, he asks the Lord to let His "merciful kindness" (or "steadfast love," *ḥesed*, see 5:7) comfort him according to the promises in His "word" (*ʾimrâ*), v. 76. He prays that the Lord will extend His "tender mercies" (or "compassions")[147] to him so that he may live and escape the threat from his enemies. He bases his prayer on his "delight" (*šaᶜaᵃšuᶜay*, see v. 24) in God's "law" (*tôrâ*), v. 77. He prays that the "proud" (or "arrogant") be openly "ashamed" (*bôš*, see 6:10)

[146]The verb *ṭapaš* occurs only here. The LXX translates ἐτυρώθη, loosely "make into cheese, curdle." The Vulgate translates *coagulatum est sicum lac*, "curdled like milk." KB, II, 379, relates the word to an Akkadian cognate, *ṭapâšu*, "to be fat" and thus "insensitive, unfeeling."

[147]The plural "compassions" intensifies the thought of the Lord's mercies.

because they have lied about him. Despite this, he will continue to "meditate" (see *śîaḥ*, 55:2) in the "precepts" (*piqqûdîm*) of the Lord, v. 78. The psalmist asks that others who "fear" (see *yirʾâ*, 2:11) the Lord and have experientially known His "testimonies" (*ʿedût*) will turn to Him in fellowship, v. 79. Finally, he prays that his heart may be "sound" (or "blameless," see *tom*, 7:8) in the Lord's "statutes" (*ḥoq*) so that he may not be "ashamed" (*bôš*, see 6:10), v. 80.

Kap

The writer expresses his devotion to the Lord. He "fainteth" (*kalâ*, see 73:26) for the "salvation" of the Lord.[148] As in v. 41, he thinks of deliverance from the threats posed by his enemies. At the same time, however, he also has "hope" (*yaḥal*, see 31:24) in God's "word" (*dabar*), v. 81. His eyes "fail" (*kalâ*), i.e., they see no hope that the promises of care in God's "word" (*ʾimrâ*) will bring the comfort he desires, v. 82. He feels like a "bottle" (better "wineskin") hanging where smoke affects it. It dries and becomes hard.[149] So the psalmist views himself as shriveled up from the pressures that surround him. Even so, he does not forget the "statutes" (*ḥoq*) of the Lord, v. 83. How many days are left in his life? The implied thought of the question is that his life will soon be complete unless the Lord delivers him. When will the Lord bring "judgment" (*mišpaṭ*)[150] on his foes, v. 84?

---

[148]Henry, p. 703, refers "salvation" to "the coming of the Messiah." While it is true that the coming of Christ will bring salvation to this earth, no context here turns the thought away from the psalmist's personal need for deliverance from his foes.

[149]Rawlinson, III, 108, considers smoking a desirable action "to toughen and harden" the wineskin. The author does not seem to express anything desirable here; it is better to view this as a negative act, shriveling up in preparation for death. Perowne, II, 358, understands the psalmist as comparing himself to a blackened wineskin, "shriveled and rendered useless by the smoke of the fire in which it is hung." Leupold, p. 841, considers the wineskin as a forgotten object, left to shrivel in the smoke. Even though God has forgotten him, he has not forgotten God's Word. It is difficult to accept these views since the psalmist elsewhere recognizes the care promised by the Lord, e.g., vv. 25, 41, 147.

[150]This is the first verse to omit a direct reference to God's Word. It is possible to understand *mišpaṭ* as a collective singular, "the judgments *of your word*." This approach would let us find God's Word in the verse, but it does force an unnatural construction upon the statement. It is easier to simply make *mišpaṭ* the object of the verse and translate with the AV. It is good to remember that the judgments of the Lord occur in harmony with His Word.

The "proud" (or "arrogant") have "dug pits," a poetical statement of the efforts made to trap the psalmist. These efforts go contrary to God's "law" (*tôrâ*) since they involve deceit and treachery, v. 85. The "commandments" (*miṣwâ*) of the Lord are "faithful," completely reliable and in opposition to others' attempts to trap the author. They persecute him with deceit. He pleads with the Lord to help him, v. 86. They had almost "consumed" (*kalâ*, see v. 81) him, but he has not spurned God's "precepts" (*piqqudîm*), v. 87. He asks the Lord to "quicken" him, cf. v. 25, bringing renewed life to his spirits, according to His "lovingkindness" (or "steadfast love," *ḥesed*, see 5:7). In response, he will keep the "testimony" (*ᶜedût*) the Lord has spoken, v. 88.

Lamed

This stanza marks the psalmist's greater reliance on God's Word. The initial verse literally reads, "Forever, O Lord; Your Word is standing in the heavens."[151] The author acknowledges the eternal nature of God's "word" (*dabar*). The Lord has "settled" it, establishing it forever throughout the universe. God's Word will never pass away, v. 89.[152] For this reason, the "faithfulness" of the Lord is forever, to "all generations" (*lᵉdor wador*, see 10:6). The psalmist implies that the promises of God expressed in His Word will never pass away.[153] In particular, He will accomplish His plan for this earth, v. 90. "They," the heaven and earth mentioned in the previous verses,

[151]Fausset, p. 368, supplies "thou art" and translates "For ever (thou art), O Lord: thy word is settled in heaven." While this is true, it goes away from the emphasis on God's Word in the psalm. Th. Booij, "Psalm 119,89–91," *Biblica* 79:4 (1998): 539–41, translates "is in command." In view of the translation as "officers" occurring widely in I Kings and II Chronicles, this is a possible view.

[152]This was Luther's favorite verse. He had it embroidered on his robe and displayed on the wall of his home. Sarah A. Cooke, *Wayside Sketches* (Salem, Ohio: Schmul Publishing Co., Inc., 1983), p. 120.

[153]This is the second verse of the psalm that does not mention God's Word. Calvin, IV, 469, translates *ᵓᵉmûnâ* as "truth." That word, however, refers more to faithfulness than to veracity. It is true because it reflects faithfully the standards of God. Verses 89–91 are a paragraph, with vv. 89 and 91 each mentioning God's Word. In addition, we see the "faithfulness" of the Lord only by comparing His work with His Word. The verse thus implies the standard of God's Word.

continue in accord with God's "ordinances" (*mišpaṭ*) (cf. 148:1–6; Jer. 31:35–36; 33:25).[154] All things in creation serve the Lord, v. 91.

Without God's "law" (*tôrâ*) as his "delights" (better "delight," *šaᶜaᶜšuᶜay*, see v. 24), "affliction" (*ᶜanî*, see 9:12) would have overcome the writer, v. 92. He will remember the "precepts" (*piqqûdîm*) that have "quickened" him in the past, cf. v. 25, reviving him in the midst of oppression, v. 93. The psalmist reminds the Lord that he belongs to Him and therefore asks the Lord to "save" him from the trials he is going through. To show his desire to do God's will, he notes that he has eagerly "sought" (*daraš*, see 9:10) His "precepts" (*piqqûdîm*), v. 94. In some unknown way, the wicked "have waited" (*qawâ*, see 25:3) to destroy him. He, however, will continue to diligently consider the "testimonies" (*ᶜedût*) of the Lord, where he finds promises to comfort him, v. 95. There is no "perfection" (*tiklâ*)[155] anywhere, but the "commandment" (*miṣwâ*) of the Lord is "exceeding broad," enough to cover every problem the author faces, v. 96.

Mêm

The author expresses his love for the "law" (*tôrâ*), so great that he thinks of the law continually through the day, v. 97. He recognizes that the "commandments" (*miṣwâ*) of the Lord have made him "wiser" (*ḥokmâ*, see 19:7) than his enemies. This is true because his meditation keeps these commands continually with him, v. 98. He has more wisdom than do his childhood teachers since he meditates on God's "testimonies" (*ᶜedût*), v. 99. He also understands more than the aged because he keeps the "precepts" (*piqqûdîm*) of God, v. 100.

The writer of the psalm has sought for purity in his life since he desires to keep God's "word" (*dabar*), v. 101. He has not turned away from the Lord's "judgments" (*mišpaṭ*) because the Lord Himself has taught him their rightness. The psalmist does not give any details of

---

[154]Delitzsch, III, 255, rejects the idea that the heavens and earth are the subject of the verb. He refers "continue" to the beings of the earth, all of whom are "obedient and humble before His judicial decisions." He concludes this from the final phrase, "all are thy servants." Dahood, III, 184, makes the subjects the "word," v. 89, and "truth," v. 90. These views are possible but are grammatically more difficult.

[155]The word *tiklâ* occurs only here. The root *kalâ*, "to end, complete," however, occurs widely, so the meaning of "perfection" is not in doubt. Soll, p. 166, translates "I have seen a limit to all things," a puzzling phrasing since the psalmist has not seen the limiting of all things.

this. The teaching likely came from earlier experiences in which he has found that God's Word is always reliable, v. 102. The "words" (*ʾimrâ*)[156] of the Lord are sweeter than honey to the writer's mouth (cf. 19:10), an indication that he loves speaking of God's Word to others, v. 103. He gains understanding through these "precepts" (*piqqûdîm*). This has led him to "hate [*śaneʾ*, see 5:5] every false way" that would lead him away from the Lord and from those actions that would please Him, v. 104.

Nûn

The "word" (*dabar*) is a "lamp" that might be carried to lighten the steps of the psalmist. It is a "light" to illuminate his path as he walks through life, v. 105. For this reason, he has sworn an oath and stated his intention to "perform it" (or "confirm it") by keeping the righteous "judgments" (*mišpaṭ*) of the Lord, v. 106.[157] The author has been greatly "afflicted" (*ʿanâ*, see 35:13), and this has oppressed him emotionally. He asks the Lord to "quicken" him, to refresh his spirits, cf. v. 25, by the promises given in His Word (*dabar*), v. 107. He further asks the Lord to "accept" (or "delight in," *raṣâ*, see 40:13) his spoken offerings of praise; cf. Hosea 14:2; Hebrews 13:15. So that he may speak correctly, he asks the Lord to teach him His "judgments" (*mišpaṭ*), v. 108.

The psalmist feels that his "soul," i.e., his life, is continually in his own hand, dependent on the decisions that he makes. For this reason, he does not forget God's "law" (*tôrâ*), v. 109. As an example of the threats he faces, the wicked have laid "a snare" (or "trap") for him. Despite this, he has not wandered away from God's "precepts" (*piqqûdîm*), v. 110. The "testimonies" (*ʿedût*) of the Lord are his "heritage" (or "inheritance") forever, since they are the source of great joy to him, v. 111. He has purposed to keep the "statutes" (*ḥoq*) of the Lord always, "even unto the end," probably referring to the end of his life, v. 112.

---

[156]The noun *ʾimratᵉka* is singular. Since the verb is plural, the word is understood best as a collective (so AV), the "words" of the Lord.

[157]Rawlinson, III, 109, translates as "the judgments of thy righteousness" and understands it as "the judgments which thy righteousness has caused thee to put forth." The view is possible; however, the identical construction for "righteous judgments" (*mišpᵉṭê ṣidqeka*) occurs in vv. 7, 62, 160, and 164. This supports the view given above.

Samek

The psalmist "hate[s]" (*śaneʾ*, see 5:5) "vain thoughts" (better "double-minded men")[158] but loves God's "law" (*tôrâ*), v. 113. He relies on the Lord to protect him from his foes by His being a hiding place and a "shield" (*magen*, see 3:3) from their attacks. The writer continues to "hope" (*yaḥal*, see 31:24) in the promises found in God's "word" (*dabar*), v. 114. He commands his enemies to leave him. He does not want their influence on his life because he intends to remain faithful to the "commandments" (*miṣwâ*) of his God, v. 115. At the same time, he prays that the Lord will "uphold" (or "sustain") him according to the promises found in His "word" (*ʾimrâ*). This will give him life, deliverance from his enemies. He also asks the Lord to keep him from becoming openly "ashamed" (*bôš*, see 6:10) of his "hope," his reliance on God's Word, v. 116. The next verse parallels v. 116. The writer again asks the Lord to hold him up that he may be safe from the attacks of others. In response, he will "have respect" (or "have regard") to the "statutes" (*ḥoq*) of the Lord, v. 117.

The author recognizes that God has "trodden down" (better "despised") those who go astray from His "statutes" (*ḥoq*). Their deceitfulness, probably in claiming to carry out God's will, is "falsehood" (or "in vain"), v. 118. The Lord puts away the wicked like "dross," an impurity that must be removed to make something pure. Because the Lord is faithful to His Word, the psalmist loves His "testimonies" (*ʿedût*), v. 119. He trembles with "fear" (or "terror," *paḥad*, see 14:5) of offending God by breaking His Word. He is "afraid" (or "in awe," *yareʾ*, see 2:11) of God's "judgments" (*mišpaṭ*), the Word by which He judges men, v. 120.[159]

ʿayin

Verses 121 and 122 do not mention God's Word directly. The writer states his personal adherence to "judgment and justice" (better

---

[158]The word *seʿaʿpîm* comes from the unused root *sʿp*, "to cleave, divide." The use here is similar to *seʿippîm* in the question "How long halt ye between two opinions?" in I Kings 18:21. Divided thought is unstable thought.

[159]Leupold, p. 848, relates God's "judgments" to "judgments . . . that God has visited upon the wicked." He later admits that the "judgments" may refer to the ordinances of God. While the view is possible, the overwhelming emphasis on God's Word in this psalm supports the view given above.

"justice and righteousness"). He therefore prays that the Lord will not allow his enemies to take him, v. 121. He asks the Lord to be the "surety" of his "servant."[160] A "surety" is a guarantee of payment. The psalmist wants the Lord to bring "good" to pass in his life by keeping the "proud" (or "arrogant") from oppressing him, v. 122. His eyes "fail," seeing no success as he looks for "salvation," i.e., deliverance from his enemies, and for the fulfillment of the "word" (*ʾimrâ*) that promises protection and has come from a righteous God, v. 123. He asks the Lord to deal with him according to His "mercy" (or "steadfast love," *ḥesed*, see 5:7) by teaching him His "statutes" (*ḥoq*), v. 124. He can ask the Lord's favor because of his position as His servant. For this reason, he asks for understanding that will let him experientially "know" the Lord's "testimonies" (*ʾedût*), v. 125.

Returning to the thought of his enemies, the psalmist asks the Lord to work on his behalf since his foes have "made void" (or "broken") God's "law" (*tôrâ*), v. 126.[161] Because his adversaries reject God's Word, he purposes all the more to love it. To show the value he gives it, he compares it to "gold" and "fine gold," gold that has been purified. His love for the Word is more than his desire for wealth, v. 127. For this reason, he "esteem[s]" (or "approves") as right all the "precepts" (*piqqûdîm*) of the Lord relating to every area of life. He "hate[s]" (*śaneʾ*, see 5:5) every way that is "false," contrary to God's Word, v. 128.

Pê

The psalmist extols the wonder of God's "testimonies" (*ʿedût*) and, for this reason, keeps them, v. 129. The "entrance" (or "opening,

[160]As in vv. 84 and 90, where the author does not mention God's Word, these verses imply it. Both "justice and righteousness" come from carrying out the standards given by God in His Word, and the psalmist has done this, v. 121. He describes himself as God's "servant," suggesting that he is one who has carried out the word of his master, v. 122.

[161]S. M. Lehrman, "Psalm 119," *JBQ* 23:1 (1995): 55–56, gives the translation "At a time of working for the Lord, they violate the Torah." He suggests that "this may be taken as a justification for the temporary abrogation of a commandment in an emergency where the life of the individual or the nation is at stake." While the translation is possible, the idea that we may set aside Scripture in an emergency cannot be sustained. This view violates the psalmist's attitude toward God's Word. He faced life-threatening situations but did not abandon his reliance on what God had spoken.

unfolding") of this "word" (*dabar*) gives spiritual light, even giving understanding to the "simple" (*petî*, see 19:7), those who know little of God's truth, v. 130. This value causes the writer to open his mouth and to pant (*šaʾap*, see 56:1) with desire for this Word. He longs for the "commandments" (*miṣwâ*) of the Lord, v. 131.

The author begins a series of four requests. He asks the Lord to "look on" (or "turn to") him and to be "merciful" (or "gracious," *ḥanan*, see 4:1) to him "as [His custom is] to do" (*mišpaṭ*)[162] to those who love His "name" (see v. 55), v. 132. He prays that the Lord will guide him through His "word" (*ʾimrâ*) so that no iniquity will control him. The next verse defines the nature of the "iniquity" as evil men, v. 133.[163] The psalmist asks the Lord to "deliver" (*padâ*, see 25:22) him from "the oppression of man" so that he will be able to keep His "precepts" (*piqqûdîm*), v. 134. In the fourth request, he requests the Lord to make His "face to shine upon thy servant" (cf. 31:16). Since no one can see the Lord's face and live (Exod. 33:20), the expression must poetically represent the blessing of the Lord. It recalls the Aaronic blessing of Numbers 6:25. The psalmist thinks especially of the Lord's teaching him His "statutes" (*ḥoq*), v. 135. The expression of his desire to know God's Word brings a sad note to his writing. He weeps "rivers of waters" over others who do not keep God's "law" (*tôrâ*), v. 136.

Ṣadê

The writer praises the Lord for His righteousness. His "judgments" (*mišpaṭ*) are also upright, agreeing with His nature as righteous, v. 137. The "testimonies" (*ʿedût*) of the Lord are righteous and very faithful, v. 138. Zeal for righteousness has "consumed" (*ṣamat*, see 18:40) the psalmist because his foes have "forgotten" (or "ignored") God's "words" (*dabar*), v. 139. The author compares God's "word" (*ʾimrâ*) to a precious metal purified by smelting (cf. notes at 12:6). The result is that the "word" is very "pure" (or greatly

[162]While *mišpaṭ* normally refers to the judgments of the Lord, it here has the sense of "custom, manner." The Lord is gracious to those who love Him. While the verse does not mention God's Word, it implies it. Only those who obey the Word can claim to love the Lord.

[163]Cohen, p. 411, calls iniquity the "infraction of the moral law." While this is possible, it seems to me that v. 134 develops the nature of the "iniquity" in v. 133.

"refined," *ṣarap*, see 12:6), with no blemishes. For this reason, he loves it, v. 140.

The psalmist is "small" (or "insignificant," *ṣaᶜîr*, see 68:27) and despised by others. In contrast with his foes, he remembers the "precepts" (*piqqudîm*) of the Lord, v. 141. The righteousness of the Lord is forever. His "law" (*tôrâ*) is therefore "true," since it would be contrary to God's nature to issue evil commands, v. 142. The author again refers to the "trouble and anguish" that he faces from his enemies. Again drawing a contrast with them, he states his "delights" (*šaᶜᵃšuᶜay*, see v. 24) in the "commandments" (*miṣwâ*) of the Lord, v. 143. Because of the righteous nature of the Lord, cf. v. 142, His "testimonies" (*ᶜedût*) are righteous forever. The psalmist prays for an understanding of them that will give him fullness of life, v. 144.

Qôp

No doubt burdened over the threat he faces, the psalmist cries out to the Lord in prayer. He pleads with the Lord to hear him and, at the same time, pledges obedience to His "statutes" (*ḥoq*), v. 145. Verse 146 parallels v. 145. The writer prays for deliverance and again states his intention to keep the Lord's "testimonies" (*ᶜedût*), v. 146. He "prevented [better 'preceded'] the dawning," rising before the morning light to pray. This may have been the first of the three times set aside for prayer each day; cf. 55:17; Daniel 6:10, 13. He confidently "hoped" (*yaḥal*, see 31:24) in the promises of protection in God's "word" (*dabar*), v. 147. He "prevents" (or "precedes") the "watches" of the night, times when he was guarding his camp.[164] He uses this time to "meditate" (see *śîaḥ*, 55:2) on God's "word" (*ᵓimrâ*), v. 148.

Because the Lord displays "lovingkindness" (or "steadfast love," *ḥesed*, see 5:7), the author asks Him to hear his prayer and to "quicken him," cf. v. 25, renewing his spirit according to His "judgment" (*mišpaṭ*), the standard of righteousness given in His Word, v. 149. Others approach him who seek "mischief," the carrying out of wicked plans. In contrast, their approach to him for wickedness takes them far from God's "law" (*tôrâ*), v. 150. His foes may approach him, but

[164]The Jews divided the night into three watches, lasting from sunset to 10 p.m. (Lam. 2:19), 10 p.m. until 2 a.m. (Judg. 7:19), and 2 a.m. until sunrise (Exod. 14:24; I Sam. 11:11).

the Lord is already near to provide protection. The promises of His "commandments" (*miṣwâ*) are true, v. 151. From "of old," dating back many years, the writer has known that the Lord has "founded" (or "established") His "testimonies" (*ᶜedût*) forever, v. 152.

Rêš

The psalmist asks the Lord to deliver him from the "affliction" (*ᶜanî*, see 9:12) he faces from his enemies. The right to prayer comes from his remembrance of God's "law" (*tôrâ*), v. 153. He asks the Lord to "plead [his] cause" (*rîb*, see 35:1), to take up his defense, and to revive his spirits; cf. v. 25, v. 154. There is no "salvation," deliverance from sin, for the wicked, because they do not carefully "seek" (*daraš*, see 9:10) the Lord's "statutes" (*ḥoq*), v. 155. Since the "mercies" (or "compassions") of the Lord are "great" (or "many"),[165] the writer asks the Lord to "quicken" him, giving him a fullness of life, cf. v. 25, according to His "judgments" (*mišpaṭ*). As in v. 149, this refers to the standards of righteousness given in God's Word, v. 156.

There are many who oppose the psalmist, seeking to do him harm. Despite this threat, he has not become discouraged or turned away from God's "testimonies" (*ᶜedût*), v. 157. He considers those who oppose him "transgressors" (or "treacherous," *bagad*, see 25:3) and is "grieved" for them (better, "loathes them"). He turns from them because they do not keep God's "word" (*ʾimrâ*), v. 158. In contrast with his foes, the psalmist loves the Lord's "precepts" (*piqqûdîm*). Because of the Lord's "lovingkindness" (or "steadfast love," *ḥesed*, see 5:7), he asks Him to "quicken" him, cf. v. 25, to give him a renewed spirit of confidence, v. 159. The first phrase is better translated, "The sum of your Word [*dabar*] is truth."[166] In every part and as a whole, God's Word is true. The statement reflects the writer's confidence in

---

[165]Either "great" or "many" gives a true statement about the "mercies" (or "compassions") of God. Since the psalmist uses *rabbîm* here and in v. 157, however, it likely has the same meaning in both places. In v. 157, it must mean "many."

[166]Fausset, III, 373–74, defends the translation "the beginning of thy word is truth." He argues that "word" should be plural if *roʾš* means "sum." The psalmist, however, has used the singular "word" over and over to refer to the whole of God's Word, e.g., vv. 9, 16, 43. The word *roʾš* often means "sum," e.g., 139:17; Exod. 30:12; Num. 4:2, 22.

what God has given to man. For this reason, God's righteous "judgments" (*mišpaṭ*) will endure forever, v. 160.

Šîn

The psalmist refers to his persecution from "princes."[167] From v. 23, it appears that these were Jewish leaders who falsely accused ("without a cause") the author. He does not fear them; he rather stands "in awe" (*paḥad*, see 14:5) of the promises given in God's "word" (*dabar*), v. 161. He "rejoic[es]" (or "exults," *śûś*, see 19:5) in God's "word" (*ʾimrâ*) as though he had found "great spoil," rich treasure. When we consider the wide span of the promises of blessing in God's Word, and the result of salvation and eternity with our Lord in heaven, God's Word is indeed a rich treasure, v. 162. The author of the psalm "hate[s]" (*śaneʾ*, see 5:5) and "abhor[s]" falsehood.[168] In contrast, he loves God's "law" (*tôrâ*), v. 163. The evidence of his love lies in his actions. He sets aside time "seven times a day" to praise the Lord because of His righteous "judgments" (*mišpaṭ*). The number "seven" here represents the many times each day (cf. 12:6; 79:12) that praise to God comes to the psalmist's heart, v. 164.

The writer recognizes that those who love the "law" (*tôrâ*) have "great peace" (cf. Prov. 3:1–2; Isa. 26:3; 32:17). The phrase "nothing shall offend them" is better "they shall have no stumbling block." God's Word keeps the believer from stumbling into sin, v. 165. The psalmist has "hoped" (or "waited") for "salvation," deliverance from his foes. While he waits, he keeps the "commandments" (*miṣwâ*) of God, v. 166. He has kept the "testimonies" (*ʿedût*) of the Lord. Having kept them, he can say that he greatly loves them, v. 167. He repeats the thought of his obedience to God. He has kept God's "pre-

---

[167]While this paragraph bears the title of "*šîn*," the individual verses begin variously with *śîn* (pronounced *seen*, vv. 161, 162, 166) or *šîn* (pronounced *sheen*, vv. 163, 164, 165, 167, 168). The *śîn* and *šîn* were originally the same letter, pronounced with two distinct sounds in different Hebrew words. The Masoretic scribes, working from the early sixth century to the mid-tenth century, added vowel points and accents to standardize the pronunciation. At that time, the scribes made the difference between the letters *śîn* and *šîn*.

[168]Rawlinson, III, 112, limits "lying" here to "false systems of worship." He specifically rejects "the habit of lying." In this context, the psalmist likely has in mind the false accusations that others have made against him, see v. 161.

cepts" (*piqqûdîm*) and "testimonies" (*ᶜedût*), knowing that all of his "ways," his thoughts and his deeds, are open to the Lord, v. 168.

Tau

Once more, the psalmist makes his "cry" (*rinnâ*, see 17:1) to the Lord, most likely bringing to the Lord his need for deliverance. He asks for understanding of God's "word" (*dabar*), possibly thinking of the promises that the Lord will protect His own, v. 169. May the Lord also accept his "supplication" (*tᵉḥinnâ*, see 6:9) for gracious deliverance. The next phrase gives the focus of his prayer. He asks the Lord to deliver him from his enemies according to the promises of His "word" (*ᵓimrâ*), v. 170. The first phrase of v. 171 is better phrased as a prayer: "Let my lips pour out [*nabaᶜ*, see 19:2] praise." This is a natural result of learning the "statutes" (*ḥoq*) of God, v. 171. Verse 172 also begins with a prayer: "Let my tongue speak of your word [*ᵓimrâ*]." Understanding the righteous nature of God's "commandments" (*miṣwâ*), the psalmist would naturally want to speak openly of them, v. 172.

The "hand" of the Lord often represents His power, e.g., v. 73. The psalmist asks the Lord to extend this power to him because he has chosen to keep the Lord's "precepts" (*piqqûdîm*), v. 173. Once more, as in v. 166, the writer states his desire for "salvation," deliverance from those who seek to destroy him. While he waits for this, his "delight" (*šaᶜᵃšuᶜay*, see v. 24) is God's "law" (*tôrâ*), v. 174. The word *ḥayâ*, here translated "let . . . live," better refers to the quickening of the psalmist's spirit; cf. v. 25. If the Lord will quicken the psalmist's spirit, he will praise Him.[169] In addition to his need for quickening, the author sees his need to have the "judgments" (*mišpaṭ*) of the Lord guide him, v. 175. Even though he has strayed like a "lost" (or "perishing") sheep, he asks the Lord to "seek" him. This straying may well refer to the psalmist's need to flee before his enemies.[170] He asks

[169]Dickson, II, 410, and Cohen, p. 416, understand the first phrase as a prayer for longer life, "that God would give him time to praise him." In view of the danger posed by his enemies, this is a possible view. I have opted for the above view because of the overwhelming use of *ḥayâ* in the psalm to refer to the renewing of the psalmist's spirits.

[170]Albert Barnes, p. 226, views this as the "confession of sin." Cohen, p. 416, likewise speaks of "the [spiritual] frailty which is part of human nature." It is inconceivable

the Lord to seek him so that he may be restored to the fold, a place of protection. He has the right to ask this because he has not forgotten the Lord's "commandments" (*miṣwâ*), v. 176.

EXCURSUS: GOD'S WORD IN PSALM 119

Psalm 119 uses ten different Hebrew words to describe God's Word.[171] The following discussion gives these words in the order of their frequency and also gives a brief indication of the special sense conveyed by each word.

1. *Law* (*torâ*), vv. 1, 18, 29, 34, 44, 51, 53, 55, 61, 70, 72, 77, 85, 92, 97, 109, 113, 126, 136, 142, 150, 153, 163, 165, 174. This word occurs twenty-five times, more than any other synonym for God's Word in the psalm. The word *torâ* refers to the Ten Commandments but also to the standards of God revealed elsewhere by the leaders of Israel and the prophets. The latter seems best in the psalm. A connotation of instruction underlies the word *torâ*. God's law thus serves to instruct man as to the standards of life the Lord requires.
2. *Word* (*dabar*), vv. 9, 16, 17, 25, 28, 42, 43, 49, 57, 65, 74, 81, 89, 101, 105, 107, 114, 130, 139, 147, 160, 161, 169. Including its plural form, *dabar* refers to God's Word twenty-three times. The word often stresses the action of God's communication to mankind.[172] In Psalm 119, however, it is not always clearly dis-

---

that the author, who has consistently stated his love for God's Word and his desire to obey, would now focus on his sins. It is more in keeping with the theme of prayer that he refer to the perilous flight his enemies have caused.

[171]Soll, p. 35, includes only eight words: *torâ*, *dabar*, *ᶜedût*, *mišpaṭ*, *ḥuqqâ*, *miṣwâ*, *piqqudîm*, and *ʾimrâ*. Burkett includes the same eight words. Rawlinson, III, 102–3, include nine words, adding *derek* to the above list. Henry, p. 685, includes ten words, adding "righteousness" and "truth" to the above words. The word that most authors omit, *ʾoraḥ*, refers to God's Word only in v. 15. A second word often omitted, *derek*, occurs by itself in vv. 3, 37. It also occurs in vv. 14, 27, 30, 32, 33 with a modifier to further define it.

[172]Earl S. Kalland, *TWOT*, I, 179, and Unger and White, p. 391, support this view.

tinguished from #8, *ʾimrâ*. While *dabar* embraces the concept of law, e.g., vv. 57, 101, 139, it also includes the promises of God, e.g., vv. 25, 65, 107.

3. *Testimony* (*ʿedût*), vv. 2, 14, 22, 24, 31, 36, 46, 59, 79, 88, 95, 99, 111, 119, 125, 129, 138, 144, 146, 152, 157, 167, 168. The word *ʿedût* occurs twenty-three times, including in v. 14 to define the word *derek* (#9, below). While the word *ʿedût* includes more than the Law elsewhere in the OT, the psalmist does not use it to refer clearly to anything else. The testimony of God's Word implies its certainty and its righteousness. God testifies to that which He knows is true and right.
4. *Judgment, ordinances* (*mišpaṭ*), vv. 7, 13, 20, 30, 39, 43, 52, 62, 75, 84, 91, 102, 106, 108, 120, 132, 137, 149, 156, 160, 164, 175. The word *mišpaṭ* occurs twenty-two times in referring to God's Word in Psalm 119. The word brings out the legal basis for God's standards. In this psalm, the word *mišpaṭ* refers to the standards God has set down in His Word, e.g., vv. 7, 62, 137, and also His promises that comfort the writer, e.g., vv. 43, 149, 156. These likely refer to the carrying out of God's standards.
5. *Statutes* (*ḥoq*), vv. 5, 8, 12, 16, 23, 26, 33, 48, 54, 64, 68, 71, 80, 83, 112, 117, 118, 124, 135, 145, 155, 171. The word *ḥoq* refers to God's Word twenty-two times, including the definition of *derek* (#9 below) in v. 33. The verb *ḥaqaq*, "to cut, engrave," underlies these words, suggesting the thought of something permanent. These words may also refer to specific commands of the Lord. As with *ʿedût* (#3 above), nothing in the psalm suggests that the psalmist thinks of anything other than the Law. More than with any other synonym, the psalmist asks the Lord to "teach" him His *ḥoq*, vv. 12, 26, 33, 124, 135; cf. also vv. 71, 171.
6. *Commandments* (*miṣwâ*), vv. 6, 10, 19, 21, 32, 35, 47, 48, 60, 66, 73, 86, 96, 98, 115, 127, 131, 143, 151, 166, 172, 176. The word *miṣwâ* occurs twenty-two times in referring to God's Word, including v. 32 where it defines the word *derek* (#9 below). The verb *ṣawâ*, "to command," underlies this word. For this reason, the noun *miṣwâ* refers to the authoritative nature of God's Word. In the psalm, *miṣwâ* refers to the commands given by God.
7. *Precepts* (*piqqudîm*), vv. 4, 15, 27, 40, 45, 56, 63, 69, 78, 87, 93, 94, 100, 104, 110, 128, 134, 141, 159, 168, 173. This word

describes God's instructions twenty-one times in the psalm, including v. 27 where it defines *derek* (#9 below). The verb root *paqad*, "to visit, inspect," indicates that this word has a connotation of care and concern in the restrictions imposed on mankind. Again, the word refers to the standards set by the law of the Lord.

8. *Word* (*ʾimrâ*), vv. 11, 38, 41, 50, 58, 67, 76, 82, 103, 116, 123, 133, 140, 148, 154, 158, 162, 170, 172. The word *ʾimrâ*, a close synonym of #2, *dabar*, occurs nineteen times. Whereas *dabar* stresses the action of God's speech, *ʾimrâ* emphasizes more the content of what He has said (see #2). There is not always a clear distinction between the two words, although *ʾimrâ* refers to God's promises more than *dabar* does, vv. 41, 50, 58, 76, 82, 116, 154, 170.
9. *Way* (*derek*), vv. 3, 14, 27, 30, 32, 33, 37. The word *derek* occurs twice clearly referring to God's Word as a "way" to be followed, vv. 3, 37.[173] There are additional times, vv. 14, 27, 30, 32, 33, in which another word defines the nature of *derek*, e.g., "the way of thy testimonies," "the way of thy precepts." The word *derek* normally refers to a path or road but often poetically describes a "way or manner of life." This is the case here where it refers to a way defined by God's Word.
10. *Way* (*ʾoraḥ*), v. 15. The word refers to God's Word only once in the psalm.[174] From the verb root *ʾaraḥ*, "to journey," it is reasonable to relate *ʾoraḥ* to travel along a path. With regard to the

[173]Soll, p. 47, rejects *derek* as a word for Torah. He notes that *derek* begins a line in the *dalet* strophe five times, but that "none of the eight undisputed Torah terms is ever used as part of the acrostic." He also points out that *derek* occurs in construct with other Torah terms (vv. 14, 27, 32, 33), while "elsewhere in Psalm 119, two Torah terms never appear in construct." Finally, he uses v. 29 as an example of the "antithesis of Torah." His arguments are correct; however, unless we accept *derek* as a Torah word, vv. 3 and 37 have no Torah word. The author uses *derek* naturally in the *dalet* strophe and in the construct phrases just as he uses *dabar* in v. 42*a* and *mišpaṭ* in v. 121 as non-Torah words.

[174]Soll, p. 47, rejects *ʾoraḥ* as a synonym for God's Word primarily because "twice it is a path of falsehood (vv 104, 128) and once an evil path (v 101)." He admits, however, that it refers "once to God's paths." The parallelism in v. 15 supports its inclusion in the list of Torah words. Murphy, p. 608, does not mention *ʾoraḥ* but makes *ʾěmûnâ*, v. 90, a tenth word to describe God's Word. The word *ʾěmûnâ*, however, has more of a sense of faithfulness or reliability. Verse 90*b* illustrates this aspect of the Lord's work.

Word of the Lord, it is a way of life. The word often parallels *derek* (#9 above), e.g., 25:4; 27:11, without a clear distinction between the two.

PSALM 120

This is the first of fifteen psalms with the title "A Song of degrees [or 'ascents']."[175] These psalms differ in nature, including community and individual lament psalms, songs of trust, wisdom psalms, and liturgical psalms. In some unknown way, they were grouped together.[176] We do not know the significance of the title.[177]

---

[175]Pss. 120–134 all have the title "A Song of degrees ['ascents']," with 122, 124, 127, 131, and 133 adding David or Solomon as the author. There is no explanation for the presence of the five psalms written by David and Solomon.

[176]Kirsten Nielsen, "Why Not Plow with an Ox and an Ass Together? Or: Why Not Read Ps 119 Together with Pss 120–134?" *SJOT* 14:1 (2000): 57, 66, argues that Pss. 120–134 were deliberately placed beside Ps. 119. This gave the readers two ways of guidance as to what was important in life. Ps. 119 stressed ethics, the need to live according to *torah*, God's Word. Pss. 120–134 stressed the importance of keeping the pilgrimages to Jerusalem. For those who could not make the trek to Jerusalem, the keeping of the law was an acceptable substitution. While the thesis is interesting, it is more likely that the placement of these psalms is coincidental. It is not certain that these psalms were written for the journey to Jerusalem (see n. 177).

[177]*Middoth* 2.5 and *Succoth* 51*b* say that psalms were chanted as the priests ascended from the court of the women to the court of the men at the temple. There were fifteen steps and they chanted a different psalm on each step. There is no evidence, however, that these were the chanted psalms. *Succoth* 53*a* gives a highly fanciful view that David sang these songs to bring water near to the surface of the earth. Leon J. Liebreich, "The Songs of Ascents and the Priestly Blessing," *JBL* 74 (1955): 33, relates the psalms to isolated words (*šalom*, *ḥanan*, *šamar*, *barak*) of the priestly blessing in Num. 6:24–26. These words, however, are common ones that occur widely. Their occurrence does not justify making a link between these psalms and the priestly blessing. Cowles, p. 497, suggests that the Jews chanted the psalms as they returned to Palestine from the Babylonian captivity. None of the psalms, however, refer to Babylon. In addition, 122:1 and 134:1 refer to the temple and five of the psalms have David or Solomon as their authors. Hirsch, II, 371, states that the psalms were "to help one to strive upward, to 'ascend' from the depths of misery in which he has fallen as the result of adverse, sad circumstances." Since the psalms include various types, this is not likely true. Delitzsch, III, 267, and Dahood, III, 194, suggest that the name comes from the climactic poetry ending several of the

Psalm 120 is an individual lament. The psalmist has faced an unknown threat. His adversaries had lied about him with the intention of stirring up rebellion. This suggests that the psalmist held a position of leadership, perhaps as king. He has cried out to the Lord for deliverance and experienced His help. The psalm does not give enough information to let us identify the author[178] or his opponents, the date,[179] or the nature of the threat to the psalmist. As with many of the psalms, it shows us the value of prayer in times of trouble.

---

psalms, where the psalmist repeats a key word, e.g., "peace," 120:6–7; "preserve," 121:7–8. The repetition is sporadic, however, not found in most of these psalms. Mays, p. 386, holds that the Jews sang these psalms as they traveled to Jerusalem for the three great feasts of the year. Oesterley, II, 500, varies this view by saying that the title "refers to the ascent of pilgrims up the hill of Zion, during which these psalms were sung, at the great festivals." Some of the psalms, however, are lament psalms and do not seem appropriate for such occasions. Clarke, p. 311, argues that these psalms relate to the fifteen degrees on Ahaz's sundial and the years added to Hezekiah's life, Isa. 38:5, 8. Hezekiah authored the ten anonymous songs. Nothing in the psalms supports the view other than the coincidence that they number fifteen and the mention of word "degrees." In addition, some of the psalms refer to a time after the Babylonian captivity. Jennings, II, 282, 284, assumes that these psalms are by "one author or guild of contemporary authors" and were sung at the temple. The view is speculative. Cuthbert C. Keet, *A Study of the Psalms of Ascents*, pp. 4ff, gives several unlikely views: indicating a vocal tone with which the psalms should be sung; Luther's view that the psalms were sung from an elevated place; singing at the end of a service as the congregation departed; and Augustine's view that the psalms encouraged raising the heart in prayer to God, among others. Keet, p. 17, has them sung as Jews traveled to Jerusalem for "offering their firstfruits at the Temple." Again, the existence of various types argues against the view. M. D. Goulder, "The Songs of Ascents and Nehemiah," *JSOT* 75 (1997): 43, argues that the psalms were responses to Nehemiah's testimony, given "to the people evening and morning through the Feast of Tabernacles." His view is speculative and rests on a contrived relationship of the psalms to the book of Nehemiah that requires a portion of that book to be displaced. Other views have also been offered. No one explanation of the title is satisfactory.

[178]Scroggie, p. 194, offers the view that Hezekiah's "songs," Isa. 38:20, are the ten anonymous Songs of degrees, one for each of the degrees on the sundial of Ahaz, Isa. 38:8. The view is speculative.

[179]Henry, III, 733, suggests that David wrote the psalm at the time "of Doeg's accusing him and the priests to Saul." He sees a similarity to Ps. 52, which was written at that time. The view is speculative. Leupold, p. 863, makes the all of these psalms postexilic, "when there was faith but not in any sense a faith of the bold and heroic type." While the date is possible, the description that the faith exhibited in these psalms is weaker than in earlier psalms is subjective.

I. The Psalmist's Prayer 1–4

1–4 The psalmist has been in "distress" (*ṣarâ*, see 9:9). At that time, he called on the Lord in prayer and received the answer to his prayer, v. 1. Verses 2–4 give the gist of his prayer. He asks the Lord to deliver him from "lying lips"[180] and from a "deceitful [*r^emîyâ*, see 32:2] tongue," the weapon of slander his adversaries have used against him. From the mention of foreigners in v. 5, these are likely heathen foes, v. 2. The writer asks rhetorically what punishment his foes should receive for their "false [*r^emîyâ*] tongue." Neither verb is passive. It is therefore appropriate to translate, "What shall He give to you, and what shall He add to you, O deceitful tongue?" v. 3. The psalmist answers his question poetically. The enemy will receive the "sharp arrows of the mighty [or 'warrior,' *gibbôr*, see 19:5]." He will be burned with the coals of the "juniper" (or "broom" shrub). This is a sparsely leaved shrub that grows in the desert regions and is often used as fuel for camping fires. Both the arrows and the coals represent severe judgment from the Lord on the psalmist's foes, v. 4.

II. The Psalmist's Lament 5–7

5–7 The psalmist laments that he dwells in "Mesech" ("Meshech"). This nation lay north of Mesopotamia, southeast of the Black Sea. Assyrian records mention trade with Meshech. We know of no reason why he would have traveled that far. It may be, however, that his flight had led him to stay briefly with a group from Meshech that had traveled south for trade purposes. The psalmist has also dwelled in the "tents of Kedar." These were a nomadic people that lived in the northwest Arabian Peninsula. This group often represents the nomadic Arabian tribes, v. 5.[181] He has stayed with those who "hate" (*śane᾿*, see

[180]Fausset, p. 375, refers this to the Samaritans who opposed the building of the temple by the Jews mentioned in v. 5. This does not explain the flight mentioned in v. 5, and the psalm does not mention the Samaritans.

[181]Kidner, pp. 430–31, suggests that Meshech and Kedar should be "coupled here as a general term for the heathen . . . figurative names for the alien company he is in: as foreign as the remotest peoples, and as implacable as his Arab kinsmen." Phillips, II, 431, makes the names symbolic "for a merciless people." Hirsch, II, 372, considers the names as setting forth a hypothetical wish. The psalmist states that it would have been better to dwell with "the Bedouins in the wilderness" than to have been among "nations who hate truth." Scroggie, III, 201, draws on the location of Meshech and Kedar in the north and south as a picture of the psalmist being

5:5) peace, their enmity toward him causing them to stir up trouble, v. 6.[182] He is for peace. They, however, reject his offers to settle the differences and engage in "war," seeking to overthrow him, v. 7.

PSALM 121

Psalm 121[183] is another "Song of degrees [or 'ascents']."[184] The psalm is also a song of trust that expresses the psalmist's confidence in the Lord. The writer refers six times to the Lord's keeping of the nation: vv. 3, 4, 5, 7 (twice), 8. Primarily because of the mistranslated question and answer in vv. 1–2, it is a familiar psalm. As with many of the psalms, we do not know the author or the occasion for writing.[185]

This is the only one of this group of psalms with the heading *šîr lammaᶜᵃlôt*, "a song for the ascents," rather than the title *šîr hammaᶜᵃlôt*, "a song of the ascents." There is no clear distinction between these titles.

The psalm makes the practical lesson that the Lord keeps those who trust Him. The psalmist goes to the Lord in prayer, vv. 1–2, because he has confidence in the Lord's power to keep him from "all

---

surrounded by heathen, a position that was "not congenial." While these views are possible, the choice of these relatively scarce names to portray a figurative thought is strange. The OT refers to Meshech only nine times, five times in Ezekiel, and mentions Kedar twelve times, eight of them in the Major Prophets.

[182]W. E. Barnes, II, 594, transliterates *rabbat*, "long," v. 6, as Rabbah, the Ammonite capital. The view is weak. The word *rab* occurs more than four hundred times elsewhere, never referring to Rabbah.

[183]The hymn "I to the Hills," from the *Scottish Psalter*, 1615, is based on this psalm.

[184]The introduction to Ps. 120 discusses the title "A Song of degrees."

[185]Henry, p. 725, attributes the psalm to David. Rotherham, p. 521, sees Hezekiah as the one lifting his eyes to the hills to see if the Assyrians were coming. Hengstenberg, III, 417, has pilgrims returning to Jerusalem singing this song in the evening after catching sight of the hills surrounding Jerusalem. Phillips, II, 435, makes vv. 1–2 the question and vv. 3–8 the answer from another speaker. He suggests Hezekiah as the first speaker and Isaiah as the one giving the answer. Jennings, II, 288, considers it postexilic. These views are speculative. The psalm does not give any clear information regarding the author or background to the psalm.

evil," v. 7. God has not changed; He is still able to protect those who follow Him.

I. The Trust of the Psalmist 1–2

1–2 The psalmist relies on the Lord for help. He announces his intention to "lift up [his] eyes" to the hills surrounding Jerusalem, where the Lord dwells in the temple. The second phrase, "from whence [*meʾayin*] cometh my help [*ʿezer*, see 20:2]," is an independent question, not the completion of 1*a*.[186] It introduces the remainder of the psalm. It is from Jerusalem that the writer's help comes, v. 1. The Lord Who created heaven and earth provides the "help" (*ʿezer*) he needs. The mention of Creation shows the power of the Lord and, thus, His ability to help, v. 2.

II. The Protection from the Lord 3–8

3–4 The psalmist addresses his readers.[187] From v. 4, we can assume that these are Israelites. The Lord will not let their foot "be moved" (or "slip," *môṭ*, see 66:9). The phrase is idiomatic for general

---

[186]John T. Willis, "An Attempt to Decipher Psalm 121:1b," *CBQ* 52:2 (1990): 250–51, considers v. 2 a "bold contrast to v. 1." In v. 1, the psalmist pretends "to consider the worship of foreign gods as a ploy over against which to affirm his trust in the help of Yahweh." Verse 2 makes the point by asking a rhetorical question. The particle *meʾayin*, however, never asks "shall" but always "whence" or "where." Gaebelein, p. 444, also understands 1*b* as a rhetorical question. He gives it a negative answer. The psalmist's help does not come from the mountains. While this may be the case, it is equally valid to let it introduce v. 2, where the psalmist gives the answer to his question. Kissane, p. 568, lets the mountains represent the whole earth. Is there "any hope of human aid?" No! Only the Lord can help. The view is possible, but it requires us to interpret the "mountains" in an unusual way. Sabourin, p. 276, makes v. 1*b* an answer from "a priest, a friend, or a relative" to someone who states his intention to look to the mountains for help. His view requires the omission of "my" in v. 1*b*, a change without textual support. Weiser, p. 746, understands v. 1 to be "the question asked by a man who sets forth on a journey." Verses 2–8 are "the utterance of the one who stays behind, speeding the other on his way." Nothing in the passage suggests a change in speakers between vv. 1 and 2.

[187]Fausset, III, 376, makes Israel speak in vv. 1–2 and the Spirit address Israel in vv. 3–8. I have made the psalmist the speaker throughout the psalm. In vv. 1–2, he states his trust in the Lord; in vv. 3–8 he assures his Israelite readers of the Lord's care. Cohen, p. 420, sees a group of pilgrims singing the psalm antiphonally. Nothing in the psalm requires this although, of course, it may have been done. David G. Barker, "'The Lord Watches Over You': A Pilgrimage Reading of Psalm 121," *BibSac* 152 (1995): 170, sees a "pilgrim" speaking in vv. 1–2 and a "priest" in vv. 3–8,

insecurity; cf. 17:5; 38:16; 94:18. The Lord will not "sleep" (*nûm*, or "be careless"), thus He is always alert to watch over His people. In both 3*a* and 3*b* the psalm writer uses the negative *ʾal*, expressing the certainty that these things will not happen, v. 3.[188] To emphasize the thought, the psalmist repeats 3*b*; the One Who "keepeth" (or "guards") Israel does not "slumber" (*nûm*, or "be careless") or "sleep" (*yašen*).[189] The psalmist changes the negative to *loʾ*, strengthening the emphatic promise of the Lord's continued care, v. 4.

5–6 The author speaks again to his readers. The Lord will keep them safe. He is a "shade" on their "right hand." The "shade" represents a protection from the sun and metaphorically shows "defense" (cf. Num. 14:9; Eccles. 7:12). This is on the "right hand," the hand that holds the weapon and is therefore not guarded by a shield, v. 5. There will be no attack or peril during the sunlight or moonlight, v. 6.[190]

7–8 The Lord will "preserve," the same root translated earlier as "keepeth" and "keeper," His people from "all evil." Nothing will happen to them that is not for their good. Even the judgments that have come upon Israel throughout history the Lord designed to draw them back to Himself. He will preserve their "soul," here referring to the life of the nation, v. 7. He will keep them when they go out and when they come in, a picture of His care in all that they do. Further, He will keep them both now and forever, throughout all time, v. 8.

---

understanding "a range of options for the identity of this second voice." Again, the psalm does not require a second voice.

[188]See G.K.C. 107 *p*, 109 *e*.

[189]Both *yašen* and *nûm* can refer to sleep. The verb *nûm*, however, can also have a metaphoric sense of being careless, Isa. 56:10. It takes that sense in both vv. 3 and 4.

[190]Among others, Moll, p. 687, and Keet, p. 29, understand the reference to sun and moon as danger from sunlight and moonlight. Moll states, "Effects similar to those manifested in sun-stroke, are produced by the moonbeams." Keet comments that "moonstroke is dangerous. The rays of the moon have been known to affect the eyes and to cause inflammation of the brain." Hengstenberg, III, 421, understands the sun and moon as representing heat and cold, figurative "for the conflicts to which the people are exposed." These views are questionable.

PSALM 122

This is the first of the Songs of "degrees" (or "ascents") to be assigned to David.[191] The better manuscripts of the LXX and the Vulgate leave the psalm anonymous, but the Dead Sea Scroll accepts David as the author. There is nothing in the psalm that disagrees with David's authorship. We do not know the circumstances behind its writing. The emphasis in the psalm rests upon Jerusalem as the place for Israel's worship. It would have been natural for David to celebrate bringing the ark of the covenant to Jerusalem with a psalm expressing his joy at the privilege of renewed worship. The existence of "gates" (v. 2), "walls," and "palaces" (v. 7) argues for a date of writing before the fall of Jerusalem to Babylon.[192] At that time, Nebuchadnezzar's army burned the city and broke down its walls, II Kings 25:9–10.

---

[191]Delitzsch, III, 276, concludes from v. 3 that the psalm belongs to the period after the rebuilding of Jerusalem. The author is an unknown person who has attended a feast and recalls here the rebuilt city. The view rests on the occurrence of Aramaic forms in vv. 3 and 4. Given the closeness of Syria to Israel, such forms are not surprising. Leupold, p. 872, finds it difficult to make David the speaker in vv. 1–2, since David has been in Jerusalem for some time after becoming king. He attributes the psalm to "a typical Israelite voicing his various sentiments . . . on what the good city meant to those who were the more faithful of the children of Israel." It is possible, however, to understand vv. 1–2 differently. Buttenwieser, p. 373, argues that *habbᵉnûyâ* is an adjective in v. 3. He translates as "rebuilt Jerusalem" and makes the psalm postexilic. The passive participle, however, may have a verbal sense as in the AV. Similar grammatical constructions with verbal senses occur at Judg. 6:28; Neh. 7:4; and Song of Sol. 4:4. Henry, p. 727, thinks that David wrote the psalm "to bring the people to be in love with Jerusalem." Prior to David, the feasts had been observed elsewhere. Now it is a new thing for the men to travel to Jerusalem. David seeks to build a new attitude among his people. Fausset, III, 377, makes David write "to conciliate the Ten northern tribes, which had been slower in recognizing him as king, to Jerusalem, the newly-constituted capital and religious centre of the nation." Hengstenberg, III, 422, suggests that pilgrims sang this song at the gates of Jerusalem, where they halted before proceeding to the temple. Rotherham, p. 523, views the psalm as Hezekiah's welcome to the northern tribes as they join in celebrating the Passover. These are possible but speculative views.

[192]Kirkpatrick, p. 739, makes the mention of walls and gates refer to the rebuilt Jerusalem in Nehemiah's time. He also understands the "house of the Lord," v. 1, as the rebuilt temple. The view leaves unanswered the question of why David's name came to be associated with the psalm. Nothing in the psalm forces us to question the title.

I. Rejoicing of the Psalmist 1–2

1–2 David rejoices at the prospect of going to worship at the "house of the Lord." The phrase refers to the Davidic tabernacle, recently moved from the house of Obed-edom after its recovery from the Philistines, II Samuel 6:12–15, v. 1. Joining himself together with others who have also come to worship, David delights that their feet "shall stand" (better "stand") within the gates of the city where they will worship, v. 2.

II. Tribute to the City 3–5

3–5 Jerusalem is "compact together" (or "joined together"). The phrase shows the strength of the city; the houses are close to one another and leave no gaps to be easily exploited, v. 3.[193] It is the place to which the tribes of Israel go. David repeats the word "tribes" to emphasize that these are the "tribes of the Lord." This is done according to the "testimony" (*ᶜedût*, see 19:7) of the Lord. The word *ᶜedût* may also stand for the Word of the Lord, e.g., 119:14, 31, 36. Here it most likely refers to the ordinance of the Lord that requires the men of Israel to journey to Jerusalem to observe the three major feasts, Deuteronomy 16:16. The men would go with thanks to the Lord's "name"[194] as they celebrated various aspects of the goodness of God, v. 4.

"Thrones of judgment" have been placed at Jerusalem, indicating its position as the civil center of the nation. The plural "thrones" is a plural of excellence, referring to the unique dignity of the throne of the king.[195] The repeated "thrones," again a plural of excellence, emphasizes its association with dispensing justice in the land, v. 5.

III. Prayer for Peace 6–9

6–9 The psalmist prays for the peace of Jerusalem. Whether he knew it or not, this is a prayer for the coming of the millennial

[193]Cohen, p. 422, and Eaton, p. 281, understand the phrase to refer to the unity of the people. While this is possible, the *puᶜal* of *ḥabar* refers elsewhere only to things, not to people, Exod. 28:7; 39:4.

[194]Note 94 at 5:11 gives a summary of the Lord's "name."

[195]Mays, p. 393, and Jennings, II, 291, understand the possible view that the thrones refer to the benches of the judges responsible for maintaining justice in the city.

kingdom. Only then will Jerusalem enjoy a continuing peace. The next phrases express the psalmist's wish: "May they prosper who love you, may peace be within your walls, and may prosperity be within your palaces [again, a plural of excellence]." The psalmist prays that the Lord will bless those who seek His blessing on Jerusalem, vv. 6–7. On behalf of others who live in the city, he now prays, "Peace be within thee." His prayer is that the city may enjoy peace, v. 8. Similarly, because of the tabernacle, located at Jerusalem, he purposes to do what he can to bring about good in the city, v. 9.

PSALM 123

Like most of the psalms in this section, this "Song of degrees [or 'ascents']" cannot be assigned to a certain author, dated, or set against a historical backdrop. In this brief lament, the psalmist represents the nation as they look to the Lord for deliverance. The fact that the heathen scorn Israel may suggest the Babylonian captivity.[196] The heathen naturally look down on the captive people and take pride in their own conquests.

I. Trust in the Lord 1–2

1–2 On behalf of the nation, the psalmist lifts up his eyes to look upon the Lord Who dwells "in the heavens." While the Lord is in fact omnipresent, the vastness and the glory of the heavens appropriately represent His dwelling, v. 1. The writer illustrates Israel's trust in the

[196]Murphy, p. 636, assigns the psalm to David. Clarke, p. 316, assigns the authorship to Hezekiah at the time of the Assyrian threat. W. E. Barnes, II, 598, transliterates *rabbat*, "exceedingly," v. 4, as Rabbah, the Ammonite capital. He places the psalmist there "surrounded by hostile and contemptuous neighbours." As in 120:6, where he translates similarly, the view is weak. The word *rab* occurs over four hundred times elsewhere but never refers to Rabbah. Jennings, p. 292, makes the psalm postexilic. The Samaritans and others offer "contemptuous opposition" to the nation. The view is possible although, eventually, Israel was able to overcome the opposition of the nations that opposed them. Delitzsch, III, 281, suggests that the psalm is "a Maccabaean Psalm." The psalm does not give enough information to let us be certain of its setting.

Lord. Servants look for some sign from their "masters" (or "master," *ʾadôn*, see 8:1), and a maiden similarly looks at her mistress for a sign.[197] In the same way, the people look to the Lord their God to send them "mercy" (or "grace," *ḥanan*, see 4:1), v. 2.

II. Prayer to the Lord 3–4

3–4 The psalmist again asks the Lord to show "mercy" (or "grace," *ḥanan*, see 4:1) to the nation. The repetition of the prayer lends emphasis to it. The people are greatly "filled with contempt" as others look down on them. This likely refers to the contempt toward Israel the nations around them displayed, v. 3. The "soul" of the nation has experienced the "scorning" (or "derision") of others who are "at ease" (or "arrogant"), and they face the contempt shown them by the "proud" (*ligʾêônîm*) v. 4.[198]

While we do not know the details of this trial, the psalmist's response still gives us practical guidance for when troubles beset us today. The psalmist approaches the omnipresent God in prayer. Although the plight of the people is such that others look down on them, the psalmist knows that he can go to the Lord in every circumstance. God still invites His children to come to Him with their burdens.

PSALM 124

This is the second of the four psalms titled "A Song of degrees [or 'ascents']" and is written by David.[199] It is a song of thanks-

[197]*NIB*, IV, 1187, considers both "master" and "mistress" to refer to God. It comments, "The feminine imaging of God here is striking." More probably, "master" and "mistress" are illustrations rather than direct references to God.

[198]The unusual word *ligʾêônîm* is normally considered as the *lamed* preposition preceding the construct of *geʾâ*, "proud," joined with the participle *yônîm*, "oppressors." Delitzsch explains it as "an intentional new formation of the poet." With either explanation, this is cruel oppression by haughty men.

[199]Delitzsch, III, 282, notes that many mss and versions omit David's name. He concludes that the author wrote this psalm "in the manner of the Davidic Psalms"

giving,[200] one in which the nation expresses its gratitude for deliverance from an unknown enemy.[201] The reference to "wrath" in v. 3 may indicate Absalom's attitude toward David. Whatever it was, the potential for overwhelming defeat was clear, vv. 3–5. The Lord's intervention not only delivered the people but also defeated their enemy, v. 7. David speaks on their behalf as he gives thanks to the Lord. With his expression of gratitude, David leaves an example for believers in this present time. It is still good to give thanks to the Lord for His many gracious actions.

I. Potential for Defeat 1–5

1–5 David expresses the threat to Israel with climactic poetry, rare in this part of the book.[202] If the Lord had not supported the nation,[203] they would have uttered the words found in vv. 3–5. If the Lord had not been with them when men rose up against them, vv. 1–2, sure defeat would have followed. Verses 3–5 give the climax to the

---

by using metaphors common to them. Since there are Aramaizing forms in the text, Delitzsch makes the psalm postexilic. The existence of Aramaic influence is not surprising, even in David's time, due to the nearness of Syria to Israel. See Judg. 5:7 (twice); Song of Sol. 1:6; 2:7 for similar grammatical constructions from early periods in Israel's history, and Ps. 122:3, 4; 133:2, 3; 144:15, also authored by David. There is no reason to reject the Jewish tradition of David's authorship.

[200]The introduction to Ps. 18 summarizes the songs of thanksgiving.

[201]Murphy, p. 637, refers the threat to "the deliverance of Israel from the pursuits of Pharaoh." Kidner, p. 436, relates the threat to the Philistine attack in II Sam. 5:17ff. Fausset, III, 378, locates it at either "the Aramaic or Syrian and Edomite war." Rawlinson, III, 205, mentions three possibilities: Saul; the Ammonites and Syrians, II Sam. 10:6–8; or Absalom, II Sam. 15:2–13. Moll, p. 613, suggests "the war with Syria and Edom," II Sam. 8:13–14. Cohen, p. 425, suggests the enmity of Sanballat, e.g., Neh. 6:1–14. This shows the impossibility of locating the background with certainty.

[202]Kidner, p. 436, understands vv. 1–2 as antiphonal. In v. 1 is a "cantor declaiming his opening line." The congregation repeats it in v. 2. While this would explain the repetition, the psalm gives no indication of a cantor and his congregation. Climactic poetry occurs elsewhere in the Psalms, e.g., 29:1–2; 93:3; 103:1–2; 148:1–6.

[203]The phrase "if it had not been the Lord" (*lûlê yᵉhwah šehayâ ʾᵃšer*) is difficult. The word *šehayâ* is explained variously: the initial *š* indicates an Aramaic influence (Delitzsch; Leupold); a pregnant construction with the two clauses contracted (Moll); or the abbreviated relative pronoun *ʾᵃšer* (BDB, p. 979). No matter which explanation we accept, the sense of the phrase is similar.

repeated thought of vv. 1–2. Their foes[204] would have "swallowed" (or "destroyed," *bala*ᶜ I, see 21:9) them "quick" (or "alive") in their "wrath" (*ʾap*, see 2:5) toward the nation. The metaphor picturesquely describes a catastrophic defeat, v. 3. David pictures the defeat as waters overwhelming drowning men or as a stream sweeping over them, v. 4. "Proud" (or "raging")[205] waters had swept over them. David uses similar word pictures, e.g., 32:6; 69:1–2; 144:7, v. 5.

II. Praise for Deliverance 6–8

6–7 David now ascribes "bless[ings]" (*barak*, see 5:12) to the Lord for delivering the people. The Lord has not given them to their foes. The phrase "prey to their teeth" pictures Israel as meat to be torn apart by the teeth of those opposed to them. The Lord has spared them from such devastation, v. 6. They have escaped like a "bird" (*ṣippôr*, see 84:3)[206] flying from the snare of a trapper. In this case, the Lord has broken the snare of their enemies and let them escape. The picture in vv. 6–7 is of the nation already caught by their foes. The Lord, however, breaks this hold and enables the escape of His people, v. 7.

8 The "help" (*ᶜezer*, see 20:2) of Israel lies in the "name of the Lord,"[207] His revealed nature. To illustrate the power available to the people, David refers to the Lord's creative work. In doing so, he underscores the Lord's omnipotence, an encouragement to the people, v. 8.

---

[204]Kidner, p. 436, introduces a "monster large enough to need only one gulp of its prey." Weiser, p. 755, refers to "powerful sea-monsters." These descriptions are fanciful. David thinks only of the overwhelming power of his enemies.

[205]Fausset, III, 379, concludes, "The term 'proud' implies that the waters are figurative [for] haughty enemies." The adjective *zêdônîm*, used only here, refers to "proud" waters, i.e., waters that are lifted up and thus raging. The waters serve as a word picture of Israel's adversaries as they swarm over the nation.

[206]Henry, III, 730, makes *ṣippôr* a "sparrow." The word, however, rather indicates the chirping of a bird. It is not specific to any one bird.

[207]A summary of the Lord's "name" is at 5:11, note 94.

PSALM 125

This "Song of degrees [or 'ascents']" expresses Israel's trust in the Lord. As with most of the psalms in this section, the title does not name an author.[208] It does not give enough information to let us be certain as to the circumstances mentioned. The nation has come through some grave peril. The psalmist describes this only generally as "the rod of the wicked," v. 3, "crooked ways," and "workers of iniquity," v. 5. The Lord, however, had kept the nation safe from this threat, and the psalmist recognizes the deliverance with these few verses.

I. Deliverance from the Wicked 1–3

1–3 The psalmist pictures the stability of those who trust the Lord by comparing them to "mount Zion." This cannot be moved but will remain forever. Those who trust the Lord are still stable. As the site where Jerusalem stands, the mountain will continue as the place from which the Lord rules in the Millennium (Isa. 2:3; 24:23; 46:13), v. 1. There are several "mountains" associated with the city. Mount Zion lies to the south of the temple, which stood on Mount Moriah. The southern part of the temple hill has the name Ophel. The original city of David stood on a mount later known as Acra. A ridge to the west of the city tapers down to the Maritime Plain. The Mount of Olives is east of the city. North of this is Mount Scopus. The Hill of Evil Counsel, thought to be the place where Judas betrayed the Lord, is southeast of the city. Just as these mountains surround Jerusalem, so the Lord surrounds His people to protect them. His protection will last forever, v. 2. The "rod [or 'scepter'] of the wicked," the influence of those who try to control Israel, will not successfully rest on "the lot of the righteous," i.e., the

---

[208]Spurgeon, p. 582, sees David as the author. Clarke, p. 319, puts the psalm at the Assyrian threat. Perowne, II, 388, dates it at the time of Nehemiah, when influential leaders of the Jews joined forces with the wicked in seeking control over the nation. Gaebelein, p. 452, sets it at the return from Babylonian captivity. Keet, p. 47, places it during "the Persian period." Delitzsch, III, 285, leaves the situation general, calling it only a time when "the people are under foreign dominion." I would follow Delitzsch, primarily because of the last verse. This says that some Jews followed the evil men who sought to take control. Just as some citizens of the United States support communism or terrorism, so some Jews cooperated with the wicked. It is not clear, however, whether Assyria, Babylon, Media-Persia, or some other nation is in view. The diversity of views shows the impossibility of setting the background.

land allotted to the nation; see Joshua 18:6, 10; 19:51. The righteous will not be forced to commit "iniquity" (*ʿawlâ*, see 7:3). Together with v. 5, the verse suggests that the wicked are in control, v. 3.

II. Reliance on the Lord 4–5

4–5 The psalmist prays on behalf of the nation. He asks the Lord to perform good works on behalf of those who are good. He explains this goodness with the additional comment that they are "upright in their hearts." Man never merits God's goodness by good works. It is the attitude of the heart that gives man the right to approach the Lord in prayer, v. 4. Those in the land who follow the "crooked ways" of Israel's enemies will receive the same judgment. The Lord will lead the wicked Israelites away, along with those who practice iniquitous actions against His people. In sharp contrast, the Lord will give peace to the nation, v. 5.[209]

PSALM 126

This "Song of degrees [or 'ascents']"[210] focuses on the nation of Israel. We do not know the author although he must have lived after the return of Judah from the Babylonian captivity.[211] He describes the nation's deliverance from Babylon. His response to this deliverance includes a picture of the Christian's response to deliverance from the bondage of sin. Just as Israel left Babylon with the determination to serve the Lord, so Christians today should have this same determination to serve Him.

---

[209]Cohen, p. 426, and Livingston, p. 428, understand the final clause as a prayer, "God preserve his Israel in peace." The phrase is a verbless clause. It is normal to supply the verb, as in the AV, NASB, and NIV. While the author no doubt focused on his own time, the principle he expresses is eschatological in nature. The Lord will one day put down all the wicked and establish this world in peace.

[210]See the discussion in the introduction to Ps. 120.

[211]Rotherham, p. 532, places the psalm in the time of Hezekiah. Livingston, p. 428, dates it "at the time when the first group of returnees entered Palestine from Babylon." The psalm does not identify its writer or the specific time of its writing.

I. Response of Israel 1–3

1–3 The phrase "turned again" is better "turned back," i.e., "brought back." The return from the Babylonian "captivity" (*šîbâ*)[212] was like a beautiful dream to Israel. Although the Lord had prophesied a seventy-year captivity (Jer. 25:11; 29:10), most of the people had forgotten this. They did not expect a fulfillment, v. 1. The return filled them with joy, bringing laughter and "singing" (*rinnâ*, better "a shout of joy," see 17:1). The subject of the verb "said" comes from among the "heathen." Seeing the new freedom of Israel, others say, "The Lord hath done great things for them." Note that the heathen often see what the Lord does for His people. The Christian's success should testify to the lost, v. 2. In addition, the people themselves acknowledge the "great things" the Lord has done for them and rejoice in His goodness, v. 3.

II. Responsibilities of Israel 4–6

4 The people offer a brief prayer that the Lord will bring back others who are still in captivity. We do not know why many remained behind in Babylon. We can speculate that age, small children, sickness, a settled life, fear of the unknown, or other things played a part. Ultimately, all we can say is that only a small number returned. These now pray that the Lord will "turn again our captivity [*šᵉbiwt*],"[213] i.e., restore the captives to the land. The phrase "as the streams in the south [or 'Negeb']"[214] is an illustration. During the dry days of summer in the Negeb, the streams in this wilderness dry up. The early

---

[212]Phillips, II, 475, understands the "captivity of Zion" as being shut up in Jerusalem by the Assyrians. *TWOT*, II, 910, follows Dahood, *Psalms*, III, 218, in translating *šîbâ* "restore the fortunes of." By doing this, the psalm becomes preexilic. Kidner, II, 439, broadens the term, referring it to restoration "from famine, or siege, captivity or plague." The AV reads *šᵉbît*, "captivity," i.e., the "returning ones." This fits well with the context. In addition, v. 4 supports the return from the captivity. There is no problem with treating the psalm as postexilic.

[213]The AV correctly follows the *qᵉrê* reading *šᵉbît*. There is debate over the meaning of the *kᵉtîb šᵉbiwt* (or *šᵉbût*). Cheyne, II, 189, translates "life." Leupold, p. 888, and Leslie, p. 127, give "fortunes." Hirsch, II, 385, and Jennings, II, 300, relate it to the captivity.

[214]The wilderness region south of Beer-sheba has the name "Negeb," a word that also means "south." The context must determine whether is should be translated "south" or transliterated "Negeb." Here, the psalmist refers to streams located in the Negeb.

fall rains fill them. In the same way, the people want others still in Babylon to fill the nation, v. 4.

5–6 The psalmist now gives a plan for successful work. The passage develops a proverbial thought. Those who "sow in tears" are those who anticipate the hard work of reestablishing themselves in the land. They have the confidence that their work will let them "reap in joy" (*rinnâ*, once more "a shout of joy"), v. 5. They go regularly[215] and weep from the exhaustive nature of their work.[216] They bear "precious seed" (better "a bag of seed"), they and will certainly come[217] with "rejoicing" (*rinnâ*, again "a shout of joy") in the harvest as they bring sheaves of wheat from the field, v. 6.[218]

PSALM 127

This is the second of two psalms associated directly with Solomon (also 72).[219] There may be a play on words in v. 2. "His beloved" (*y^adîdô*, see 45, title) is from the same root as "Jedidiah" (*y^edîdyah*), the name given to Solomon meaning "beloved of the Lord" (II Sam. 12:25). The psalm is a wisdom psalm that instructs the nation and

---

[215]The imperfect verb from *halak* with its infinitive absolute indicates a continuing action. G.K.C. 113 *u*.

[216]Anderson, II, 866, and Weiser, p. 762, suggest that the sowing of crops was associated with ceremonies commemorating the death of one of the gods. Weeping accompanied the sowing. It is unlikely, however, that the psalmist would have referred to a heathen custom here. He rather simply takes note of the strenuous nature of the work that results in a harvest.

[217]The imperfect verb from *bô᾽* follows its infinitive absolute, giving emphasis to the action. G.K.C. 113 *p*.

[218]The last two verses are often quoted in support of soulwinning efforts. While they do not apply directly to evangelism, they give a principle of work that is true in every area. Those who labor will see fruit from their labors. This is as true in evangelism as it is in other areas of life.

[219]Henry, III, 734, makes David the author, writing "for Solomon." The *lamed* preposition, however, is commonly used to introduce the author. Cf. G.K.C. 129 *c*. Delitzsch, III, 290, 292, suggests that Solomon's name was added only because of the allusion to Jedidiah, v. 2, and the "Proverbs-like form of the Psalm." Cohen, p. 428, thinks that Solomon's name was added because of the reference to the "house," v. 1. These views are speculative. We have no reason to doubt the accuracy of the title.

present-day believers. Whether building a house, securing a city against attack, or rearing children, God's people must rely on Him. Solomon must have penned the psalm before his own departure from the ways of the Lord.[220]

I. Trusting the Lord 1–2

1–2 Solomon uses the building of a house as an example of a time for relying upon the Lord.[221] It may be, although the psalm does not say, that the king was engaged in building either the temple or his own palace (I Kings 9:10). He recognizes the need for having the Lord's blessings upon one's work. Otherwise, the work is "vain" (*šawᵓ*, see 12:2). The same is true in guarding a city against attack. It is "vain" (*šawᵓ*) for the watchman to go about his rounds with no concern for the Lord's protection, v. 1.[222] To rise early, stay up late, or to eat the "bread of sorrows," food that has comes from hard labor, is equally "vain" (*šawᵓ*). All such effort is without lasting value unless the Lord guides it. The threefold use of *šawᵓ* emphasizes the thought of neglecting the Lord. The Lord gives blessed sleep to His "beloved,"[223] a gift that allows the neglect of fruitless self-effort, v. 2.[224]

II. Blessing of Children 3–5

3–5 Solomon now turns to the family, one of the greatest blessings God bestows. The gift of children is an inheritance from the Lord.

---

[220]In addition to Pss. 72 and 127, where Solomon's name appears in the title, it is likely that he also authored Ps. 132. While his name does not appear there, the content of the psalm suggests the dedication of the temple.

[221]The city of Edinburgh takes its motto from this verse: *nisi Dominus frustra*, "Except the Lord, it is in vain."

[222]In the OT, the Jews observed three night watches: the beginning (Lam. 2:19), from sunset until 10 p.m.; the middle, between 10 p.m. and 2 a.m. (Judg. 7:19); and the morning, from 2 a.m. until sunrise (Exod. 14:24).

[223]Among others, Gaebelein, p. 457, and Alexander, p. 526, understand that God gives His blessings while the godly sleep. This does not commend slothfulness but rather suggests that God blesses the godly without their effort. While the view is possible, the psalm leaves it unsaid and thus uncertain. In view of the emphasis on work elsewhere in Solomon's writings, e.g., Prov. 18:9; 20:11, I prefer the thought of the peace that comes from relying on the Lord.

[224]The initial "so" translates *ken*. Leupold, p. 894, derives this from *kûn* and translates it as a noun, "what is right." This is unlikely, however, since it requires supplying the thought of time later in the verse ("while he sleeps").

They are His reward. The wicked have children as well as the godly. To the godly, however, children have a special position not known by the wicked. They come from the Lord, v. 3. A "mighty man" (*gibbôr*, see 19:5), a warrior, sends forth arrows. In the same way, the young man brings forth children. Just as the arrows defend the warrior, so children defend their father in his sickness or old age, v. 4.[225] The "man" (*geber*, see 34:8) whose "quiver" is full, the image coming from the warrior in v. 4, is "happy" (or "blessed," *ʾašrê*, see 1:1). Such men will not be publicly "ashamed" (*bôš*, see 6:10) when speaking with their adversaries in the gate of the city. The children will support their father's position in the matters at hand, v. 5.[226]

PSALM 128

Neither the title nor the psalm is clear as to the background, the author, the purpose, or the date of writing.[227] The psalm is a wisdom psalm that teaches the people about the blessings that come from following the Lord. The author first describes the personal blessings of

[225]Daniel J. Estes, "Like Arrows in the Hand of a Warrior (Psalm CXXVII)," *VT* 40:3 (1991): 310, sees the comparison differently. As the archer guides his arrows toward the target, so the father guides his children to take their place in society. The view is possible.

[226]Perowne, II, 396, and W. E. Barnes, II, 606, consider this a lawsuit. Weiser, p. 766, suggests that the children help their father "gain vindication in the face of every sort of lie." Leslie, p. 426, suggests that the sons are ready to fight for their father to protect him from the miscarriage of justice. Ewald, II, 166, makes the sons "the strongest protection of the house and the ageing parents." Hengstenberg, III, 450, has the sons "managing the affairs of their fathers." Hirsch, II, 388, sees the sons as defending an insult to their parents. From this variety of suggestions, it is clear that we cannot be dogmatic. In some way, the sons defend their father.

[227]Clarke, p. 323, places it at the time of the Assyrian threat. Anderson, II, 869, has the postexilic author, a priest, write at the Feast of Tabernacles. Leupold, p. 895, sets the psalm in the time of Nehemiah. He feels that the psalm emphasizes the family because of the "scarcity of population" in the land. Fausset, III, 382, places it a little earlier, after the return from Babylon and during Samaritan opposition. From the promise of blessing coming from the temple and the prosperity of Jerusalem, v. 5, and of peace, v. 6, I would locate the psalm earlier rather than later, perhaps during Solomon's reign.

the godly person. He then moves to the extended blessings that come to the nation and to the descendants of the godly.

I. Personal Blessings of the Godly 1–4

1–2 Everyone who "feareth the Lord" (see *yir᾿ê yᵉhwah*, 15:4) is "blessed" (*᾿ašrê*, see 1:1). As is normal in the Psalms, the word *᾿ašrê* is plural. This emphasizes the blessedness that comes to the godly man. As the result of his reverence for the Lord, he walks in godly ways, v. 1. He will be productive, bringing forth fruit to eat from his labors. He will be "happy" (better "blessed," *᾿ašrê*),[228] and things will go well with him, v. 2.

3–4 The psalmist now turns to the family blessings that God will give to His children. The wife of the godly man is a "fruitful vine." Like a vine, she will bear fruit "by the sides of" (better "within") the house. Her children will be like "olive plants [see *šatal*, 1:3]" placed around the "table" (*šulḥan*, see 23:5). The olive tree, with its green and silver leaves and its valuable black olives, is a picture of fruitfulness and blessing (52:8; Jer. 11:16; Hos. 14:6), v. 3. This mighty man (*geber*, see 34:8) who "feareth the Lord" (see 15:4) will be "blessed" (*barak*, see 5:12) by Him. The promise still holds true. Those who reverence the Lord will receive His blessing, v. 4.

II. Extended Blessings of the Godly 5–6

5–6 The psalmist now looks to the future blessings that will come from the Lord. He will "bless" (*barak*) the godly person "out of" (better "from") "Zion," standing here for Jerusalem, the location of the temple where the Lord dwelt. The godly will see the prosperity of Jerusalem, the capital and thus representing the nation, during the rest of his life, v. 5. He will also live to see his descendants. The AV supplies the conjunction *and*. The final phrase stands by itself as a benedictory prayer for the nation: "Peace be upon Israel," v. 6.

---

[228]This is the only place in Psalms that the word *᾿ešer* is in construct to a pronominal suffix. It is still plural and thus emphatic. As with 1:1 (and everywhere else the word appears), I prefer the translation "blessed." Happiness is transitory. True blessedness remains despite the circumstances.

PSALM 129

The psalm is a community lament.[229] The unknown author writes on behalf of the nation. He refers to "Israel" speaking, v. 1, and to those who "hate Zion," v. 5. Although he pronounces an imprecation upon Israel's foes, v. 6, the imprecation does not come to the level of those in the imprecatory psalms.[230] At the time of the writing, Israel is no longer a young nation, vv. 1–2. The likely time of writing is after the return from the Babylonian captivity, when the nation faced opposition from surrounding nations. In the time of Zerubbabel, the opposition came from Syria (Ezra 4:7, "Syrian tongue"). During the leadership of Nehemiah, the opposition involved Samaria to the north, Arabs to the south, Ammonites to the east, and Philistines ("Ashdodites") to the west (Neh. 4:2, 7). Either of these times fit the opposition referred to in the psalm.[231]

The psalm presents a picture of the implacable nature of God's enemies. They afflict God's people, vv. 1–3, and bind them to restrict their freedom, v. 4. They hate them, v. 5, and refuse to pronounce blessings on them, v. 8. It should not surprise Christians that the world opposes them. This has always been the way of those who reject God's presence in their lives.

I. The Oppression and the Deliverance 1–4

1–3 The psalmist pictures Israel as speaking of its past persecution. The nation has been "afflicted" (*ṣarar*, see 31:9) "many a time" (or "greatly") ever since "youth," the early days when Israel suffered

[229]Leslie, p. 128, views the psalm as one of thanksgiving, possibly connected with the fall New Year festival. The mood of the psalm, however, is too somber to classify it this way.

[230]The introduction to Ps. 35 discusses the imprecatory psalms.

[231]Oesterley, II, 523, sets it at Assyria's defeat in the time of Hezekiah. Calvin, V, 120, places the psalm later, after Antiochus Epiphanes, when Syria was Israel's enemy. Evidence from the Dead Sea scrolls, however, indicates that the Psalms existed before this time. The psalm does not let us be dogmatic as to the date of its writing. Weiser, p. 772, does not see "a concrete historical situation." He rather sees "the cultic rite of the representation of history as the history of salvation. This view is subjective, not naturally drawn from the psalm. Fausset, p. 383, refers the plowing of v. 3 to that done by Titus as he plowed under the temple site after his conquest of Jerusalem in AD 70. The lament refers to history, however, and does not prophesy future calamity.

bondage in Egypt, v. 1. Others have "afflicted" (*ṣarar*) them but have not "prevailed" over them. While others may have overcome Israel, this was always temporary. The Lord used these times to punish the nation and to teach them their need of living for Him. When the punishment was over, the nation took control of itself once more, v. 2. The psalmist compares these afflictions to long furrows plowed on the back of the nation, v. 3.

4 The Lord is righteous and has not cast away the nation. He has remained faithful to His covenant. In each time of persecution, He has cut in two the cords that have bound Israel,[232] bringing freedom to the nation, v. 4.

II. The Imprecation and the Result 5–8

5–7 The psalmist prays for judgment on the nation's foes.[233] May those who "hate [*śane*ʾ, see 5:5] Zion," the holy city representing the nation, be "confounded" (or "ashamed," *bôš*, see 6:10), v. 5. May they be as the withered "grass upon the housetops." Some of the flat-roofed houses were covered with dirt for insulation. Grass would grow there during the rainy season. When the heat comes, however, the new grass with its shallow root system withers and dies before "it groweth up" (or "it is plucked up"), v. 6.[234] There is not enough to fill the hand of a "mower" (or "reaper") as he grasps them to cut.[235] One

[232]Kissane, p. 585, and Clarke, p. 324, suggest that the cutting is of the traces that bind the animal to the plow. Cutting them spoils the enemy's plowing of Israel. This is a possible view.

[233]Leupold, p. 901, treats the verbs as normal imperfects and considers the whole passage as a prediction of what will befall those who hate Zion. This is grammatically possible. However, the same verbs occur regularly in the Psalms as cohortatives or jussives (*yebošû*, at least eleven times, e.g., 6:10; 35:4; *yissogû*, only four times, all jussives, 35:4; 40:14; 70:2; 78:57). This evidence argues that the verse is a prayer.

[234]The verb translated "groweth up" (*šalap*) occurs twenty-three times elsewhere, twenty-one in connection with drawing a sword or dagger. The two other times (Ruth 4:7, 8) refer to drawing off a shoe. The word never refers to growing. With the LXX translating ἐκσπασθῆναι, and the Vulgate, *priusquamevellatur*, the evidence supports the idea of plucking the grass out of the dirt.

[235]Delitzsch, III, 300, argues that grass "can be pulled up just as well when it is withered as when it is green." For this reason, he translates *šalap* as "shooteth up," bringing forth ears or blossoms. I disagree with his reasoning. Grass is not easily pulled up when it has withered since the ground is harder. There is also no support for the translation "shooteth up."

who tries to "bind" (or "gather") sheaves of the grass will not find enough to fill the fold of his robe at the bosom (cf. Neh. 5:13), v. 7.

8 The thought of reaping suggests the practice of invoking God's blessings on others during the harvest (Ruth 2:4). Those who pass by Israel's foes, however, do not seek the Lord's "blessing" (see *barak*, 5:12) on them. They will not "bless" (*barak*) them in "the name of the Lord"[236] by asking the Lord to favor them, v. 8.

PSALM 130

This "Pauline Psalm"[237] is a penitential psalm, an individual lament in which the psalmist grieves over his own sin; cf. v. 3.[238] We do not know the author or the background to the writing.[239] Since the psalm uses Hebrew words that occur elsewhere only in later books,[240] it is probable that it comes from the later period of Israel's history. The details are left vague, giving the psalm a general application to all who express sorrow for their sins. In every case, there is forgiveness with the Lord for the repentant sinner.

I. Expression of Grief 1–4

1–2 The psalmist pours out his heart to the Lord "out of the depths" of his misery over his sin. The picture is of someone caught in floodwaters that threaten to overwhelm him. He grieves over his sin but realizes that only the Lord can deliver him from its consequences, v. 1. The psalmist pleads with the Lord to hear his prayer. The reference to his "voice" makes it likely that he prayed audibly.

---

[236]Note 94 at 5:11 gives a summary of the Lord's "name."

[237]See the introduction to Ps. 32.

[238]The penitential psalms include Pss. 6, 32, 38, 51, 102, 130, and 143.

[239]Henry, III, 739, makes David the author. Clarke, p. 325, assigns it to Hezekiah. Rawlinson, III, 246, places the psalm during the Captivity, while Cohen, p. 433, dates it during the time of Nehemiah. There is not enough information to be certain of the author's identity.

[240]The word *qaššub*, "attentive," v. 2, occurs only in II Chron. 6:40; 7:15; and Neh. 1:6, 11. The word *sᵉlîḥâ*, "forgiveness," v. 4, occurs only in Neh. 9:17 and Dan. 9:9.

The description of his prayer as "supplications" (*taḥ*^{a}*nun*, see 28:2) suggests that he was caught up emotionally in his plea for forgiveness, v. 2.

3–4 The author acknowledges the greatness of his sin. If the Lord kept a record of man's iniquities, who would be able to stand before Him? The rhetorical question requires the answer that no one could stand before the Lord. The Lord does not ignore man's sin, but He does take into account man's attitude toward sin. Where there is repentance and confession, the Lord forgives. Without this gracious action, no one would be able to stand before the Lord, v. 3. The psalmist refers to this forgiveness, an act of mercy that leads the Lord to be "feared" (or "reverenced"), v. 4.

II. Anticipation of Mercy 5–8

5–6 The psalmist eagerly "wait[s]" (*qawâ*, see 25:3) for the Lord to work on his behalf. His "soul," he himself, "wait[s]" (*qawâ*) for this gracious action. While he waits, he finds "hope" (*yaḥal*, see 31:24), confidence based on God's "word," the many promises of mercy toward His people, v. 5. The writer repeats the thought of waiting, this time illustrating it from the picture of the watchmen who wait for the dawn. Lonely and sleepy, facing the blackness of night and possible bad weather, the watchman looks eagerly for the morning. The psalm writer's anticipation is greater than that of the watchmen who look for the rising of the sun, v. 6.

7–8 The author now addresses the nation. They also need to "hope" (*yaḥal*) in the Lord; He is the source of "mercy" (or "steadfast love," *ḥesed*, see 5:7) and abundant "redemption" (see *padâ*, 25:22), v. 7. He will "redeem" (*padâ*) Israel from all their "iniquities," the times they have deviated from God's Word. The word "all" indicates that the forgiveness will be complete, v. 8.

PSALM 131

This short song of David[241] expresses his confidence in God. Although king of the nation, he does not rely upon his own resources and abilities. He turns from these to trust in the Lord. We do not know the circumstances that called David to write.[242] It is possible that he faced one of the many crises in his life. In any case, he sets down his attitude of reliance on the Lord. In this, he sets an example for believers in all ages.

I. David's Prayer 1

1 David's prayer is negative, a denial of pride. His heart is not "haughty" (or "arrogant"). His eyes are not "lofty," raised to look on higher things such as wealth or position. He does not presumptuously "exercise" himself in great matters or things too "high" (or "difficult," *pala*ᵓ, see 9:1) for him. In this context, this refers to goals set simply for self-glorification.[243] David was the king. Necessarily, he dealt with great matters. He states here his refusal to seek after things purely to satisfy his pride, v. 1.[244]

---

[241]*NIB*, IV, 1208, and Mays, p. 408, note that the translation of the NRSV ("My soul is like the weaned child that is with me") argues that a woman authors this psalm. The reference to a weaned child with his mother does not mean that the mother speaks here. This is an illustration of David's contentment. It is inconceivable that the Jews would have accepted a psalm written by a woman. Delitzsch, III, 305, makes the author refer to David only because he "is the model of the state of mind which the poet expresses here." Rotherham, p. 541, accepts David as starting the psalm but has Hezekiah finish it. As short as this psalm is, it is doubtful that it took two men to complete. Leupold, pp. 908–9, thinks that it is not necessary to insist on David as the author since the words "of David" are missing in some mss. He makes the psalm postexilic. There is nothing in the psalm, however, that argues against David's authorship. The fact that the author exhorts Israel, v. 3, suggests that he must have held a high place in the nation.

[242]Henry, III, 740, makes the psalm an answer to the charges that David "sought the kingdom, in the pride of his heart," I Sam. 18:8; 20:31. While possible, nothing in the psalm lets us be dogmatic about its background.

[243]Bernard P. Robinson, "Form and Meaning in Psalm 131," *Biblica* 79:2 (1998): 182, aptly notes that the reference to "heart" and "eyes" is synecdoche, standing for the whole person. These parts, however, specially refer to pride: "He is not haughty in his heart . . . he is not lifted up in respect of his eyes."

[244]Keet, p. 82, refers the "great matters" to "problems of Greek philosophy which were beginning to exercise the Hebrew mind." The view ignores the title that assigns the psalm to David.

II. David's Trust 2

2 The verse can be rendered, "As a weaned child[245] with his mother, as the weaned child is my soul with me." David compares his behavior to that of a child that has been weaned from his mother's breast. Though he now has been separated from his mother, he still finds comfort with her. He remains in his mother's arms, not seeking to be nursed but content simply to be with her. David has "behaved [or 'stilled'] and quieted" himself like a weaned child that relies on its mother. The picture shows David's need of the Lord. He repeats the thought to emphasize his trust in the Lord, v. 2.

III. David's Exhortation 3

3 David exhorts Israel to turn from pride and self-gratification.[246] They should confidently "hope" (*yaḥal*, see 31:24) in the Lord. The king has seen the value of such trust in his own life. He therefore urges Israel to rely on the Lord both for immediate and for eternal needs, v. 3.

PSALM 132

When Israel first occupied Palestine, they located the tabernacle at Shiloh (Judg. 18:31), about ten miles north of Bethel and east of the road leading from Bethel to Shechem (Judg. 21:19). During the wars with Philistia, Shiloh was destroyed (Jer. 7:12, 14), an act confirmed by archaeology. When the Israelites brought the ark of the covenant to be with the army, the Philistines captured it and took it to Ashdod (I Sam. 5:1), one of their principal cities. For seven months, the Lord sent repeated calamities to the Philistines until they realized their need to return the ark to Israel. Israel kept it in Kirjath-jearim, a city located on the border between Judah and Benjamin about eight

[245]The phrase "weaned child" translates the passive participle of *gamal*, "to recompense, complete," see 7:4. It refers here to the child who has completed nursing and now lies content in his mother's arms.

[246]Leslie, p. 410, understands v. 3 as "a congregational prayer." Nothing in the verse requires us to introduce a new subject at this point.

miles west of Jerusalem. It remained there for twenty years (I Sam. 7:2) until David brought it to Jerusalem (II Sam. 6:1–15), where he had built a tabernacle for it (II Sam. 6:17). Later, Solomon replaced the temporary tabernacle structure with a more permanent temple. This is the likely time for Solomon to write the psalm. Although his name does not appear in the psalm, the author displays an intimate knowledge of David that could only have come from a close association with him. In addition, vv. 8–10 closely parallel Solomon's prayer (II Chron. 6:41–42).

This psalm recounts David's effort to locate the ark so that Israel could once more worship at the tabernacle. His actions illustrate his faithfulness to the Lord. Solomon recalls the Lord's promise to David. On this basis, he asks the Lord to bless him, his descendants, and the nation.[247]

There is an emphasis on the blessing God gives to faithfulness. He will remember His covenant, vv. 11–12. He will dwell in Jerusalem and provide the material needs of His people, vv. 14–15. He will give spiritual blessing that causes great rejoicing among the people, v. 16. He will strengthen the kingdom of David, letting it burn brightly under the leadership of Messiah, v. 17. The foes of Messiah will suffer shame but His rule will prosper, v. 18. God still blesses faithfulness among His people.

I. A Restored Worship 1–9

1–5 Solomon asks the Lord to remember David. Omitting the supplied "and," Solomon notes the "afflictions" (*ᶜanâ*, see 35:13) that David endured. He thinks of the difficulties that David faced as he sought to bring the ark to Jerusalem: the lack of advice by the priests

---

[247]Clarke, p. 327, gives Hezekiah as the author. Oesterley, II, 549–50, makes the psalm "composed by a court official in the name of the king. . . . [in] the later period of the monarchy." Fausset, III, 385, makes the author an unknown writer in postexilic times. He quotes from David and Solomon. There is no reason to stress the kingly line of David, however, unless it existed. Following the return, Israel was still subject to Babylon, then to the Medo-Persian alliance, and did not have a king. *NIB*, IV, 1211, also makes the psalm postexilic. He sees vv. 17–18 as suggesting that Israel has no king. These verses, however, may be understood differently (see comments). Ewald, II, 239, refers the psalm to Zerubbabel. While the psalm mentions David four times, it does not name him as the author. The parallelism of vv. 8–10 with II Chron. 6:41–42 suggests Solomonic authorship.

(I Chron. 15:11–13) and the death of Uzza (I Chron. 13:9–10), v. 1. Despite this, David swore to the Lord, v. 2,[248] that he would not rest, vv. 3–4,[249] until he had made a "habitation" (*miškanôt*, lit. "tabernacles") for the Lord to dwell in. The plural of majesty is appropriate in referring to God's dwelling on earth. Since David was a man of war, the Lord did not let him build the temple. He rather placed it in a tent (II Sam. 6:17), following the pattern given earlier to Moses. He did, however, collect materials for Solomon to use in its building (I Chron. 28:14–18), v. 5.

6–7 The people had heard of "it," the ark of the covenant,[250] when they were in "Ephratah," the region near Kirjath-jearim where the ark first rested after its return from Philistia.[251] They found the ark in the "fields of the wood [*yaᶜar*],"[252] in Kirjath-jearim (*qiryat yᵉᶜarîm*), v. 6. Having brought it to Jerusalem, the people anticipate going to "his" (or "His") dwelling and worshiping at the ark, God's footstool, v. 7.[253]

8–9 Solomon calls upon the Lord to rise up and enter into the temple, His resting place on the earth. May He and the ark of His covenant come into the temple, v. 8.[254] May the priests carry out their

---

[248]Neither I Sam. nor I Chron. records David's oath. I Chron. 13:1–3 tells us that David spoke with many leaders in preparation for bringing the ark to Jerusalem. His desire to bring the ark to his capital city is clear. David likely had told Solomon of his oath as he charged his son to build a temple for the ark, I Chron. 28:9–10.

[249]The pledge to avoid sleep is idiomatic, cf. Prov. 6:4. Actually, three months elapsed before the ark arrived in Jerusalem, II Sam. 6:11–15.

[250]The suffix "it" is feminine in form while *ʾᵃrôn*, "ark," is masculine. Kissane, p. 592, makes the pronoun refer to David's "oath," v. 2, a feminine word. Moll, p. 629, refers the pronoun "it" to v. 7. The 3fs pronoun may refer generally to the verbal thought of the preceding sentence. G.K.C. 135 *p*. That thought here is of "an habitation for the mighty God of Jacob," i.e., the ark.

[251]Eaton, p. 292, and Alexander, p. 532, understand "Ephratah" as another name for Bethlehem, the city of David's birth, located about ten miles west of Kirjath-jearim. David heard of the ark when he was in Bethlehem. This is a possible view.

[252]The word *yaᶜar* is from the same root as *yᵉᶜarîm*. This leads to the natural thought that Solomon refers to *qiryat yᵉᶜarîm*, "the city of forests," where the ark rested. Delitzsch, III, 313, notes that Shobal, the founder of Kirjath-jearim, was the grandson of Ephratah, I Chron. 2:50. It is likely that Ephratah's name became attached to the region.

[253]The ark of the covenant is elsewhere called God's footstool, I Chron. 28:2; Ps. 99:5. Although filling the universe, He rested on the ark so that His glory appeared there between the cherubs.

[254]Delbert R. Hillers, "Ritual Procession of the Ark and Ps 132," *CBQ* 30:1 (1968): 51, understands the *lamed* preposition as "from." He translates "Arise, O

ministry in righteousness. May the "saints [*ḥasîd*, see 4:3] shout for joy [*ranan*, see 5:11]" as they engage in the restored worship, v. 9.

II. A Recalled Promise 10–12

10–11 Returning to David's life again, Solomon asks the Lord to remember His covenant with the king (II Sam. 7:12–16). In light of His promises to bless the descendants of David, he asks the Lord not to turn His "anointed" (*mašîaḥ*, see 2:2), himself, away when he comes to worship.[255] He does not appeal to the Lord on the basis of his own merit but rests his plea on the Word of God, v. 10. He refers to the covenant again, the repetition giving emphasis to his reliance on God's promise, v. 11.

12 Solomon does not take the promise for granted. He recognizes that David's children must maintain a wholesome relationship to the Lord. If they sin, they will suffer judgment; cf. 89:30–35. If they follow God's Word, however, they will have His continued blessing on their rule, v. 12.

III. A Renewed Blessing 13–18

13–16 The underlying reason for God's blessing on David is that He has chosen "Zion," Jerusalem, for His own dwelling, v. 13. He has appointed it as His resting place forever. He will dwell there since it is the place He desires as His own, v. 14. He will "abundantly bless"[256] the nation by providing its food. He will satisfy even the poor with "bread," food to meet their needs, v. 15.[257] He will clothe

---

Yahweh, from your resting-place," and makes this "a call for God to intervene on behalf of the king." While the *lamed* preposition may mean "from," this is rare compared with its normal sense of "to, into, for, until." In addition, the context of vv. 7, 9, speaks of worship in the tabernacle.

[255]Leupold, p. 914, and Hengstenberg, III, 465, make the "anointed" refer to David. While there is no question that David was the initial anointed one, it is not likely that Solomon would pose the potential of God's turning away from the dead king. Solomon is now the "anointed" ruler. This description commonly applied to kings, I Sam. 24:10; 26:9, 11, 16, 23; II Sam. 1:14, 16; Isa. 45:1. Solomon applies the term to himself in his prayer in II Chron. 6:42, a verse that is close to v. 10.

[256]The verse repeats the root *barak*, see 5:12: "blessing, I will bless." This is a common way of emphasizing the thought, leading to the phrasing "abundantly bless."

[257]Murphy, p. 652, spiritualizes the promise of provision as "full and free salvation." There is no need for this. Verse 16 promises spiritual blessings. Verse 15 deals

the priests with "salvation," which they may in turn convey to the people by ministering to them. The "saints" (*ḥasîd*, see 4:3) will "shout aloud for joy" (*ranan*, see 5:11). The fulfillment of the paragraph lies in the Millennium. It is then that the Lord will dwell in Zion "for ever." It is then that the nation will receive abundant "provision." It is then that the priests will personally possess "salvation" and the saints "shout for joy." While there have been partial fulfillments in history, the ultimate satisfaction of these promises is yet future, v. 16.

17–18 The Lord will make the "horn [*qeren*, see 18:2] of David to bud." The "horn" generally represents strength and may represent a kingdom; cf. Dan. 7:7, 8, 24. Here, the strength of David is his kingdom. Its budding represents its growth as the Lord blesses it. The ultimate blessing of growth occurs when the nation brings forth the Messiah. Zacharias's statement in Luke 1:69 comes from this verse. The Lord has also ordained a lamp, a continuing flame to signify its existence. This is for His "anointed" (*mašîaḥ*, see 2:2), the reigning descendant of King David. The promise not only includes the kings of Judah in the OT but also extends to the rule of Jesus Christ, the ultimate Anointed One, v. 17. The Lord will bring public "shame" (*bošet*, see *bôš*, 6:10) upon the enemies of David. Upon "himself," Messiah, the crown that signifies rule will continue to "flourish" (or "prosper," *ṣûṣ*, see 72:16), v. 18.

PSALM 133

This is the last of the songs of degrees (or "ascents") written by David.[258] It is a wisdom psalm that emphasizes the need for harmony

---

with the material needs of the people.

[258]Delitzsch, p. 317, rejects David's authorship. He notes that the Targum and *Codex Vaticanus* lack David's name. Further, he asserts that the participle *šeyyored* in v. 2 is an Aramaic construction. See the introduction to Ps. 124, note 200, for a discussion of Aramaic influence. The omission of David's name from the Targum and *Vaticanus* is not conclusive. There is much variation from the MT in these translations. Some versions of the LXX and Vulgate include David's name.

between God's people.[259] David makes this thought with a brief statement and two word pictures to illustrate it. The psalm does not give its background. It is a reasonable conjecture that David wrote it after bringing the Ark of the Covenant to Jerusalem. This let Israel keep the command that all men should join together in worship at the Feasts of Passover, Pentecost, and Tabernacles (Deut. 16:16).[260]

I. The Blessing of Unity 1

1 David clearly states the theme of the psalm. "How good [*mah-ṭôb*] and how pleasant [or how 'delightful,' *mah-naʿîm*]" is unity among brethren! The particle *mah* in both cases emphasizes the exclamation, expressing David's wonder at the harmony among the people. While the unity may have come from the common goal of worshiping the Lord, unity of every kind among believers is likewise good. Unity of purpose, unity in fellowship between obedient believers, unity in goals, and other forms of unity should also mark Christianity, v. 1.

II. The Illustrations of Unity 2–3

2 The common bond of worship leads David to introduce the anointing of the high priest as an illustration. At the institution of the priestly ministry, a special blend of oil and spices was prepared (Exod. 30:25–33). Aaron and his sons were set apart by an anointing of the oil (Exod. 30:30). The oil ran down upon his beard, which

[259]This psalm was sung at the ordination of John Gill, author of an exposition of the complete Bible, at the time of his installation as pastor of the Baptist church at Kettering, England.

[260]Clarke, p. 329, suggests the possibility that the psalm deals with the unity established when Israel joined Judah in accepting David's rule. Shortly after, David captured Jerusalem and made it his capital, II Sam. 5:1–9. The view is possible. Henry, III, 745, refers the unity to David's family. With many sons by many wives, jealousy and quarrels would naturally have arisen. David exhorts unity. The view is too restrictive. Cohen, p. 439, suggests that it relates to Nehemiah's efforts to increase the population of Jerusalem. This places the psalm too late for David's authorship. Oesterley, II, 534–35, argues that in early days, married children continued to live with the family. Later, they set up their home apart from the family, breaking the unity of the family. This psalm extols the virtues of the old way. The view is speculative.

extended "to the skirts [or 'edge,' the upper hem] of his garments."[261] The garments were also sprinkled with oil (Exod. 29:21, 29). David had seen the anointing of priests and could picture what the anointing of Aaron had been like. This flowing of oil from the top of his head along the beard to the priestly garments represents the unity that flowed from one person to the next as they worshiped together, v. 2.

3 With his second illustration, David draws on the anointing of the mountains with moisture from heaven. David uses the word "dew" poetically to represent all of the moisture received on the mountains (Gen. 27:28; Song of Sol. 5:2). He mentions Mt. Hermon as the dominant mountain of the land (see 89:12).[262] Other mountains also receive this moisture. It flows down the mountains to form the rivers and streams that give life to the crops. This is the blessing commanded by the Lord that brings continuing life to the land. It also pictures the spiritual blessing of life that comes to those united by faith in Jesus Christ, v. 3.

PSALM 134

This last of the songs of degrees (or "ascents") has no certain background. We can infer that the author was a priest since he speaks of the priestly ritual.[263] His name, however, must remain unknown.

---

[261]Horne, p. 602, and Keet, p. 104, make the picture one of uniting the whole nation. To portray this, they make the oil run down to the lower hem of Aaron's robe. Kirkpatrick, p. 770, has the oil flowing onto the shoulders and breast, where the names of the tribes were located. Phillips, II, 541, sees the oil as flowing "to the skirts of Aaron's garment." This pictures "Christ in His mercy," extending grace down to the earth. All of these views require a large amount of oil and are therefore unlikely.

[262]Rodd, p. 105, suggests the possible view that the phrase "dew of Hermon" proverbially represented "specially heavy dew." Since the phrase does not occur again, we cannot verify the suggestion.

[263]Sabourin, p. 410, and Clarke, p. 331, suggest that vv. 1–2 are the address of the people to the priests and Levites, with v. 3 being the response of the priests to the people. We know nothing of such an antiphonal ceremony in the Jewish ritual. While this is possible, it is speculative. Ewald, II, 168, thinks that v. 3 speaks of the author

He wrote before the destruction of the temple, but nothing indicates the time or situation that he faced.[264]

I. Exhortation for the Priests 1–2

1–2 The author is likely the high priest. He charges the priests to "bless" (*barak*, see 5:12) the Lord, i.e., to ascribe blessings to Him. The phrase "servants of the Lord" describes the priests as they carry out their responsibilities.[265] This involves standing at night in the temple.[266] The OT refers to evening service at the tabernacle (Lev. 8:35; I Chron. 9:33; 23:30). Other references to standing in the temple refer to priestly service (e.g., 135:2; II Chron. 35:5). Priests kept the sacrificial fire burning and baked the morning meal offering. The psalmist may also have had in mind some special national ceremony. The reference to prayer in v. 2 suggests some spiritual service rather than some routine action. We know nothing certain, however, of the service. Standing "in" the temple necessarily involved the priests, v. 1. They "lift up their hands" in prayer[267] "in [or "to"] the sanctuary."[268] As they do this, they "bless [*barak*] the Lord," the One Who dwells in the temple. This again speaks of the blessings the Lord possesses: His power, knowledge, presence, etc., v. 2.

"in opposition to the Levites" and makes the author a layman. Verse 3, however, need not be interpreted this way.

[264]Kirkpatrick, p. 712, dates the psalm after the rebuilt temple of Nehemiah's time. Verse 3 argues for an earlier date, however, since the Lord no longer dwelled in the temple at that time; cf. Ezek. 10:18–19.

[265]Leupold, p. 922, includes "laymen as well as priests" among those who bless the Lord. He admits, however, that to "stand before the Lord is a technical expression which signifies some type of official service of God in the sanctuary." For this reason, I would limit the term "servants of the Lord" to the priests.

[266]*Menahoth* 110*a* holds that this refers to those devoting themselves to the study of the Torah. Calvin, V, 167, mentions the possibility that the Levites stood because only the high priest sat in the temple. Neither view has much to commend it.

[267]See 28:2 for a discussion of lifting the hands in prayer.

[268]Since the Hebrew does not give the preposition, something must be supplied to complete the phrase. Adding the word *to* smoothly flows into the last part in which the priests "bless the Lord, Who dwells in the holy of holies." The LXX and Vulgate translate this way.

II. Blessing of the Lord 3

3 The author now pronounces a blessing upon the priests for their faithful service. May the Creator God, the Maker of the heavens and the earth, "bless" (*barak*) them. This blessing will naturally come from "Zion," the Lord's presence in the holy of holies in the temple located in Zion, Jerusalem. As a practical application of the psalm, such blessings will come on those who faithfully serve the Lord today, v. 3.

PSALM 135

This psalm is one of several that relate the history of Israel.[269] The psalmist relies on the work of the Lord on Israel's behalf as the basis for praising Him. The unknown author wrote after Israel was settled in the land, vv. 10–11. The statement in v. 21 that the Lord dwells in Jerusalem sets it before the captivity and the destruction of the city. Other than these few facts, we know nothing of the author, the background to the psalm, or the date of its writing.[270]

I. The Praise of the Lord 1–4

1–3 The psalm begins and ends with a note of praise, *hal^{e}lû·yah*, making it one of the "Hallelujah psalms."[271] The praise should

---

[269]The historical psalms include Pss. 78, 105, 106, 135, and 136. While other psalms mention events from Israel's past, these psalms have a greater emphasis on the nation's history.

[270]Scroggie, IV, 11, identifies Hezekiah as the author or the collector and editor. While possible, the view is speculative. Clarke, p. 332, suggests Ezra as the author. Jennings, II, 321, makes the psalm postexilic. These two views place it after the rebuilt temple. If so, the psalm skips the judgment period of the nation and focuses solely on its history a century or more before. Sabourin, p. 190, considers it late, "its author having borrowed material from other psalms." Similarities with other psalms do not prove that this psalm is late. The discussion takes up the similarities as they occur.

[271]Pss. 106, 111, 112, 113, 135, 146, 147, 148, 149, and 150 begin with the phrase *hal^{e}lû·yah*. Of these, all but 111 and 112 begin and end with the phrase.

include the "name of the Lord,"[272] His nature as revealed to man. The phrase "servants of the Lord" refers to the priests and Levites.[273] These should praise the Lord, v. 1. Those who "stand in the house of the Lord"[274] and in the temple courts as they serve Him, v. 2,[275] should offer praise. He is good and therefore worthy of praise. They should "sing praises" (*zamar*, see 7:17) to His "name" (see v. 1) since it is "pleasant" (or "delightful"). The repetition of the command to praise the Lord makes the command emphatic, v. 3.[276]

4 The verse makes the transition to the next section. The Lord has chosen "Jacob," the progenitor of the nation and therefore representing Israel. He has chosen him for Himself to be his "peculiar [or 'special,' *sᵉgullâ*] treasure."[277] The following verses show some of the Lord's work in bringing the nation into existence, v. 4.

II. The Work of the Lord 5–18

5–7 The psalmist magnifies the Lord. He knows that *yᵉhwah* is great and that therefore the "Lord" (*ʾadôn*, see 8:1) is above all the others which men consider gods, v. 5. The Lord has done whatever pleased Him. He has carried out His work in the heaven above, in the earth and sea, and in the deeps below, v. 6. As examples of His work in nature, the psalmist mentions the Lord's work in bringing clouds

[272]Note 94 at 5:11 summarizes the Lord's "name."

[273]Kissane, p. 599, and Leslie, p. 196, include the people as "servants of the Lord" since they came into the temple courtyard. The phrase "stand in the house of the Lord" suggests the priests and Levites. The reference to the courts of the temple is simply synonymous parallelism.

[274]Cf. the discussion of 134:1 for the phrase "stand in the house of the Lord."

[275]Cheyne, II, 204, makes vv. 1–2 an independent psalm that accompanies Ps. 134. He bases the view on the form of v. 3, a subjective conclusion. It is not unusual for separate verses in a psalm to call for praise of the Lord, e.g., 147:1, 12; 148:1, 2, 3, 4, 5, 7, 13, 14, and every verse in Ps. 150.

[276]Verse 1 repeats, with a change in the order, the threefold call to praise in 113:1. It is not possible to say that one psalm quotes from the other. Both may have developed the call to praise from a common source.

[277]The word *sᵉgullâ* occurs in the Psalms only here. Elsewhere, The OT teaches that God sovereignly chose Israel as He selected them out of the whole world, Exod. 19:5. Israel therefore had an obligation to keep the Lord's commandments, Deut. 26:18, and to be holy, Deut. 7:6; 14:2. When the Lord judges the earth, He will not forget Israel, Mal. 3:17 ("jewels").

from distant points on the horizon, bringing lightning in the rainstorm, and creating wind, v. 7.

8–9 The Lord has also worked in Israel's history. He killed the firstborn in Egypt (Exod. 12:29), v. 8. He sent "tokens" (i.e., religious signs, *ʾôt*, see 65:8) and miracles, the plagues of Egypt (Exod. 7–12), to convince Pharaoh and his servants to let the nation go, v. 9.

10–12 The Lord then led Israel through the wilderness to the Promised Land. He gave them victory over "great nations" with "mighty kings," v. 10. With the Lord's blessing they defeated Sihon, king of the Amorites (Num. 21:23–24), Og, king of Bashan (Deut. 3:1–4), and numerous foes in Canaan (e.g., Josh. 6:20–21; 11:1–8), v. 11. He gave the land to the nation as its "heritage," fulfilling the promise made long before to Abraham (Gen. 12:7), v. 12.[278]

13–14 The "name" (see v. 1) of the Lord, the revelation of His nature, is an everlasting name. The remembrance of the Lord will continue "throughout all generations" (*lᵉdor wador*, see 10:6), v. 13. He will "judge" the nation, setting up His government and enforcing His laws. He will "repent himself concerning [or 'have compassion on'] his servants" as He cares for their needs, v. 14.

15–18 The final paragraph of this passage is almost identical to 115:4–8.[279] The passage has a chiastic structure:

A The idols of the heathen are silver and gold,
B the work of men's hands, v. 15.
C They have mouths, but they speak not;
D Eyes have they, but they see not, v. 16.
D¹ They have ears, but they hear not;
C¹ Neither is there (*yeš*, see 7:3) any breath in their mouths, v. 17.
B¹ They that make them are like unto them:
A¹ So is every one that trusteth in them, v. 18.

The thought progresses from idolatry to making the idols to the weakness of the idols and then reverses this order. The passage shows the utter futility of worshiping weak deities. Those who make idols their gods will likewise become weak.

[278]The passage is similar to 136:17–22. We do not know which of these was written first. Both may have quoted from some other document, or the same author may have written both.

[279]Once more, it is not possible to say whether both psalms had the same author, if one author quotes from another, or if both quoted from a common source.

III. The Blessing of the Lord 19–21

19–21 The psalm ends as it began with a call to praise the Lord. The psalmist calls upon the whole nation to "bless [*barak*, see 5:12] the Lord," to ascribe to the Lord those attributes that belong to Him and to express appreciation for His goodness. The "house of Aaron," the priests, should "bless" (*barak*) the Lord, v. 19. The "house of Levi" refers to the Levitical workers in the temple. They should also "bless" (*barak*) Him. All who "fear the Lord" (*yir*ʾ*ê y*ᵉ*hwah*, see 15:4), giving reverence to God, should "bless" Him (*barak*), v. 20. The Lord should be "blessed" (*barak*) from all who dwell in Jerusalem. The final "praise ye the Lord" is the familiar *hal*ᵉ*lû-yah*, the word that begins the psalm, v. 21.[280]

Both the first and last paragraphs, vv. 1–3, 19–21, call the people to praise the Lord. The middle portion of the psalm, vv. 4–18, gives selected examples of God's work on behalf of the nation. This provides the reason for praising the Lord, which gives a pattern that believers should still follow. Since God has worked on our behalf, we should be faithful in offering our praise to Him.

PSALM 136

The psalm is both a song of thanksgiving and a historical review of the Lord's work on behalf of the nation.[281] The obvious poetical structure in which it repeats the call of praise twenty-six times has led to the name of the "Great Hallel," the great psalm of praise.[282] The pattern demands a liturgical use.[283] After each statement by

[280]The final passage is similar to 115:9–11 and to 118:2–4. With the thought occurring this often, it may have been a common saying in Israel.

[281]The introduction to Ps. 18 summarizes the songs of thanksgiving. The introduction to Ps. 78 briefly discusses the historical psalms.

[282]This name reflects the nature of the psalm although the word *hal*ᵉ*lû* does not occur in it. The name comes from the Talmud, *Pesaḥîm* 118*a*, where the twenty-six verses are said to reflect the twenty-six generations of man from the Creation to the giving of the Law at Mt. Sinai.

[283]The Jews recite this psalm in the Sabbath morning service and during the Passover Feast, *NEJ*, p. 627.

the priests, the congregation (or a selected group of priests) would respond, "for his mercy [or 'steadfast love,' *ḥesed*, see 5:7] endureth for ever." Aside from this use in the nation's worship, there is no indication of the author.[284] The psalm comes from the time when Israel is in the land and likely during the time before the destruction of the temple.[285] It is similar in part to Psalm 135, but we cannot certainly say that the same man wrote both psalms.

It is impossible to read the psalm carefully without noting that God's mercy is unfailing. At all times and in all circumstances, those who have accepted Jesus Christ as their Savior may confidently rely on the mercy of God. We may not always understand why the Lord allows certain events. We can rest secure, however, that God will extend His promised mercies to us.

I. The Thanksgiving to the Lord 1–3

1–3 The psalmist sets the tone with an imperative: "Give thanks unto the Lord." The Lord is a good God and therefore worthy of our thanksgiving. His "mercy" (or "steadfast love," *ḥesed*) is unending, v. 1. The psalmist repeats the exhortation twice, each time showing the exalted position of the Lord. He is God above all the gods that men may worship. He is the "Lord" (*ʾadôn*, see 8:1) of all the "lords" who control men. Despite this exalted position, He continues to show His steadfast love to mankind, vv. 2–3.

II. The Work of the Lord 4–26

A. God's Work in Creation 4–9

4–5 Having established the supreme position of the Lord, the psalmist now illustrates His power by describing some of His work. He is, first of all, the Creator of all things. He has done the "great wonders [*palaʾ*, see 9:1]" of Creation by Himself. Remembering that

---

[284]Phillips, II, 563, assigns the psalm to Hezekiah. Clarke, p. 333, tentatively suggests Ezra as the author. Any suggestion is speculative since the psalm gives no historical material to relate to an individual.

[285]Leupold, p. 929, assigns the psalm to a "late date." Anderson, II, 894, calls it "post-Exilic." Neither man gives evidence to support his view. Since the psalm is historical and says nothing about the deliverance from the Babylonian captivity, I would set it in preexilic times.

all of the nations surrounding Israel worshiped many gods, this is a unique idea. The Lord alone carried out the wonders of Creation, v. 4. He did this with "wisdom" (or "understanding," *t^ebûnâ*, see 49:3), knowing the interrelationships in the heavens and framing them all to accomplish His purposes, v. 5.

6–9 He is the One Who spread out the earth over the waters (Gen. 1:9–10), v. 6. He made the "great lights" in the heavens, the sun that dominates the day and the moon and stars that fill the night sky (Gen. 1:14–18). In all this, He continues His steadfast love for man, vv. 7–9.

B. God's Work in Deliverance 10–16

10–12 The psalmist turns to the deliverance of Israel from their bondage in Egypt. As the climax of the plagues brought on the Egyptians, the Lord took the firstborn of both men and animals (Exod. 12:12, 29). Although this seems harsh, it was necessary in order to free the nation from the control of the Pharaoh, who had ignored the nine previous plagues. As such, the death of the firstborn represented the steadfast love of the Lord for His people, v. 10. Israel was now able to leave Egypt (Exod. 12:31–33, 37–41), v. 11, as the Lord worked on their behalf with "a strong hand" and "a stretched out arm" (Exod. 13:14). The "hand" and "arm" of the Lord represent His power (89:13, 21; 98:1), v. 12.

13–16 In bringing Israel out of Egypt, the Lord led them directly to the Red Sea. When Pharaoh ordered his army to bring the people back, they seemed to be trapped. This, however, was a chance for the Lord to show His power. He divided the Red Sea and directed Israel to pass over through the channel (Exod. 14:21–22), a clear portrayal of His steadfast love for the nation, vv. 13–14. When Pharaoh ordered his army to follow Israel through, the Lord allowed their army partially across. Then He let the waters sweep over the Egyptians, drowning that entire group of soldiers (Exod. 14:23–28). Once more, the Lord showed His love for His people by delivering them from this military threat, v. 15. He then led the nation through the wilderness by the cloudy pillar and the pillar of fire (Exod. 13:21–22), v. 16.

C. God's Work in Victory 17–22

17–22 As Israel approached the Land of Promise, heathen nations opposed them. The Lord gave them victory over these kings, v. 17.

They put to death the kings that formerly held great power (Num. 31:8; Josh. 10:22–27), v. 18, including Sihon, king of the Amorites, and Og, king of Bashan (Num. 21:23–24, 33–35), vv. 19–20. Israel took these lands as their "heritage" (or "inheritance," Gen. 12:7). All of this showed God's love toward the nation, vv. 21–22.[286]

D. God's Work in Caring for Israel 23–26

23–26 The final section of the psalm summarizes God's care for the people. He remembered them in their "low estate," their slavery in Egypt, v. 23. He "redeemed" (better "rescued") the nation from their Egyptian oppressors, v. 24. He gave them food throughout their wilderness wanderings, v. 25. The psalmist closes by urging others to express their gratitude to the "God of heaven."[287] He is worthy since His steadfast love is unfailing, v. 26.

PSALM 137

Psalm 137 is one of the latest songs of the book. It clearly refers to the Babylonian captivity, a low point in Israel's history. It is a community lament, reflecting the sorrow of the people over the events that have placed them in bondage. Because of the nature of the cry for vengeance, the psalm is considered an imprecatory psalm.[288] We do not know the author[289] or reason for writing. The writer focuses on

---

[286]Verses 17–22 are similar to Ps. 135:10–12. The same author may have written both psalms, one writer may have quoted from the other, or both may have quoted from a common source.

[287]VanGemeren, p. 826, calls the phrase "a relatively late designation of the Great King of Kings." He cites Ezra 1:2; Neh. 1:4; 2:4; and Dan. 2:44. None of these use *ʾel* as the name for God but, rather, *ʾĕlohê*, or in Daniel, *ʾĕlah*, an Aramaic word. Since the same phrase occurs with *ʾĕlohê* in Gen. 24:3, 7, it is not a late name for God.

[288]Within the group of imprecatory psalms, 35, 59, 69, 70, 109, and 140 are individual laments and 58, 83, and 137 are community laments. The introduction to Ps. 35 discusses reasons that may have justified the imprecations.

[289]The LXX has the title "*Belonging* to David, *a psalm of* Jeremiah," i.e., a Davidic type of song written by Jeremiah. The Vulgate is similar. This is clearly wrong since Jeremiah finished his life in Egypt and did not go into the Babylonian captivity. Phillips, II, 574, sees the author as an unknown Jew who had returned from Babylon

music (vv. 2–6), suggesting that he was a temple musician, perhaps one of those exiled in the later part of the Captivity, ca. 586 BC.

I. The Distress over Israel's Captivity 1–3

1–3 The psalmist looks back to the years of bondage in Babylon. The phrase "rivers of Babylon" refers to the Tigris and Euphrates rivers that border the land as well as to the many smaller rivers that feed the two larger rivers.[290] Irrigation canals also crisscrossed Babylon. These would have been natural gathering places for groups of people. The captives met there to weep, expressing their personal grief and also recognizing the downfall of the nation, v. 1. Since this was not a time for joy, they stored their "harps" (or "lyre," *kinnôr*, see 33:2) by hanging them on the "willows" (or "poplars," *ᶜᵃrabîm*), v. 2. Their captors harassed them by requiring them to sing. "They that wasted" Israel (or their "tormentors," *tôlal*)[291] required "songs of Zion," songs that forced the Jews to recall the loss of their homeland, v. 3.

II. The Devotion for Israel's Home 4–6

4–6 The rhetorical question requires a negative answer. In bondage, cut off from their homeland, the Jews have no incentive to sing of the Lord. It would be hard for them to sing of their God in this "strange [*nekar*, see 18:44] land." The heathen who surrounded them thought that their gods were greater than Israel's God. They would not see the captivity as judgment for Israel's sin, v. 4. While he cannot sing of God's greatness, the psalmist determines not to forget God's dwelling. To show this, he invites judgment: "If I forget . . . Jerusalem, let my right hand forget her cunning [or 'skill']," likely referring to the hand's ability to play the harp, v. 5.[292] The first two phrases in

---

before the Captivity. Hezekiah added the psalm to Israel's collection of hymns. The view is speculative.

[290]The OT also refers to the Chebar and Ulai rivers, Ezek. 1:3; Dan. 8:2. These are lesser rivers or canals that we cannot locate with certainty.

[291]This is the only place that *tôlal* occurs in the OT. The parallelism with "they that carried us away captive" requires a similar meaning. The AV follows the Targum reading *šalal*, "to waste, plunder."

[292]Schneir Levin, "Let My Right Hand Wither," *Judaism* 45:3 (1996): 285–86, gives a medical sense to v. 5*b*–6*a*: "Let my right arm palsy, let my tongue stick to my palate." He relates this to a stroke or to cerebral palsy. While v. 6*a* is close to the

v. 6 should be reversed. May he lose his ability to sing if he forgets Jerusalem, if he does not "prefer" (or "exalt") it as his chief joy. This focus on Jerusalem is appropriate, since this was the place where God dwelled on earth in OT times and will one day dwell again, v. 6.

III. The Doom of Israel's Foes 7–9

7–9 The writer asks the Lord to remember the day in which Jerusalem fell. The Edomites joined with Babylon in the attack upon Israel.[293] Their thought was to "rase it, rase it," i.e., to lay bare its foundations, v. 7. The psalmist pronounces judgment on the "daughter of Babylon," the people of a nation "to be destroyed" (*šadad*, see 17:9). This is poetic in nature, giving to them as they have "served" (*gamal*, see 7:4) Israel. The one who brings this on them will be "happy" (or "blessed," *ʾašrê*, see 1:1). The intensive plural suggests the great satisfaction that will belong to the one leading this victory, v. 8. The author repeats the intensive plural *ʾašrê*, a further indication of the joy that will come at Babylon's fall. The parallelism between 8*b* and 9 suggests that the Babylonians had treated Israel's children with cruelty. In ancient times, putting a son to death was an act of war (cf. Isa. 13:16; Hos. 13:16). It prevented a warrior from growing up to avenge his nation. The imprecation does not advocate cruelty; it simply recognizes the poetic judgment that Babylon will receive, v. 9.

The early verses show the impact that judgment for sin has upon one's testimony. Even while remembering God and His dwelling place in the temple at Jerusalem, vv. 4–6, the captives could not sing joyous songs of praise to Him, vv. 1–3. They still, however, have the confidence that God has not left them. They turn to Him in prayer as they seek deliverance, vv. 7–9. These illustrations are still true. Judgment robs the believer of his joyous relationship to the Lord. It should not rob him, however, of the presence of God, nor of His willingness to respond to the prayers of His children.

---

text, v. 5*b* is debatable. The word *šakaḥ*, "forget," occurs twice. It is unlikely that the psalmist would give the same word such radically different meanings. It is true that some authors suggest "wither" as a translation for *šakaḥ*, e.g., Dahood, III, 271; Harman, p. 428. This still supports the inability to play the harp. To go beyond this to a medical diagnosis is speculative.

[293]Ezekiel 35:5 accuses Edom of "perpetual hatred" against Israel. Such passages as Ezek. 25:12 and Obad. 10–14 show the continuing enmity of Edom toward Israel.

PSALM 138

The psalm begins a series of eight Davidic psalms. The compiler of Book V has grouped these together in this part of the book because of their common authorship. We know nothing of the background to this psalm. Verses 3 and 7 suggest that David has just come through some trouble.[294] The obvious note of praise sounded in these verses agrees with what we see elsewhere in the psalms attributed to David, so there is no reason to question his authorship.[295] The note of praise is also the reason for classifying the psalm as a song of thanksgiving.[296]

I. Vow of David 1–3

1–3 David begins with a clear vow that he will praise the Lord with his whole being. He will "sing praise [*zamar*, see 7:17] before the gods" (*ᵓelohîm*). Since David knew full well that there was only one true God, the word *ᵓelohîm* must be understood here to refer to judges or other civil leaders of Israel (cf. Exod. 21:6; 22:8). David's pledge to praise the Lord will be public, before others who govern the nation, v. 1.[297]

---

[294]Clarke, p. 336; Moll, p. 644; and Fausset, III, 392, suggest that the psalm recalls the covenant made by God with David in II Sam. 7. The view rests on understanding "word" as "promise" in v. 2, a possible meaning. The view also requires that the mention of trouble in vv. 3 and 7 refer to a threat on David's life that would prevent the fulfillment of the covenant. This is a possible interpretation although the psalm does not clearly state it. Phillips, II, 582, dates the psalm "at the time of Absalom's rebellion," a possible but not provable view.

[295]Delitzsch, III, 338, identifies the author as someone who writes "as it were out of the soul of David." The view is speculative and unsupported by the psalm. Cohen, p. 449, notes that some mss of the LXX include "of Haggai and Zechariah" in the title. From this, he concludes that it was originally by David but "was re-edited for liturgical use after the Restoration." On subjective grounds Ewald, II, 187, assigns the psalm to Zerubbabel. Kirkpatrick, p. 783, makes the psalm postexilic. Nothing in the psalm argues against David's authorship. For the heading, "Psalm of David," see the introduction to Psalm 25.

[296]The introduction to Ps. 18 summarizes the songs of thanksgiving.

[297]Dahood, III, 276, refers *ᵓelohîm* to the "deities of the heathen kings mentioned in v. 4." Calvin, V, 199, understands the "gods" as angels. The LXX translates *ᵓelohîm* by ἀγγέλων and the Vulgate does so by *angelorum*, both "angels." Hirsch, II, 429, refers to the gods of other nations. David, however, would not have thought of these deities as watching him as he worshiped in Israel. Weiser, pp. 797–98, translates,

In carrying out his praise of the Lord, David states his intention to worship toward the Lord's "holy temple." The "temple" (*hêkal*, see 5:7) here refers to the tabernacle he had brought to Jerusalem (II Sam. 6:12–15). He worships toward it because it was the earthly dwelling of the Lord. He will praise the Lord's "name," i.e., the nature of the Lord,[298] because of His "lovingkindness" (or "steadfast love," *ḥesed*, see 5:7) and the truth of His Word. To develop this last thought, David notes that the Lord has magnified His Word above His name. The thought is that the Lord completely fulfills His Word. To fail in this would be to go contrary to His nature as a faithful God, v. 2. Christians still have this confidence. God's Word is sure.

David refers to some crisis in which he has cried out to the Lord for protection. The Lord has answered his prayer by giving him inner strength. While we do not know the details of this incident, it likely refers to the trouble that David mentions in v. 7. In some way, David's enemies threatened him. The Lord, however, sustained him in the trial, v. 3.

II. Prophecy of David 4–6

4–6 David extends his personal experience to "all the kings of the earth." They will also praise the Lord when they hear His words. This is a millennial promise, looking forward to the time when all of the nations will look to the Lord as the King, v. 4. They will sing songs of praise to Him, recognizing the greatness of His glory, v. 5. Despite this greatness, the Lord will humble Himself to meet the needs of the lowly (cf. Isa. 57:15). He will not, however, draw near to help the proud. He knows them from "afar" but keeps them at a distance, v. 6.

III. Confidence of David 7–8

7–8 Knowing the nature of the Lord, David now expresses his confidence that the Lord will help him in his present trial. Although "trouble" (*ṣarâ*, see 9:9) surrounds David, he knows that the Lord

---

"I will sing thy praise before God." This is an improbable way of understanding the verse. Ewald, II, 187, understands the phrase "before the gods" as "in the sight of God" and interprets it as worship at the temple. This limits David's worship, an unlikely view.

[298]Note 94 at 5:11 summarizes the "name" of the Lord.

will "revive" (or "preserve") him. The Lord will stretch out His hand, the hand that represents strength (17:7; 18:35), against the "wrath" (*ʾap*, see 2:5) of David's enemies. The Lord's "right hand" will "save" (or "deliver") David from the threat against his life, v. 7. The Lord will "perfect" (or "complete") His will concerning David. The Lord's "mercy" (or "steadfast love," *ḥesed*) is everlasting. With this knowledge, David closes with a prayer that the Lord will not "forsake" (*rapaʾ*, see 37:8) him, v. 8.

PSALM 139

This psalm beautifully praises God for Who He is and what He has done. David acknowledges the omniscience of God (vv. 1–6), tells of His omnipresence (vv. 7–12), and illustrates His omnipotence (vv. 13–18). Seeing the greatness of God, David can only cast himself upon the Lord for deliverance from his enemies and purpose to live a pure life of dedication to Him (vv. 19–24). These truths still stand. God is omniscient, omnipresent, and omnipotent and is therefore worthy of praise.

The song is for the "chief musician," the director of the music in Israel's worship. David anticipated that the priests would use the psalm in the tabernacle worship.[299] It is clear from the final part that David faced enemies. Other than this, we know nothing of the background of the writing.

[299]*Codex Alexandrinus* of the LXX makes the author Zechariah in the Captivity. For this reason, Leupold, p. 942, gives the inscription of the MT a "loose sense—a psalm in the spirit of David." The evidence for the view is weak. Buttenwieser, p. 541, relies on the common use of rare words and phrases occurring here and in Job to make this "another work of the author of the Job drama." Rather than common authorship, this argues that both works are early, from the same period of time. Cohen, p. 451, and Delitzsch, III, 343, rely on Aramaisms in the text to set aside David's authorship and date the psalm as postexilic. Aramaism, however, occurs in other early writings. See note 199 at Ps. 124 for a discussion of this.

I. The Omniscience of God 1–6

1–5 David acknowledges that God has "searched" him, thoroughly examining his inner being. God therefore has "known" (*yada*ᶜ, see 1:6) him for what he is, v. 1. He knows David when he sits and when he rises, i.e., whatever he does when he is awake. He understands David's thoughts "afar off," even before they are fully developed, v. 2.[300] The Lord "compasseth" (or "sifts") his "path," separating the good from the bad activities. He knows David's "lying down," his rest. He knows all of David's ways, v. 3. The Lord knows David's every word even before he speaks it. This completes God's knowledge of David—his thoughts (v. 2), his actions (v. 3), and now his speech, v. 4. Because the Lord knows David so intimately, He can protect and guide him. He has "beset" (or "enclosed") David behind and before and has placed His hand on him to guide him (cf. v. 10), v. 5.

6 The knowledge possessed by the Lord is too wonderful for David to comprehend. It is inaccessibly "high" (*śagab*, see 20:1), exalted knowledge and therefore unreachable for David. Even though he is the king, with advisors and many other human resources available to him, he cannot attain this kind of knowledge, v. 6.

II. The Omnipresence of God 7–12

7–12 David now focuses on the presence of God. He asks rhetorically if there is any place he can go away from the Lord. He answers this question in vv. 8–12 by giving examples to show that the Lord is present everywhere, v. 7. If David ascends into heaven, God is there. If David were to "make [his] bed in hell" (or "spread out Sheol," see *š*ᵉ*ʾôl*, 6:5)[301] as his resting place, the Lord would be there as well, v. 8. If he takes "the wings of the morning [or 'dawn']," the rays of light flying across the earth as it turns; if he dwells in the farthest parts of the sea, v. 9; even in those remote places the Lord would continue to

[300] Th. Booij, "Psalm CXXXIX: Text, Syntax, Meaning," *VT* 54:1 (2005): 3, understands "afar off" as a reference to time. The Lord has known David's thoughts "of old, long before." This is a possible view.

[301] Henry, p. 757, understands Sheol as in "the very centre" of the earth or as "the place of the damned." Neither view is correct. In the OT, Sheol simply represents the place of the dead. This may be the grave or the places of the wicked or godly spirits after death. David here waxes poetic as he describes his inability to flee from God's presence.

guide and protect him with His "right hand," symbolic of His power (cf. 138:7, 8), v. 10. If he says to himself,[302] "The darkness shall cover [*šûp*][303] me" and "The night shall be light about me" (with the sense "The night will replace the light about me"), v. 11, the Lord will still be with him. "The darkness hideth not from thee."[304] The night shines like the day to the Lord, with both alike to Him, v. 12.

III. The Omnipotence of God 13–18

13–16 David now turns his thoughts to the creative work of God. To illustrate this, he looks at his own birth. The Lord has "possessed my reins" (better "created my inner parts," *kilyâ*, see 7:9).[305] The Lord has "covered" (better "woven")[306] David in the womb as He created David's unique design, v. 13. David responds with praise as he considers that he has been "fearfully [or 'awesomely'] and wonderfully made."[307] The Lord's works are "marvellous" (*pala*ᵓ, see 9:1). Earlier (v. 6), David has acknowledged his inability to comprehend the

[302]Booij, p. 4, says that v. 11*a* should be translated as a simple statement: "And so I say . . ." The grammar is open to question, and the AV is defensible.

[303]The verb *šûp*, "bruise, crush," is awkward here. It portrays the conquest of the night as though the darkness overwhelms David by cutting off light from him. Rawlinson, III, 314, lets the darkness picture "the deepest gloom" but this is foreign to the context.

[304]David makes an interesting play on words in the phrase: *ḥošek lo*ᵓ *yaḥšîk mimmeka*, "the darkness is not dark to you."

[305]*TWOT*, I, 440–41, understands *kilyâ* as "a figure for the entire body." This is possible. The word *kilyâ* represents the kidneys but often poetically stands for the inner being. The word occurs four other times in the Psalms, 7:9; 16:7; 26:2; and 73:21, all describing the inner being. Here, however, where David uses *kilyâ* as something created, a physical part of the body, or the body itself, may be meant. This parallels the "weaving" of the design that was David, v. 13*b*.

[306]Fausset, p. 395, and Morris, p. 83, translate the verb as *sakak* I, "covered," understanding it as "protected." The translation is possible. The context, however, argues for understanding the verb as *sakak* II, "to weave," found elsewhere at Job 10:11.

[307]The MT of the phrase "fearfully and wonderfully made" reads *nôra*ᵓ*ôt niplêtî*, lit. "awesomely wonderful." The word *niplêtî* is from the root *palâ*, generally considered a form of *pala*ᵓ (so BDB, p. 811). C. John Collins, "Psalm 139:14: 'Fearfully and Wonderfully Made'?" *Presbyterion: Covenant Seminary Review* 25:2 (1999): 117–19, understands *palâ*, as a distinct root, "to be set apart, distinguished." From this, he translates "awesomely distinguished" (as a member of the covenant people). The context, however, is about the psalmist's being created. Translating as "awesomely wonderful" fits better into this emphasis.

knowledge the Lord possesses. Now, however, he states that he does recognize the wonderful nature of what God has done, v. 14.[308]

David recognizes that he was not hidden from the Lord even "when [he] was made in secret," when he was conceived. At that time he was "curiously wrought" (*raqam*). The verb *raqam* refers to skilful weaving; cf. v. 13. David thinks of the skill with which the Lord has created him "in the lowest parts of the earth." From the parallelism with the word "secret," this phrase refers again to his conception, an act carried out in a hidden part of this world, v. 15. The Lord was fully aware of David's "substance, yet being unperfect [*golmî*]," still in its embryonic state, not fully developed.[309] The phrase "in continuance" is lit. "days." The Lord has written in a book the days of David's life before these days came to pass. The Lord had a calling for him even before his birth, v. 16.

17–18 These thoughts of God's work on his behalf are "precious" to David. The "sum" (or "total") number of them is "great," numerous, v. 17. If he were to try counting them, they would be more than the number of the grains of sand. For this reason, when David is awake, he is "still with" the Lord, meditating on what the Lord has done for him, v. 18.

IV. The Reliance on God 19–24

19–22 The final section gives the application of the psalm. In view of the greatness of God, developed in the earlier verses, David relies on Him for deliverance from his enemies. The statement "Surely thou wilt slay the wicked" is better phrased as a prayer: "O that you would slay the wicked." David directs his prayer to "God" (*ʾĕlôah*, see 18:31). With the confidence that God will defend him, David tells the "bloody men [*ʾĕnôš*, see 8:4]," likely referring to those who murdered others in the rebellion against David, to "depart" from him,

---

[308]While it makes no difference in the sense, the phrase "marvellous are thy works" is better "thy works are marvelous." See the discussion of the *nipʿal* participle of *palâ* at 75:1.

[309]The word *golmî* occurs only here. The Vulgate translates *imperfectum*, "unfinished," and the LXX ἀκατέργαστόν, "unwrought, rough." Since the context refers to the conception and development of the unborn child, it is appropriate to refer the thought to the undeveloped child, the embryo. As such, the passage bears on the contemporary argument over abortion. Life does begin in the womb.

v. 19. These "enemies" (*ʿareyka*)[310] "speak against [God] wickedly" (or "speak of you for wickedness"), using God's name to justify their evil actions. They "take [God's] name in vain," better "lift up [God's] name for vanity [or 'without purpose,' *šawʾ*, see 12:2]," v. 20.[311]

David "hate[s]" (*śaneʾ*, see 5:5) those who "hate" (*śaneʾ*) the Lord. He "[is] grieved with" (or "loathes") those who set themselves against God, v. 21. He "hate[s]" (*śaneʾ*) them with "perfect [or 'complete'] hatred," a hatred free from any desire to limit God's judgment. He considers them his personal enemies, v. 22.

23–24 David closes the psalm with a prayer of dedication. He asks the Lord to search his "heart," his innermost being. He urges the Lord to "try" him, to examine him, and to know his "thoughts" (or "anxious thoughts," *śarʿap*, see 94:19), v. 23.[312] If his heart contains any "wicked way" (lit. "way of sorrow"), i.e., wickedness that will lead to grief over his sin, David asks for guidance in the way that leads to everlasting life, v. 24.

PSALM 140

As with many of his songs, David writes Psalm 140 for the "chief musician" (*mᵉnaṣṣeaḥ*, see 4, intro.) of the tabernacle. It is an impre-

---

[310]The word *ʿareyka* is difficult. Symmachus, Jerome, and the Targum understood *ʿar* as an Aramaism, "enemy." This has support from I Sam. 28:16. Perowne, II, 446, reads *ʿaleyka*, a change with some textual support. Bratcher and Reyburn, p. 1131, support this view.

[311]There is no object of the verb "lift up." Rawlinson, III, 315, suggests "lift up [their soul]" as in prayer. Anderson, II, 912, understands the verb as a passive participle and translates "lift themselves up." These views are possible. I have let the phrase parallel the first part of the verse and supplied "your name" as best referring to the Lord. Gene Rich, "The Integrity of the Text of Psalm 139:20b," *CBQ* 46:1 (1984): 30, notes that the word "vain" (*laššawʾ*) may also mean "destruction." He translates, "They have carried away thy cities to destruction." While possible, the translation "destruction" conveys a decidedly minor component of meaning. This translation does not occur elsewhere in the AV.

[312]Using a Maori melody, Edwin Orr wrote the hymn "Search Me, O God." The first verse comes from vv. 23–24 of this psalm.

catory psalm;[313] David faces an unknown threat. He refers to evil and violent men, v. 1; to false accusations, v. 3; to an attempted overthrow of his ways, v. 4; and to traps, perhaps ambushes, v. 5. A king who ruled for forty years must have faced many potential coups. We do not know enough about David's life to place this at a specific time.[314] By not identifying the danger, the psalm becomes a model prayer for today's believers who face trials that come to them from the wicked.

I. David's Prayer for Deliverance 1–3

1–3 The first four parts of the psalm are the four stanzas of a single hymn. All give part of David's prayer, a prayer broken by three interjections of "selah." Each of these calls the reader to briefly stop and meditate on what has been said: the *danger* of the threat, v. 3; the *deviousness* of the threat, v. 5; and the *determination* of those who threaten, v. 8. The fourth part of the prayer expresses David's personal *desire* and thus does not end in "selah."

David pleads with the Lord to "deliver" (better "rescue") him from "the evil man [*ʾadam*]" and "the violent man [*ʾîš*]."[315] Since David later uses plural pronouns, the word "man" is a collective in both places, though he uses different words to represent all his foes. These are "evil" and "violent" (*ḥamas*, see 7:16) men, v. 1. They "imagine mischiefs" (or "plan evil"). They are "gathered together for" (or "stir up") "war" (lit. "wars") against David. The plural "wars" may indicate repeated efforts to overthrow David from his rule over the nation, v. 2. They have spoken vicious words against David. They have sharpened their tongues like a "serpent" (*naḥaš*); cf. 52:2; 57:4. The "poison" (*ḥemâ*, see 6:1) of "adders" (*ʿakšûb*) is in their speech.[316] Paul

---

[313]The imprecatory psalms include individual laments in Pss. 35, 59, 69, 70, 109, and 140, and community laments in Pss. 58, 83, and 137. The introduction to Ps. 35 discusses the imprecatory psalms. In Ps. 140, the imprecations in vv. 10–11 grow out of David's individual lament to God.

[314]Rotherham, p. 571, dates it during David's service in Saul's court. Alexander, p. 550, relates it to the time Saul threw a spear at him; cf. I Sam. 18:10–11; 19:9–10. Jennings, II, 342, places it at the time of Doeg. Delitzsch, III, 356, relates the psalm to Absalom's rebellion, II Sam. 15–18, or to the rebellion of Sheba, II Sam. 20. The psalm does not give enough information to let us be certain.

[315]See note 312 at 22:6 for the contrast between *ʾadam* and *ʾîš*.

[316]David uses the words *naḥaš* and *ʿakšûb* poetically. The word *naḥaš* is the most general word for "serpent" or "snake." The word *ʿakšûb* occurs only here. The LXX

uses this last phrase in Romans 3:13 to describe the unsaved person. James 3:8 may also allude to the verse. The word "selah" draws attention to David's plight, v. 3.

II. David's Prayer for Preservation 4–5

4–5 David now asks the Lord to keep him safe from the attacks of his foes. These are "wicked," opposed to righteous ways, and "violent" (*ḥamas*). Their goal is to "overthrow [David's] goings" (or "trip [his] feet"), idiomatic for interfering with his plans, v. 4. These proud enemies have hidden a snare of cords for David. They have spread a net to capture him. They have set "gins" (or "traps," *moqᵉšîm*, see 18:5) to snare him. The word "selah" again calls attention to the difficulties facing David, v. 5.

III. David's Prayer for Protection 6–8

6–8 David has called upon the Lord as his God. The name suggests the power of God, something David needs as he confronts his enemies. He asks the Lord (*yᵉhwah*), the name of God as He interacts with His people, to hear his "supplications" (*taḥᵃnûn*, see 28:2), the cries of his heart, v. 6. David directs his prayer to the mighty God, his master, the "strength of [his] salvation," i.e., the strong One Who is able to deliver. He has "covered" (*sakak*, see 5:11) David's "head" in past days of "battle" (*našeq*, better "armor"). The phrase idiomatically describes the day when men put on their armor in preparation for battle. The head, of course, is a critical part of the body. A wound there can be fatal. The Lord, however, has shielded David from those who attack, v. 7. Based on this past protection, David now asks for continuing protection from his adversaries. He asks the Lord not to let them achieve their desires. Likewise, he asks the Lord not to advance their "wicked device [or 'plans']." Such success would lift them up in pride.[317] For the final time, David uses "selah" to call attention to the wicked, v. 8.

---

translates it as ἀσπίδων, "asps." From the parallelism, it must refer to some poisonous serpent.

[317]The MT does not have the word "lest." The phrase is simply "they will be high," i.e., become proud.

IV. David's Prayer for Victory 9–11

9–11 While the Lord has protected his "head," David now asks that the "head" of his foes be unprotected. He prays that the "mischief" (or "trouble," *ᶜamal*, see 7:14) they speak of would come on them, v. 9. David pronounces an imprecation on his enemies. He desires that "burning coals" would fall on them. He asks that they would be cast into "the fire" and into "deep pits" (or "watery pits," *mahᵃmorôt*)[318] from which they would not be able to escape. The prayer is a poetic statement of judgment.[319] It should be understood as a picturesque statement of punishment, v. 10.[320] David prays that the "evil speaker" (lit. "man of tongue") would not be established. From the context of vv. 3 and 9, this "man of tongue" is one who has slandered David, lying about his character or actions. David expects the "violent man" (*ḥamas*, see 7:16) to face evil that will "overthrow" (*madḥepot*)[321] him (con. v. 4). The word "overthrow" is a plural of amplification, intensifying the thought, v. 11. The Lord will care for the "afflicted" (*ᶜanî*, see 9:12) and "maintain the right" (or "justice") for the poor. There is no need to end this paragraph with "selah" since David no longer speaks of his peril. In addition, there is a clear change of thought between vv. 11 and 12.

---

[318]The word *mahᵃmorôt* occurs only here. Its meaning of "watery pits" (or "miry pits") comes from an Arabic cognate *hamara*, "pour, pour out."

[319]Rawlinson, III, 328, interprets the verse as a literal statement of judgment. The "fire" is "the fire prepared to receive the wicked." The view faces the difficulty of reconciling the "burning coals" and the "watery pits" with the fires of hell. We know nothing of burning coals in hell, and the Bible does not portray it as a watery pit. Henry, p. 761, understands the "burning coals" as symbolizing judgment from heaven and "the fire" as literal hell. It is doubtful if the same verse should be symbolic in one part and literal in the next.

[320]*NIB*, IV, 1240, appropriately comments that the psalmist's prayer "is not a request for personal revenge." It is rather a request for justice.

[321]The word *madḥepot* occurs only here. Leslie, p. 343, translates "thrust upon thrust." Clarke, p. 340, is similar, "blow on blow." The NASB follows this but interprets it as "speedily." Delitzsch, III, 360, draws on the root *dḥp,* "to drive, hasten," and interprets as "forced marches," which he translates as "violent haste." Rawlinson, III, 328, understands it as "destructions." The phrase lit. reads, "Evil shall hunt the man of violence for drivings." I interpret "drivings" as "driving him down," i.e., overthrowing him.

V. David's Expression of Confidence 12–13

12–13 David anticipates the victory the Lord will give. He knows from experience (*yadaᶜ*, see 1:6) that the Lord will sustain the "afflicted" (*ᶜanî*, see 9:12). It is clear but unstated that David thinks of the righteous who are afflicted. In addition, the Lord will extend "right" (better "justice") to the poor, v. 12. For this reason, the righteous will offer thanks to the "name" of the Lord, the Lord as revealed in His nature.[322] The upright will continually dwell in the presence of the Lord, v. 13.

PSALM 141

David faces some unknown threat[323] that causes him to lament his circumstances. He displays unusual spiritual maturity, vv. 2–5. The threat includes others beside David, v. 7. This suggests a time during the latter part of David's reign. Despite the seriousness of his situation, he maintains his trust in the Lord. He first prays, then expresses his expectation of victory over his enemies, and finally states his continuing faith that the Lord will deliver him. David's response gives an example for believers to follow in difficult trials.

I. The Prayer of David 1–4

1–2 David pleads with the Lord to hear his "cry" (or "call"). He asks for a speedy response, likely because of the seriousness of the threat. The phrase "give ear unto my voice" pictures the Lord's

[322]Note 94 at 5:11 discusses the "name" of the Lord.

[323]Clarke, p. 341, sets the psalm during Saul's pursuit of David, I Sam. 24:1–7. Horne, p. 625, dates it just before David's flight to Achish in Gath. Jennings, II, 345, places it during Absalom's rebellion. Fausset, III, 398, sees v. 7 as indicating that the problem "is national, not merely individual." Any threat to David as king of the nation would also affect the whole land. Dahood, III, 309, assigns the psalm to "an Israelite living in the North Israelite dispersion after the fall of Samaria." The view, of course, sets aside the title. *NIB*, IV, 1244, refers to the author as "she or he." The context of vv. 4–5, however, argues against feminine authorship. In any case, it is unlikely that the Jews would have accepted a psalm written by a woman.

hearing his prayer (77:1; 86:6), v. 1. David compares his prayer to incense; just as the odor wafts upward for God to smell, so his prayer ascends up to God's ears (cf. Rev. 5:8; 8:3–4). May the lifting of his hands in prayer be as the evening sacrifice, acceptable to the Lord.[324] Because the Jews burned incense in the evening (Exod. 30:8) at the time of the evening sacrifice, the early church included this psalm in its liturgy, using it as the evening hymn, v. 2.[325]

3–4 As he approaches the Lord, David acknowledges his need for personal purity. Knowing the threat of his enemies would lead to a natural desire to curse them or to retaliate in some evil way. David, however, asks the Lord to guard him from such actions. He asks the Lord to set a guard upon his speech in order to keep him from wicked words (17:3–4; 39:1), v. 3. He prays that the Lord will keep him from wickedness toward his foes. May the Lord keep him from the same kind of actions. The phrase "eat of their dainties [or 'delicacies']" poetically portrays taking part in the wicked works of his adversaries, v. 4.[326]

II. The Judgments of the Lord 5–6

5 David's foes have apparently criticized him. He recognizes that a blow from a righteous man would be a "kindness" (or "act of steadfast love," *ḥesed*, see 5:7; cf. Prov. 9:8–9; 27:6). The reproof of a righteous man would be as an anointing of oil, which David would willingly receive.[327] Although the Lord may chasten him in these ways, his "prayer" (*t^epillâ*, see 4:1) will continue against the "calamities" (or "wicked actions") of his foes, v. 5.

6 David anticipates the judgment of his foes. Their "judges," i.e., their leaders, will be "overthrown[328] in stony places [or 'by the sides

---

[324]See 28:2 for a discussion of lifting the hands in prayer.

[325]Gregory, *Apostolic Constitutions* ii.59.

[326]Calvin, V, 236, and Eaton, p. 304, understand this as an invitation for David to join his foes in fellowship, meant to win him to their side. The view is possible. I prefer to make the delicacies a poetical picture of the wicked actions of David's foes. This parallels the first half of the verse.

[327]The phrase "It shall be an excellent oil, which shall not break my head" is rough. Something like "It is *as* oil *on my* head. Let not my head refuse it" is appropriate.

[328]Horne, p. 627, translates "overthrown" (*šamaṭ*) as "dismissed," a sense it does not clearly have. He refers this to David's sparing of Saul at two different times and

of the rock,' a cliff]," a poetic picture of their judgment. The followers of these wicked men will then hear the words of David and know that they are "sweet" (or "pleasant"), v. 6.[329]

III. The Confidence in the Lord 7–10

7–8 There is no need to reverse the clauses as in the AV. As when "one cutteth and cleaveth wood upon [or 'plows and breaks open'] the earth," so the bones of David's friends are scattered at the opening of their "grave" (*šᵉʾôl*, see 6:5), v. 7.[330] For this reason, David looks to the Lord as His source of strength. He puts his "trust" (*ḥasâ*, see 2:12) in the Lord and prays that He not leave him "destitute" without a defense, v. 8.

9–10 David asks the Lord to keep him from the traps his foes have laid for him. There is no significant difference between "snares" and "gins." Both portray the plans David's enemies have laid to entrap him, v. 9. David prays a brief imprecation upon his adversaries. May they fall victim to their own plans while he "withal escape[s]" (or "altogether [i.e., completely] passes by") without being taken, v. 10.

---

his kind words in withholding judgment. It is a strain to interpret the text this way.

[329]Fausset, III, 399, and Phillips, II, 616, understand the pronoun "they" to refer to the leaders. Faced with the prospect of death, they listen finally to David's words. While this is possible, the judgment of being thrown from a cliff seems to picture the death of the leaders. Without leadership, "they," their followers, listen to the words of the righteous. Cohen, p. 459, sees the wicked leaders admitting David's words to be pleasant before they are thrown over a cliff. The order of the verse is against this.

[330]The phrase "our bones" is difficult because of the personal pronoun. On weak evidence, John Barclay Burns, "An Interpretation of Psalm CXLI 7*b*," *VT* 22:2 (1972): 245–46, emends to the third person pronoun, "their." He refers the phrase to "the Canaanite god Mot whose gaping jaws and insatiable appetite" lead him to pick the bones of the saints clean and scatter them beside Sheol. Nothing in the text refers to Mot. The NIV translates as though David's foes are speaking, "They will say . . . our bones have been scattered." Albert Barnes, III, 308, understands the phrase as poetic. "David and his followers" are like bones scattered about the graves, "weak, feeble, disorganized." Phillips, II, 617, makes this a reference to the "discovery of a mass grave" that sparks David's words. Horne, p. 628, is specific, referring this to the slaughter of priests by Doeg. Hirsch, II, 454, makes this a picture of "Israel dispersed throughout the wide world." Some mss of the LXX change the pronoun to "their." Leupold, p. 957, and Delitzsch, III, 366, understand the statement as one of hope. The buried bones of the righteous await the resurrection. The view requires an interpretation that is not clear from the text. If we connect vv. 7 and 8, the verse gives an introduction to David's prayer.

PSALM 142

The psalm is a "Maschil" (*maśkîl*, see 32, title), a psalm for meditation that leads to wisdom. David composed this individual lament "when he was in the cave," which may have been during his flight from Saul; cf. the title of Psalm 57. David hid first in the cave near the town of Adullam, I Samuel 22:1, then later in the cave in the wilderness of En-gedi, I Samuel 24:1–3.[331] Since David sees himself without the help of others, v. 4, it is appropriate to place the incident during David's flight from Saul, before others gather to his side. The cave of Adullam falls into this time. From the cave, David offers his "prayer" (*tᵉpillâ*, see 4:1) to the Lord.

As St. Francis of Assisi lay dying, with a weak voice, he began reciting Psalm 142. Others who were keeping vigil with him in his last moments joined with him. His voice trailed off as he died.[332]

I. The Expression of David's Sorrow 1–2

1–2 Although we do not know the nature of David's problem, we do know how he reacted to the threat. He "make[s] . . . supplication" to the Lord (or "ask[s] mercy," *ḥanan*, see 4:1). In so doing, he gives us an example of how we should respond to difficulties in life. God has given the resource of prayer to His children. Verses 1*a* and 1*b* mention prayer in poetic variation, v. 1. David pours out his "complaint" (*śîaḥ*, see 55:2) before the Lord. In showing his "trouble" (*ṣarâ*, see 9:9) to the Lord, David apparently describes his situation, v. 2.

II. The Nature of David's Sorrow 3–4

3–4 Whatever David's problem, his spirit "was overwhelmed" (or "fainted") because of it. Yet he was confident that the Lord knew his "path," the situation he faced. His enemies had sought to lay a trap for him, v. 3. The "right hand" is the side where David would expect to find those who supported him; cf. 16:8; 110:5. Now, however, he looks to his right and sees no one. Potential "refuge" (*manôs*, see

---

[331]Fausset, III, 400, and Phillips, II, 621, suggest the cave of Adullam. Rotherham, p. 578, identifies the cave as that of En-gedi.

[332]Omer Englebert, *Saint Francis of Assisi*, trans. and ed. Edward Hutton (New York: Longmans, Green and Co., 1950), pp. 312–13.

59:16), a place to which he may flee, has "failed" (*ᵓabad*, see 1:6) him. There is no one who seriously "cares" (*daraš*, see 9:10) for him, v. 4.

III. The Deliverance from David's Sorrow 5–7

5–7 Though man has forsaken David, the Lord is still there to defend him. David cries out to Him as his "refuge" (*maḥseh*, see 14:6) and "portion" in life. This is the correct place to find a resource. While it is encouraging to have others supporting you, no one can take the place of the Lord, v. 5. David asks the Lord to hear his "cry" (*rinnâ*, see 17:1). He asks Him for freedom from his "persecutors" (or "those who pursue"). They have brought David "very low." He does not have the strength to overcome them, v. 6. David asks the Lord to deliver him "out of prison," a metaphor describing the trial that has constrained his freedom.[333] He will then praise the Lord's "name,"[334] His nature as a prayer-answering God.[335] The "righteous," those who follow the Lord, will then surround David. This will take place because God will "deal bountifully" (*gamal*, see 7:4) with him, v. 7.

PSALM 143

Martin Luther considered this psalm a "Pauline Psalm" since it expressed Pauline doctrine so clearly.[336] Because of v. 2, the church

[333]This is the only time that "prison" occurs in the Psalms, so we must understand it from the context. Robinson, p. 135, perceives the prison as an actual prison. Neale, IV, 355, and Cowles, p. 535, refer it to the actual cave in which David was shut up. This is a possible view. *NIB*, IV, 1247, makes it designate the Exile. This requires that we reject David's authorship. Dahood, III, 319, relates the "prison" to Sheol. This leads to the question of why David does not use the word *šeᵓôl* when he often uses it elsewhere, e.g., 6:5 ("grave"); 9:17 ("hell").

[334]Note 94 at 5:11 gives a summary of the Lord's "name."

[335]Notice the three affirmations David makes about the Lord: "thou knewest my path," v. 3; "thou art my refuge and my portion," v. 5; and "thou shalt deal bountifully with me," v. 7. God knows His own, He protects His own, and He blesses His own.

[336]See the introduction to Ps. 32.

considers it a penitential psalm.[337] David laments some personal sin and the judgment that has followed. Although we cannot be certain of the background, David's sin that brought about the later rebellion of Absalom (II Sam. 12:10) may well have led to this prayer.[338]

It is worth noting that David's sin has caused the judgment he laments. Without repentance, sin always brings punishment, either in this life or in the life to come. David expresses his trust in the Lord, an indication that he has repented of his sin and sought forgiveness.[339] This is the only basis upon which God's people can approach the Lord today when they find themselves being judged for their sin.

I. Description of David's Plight 1–6

1–2 David goes to the Lord in "prayer" (*t^e^pillâ*, see 4:1). He bases his "supplications" (*taḥ^a^nûn*, see 28:2) on the Lord's faithfulness and righteousness to His promise (II Sam. 7:12–16), v. 1. He asks the Lord not to bring judgment on him. All have sinned. The second part of the verse is better "no living man is righteous." The fact that others have sinned does not excuse David. It does, however, recognize that all men are guilty before God, v. 2.

3–4 David turns to the threat that confronts him. His enemy has "persecuted [his] soul," seeking his life. The enemy has "smitten" (or "crushed," see *dak*, 9:9) David's life "down to the ground" in his attempt to put him to death. David has dwelled in the darkness of caves like others who dwell forever in the darkness of the grave, v. 3. This persecution has discouraged him. His heart is "desolate" (or "appalled," *šamem*, see 40:15), v. 4.

5–6 When David recalled the past, he meditated on the works of the Lord. He "muse[d]" (see *śîaḥ*, 55:2) on "work" of God's "hands." These speak metaphorically here of the creative power of God, v. 5. Since God is still powerful, David reaches out his hands to the Lord

---

[337]The seven penitential psalms include Pss. 6, 32, 38, 51, 102, 130, and 143.

[338]Henry, III, 766, places the psalm during Saul's attempt to capture David. Moll, p. 659, and Clarke, p. 344, date it at the time of Absalom's rebellion. The LXX and Vulgate support this view. Cohen, p. 462, considers it postexilic. Fausset, III, 401, connects the psalm with II Sam. 7 on the basis of the phrase "servant of the Lord" in vv. 2 and 12. This is tenuous ground for the conclusion.

[339]Thomas Bilney, burned at the stake during the reign of Henry VIII, recited this psalm as he faced his martyrdom.

in prayer.[340] His thirst for God was as thirst for water in a "thirsty" (^{ca}*yepâ*, or "parched")[341] land. The word "selah" calls attention to David's situation, v. 6.

II. Summary of David's Prayer 7–12

7–8 David prays for a speedy answer to his petition because his spirit "faileth" (*kalâ*, see 73:26), is discouraged. He asks that the Lord would not hide His face from him. This would make David like others who have gone into the "pit" (*bôr*, see 7:15), i.e., the grave, v. 7. He asks to hear of the Lord's "lovingkindness" (or "steadfast love," *ḥesed*, see 5:7) "in the morning," when the new day of peace ends the "darkness" (v. 3) of his trial.[342] He has placed his trust in the Lord. He asks for guidance since he has sought divine help with his prayer, v. 8.

9–10 David pleads for deliverance from his enemies. He has fled to the Lord for protection, v. 9. Again, he asks for divine guidance, because he wants to do God's will. God's Spirit is good. David seeks to be directed into "the land of uprightness [*mîšôr*, see 26:12]," the path of justice, v. 10.[343]

340See 28:2 for a discussion of lifting the hands in prayer.

341Stefan Paas, "A Textual Note on Psalm 143,6 (אֶרֶץ־עֲיֵפָה - » a weary land «?)" *ZAW* 113:3 (2001): 418, revocalizes *ʿyph* and derives it from *ʿyp* II, "to be dark." He translates "a dark land," which he refers to "the nether world," i.e., death. While the root *ʿyp* may indeed refer to darkness, it is rare, occurring clearly only in Job 10:22 and Amos 4:13. This is a psalm attributed to David, also the author of Ps. 63, where the root *ʿyp* occurs in v. 1, its only other occurrence in the Psalms. The root occurs widely outside of the Psalms. While Paas's view is possible, I prefer the more common usage here.

342Fausset, III, 402, associates the "morning" with "salvation, as the favourable season for granting it." He cites 59:16; 90:14; and 96:5 (marg.) in support of this view. This is selective support. The word also occurs thirteen other times in the Psalms, often referring to a time. Ps. 59:16 supports the above view. Anderson, II, 929, suggests "salvation (i.e. oracles of deliverance) was usually made known in the temple liturgy at the break of day." The view is speculative; nothing in the OT describes such ritual. Dahood, III, 325, is also speculative in making the "morning" picture the dawn of resurrection and immortality. Perowne, II, 461, sees "morning" as "early, soon," a possible view.

343Cohen, p. 463, and Perowne, II, 461, translate *mîšôr* as "level [or 'even'] ground," a place where one is less prone to stumble or stray. Dahood, III, 326, translates similarly but refers it to "the celestial abode of the just." The word occurs elsewhere in 26:12; 27:11; 45:6; and 67:4. In my judgment, the word refers to some aspect of righteousness in each case. I take it this way here.

11–12 For the sake of the Lord's "name,"[344] His reputation, David asks that He "quicken" him, reviving his discouraged spirit. For the sake of the Lord's "righteousness," His faithfulness to His word, David asks Him to deliver him from the "trouble" (*ṣarâ*, see 9:9), the emotional stress, caused by his foes, v. 11. Out of the Lord's "mercy" (or "steadfast love," *ḥesed*), David asks the Lord to "cut off" (*ṣamat*, see 18:40) his enemies, to "destroy" (*ʾabad*, see 1:6) those who "afflict" (*ṣarar*, see 31:9) him. He closes by reminding the Lord that he is His "servant," v. 12.

PSALM 144

Psalm 144 is the last of nine psalms with the simple inscription *lᵉdawid*, all of which supply words to obtain "*A Psalm* of David."[345] The heading agrees with the mention of David in v. 10. We do not know the circumstances that led to writing the psalm.[346] David now rules the nation, cf. v. 2. There was undoubtedly some military conquest in which David had seen the Lord deliver Israel; cf. vv. 1, 10. Verses 7–8, 11, indicate that a plot had been developed against David. The double reference to "strange children," vv. 7, 11, suggests that the plot involved people outside of Israel. No matter what the occasion for writing, David speaks of ideal times in vv. 12–15, a passage that suggests the millennial reign of the Lord.

---

[344]Note 94 at 5:11 gives a summary of the Lord's "name."

[345]For the heading "Psalm of David," see the introduction to Ps. 25.

[346]The LXX adds the words "according to Goliath" to the heading. Leupold, p. 969, thinks that the psalm "may have been written at a later date with the Goliath incident as a general background." Delitzsch, III, 379, likewise relates the psalm to David's victory over Goliath. This view, however, does not allow for the plot referred to in vv. 7–8, 11. Murphy, p. 678, dates it at the time of David's conquest of Jerusalem. Phillips, II, 638, dates the psalm after Absalom's death, when David is back on the throne. Oesterley, II, 569, understands the reference to David to indicate a date in "the monarchial period," possibly during the reign of Hezekiah. *NIB*, VI, 1254, understands the psalm as "a rereading of Psalm 18," written after the close of the Davidic monarchy. The view ignores the early tradition expressed in the title. The psalm itself leaves the background indefinite.

I. Prayer for Deliverance 1–8

A. The Strength of the Lord 1–2

1–2 David praises the Lord in Whom he trusts. He describes the "blessed[ness]" (*barak*, see 5:12) of the One Who has given him "strength" (*ṣûr*, see 18:2). The Lord has taught David how to go into battle, v. 1. In addition, the Lord is David's "goodness" (or "steadfast love," *ḥesed*, see 5:7). He is David's "fortress," his "high tower" (*miś-gab*, or "refuge," see 9:9), and the One Who delivers him from peril. He is David's "shield" (*magen*, see 3:3), his defense, and the One in Whom he puts his "trust" (*ḥasâ*, see 2:12). He is the One Who "sub-dues" David's "people" (*ᶜammî*)[347] under his rule. David expresses his reliance on the Lord's ability to keep peace among his people, v. 2.[348]

B. The Weakness of Man 3–4

3–4 In comparison with the strength of the Lord, David sees him-self as weak. He rhetorically asks why the Lord has bothered with mankind. Why has He taken note of "the son of man [*ᵓᵉnôš*, frail man, see 8:4]," v. 3? Man is like "vanity" (*hebel*, "a breath," see 31:6) with little substance. He is like "a shadow that passeth away." As the sun moves along its course, the shadows move with it and eventually van-ish, v. 4.

C. The Work of Deliverance 5–8

5–6 David prays that the Lord will intervene. Poetically, he asks the Lord to "bow [or 'thrust aside'] thy heavens" and come to his aid. When the Lord will "touch the mountains," they will burst into fire showing His presence (cf. 104:32; Exod. 19:18), v. 5.[349] He appeals

---

[347]The Syriac, Targum and several mss read the plural *ᶜamîm*. Livingston, p. 449, accepts this reading and refers it to the "surrounding nations." While this may be the case, it is not the only possible view. Even if we adopt the plural, David may simply refer to the various groups plotting against him, vv. 7–8, 11.

[348]Fausset, III, 403, understands "subdues my people" to include both Israel and "*all the heathen to be subdued under the Son of David in due time*." The context does not support a messianic application at this point. Delitzsch, III, 381, refers the phrase to "God-given power." David, not yet king, expresses his "hope that Jahve will grant him deeds of victory which will compel Israel to submit to him." The view is possible although the psalm seems to speak of David as already ruling.

[349]Hengstenberg, III, 531, and Fausset, III, 403, make the "mountains" symbolize kingdoms of the world that oppose God. He burns them in judgment. The symbol-

to the Lord to send lightning to scatter his foes. The "arrows" of the Lord poetically represent different weapons brought against His foes, cf. 7:13; 45:5, v. 6.

7–8 "Send thine hand" (better "Stretch out your hands"), extending power, David asks the Lord. He needs the Lord to "rid" him (better "set [him] free") and to "deliver [him] out of great waters." David thinks here of the waters of judgment that sweep over nations; cf. 18:16. These are "strange [*nekar*, see 18:44] children," people from another nation who oppose David, v. 7. They speak "vanity" (*šawʾ*, see 12:2), that which has no substance, and their "right hand" is lifted up in "falsehood" (*šeqer*), lying oaths.[350] The description fits that of a nation that has violated some covenant with David. Though they have sworn to carry out certain provisions, they speak deceitfully and take an oath they have no intention to keep, v. 8.

II. Praise to the Deliverer 9–11

9–11 David pledges to sing a "new song" of praise to the Lord.[351] He will "sing praises" (or "make music," *zamar*, see 7:17) on a "psaltery [*nebel*, see 33:2] and an instrument of ten strings" (better "upon a harp of ten strings," see 33:2). The *nebel* had its strings arranged on a rounded frame, v. 9. The Lord is the One Who "giveth salvation," i.e., delivers kings from their trials. David himself is an example of this deliverance. The Lord has delivered him from the "hurtful sword," the threat against him, v. 10. On the basis of this past deliverance, David asks for continued deliverance by the Lord. Identically repeating part of v. 7 and all of v. 8, David asks the Lord to rescue him from the "strange [*nekar*] children," the foreigners who speak "vanity" (*šawʾ*, see 12:2), deceitful and harmful words, v. 11.

---

ism is arbitrary, avoiding the pattern set at Mt. Sinai. Weiser, p. 824, suggests the possible view that the psalmist prays for a theophany, as at Sinai. Since "theophany" implies a visible manifestation of the Lord, I would not go this far.

[350]In the Talmud, *Baba Bathra* 45*a* understands the "hand of falsehood" as a hand that takes that which is not its own. In the Psalms, however, *šeqer* normally refers to lying, e.g., 27:12; 52:3.

[351]Ps. 33:3 discusses the phrase "new song."

III. Prospect of the Delivered 12–15

12–14 David's vision of the immediate future now expands into a view of the millennial kingdom. At that time, Israel's "sons" will be as fully grown plants, mature and healthy. Their "daughters" will be "corner stones, polished after the similitude of a palace" (or "pillars, carved for the pattern of a palace"). Both word pictures present the prospect of successful lives for the Israelites' offspring, v. 12. David continues to describe the blessing of the land. The granaries will be full. The sheep will bring forth abundantly, with "thousands and ten thousands in our streets [better 'fields']," v. 13. The "oxen" (or "cattle") will "be strong to labour" (better "be heavily laden") as they carry the possessions and wealth of the nation, v. 14*a*.

The final part of v. 14 begins a new thought. There will be "no breaking in," no breach made by an enemy in the walls of Jerusalem. There will be no "going out," no foreign captivity. There will be no "complaining" (or "outcry") in the streets. The picture is of a nation at peace with no concern over war, v. 14*b*.

15 The people who enjoy this situation are "happy" (*ʾašrê*, better "blessed," see 1:1). The nation whose mighty God is the Lord, Who interacts with them to bring such a condition about, is indeed "happy" (*ʾašrê*, again "blessed"). While the verse does not say this, the picture is of faithful Israel, now trusting Jesus Christ as Savior and enjoying the blessings of the kingdom age. The world is free from the curse of sin, and the rule of the Lord ensures an age of peace, v. 15.

PSALM 145

The psalm is one of pure praise to the Lord. It is the first of a sequence of psalms, which extends to the end of the book, that act as a doxology. The repetition of key words and phrases emphasizes this theme.[352] David may have written the psalm following some great

[352]The words "bless," vv. 1, 2, 10, 21; "praise," vv. 2, 3; "speak," vv. 6, 11; and "talk," vv. 11, 21, show man's responsibility. The phrase "for ever and ever," vv. 1, 2, 21, shows the duration of man's praise by each "generation," vv. 4 (twice), 13 (twice). The Lord is worthy of this praise. He is "great," vv. 3 (twice), 6, 8; "glori-

victory over one of the nation's enemies. If so, we can only speculate on the event. Such praise to God, however, is appropriate in every circumstance. Believers in this age still do well to develop an attitude of praise to the Lord.

The psalm is an acrostic[353] with the *nûn* line missing.[354] One of the copies found at Qumran, along with one ms of the LXX, the Vulgate, and the Syriac translations, include a *nûn* line.[355] An early translator probably adapted the line from v. 17 to complete the poem.

I. The Praise and Blessing of the Lord 1–7

1–3 David announces his intention to exalt God, his "king." This address is significant. David, the earthly king, recognizes the Lord as King over all. David will "bless" (*barak*, see 5:12) the "name" of the Lord,[356] His nature, forever, v. 1. He will ascribe "bless[ings]" (*barak*)

---

ous," v. 5 (cf. His glorious kingdom, vv. 11, 12), and with "majesty," vv. 5, 12. He is "good," vv. 7, 9; "righteous," vv. 7, 19; and merciful, vv. 8, 9. He is powerful, vv. 4, 11, 12, and carries out His "works," vv. 4, 9, 10, 17. His "kingdom" will be everlasting, vv. 11, 12, 13 (twice).

[353]Pss. 9, 10, 25, 34, 37, 111, 112, and 119 are also acrostics. *NIB*, IV, 1258, suggests that the first Hebrew letters of vv. 11–13 "combine to spell . . . the Hebrew root from which the words 'king' (*melek*) and 'kingdom' (*malkût*) are derived." He concedes that this may be coincidental but then states that "it was probably intended by the clever poet who carefully structured Psalm 145. Its effect is to further emphasize the message that God is king." The letters *mêm*, *lamed*, and *kap* naturally occur in sequence. If the psalmist intends to create an acrostic poem, he has no other choice.

[354]Clarke, p. 348, notes that "the omission of 'Nun' here is a reminder that the fulness of praise is not yet reached until the voices of the heavenly saints, including the Church, join in." While this idea is devotional, irregular acrostics are more common than regular ones. The psalmist may have been distracted or unable to think of a word to express what he wanted to say. Hengstenberg, III, 535, suggests that the omission was deliberate in order to obtain "three strophes, each of seven verses." Verse 14, however, fits better into the final section, making the strophes uneven. *Berakoth* 4*b* suggests that the *nûn* line is missing "because the fall of Israel's enemies begins with it." This refers to Amos 5:2, where the statement begins with *nplh*. Barnabas Lindars, "The Structure of Psalm CXLV," *VT* 39 (1989): 28–30, includes the *nûn* line to make the three central lines begin "with the letters MLK in reverse." This supposedly reflects the emphasis on "kingdom" in vv. 11–13. The view is contrived. The word spelled in reverse and a "central" paragraph that is not central argue against it.

[355]The line reads, *Ne*^{æ}*man y*^{e}*hwah b*^{e}*kol·d*^{e}*barayw w*^{e}*ḥasîd b*^{e}*kol·ma*^{ca}*śayw*. This translates, "The Lord is faithful in all His words and steadfastly loving in all His works." Many modern versions include this as 13*b* (NAB, NIV, NRSV) or 14*a* (REB).

[356]See note 94 at 5:11 for a brief summary of the Lord's name.

to the Lord each day and praise His "name," again His nature, forever, v. 2. The Lord is "great" (or "majestic") and "greatly to be praised" (or "greatly worthy of praise"). Such majesty cannot be comprehended, v. 3.

4–7 As each "generation" (*dôr lᵉdôr*, cf. 10:6) of believers give "praise" (*šabaḥ*, see 63:3) to the Lord for His works, they tell the next generation about His "mighty acts" (or "power"). They "declare" (or "proclaim") openly the mighty works of God, v. 4. David himself pledges to "speak" (better "meditate," *śîaḥ*, see 55:2) about the glorious "honour" (or "majesty," *hadar*, see 8:5) of God's "majesty" (or "splendor," *hôd*, see 8:1) and of His "wondrous works" (*palaʾ*, see 9:1), v. 5. The "men" of each generation, mentioned in v. 4, will speak of the power of the "terrible" (or "awesome") actions of the Lord. David will also recount the greatness of God, v. 6. The men of each generation will "abundantly utter" (*nabaᶜ*, see 19:2) the "memory" (or "remembrance") of God's abundant goodness. They will "sing" (*ranan*, see 5:11) of His righteousness, v. 7.

II. The Nature and Kingdom of the Lord 8–13

8–9 The Lord is "gracious" (see *ḥanan*, 4:1) and "full of compassion" (or "merciful"). He is slow to "anger" (*ʾap*, see 2:5) and displays great "mercy" ("steadfast love," *ḥesed*, see 5:7), v. 8. He is good to all (cf. Matt. 5:45) and imparts mercy to every living creature, v. 9.

10–13 The "works" of the Lord will praise Him. The "saints" (*ḥasîd*, see 4:3) will "bless" (*barak*) Him, v. 10. They will speak of the coming glory of His reign. They will talk about His "power," in this context His ability to subdue all who oppose Him and to establish His rule over the earth, v. 11. They will tell others of His "mighty acts" (or "power," see v. 4). They will speak of the glorious "majesty" (*hadar*, see 8:5) of His reign on the earth, v. 12. His reign will be "everlasting," and His "dominion" over the nations will continue through "all generations" (*dor wador*, cf. 10:6), v. 13.

III. The Care and Work of the Lord 14–21

14–16 The previous verses have introduced the millennial reign. David now develops the nature of this period. The Lord watches over the weak of the earth. He "upholdeth" (or "supports") those who fall over the obstacles of life. He raises up those who are bowed down by cares, v. 14. The eyes of all people look to Him to supply their needs. He provides their "meat" (or "food") at the proper time, v. 15. He opens His hand to dispense that which satisfies the desires of all living creatures, v. 16.

17–20 The Lord is righteous and "holy" (or "merciful," *ḥasîd*, see 4:3) in all that He does, v. 17. He is near to those who sincerely call upon Him in prayer, v. 18. He will satisfy the desires of those who "fear" (or "revere," see *yirʾâ*, 2:11) Him. He will hear their cry in times of trouble and will deliver them, v. 19. He "preserveth" (or "keeps") those who love Him. In contrast, He will completely "destroy" the wicked, v. 20.

21 In the light of all that God has done and will do for His own, David pledges to praise the Lord. He urges "all flesh," others of mankind, to ascribe "bless[ings]" (*barak*, see 5:12) to the holy "name" (see v. 1) of the Lord "for ever and ever" (cf. vv. 1, 2), v. 21.

PSALM 146

Psalms 146–148 begin and end with the word *halᵉlû·yah*, "praise ye the Lord." For this reason, they have been called the "Hallel" psalms.[357] The psalm begins the theme of praise to the Lord that concludes the book in Psalms 146–150. We do not know the author[358] or the background to the writing of the psalm. The references to freeing prisoners, v. 7, and protecting strangers, v. 9, may refer to ending the Babylonian Captivity. If so, the date of the psalm lies after the return to Palestine. The author refers to God as the Creator and gives

[357]Psalms 106, 113, 135, 149, and 150 also begin and end with *halᵉlû·yah*, but no special name indicates this.

[358]Since Pss. 145–150 all praise the Lord, Henry, III, 772, 776, makes David the author of all these psalms. While this may be true, David is not the only biblical writer to praise the Lord, e.g., Asaph, Ethan, Solomon. Without giving reasons, Calvin, V, 284, also accepts Davidic authorship. It is unlikely that David would write 3*a*. The LXX attributes Ps. 146 to Haggai and Zechariah. Fausset, III, 406, accepts this and makes it a psalm for the dedication of the wall about Jerusalem. Rotherham, p. 591, sees Hezekiah as the principal author with Nehemiah adding vv. 3–4. The view is subjective, unsupported by the psalm.

numerous examples of His care for mankind, vv. 6–10. From these illustrations, it is likely that no single event caused the psalmist to write. He simply praises the God Who cares for His own.

I. The Call to Praise 1–2

1–2 The introductory part of the psalm strikes a note of praise. The author follows the familiar *hal*^{e}*lû·yah*, "praise ye the Lord," with his personal statement of praise, v. 1. He then pledges praise to the Lord throughout his life. He will "sing praises" (*zamar*, see 7:17) to the Lord as long as he lives, v. 2.

II. The Weakness of Man 3–4

3–4 Perhaps by way of contrast with his planned description of God's power in vv. 5–10, the psalmist describes the futility of relying on man. There should be no trust in "princes," those who hold positions of influence and leadership. Neither should there be trust in "the son of man," here a general term for mankind, who lack the ability to "help" (or "deliver") in times of trouble, v. 3. Such are mortal men. His "breath goeth forth" (or "spirit departs"), and he returns to the earth from which he came (Gen. 2:7). On the day of his death, his thoughts "perish" (*ʾabad*, see 1:6), coming to an end in this life, v. 4.

With the contrast between vv. 3–4 and vv. 5–10, the psalmist makes a practical application that still holds true. Rather than trusting in other men, Christians should place their faith in the Lord. He alone has the power to deliver His children. It is no wonder that the psalmist begins with a note of praise, vv. 1–2. Our Lord is worthy of this.

III. The Power of God 5–10

5–7*b* The psalmist now begins to justify the exhortation of v. 1. God is worthy of praise because He is a God of power, faithfulness, justice, and love. "Happy" (or "Blessed," *ʾašrê*, see 1:1) is the man that has this God as his "help" (*ʿezer*, see 20:2) and who has placed his "hope" for the future in Him, v. 5. God has displayed His power in the creation of all things. He shows His faithfulness in keeping "truth" forever, His word to those who follow Him, v. 6. He brings about "judgment" (better "justice") for the oppressed and gives food to the hungry, v. 7*a*, *b*.

7*c*–10 A series of declarative statements shows God's worthiness to receive praise. He frees those who have been unjustly imprisoned, v. 7*c*. He gives spiritual sight to those who cannot see. This must have a metaphorical sense as in Numbers 22:31; II Kings 6:17, since no blind were healed in the OT, John 9:32. He gives encouragement to those bowed down with the troubles of life and loves those who are righteous, v. 8. He protects strangers and eases the burdens of orphans and widows. In sharp contrast, He interferes with the plans of the wicked. The ultimate fulfillment of these promises will come in the Millennium, v. 9. The God of Israel will reign forever, throughout "all generations" (*l^{e}dor wador*, see 10:6). With this the psalmist concludes his argument. This God is worthy of praise, v. 10.

PSALM 147

The theme of praise to the Lord continues with this psalm.[359] As Psalms 146 and 148 do, it opens and closes with *hal^{e}lû·yah*, "praise ye the Lord." We do not know the author.[360] He likely was one who had returned from the Captivity and wrote the psalm to praise the Lord for graciously restoring the nation.[361] Each of the three sections

[359]The LXX divides the psalm; Ps. 146 includes vv. 1–11, and Ps. 147 includes vv. 12–20. This brings the numbering of the LXX back into agreement with the traditional numbering. The LXX assigns both psalms to Haggai and Zechariah, an early tradition for which there is no evidence. See the introduction to Ps. 10 for additional comment on the numbering of the Psalms in the LXX. While Livingston, p. 454, looks on the division with favor, no Hebrew ms supports it. It is also a single psalm in the Syriac version.

[360]Since Pss. 145–150 all praise the Lord, Henry, III, 772, 779, makes David the author of all these psalms. He locates the psalm at the building up of Jerusalem in David's time. While the view is possible, David is not the only biblical writer to praise the Lord, e.g., Asaph, Ethan (or Jeduthun), and the sons of Korah. Phillips, II, 668, tentatively suggests Zechariah as the author. The psalm does not let us be dogmatic as to its authorship.

[361]Note the reference to building the city, gathering "the outcasts of Israel," v. 2, and strengthening the gates of the city, v. 13, all of which may refer to the returned nation. These references cause Ewald, II, 320, and Sabourin, p. 193, to date the psalm at the dedication of the walls, Neh. 12:27–43.

of the psalm begins with a call to praise the Lord (vv. 1, 7, 12). For His greatness, vv. 1–6, His providential care, vv. 7–11, and His infallible Word, vv. 12–20, God is worthy of man's praise.

I. The Greatness of the Lord 1–6

1–3 After calling for praise to the Lord, the psalmist gives reasons for his exhortation. It is "good" and "pleasant" (or "delightful"). It is "comely" (or "fitting") to "sing praises" (*zamar*, see 7:17) to Him, v. 1. To illustrate the appropriateness of praise, the psalmist cites several of the Lord's actions. The Lord has built up Jerusalem. From the context of gathering the "outcasts of Israel" and strengthening the "gates" (v. 13), this refers to the rebuilding described in Nehemiah, v. 2. He heals those who are "broken in heart," grieving over various problems, and binds up their "wounds" (or "sorrows"),[362] v. 3.

4–6 The passage continues to show the worth of the Lord to receive praise. He both counts and names the stars, impossible for man but a routine exercise for the omniscient God. Remembering that names in the OT have significance, this action by the Lord suggests that He identifies the stars in a way that reflects the unique nature of each one, v. 4. He is indeed great and "of great [or 'abundant'] power. His "understanding" (*tᵉbûnâ*, see 49:3) is "infinite" (or "without number"), v. 5. With this power and wisdom, the Lord "lifteth up" (or "restores") the "meek" (or 'afflicted,' see *ʿanî*, 9:12).[363] At the same time, He casts "down to the ground" those who are wicked, v. 6.

II. The Care of the Lord 7–11

7–9 The second call to praise focuses on the Lord's care for the earth and for His own. We should give "thanksgiving" (*tôdâ*, see 26:7) to the Lord in song. We should "sing praise" (*zamar*, see 7:17) to God accompanied by the "harp" (or "lyre," *kinnôr*, see 33:2), v. 7. He spreads the clouds over the skies to give the rain for the earth

[362]From the parallelism, the "wounds" here are emotional in nature. Leupold, p. 989, refers them to grief over sin. Hengstenberg, III, 546, makes them "spiritual wounds." Since nothing in the psalm limits the "breaking in heart" to the spiritual realm, I would take the word in a broader sense as including all sorts of sorrows.

[363]Leupold, p. 990, translates *ʿᵃnawîm* as "meek," and Hirsch, II, 483, as "humble." These are possible translations. I have translated "afflicted" as more appropriate for one that is restored.

(Matt. 5:45). He makes grass grow for the animals that graze on the "mountains" (or "hills"), v. 8. He provides food for the animals as well as the young ravens when they call to indicate their hunger, v. 9.

10–11 The Lord "delighteth" (*ḥapeṣ*, see 18:19) not in the strength furnished by a horse. He finds no "pleasure" (*raṣâ*, see 40:13) in the legs that carry man long distances, v. 10. Rather than the strength that comes from this world, the Lord finds "pleasure" (*raṣâ*) in those who rely on Him. He delights in those who "fear" (see *yirʾâ*, 2:11) Him, giving Him reverence, and who place their "hope" (*yaḥal*, see 31:24) in His "mercy" (or "steadfast love," *ḥesed*, see 5:7), v. 11.

III. The Word of the Lord 12–20

12–14 The psalmist calls upon those who live in Jerusalem to "praise" (*šabaḥ*, see 63:3) the Lord. To emphasize this need, he repeats his exhortation to "Zion," again referring to Jerusalem; cf. 2:6; 9:11, v. 12. The Lord has "strengthened" (*ḥazaq*, see 27:14) the "bars of thy gates," a major defense against an enemy. He has "blessed" (*barak*, see 5:12) the "children" (or "people") dwelling there, v. 13. He gives peace to the land, likely referring to Nehemiah's success in overcoming the threat posed by his foes. The Lord has also blessed the land with an abundant harvest of the "finest" (*ḥeleb*, see 17:10) wheat, v. 14.

15–17 The psalmist now describes what the Lord has accomplished through His word. He sends His command to the earth, and it goes swiftly to carry out His will, v. 15. He gives snow so that the land appears covered with wool. Conversely, He scatters the "hoarfrost" (or "frost") on the ground as though it were ashes blown away by the wind, v. 16. He "casteth forth" (or "casts down") ice as "morsels" (or "tiny bits"). Yet this builds up to create a frigid climate that no one can stand against, v. 17.

18–20 The reverse is also true. The Lord sends His command and melts (see *masâ*, 6:6) the ice. He sends winds to blow and waters to flow in the streams and rivers, v. 18. He speaks to Jacob, representing the nation, giving His "statutes" and "judgments" to the nation, v. 19. He has not done this for any other nation. He has not revealed His "judgments," His standards for life, to any other group. In the light of this, the psalmist closes appropriately: *halᵉlû·yah*, "praise ye the Lord," v. 20.

PSALM 148

Coming as it does toward the end of the book, this psalm is appropriately a total song of praise. The word *halᵉlû*, "praise," occurs twelve times, governing thirty-one groups giving praise. The unknown author[364] calls upon a wide range of subjects to praise the Lord. These begin with objects of nature, move to include various groups within mankind, and climax with praise to the Lord for exalting His people Israel.

I. Praise from the Heavens 1–6

1–4 As with the other psalms at the end of the book (146–150), this psalm begins and ends with *halᵉlû yah*, "praise ye the Lord." Praise should come to the Lord "from the heavens" and "in the heights." These general terms include both angelic praise and the praise that comes from the universe, v. 1. The "angels" and the "hosts" (*ṣᵉbaʾôt*, see 24:10) both refer to the angelic host (I Kings 22:19; Isa. 6:3) that praises God. The angels are powerful enough to delude one into trying to usurp God's place (Isa. 14:12–14) and are great enough to entice men into worshiping them (Col. 2:18). Nonetheless, they were created to serve God (Col. 1:16). Their Hebrew name, *malʾak*, means "messenger," suggesting their role of service to the Lord. As such, they should praise Him. Revelation 5:11–12 develops the praise of the Lord that comes from the angels, v. 2. The sun, moon, and stars should praise Him. These are the first of several inanimate objects that the psalmist calls on to praise the Lord. All of these give praise by their existence. Just as a work of art testifies to the creativity of its maker and a symphony to the talent of its composer, so these inanimate objects praise the God Whose wisdom and power brought them into being, v. 3. As in 68:33, the "heav-

[364]The author of the psalm and the time of writing are not known. Since Psalms 145–150 all praise the Lord, Henry, III, 772, makes David the author of all these psalms. His argument overlooks that fact that other biblical writers also praise the Lord, e.g., Asaph, Ethan (or Jeduthun), the sons of Korah. David may have authored this psalm but we cannot be certain. Sabourin, p. 193, makes the psalm postexilic, possible but not provable. We can say that the psalm is earlier than the apocryphal *Song of the Three Children*, written ca. mid-third century BC. The last half of this expands Ps. 148 and relates it to the three Israelites in the fiery furnace in Dan. 3.

ens of heavens" are the highest parts of earth's atmosphere.[365] These and the waters of the clouds that float high in the sky should likewise praise the Lord, v. 4.

5–6 These created beings and objects mentioned in vv. 2–4 should praise the "name"[366] of the Lord, His nature as a powerful and omniscient God. He "created" (*bara*ʾ, see 51:10) them with His word (Gen. 1:3, 6, 9, 11, 14, 20, 24), v. 5. He has established them forever. The divine decree that brought them into being will never pass away, v. 6.

II. Praise from the Earth 7–10

7–10 The author now turns from the heights to the praise that comes from the depths of the earth. "Dragons" (or "sea creatures," *tannîn*, see 44:19) and other creatures in the "deeps" of the waters should praise the Lord, v. 7. Fire, hail, snow, "vapours" (lit. "smoke"), and the winds of storms all carry out the word of God and thereby give praise to Him, v. 8. The mountains and hills, the fruit-bearing trees and mighty cedars that represent the other trees, v. 9, the "beasts [*ḥay*] and all cattle [*b*ᵉ*hemât*],"[367] wild and domesticated animals, the animals that creep, and the birds all praise God by their existence, v. 10.

III. Praise from Mankind 11–14

11–12 The final group offering praise to God includes various classes of mankind. Praise should come to the Lord from kings and the common people, "princes" (representing highly placed leaders) and judges, v. 11, young men and women, older men and children. These representative groups show that all mankind should praise the Lord, v. 12.

13–14 The psalmist repeats the command to praise the Lord and then briefly justifies it. As in v. 5, praise should go to the "name" of

---

[365]Leupold, p. 997, understands the "heavens of heavens" as "the dwelling place of God Himself." He takes the waters "above the heavens" as an unlimited source of water above the clouds. Jennings, II, 370, sees the phrase as describing "the boundless depth of the heavens." Kissane, p. 651, makes the phrase refer to the "firmament which divided the waters above from the waters below." The parallelism of the verse, along with similar phrases in 68:33; 57:5, 11; and 113:4, argues that both phrases refer to the upper atmosphere of the earth.

[366]Note 94 at 5:11 gives a summary of the Lord's "name."

[367]See 50:10, note 96.

the Lord. It is "excellent" (or "exalted," *śagab*, see 20:1). His "glory" (*hôd*, see 8:1) is higher than the whole creation, v. 13. This elevated God has "exalted" (or "raised up") the "horn" (*qeren*, see 18:2) of His people. As is often the case, the "horn" represents strength. It indicates here a "strong one," a mighty king for the nation, a forward look at Messiah's rule.[368] This is truly reason for "praise" (*tᵉhillâ*)[369] from all the "saints" (or "godly ones," *ḥasîd*, see 4:3). That this includes "the children of Israel" suggests the future reign when the Lord rules from among His people, a nation "near unto him." On this thought, the psalmist appropriately concludes, *halᵉlû-yah*, "Praise ye the Lord," v. 14.

PSALM 149

The psalm is another of the Hallelujah psalms.[370] The unknown psalmist[371] begins by praising the Lord and closes with a renewed dedication to Him. No clue in the psalm identifies either the author or the occasion for writing.[372] The psalm is clearly messianic, looking forward to the millennial reign of the Lord. In view of this subject, it is appropriate to give praise to the Lord.

---

[368]Murphy, p. 699, considers the horn to represent Israel's "power and place among the nations" after its return from captivity. I have given it an eschatological sense since the rest of the verse seems better to focus on the Millennium. Even after the return, Israel was weak and subject to Babylonian authority. W. E. Barnes, II, 672, refers the horn to Simon the son of Onias, mentioned in Ecclus. 50:1–21. Aside from the difficulty of fixing the date of Simon, this view would place the psalm in the intertestamental period, not a probable date.

[369]This is the only time that *tᵉhillâ* occurs in the psalm. The other twelve occurrences of "praise" use the word *halᵉlû*. Both words come from the same Hebrew root.

[370]See 106:1 for a brief summary of these psalms.

[371]Henry, III, 772, assigns the psalm to David because of its theme of praise to the Lord. While this is possible, it is also speculative.

[372]Various authors, e.g., Cohen, Livingston, date the psalm in the time of Nehemiah. It praises the Lord for restoring the people to the Promised Land. This is a possible view, although the psalm is not clear enough to let us be certain. The verses that speak of Israel's deliverance may as well point to other deliverances by the Lord.

I. Praising the Lord for Past Deliverance 1–5

1–3 The psalmist issues a general call to Israel, "Praise ye the Lord" (*hal^e^lû yah*). They should sing a "new song" of praise to Him.[373] The phrase "congregation of saints" (or "assembly of holy ones [*ḥasîd*, see 4:3]") suggests the cause for praise. This is a group of people who have been made holy by the gracious work of the Lord. They should therefore offer praise to Him. This is the first hint that the psalm looks forward to the millennial reign of Christ when redeemed Israel worships Him, v. 1. Israel should rejoice in the Lord as their Creator[374] and also as their King. He has chosen them out of the creation to rule them as His special people. Israel's continued sin has kept them from rejoicing in the Lord as their King. The fulfillment of this lies in the future, after Israel's redemption and the Lord's return to set up His kingdom over the earth, v. 2. Dancing has historically been a way to express joy; cf. II Samuel 6:16; Psalm 30:11; 150:4. They do this as they rejoice in the Lord's "name."[375] They will "sing praises" (or "make music," *zamar*, see 7:17) with the "timbrel" (*top*, see 81:2) and "harp" (or "lyre," *kinnôr*, see 33:2), v. 3.

4–5 The Lord is pleased with His people, the setting again pointing to the salvation of the nation. They have turned from their sins and now worship the Lord. He responds with "pleasure" (*raṣâ*, see 40:13). He will "beautify" (or "glorify") the "meek" (or "afflicted," see *ᶜanî*, 9:12) with "salvation," deliverance from judgment upon them for their sins, v. 4. In response, the psalmist again calls the "saints" (or "holy ones," *ḥasîd*, see 4:3) to praise the Lord. Let them rejoice in "glory" (or "honor"), i.e., the salvation their Lord has given them. Even when they lie on their "beds" (*miškab*)[376] for the night's rest, they should "sing aloud," (*ranan*, see 5:11), praising Him for Who He is and what He has done, v. 5.

---

[373]Psalm 33:3 discusses the phrase "new song."

[374]The phrase "him that made him" translates a plural participle. The plural is a plural of excellence, appropriate when referring to the Lord.

[375]Note 94 at 5:11 summarizes the sense of the Lord's "name."

[376]Kidner, p. 489, translates *miškab* as "couches" and suggests that this is "reclining at a festal meal." The word *miškab*, however, regularly indicates a bed. Of the forty-six times it occurs in the OT, only at Job 7:13 is the word translated "couch."

II. Praising the Lord for Future Victory 6–9

6–9 Redeemed Israel both praises the Lord and serves Him. "High praises" are in their speech but also a "two-edged sword"[377] in their hands. The picture is of a nation going to war against the enemies of God. This suggests the Battle of Armageddon at the close of the Tribulation; cf. Zechariah 14:3; Revelation 17:14; 19:11–21, v. 6. The nation accompanies the Lord as He brings "vengeance" (*n*ᵉ*qamâ*, see 18:47) on wicked mankind, v. 7, when their kings become captives. While events of this kind happened on a limited scale in the OT, the context here suggests a different time. This is a time when Israel has accepted Jesus Christ as Savior and therefore praises the Lord for salvation. It is a time when the "heathen" and the "people," both plural words, receive judgment. It is a time when "kings" and "nobles," again plural words, become captives, v. 8. The Lord executes judgment upon the wicked. The phrase "this honour [*hadar*, see 8:5] have all his saints" is better "this is an honor for all His holy ones [*ḥasîd*, see 4:3]." Israel receives glory in God's kingdom while their enemies receive judgment. Since this speaks of the fulfillment of God's plan for mankind, it is right to end with a note of praise to the Lord, v. 9.

PSALM 150

The psalm is a doxology of praise to the Lord.[378] Every verse repeats the command to praise the Lord, with variations of *halal*

---

[377]The phrase is lit. "a sword of mouths." The word "mouths" refers to an opening. Here, it refers to the sword opening on either side, its cutting edge ready to devour its target; cf. Judg. 3:16. Phillips, II, 694, and Kidner, p. 490, understand the "sword" as "the Word of God." The context rather supports a literal battle in which the Lord and the saints overcome the wicked nations of the earth. Hirsch, II, 494, spiritualizes the "two-edged sword." He refers it to "the high praises with which they commit both their acts and their destiny to the Lord." The thought is devotional but impossible to defend. VanGemeren, p. 878, suggests that this refers "to a kind of sword dance . . . symbolic of the attitude of joyous expectation." The view is speculative, without support elsewhere.

[378]The hymn "Praise the Lord Who Reigns Above," by Charles Wesley, paraphrases the whole psalm. The hymn first appeared in a collection of hymns published in 1743. Although Wesley wrote the music, he adapted it from a tune by J. A.

occurring thirteen times. We do not know the author of the psalm[379] or the date of its writing. The author likely wrote it for some service of praise at the temple.[380] Because of its nature as a psalm of praise, it has traditionally closed the book.[381] Its theme, however, should continue to resound from the lips of those who love the Lord.

I. The Object of Praise 1–2

1–2 Continuing the pattern seen in Psalms 146–149, the psalm begins and ends with *halᵉlû·yah*, "Praise ye the Lord." Because of Who He is, what He has done, and especially what He means to those who know Jesus Christ as their Savior, it is appropriate to offer Him praise. The psalmist urges others to praise the Lord in His "sanctuary." From the parallelism with 1*b*, this is likely the heavenly tabernacle.[382] Every living creature will praise the Lord in heaven (Rev. 5:11–13; 19:1–6). The phrase "firmament of his power" is lit. "His mighty expanse," a reference to the heavens, v. 1. With two short phrases, the psalmist justifies his call to praise. We praise the Lord because of His "mighty acts." The phrase is not specific, but the act of creation alone is enough to bring about praise to the mighty God. We praise Him also because of His "excellent [or 'abundant'] greatness," above all created beings and above the creation itself in His splendor and magnificence, v. 2.

Greylinghausen. The introduction to Ps. 103 discusses the hymn "Praise Ye the Lord, the Almighty," which is partially based on this psalm.

[379]Henry, III, 772, relies on the common theme of praise in Pss. 146–150 to make David the author of all these psalms. This may be true—we cannot tell—but David is not the only biblical writer to praise the Lord, e.g., Solomon, the sons of Korah, Asaph.

[380]Fausset, III, 411, connects the psalm with the dedication of the walls in Nehemiah's time. While this is possible, nothing in the psalm makes this certain.

[381]Each of the five books in Psalms ends with a doxology of praise to the Lord for His faithfulness. See also 41:13; 72:19; 89:52; and 106:48.

[382]Among others, Harman, p. 453, and Hirsch, II, 496, refer this to the earthly sanctuary, a possible view. Clarke, p. 357, understands it as the millennial temple. Jennings, II, 375, makes it "the whole earth." Better parallelism with 1*b* comes from making it the heavenly temple. Horne, p. 657, and Briggs, II, 544, refer *qodeš* to the nature of the Lord. Horne translates as "holiness" and Briggs as "sanctity." The parallelism, however, argues for a location for praise rather than an attribute of God.

II. The Manner of Praise 3–6

3–5 The psalmist now begins a listing of instruments from which praise to the Lord should come. While a long list, it is only representative of those musical instruments that make sounds of praise to God. There is the ram's horn "trumpet" (*šôpar*, see 47:5), the "psaltery" (or "harp," *nebel*, see 33:2), and the "harp" (or "lyre," *kinnôr*, see 33:2), v. 3. There is the "timbrel" (or "tambourine," *top*, see 81:2) accompanied by dancing, a means of expressing joy, 30:11; 149:3. There are "stringed instruments" and "organs" (or "flute," *ᶜûgab*),[383] v. 4. "Loud cymbals" and "high sounding [or 'resounding,' *tᵉrûᶜâ*, see 27:6] cymbals" create notes of praise to the Lord, v. 5.

6 Along with the instrumental praise, there is also vocal praise.[384] This comes from all living creatures—humans and animals (148:7, 10–11; Rev. 5:13)—as they offer their praise to the Lord. It is appropriate to end the psalm with the praise of living beings as opposed to the lifeless instruments in the earlier verses. On this note, the psalmist ends the book: *halᵉlû-yah*, "Praise ye the Lord," v. 6.

[383]This is the only occurrence of *ᶜûgab* in the psalms. The word comes from *ᶜagab*, "to lust, show inordinate affection." The connection with the flute or pipe apparently lies in the instrument's ability to create a sensuous mood with music. Scroggie, IV, 154, tentatively suggests that "it consisted of a collection of reeds." Delitzsch, III, 415, calls it a "shepherd's pipe." Rawlinson, III, 417, understands it as a "double pipe."

[384]Leupold, p. 1006, claims that "musical instruments did not seem to be used to accompany human voices." Such passages as 33:1–3; 71:22–23; 81:1–3; and 98:4–6 join singing and instruments.

BIBLIOGRAPHY

Commentaries and Other Books on Psalms

Alexander, Joseph Addison. *Commentary on Psalms*. 1873. Reprint, Grand Rapids, Mich.: Kregel Publications, 1991.

Anderson, A. A. *The Book of Psalms*. 2 vols. In *New Century Bible Commentary*. Grand Rapids, Mich.: Wm. B. Eerdmans Publishing Company, 1989.

Ballard, H. Wayne, Jr., and W. Dennis Tucker Jr., eds. *An Introduction to Wisdom Literature and the Psalms*. Macon, Geo.: Mercer University Press, 2000.

Barnes, Albert. *Notes on the Old Testament: Psalms*. 3 vols. Reprint, Grand Rapids, Mich.: Baker Book House, 1950.

Barnes, W. E. *The Psalms with Introduction and Notes*. 2 vols. In *Westminster Commentaries*, edited by Walter Lock and D. C. Simpson. London: Methuen & Co., Ltd., 1931.

Bratcher, Robert G., and William D. Reyburn. *A Translator's Handbook on the Book of Psalms*. New York: United Bible Societies, 1991.

Briggs, Charles Augustus, and Emilie Grace Briggs. *A Critical and Exegetical Commentary on the Book of Psalms*. 2 vols. Edinburgh: T. & T. Clark, 1906.

Bullock, C. Hassell. *Encountering the Book of Psalms: A Literary and Theological Introduction*. Grand Rapids, Mich.: Baker Academic, 2001.

Burkett, Ken. *Psalm 119: A Thematic and Literary Analysis*. PhD dissertation, Bob Jones University, 1994.

Buttenwieser, Moses. *The Psalms*. In *The Library of Biblical Studies*, edited by Harry M. Orlinsky. New York: Ktav Publishing House, Inc., 1969.

Calvin, John. *Commentary on the Book of Psalms*. Translated by James Anderson. 5 vols. Grand Rapids, Mich.: Wm. B. Eerdmans Publishing Company, 1949.

Cheyne, T. K. *The Book of Psalms*. 2 vols. London: Kegan Paul, Trench, Trübner & Co., Ltd., 1904.

Clarke, Arthur G. *Analytical Studies in the Psalms*. Kilmarnock, Scotland: John Ritchie Ltd., n.d.

Cohen, A. *The Psalms*. In *Soncino Books of the Bible*, edited by A. Cohen. London: The Soncino Press, 1969.

Crenshaw, James L. *The Psalms: An Introduction*. Grand Rapids, Mich.: Wm. B. Eerdmans Publishing Company, 2001.

Dahood, Mitchell. *Psalms*. 3 vols. In AB, edited by William Foxwell Albright and David Noel Freedman. Garden City, N.Y.: Doubleday & Company, Inc., 1965.

The Dead Sea Psalms Scroll. Edited by J. A. Sanders. Ithaca, N. Y.: Cornell University Press, 1967.

Delitzsch, Franz. *Psalms*. Translated by Francis Bolton. 3 vols. In *Commentary on the Old Testament*. 1871. Reprint, Grand Rapids, Mich.: Wm. B. Eerdmans Publishing Company, 1978.

Dickson, David. *A Commentary on the Psalms*. 2 vols. Reprint, London: The Banner of Truth Trust, 1959.

Eaton, J. H. *Psalms*. London: SCM Press Ltd., 1967.

Ewald, Heinrich A. V. *Commentary on the Psalms*. Translated by E. Johnson. 2 vols. London: Williams and Norgate, 1880.

Fausset, A. R. *Job—Isaiah*. Vol. 3 in *A Commentary: Critical, Experimental and Practical on the Old and New Testaments*. 1866. Reprint, Grand Rapids, Mich.: Wm. B. Eerdmans Publishing Company, 1967.

Gaebelein, Arno C. *The Book of Psalms: A Devotional and Prophetic Commentary*. Neptune, N.J.: Loizeaux Brothers, 1939.

Goldingay, John. *Songs from a Strange Land: Psalms 42–51*. In *The Bible Speaks Today*, edited by J. A. Motyer and John R. W. Stott. Downers Grove, Ill.: InterVarsity Press, 1978.

Harman, Allan M. *Commentary on the Psalms*. Fearn, Ross-shire, Scotland: Geanies House, 1998.

Hengstenberg, E. W. *Commentary on the Psalms*. 3 vols. In *Clark's Foreign Theological Library*. Edinburgh: T. & T. Clark, 1876.

Henry, Matthew. *An Exposition with Practical Observations of the Book of Psalms*. Vol. 3, *Commentary on the Whole Bible*. 1710. Reprint, New York: Fleming H. Revell Company, 1935.

Hirsch, Samuel Raphael. *The Psalms*. Translated by Gertrude Hirschler. 2 vols. New York: Feldheim Publishers, 1976.

Horne, George. *Commentary on the Book of Psalms*. Edinburgh: Thomas Nelson and Peter Brown, 1831.

Jennings, A. C. *The Psalms*. 2 vols. London: Macmillan and Co., 1884.

Keet, Cuthbert C. *A Study of the Psalms of Ascents*. London: Mitre Press, 1969.

Kidner, Derek. *Psalms 1–72*. In *The Tyndale Old Testament Commentaries*, edited by D. J. Wiseman. Downers Grove, Ill.: InterVarsity Press, 1973.

———. *Psalms 73–150*. In *The Tyndale Old Testament Commentaries*, edited by D. J. Wiseman. Downers Grove, Ill.: InterVarsity Press, 1973.

Kirkpatrick, A. F. *The Book of Psalms*. In *The Cambridge Bible for Schools and Colleges*. London: Cambridge University Press, 1939.

Kissane, Edward J. *The Book of Psalms*. Dublin, Ireland: Browne and Nolan Limited, 1964.

Lawson, Steven J. *Psalms 1–75*. In *Holman Old Testament Commentary*, edited by Max Anders and Steven J. Lawson. Nashville, Tenn.: Broadman & Holman Publishers, 2003.

Leslie, Elmer A. *The Psalms*. New York: Abingdon-Cokesbury Press, 1949.

Leupold, H. C. *Exposition of the Psalms*. Grand Rapids, Mich.: Baker Book House, 1959.

Livingston, George Herbert. *The Book of Psalms 73–150*. Vol. 2, *WBC*, edited by Charles W. Carter and Lee Haines. Grand Rapids, Mich.: Wm. B. Eerdmans Publishing Company, 1968.

Luther, Martin. Vols. 12–14, *Luther's Works*, edited by Jaroslav Pelikan. Translated by L. W. Spitz Jr. *et al*. St. Louis, Mo.: Concordia Publishing House, 1959.

Mays, James Luther. *Psalms*. In *Interpretation: A Bible Commentary for Teaching and Preaching*. Louisville, Ky: John Knox Press, 1994.

McCann, J. Clinton. *A Theological Introduction to the Book of Psalms: The Psalms as Torah*. Nashville, Tenn.: Abingdon Press, 1993.

———. *The Book of Psalms*. Vol. 4, *The New Interpreter's Bible*, edited by Bruce C. Birch, Katheryn Pfisterer Darr, and David L. Peterson. Nashville, Tenn.: Abingdon Press, 1996.

Moll, Carl Bernhard. *The Psalms*. In *Commentary on the Holy Scriptures*, edited by John Peter Lange. Translated by Charles A. Briggs *et al.* Reprint, Grand Rapids, Mich.: Zondervan Publishing House, 1960.

Morris, Henry M. *Sampling the Psalms*. San Diego, Calif.: Creation-Life Publishers, 1978.

Murphy, James G. *A Critical and Exegetical Commentary on the Book of Psalms*. Based on work by Warren Draper. 1876. Reprint, Minneapolis, Minn.: James Family Publishing, 1977.

Oesterley, W. O. E. *The Psalms*. 2 vols. New York: The Macmillan Company, 1939.

Perowne, J. J. Stewart. *Commentary on the Psalms*. 3 vols. 1878–79. Reprint, Grand Rapids, Mich.: Kregel Publications, 1989.

Phillips, John. *Exploring Psalms: An Expository Commentary*. 2 vols. Grand Rapids, Mich.: Kregel Publications, 2002.

Rawlinson, G. *Psalms*. 3 vols. In *The Pulpit Commentary*, edited by H. D. M. Spence and Joseph S. Exell. New York: Funk & Wagnalls Company, n.d.

Ridderbos, Nicolaas H. "The Psalms: Style-Figures and Structure." Vol. 13, *Oudtestamentische Studiën*. Leiden: E. J. Brill, 1963.

Rodd, Cyril A. *Psalms 1–72*. In *Epworth Preacher's Commentaries*, edited by Norman H. Snaith and S. Clive Thexton. London: The Epworth Press, 1963.

Rotherham, Joseph Bryant. *Studies in the Psalms*. London: H. R. Allenson, Ltd., 1911.

Sabourin, Leopold. *The Psalms: Their Origin and Meaning*. New York: Alba House, 1974.

Scroggie, W. Graham. *The Psalms*. 4 vols. London: Pickering & Inglis, Ltd., 1950.

Soll, Will. *Psalm 119: Matrix, Form, and Setting*. No. 23, The Catholic Biblical Quarterly Monograph Series. Washington, D.C.: The Catholic Biblical Association of America, 1991.

Spurgeon, Charles H. *The Treasury of David*. Edited by David Otis Fuller. Grand Rapids, Mich.: Kregel Publications, 1968.

The Targum of Psalms. Translated and edited by David M. Stec. In *The Aramaic Bible*. Collegeville, Minn.: Liturgical Press, 2004.

Thirtle, James William. *The Titles of the Psalms: Their Nature and Meaning Explained*. London: Henry Frowde, 1904.

Thompson, W. Ralph. *The Book of Psalms 1–72*. Vol. 2, *WBC*, edited by Charles W. Carter and Lee Haines. Grand Rapids, Mich.: Wm. B. Eerdmans Publishing Company, 1968.

VanGemeren, Willem A. *Psalms*. Vol. 5, *The Expositor's Bible Commentary*, edited by Frank E. Gaebelein. Grand Rapids, Mich.: Zondervan Publishing House, 1991.

Weiser, Artur. *The Psalms*. Translated by Herbert Hartwell. In *The Old Testament Library*, edited by G. Ernest Wright, John Bright, James Barr, and Peter Ackroyd. London: SCM Press, Ltd., 1965.

White, R. E. O. *A Christian Handbook to the Psalms*. Exeter, Devon, Great Britain: The Paternoster Press; Grand Rapids, Mich.: Wm. B. Eerdmans Publishing Company, 1984.

General Works

Herodotus. *The Histories*. Translated by Robin Waterfield. New York: Oxford University Press, 1998.

Josephus. *The Works of Josephus: New Updated Edition*. Translated by William Whiston. Peabody, Mass.: Hendrickson Publishers, Inc., 2000.

Robinson, Theodore H. *The Poetry of the Old Testament*. London: Gerald Duckworth & Co. Ltd., 1947.

Unger, Merrill F., ed. *Unger's Bible Dictionary*. Chicago: Moody Press, 1957.

Wigoder, Geoffrey, ed. *NEJ*. Washington Square, N.Y.: New York University Press, 2002.

Linguistic Aids

Harris, R. Laird, ed. *TWOT*. 2 vols. Chicago: Moody Press, 1980.

Hulst, A. R. *OTTP*. Leiden: E. J. Brill, 1960.

Lisowsky, Gerhard. *Konkordanz zum Hebräischen Alten Testament*. Stuttgart: Wurttembergische Bibelanstalt, 1958.

Gesenius, Wilhelm. *Gesenius' Hebrew Grammar*. Edited by E. Kautzsch. Translated by A. E. Cowley. Oxford: Clarendon Press, 1970.

Holladay, William L. *A Concise Hebrew and Aramaic Lexicon of the Old Testament*. Grand Rapids, Mich.: Wm. B. Eerdmans Publishing Company, 1971.

Koehler, Ludwig, and Walter Baumgartner. *The Hebrew and Aramaic Lexicon of the Old Testament*. Revised by Walter Baumgartner and Johann Jakob Stamm. Translated and edited by M. E. J. Richardson. New York: E. J. Brill, 1995.

Unger, Merrill F., and William White Jr., eds. *Nelson's Expository Dictionary of the Old Testament*. Nashville, Tenn.: Thomas Nelson Publishers, 1980.

Waltke, Bruce K., and M. O'Connor. *An Introduction to Biblical Hebrew Syntax*. Winona Lake, Ind: Eisenbrauns, 1990.

Williams, Ronald J. *Hebrew Syntax: An Outline*. Toronto: University of Toronto Press, 1974.

Periodicals

Allen, Ronald B. "Psalm 87, A Song Rarely Sung." *BibSac* 153 (1996): 131–40.

Ashburn, Daniel G. "Creation and the Torah in Psalm 19." *JBQ* 22:4 (1994): 241–48.

Barker, David G. "The Waters of the Earth: An Exegetical Study of Psalm 104:1–9." *GTJ* 7:1 (1986): 57–80.

Barré, Michael L. "The Seven Epithets of Zion in Ps 48,2–3." *Biblica* 69:4 (1988): 557–63.

Beckwith, Roger T. "The Early History of the Psalter." *TB* 46:1 (1995): 1–27.

Bellinger, W. H., Jr. "The Interpretation of Psalm 11." *EQ* 56:2 (1984): 95–101.

Benedetto, Robert. "Psalm 84." *Interp* 51:1 (1997): 57–61.

Berlin, Adele. "Psalm 118:24." *JBL* 96:4 (1977): 567–68.

Boesak, Willa. "Psalm 82: God amidst the gods." *Journal of Theology for Southern Africa* 64:1 (1988): 64–68.

Booij, Thijs. "Psalm 104,13b: 'The Earth is Satisfied with the Fruit of Thy Works.'" *Biblica* 70:3 (1989): 409–12.

———."Psalm 119,89–91." *Biblica* 79:4 (1998): 539–41.

———. "Psalm CI 2—'When Wilt Thou Come to Me?'" *VT* 38:4 (1988): 458–62.

———. "The Role of Darkness in Psalm CV 28." *VT* 39:2 (1989): 209–14.

———. "Psalm CX: 'Rule in the Midst of Your Foes!'" *VT* 41:4 (1991): 396–407.

———. "Psalm CXXXIX: Text, Syntax, Meaning." *VT* 54:1 (2005): 1–19.

Burns, John Barclay. "An Interpretation of Psalm CXLI 7*b*." *VT* 22:2 (1972): 245–46.

Ceresko, Anthony R. "A Poetic Analysis of Ps 105, with Attention to Its Use of Irony." *Biblica* 64:1 (1983): 20–46.

———. "The ABCS of Wisdom in Psalm XXXIV." *VT* 35:1 (1985): 99–104.

———. "A Note on Psalm 63: A Psalm of Vigil." *ZAW* 92:3 (1980): 435–36.

Childs, Brevard S. "Psalm Titles and Midrashic Exegesis." *JSS* 16:2 (1971): 137–50.

Cohn, Herbert. "Hinds in Psalm 29." *JBQ* 24:4 (1996): 258–59.

Collins, C. John. "Psalm 139:14: 'Fearfully and Wonderfully Made'?" *Presbyterion*: *Covenant Seminary Review* 25:2 (1999): 115–20.

Craig, Kenneth M., Jr. "Psalm 82." *Interp* 41:3 (1995): 281–84.

Custer, Stewart. "New Testament Quotations from Psalms." *BV* 4 (1970): 117–25.

———. "Contrasts in Character." *BV* 4 (1970): 79–82.

Dahood, Mitchell J. "A Note on Psalm 15,4 (14,4)." *CBQ* 16:3 (1954): 302.

Davis, Ellen F. "Psalm 98." *Interp* 46:2 (1992): 171–75.

Dijkstra, Meindert. "He Pours the Sweet Wine Off, Only the Dregs Are for the Wicked. An Epigraphic Note on *mizzoeh* in Psalm 75,9." *ZAW* 107:2 (1995): 296–300.

Du Preez, Jannie. "Interpreting Psalm 47." *Missionalia* 25:3 (1997): 308–23.

———. "The Missionary Significance of Psalm 117 in the Book of Psalms and in the New Testament." *Missionalia* 27:3 (1999): 369–76.

Durham, John I. "The King as 'Messiah' in the Psalms." *RevEx* 81:3 (1984): 425–35.

Earwood, Greg C. "Psalm 46." *RevEx* 86 (1989): 79–86.

Eder, Asher. "Psalm 91 as Responsory." *JBQ* 28:2 (2000): 117–18.

Emerton, J. A. "How Does the Lord Regard the Death of His Saints in Psalm CXVI.15?" *JTS* 34:1 (1983): 146–56.

———. "The Problem of Psalm LXXXVII." *VT* 50:2 (2000): 183–99.

Estes, Daniel J. "Like Arrows in the Hand of a Warrior (Psalm CXXVII)." *VT* 41:3 (1991): 304–11.

Fokkelman, J. P., and Gary A. Rendsburg. "נגדה נא לכל עמו (Psalm CXVI 14B, 18B)." *VT* 53:3 (2003): 328–36.

Goulder, M. D. "The Songs of Ascents and Nehemiah." *JSOT* 75 (1997): 43–58.

Greenstein, Edward L. "Yhwh's Lightning in Psalm 29:7." *Maarav* 8 (1992): 49–57.

Hannay, Margaret P. "'Psalms done unto metre': The Common Psalms of John Milton and the Bay Colony." *Christianity and Literature* 32:3 (1983): 19–29.

Harris, Murray J. "The Translation of Elohim in Psalm 45:7–8." *TB* 35 (1984): 65–89.

Heinemann, Mark H. "An Exposition of Psalm 22." *BibSac* 147 (1990): 286–308.

Herr, Larry G. "An Off-Duty Archaeologist Looks at Psalm 23." *BibRev* 8:2 (1992): 44–51.

Hillers, Delbert R. "Ritual Procession of the Ark and Ps 132." *CBQ* 30:1 (1968): 48–55.

Hofreiter, Paul. "Johann Sebastian Bach and Scripture: 'O God, from Heaven Look Down.'" *CTQ* 59:1–2 (1995): 67–92.

Holliday, William L. "A New Proposal for the Crux in Psalm II 12." *VT* 28:1 (1978): 110–12.

Hustad, Donald P. "The Psalms as Worship Expression: Personal and Congregational." *RevEx* 81:3 (1984): 407–24.

Janzen, J. Gerald. "Another Look at Psalm XII 6." *VT* 54:2 (2004): 157–64.

Jarick, John. "The Four Corners of Psalm 107." *CBQ* 59:2 (1997): 270–87.

Johnson, Elliot E. "Hermeneutical Principles and the Interpretation of Psalm 110." *BibSac* 149 (1992): 428–53.

Konkel, August. "The Exaltation of the Eternal King." *Didaskalia* 1:2 (1990): 14–22.

———. "The Sacrifice of Obedience." *Didaskalia* 2:2 (1991): 2–11.

Kselman, John S. "Two Notes on Psalm 37." *Biblica* 78:2 (1997): 252–54.

———. "A Note on LR'WT in Ps 40,13." *Biblica* 63:4 (1982): 552–54.

———. "A Note on Psalm 85:9–10." *CBQ* 46:1 (1984): 23–27.

Kselman, John S., and Michael L. Barré. "A Note on *ʾelem* in Psalm LVIII 2." *VT* 54:3 (2004): 400–402.

Laney, J. Carl. "A Fresh Look at the Imprecatory Psalms." *BibSac* 138 (1981): 35–45.

Layton, Scott C. "Jehoseph in Ps 81,6." *Biblica* 69:406–11.

Lee, Archie C. C. "The Context and Function of the Plagues Tradition in Psalm 78." *JSOT* 48:84–85.

Lehrman, S. M. "Psalm 119." *JBQ* 23:1 (1995): 55–56.

Leveen, Jacob. "A Displaced Verse in Psalm XLI." *VT* 1 (1951): 65–66.

Levenson, J. D. "A Technical Meaning for *N^{C}M* in the Hebrew Bible." *VT* 35:1 (1985): 61–67.

Levin, Schneir. "Let My Right Hand Wither." *Judaism* 45:3 (1996): 285–86.

Lewis, Joe O. "An Asseverative לא in Psalm 100 3?" *JBL* 82:2 (1963): 216.

Liebreich, Leon J. "The Songs of Ascents and the Priestly Blessing." *JBL* 74 (1955): 33–36.

Lindars, Barnabas. "The Structure of Psalm CXLV." *VT* 39 (1989): 23–30.

Longman, Tremper, III. "Psalm 98: A Divine Warrior Victory Song." *JETS* 27:3 (1984): 267–74.

Luc, Alex. "Interpreting the Curses in the Psalms." *JETS* 42:3 (1999): 395–410.

Lundblom, Jack R. "Psalm 23: Song of Passage." *Interp* 40:1 (Jan. 1986): 5–16.

McCambley, Casimir. "On the Sixth Psalm, Concerning the Octave by Saint Gregory of Nyssa." *Greek Orthodox Theological Review* 32:1 (1987): 39–50.

McKay, J. W. "Psalms of Vigil." *ZAW* 91:1 (1979): 229–47.

Macintosh, A. A. "Psalm XCI 4 and the root רחס." *VT* 23 (1973):56–62.

Marlowe, W. Creighton. "'Spirit of Your Holiness' (רוּח דְשְׁךָ) in Psalm 51:13." *TJ* ns 19 (1998): 29–49.

Mays, James L. "Prayer and Christology: Psalm 22 as Perspective on the Passion." *Theology Today* 42:3 (1985): 322–31.

Merrill, A. L. "Psalm XXIII and the Jerusalem Tradition." *VT* 15 (1965): 354–60.

Mosca, Paul G. "Once Again the Heavenly Witness of Ps 89:38." *JBL* 105:1 (1986): 27–37.

Nielsen, Kirsten. "Why Not Plow with an Ox and an Ass Together? Or: Why Not Read Ps 119 Together with Pss 120–134?" *SJOT* 14:1 (2000): 56–66.

Mullen, E. Theodore, Jr. "The Divine Witness and the Davidic Royal Grant: Psalm 89:37–38." *JBL* 102:2 (1983): 207–18.

Ogden, Graham S. "Translating Psalm 10.11." *Bible Translator* 42:2 (1991):231–33.

Paas, Stefan. "A Textual Note on Psalm 143,6 (אֶרֶץ־עֲיֵפָה - » a weary land «?)." *ZAW* 113:3 (2001): 415–18.

Petuchowski, Jakob J. "'*Hoshiᶜah Na*' in Psalm CXVIII 25, — A Prayer for Rain." *VT* 5:266–71.

Prinsloo, Gert T. M. "Man's Word—God's Word: A Theology of Antithesis in Psalm 12." *ZAW* 110:3 (1998): 390–402.

Prinsloo, W. S. "Psalm 82: Once Again, Gods or Men." *Biblica* 76 (1995): 219–28.

Raabe, Paul R. "Deliberate Ambiguity in the Psalter." *JBL* 110:2 (1991): 213–27.

Rendsburg, Gary. "Hebrew *rḥm* = 'Rain.'" *VT* 33:3 (1983): 357–62.

———. "Psalm CX 3b." *VT* 49:4 (1999): 548–53.

Rice, Gene. "The Integrity of the Text of Psalm 139:20b." *CBQ* 46:1 (1984): 28–30.

Roberts, J. J. M. "A New Root for an Old Crux, Ps. XXII 17c." *VT* 23 (1973): 247–52.

Robinson, A. "Three Suggested Interpretations in Ps. LXXXIV." *VT* 24 (1974): 378–81.

Robinson, Bernard P. "Form and Meaning in Psalm 131." *Biblica* 79:2 (1998): 180–97.

Slotki, Judah Jacob. "Psalm XLIX 13, 21 (AV 12, 20)." *VT* 28:3 (1978): 361–62.

Smith, Mark S. "The Invocation of Deceased Ancestors in Psalm 49:12c." *JBL* 112:1 (1993): 105–7.

Snaith, Norman H. "Selah." *VT* 2:3 (1952): 43–56.

Strugnell, John, and Hanan Eshel. "Psalms 9 and 10 and the Order of the Alphabet." *BibRev* 17:3 (2001): 41–44.

Sutcliffe, Edmund F. "A Note on Psalm CIV 8." *VT* 2:2 (1952): 177–79.

Tarazi, Paul Nadim. "An Exegesis of Psalm 93." *St Vladimir's Theological Quarterly* 35 (1991): 137–48.

Tate, Marvin E. "The Interpretation of the Psalms." *RevEx* 81:3 (1984): 363–75.

Trull, Gregory V. "An Exegesis of Psalm 16:10." *BibSac* 161 (2004): 304–21.

Tsevat, Matitiahu. "God and the Gods in Assembly. An Interpretation of Psalm 82." *HUCA* 40–41 (1970): 123–37.

Tsumura, David Toshio. "Twofold Image of Wine in Psalm 46:4–5." *JQR* 71:3 (1981): 167–75.

Tur-Sinai, N. H. "Unverstandene Bibelworte I." *VT* 1 (1951): 307–9.

Vogt, E. "The 'Place of Life' of Ps 23." *Biblica* 34 (1953): 195–211.

Weir, J. Emmette. "The Perfect Way, A Study of Wisdom Motifs in Psalm 101." *EQ* 53:1 (1981): 54–59.

Wernberg-Møller, P. "Two Difficult Passages in the Old Testament." *ZAW* 69:1 (1957): 69–73.

White, R. E. O. "The Student's Psalm?" *ET* 102:2 (1990): 71–74.

Whitekettle, Richard. "Bugs, Bunny, or Boar? Identifying the *Zîz* Animals of Psalms 50 and 80." *CBQ* 67:2 (2005): 250–64.

Whitley, Charles. "The Text of Psalm 90,5." *Biblica* 63:4 (1982): 555–57.

Willis, John T. "An Attempt to Decipher Psalm 121:1b." *CBQ* 52:2 (1990): 241–51.

Willis, Timothy M. "A Fresh Look at Psalm XXIII 3*a*." *VT* 37 (1987): 104–6.

Wilson, Gerald H. "A First Century C.E. Date for the Closing of the Book of Psalms." *JBQ* 28:2 (2000): 102–10.

Zink, J. K. "Uncleanness and Sin: A Study of Job XIV 4 and Psalm LI 7." *VT* 17:3 (1967): 354–61.

Zolli, Eugene. "*Kerum* in Ps. 12:9: A Hapax Legomenon." *CBQ* 12:1 (1950): 7–9.

LIST OF HEBREW WORDS

ʾ

ʾabad 1:6
ʾebyôn 72:13
ʾadôn 8:1
ʾaddîr 8:1
ʾadam 22:6
ʾahab 78:68
ʾwl 38:5
ʾôt 65:8
ʾaḥ^{a}rît 37:37
ʾaṭad 58:9
ʾîyîm 72:10
ʾîš 22:6
ʾ^{e}lôah 18:31
ʾ^{e}lohîm 7:1
ʾalaḥ 14:3
ʾ^{e}lîlîm 96:5
ʾummîm 117:1
ʾamaṣ 27:14
ʾ^{e}nôš 8:4
ʾ^{a}naḥâ 6:6
ʾap 2:5
ʾarbeh 78:46
ʾ^{a}rî 7:2
ʾ^{a}rešet 21:2
ʾašam 5:10
ʾašrê 1:1

b
bagad 25:3
bahal 2:5
bôr 7:15
bôš 6:10
bakaʾ 84:6
b^{e}lîyaʿal 18:4
balaʿ I 21:9
balaʿ II 55:9
baʿar 49:10
bar 2:12
baraʾ 51:10
barak 5:12
baśar 40:9

g
gibbôr 19:5
geber 34:8
gôyim 117:1
gûr 5:4
gîl 16:9
galgal 77:18
galal 37:5
golmî 139:16
gamal 7:4
gittît 8, intro.

d
d^{e}ḥî 56:13
dak 9:9
dal 41:1
darak 7:12
daraš 9:10
dašen 20:3

h
hebel 31:6
hagâ 1:2
hagîg 5:1
higgayôn 9:16
hadar 8:5
hôd 8:1
hawâ 5:9
hût 62:3
hêkal 5:7
hol^{e}lîm 5:5
haras 11:3

z
z^{e}bul 49:14
zahar 19:11
zûr 44:20
zîz 50:11
zullût 12:8
zamar 7:17
zimrâ 81:2
zaʿam 38:3

ḥ
ḥebel 16:6
ḥag 81:3
ḥodeš 81:3
ḥazaq 27:14
ḥaṭaʾ 4:4
ḥîdâ 49:4
ḥkm 19:7
ḥeleb 17:10
ḥeled 17:14
ḥelkâ 10:8
ḥalal I 87:7
ḥalal II 55:20
ḥalaṣ 7:4
ḥemâ 6:1
ḥamas 7:16
ḥ^{a}nît 35:3

s
*s*ᵉ*gullâ* 135:4
sôd 25:14
soḥerâ 91:4
sok 27:5
sakak 5:11
selâ 3, intro.
*sela*ᶜ 18:2
*se*ᶜᵃ*pîm* 119:113
sapap 84:10

ᶜ

ᶜ*ebrâ* 7:6
ᶜ*edût* 19:7
ᶜᵃ*dî* 32:9
ᶜ*ûgab* 150:4
ᶜ*ûd* 20:8
ᶜ*awlâ* 7:3
ᶜ*awon* 18:23
ᶜ*ezer* 20:2
ᶜ*elyôn* 7:17
ᶜ*amal* 7:14
ᶜ*anâ* 35:13
ᶜ*anaw* 9:12
ᶜ*anî* 9:12
ᶜ*aṣûm* 10:10
ᶜ*aqeb* 49:5
ᶜ*iqqeš* 18:26
ᶜ*arob* 78:45
ᶜ*arak* 5:3

p
padâ 25:22
pûn 88:15
paḥad 14:5
*pala*ᵓ 9:1
palal 5:2
pissâ 72:16
paqad 8:4
paraḥ 72:7
paras 69:31
*peša*ᶜ 5:10
petî 19:7
patal 18:26
peten 58:4

ṣ
*ṣ*ᵉ*ba*ᵓ*ôt* 24:10
ṣedeq 9:4
ṣûṣ 72:16
ṣûr 18:2
ṣelem 39:6
ṣalmawet 23:4
ṣamat 18:40
ṣinnâ 5:12
*ṣa*ᶜ*îr* 68:27
*ṣa*ᶜ*aq* 34:17
ṣippôr 84:3
ṣarâ 9:9
ṣarap 12:6
ṣarar 31:9

q
*qa*ᵓ*at* 102:6
qawâ 25:3
qûm 1:5
qinyan 104:24
qarob 15:3
qeren 18:2

r
*ro*ᵓ*š* 69:21
ragaz 4:4
ragal 15:3
rigmâ 68:27
ragaš 2:1
radâ 49:14
*r*ᵉ*wayâ* 23:5
*rûa*ᶜ 41:11
rûš 82:3
raḥam 18:1
raḥas 45:1
rîb 35:1
rokes 31:20
*r*ᵉ*mîyâ* 32:2
remîm 22:21
rinnâ 17:1
ranan 5:11
*ra*ᶜ 7:9
*rea*ᶜ 12:2
*r*ᵉ*pa*ᵓ*îm* 88:10
raṣâ 40:13
raqam 139:15
*raša*ᶜ 1:1

ś
śagab 20:1
śaṭam 55:3
śîaḥ 55:2
śîś 19:5
śamaḥ 16:9
*śane*ᵓ 5:5
*śar*ᶜ*ap* 94:19
śaq 30:11

š
*ša*ᵓᵃ*gâ* 22:1
*š*ᵉᵓ*ôl* 6:5
*ša*ᵓ*ap* 56:1
šabaḥ 63:3
šabar 3:7
*š*ᵉ*gî*ᵓ*ôt* 19:12
šiggayôn 7, intro.

šadad 17:9
šadday 68:14
šawʾ 12:2
šôʾâ 35:8
šawʿî 5:2
šûp 139:11
šôpar 47:5
š^{e}ḥît 107:20
šaḥal 91:13
šaḥat (noun) 7:15
šaḥat (verb) 14:1
šîr 30, intro.
šulḥan 23:5
šalîš 80:5
š^{e}mînît 6, intro.
šamem 40:15
šaʿ^{a}šuʿay 119:24
š^{e}pattayim 68:13
š^{e}rîrût 81:12
šatôt 11:3
šatal 1:3

t

t^{e}bûnâ 49:3
tôdâ 26:7
tawâ 78:41
tôlal 137:3
tôr 74:19
taḥ^{a}nûn 28:2
t^{e}ḥinnâ 6:9
tiklâ 119:96
tom 7:8
tamam 18:25
tannîm 44:19
top 81:2
t^{e}pillâ 4:1
tiqwâ 9:18
t^{e}rûʿâ 27:6